FUNDAMENTALS OF
Cognition

9/2012

FUNDAMENTALS OF
Cognition

Second Edition

Michael W. Eysenck

Ψ **Psychology Press**
Taylor & Francis Group

HOVE AND NEW YORK

UNIVERSITY OF CHICHESTER

First published 2012
by Psychology Press
27 Church Road, Hove, East Sussex BN3 2FA

Simultaneously published in the USA and Canada
by Psychology Press
711 Third Avenue, New York NY 10017

www.psypress.com

Psychology Press is an imprint of the Taylor & Francis Group, an informa business

British Library Cataloguing in Publication Data
A catalogue record for this book is available from the British Library

Library of Congress Cataloging in Publication Data
Eysenck, Michael W.
    Fundamentals of cognition / Michael W. Eysenck. — 2nd ed.
        p. cm.
    Includes bibliographical references and index.
     ISBN 978–1–84872–070–1 (hbk)—ISBN 978–1–84872–071–8 (soft cover)
    1. Cognition. I. Title.

    BF311.E938 2011   2011021508
    153—dc23

ISBN: 978–1–84872–070–1 (hbk)
ISBN: 978–1–84872–071–8 (pbk)

Typeset in Sabon by Newgen Imaging Systems (P) Ltd
Cover design by Andrew Ward
Printed and bound in Slovenia.

To Maria with love

A professor is someone who talks in other people's sleep.
(Anonymous)

Contents

Preface

Cognitive psychology is concerned with the processes that allow us to make sense of the world around us and to make (reasonably) sensible decisions about how to cope with everyday life. As such, it is of huge importance within psychology as a whole. The advances made by cognitive psychology have permeated most of the rest of psychology – areas such as abnormal psychology and social psychology have been transformed by the cognitive approach. As a cognitive psychologist myself, I may be biased. However, I genuinely believe that cognitive psychology is at the heart of psychology.

The Chinese have a saying, "May you live in interesting times." It has been my good fortune during my career to see cognitive psychology become more and more interesting. One important reason is that there has been a substantial increase in research showing the relevance of the cognitive approach in the real world. Examples discussed in this book include the following: security scanning at airports, why fingerprinting experts make mistakes, the misinterpretations of patients with anxiety disorders, the fallibility of eyewitness testimony, how you can tell when someone is lying, and why our reasoning is often very illogical.

Another important reason why cognitive psychology has become increasingly interesting is that technological advances now permit us to observe the brain in action in great detail. You have probably seen the fruits of such research in the brightly colored pictures of the brain to be found within the covers of numerous magazines. In this book, there is much coverage of the exciting discoveries based on brain imaging.

I would like to express my gratitude to all those who helped in the preparation of this book. They include several people working for Psychology Press: Lucy Kennedy, Becci Edmondson, Tara Stebnicky, Sharla Plant, and Mandy Collison. In addition, thanks are due to those who kindly took time to review a draft of this book (Bruce Bridgeman, Jerwen Jou, Dawn Morales, Susan Dunlap, Jon May, Mitchell Longstaff, Jelena Havelka, and Matt Field). Finally, I owe a huge debt of gratitude to my wife, Christine, who devoted hundreds of hours to tracking down the numerous articles that form the basis of this book.

This book is deservedly dedicated to my mother-in-law. She has made huge contributions to our family and has devoted herself wholeheartedly to the well-being of her three grandchildren (Fleur, William, and Juliet).

Michael W. Eysenck
Hong Kong, China

Chapter 1

Contents

Introduction to cognitive psychology

INTRODUCTION

There is more general interest than ever in understanding the mysteries of the human brain and the mind. So far as the media are concerned, numerous television programs, movies, and books have been devoted to the more dramatic aspects of the brain and its workings. You must have seen pretty colored pictures of the brain in magazines, revealing which parts of the brain are most active when people are engaged in various tasks. So far as science is concerned, there has been an explosion of research on the brain by scientists from several disciplines including cognitive psychologists, cognitive neuroscientists, biologists, and so on.

How does all of this relate to cognitive psychology? Cognitive psychology is concerned with the processes involved in acquiring, storing, and transforming information. Let's make that more concrete by focusing on what you are

---

Learning Objectives

After studying Chapter 1, you should be able to:

- Define "cognition," and identify which types of mental processes are studied in cognitive psychology.
- Explain why introspection is not a good method for understanding these mental processes.
- Discuss the advantages and disadvantages of the behaviorist approach to studying human cognition.
- Describe the uses and limitations of the four main methods/approaches used in cognitive psychology – experimental cognitive psychology; cognitive neuroscience; cognitive neuropsychology; and computational cognitive science.
- Define, compare, and contrast "bottom-up" and "top-down" processes.
- Define, compare, and contrast "serial" and "parallel" processes.

Key Term
Textisms: the new abbreviations (often involving a mixture of symbols and letters) used when individuals produce text messages.

currently doing. In the next paragraph, the italicized words indicate some of the main aspects of human cognition.

You are using *visual perception* to take in information from the printed page, and hopefully you are *attending* to the content of this book. As a result, *learning* is taking place. In order for this to happen, you must possess good *language skills* – you wouldn't learn much if you tried to read a textbook written in an unfamiliar language! Your reading benefits from having *stored knowledge* relevant to the material in this book. There may also be an element of *problem solving* as you relate what is in the book to the possibly conflicting information you learned previously. Finally, the acid test of whether your learning has been effective and has led to *long-term memory* comes when you are tested on your knowledge of the material contained in this book.

The italicized words in the previous paragraph form the basis of much of the coverage of cognitive psychology in this book. If you look at the titles of the various chapters, you may feel cognitive psychology can be neatly divided up into various categories (e.g., attention; perception; language). However, it is important to realize that all the categories *interact* with each other. For example, language isn't totally irrelevant to the other categories. Much of what we learn and remember is language-based, and language is heavily involved in most of our thinking and reasoning.

In the Real World 1.1: *Text messaging*

As we will see throughout this book, cognitive psychology is very relevant to everyday life. For example, consider the huge increase in recent years in the number of text messages sent from one cell phone to another. Millions of people use **textisms** (abbreviations and symbols in place of whole words) when texting. This has caused controversy because of fears that the frequent use of textisms is having a negative effect on the language skills of children and young adults.

Is texting having a damaging effect? Most of the evidence indicates that texting and the use of textisms have a positive effect. A good command of grammar and sentence structure is needed to communicate effectively via text messages. Texting provides useful practice in reading and writing (Crystal, 2008).

Plester et al. (2009) found that children aged 10 to 12 who were best at using textisms were also the best at ordinary spelling and writing. This doesn't prove that using textisms benefits language skills. However, Plester et al. argued that using textisms leads children to focus on the sounds of words and on their spellings.

There may be limits on the benefits of texting and textisms. Rosen et al. (2010) found that young adults who texted the most performed the best when asked to write informally about happiness. However, the high texters performed poorly when writing a formal letter to a company. Rosen et al. argued that a potential disadvantage with extensive texting is that it can promote an excessively "loose" and informal approach to written communications.

Research Activity 1.1: *Textisms*

To what extent have textisms been absorbed into language? We will consider this issue based on a study by McWilliam et al. (2009). The task involves naming the colors in which list items are presented as rapidly as possible. That is what you need to do for each list in turn, recording the total time taken to work through the entire list. Before you start, note that the first list consists of textisms: GR8 = great; 2MRW = tomorrow; CUL8R = see you later; WTUUP2 = what are you up to?

LIST 1	LIST 2	LIST 3
GR8	DEAL	#$&!+
CUL8R	DOUBLE	£#@
WTUUP2	TOP	#$&!+
2MRW	PLANE	?&%@£=
WTUUP2	DEAL	£#@
GR8	TOP	#$&!+
WTUUP2	DOUBLE	$+?%
2MRW	TOP	$+?%
GR8	DEAL	£#@
CUL8R	PLANE	$+?%
2MRW	DOUBLE	#$&!+
WTUUP2	TOP	£#@
WTUUP2	DEAL	#$&!+
CUL8R	DOUBLE	?&%@£=
GR8	DEAL	?&%@£=
CUL8R	PLANE	$+?%
WTUUP2	DOUBLE	?&%@£=
GR8	TOP	£#@
2MRW	DOUBLE	$+?%
2MRW	DOUBLE	#$&!+
GR8	TOP	?&%@£=
CUL8R	PLANE	£#@
2MRW	DOUBLE	$+?%
WTUUP2	TOP	#$&!+
CUL8R	PLANE	#$&!+
2MRW	DOUBLE	?&%@£=
WTUUP2	DEAL	?&%@£=
GR8	DOUBLE	$+?%
CUL8R	DEAL	#$&!+
CUL8R	TOP	£#@
2MRW	PLANE	$+?%
WTUUP2	PLANE	£#@
CUL8R	PLANE	#$&!+
GR8	DEAL	£#@
2MRW	TOP	$+?%
WTUUP2	PLANE	?&%@£=
WTUUP2	DOUBLE	£#@
GR8	DEAL	?&%@£=
CUL8R	DEAL	?&%@£=
WTUUP2	TOP	$+?%
2MRW	PLANE	#$&!+
GR8	TOP	#$&!+
2MRW	DOUBLE	$+?%
GR8	DEAL	?&%@£=
CUL8R	PLANE	£#@
2MRW	PLANE	?&%@£=
CUL8R	DEAL	£#@
GR8	TOP	$+?%

McWilliam et al. (2009) found that their participants took significantly longer to name the colors when they used textisms (List 1) than when they used real words (List 2) or symbol strings (List 3). Thus, textisms attracted more attention and processing effort than words or symbols strings and this caused color-naming times to increase. These findings suggest (but don't prove) that textisms (at least among the university students they tested) have indeed been absorbed into the language.

HISTORY OF COGNITIVE PSYCHOLOGY

We can date the origins of cognitive psychology to the ancient Greek philosopher Aristotle (384–322 BC), who was perhaps the cleverest person that ever lived. He was interested in several topics relevant to psychology, including imagery and learning (Leahey, 2003). For example, Aristotle argued that people, events, and things tend to be linked and remembered on the basis of three laws of association: contiguity or closeness; similarity; and contrast. For instance, seeing Donna can make us think of Jack for three reasons:

1. We've previously seen Donna and Jack together (law of contiguity).
2. Donna and Jack resemble each other (law of similarity).
3. Donna and Jack are very different (law of contrast).

INTROSPECTION

Aristotle thought that **introspection** (the systematic investigation of one's own thoughts) was the only way of studying thinking. Two thousand years later there was still much enthusiasm for using introspection. Oswald Külpe (1862–1915) founded the Würzburg School, which was dedicated to the use of introspection. Participants focused on a complex stimulus (e.g., a logical problem), after which they reported their conscious thoughts during the task. This revealed that people consciously think about sensations, feelings, images, conscious mental sets, and thoughts.

Introspection is now a much less popular way of studying human cognition than it used to be. Why is that? One problem is that it isn't possible to check the accuracy of the conscious thoughts people claim to have. Külpe argued that people sometimes have "imageless thoughts," whereas another prominent psychologist (E. B Titchener) claimed that *all* thoughts have images. This controversy couldn't be resolved by introspection.

Another major problem with introspection was pointed out even before the Würzburg School had been set up. According to the British scientist Francis Galton (1883), the position of consciousness "appears to be that of a helpless spectator of but a minute fraction of automatic brain work."

Our behavior is often influenced by processes occurring *outside* of consciousness (see also Chapter 3). Nisbett and Wilson (1977) discussed an experiment in which participants were presented with a horizontal array of essentially identical stockings. They decided which pair was best and then indicated *why* they had chosen that particular pair. Participants typically justified their choices by claiming the chosen pair was slightly superior in color or texture. This introspective evidence was well wide of the mark. In fact, most participants chose the right-most pair – their choices were actually influenced

Key Term

Introspection:
a careful examination and description of one's own inner mental thoughts and states.

by relative spatial position. However, even when they were specifically asked whether the position of the selected pair of stockings in the array might have influenced their choice, they vehemently denied it.

Some motivational processes are outside conscious awareness. Pessiglione et al. (2007) gave participants the task of squeezing a handgrip to earn money. Immediately before each trial, the money that could be earned was indicated by a £1 (about $1.50) or 1 pence (about 1.5 cents) coin presented on the screen. The coin was clearly visible or it was subliminal (below the level of conscious awareness). Participants squeezed harder on high-reward trials even when the reward wasn't consciously visible, and there was more activation in brain areas associated with reward processing. Thus, motivation can be influenced by unconscious processes.

In sum, there are four major problems with relying heavily on introspective evidence:

1. We are largely unaware of many of the processes influencing our motivation and behavior.
2. Our reports of our conscious experience may be distorted (deliberately or otherwise). For example, we may pretend to have more positive thoughts about someone than is actually the case.
3. There is a delay between having a conscious experience and reporting its existence. As a result, we may sometimes forget part of our conscious experience before reporting it (Lamme, 2003).
4. We are generally consciously aware of the *outcome* of our cognitive processes rather than those *processes* themselves (Valentine, 1992). For example, what is the name of the person who became American President after George W. Bush? I imagine you rapidly thought of Barack Obama, but without any clear idea of how you produced the right answer.

BEHAVIORISM

The dominant approach to psychology throughout most of the first half of the twentieth century was behaviorism. **Behaviorism** started in the United States in 1913. Its central figure was John Watson (1878–1958), who was determined to make psychology an experimental science. He argued that the best way of achieving that goal was by carrying out well-controlled experiments under laboratory conditions.

According to Watson, psychologists should focus on observable stimuli (aspects of the immediate situation) and observable responses (behavior produced by the participants in an experiment). Learning occurs when an association is formed between a stimulus and a response. Terms referring to mental events can't be verified by reference to observable behavior, and so should be abandoned. Watson (1913, p. 165) wanted behaviorism to be an approach that would "never use the terms consciousness, mental states, mind, content, introspectively verifiable, and the like."

It is helpful in understanding Watson's approach to focus on one of his key assumptions: "The behaviorist ... recognizes no dividing line between man and brute" (Watson, 1913, p. 158). This is an important assumption, because you can't obtain introspective evidence from other species, nor can you study their mental states.

Key Term
Behaviorism: an approach to psychology that emphasizes a rigorous experimental approach and the role of conditioning in learning.

Watson had spent several years prior to 1913 involved in animal research. He found he could conduct proper experiments on other species with no reliance on introspection.

The American psychologist Burrhus Frederic Skinner (1904–1990) was the most influential behaviorist of all. He focused on operant conditioning, a form of learning in which behavior is controlled by its consequences. We learn to produce responses followed by reward or positive reinforcement and to avoid producing responses followed by unpleasant or aversive consequences. Operant conditioning is important, but it fails to account for complex human cognition (e.g., problem solving; reasoning; creativity).

Skinner agreed with Watson that the behaviorists' emphasis on *external* stimuli and responses should be accompanied by a virtual ignoring of *internal* mental and physiological processes. This had bizarre consequences. As Murphy and Kovach (1972) pointed out, "It is for the behaviorist no more intelligible to say that we think with the brain than to say that we walk with the spinal cord."

Not all behaviorists agreed with Watson and Skinner that internal processes and structures should be ignored. A prominent opponent of that position was Tolman (1948). He carried out studies in which rats learned to run through a maze to a goal box containing food. When he blocked off the path the rats had learned to use, they rapidly learned to follow alternative paths leading in the right general direction. This suggested the rats had an internal cognitive map indicating the approximate layout of the maze and were not simply learning a sequence of responses.

Evaluation

- ➕ The behaviorists argued that it was desirable for psychology to become a fully-fledged science.

- ➕ Their claim that the careful observation of behavior in controlled settings under experimental conditions is of fundamental importance is still valid a century later (Fuchs & Milar, 2003).

- ➖ The behaviorists understated the impact of internal factors (e.g., past experience; goals) on behavior. Skinner argued that our behavior is controlled by *current* rewards and punishments. If that were the case, we would be like weather vanes blown about by changes in the rewards and/or punishments in the environment (Bandura, 1977).

- ➖ Most human behavior doesn't simply involve learning to associate certain stimuli with certain responses. For example, when we speak, we generally plan what we are going to say several words ahead of the words we are uttering. This involves complex internal processes that are neither stimuli nor responses.

COGNITIVE PSYCHOLOGY

Cognitive psychology, with its emphasis on understanding *internal* processes and structures, is very different from behaviorism. Indeed, it is common to talk about the "cognitive revolution" that overthrew behaviorism (e.g., Hobbs & Burman, 2009). However, we mustn't exaggerate the differences. Both approaches attached great importance to the use of a scientific approach and the experimental method. In addition, we have seen that some behaviorists (e.g., Tolman) were interested in internal processes. Thus, what happened as behaviorism gave way to cognitive psychology was "rapid, evolutionary change" (Leahey, 1992) rather than a revolutionary change.

It is almost as pointless to ask "When did cognitive psychology start?" as it is to inquire "How long is a piece of string?" The reality is that several psychologists made early contributions to cognitive psychology, but their efforts were mostly unsystematic and uncoordinated.

Many of the pioneers in cognitive psychology focused on memory. For example, Hermann Ebbinghaus (1850–1909) carried out numerous well-controlled studies of forgetting (Zangwill, 2004). He used nonsense syllables (e.g., KEB) designed to lack meaning so that he could obtain a relatively "pure" measure of forgetting. In fact, some meaning can be attached to almost any nonsense syllable (e.g., KEB might remind you of kebab). In spite of that, Ebbinghaus (1885) established that forgetting is especially rapid shortly after learning, with the rate of forgetting decreasing after that (Chapter 5).

Hugo Münsterberg (1863–1916) was interested in eyewitness testimony and wrote a book (*On the Witness Stand*, 1908) about it. In this book he discusses one of the earliest experiments in cognitive psychology. A fake murder was staged during a lecture. A student drew a revolver and a second student rushed at him. Professor Liszt stepped between them and the revolver went off. The students who witnessed this event made many errors in recalling the event, including adding nonexistent elements.

The English psychologist Sir Frederic Bartlett (1886–1969) made an outstanding contribution to memory research (Pickford & Gregory, 2004). In his book *Remembering: An Experimental and Social Study* (1932), Bartlett argued that human memory is an active process. We recall events so as to make them *consistent* with our preexisting knowledge and experience. This will often lead to systematic errors and distortions in memory (see Chapter 9).

Towards the end of the nineteenth century, there was rapid economic development in North America. The construction of a national railroad system meant that people were traveling more and it became increasingly important to improve communication systems. These developments led William Bryan and Noble Harter (1897, 1899) to study learning in Morse code telegraph operators working for Western Union. Not surprisingly, they found that these operators became increasingly efficient at both receiving and sending messages in Morse code. More importantly, the operators' ability to receive messages showed some periods of rapid improvement with other periods of no improvement (plateaus) in between. The operators initially became skilled at identifying individual letters. After that, they required a period of learning before mastering the ability to identify syllables and whole words.

The American William James (1842–1910) was possibly the most influential early contributor to cognitive psychology (Hunter, 2004). His greatest

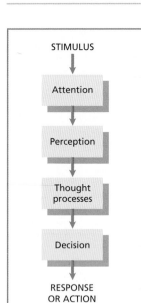

STIMULUS

Attention

Perception

Thought processes

Decision

RESPONSE OR ACTION

Figure 1.1   An early version of the information-processing approach.

contributions came in his book *Principles of Psychology* (1890), which contains numerous fascinating insights into a host of topics including consciousness, attention, emotion, memory, and reasoning. William James argued that we are shaped as individuals by our actions and habits. In his own words, "Sow an action, and you reap a habit; sow a habit, and you reap a character; sow a character, and you reap a destiny" (quoted in Hunter, 2004, p. 493).

The year 1956 was of critical importance in the emergence of cognitive psychology (Thagard, 2005). During this year, several researchers who were to become highly influential cognitive psychologists made major contributions. At a meeting at the Massachusetts Institute of Technology, Noam Chomsky gave a paper on his theory of language, George Miller presented a paper on short-term memory (Miller, 1956), and Newell and Simon discussed their approach to problem solving (Newell et al., 1958). In addition, the first systematic attempt to consider concept formation from a cognitive perspective was reported (Bruner et al., 1956).

Information-processing approach

At one time, most cognitive psychologists subscribed to the information-processing approach. A version of this approach popular about 45 years ago is shown in Figure 1.1. A stimulus (an environmental event such as a problem or a task) is presented. This stimulus causes various internal cognitive processes to occur, which finally lead to the desired response or answer. Processing directly affected by the stimulus input is often described as **bottom-up processing**. It was typically assumed that only one process occurs at any moment in time. This is known as **serial processing** – it means that one process is completed before the next one starts.

We can see more clearly what was involved in the information-processing approach by considering the model of human memory put forward by Richard Atkinson and Richard Shiffrin (1968; see Figure 1.2 and Chapter 4). They argued that we possess a separate sensory store for each of the sense modalities (e.g., vision; hearing).

With our limited processing capacity, there is generally too much information in the sensory stores for us to attend to all of it. Accordingly, we attend to only *some* of the available information, which then proceeds to the short-term store. This store has limited capacity and information doesn't remain in it for long. However, if we rehearse (say over to ourselves) information in the short-term store, some of it will be transferred to the long-term store.

Atkinson and Shiffrin's (1968) multistore model is discussed more fully in Chapter 4. However, three points are worth making here. First, the arrows pointing to the right reveal the importance of bottom-up processing in the

Figure 1.2   The multistore model of memory.

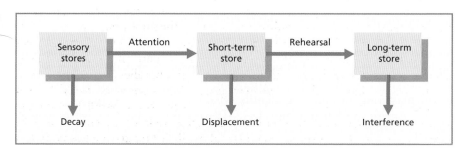

Sensory stores — Attention → Short-term store — Rehearsal → Long-term store

Decay   Displacement   Interference

model. Second, it is assumed that attentional processes determine which fraction of the information available in the sensory stores enters the short-term store. Presumably top-down processes such as our goals and expectations influence what we attend to, but these processes are deemphasized in the model.

Third, let's focus on the notion that information enters the short-term store *before* the long-term store. Suppose you see the word "yacht" and start rehearsing it in the short-term store. How do you know it has an odd pronunciation? You must have obtained its pronunciation from long-term memory *before* rehearsing it. Thus, we seem to need an arrow pointing from the long-term store to the short-term store to explain what is happening. This is another example of top-down processes being deemphasized.

Limitations

The information-processing approach provides a drastic *oversimplification* of a complex reality. It is nearly always the case that processing is not exclusively bottom-up but also involves top-down processing (as we saw with the multistore model). **Top-down processing** is processing influenced by the individual's expectations and knowledge rather than simply by the stimulus itself. Look at the triangle shown in Figure 1.3 and read what it says. Unless you are familiar with the trick, you probably read it as, "Paris in the spring." If so, look again, and you will see the word "the" is repeated. Your expectation that it was the well-known phrase (top-down processing) dominated the information actually available from the stimulus (bottom-up processing).

Figure 1.3 Demonstration of top-down processing.

Most cognition involves bottom-up *and* top-down processing. A very clear demonstration comes from a study by Bruner and Postman (1949), which can be seen on YouTube (Red Spade experiment: Jerome Bruner & Leo Postman). In this study, participants expected to see conventional playing cards presented very briefly. When red spades or clubs were presented, some participants saw the color as brown, purple, or rusty black. There was an almost literal blending of the red color stemming from bottom-up processing and the black color stemming from top-down processing due to the expectation that spades and clubs will be black.

More recent evidence that top-down processes influence color perception comes from Mitterer and de Ruiter (2008). Objects that can be almost any color (e.g., socks) were presented in an ambiguous hue intermediate between yellow and orange. The object was more likely to be perceived as orange when observers had previously seen an "orange" object (e.g., goldfish; carrot) in the same hue than when they had seen a "yellow" object (e.g., lemon; banana) in that hue. Thus, color perception depends in part on top-down processes based on world knowledge.

The traditional information-processing approach was also oversimplified in assuming that processing is necessarily serial. In numerous situations, some of the processes involved in a cognitive task occur at the same time – this is **parallel processing**. As we will see repeatedly in this book, several different brain areas are usually active at the same time when someone performs a complex task. That is what we would expect if most processing is parallel rather than serial.

It is often hard to know whether processing is serial or parallel (or a mixture of the two). However, we are more likely to use parallel processing when performing a much-practiced task than one we have just started to learn (see Chapter 11). For example, someone taking their first driving lesson finds it

Key Terms
Top-down processing: stimulus processing that is determined by expectations, memory, and knowledge rather than directly by the stimulus.
Parallel processing: two or more processes occurring simultaneously; see **serial processing**.

almost impossible to steer accurately and to pay attention to other road users at the same time. In contrast, an experienced driver finds it easy and can even hold a conversation as well.

Section Summary

Introspection

- Introspection was much used to study thinking before the advent of behaviorism. It is limited because many cognitive processes occur below the level of conscious awareness, and conscious reports are sometimes distorted.

Behaviorism

- Behaviorism (dominant in the first half of the twentieth century) emphasized a scientific approach based on observable stimuli and responses. It was limited because it exaggerated the importance of current rewards and punishments as factors influencing behavior and minimized the importance of goals and past experience.

Cognitive psychology

- Cognitive psychology extended behaviorism by focusing on *internal* processes and structures as well as *external* stimuli and responses. There were many early pioneers in cognitive psychology, of whom William James probably had the greatest long-term impact. In the 1950s and 1960s, cognitive psychologists put forward information-processing theories that emphasized bottom-up, serial processes. Such theories were oversimplified, and were gradually replaced by theories that recognized the importance of top-down and parallel processes.

CONTEMPORARY COGNITIVE PSYCHOLOGY

I discuss up-to-date theory and research in cognitive psychology throughout this book. One of cognitive psychology's most distinctive features is the use of several approaches to increase our understanding of human cognition. There are four major approaches, each with its own strengths (see below).

1. *Experimental cognitive psychology:* This approach involves carrying out experiments on healthy individuals (often college students). Behavioral evidence (e.g., participants' level of performance) is used to shed light on internal cognitive processes.
2. *Cognitive neuroscience:* This approach also involves carrying out experiments. However, it extends experimental cognitive psychology by using evidence from brain activity (as well as from behavior) to understand human cognition.
3. *Cognitive neuropsychology:* This approach also involves carrying out experiments. Although the participants are brain-damaged patients, it is hoped the findings will increase our understanding of cognition in healthy individuals as well. Cognitive neuropsychology was originally closely linked to cognitive psychology but has recently also become linked to cognitive neuroscience.

4. *Computational cognitive science:* This approach involves developing computational models based in part on experimental findings to explain human cognition.

Is one of these approaches better than any of the others? The answer is "No." Each approach has its own strengths and weaknesses (see below). As a result, researchers increasingly use two or more of these approaches to shed as much light as possible on the complexities of human cognition. Hence the dividing lines among these four approaches are becoming increasingly blurred.

EXPERIMENTAL COGNITIVE PSYCHOLOGY

For many decades, nearly all research in cognitive psychology involved carrying out experiments on healthy individuals under laboratory conditions. Such experiments are typically tightly controlled and "scientific." Researchers have shown great ingenuity in designing experiments to reveal the processes involved in attention, perception, learning, memory, and so on. As a result, the findings of experimental cognitive psychologists have played a major role in the development and subsequent testing of most theories in cognitive psychology.

Experimental cognitive psychologists typically obtain measures of the speed and accuracy of task performance. They want to use such behavioral measures to draw *inferences* about the internal processes involved in human cognition. Below we consider one example of this kind of approach.

An important phenomenon in cognitive psychology is the Stroop effect (Stroop, 1935). Participants name the colors in which words or letter strings appear. Performance is fast and accurate when words congruent with the colors (e.g., BLUE printed in blue; RED printed in red) or neutral letter strings (e.g., FPRSM) are used. However, participants are much slower when words incongruent with the colors (e.g., BLUE printed in red) are used – this is the **Stroop effect** (MacLeod, 2005).

Why does the Stroop effect occur? We are so familiar with reading words that time-consuming conflict resolution is needed on incongruent trials. However, an additional mechanism is also involved. Kane and Engle (2003) compared performance on incongruent trials when 75% of the total trials were congruent and when 0% were congruent. They argued that it would be much harder to maintain the task goal ("Ignore the word and respond to the color") in the former condition because the correct response could be produced on most trials by simply reading the word. As predicted, the error rate was much higher in the 75% condition than the 0% condition (14% vs. 3%).

We will see the huge contribution experimental cognitive psychology has made to our understanding of human cognition throughout this book. However, a concern is that how people behave in the laboratory may differ from how they behave in everyday life. In other words, laboratory research may be low in **ecological validity** – the extent to which the findings of laboratory studies are applicable to everyday life.

Two points need to be made here. First, it is far better to carry out well-controlled experiments under laboratory conditions than poorly controlled experiments under naturalistic conditions. It is precisely because it is considerably easier for researchers to exercise experimental control in the laboratory that so

Key Terms

Stroop effect:
the finding that naming the colors in which words are printed takes longer when the words are conflicted color words (e.g., the word RED printed in green).

Ecological validity:
the extent to which research findings (especially laboratory ones) can be generalized to the real world.

Key Term
Cognitive neuroscience: an approach that aims to understand human cognition by combining information from brain activity and behavior.

much research is laboratory-based. Second, more and more research in cognitive psychology has direct real-world applicability. Such research is highlighted in nearly every chapter of this book.

COGNITIVE NEUROSCIENCE

Much can be discovered about human cognition by obtaining behavioral evidence. However, what is exciting about **cognitive neuroscience** is that it provides us with information about brain activity during performance of cognitive tasks as well as behavioral evidence. As we will see, much research in cognitive neuroscience involves the use of various brain-imaging techniques while participants perform a cognitive task.

To understand research involving functional neuroimaging, we must consider how the brain is organized and how the different areas are described. There are various ways of describing specific brain areas. Below we will discuss two of the main ones.

First, the cerebral cortex is divided into four main divisions or lobes (see Figure 1.4). There are four lobes in each brain hemisphere: frontal, parietal, temporal, and occipital. The frontal lobes are divided from the parietal lobes by the central sulcus (sulcus means furrow or groove), the lateral fissure separates the temporal lobes from the parietal and frontal lobes, and the parieto-occipital sulcus and pre-occipital notch divide the occipital lobes from the parietal and temporal lobes. The main gyri (or ridges; gyrus is the singular) within the cerebral cortex are shown in Figure 1.4.

Researchers use various terms to describe more precisely the brain area(s) activated during the performance of a given task:

- *dorsal:* superior or towards the top
- *ventral:* inferior or toward the bottom
- *anterior:* toward the front
- *posterior:* toward the back
- *lateral:* situated at the side
- *medial:* situated in the middle.

Figure 1.4   The four lobes, or divisions, of the cerebral cortex in the left hemisphere.

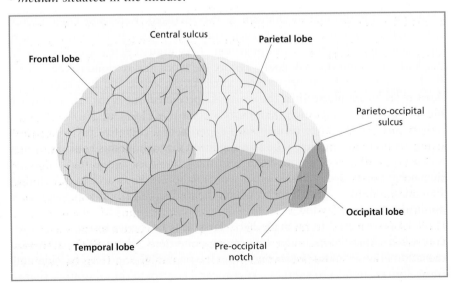

Central sulcus

Parietal lobe

Frontal lobe

Parieto-occipital sulcus

Occipital lobe

Temporal lobe

Pre-occipital notch

Second, the German neurologist Korbinian Brodmann (1868–1918) produced a map of the brain based on variations in the cellular structure of the tissues (see Figure 1.5). Many (but not all) of the areas identified by Brodmann correspond to functionally distinct areas. We will often refer to areas such as BA17, which simply means Brodmann Area 17.

Dramatic technological advances in recent years mean we now have many ways of obtaining detailed information about what the brain is doing when we perform numerous tasks. We can work out *where* and *when* in the brain activity occurs.

Why is such information useful? First, it allows us to work out the order in which different parts of the brain become active when someone is performing a task. This may provide valuable insights into the processes involved in task performance.

Second, it allows us to find out whether two tasks involve the same parts of the brain in the same way, or whether there are important differences. For example, there has been some controversy as to whether the processes involved in recognizing faces are the same as those involved in recognizing objects. Evidence from brain-imaging studies indicates that somewhat different brain areas are involved, which strongly suggests that the processes used in face recognition differ slightly from those used in object recognition.

Many techniques are used to study patterns of brain activity when someone is performing a task. These techniques vary in spatial resolution (precision with which the area of brain activity can be measured) and temporal resolution (precision with which the timing of brain activity can be assessed). Below we will consider briefly some of the main ones.

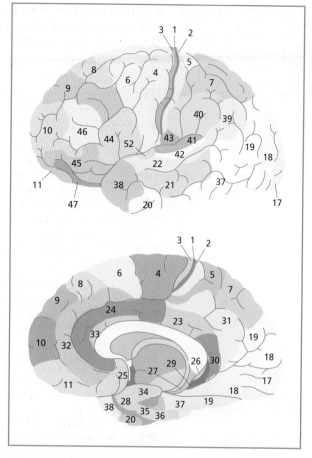

Figure 1.5   The Brodmann areas of the brain on the lateral (top) and medial (bottom) surfaces.

Event-related potentials

The electroencephalogram (EEG) is based on recordings of electrical brain activity measured at the surface of the scalp. Very small changes in electrical activity within the brain are picked up by scalp electrodes. However, spontaneous or background brain activity sometimes obscures the impact of stimulus processing on the EEG recording. This problem can be solved by presenting the same stimulus several times. After that, the segment of EEG following each stimulus is extracted and lined up with respect to the time of stimulus onset. These EEG segments are then simply averaged to produce a single waveform. This method produces **event-related potentials** (ERPs) from EEG recordings and allows us to distinguish genuine effects of stimulation from background brain activity.

Key Term
Event-related potentials (ERPs): the pattern of electroencephalograph (EEG) activity obtained by averaging the brain responses to the same stimulus (or similar stimuli) presented repeatedly.

ERPs have poor spatial resolution but their temporal resolution is excellent. Indeed, they can often indicate when a given process occurred to within a few milliseconds. However, there are limitations with the use of ERPs. Remember that a given stimulus needs to be presented several times in order to produce consistent ERPs. That works well when participants process the stimulus in the same way on each trial, but is inappropriate when processing differs over trials. For example, it may take some time to work out the anagram HCRIA the first time you see it, but is likely to involve far less processing on subsequent trials.

Positron emission tomography (PET)

Positron emission tomography (PET) is based on the detection of positrons (the atomic particles emitted by some radioactive substances). Radioactively labeled water (the tracer) is injected into the body, and rapidly gathers in the brain's blood vessels. When part of the cortex becomes active, the labeled water moves rapidly to that place. A scanning device next measures the positrons emitted from the radioactive water. A computer then translates this information into pictures of the activity levels in different brain regions. It sounds dangerous to inject a radioactive substance. However, tiny amounts of radioactivity are involved, and the tracer has a half-life of only 2 min.

PET has reasonable spatial resolution, in that any active area within the brain can be located to within 5–10 mm. However, it suffers from various limitations. First, PET scans indicate the amount of activity in each region of the brain over a period of 30–60 s. Thus, PET has very poor temporal resolution.

Second, PET is an invasive technique because participants are injected with radioactively labeled water. This makes it unacceptable to some potential participants.

Functional magnetic resonance imaging (fMRI)

In magnetic resonance imaging (MRI), radio waves are used to excite atoms in the brain. This produces magnetic changes detected by a very large magnet (weighing up to 11 t) surrounding the patient. These changes are then interpreted by a computer and turned into a very precise three-dimensional picture. MRI scans can be obtained from numerous different angles but only tell us about the *structure* of the brain rather than about its *functions*.

Cognitive neuroscientists are generally more interested in brain functions than brain structure. Happily, MRI technology can provide functional information in the form of functional magnetic resonance imaging (fMRI). What is measured in fMRI is based on assessing brain areas in which there is an accumulation of oxygenated red blood cells suggestive of activity. Technically, this is the BOLD (blood oxygen-level-dependent contrast) signal. Changes in the BOLD signal produced by increased neural activity take some time, so the temporal resolution of fMRI is about 2 or 3 s. However, its spatial resolution is very good (approximately 1 mm). Since the temporal and spatial resolutions of fMRI are both much better than those of PET, fMRI has largely superseded PET.

Magneto-encephalography (MEG)

Magneto-encephalography (MEG) involves using a superconducting quantum interference device (SQUID) to measure the magnetic fields produced by electrical brain activity. The technology is complex because the size of the magnetic field

---

Key Terms

Positron emission tomography (PET):
a brain-scanning technique based on the detection of positrons; it has reasonable spatial resolution but poor temporal resolution.

Functional magnetic resonance imaging (fMRI):
a brain-imaging technique based on imaging blood oxygenation using an MRI scanner; it has very good spatial resolution and reasonable temporal resolution.

Magneto-encephalography (MEG):
a noninvasive brain-scanning technique based on recording the magnetic fields generated by brain activity; it has excellent temporal resolution and reasonably good spatial resolution.

created by the brain is extremely small relative to the earth's magnetic field. However, MEG has excellent temporal resolution (at the millisecond level) and its spatial resolution can be reasonably good. It is very expensive and one-third of participants in one study (Cooke et al., 2007) reported that the experience was "a bit upsetting." The same proportion reported side-effects such as muscle aches and headaches.

Brain imaging in practice

We can see the potential value of brain imaging by considering concrete examples of its use in research. First, cognitive neuroscientists are starting to work out what we are looking at just by considering our brain activity. For example, Kay et al. (2008) presented two individuals with 120 natural images and fMRI was used to assess patterns of brain activity. The fMRI data permitted correct identification of the image being viewed on 92% of the trials for one participant and on 72% of trials for the other. This is remarkable given that chance performance would be 1/120 or 0.8%!

A similar approach also using fMRI has been used with a visual imagery task (Reddy et al., 2010). Participants formed visual images of objects belonging to four categories (food, tools, faces, buildings). The visual images were correctly categorized from fMRI data on 50% of trials (chance performance = 25%).

Why is research on "brain reading" important? It may prove very useful for identifying what people are dreaming or thinking about. More generally, it can reveal our true feelings about other people. For example, consider the emotion of love and the expression, "Love hurts." Chen et al. (2010) showed participants animated stimuli of hands or feet in painful situations and asked them to imagine it was their romantic partner, a stranger, or themselves in those situations. The brain activation when it was themselves in those situations was much more similar to the brain activation when it was their loved one than when it was a stranger. Thus, love makes us experience pain in a loved one similarly to experiencing ourselves in pain.

Zeki and Romaya (2010) asked people to look at photographs of someone they were deeply in love with as well as photographs of good friends of the same sex as their partner. Brain areas including the insula, the anterior cingulate, and the hypothalamus were more activated when the photograph was of the loved one rather than a friend. The pattern of activation was very similar in men and women and for homosexual as well as heterosexual relationships. This suggests that the same "love network" is involved in all cases.

Zeki and Romaya (2010) also found that love was associated with reduced activation in parts of the prefrontal cortex involved in judgment. This suggests that "love is blind," leading us to be less judgmental about those we love.

Evaluation

Brain-imaging techniques (and ERPs) provide useful information about the timing and location of brain activation during performance of an enormous range of cognitive tasks. Such information (when combined with behavioral evidence) has proved of much value in increasing our understanding of human cognition. We will consider numerous examples in the course of this book. However, brain-imaging techniques don't provide a magical solution. The crucial point is that it is often hard to *interpret* the findings from brain-imaging studies. We will consider *three* reasons why that is the case.

First, when researchers argue that a given brain region is active during the performance of a task, they mean it is active relative to some baseline. What is an appropriate baseline? We might argue that the resting state (e.g., participant sits with his/her eyes shut) is a suitable baseline condition. However, the brain is very active even in the resting state and performing a task increases brain activity by 5% or less. Indeed, the brain is very active even when someone is in a coma, under anesthesia, or in slow-wave sleep (Boly et al., 2008). Thus, most brain activity we observe reflects basic brain functioning.

The common expectation is that task performance produces *increased* brain activity reflecting task demands. In fact, however, there is often *decreased* brain activity in some brain regions (Raichle & Snyder, 2007). Decreased activity is especially likely when the current task requires considerable effort, and so there is reduced ability to engage in nontask processing. The take-home message is that brain functioning is much more complex than often assumed.

Second, brain-imaging techniques indicate there are *associations* between patterns of brain activation and behavior. For example, performance on a reasoning task may be associated with activation of the prefrontal cortex at the front of the brain. Such associations are hard to interpret. We can't be certain that involvement of the prefrontal cortex is necessary or essential for performance of the task. Perhaps anxiety caused by thoughts of possible failure on the reasoning task causes activation of that brain area.

Third, most brain-imaging research is based on the assumption of **functional specialization** – the notion that each brain region is specialized for a different function. In fact, matters are often much more complex. The performance of a given task is often associated with activity in several different brain regions, and this activity is often integrated and coordinated. It is harder to identify brain networks involving coordinated brain activity than to pinpoint specific regions especially active during task performance (Ramsey et al., 2010).

COGNITIVE NEUROPSYCHOLOGY

Sadly, millions of people around the world have a **lesion** – structural damage to the brain caused by injury or disease. As a result, they have problems with cognitive processing. What do you think of the idea of studying such brain-damaged patients in order to understand normal human cognition? It doesn't sound very promising, does it? However, I will try to convince you of the value of this approach, which is generally known as cognitive neuropsychology.

I had assumed for several years that whether or not I had broadband access on my computer at home depended solely on the strength of the signal reaching it. However, one day my gray cat Lulu flopped out over the entire keyboard, causing me to lose broadband access. This malfunction led me to the discovery that pressing two specific keys at the same time (which Lulu had managed to do) switched off broadband access. Thus, I learned something useful about the workings of my computer only after it started malfunctioning.

Numerous fascinating conditions produced by brain damage are considered in this book. Here I will mention just two. First, there is blindsight, a puzzling condition discussed more fully in Chapter 2. Patients with blindsight deny they can see objects presented to the "blind" parts of their visual field, and so we might assume they have *no* perceptual abilities in those areas. However, their performance is reasonably good when they guess whether a stimulus is in one of

---

Key Terms

Functional specialization:
the assumption (only partially correct) that cognitive functions (e.g., color processing; face processing) occur in specific brain regions.

Lesion:
a structural alteration within the brain caused by disease or injury.

two locations, or whether a stimulus is present or absent! Thus, various visual processes can operate with some efficiency in the absence of any conscious experience of seeing.

Second, there is prosopagnosia or face blindness (see Chapter 2 for a detailed account). Patients with this condition suffer much embarrassment because they can't recognize faces. As a result, they are in constant danger of greeting total strangers as long-lost friends or ignoring close friends. Intriguingly, the perceptual impairment is not general, and so the problem is *not* simply one of poor eyesight. Prosopagnosics are reasonably good at recognizing most objects other than faces, suggesting that part of the brain is specialized for face recognition.

Major assumptions

Here we discuss some of the main theoretical assumptions of cognitive neuropsychology (Coltheart, 2001). One such assumption is that of **modularity**, meaning that the cognitive system consists of numerous modules or processors operating relatively independently of each other. It is assumed these modules respond to only *one* particular class of stimuli. For example, there may be a face-recognition module responding only when a face is presented.

There is some support for the modularity assumption. For example, consider the processing of visual stimuli. As we will see in Chapter 2, different aspects of visual stimuli (e.g., color; form; motion) are processed in different, specific brain areas.

Another important assumption is that the way the modules or processors are organized is very similar across people. If this assumption is correct, then we can generalize the information obtained from one brain-damaged patient to draw conclusions about the organization of modules in other people. If the assumption is incorrect, then the findings from a single brain-damaged patient won't generalize.

A final important assumption is that of subtractivity. The basic idea is that brain damage impairs one or more modules, but can't lead to the development of any new ones. As a result, the study of brain-damaged patients with damage to module X can provide very useful information about that module's role in healthy human cognition.

One way cognitive neuropsychologists understand how the cognitive system works is by searching for dissociations. A **dissociation** occurs when a patient performs at the same level as healthy individuals on one task but is severely impaired on a second one. For example, patients with amnesia (a condition associated with severe memory problems) perform very poorly on tasks involving long-term memory. However, they perform as well as healthy individuals on tasks involving short-term memory (see Chapter 5).

The above findings suggest that long-term memory and short-term memory involve separate modules. Alternatively, it could be argued that brain damage reduces the ability to perform difficult (but not easy) tasks, and that long-term memory tasks are more difficult than short-term memory ones. However, researchers have found other patients with very poor performance on most short-term memory tasks but intact long-term memory (Chapter 5). This gives us a **double dissociation**: Some patients perform at the healthy level on task X but are impaired on task Y, with others showing the opposite pattern. This double dissociation provides strong evidence that there are separate short-term and long-term memory systems.

Key Terms

Modularity:
the assumption that the cognitive system consists of several fairly independent or separate modules or processors, each of which is specialized for a given type of processing (e.g., face processing).

Dissociation:
as applied to brain-damaged patients, intact performance on one task but severely impaired performance on a different task.

Double dissociation:
the finding that some individuals (often brain-damaged) have intact performance on one task but poor performance on another task, whereas other individuals exhibit the opposite pattern.

An important issue cognitive neuropsychologists have addressed is that of whether to focus on individuals or groups in their research. In research on healthy individuals, we can have more confidence in our findings if they are based on fairly large groups of participants. However, the group-based approach is problematical when applied to brain-damaged patients because patients with apparently the same condition typically differ in the pattern of impairment. Indeed, every patient can be regarded as unique just as snowflakes are different from each other (Caramazza & Coltheart, 2006). As a result, group data can be confusing and very hard to interpret.

Transcranial magnetic stimulation (TMS)

The ideal kind of lesion for researchers seeking to understand human cognition would, first, be small and would affect only *one* module. Second, it would last only briefly so that it was easy to compare performance with that module functioning and not functioning. Third, the researcher should be able to decide precisely *which* brain area was to receive a brief lesion. It might sound impossible to achieve this ideal, but the technique we are about to discuss comes close to doing so. It does *not* involve brain-damaged patients. However, it resembles traditional cognitive neuropsychology in that the emphasis is on patterns of performance resulting from inactivation of various brain areas.

In **transcranial magnetic stimulation (TMS)**, a coil (often in the shape of a figure of eight) is placed close to the participant's head. Then, a very brief (less than 1 ms) but large magnetic pulse of current is run through it. This causes a short-lived magnetic field producing electrical stimulation of the brain. This generally leads to inhibited processing activity in the affected area (often about 1 cm³ in extent). In practice, several magnetic pulses are usually administered in a fairly short period of time; this is repetitive transcranial magnetic stimulation (rTMS).

Why are TMS and rTMS useful? If TMS applied to a particular brain area leads to impaired task performance, we can conclude that brain area is necessary for task performance. Conversely, if TMS has *no* effect on task performance, then the brain area affected by it isn't needed to perform the task effectively. What is most exciting about TMS is that it can reveal that activity in a particular brain area is *necessary* for normal levels of performance on some task.

A limitation with TMS is that it isn't clear exactly how much cortical area it affects or what its effects are on the brain. It mostly *reduces* activation in the brain areas affected (inhibitory effect), which fits with the notion that its effects resemble those of a temporary lesion. However, TMS can also *increase* brain activation (excitatory effect), especially shortly after administration (Bolognini & Ro, 2010). In either case, it is assumed that disruptive effects of TMS on a cognitive task indicate that the brain area affected is required for effective performance of that task (Ziemann, 2010).

Evaluation

➕ Cognitive neuropsychology and TMS both permit the identification of brain areas necessary for the performance of a given task (Fellows et al., 2005).

➕ TMS is a flexible technique that can be used to disrupt activity of numerous brain areas.

+ Double dissociations with brain-damaged patients provide strong evidence for various major processing modules.

− It would be relatively easy to interpret findings from patients if the brain damage were limited to a *single* module. In fact, however, brain damage often affects several modules, which complicates the interpretation of findings.

− TMS can only be applied to surface structures of the brain and it is hard to know how much of the brain is affected.

− The effects of TMS on the brain are complex. It generally produces inhibitory effects but can also produce excitatory effects.

COMPUTATIONAL COGNITIVE SCIENCE

Another way to study cognition is by constructing artificial systems doing some of the same things as brains – this is computational cognitive science. Let's start by distinguishing between computational modeling and artificial intelligence. **Computational modeling** involves programming computers to model (or mimic) some aspects of human cognitive functioning. In contrast, artificial intelligence involves constructing computer systems that produce intelligent outcomes, but the processes involved are typically very different from those used by humans.

Artificial intelligence was used to construct a chess program known as Deep Blue that in 1997 beat the then World Champion, Garry Kasparov, in the second of two matches. It did so by considering 200 million chess positions per second, which is radically different from the approach adopted by human chess players.

I will focus on computational modeling rather than artificial intelligence because it is of more direct relevance to understanding human cognition. My coverage of computational modeling will be fairly brief for two main reasons. First, computational models tend to be complex, and so it is only feasible to provide some of the flavor of such models in this book. Second, the computational cognitive science approach (with several outstanding exceptions) has probably contributed rather less to our understanding of human cognition than the three other approaches I have already discussed.

Computational cognitive scientists often rely heavily on one or more previous relevant theories or models when developing their own computational models. What is the point of taking an existing theory and implementing it as a program? One important reason is that theories only expressed verbally often contain hidden assumptions or vague terms. This is much less likely to happen with a computer program because *all* the details need to be spelled out.

Let's consider a concrete example of an influential model that was expressed verbally and omitted many details. As discussed earlier, Atkinson and Shiffrin (1968) put forward a model of memory in which it was assumed that rehearsal (saying to-be-learned material to oneself) leads to the long-term storage of the information being rehearsed. More specifically, the more times a word is rehearsed, the better it is remembered over time (see Chapter 4).

Key Term

Computational modeling:
this involves constructing computer programs that will simulate or mimic some aspects of human cognitive functioning.

Atkinson and Shiffrin's model was used to account for findings from studies in which a list of words was presented. This was followed by the participants writing down as many list words as possible in any order. If we wanted to make precise predictions, we would need to know the following (at least): How long does it take to rehearse one word? How many words are rehearsed together? How rapidly does information about a rehearsed word accumulate in long-term memory? Atkinson and Shiffrin (1968) didn't provide answers to most of these questions. However, they would need to be answered to produce an adequate computer model.

Most theories within cognitive psychology are relatively specific in their application. For example, there are theories concerned with short-term memory (see Chapter 4) or with drawing inferences in language comprehension (see Chapter 8). It would be of enormous value to develop broad theories of cognition revealing the overall structure of the human cognitive system. Some progress in this direction has been made by computational cognitive scientists as discussed below.

John Anderson has produced several versions of a broad-based theoretical approach – his Adaptive Control of Thought – Rational (ACT-R) model. The most recent version was put forward by Anderson et al. (2008). It is based on the assumption that the cognitive system consists of several modules, each performing its own specialized operations fairly independently of the other modules. Here are four of the main modules, each of which can be used across numerous tasks:

1. *Retrieval module:* Maintains the retrieval cues needed to access stored information.
2. *Goal module:* Keeps track of an individual's intentions and controls information processing.
3. *Imaginal module:* Changes problem representations to facilitate problem solution.
4. *Procedural module:* Uses various rules to determine what action will be taken next; it also communicates with the other modules.

What is especially exciting about Anderson et al.'s (2008) version of ACT-R is that it combines computational cognitive science with cognitive neuroscience. What that means in practice is that the brain areas associated with each module are identified (see Figure 1.6).

Connectionism

Over the past 30 years or so, there has been much interest in connectionist networks or parallel distributed processing (PDP) models. This interest started with books by Rumelhart et al. (1986) and by McClelland et al. (1986). **Connectionist networks** make use of elementary units or nodes connected together in various structures or layers.

We will focus here on *two* key features of many connectionist networks. First, in contrast to many other kinds of computational models, connectionist networks show evidence of learning. One way this learning occurs is by backward propagation of errors. Back-propagation is a learning mechanism in which the responses produced by a connectionist network are compared

Key Term

Connectionist networks: these consist of units or nodes that are connected in various layers with no direct connection from stimulus to response.

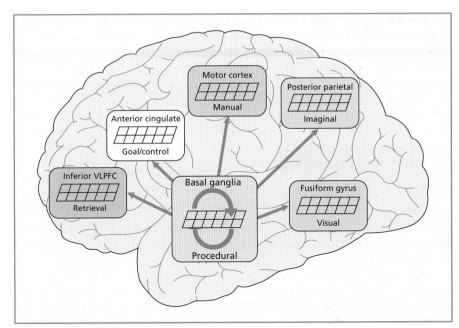

Figure 1.6 The main modules of the ACT-R (Adaptive Control of Thought – Rational) cognitive architecture with their locations within the brain. VLPFC = ventrolateral prefrontal cortex. Reprinted from Anderson et al. (2008), Copyright © 2008, with permission from Elsevier.

with the correct ones. This feedback is used to improve the accuracy of the network's subsequent responses.

Sejnowski and Rosenberg (1987) produced a connectionist network called NETtalk. It was given 50,000 trials to learn the spelling–sound relationships of a set of 1000 words. After this training, NETtalk achieved 95% success in identifying the sounds of the words on which it had been trained. It was also 77% correct on a further 20,000 words. This is fairly impressive. However, the 50,000 trials it needed indicate that NETtalk learns more slowly than the average child!

Second, most theories in cognitive psychology are based on the assumption that knowledge (e.g., about a word or concept) is represented in a given location. In contrast, several connectionist models (e.g., the parallel distributed processing approach of Rumelhart et al., 1986) are based on the assumption that knowledge is represented in a *distributed* way throughout the network. It has sometimes been claimed that the structure of such connectionist networks resembles the organization of neurons in the brain. However, this has been disputed. Each cortical neuron is connected to only 3% of the neurons in the surrounding square millimeter of cortex. In contrast, it is assumed in most connectionist networks that the basic units are much more interconnected.

There are some problems with the assumption that concept representations are distributed within the brain. Suppose you were presented with two words at the same time. That would cause numerous units or nodes to become activated, making it hard (or even impossible) to decide which units or nodes belonged to which word (Bowers, 2002).

There is also evidence that much information is stored in a given location in the brain (Bowers, 2009). For example, Quiroga et al. (2005) discovered a neuron in the temporal lobe that responded strongly when pictures of the actress Jennifer Aniston were presented. However, it didn't respond when pictures of other famous people were presented. These findings don't rule out the possibility that much of our knowledge of Jennifer Aniston is distributed within the brain.

Some connectionist models assume there is *local* rather than distributed representation of knowledge. We will encounter some such models in the course of this book. Examples include the reading model of Coltheart et al. (2001; see Chapter 9) and the model of speech production put forward by Dell (1986; see Chapter 10).

Evaluation

➕ The greatest strength of computational models is that the underlying theoretical assumptions are spelled out with precision. This is typically *not* the case with traditional theories expressed purely in verbal terms.

➕ Some computational models (e.g., ACT-R; Anderson et al., 2008) are much more comprehensive in scope than most traditional noncomputational models and theories.

➕ The combining of computational cognitive science and cognitive neuroscience (e.g., ACT-R, Anderson et al., 2008) is an exciting development.

➕ It is assumed within the connectionist approach that human cognition involves considerable parallel processing. That assumption is supported by brain-imaging data which generally indicate that several brain areas are active at any given time.

➖ Many computational models don't make new predictions and have limited applicability (Anderson & Lebiere, 2003).

➖ Computational models deemphasize motivational and emotional factors. As the British psychologist Stewart Sutherland said jokingly, he would believe that computers are like humans if one tried to run away with his wife.

COMBINING APPROACHES

We can see the usefulness of combining information from experimental cognitive psychology, cognitive neuroscience, and cognitive neuropsychology by considering a concrete example. For many years, there has been controversy concerning the relationship between visual perception and visual imagery (see Chapter 2 for a detailed discussion). Stephen Kosslyn and his colleagues (e.g., Kosslyn & Thompson, 2003) argue that visual imagery typically involves the same processes as visual perception. In contrast, Pylyshyn (e.g., 2003) argues that visual imagery doesn't involve the same processes as visual perception, but instead depends on abstract forms of thinking and knowledge.

If Kosslyn is right, we can make three major predictions. First, people should scan visual images in a similar way to visual arrays (behavioral evidence). Second, the brain areas activated during visual imagery should overlap considerably with those activated during visual perception (brain-imaging evidence). Third, brain-damaged patients with severely impaired visual perception should also have impaired visual imagery, and vice versa (cognitive neuropsychological evidence).

Borst and Kosslyn (2008) compared visual perception with visual imagery. In the perception condition, participants scanned over dots visible in front of them. In the imagery condition, they scanned over dots they imagined. As the distance to be scanned increased, there was a similar increase in scanning time in the two conditions.

The early stages of visual perception involve regions in the occipital area at the back of the brain (BA17 and BA18). If visual imagery tasks produce activation in BA17 and BA18, Kosslyn's theoretical approach receives support but Pylyshyn's does not. In fact, visual imagery is often associated with much activation in BA17 and BA18 (Kosslyn & Thompson, 2003). More generally, visual imagery is typically associated with activation in about two-thirds of the brain areas activated during visual perception (Kosslyn, 2004).

The notion that visual imagery involves many of the same processes as visual perception can also be tested by using repeated transcranial magnetic stimulation (rTMS). If BA17 is necessary for visual imagery, then magnetic stimulation applied to it should impair performance on a visual imagery task. Precisely that finding was reported by Kosslyn et al. (1999).

Many brain-damaged patients with impaired visual imagery also have impaired visual perception, and vice versa (Bartolomeo, 2002). Such patients provide support for Kosslyn's theory. However, other patients have very poor visual imagery but essentially intact visual perception, or impaired visual perception but good visual imagery (Bartolomeo, 2008).

In sum, three different kinds of evidence all suggest there are major similarities between visual perception and visual imagery. The totality of the evidence provides much more support for Kosslyn's theory than could be obtained from one kind of evidence on its own. The evidence from brain-damaged patients suggests there are also important differences between perception and imagery. We can use behavioral and brain-imaging evidence to identify those differences more clearly (see Chapter 2).

COMBINING FINDINGS

The research literature in psychology consists of literally millions of experiments and studies (as textbook writers discover to their cost!). There are often hundreds of published articles on very narrow and specific research topics. How can we make sense of the multitude of findings? An increasingly influential answer is to use meta-analyses. A **meta-analysis** involves combining the data from a large number of similar studies into one very large analysis. Numerous meta-analyses are discussed throughout this book because they have the great advantage of providing a coherent overall picture of research on any given topic.

What are the potential problems with meta-analyses? Sharpe (1997) identified three:

1. The "Apples and Oranges" problem: Studies that aren't very similar to each other may nevertheless be included within a single meta-analysis.
2. The "File Drawer" problem: It is generally harder for researchers to publish studies with nonsignificant findings. Since meta-analyses often ignore unpublished findings, the studies included may not be representative of the studies on a given topic.

Key Term
Meta-analysis: a form of statistical analysis based on combining the findings from numerous studies on a given issue.

3. The "Garbage in–Garbage out" problem: Many psychologists carrying out meta-analyses include all the relevant studies they can find. This means that very poor and inadequate studies are often included along with high-quality ones.

Note that the above three problems are identified as *potential* problems. Cognitive psychologists and neuroscientists have become increasingly sophisticated in the ways they carry out meta-analyses, as a result of which there are now fewer problems than in the past. The "Apples and Oranges" and "Garbage in–Garbage out" problems can be greatly reduced by setting up precise criteria that have to be met for any given study to be included in the meta-analysis. There are mechanisms for estimating the extent of any "File Drawer" problem. For example, it can be reduced by asking researchers in the area of the meta-analysis to supply their unpublished data.

Section Summary

Experimental cognitive psychology

- Experimental cognitive psychologists carry out well-controlled laboratory studies on healthy individuals. They use behavioral measures to draw inferences about the internal processes involved in cognition. Some of this research possesses only limited ecological validity.

Cognitive neuroscience

- Much research in cognitive neuroscience involves assessing brain activity as well as behavior during task performance. Various techniques (e.g., PET; fMRI) allow us to work out *where* and *when* in the brain activity is occurring. These techniques reveal associations between patterns of brain activity and behavior, but don't establish that any given brain area is *essential* for task performance.

Cognitive neuropsychology

- Cognitive neuropsychology involves studying the performance of brain-damaged patients on cognitive tasks to increase our understanding of cognition in healthy individuals. Strong evidence for the existence of separate modules or processors comes from double dissociations – some patients are impaired on task X but not task Y, and others show the opposite pattern. Brain damage is often so extensive that it is hard to interpret the findings. However, it is possible to disrupt the functioning of a small brain area very briefly using transcranial magnetic stimulation.

Computational cognitive science

- Computational modeling has been used to develop explicit models of human cognition including cognitive architectures. Connectionist models are able to learn and are based on the assumption that there is considerable parallel processing. Computational models sometimes fail to generate new predictions.

Combining approaches

- It is valuable to combine information from different approaches. For example, converging evidence from experimental cognitive psychology, cognitive neuroscience, and cognitive neuropsychology indicates there are major similarities between visual perception and visual imagery.

> **Combining findings**
> • It is possible to make more coherent sense of the large research literature by carrying out meta-analyses combining numerous findings in a single statistical analysis. Meta-analyses can be misleading because of the Apples and Oranges, File Drawer, and Garbage in–Garbage out problems. However, all these problems can be reduced or eliminated.

STRUCTURE OF THE BOOK

Human cognition involves numerous different processes, most of which interact with each other in complex ways. The existence of such complex interactions poses a challenge for textbook writers. For example, Chapters 8 and 9 in this book are devoted to language, but it would be ludicrous to argue that language is totally irrelevant to the processes discussed in the other chapters. Much of the information we learn and remember is language-based, and language is heavily involved in most of our thinking and reasoning. It is nevertheless the case that only the topics considered in the language chapters focus *directly* on attempts to understand the nature of language itself.

CHAPTER BY CHAPTER

Chapter 2 is concerned with perception and especially with the processes that enable us to make sense of the visual and auditory stimuli we encounter. Chapter 3 is concerned with attention and consciousness, which both share close links with perception. What we perceive and are consciously aware of at any given moment tends to be those aspects of the environment to which we are directing our attention. Chapter 3 also focuses on multitasking, which has become increasingly important in our 24/7 lifestyles.

Memory is of vital importance within human cognition. Without memory, we wouldn't be able to make any sense of our environment, to use language, or to engage in problem solving and reasoning. More generally, we wouldn't benefit from experience. Chapters 4, 5, and 6 are devoted to human memory. Chapter 4 focuses on short-term memory, which involves retaining information for a few seconds. Short-term memory is essential to us in several ways. It allows us to retain information about some aspects of a problem while focusing on other aspects. It also allows us to remember what a speaker said at the start of a sentence as he/she moves toward the end of it.

Long-term memory is the subject matter of Chapter 5. Our long-term memories are remarkably diverse. They encompass personal memories of events in which we have been involved, general knowledge, and knowledge of how to perform many skills. Chapter 6 is concerned with everyday memory. This includes our autobiographical memories for the important events of our lives, eyewitness testimony, and our ability to remember to perform actions (e.g., meeting a friend) at the appropriate time.

Chapter 7 is concerned with general knowledge. We use semantic memory to store a huge amount of information about the world, and the ways such information is stored are discussed in detail.

Chapter 8 focuses on our understanding of language and deals with both written and spoken language. Language comprehension is of crucial importance in everyday life, and the surprisingly complex processes involved are dealt with in this chapter.

Chapter 9 is concerned with language production. It covers speech production and writing, both of which are designed for communication with others. As we will see, much can be learned about the processes underlying speech production by considering the kinds of errors made by speakers.

Chapter 10 has problem solving and expertise as its central focus. The issues discussed include the processes we use to solve complex problems, the nature of scientific discovery, and what is involved in developing a high level of expertise.

Chapter 11 is devoted to decision making and reasoning, both of which are of major importance in our everyday lives. A common theme is that people surprisingly often make use of simple rules of thumb when engaged in decision making or reasoning.

Chapter 12 deals with cognition and emotion. How we interpret the present situation helps to determine our emotional state. In addition, our current emotional state or mood (e.g., anxious; depressed; happy) has systematic effects on memory, judgment, decision making, and reasoning.

In sum, this book covers all the main areas within human cognition, with an emphasis on the everyday relevance of the topics discussed. Throughout the book, I will use information from behavioral research, brain-imaging research, and research on brain-damaged patients to try to build up a reasonably complete understanding of human cognition.

Essay Questions

1. What are the major highlights in the development of cognitive psychology?
2. Why is the information-processing approach of the 1960s no longer highly regarded?
3. Describe the major approaches to understanding human cognition.
4. Why has there been a dramatic increase in research within cognitive neuroscience? What are the limitations with this approach?

Further Reading

- Cacioppo, J. T., Berntson, G. G., & Nusbaum, H. C. (2008). Neuroimaging as a new tool in the toolbox of psychological science. *Current Directions in Psychological Science, 17*, 62–67. This article provides an overview of brain-imaging research and introduces a special issue devoted to that area.
- Eysenck, M. W., & Keane, M. T. (2010). *Cognitive psychology: A student's handbook* (6th ed.). New York, NY: Psychology Press. Chapter 1 of this textbook contains a detailed account of the major approaches to human cognition.
- Gazzaniga, M. S., Ivry, R. B., & Mangun, G. R. (2009). *Cognitive neuroscience: The biology of the mind* (3rd ed.). Michael Gazzaniga and his coauthors provide a comprehensive and up-to-date account of research in cognitive neuroscience.
- Leahey, T. H. (2003). Cognition and learning. In D. F. Freedheim (Ed.), *Handbook of psychology, Vol. 1: The history of psychology* (pp. 109–133). Hoboken, NJ: Wiley. The fascinating history of the development of cognitive psychology is described in detail in this chapter.
- Patterson, K., & Plaut, D. C. (2009). "Shallow draughts intoxicate the brain": Lessons from cognitive science for cognitive neuropsychology. *Topics in Cognitive Science, 1*, 39–58. Karalyn Patterson and David Plaut discuss the major assumptions of cognitive neuropsychology and assess their validity.

Chapter 2

Contents

Perception

2

INTRODUCTION

The focus of this chapter is on perception. What do we mean by "perception"? According to Sekuler and Blake (2002, p. 621), it is "the acquisition and processing of sensory information in order to see, hear, taste, or feel objects in the world; it also guides an organism's actions with respect to those objects." In this chapter, we will be considering our two most important senses: vision and hearing.

VISUAL PERCEPTION

Visual perception is of enormous importance in our everyday lives. It allows us to move around freely, to recognize people, to read magazines and books, to admire the wonders of nature, and to watch movies and television. It is very important for visual perception to be accurate – if we misperceive how close cars are as we cross the road, the consequences can be fatal. As a result, far more of the human cortex is devoted to vision than to any other sensory modality.

Visual perception generally seems so simple and effortless that we are in danger of taking it for granted. In fact, it is very complex, with numerous processes being involved in transforming and interpreting sensory information. Supporting evidence comes from the efforts of researchers in artificial intelligence who have tried to program computers to "perceive" the environment. As yet,

Learning Objectives

After studying Chapter 2, you should be able to:

- Compare and contrast imagery and perception.
- Describe how mental rotation tasks are used to inform us about visual imagery and visual perception.
- Explain how the two visual systems reconcile differences between perception (optical illusions) and reality so that our actions achieve their goal.
- Explain what change blindness phenomena tell us about human attention and perception.
- Relate the phonemic restoration effect in speech perception to top-down and bottom-up processing.
- Define face recognition, and describe what studies of prosopagnosic patients find about where and how face recognition occurs in the brain.
- Define perceptual organization, pattern recognition, and object recognition, and describe the theories that account for each of these processes.

no computer can match more than a fraction of the skills of visual perception possessed by nearly every sighted adult human.

Several important questions concerning visual perception are discussed in this chapter. In a world of overlapping objects, how do we decide where one object ends and another begins? How do we make sense of ambiguous two-dimensional stimuli (e.g., handwriting)? How do we decide whether the object in front of us is a cat or a dog? How do we recognize individual faces given that most faces are broadly similar (e.g., they have two eyes, a nose, a mouth, and so on)? How similar is visual imagery to visual perception? Why are we susceptible to many visual illusions in the laboratory when our everyday visual perception is so accurate? Why do we often fail to detect changes in our visual environment? Is vision possible in the absence of conscious awareness?

AUDITORY PERCEPTION

Auditory perception is also extremely important in our everyday lives. It enables us to understand what friends are saying and to make sense of movies and television programs. Auditory perception is also valuable for listening to (and enjoying) music, identifying animal noises, realizing a car is approaching rapidly behind us, and so on.

Speech perception is by far the most important use to which we put our auditory system, and so that will be the central focus in our coverage of auditory perception. Most of us are very good at understanding what other people are saying even when they speak in a strange dialect and/or ungrammatically. It is easy to take our ability to understand the speech of others for granted. Indeed, in view of the enormous experience we have all had in using the English language and listening to other people, speech perception may seem remarkably easy.

As we will see later, speech perception is much more of an achievement than it appears. One of the most difficult problems is to divide the almost continuous sounds we hear into separate words. How we solve that problem (and several others) in speech perception is discussed later.

Speech perception can be especially difficult in a crowded room in which lots of people are speaking and perhaps music is playing as well. In such conditions, how do we focus on what our friend is saying? That problem is one of selective attention and is discussed in Chapter 3.

PERCEPTUAL ORGANIZATION

It would probably be fairly easy to work out accurately which parts of the visual information presented to us belong together and thus form objects if those objects were spread out in space. Instead, the visual environment is often complex and confusing, with many objects overlapping others and so hiding parts of them from view. As a result, it can be difficult to achieve perceptual segregation of visual objects.

The first systematic attempt to study perceptual segregation (and the perceptual organization to which it gives rise) was made by the Gestaltists. They were German psychologists (including Koffka, Köhler, and Wertheimer), most of whom emigrated to the United States before the Second World War. Their fundamental principle was the **law of Prägnanz**, according to which we typically perceive the simplest possible organization.

Key Term
Law of Prägnanz: the notion that the simplest possible organization of the visual environment is what is perceived; proposed by the Gestaltists.

The Gestaltists put forward several other laws, but most of them are examples of the law of Prägnanz (see Figure 2.1). The fact that three horizontal arrays of dots rather than vertical groups are seen in Figure 2.1(a) indicates that visual elements tend to be grouped together if they are close to each other (the law of proximity).

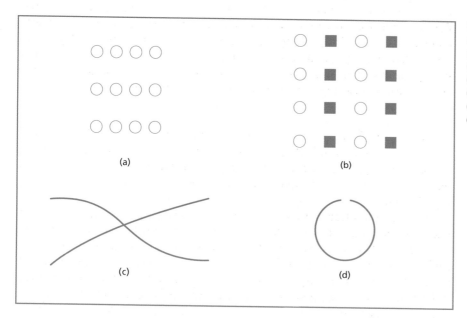

Figure 2.1 Examples of the Gestalt laws of perceptual organization: (a) the law of proximity; (b) the law of similarity; (c) the law of good continuation; and (d) the law of closure.

Research Activity 2.1: *Gestalt laws in conflict*

Have a look at the three displays in Figure 2.2 and decide how you would group the stimuli in each case. You can then compare your judgments with those obtained by Quinlan and Wilton (1998) in a study using very similar stimuli. In their study, about half the participants grouped the stimuli in (a) by proximity or closeness and half by similarity of shape. In (b) and (c), most participants grouped by similarity of color rather than similarity of shape or proximity.

This Research Activity focuses on what happens when different laws of organization are in conflict, an issue deemphasized by the Gestaltists. According to Quinlan and Wilton (1998), the visual elements in a display are initially grouped or clustered on the basis of proximity or closeness. However, when grouping based on proximity produces mismatches both within and between clusters (b and c), then observers favor grouping on the basis of similarity of color rather than proximity.

Figure 2.2 (a) Display involving a conflict between proximity and similarity; (b) display with a conflict between shape and color; (c) a different display with a conflict between shape and color. All adapted from Quinlan and Wilton (1998).

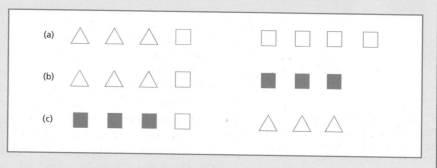

Key Term

Figure–ground organization:
the division of the visual environment into a figure (having a distinct form) and ground (lacking a distinct form); the contour between figure and ground appears to belong to the figure, which stands out from the ground.

Figure 2.1(b) shows the law of similarity, which states that elements will be grouped together perceptually if they are similar. Vertical columns rather than horizontal rows are seen because the elements in the vertical column are the same whereas those in the horizontal rows are not.

We see two lines crossing in Figure 2.1(c) because according to the law of good continuation we group together those elements requiring the fewest changes or interruptions in straight or smoothly curving lines. Finally, Figure 2.1(d) shows the law of closure, according to which missing parts of a figure are filled in to complete the figure. Thus, a circle is seen even though it is actually incomplete.

Kubovy and van den Berg (2008) confirmed the importance of grouping by proximity and of grouping by similarity. They also found that the *combined* effects on grouping of proximity and similarity were equal to the sum of their separate effects.

The Gestaltists emphasized **figure–ground segregation** in perceptual organization. One part of the visual field is identified as the figure, whereas the rest is less important and forms the ground. The Gestaltists claimed that the figure is perceived as having distinct form or shape, whereas the ground lacks form. In addition, the figure is perceived in front of the ground, and the contour separating the figure from the ground belongs to the figure. Check the validity of these claims by looking at the faces–goblet illusion (see Figure 2.3).

There is more attention to (and processing of) the figure than of the ground. Weisstein and Wong (1986) flashed vertical lines and slightly tilted lines onto the faces–goblet illusion, and observers decided whether the line was vertical. Performance was much better when the line was presented to what the observers perceived as the figure rather than to the ground.

FINDINGS

The Gestaltists used artificial figures, and it is important to see whether their findings apply to more realistic stimuli. Elder and Goldberg (2002) presented observers with pictures of natural objects. Proximity or closeness was a very powerful cue when deciding which contours belonged to which objects. In addition, the cue of good continuation made a positive contribution.

According to the Gestaltists, figure–ground segregation depends very little on past knowledge and experience. That led them to deemphasize the role of experience. In a study by Schwarzkopf et al. (2009), observers were presented with atypical shape contours that were hard to interpret. However, the observers showed rapid and flexible learning leading to a rapid improvement in performance.

The Gestaltists assumed that figure–ground segregation occurs very *early* in visual processing and so always precedes object recognition. These assumptions were tested by Grill-Spector and Kanwisher (2005). Photographs were presented for between 17 ms and 167 ms followed by a mask. On some trials, participants performed an object detection task based on deciding whether the photograph contained an object. This was done to assess figure–ground segregation. On other trials, participants carried out an object categorization task (e.g., deciding whether the photograph showed an object from a given category such as "car"). Surprisingly, reaction times and error rates on the two tasks were extremely similar.

In another experiment, Grill-Spector and Kanwisher (2005) asked participants to perform the object detection and categorization tasks on each

Figure 2.3 An ambiguous drawing that can be seen either as two faces or as a goblet.

trial. When the object was not detected, categorization performance was at chance level; when the object was not categorized accurately, detection performance was at chance.

The above findings imply that the processes involved in figure–ground segregation resemble those involved in object recognition. However, that isn't always the case. Mack et al. (2008) also compared performance on object detection (i.e., is an object there?) and object categorization (i.e., what object is it?) tasks. However, they used conditions in which objects were inverted or degraded to make object categorization harder. In those conditions, object categorization performance was significantly worse than object detection. Thus, object categorization is more complex and can involve somewhat different processes from those involved in object detection.

Evaluation

+ The Gestaltists correctly argued for the importance of organization in visual perception.

+ The Gestaltists discovered several important aspects of perceptual organization, most of which are relevant with natural scenes.

− The Gestaltists deemphasized the role of experience and knowledge in perceptual organization.

− The Gestaltists were wrong to argue that figure–ground segregation always occurs before object recognition.

− There was a failure to explain the perceptual phenomena identified by the Gestaltists – *why* do we perceive the simplest possible organization of the visual information available to us?

Section Summary

• According to the Gestaltists, we typically perceive the simplest possible organization when presented with a visual display. They correctly argued that factors such as proximity and similarity were important, but didn't focus on what happens when such factors conflict. The Gestaltists identified figure–ground segregation as central to perceptual organization, but largely ignored the role of past experience in determining the form it takes. The Gestalists provided useful descriptions of perceptual phenomena but had less success in explaining those phenomena.

PATTERN RECOGNITION

We spend much of our time (e.g., when reading) engaged in pattern recognition – the identification or categorization of two-dimensional patterns. Much research on pattern recognition has addressed the issue of how alphanumeric patterns (alphabetical and numerical symbols) are recognized. A key issue here is the *flexibility* of the human perceptual system. For example, we can recognize the letter "A" rapidly and accurately across large variations in orientation, typeface, size, and writing style.

Why is pattern recognition so successful? At a general level, it is clear that it involves *matching* information from the visual stimulus with information stored in memory. Some of the main processes involved are discussed below.

TEMPLATE THEORIES

According to template theories, we have templates (forms or patterns stored in long-term memory) corresponding to each of the visual patterns we know. A pattern is recognized on the basis of which template provides the closest match to the stimulus input. This kind of theory is simple. However, it isn't very realistic in view of the enormous variations in visual stimuli allegedly matching the same template.

A modest improvement to the basic template theory is to assume that the visual stimulus undergoes a normalization process. This process produces an internal representation of the visual stimulus in a standard position (e.g., upright), size, and so on *before* the search for a matching template begins. Normalization would help pattern recognition for letters and digits. However, it is improbable it would consistently produce matching with the appropriate template.

Another way of improving template theory would be to assume that there is more than one template for each letter and digit. This would permit accurate matching of stimulus and template across a wider range of stimuli, but at the cost of making the theory more complex.

In sum, template theories are ill-equipped to account for the flexibility shown by people when recognizing alphabetical and numerical symbols. The limitations of template theories are especially obvious when the stimulus belongs to an ill-defined category for which no single template could possibly suffice (e.g., buildings).

FEATURE THEORIES

According to feature theories, a pattern consists of a set of specific features or attributes (Jain & Duin, 2004). For example, feature theorists might argue that the key features of the letter "A" are two straight lines and a connected cross-bar. This kind of theoretical approach has the advantage that visual stimuli varying greatly in size, orientation, and minor details can be identified as instances of the same pattern.

The feature-theory approach has been supported by studies of visual search in which a target letter has to be identified as rapidly as possible. Neisser (1964) compared the time taken to detect the letter "Z" when the distractor letters consisted of straight lines (e.g., W, V) or contained rounded features (e.g., O, G) (see Figure 2.4). Performance was faster in the latter condition because the distractors shared fewer features with the target letter Z.

Most feature theories assume that pattern recognition involves specific processing followed by more global or general processing to integrate information from the features. However, global processing can *precede* more specific processing. Navon (1977) presented observers with stimuli such as the one shown in Figure 2.5. In one experiment, observers decided whether the large letter was an "H" or an "S"; on other trials, they decided whether the small letters were Hs or Ss.

What did Navon (1977) find? Performance speed with the small letters was greatly slowed when the large letter differed from the small letters. In contrast, decision speed with the large letter was *not* influenced by the nature of the small letters. Thus, as Navon expressed it, we often see the forest (global structure) before the trees (features) rather than the other way round.

Dalrymple et al. (2009) replicated the above finding when the small letters were very small and close together. However, processing was faster at the level of the small letters than the large letter when the small letters were larger and spread out. In this condition, it was harder to identify the large letter.

Feature detectors

If the presentation of a visual stimulus leads initially to detailed processing of its basic features, we might be able to identify cells in the cortex involved in such processing. Relevant evidence was obtained in the Nobel prize-winning research of Hubel and Wiesel (1962). They studied cells in parts of the occipital cortex (at the back of the brain) associated with the early stages of visual processing. Some cells responded in two different ways to a spot of light depending on which part of the cell was affected:

1. An "on" response with an increased rate of firing when the light was on.
2. An "off" response with the light causing a decreased rate of firing.

Hubel and Wiesel (e.g., 1979) discovered two types of neuron in primary visual cortex: simple cells and complex cells. Simple cells have "on" and "off" regions with each region being rectangular in shape. These stimuli respond most to dark bars in a light field, light bars in a dark field, or straight edges between areas of light and dark. Any given simple cell only responds strongly to stimuli of a particular orientation. Thus, the responses of these cells could be relevant to feature detection.

Complex cells differ from simple cells in that they respond more to moving contours. There are many more complex cells than simple ones. Finally, there are end-stopped cells. Their responsiveness depends on stimulus length and orientation.

All these types of cell are involved in feature detection. However, we mustn't exaggerate their usefulness. These cells provide *ambiguous* information because they respond in the same way to different stimuli. For example, a cell may

LIST 1	LIST 2
IMVXEW	ODUGQR
WVMEIX	GRODUQ
VXWIEM	DUROQG
MIEWVX	RGOUDQ
WEIMXV	RQGOUD
IWVXEM	UGQDRO
IXEZVW	GUQZOR
VWEMXI	ODGRUQ
MIVEWX	DRUQGO
WXEIMV	UQGORD

Figure 2.4 Illustrative lists to study letter search: The distractors in List 2 share fewer features with the target letter Z than do the distractors in List 1.

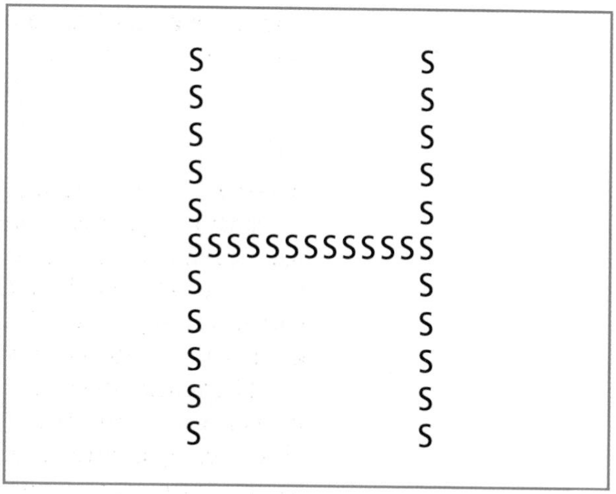

Figure 2.5 The kind of stimulus used by Navon (1977) to demonstrate the importance of global features in perception.

respond equally to a horizontal line moving rapidly and a nearly horizontal line moving slowly.

More recent research has identified neurons that respond in a much more specific and unambiguous fashion (Mather, 2009). Some of these neurons respond only to stimuli having a specific orientation, or a specific location in the visual field, or having a specific spatial frequency.

Context

Stimulus features play an important role in pattern recognition. However, as discussed in more detail shortly, feature theories deemphasize the effects of context and of expectations. Weisstein and Harris (1974) used a task involving detection of a line embedded in a briefly flashed three-dimensional form or in a less coherent form.

According to feature theorists, the target line should *always* activate the same feature detectors. As a result, the coherence of the form in which it is embedded shouldn't affect detection. In fact, however, target detection was best when the target line was part of a three-dimensional form. Weisstein and Harris called this the "object superiority effect." This effect occurs because the context provides useful information concerning the target stimulus. It also makes the target stimulus more perceptible (Loverock, 2007).

TOP-DOWN PROCESSES

Feature theories of pattern recognition emphasize bottom-up processes. However, top-down processes also play an important role. Consider, for example, the **word superiority effect** (Reicher, 1969). A letter string is presented briefly followed by a pattern mask that inhibits further processing of the letter string. Participants decide which of two letters was presented in a given position (e.g., the third letter). Performance is better when the letter string forms a word than when it does not – this is the word superiority effect.

The word superiority effect suggests that information about the word presented can facilitate identification of its letters. In other words, there are top-down effects from the word level of processing to the letter level.

There is also a pseudoword superiority effect: Letters are easier to identify when presented in pseudowords (pronounceable nonwords such as "MAVE") than in unpronounceable nonwords (Carr et al., 1978). *What* produces this effect? There is some overlap between the spelling patterns in the pseudoword and genuine words (e.g., "SAVE"; "GAVE"). This overlap benefits identification of the letters in the pseudoword in a top-down fashion.

Grainger and Jacobs (2005) argued that the pseudoword superiority effect depends on the extent to which the pseudoword is misperceived as a word. They obtained support for their viewpoint in a study on French participants. One pseudoword they presented was AVROL. The only genuine French word closely resembling AVROL is AVRIL (French for April). When participants decided whether the second letter of the pseudoword was V or T, they showed a pseudoword superiority effect because the second letter of the genuine word AVRIL is also V.

In contrast, Grainger and Jacobs (2005) obtained a pseudoword *inferiority* effect when participants decided whether the fourth letter of AVROL was O or I. In this condition, misperceiving AVROL as AVRIL led many participants to misidentify the letter.

| Key Term

Word superiority effect: the finding that a target letter is detected faster when presented in words than in **nonwords**.

In the Real World 2.1: *Fingerprinting*

Pattern-recognition techniques are extremely important in the real world. For example, finger printing assists in the identification of criminals. The criminal's fingerprint (the latent print) provides a pattern that is matched against stored fingerprint records.

How does fingerprint identification work in criminal cases? It involves computer systems and human experts working together. Automatic fingerprint identification systems (AFIS) scan through huge databases (e.g., the FBI has the fingerprints of over 60 million persons). This produces a small number of possible matches to the fingerprint(s) obtained from the scene of the crime ranked in terms of similarity to the criminal's fingerprint. Experts then decide whether any fingerprint in the database matches the criminal's.

AFIS focuses on features at two levels (Jain et al., 2010). At a general level, there are three basic fingerprint patterns: loop; arch; whorl (circle), with about two-thirds of individuals having the loop pattern (see Figure 2.6).

Fingerprints also contain more specific features. We have patterns of ridges and valleys known as friction ridges on our hands. Of particular importance are minutiae points - locations where a friction ridge ends abruptly or a ridge divides into two or more ridges. There are typically between 20 and 70 minutiae points in a fingerprint, and this information is stored in a database (Jain et al., 2010). The expert is provided with information about feature or minutiae similarity from AFIS but also makes use of microfeatures (e.g., sweat pores; the width of particular ridges) (Dror & Mnookin, 2010).

Do you share the common belief that fingerprint identification is almost infallible? In fact you shouldn't, even though it is probably more accurate than any other identification method except DNA (Spinney, 2010). Decide whether the two fingerprints shown in Figure 2.7 come from the same person. Four fingerprinting experts decided both fingerprints came from the same person, namely, the bomber involved in the terrorist attack on Madrid on 11 March 2004. In fact, the fingerprints come from two different individuals. The left one is from the Madrid bomber, but the right one comes from Brandon Mayfield, an Oregon lawyer who was falsely arrested.

Fingerprint misidentification is common in the laboratory. Langenburg et al. (2009) studied the effects of context (e.g., alleged conclusions of an internationally respected expert) on fingerprint identification. Experts and non-experts were both influenced by contextual information, but non-experts were influenced more. Dror and Rosenthal (2008) presented five experts with pairs of fingerprints they had judged as matching or not matching several years earlier. About 10% of the time, their two judgments differed.

Why do experts make mistakes in fingerprint identification? First, their judgments are influenced by irrelevant and misleading information (Langenburg et al., 2009). Cole (2005) reviewed real-life cases involving fingerprint misidentification by experts. In more than 50% of the cases, the original expert misidentification was confirmed by one or more additional experts.

Figure 2.6   The loop pattern (found in 60%–65% of individuals) involves ridges curving back (left); the whorl pattern (30%–35%) involves central ridges turning through at least one complete turn (center); the arch pattern (5%) involves ridges running across the pattern with no backward turn (right).

Dror et al. (2006) asked experts to judge whether two fingerprints matched, having told them incorrectly that the prints were the ones mistakenly matched by the FBI as the Madrid bomber. Unknown to these experts, they had judged these fingerprints to be a clear and definite match several years earlier. However, when provided with misleading information about the Madrid bomber, 60% of the experts now judged the prints to be definite nonmatches! Thus, top-down processes triggered by contextual information can distort fingerprint identification.

Second, a criminal's fingerprints can now be compared against hugely more stored prints than previously. This greatly increases the chances of discovering an incorrect print extremely similar to that of the criminal. As a result, experts should require more evidence of similarity before deciding they have found a match (Dror & Mnookin, 2010). However, that isn't happening. Charlton et al. (2010) found that fingerprint experts had a strong desire to resolve cases (especially major crimes), which can increase misidentifications.

In sum, fingerprint identification depends heavily on comparing features at different levels of specificity (bottom-up processing). Errors occur because experts are influenced by misleading contextual information (top-down processing) and because the degree of similarity they require before deciding they have found a match is insufficiently stringent.

Figure 2.7 The FBI's mistaken identification of the Madrid bomber. The fingerprint from the crime scene is on the left. The fingerprint of the innocent suspect (positively identified by various fingerprint experts) is on the right. From Dror et al., 2006. Copyright © 2006, with permission from Elsevier.

In sum, pattern recognition doesn't depend solely on bottom-up processing involving features or other aspects of visual stimuli. Top-down processes are often important. We will see more evidence of the importance of top-down processes in pattern recognition in the next section.

MEDICAL DIAGNOSIS

Another real-world area in which pattern recognition is extremely important is that of doctors making medical diagnoses from X-rays. Indeed, it can literally be a matter of life or death.

Much research has compared the pattern-recognition performance of medical experts with that of novice or non-expert ones (see Chapter 10). Unsurprisingly, experts possess much more relevant knowledge than non-experts and this knowledge allows them to produce more accurate diagnoses (Norman, 2005).

Pattern recognition can involve analytic or implicit reasoning (Engel, 2008). Analytic reasoning is relatively slow and deliberate, whereas implicit reasoning is fast and automatic. Medical experts make much use of implicit reasoning. In one study (Kundel et al., 2007), doctors were shown complex mammograms, some of which revealed the presence of breast cancer. The cancer was fixated on average in just over 1 s. The most expert doctors generally fixated the cancer almost immediately, whereas the non-expert ones took somewhat longer.

The findings of Kundel et al. (2007) suggest that experts are more likely than non-experts to use implicit reasoning, whereas the non-experts made more use of analytic reasoning. However, other evidence indicates that medical experts often start with fast, automatic processes but cross-check their diagnoses with analytic ones (McLaughlin et al., 2008).

Section Summary

Template theories

- Template theories assume we recognize a visual stimulus by matching it to the template or stored pattern it most resembles. Such theories can't easily account for human flexibility in pattern recognition.

Feature theories

- Some feature theories assume that pattern recognition involves specific feature processing followed by more global or general processing. However, global processing can precede more specific processing. In addition, feature theories deemphasize the effects of context and expectations.

Top-down processes

- The word superiority effect depends on top-down processes involving word-based information. Similar processes are involved in the pseudoword superiority effect, in which pseudowords are misperceived as words.

Fingerprinting

- Fingerprint identification involves experts using information about feature or minutiae similarity plus various microfeatures (e.g., sweat pores). Experts make mistakes because their judgments are influenced by irrelevant and misleading information. In addition, their criteria for accepting similar fingerprints as matching are sometimes insufficiently stringent when highly motivated to resolve a criminal case.

Medical diagnosis

- Medical experts make more use than non-experts of implicit or automatic processes when engaged in pattern recognition during diagnosis. However, they generally cross-check their proposed diagnosis with analytic or deliberate processes.

VISUAL OBJECT RECOGNITION

Thousands of times every day we identify or recognize objects in the world around us. At this precise moment, you are aware that you are looking at a book (possibly with your eyes glazed over). If you raise your eyes, then perhaps you can see a wall, windows, and so on in front of you. It probably seems incredibly easy to recognize common objects. In fact, visual object recognition is much more complex than you might imagine. For example, many objects (e.g., chairs; houses) vary enormously in their visual properties (e.g., color, size, shape) and yet we can still recognize them.

We can also recognize many objects over a wide range of viewing distances and orientations. For example, most plates are round but we can identify plates seen from an angle so they appear elliptical. We are also confident that the ant-like creatures we can see from the window of a plane during its descent are actually people. In sum, there is much more to object recognition than might initially be supposed (than meets the eye?).

RECOGNITION-BY-COMPONENTS THEORY

What processes are involved in object recognition? An influential answer was provided by Irving Biederman (1987) in his recognition-by-components theory. He argued that objects consist of basic shapes or components known as **geons** (geometric ions). Examples of geons are blocks, cylinders, spheres, arcs, and wedges.

How many geons are there? According to Biederman (1987), there are about 36 different geons. That may sound suspiciously few to provide descriptions of all the objects we can recognize and identify. However, we can identity enormous numbers of spoken English words even though there are only about 44 phonemes (basic sounds) in the English language. This is because they can be arranged in almost limitless combinations.

The same is true of geons – the reason for the richness of the object descriptions provided by geons stems from the different possible spatial relationships among them. For example, a cup can be described by an arc connected to the side of a cylinder. A pail can be described by the same two geons but with the arc connected to the top of the cylinder.

Geon-based information about common objects is stored in long-term memory. As a result, object recognition depends crucially on the identification of geons. Of major importance, an object's geons can be identified from numerous viewpoints. Thus, object recognition should generally be easy unless one or more geons are hidden from view. In other words, it is viewpoint-invariant.

The assumption that object recognition is viewpoint-invariant was tested by Biederman and Gerhardstein (1993). Object naming was facilitated as much by two different views of an object as by two identical views even when there was an angular difference of 135° between the views. These findings suggest that object recognition is viewpoint-invariant. However, we will see shortly that is often *not* the case.

We are most sensitive to those visual features of an object directly relevant to identifying its geons. *How* have we developed this sensitivity? Perhaps our everyday experience with simple manufactured objects (e.g., cylinders; funnels; spherical objects; bricks) is of major importance.

In fact, there is evidence against the above explanation. Consider the Himba, a seminomadic people in Northwestern Namibia. They have very little exposure to manufactured objects. In spite of that, they are as sensitive to geon-relevant information as individuals living in the developed world (Lescroart et al., 2010). What seems to matter is exposure to a great variety of naturally occurring objects in the world around us.

Key Term
Geons: basic shapes or components that are combined in object recognition; an abbreviation for "geometric ions" proposed by Biederman.

How do we recognize objects when only some of the relevant visual information is available? According to Biederman (1987), the concavities (hollows) in an object's contour provide especially useful information. He obtained support for this view in an experiment in which observers were presented with degraded line drawings of objects (see Figure 2.8). Object recognition was much harder to achieve when parts of the contour providing information about concavities were omitted than when other parts of the contour were deleted.

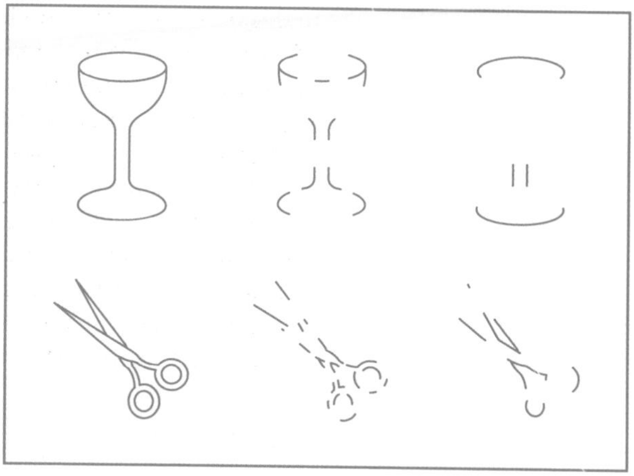

Recognition-by-components theory strongly emphasizes bottom-up processes in object recognition. However, top-down processes depending on factors such as expectation and knowledge are often important, especially when object recognition is difficult. For example, Viggiano et al. (2008) found that observers relied more on top-down processes when animal photographs were blurred than when they weren't blurred. This happened because there was less information for bottom-up processes to make use of with the blurred photographs.

Figure 2.8   Intact figures (left), with degraded line drawings either preserving (center) or not preserving (right) parts of the contour providing information about concavities. Adapted from Biederman (1987).

Evaluation

⊕ It is plausible that geons or geon-like components are involved in object recognition.

⊕ The identification of concavities is of major importance in object recognition.

⊖ The theory only accounts for fairly unsubtle perceptual discriminations. For example, it allows us to decide whether an animal is a dog or a cat, but not whether it is our dog or cat.

⊖ It is assumed within the theory that objects consist of invariant geons. However, object recognition is actually much more flexible than that. For example, the shapes of some objects (e.g., clouds) are so variable that they don't have identifiable geons.

⊖ The theory is based on the assumption that the processes in object recognition are viewpoint-invariant. We will shortly see that this is very often not the case.

⊖ As the theory assumes, bottom-up processes are very important in object recognition. However, top-down processes are also important when object recognition is difficult.

DOES VIEWPOINT AFFECT OBJECT RECOGNITION?

Form a visual image of a bicycle. Your image probably involved a side view in which the two wheels of the bicycle can be seen clearly. We can use this example to discuss an important controversy. Suppose some people were presented with a picture of a bicycle shown in the typical view as in your visual image, whereas other people were presented with a picture of the same bicycle viewed end-on or from above. Both groups are instructed to identify the object as rapidly as possible. Would the group given the typical view of a bicycle perform this task faster than the other group?

Biederman (1987) claimed that object recognition is equally rapid and easy regardless of the angle from which an object is viewed. In other words, he assumed that object recognition is viewpoint-invariant. As we have just seen, Biederman and Gerhardstein (1993) obtained evidence supporting that assumption. However, other theorists (e.g., Friedman et al., 2005) argue that object recognition is generally faster and easier when objects are seen from certain angles. Such theorists favor the view that object recognition is viewpoint-dependent.

As you have probably guessed, object recognition is sometimes viewpoint-dependent and sometimes viewpoint-invariant. According to Tarr and Bülthoff (1995), viewpoint-invariant mechanisms are typically used when object recognition involves making easy discriminations (e.g., between cars and bicycles). In contrast, viewpoint-dependent mechanisms are more important when the task requires difficult within-category discriminations (e.g., between different makes of car; between faces).

Evidence consistent with the above general approach was reported by Tarr et al. (1998). They considered recognition of the same 3-D objects under various conditions. Performance was close to viewpoint-invariant when the object recognition task was easy (e.g., detailed feedback after each trial). However, it was viewpoint-dependent when the task was difficult (e.g., no feedback provided).

One factor influencing the extent to which object recognition is viewpoint-dependent is the amount of information available to the observer. For example, consider face recognition. Face recognition is typically strongly viewpoint-dependent (Burke et al., 2007). However, faces in most research have been presented two-dimensionally on computer monitors. In contrast, we perceive faces in three dimensions in our everyday lives. Burke et al. found that face recognition was much less strongly viewpoint-dependent with three-dimensional faces than with two-dimensional ones.

Cognitive neuroscience

The notion that object recognition can be either viewpoint-invariant or viewpoint-dependent has received support from research in cognitive neuroscience. Visual processing proceeds through several areas in the occipital lobe at the back of the brain and finishes up in the inferotemporal cortex, which is of crucial importance in visual object recognition (Peissig & Tarr, 2007).

Suppose we consider neuronal activity in inferotemporal cortex while observers are presented with objects having various angles, sizes, and so on. Neurons vary in invariance or tolerance (Ison & Quiroga, 2008). Neurons responding almost equally strongly to a given object regardless of its orientation, size, and so on possess high invariance or tolerance. In contrast, neurons responding most strongly to an object in a specific orientation or size have low invariance.

We need to be careful when relating evidence about neuronal selectivity and tolerance to theories of object recognition. In general terms, however, inferotemporal neurons having high invariance or tolerance seem consistent with theories claiming that object recognition is viewpoint-invariant. In similar fashion, inferotemporal neurons having low invariance appear to fit with theories claiming that object recognition is viewpoint-dependent. Thus, the findings from cognitive neuroscience suggest that object perception can be viewpoint-dependent or viewpoint-invariant.

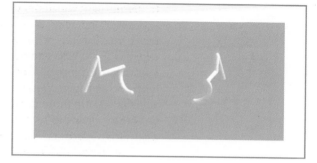

Figure 2.9 Example images of a "same" pair of stimulus objects. From Foster and Gilson (2002) with permission from The Royal Society London.

Viewpoint-dependent and viewpoint-invariant processes

It is an oversimplification to assume that object recognition in a given situation necessarily involves only viewpoint-invariant or viewpoint-dependent processes. Some theorists (e.g., Foster & Gilson, 2002; Hayward, 2003) argue that viewpoint-dependent and viewpoint-invariant information is generally combined cooperatively to produce object recognition.

Evidence that the two kinds of information can be used at the same time in object recognition was reported by Foster and Gilson (2002). Observers saw pairs of simple three-dimensional objects formed from connected cylinders (see Figure 2.9). Their task was to decide whether the two images showed the same object or two different objects. When two objects were different, they could differ in terms of a viewpoint-invariant feature (e.g., number of parts) and/or various viewpoint-dependent features (e.g., part length; angle of join between parts).

Foster and Gilson's (2002) key finding was that observers used both kinds of information. This suggests that we make use of all available information in object recognition rather than confining ourselves to only some of the information.

DISORDERS OF OBJECT RECOGNITION

Insights into the processes involved in object recognition have been obtained by studying brain-damaged patients having deficient object recognition. Such patients suffer from visual agnosia. This is a condition in which there are great problems in recognizing visual objects even though visual information reaches the visual cortex.

There are substantial differences among patients with visual agnosia in the specific problems they have with object recognition. Historically, much importance was attached to a distinction between two forms of impairment in object recognition:

1. **Apperceptive agnosia**: Object recognition is impaired because of deficits in perceptual processing.
2. **Associative agnosia**: Perceptual processes are essentially intact, but there are difficulties in accessing relevant knowledge about objects from long-term memory.

According to this view, the problems with object recognition occur at an *earlier* stage of processing in apperceptive agnosia than in associative agnosia.

Key Terms

Apperceptive agnosia: this is a form of visual agnosia in which there is impaired perceptual analysis of familiar objects.

Associative agnosia: this is a form of visual agnosia in which perceptual processing is fairly normal but there is an impaired ability to derive the meaning of objects.

How can we distinguish between apperceptive agnosia and associative agnosia? One way is to assess patients' ability to copy objects they can't recognize. Patients who can copy objects are said to have associative agnosia, whereas those who can't have apperceptive agnosia. A test often used to assess apperceptive agnosia is the Gollin picture test. On this test, patients are presented with increasingly complete drawings of an object. Those with apperceptive agnosia require more drawings than healthy individuals to identify the objects.

How clear-cut is the distinction between apperceptive agnosia and associative agnosia? Delvenne et al. (2004) argued there are deficits in perceptual processing even in associative agnosia, but these deficits are too subtle to be detected by standard tests.

However, Anaki et al. (2007) found an apparent exception. They studied DBO, a 72-year-old man with associative agnosia who had very poor ability to access stored information about objects. For example, he found it very hard to name famous faces or to realize there was a connection between two famous faces. However, his perceptual processing seemed intact (e.g., he had intact immediate recognition memory for faces whose external features had been deleted).

Another patient with relatively pure associative agnosia is DJ (Fery & Morais, 2003). He recognized only 16% of common objects presented visually, indicating he couldn't easily access stored information about the forms and shapes of objects. In spite of DJ's problems, several processes relating to object recognition seemed essentially intact. He was correct on 93% of trials on a hard animal-decision task requiring a decision as to which one out of various drawings was an animal. On this task, the non-animals were actual animals with one part added, deleted, or substituted (see Figure 2.10).

The distinction between apperceptive and associative agnosia is oversimplified. Consider patients having apperceptive agnosia. Many of them have problems at early stages of perceptual processing (Riddoch & Humphreys, 2001). For example, Riddoch et al. (2008) studied a patient (SA), a hospital clerical worker with apperceptive agnosia. She had great difficulties in shape discrimination (e.g., discriminating between rectangles and squares) and in copying complex drawings.

Other patients with apperceptive agnosia have problems at a later stage of processing. Consider HJA, a male patient with apperceptive agnosia. He performed well on tasks involving shape discrimination and copying drawings, but found

Figure 2.10 Examples of animal stimuli: (from top to bottom) with a part missing, the intact animal, with a part substituted, and with a part added. From Fery and Morais (2003).

it very hard to integrate visual information (Riddoch et al., 2008). In his own words, "I have come to cope with recognizing many common objects, if they are standing alone. When objects are placed together, though, I have more difficulties. To recognize one sausage on its own is far from picking one out from a dish of cold foods in a salad" (Humphreys & Riddoch, 1987).

Some patients with visual agnosia have severe problems with top-down processes based on knowledge (Rizzi et al., 2010). Foulsham et al. (2009) studied CH, a 63-year-old woman apparently suffering from apperceptive agnosia. She had to decide whether a piece of fruit was present in photographs of everyday scenes, a task on which her performance was poor. Inspection of CH's eye movements revealed that she failed to focus on areas most likely to contain a piece of fruit. Thus, she couldn't use top-down knowledge of the structure of visual scenes to guide her eye movements.

In sum, research on brain-damaged patients provides strong evidence that object recognition involves several stages of processing (Riddoch & Humphreys, 2001). One of the early stages involves form and shape processing, a stage at which many apperceptive agnosics experience problems. The next stage involves integrating or combining information about an object's features, a stage at which apperceptive agnosics such as HJA and SA have problems.

The final stage of object recognition involves observers gaining access to semantic knowledge about objects after they have formed a detailed structural description of those objects. Some patients with associative agnosia (e.g., DBO; DJ) have problems at this stage of processing.

Section Summary

Recognition-by-components theory

- According to Biederman's theory, object recognition involves the identification of an object's geons (basic shapes). It is also assumed within the theory that object recognition is viewpoint-invariant and that concavities facilitate geon identification. The theory minimizes the importance of top-down processes and only accounts for unsubtle perceptual discriminations.

Does viewpoint affect object recognition?

- Viewpoint-invariant mechanisms are typically used when object recognition is easy whereas viewpoint-dependent mechanisms are used when it is difficult. Consistent with this view, some neurons in inferotemporal cortex are sensitive to an object's orientation whereas others are not. Viewpoint-dependent and viewpoint-invariant mechanisms are often used jointly to facilitate object recognition.

Disorders of object recognition

- Research on patients with visual agnosia suggests that object recognition involves several processing stages. Some patients have impaired processing at an early stage (form and shape discrimination). Others have impaired processing at the next stage (integration of visual information). Still other patients have problems with accessing stored knowledge about objects. Patients can also have problems in accessing knowledge about the structure of visual scenes to guide their eye movements.

FACE RECOGNITION

Recognizing faces is of enormous importance in our lives. We can sometimes identify people from their physique, the way they walk, or their mannerisms. Most of the time, however, we simply look at their faces. Form a visual image of someone important in your life. Your image probably contains fairly detailed information about their face and its special features.

In view of its great importance, we would expect face recognition to occur rapidly. Hsiao and Cottrell (2008) carried out a study on face recognition in which observers were allowed one, two, three, or unlimited eye fixations on each face. Face-recognition performance was above chance even with only one fixation, and was as good with two fixations as with three or unlimited fixations. On average, the first fixation was just to the center of the nose and the second fixation was around the center of the nose. This emphasis on the nose presumably occurs because the nose is close to the center of the face.

Face recognition plays a crucial role in many court cases. Hundreds (perhaps thousands) of innocent people have been locked up in prison because eyewitnesses mistakenly claimed to recognize them as the person who committed a crime. We know this because DNA has shown conclusively that the person found guilty of a crime didn't commit it (see Chapter 6).

Why do eyewitnesses sometimes identify the wrong person? The most important reason is that face recognition is often rather difficult. In one study (Davis & Valentine, 2009), participants watched moving video images resembling those captured by closed-circuit television (CCTV). The participants decided whether individuals physically present were the same as those shown in the video images. Participants made many errors even when high-quality close-up images were used.

Kemp et al. (1997) provided college students with credit cards containing their photograph. The students were told to buy some goods in a supermarket and then present their photo ID to the cashier. When the students used the correct card, the cashier accepted it 93% of the time. However, when students presented the card of someone else who looked similar to them, the cashier accepted the incorrect card 64% of the time!

Does face recognition involve different processes from object recognition? Most of the evidence supports the notion that faces are processed differently from other objects. We will start by considering research on healthy individuals followed by findings from brain-damaged patients. Finally, we consider theoretical approaches to understanding face recognition.

FACE VS. OBJECT RECOGNITION

How does face recognition differ from the recognition of other objects? An important part of the answer is that face recognition involves more holistic processing (combining or integrating information across the whole object). Information about specific features of a face can be unreliable because different individuals share similar facial features (e.g., eye color) or because an individual's features can change (e.g., skin shade; mouth shape). This makes it desirable for us to process faces holistically.

In the part–whole effect, memory for a face part is more accurate when it is presented within the whole face rather than on its own. Farah (1994)

Research Activity 2.2: *Composite face illusion*

You can obtain a sense of another illusion (the composite face illusion) found with faces but not other objects by looking at Figure 2.11. First look at the top row and ask yourself whether the top halves of the faces (above the white line) are the same or different. Then look at the bottom row and perform exactly the same task.

In fact, the top halves are identical in both rows. However, you probably took longer and/ or made the wrong decision with respect to the top row. The difference between the two rows is that the bottom halves differ in the top row but are identical in the bottom row. The top halves look slightly different in the top row because it is natural to integrate information from both half faces in a holistic way.

Figure 2.11 The composite face illusion. All the top halves of the faces are identical. However, when aligned with distinct bottom halves (see top row), they appear slightly different. This occurs because faces are perceived as an integrated whole. When the top halves of the faces are aligned with identical bottom parts (bottom row), it is more obvious that the top halves are the same. From Kuefner et al. (2010). Copyright © 2010, with permission from Elsevier.

studied this effect. Participants were presented with drawings of faces or houses, and associated a name with each face and each house. After that, they were presented with whole faces and houses or with only a single feature (e.g., mouth; front door).

Recognition performance for face parts was much better when the whole face was presented rather than only a single feature. This is the part–whole effect. In contrast, recognition performance for house features was very similar in whole- and single-feature conditions.

Research Activity 2.2 gave you some insight into the composite face illusion. In this illusion, participants are presented with composite faces (two half faces of different individuals) and these two half faces are aligned or misaligned along the horizontal axis. Performance on tasks requiring perception of only one half face is impaired when the half faces are aligned compared to when they are misaligned (e.g., Young et al., 1987). This composite illusion is typically not found with non-face objects (McKone et al., 2007), suggesting there is less holistic processing with objects.

Why does the composite face illusion exist? At a general level, we have a strong tendency to fuse together two aligned face halves. Taubert and Alais (2009) found that there was more evidence of holistic processing when faces were misaligned along the vertical axis than when they were misaligned along the horizontal axis. They argued that this occurred because vertically misaligned faces are more biologically plausible than horizontally misaligned ones.

According to Gauthier and Tarr (2002), many of the findings pointing to major differences between face and object processing shouldn't be taken at face value (sorry!). According to them, it is crucially important that most people have far more *expertise* in recognizing individual faces than the individual members of other categories. There is only modest support for this viewpoint (McGugin & Gauthier, 2010; see below).

Prosopagnosia:
a condition mostly caused by brain damage in which there is a severe impairment in face recognition with little or no impairment of object recognition; popularly known as "face blindness."

Fusiform face area:
an area within the inferotemporal cortex that is associated with face processing; the term is somewhat misleading given that the area is also associated with the processing of other categories of visual objects.

FACE BLINDNESS: PROSOPAGNOSIA

If face processing differs substantially from object processing, we might expect to find some brain-damaged individuals with severely impaired face recognition but not object recognition. Such individuals exist. They suffer from a condition known as **prosopagnosia** (pros-uh-pag-NO-see-uh), coming from the Greek words meaning "face" and "without knowledge."

Patients with prosopagnosia (often referred to as face blindness) have enormous problems with faces. JK, a woman in her early 30s, described an embarrassing incident caused by her prosopagnosia: "I went to the wrong baby at my son's daycare and only realized that he was not my son when the entire daycare staff looked at me in horrified disbelief" (Duchaine & Nakayama, 2006, p. 166).

Some (but by no means all) prosopagnosics have very good object recognition. Duchaine (2006) studied a prosopagnosic called Edward, a 53-year-old married man with two PhDs who did very poorly on several tests of face memory. In contrast, he performed slightly better than healthy controls on most memory tasks involving nonface objects, even when the task involved recognizing individual members within categories.

Why do prosopagnosics have very poor face recognition but reasonable object recognition? One explanation is that they have suffered damage to a part of the brain specialized for processing faces. Another possibility is that face recognition is simply much harder than object recognition. Face recognition involves distinguishing among members of the same category (i.e., faces), whereas object recognition generally only involves identifying the relevant category (e.g., cat; car). However, the findings of Duchaine (2006) cast doubt on that explanation.

We would have strong evidence that face recognition involves different processes from object recognition if we discovered patients with intact face recognition but impaired object recognition. Moscovitch et al. (1997) studied CK, a man with impaired object recognition. He performed as well as controls on face-recognition tasks regardless of whether the face was a photograph, a caricature, or a cartoon provided it was upright and the internal features were in the correct locations.

In sum, while most prosopagnosics have somewhat deficient object recognition, others have essentially intact object recognition even with difficult object-recognition. Surprisingly, a few individuals have reasonably intact face recognition in spite of severe problems with object recognition. These findings suggest that different processes (and brain areas) underlie face and object recognition.

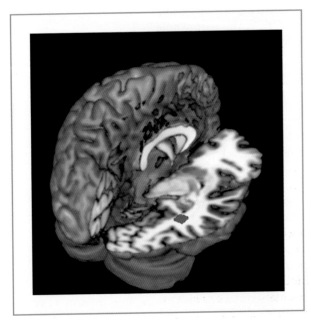

Figure 2.12 Approximate location of the fusiform face area in the right hemisphere, viewed from the back. From Ward (2010).

FUSIFORM FACE AREA

Which brain region is specialized for face processing? The **fusiform face area** in the inferotemporal cortex has (as its name strongly implies!) been identified as such a brain region (see Kanwisher & Yovel, 2006, for a review). This area (shown in Figure 2.12) is frequently damaged in patients with prosopagnosia (Barton et al., 2002).

The fusiform face area typically responds at least twice as strongly to faces as to other objects in brain-imaging studies (McKone et al., 2007). Downing et al. (2006) presented participants with faces, scenes, and 18 object categories (e.g., tools, fruits, vegetables). The fusiform face area responded significantly more strongly to faces than to any other stimulus category.

Gauthier and Tarr (2002) argued that the fusiform face area is NOT specific to face processing. Instead, they claimed it is used for processing *any* object category for which the observer possesses real expertise. Most evidence is inconsistent with this claim. McKone et al. (2007) reviewed studies that considered whether the effects of expertise with various objects are greatest in the fusiform face area. In fact, larger effects were reported *outside* the fusiform face area than *inside* it.

We need to avoid exaggerating the importance of the fusiform face area in face processing. Grill-Spector et al. (2006) found the fusiform face area is NOT used exclusively for face processing. Observers saw faces and three categories of objects (animals, cars, and abstract sculptures). More high-resolution voxels (small volume elements in the brain) in the fusiform face area were selective to faces than to any of the object categories. However, the differences were not dramatic. The average number of voxels selective to faces was 155 compared to 104 (animals), 63 (cars), and 63 (sculptures).

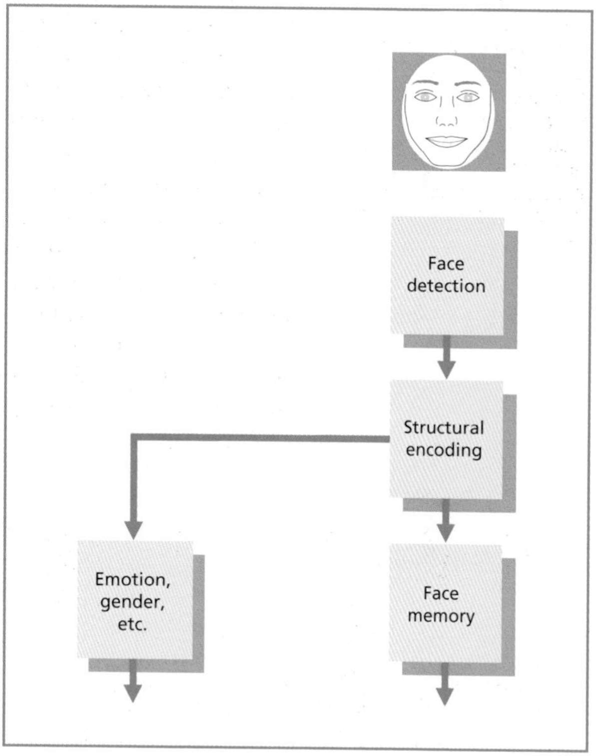

THEORIES OF FACE RECOGNITION

Several theories of face recognition have been put forward. The single most influential theory is that of Bruce and Young (1986). According to that theory, when we look at a familiar face, we first access familiarity information followed by personal information (e.g., the person's occupation), followed by the person's name.

A modified (and simplified) version of that theory was proposed by Duchaine and Nakayama (2006), and will be discussed here (see Figure 2.13). Initially, observers decide whether the stimulus they are looking at is a face (face detection). This is followed by processing of the face's structure (structural encoding), which is then matched to a memory representation (face memory). The structural encoding of the face can also be used for recognition of facial expression and gender discrimination.

We will consider three major assumptions of this theoretical approach. First, the initial stage of processing involves deciding whether the stimulus at which we are looking is a face (face detection). Earlier we discussed a prosopagnosic called Edward who had extremely poor face recognition. In

Figure 2.13 Simplified version of the Bruce and Young (1986) model of face recognition. Face detection is followed by processing of the face's structure, which is then matched to a memory representation (face memory). The perceptual representation of the face can also be used for recognition of facial expression and gender discrimination. Reprinted from Duchaine and Nakayama (2006), Copyright © 2006, with permission from Elsevier.

spite of his problems with later stages of face processing, he detected faces as rapidly as healthy individuals (Duchaine, 2006).

Second, *separate* processing routes are involved in the processing of facial identity (who is the person?: face memory) and facial expression (what is he/she feeling?). It follows that some individuals should show good performance on facial identity but poor performance on identifying facial expression, whereas others should show the opposite pattern. These two patterns were reported by Young et al. (1993).

Humphreys et al. (2007) reported very clear findings in three individuals with prosopagnosia. All three had poor ability to recognize faces, but their ability to recognize facial expressions (even the most subtle ones) was comparable to that of healthy individuals.

Third, it is assumed that we retrieve personal information about a person *before* recalling their name. The person's name can *only* be recalled provided that some other information about him/her has already been recalled. Young et al. (1985) asked people to keep a diary record of problems they experienced in face recognition. There were 1008 incidents in total, but people *never* reported putting a name to a face while knowing nothing else about that person. In contrast, there were 190 occasions on which someone remembered a reasonable amount of information about a person but not their name.

In spite of Young et al.'s (1985) findings, the assumption that the processing of names *always* occurs after the processing of personal information (e.g., occupation) is too rigid. Brédart et al. (2005) found that members of a Cognitive Science Department could name the faces of their close colleagues faster than they could retrieve personal information about them. This occurred because the participants had been exposed so often to the names of their colleagues.

In sum, there is good support for the various processing components identified within the theoretical approach initiated by Bruce and Young (1986). More specifically, it is valuable to distinguish between the processing of facial identity and facial expression. It is typically harder to retrieve someone's name than to retrieve personal information about them. However, this isn't always the case even though that is the prediction from the theory.

SUPER-RECOGNIZERS

We saw earlier that some individuals (especially those with prosopagnosia) have extremely poor face-recognition ability. There is also evidence for individuals having exceptional face-recognition ability. Russell et al. (2009) identified four individuals who claimed to have significantly better than average face recognition ability. For example, one of them said, "It doesn't matter how many years pass, if I've seen your face before I will be able to recall it. It only happens with faces" (Russell et al., 2009, p. 253).

All four individuals performed at a very high level on several tasks involving face recognition. For example, one task involved identifying famous people when shown photographs of them before they were famous (often when they were children). Russell et al. (2009) called these individuals "super-recognizers."

Genetic factors probably help to explain the existence of super-recognizers. Wilmer et al. (2010) studied face recognition in identical twins (who share 100% of their genes) and fraternal twins (who share 50% of their genes). The face-recognition performance of identical twins was much more similar than

Section Summary

Face vs. object recognition

- Phenomena such as the part–whole effect and the composite illusion indicate that face recognition involves holistic processing to a greater extent than does object recognition. However, it has been argued that these phenomena simply reflect our expertise with faces.

Face blindness

- Many patients with prosopagnosia or face blindness have essentially intact object recognition. Other patients have deficient object recognition but intact face recognition. These findings suggest that face recognition involves different processes from object recognition.

Fusiform face area

- The fusiform face area has been identified as being of special importance for face processing. Supporting evidence comes from prosopagnosics who generally have damage to this area. Brain-imaging studies on healthy individuals indicate that the area is used in object recognition as well as face recognition.

Theories of face recognition

- Bruce and Young (1986) and Duchaine and Nakayama (2006) argued that several different processes are involved in face recognition. There is reasonable evidence for processing components including face detection, facial identity, and facial expression. Names are generally (but not always) retrieved more slowly than other kinds of personal information.

Super-recognizers

- Super-recognizers have exceptional face-recognition ability. Twin studies indicate that genetic factors strongly influence face-recognition ability, which may help to account for the existence of super-recognizers.

that of fraternal twins. This finding suggests that genetic factors influence face-recognition ability.

VISUAL IMAGERY AND VISUAL PERCEPTION

Close your eyes for a few moments and imagine the face of someone very important in your life. What did you experience? Many people claim that forming visual images is like "seeing with the mind's eye," suggesting there are important similarities between imagery and perception.

There are also important differences between imagery and perception. Visual imagery involves forming a mental representation of an object in the absence of the relevant stimulus in the environment and so relies totally on top-down processes. In contrast, visual perception depends heavily on bottom-up processes. Note that this issue is discussed briefly in Chapter 1.

If visual imagery and perception are similar, why don't we confuse them? In fact, a few people show such confusions – they suffer from hallucinations in which what they believe to be visual perception occurs in the absence of the

Key Term

Charles Bonnet syndrome:
a condition in which individuals with eye disease form vivid and detailed visual hallucinations that are mistaken for visual perception.

appropriate environmental stimulus. Hallucinations are common in individuals with **Charles Bonnet syndrome**, a condition associated with eye disease in which detailed visual hallucinations not under the patient's control are experienced. One sufferer reported the following hallucination: "There's heads of 17th century men and women, with nice heads of hair. Wigs, I should think. Very disapproving, all of them. They never smile" (Santhouse et al., 2000).

ffytche et al. (1998) found that patients with Charles Bonnet syndrome had increased activity in brain areas specialized for visual processing when hallucinating. In addition, hallucinations in color were associated with increased activity in brain areas specialized for color processing, hallucinations of faces were related to increased activity in regions specialized for face processing, and so on. Thus, the hallucinations experienced by patients with Charles Bonnet syndrome probably involve the same (or similar) processes to those involved in visual perception.

Very few people experience hallucinations. Indeed, anyone (except those with eye disease) suffering from numerous hallucinations is unlikely to remain at liberty for long! *Why* don't most of us confuse images with perceptions? One reason is that we often deliberately construct images, which is not the case with perception.

Another reason is that images typically contain much less detail than perception. Harvey (1986) found that participants rated their visual images of faces as most similar to photographs of the same faces from which the sharpness of the edges and borders had been removed.

Why is visual imagery useful to us? According to Moulton and Kosslyn (2009, p. 1274), imagery "allows us to answer 'what if' questions by making explicit and accessible the likely consequences of being in a specific situation or performing a specific action." For example, car drivers may use imagery to predict what will happen if they make a particular maneuver and top golfers use mental imagery to predict what would happen if they hit a certain shot.

THEORIES

What is the nature of visual imagery? The assumption that visual imagery resembles visual perception is popular. Stephen Kosslyn (e.g., 1994, 2005) has put forward an extremely influential theory based on that assumption. It is known as perceptual anticipation theory because the mechanisms used to generate images involve processes used to anticipate perceiving stimuli. Thus, the theory assumes there are close similarities between visual imagery and visual perception.

More specifically, visual images are depictive representations – they are like pictures or drawings in that the objects and parts of objects contained in them are arranged in space. Information within an image is organized spatially in the same way as information within a percept. Thus, for example, a visual image of a desk with a computer on top of it and a cat sleeping beneath it would be arranged so that the computer was at the top of the image and the cat at the bottom.

Where in the brain are these depictive representations formed? Kosslyn argues that they are formed in a brain area in which the spatial organization of brain activity resembles that of the imagined object. According to Kosslyn and Thompson (2003), depictive representations are created in early visual cortex in the occipital area at the back of the brain. Early visual cortex consists of primary visual cortex (also known as BA17 or V1) and secondary visual cortex (also known as BA18 or V2).

Kosslyn and Thompson (2003) used the term "visual buffer" to refer to the brain areas in which the depictive representations are formed, among which Areas 17 and 18 are of special importance. This visual buffer is used in visual perception as well as visual imagery; indeed, Areas 17 and 18 are of great importance in the early stages of visual processing.

In perception, processing in the visual buffer depends primarily on external stimulation. In contrast, visual images in the visual buffer depend on nonpictorial, propositional information stored in long-term memory. Visual long-term memories of shapes are stored in the inferior temporal lobe, whereas spatial representations are stored in posterior parietal cortex (see Figure 2.14).

We can compare Kosslyn's perceptual anticipation theory with the propositional theory of Zenon Pylyshyn (e.g., 2002, 2003). According to Pylyshyn, performance on mental imagery tasks does *not* involve depictive or pictorial representations. Instead, what is involved is tacit knowledge (knowledge not generally accessible to conscious awareness).

More specifically, tacit knowledge is "knowledge of what things would look like to subjects in situations like the ones in which they are to imagine themselves" (Pylyshyn, 2002, p. 161). This knowledge is in the form of propositions, which represent meaning in an abstract form. Thus, participants given an imagery task base their performance on relevant stored knowledge rather than visual images.

The exact nature of the tacit knowledge allegedly involved in visual imagery is puzzling, because Pylyshyn has not provided a very explicit account. However, there is no reason within his theory why early visual cortex would be involved when someone forms a visual image.

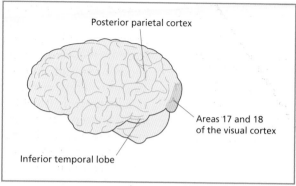

Figure 2.14   The approximate locations of the visual buffer in BA17 and BA18, of long-term memories in the inferior temporal lobe, and of spatial representations in posterior parietal cortex, according to Kosslyn and Thompson's (2003) anticipation theory.

IMAGERY RESEMBLES PERCEPTION

If visual perception and visual imagery involve similar processes, they should influence each other. There should be *facilitative* effects if the content of the perception and the image is the same but *interference* effects if the content is different. As we will see, both predictions have been supported.

So far as facilitation is concerned, we will consider a study by Pearson et al. (2008). They studied **binocular rivalry** – when two different stimuli are presented one to each eye, only *one* is consciously perceived at any given moment. If one of the stimuli is presented shortly beforehand, that increases the chances it will be perceived in the binocular rivalry situation.

Pearson et al. (2008) obtained the predicted findings when observers initially *perceived* a green vertical grating or a red horizontal grating. This facilitation effect was greatest when the orientation of the grating under binocular rivalry conditions was the same as the initial orientation and least when there was a large difference in orientation.

Pearson et al. (2008) also considered what happened when the initial single grating was *imagined* rather than perceived. The pattern of facilitation in binocular rivalry was remarkably similar to that observed when the initial single grating was perceived. These findings suggest that visual imagery involves similar processes to visual perception.

So far as interference is concerned, we will focus on a study by Baddeley and Andrade (2000). Participants rated the vividness of visual or auditory images under control conditions (no additional task) or while performing a second task. This second task involved visual/spatial processes or verbal processes (counting aloud repeatedly from 1 to 10). The visual/spatial task reduced the vividness of visual imagery more than that of auditory imagery because some of the same mechanisms were involved on the visual/spatial task and visual imagery task.

Brain imaging

If visual imagery and visual perception involve similar processes, we would expect similar brain areas to be activated when people engage in tasks involving imagery or perception. Note that I said similar rather than identical – the fact that visual perception involves bottom-up processes but visual imagery does not means that no-one would expect precisely the same brain areas to be involved.

According to Kosslyn (1994, 2005), much processing associated with visual imagery occurs in early visual cortex (Areas 17 and 18), although several other brain areas are also involved. Kosslyn and Thompson (2003) considered numerous studies in which activation of early visual cortex was assessed. Tasks involving visual imagery were associated with activation of early visual cortex in about half the studies reviewed. This is impressive evidence that visual imagery can involve very similar processes to those used in visual perception.

Kosslyn and Thompson (2003) identified three factors influencing whether early visual cortex was activated during visual imagery:

1. *The nature of the task:* Imagery tasks requiring participants to inspect fine details of their visual images were much more likely to be associated with activity in early visual cortex than were other imagery tasks.
2. *Sensitivity of brain-imaging technique:* There was more evidence that early visual cortex was involved in visual imagery when more sensitive brain-imaging techniques (e.g., fMRI) were used than when less sensitive ones (e.g., PET) were used.
3. *Shape-based vs. scanning tasks:* Early visual cortex was more likely to be involved when the imagery task required processing of an object's *shape* than when the emphasis was on imagining an object in motion. As we will see shortly, spatial processing (required to imagine an object in motion) involves different brain areas from visual processing.

The finding that activation in early visual cortex is often associated with visual imagery provides no guarantee it is *essential* for visual imagery. More convincing evidence was reported by Kosslyn et al. (1999). Participants memorized a stimulus containing four sets of stripes, after which they formed a visual image of it and compared the stripes (e.g., in terms of their relative width). Immediately before performing the task, some participants received repetitive transcranial magnetic stimulation (rTMS; see Glossary) applied to Area 17 (V1). rTMS significantly impaired performance on the imagery task, thus showing it is causally involved in imagery.

Showing that the brain areas involved in visual imagery are often the same as those involved in visual perception doesn't prove that imagery and perception involve the same processes. However, the findings of Klein et al. (2004) provide some reassurance. Participants were presented with flickering black-and-white, bow-tie shaped stimuli with a horizontal or a vertical orientation in the perceptual condition. In the imagery condition, they imagined the same bow-tie shaped stimuli.

What did Klein et al. (2004) find? Unsurprisingly, there was more activation within early visual cortex in the vertical direction when the stimulus was in the vertical orientation and more in the horizontal direction when it was in the horizontal orientation. Dramatically, the same pattern was also the case in the imagery condition. This provides evidence that the processes involved in visual imagery closely approximate those involved in visual perception.

Ganis et al. (2004) compared patterns of activation across most of the brain in visual perception and imagery. There were two main findings. First, there was extensive overlap in the brain areas associated with perception and imagery. This was especially so in the frontal and parietal areas, perhaps because perception and imagery involve similar cognitive control processes.

Second, the brain areas activated during imagery formed a subset of those activated during perception, especially in temporal and occipital regions. Thus, visual imagery involves only *some* of the processes involved in visual perception. It has been estimated (Kosslyn, 2005) that visual imagery tasks are associated with activation in about two-thirds of the brain areas activated during visual perception. Perception necessarily involves more low-level organization than imagery, and imagery relies more heavily on memory and top-down processes.

IMAGERY DOES *NOT* RESEMBLE PERCEPTION

In spite of the findings discussed above, there are important differences between visual imagery and visual perception. For example, imagine a cube balanced on

Research Activity 2.3: *Rotating images*

Have a look at Figure 2.15, which contains the outlines of three objects. Start with the object on the left and form a clear image of it. When you have done so, close your eyes, mentally rotate the image by 90 degrees clockwise, and decide what you see. Then repeat this exercise with the other two objects. When you have done that, see what happens when you actually rotate the book through 90 degrees. You should find it easy to identify the objects when you perceive them even though you probably couldn't when you only imagined rotating them.

Slezak (1991, 1995) carried out research using stimuli very similar to those shown in Figure 2.15. No observers reported seeing the objects. This *wasn't* a deficit in memory – participants who sketched the image from memory and then rotated it saw the new object.

What can we learn from this Research Activity and the work of Slezak (1991, 1995)? The take-home message is that there is a clear-cut difference

Figure 2.15 Slezak (1991, 1995) asked participants to memorize one of the above images. They then imagined rotating the image 90° clockwise and reported what they saw. None of them reported seeing the figures that can be seen clearly if you rotate the page by 90° clockwise. Left image from Slezak (1995), center image from Slezak (1991), right image reprinted from Pylyshyn (2003), reprinted with permission from Elsevier and the authors.

between imagery and perception. More specifically, the information contained in images can't be used as *flexibly* as visual or perceptual information.

one corner and then cut across the equator. What is the shape of the cut surface when the top is cut off? Most students say it is a square (Ian Gordon, personal communication), but in fact it is a regular hexagon. This suggests that images often consist of simplified structural descriptions omitting important aspects of the object being imagined.

Brain damage

If visual perception and visual imagery involve the same mechanisms, brain damage should have similar effects on perception and imagery. That is often the case (Bartolomeo, 2002, 2008). However, there are many exceptions. Moro et al. (2008) studied two brain-damaged patients. Patient 1 was a 29-year-old woman who worked as a clerk and Patient 2 was a 23-year-old man who was a factory worker. Both had essentially intact visual perception but impaired visual imagery.

What was the nature of their imagery impairment? They were very poor at drawing objects from memory even though they could copy the same objects when shown a drawing (see Figure 2.16). When patient 2 described a guitar he said: "You play it with one hand here and the other hand here [he moved his hands accordingly] but its shape … I don't know."

Patients (including those studied by Moro et al., 2008) with impaired visual imagery but intact visual perception have damage to the left temporal lobe. This happens because much of our knowledge of concepts (including objects) is stored there (Patterson et al., 2007).

What do the above findings mean? It is likely that visual images are generated from information stored in the temporal lobes. However, this generation process is not needed (or is much less important) for visual perception.

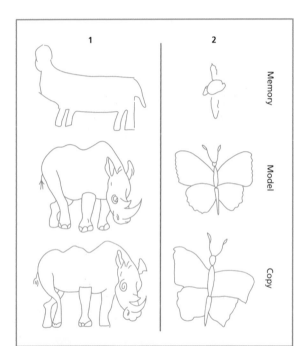

Figure 2.16 Drawings from memory (top row) and from copy (bottom row) by Patient 1 (29-year-old woman) on the left and by Patient 2 (23-year-old man) on the right. The drawings that were copied are shown in the middle. From Moro et al. (2008). Copyright © 2008, with permission from Elsevier.

Other patients have intact visual imagery but impaired visual perception (Bartolomeo, 2002, 2008). In **Anton's syndrome** ("blindness denial"), blind people are unaware they are blind and may confuse imagery with actual perception. Goldenburg et al. (1995) described a patient with Anton's syndrome, nearly all of whose primary visual cortex had been destroyed. In spite of that, the patient generated visual images so vivid they were mistaken for real visual perception. Zago et al. (2010) reported similar findings in another patient with Anton's syndrome having total damage to primary visual cortex.

In sum, there are important differences between the processes and brain areas involved in visual imagery and visual perception. This conclusion is supported by evidence that some brain areas are more important for perception than for imagery, and vice versa. In general, the information available in visual perception is more detailed and can be used more flexibly than that available in visual images.

Key Term

Anton's syndrome: a condition in which blind patients mistakenly believe that visual imagery is actually visual perception.

MENTAL ROTATION

So far we have considered the processes involved when someone forms a *static* mental image of a face or some other object. However, our imagery abilities can be used in many other ways. We can form images in other sense modalities; for example, imagining the sounds of church bells or the taste of our favorite food. In addition, we possess powers of spatial ability – we can close our eyes and imagine the layout of familiar rooms.

We can also imagine what would happen if some object were *rotated* from one orientation to another. For example, you may have had the frustrating experience of trying to fit several suitcases into a small car trunk. Perhaps you solved the problem by imagining what would happen if some suitcases were rotated into a different position. As we will see, much research has considered the processes involved in mental rotation.

How can we show that people use mental rotation to perform the task in the Research Activity? This question was addressed by Shepard and Metzler (1971), who carried out classic research on mental rotation using stimuli such as those in the Research Activity. Their central assumption was as follows: If we use mental rotation, the time taken to decide whether two objects are identical will be longer the more rotation that is required. Shepard and Metzler found strong support for this assumption whether rotation was required in two dimensions or in three.

What role does mental rotation play in our everyday lives? We need good spatial processing

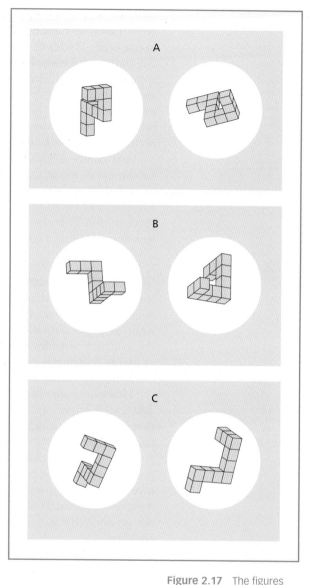

Figure 2.17 The figures in A are the same, differing only with respect to an 80° rotation in the picture plane. The figures in B are also the same. They differ only with respect to an 80° rotation in depth. The figures in C are different – they cannot be rotated to appear identical. From Shepard and Metzler (1971). Reprinted with permission from AAAS.

Research Activity 2.4: *Mental rotation*

Have a look at the pairs of objects shown in Figure 2.17. Decide in each case whether the two objects in each pair are identical or mirror images of each other. In addition, keep a record of how long it took you to make each decision.

When you have done that, ask yourself how you did it. Most people report that they engaged in mental rotation – one object was rotated mentally until it was easy to compare directly with the other one. It probably took you about 3 s with the pairs of shapes in A and B – this is consistent with the notion that you made use of time-consuming mental rotation.

skills to move successfully around the environment. The ability to perform mental rotation rapidly and accurately is an indication of such processing skills. In one study (Fields & Shelton, 2006), there were two virtual environments (a city park and a zoo). Participants viewed survey movies of each environment recorded from 700 feet above the ground in virtual space. After that, they answered questions designed to assess their knowledge of the layout of each environment (e.g., "Imagine you are standing at the clock tower, facing the fountain. Point to the carousel"). Performance was better among those who performed well on a mental rotation test than those who did not.

Astronauts typically experience disorientation when in space. The conditions in which they work mean they need good mental rotation abilities to recognize objects seen from non-upright orientations (Kornilova, 1997). Menchaca-Brandan et al. (2007) developed a virtual reality simulation of a space station. Participants obtaining good scores on a mental rotation test were best at controlling a robot arm around the workspace.

Gender differences

It is often believed that there are large gender differences in various cognitive abilities. Females are thought to outperform males on tests of verbal ability whereas males outperform females in terms of mathematical ability. In fact, the evidence provides only very modest support for these beliefs. When the available evidence is considered, there are only small and inconsistent gender differences in verbal and mathematical ability (Hyde, 2005).

However, males often outperform females on tests of spatial ability (Hyde, 2005; see Chapter 4). There are various reasons for this gender gap. The fact that males devote much more time than females to video games is an important factor (Terlecki & Newcombe, 2005).

One of the largest gender differences is in mental rotation, with males generally performing better than females (Hyde, 2005). In a cross-cultural study involving 53 countries (Lippa et al., 2010), males significantly outperformed females on a mental rotation task in every country. For reasons that are unclear, the gender difference was greater in countries having a high level of gender equality.

How can we explain the gender difference in mental rotation ability? It has been argued that the findings are consistent with a hunter-gatherer theory (e.g., Silverman et al., 2007). According to this theory, men in our ancestral past went out hunting and needed expert spatial skills to find their way back home. In contrast, women historically needed different spatial skills to gather plant resources.

As predicted on the hunter-gatherer theory, women in 35 out of the 40 countries studied by Silverman et al. scored higher than men on memory for object locations. Further support for the theory was reported by Pacheco-Cobos et al. (2010). They found that Mexican women gathered mushrooms in the natural environment with less energy expenditure than Mexican men.

Social factors help to explain why males generally outperform females in mental rotation. Moè (2009) obtained the typical finding with standard instructions. However, when the instructions indicated that women were better than men at mental rotation, there was no gender difference in performance (Moè, 2009). This latter finding may have occurred because the instructions served to invalidate the gender stereotype that females are not as good as men at spatial skills.

Cherney (2008) assessed the effects of 4 h of practice with computer games on mental rotation. Performance improved substantially on two tests of mental rotation even after this limited amount of practice. Of most importance here, the performance improvement was significantly greater for female participants than for male ones. Thus, exposure to appropriate forms of practice can reduce (or eliminate) gender differences in mental rotation.

Cognitive neuroscience

The primary visual cortex in the occipital region of the brain and the temporal lobes (associated with the storage of object and concept information) are both important in visual imagery (Kosslyn & Thompson, 2003). In contrast, mental rotation involves spatial and motor processing (involving imagining object manipulation). Thus, the brain areas most associated with mental rotation should differ substantially from those associated with visual imagery.

Zacks (2008) reviewed 19 brain-imaging studies of mental rotation. The parietal region was activated during mental rotation, especially parts of the posterior parietal lobe such as BA7 and the intraparietal sulcus (see Figure 2.18). There was increased activation in those areas with increasing amounts of mental rotation. These findings are as expected given that parietal areas contain spatial maps and are associated with spatial processing (Thompson et al., 2009). Note that the posterior parietal region is generally *not* activated during visual imagery tasks (Kosslyn, 2005).

The discovery that parietal areas are activated during mental rotation tasks doesn't show these areas are *necessary* for mental rotation. Stronger evidence can be obtained by using transcranial magnetic stimulation (TMS; see Glossary) to produce brief inhibition of processing in the parietal region. When this was done, performance on mental rotation tasks was impaired (Aleman et al., 2002; Harris & Miniussi, 2003). This suggests that parietal regions are essential for efficient mental rotation.

Zacks (2008) also found that motor areas in the posterior frontal cortex were often activated during mental rotation. This often happens because there

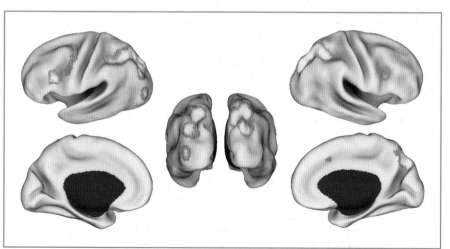

Figure 2.18 Brain regions in the meta-analysis that responded during mental rotation tasks. Brighter colors indicate stronger responses. From Zacks (2008). Copyright © 2008. Reproduced with permission from MIT Press and Cognitive Neuroscience Institute.

is mental simulation of the physical actions involved in object rotation. Such mental simulation should be greater when there is mental rotation of hands than of other objects (e.g., letters). In one study (Tomasino et al., 2005), transcranial magnetic stimulation applied to posterior frontal cortex impaired mental rotation of hands but not of letters.

In sum, cognitive neuroscientists have provided evidence that the processes involved in mental rotation differ substantially from those involved in visual imagery. More specifically, mental rotation involves brain areas known to be involved in spatial processing and others involved in motor simulation.

Section Summary

- Patients with Charles Bonnet syndrome experience detailed visual hallucinations. Areas specialized for visual processing are activated when these patients hallucinate. Visual imagery fulfills the function of predicting future perception.

Theories

- According to Kosslyn, there are close similarities between visual imagery and visual perception. Information within an image is organized spatially in the same way as information within a percept. Pylyshyn argues that mental imagery relies on relevant abstract stored knowledge. The common finding that early visual cortex is activated during visual imagery supports Kosslyn's viewpoint. Evidence that visual imagery and visual perception can have mutually facilitatory or interfering effects also supports his position. However, the existence of patients with intact visual perception but impaired visual imagery and vice versa is more consistent with Pylshyn's position. Images differ from percepts in being less detailed and less flexible.

Mental rotation

- Males generally outperform females on mental rotation tasks. A hunter-gatherer theory provides a partial account of this finding. However, social factors (e.g., gender stereotypes) and greater relevant practice by males are also involved. The brain areas associated with mental rotation differ from those associated with visual imagery. More specifically, mental rotation involves brain areas associated with spatial processing and mental simulation.

PERCEPTION AND ACTION

The visual system is of great value in allowing us to construct an accurate internal model of the world around us. When we look around us, we are generally very confident that what we can see corresponds precisely to what is actually there. Indeed, the human species would have become extinct a very long time ago if we perceived the environment inaccurately! If we thought the edge of a precipice was further away than was actually the case, our lives would be in danger. In spite of these arguments in favor of accurate visual perception,

Research Activity 2.5: *Visual illusions*

Have a look at the two figures in Figure 2.19(a) and decide which of the two vertical lines is longer. Nearly everyone says the vertical line on the left looks longer than the one on the right. In fact, they are the same length, as can be confirmed by using a ruler (this is the Müller-Lyer illusion).

Now have a look at the two rectangles in Figure 2.19(b) and decide which is larger. Most people say rectangle A is larger than B, but they are in fact the same size (this is the Ponzo illusion).

These are just two out of literally hundreds of visual illusions. How can we explain them? Perhaps we treat two-dimensional illusion figures as if they were three-dimensional (Gregory, 1973). For example, the long lines in the Ponzo illusion look like railway lines or the edges of a road receding into the distance. As a result, rectangle A can be seen as further away from us than rectangle B. If it were a three-dimensional scene, then rectangle A would be larger than rectangle B.

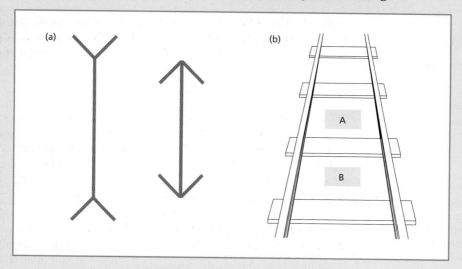

Figure 2.19   (a) The Müller-Lyer illusion. (b) The Ponzo illusion.

psychologists have found we are subject to numerous visual illusions, some of which are discussed in Research Activity 2.5.

The existence of the Müller-Lyer, Ponzo, and other illusions leaves us with an intriguing paradox. How has the human species survived given that our visual perceptual processes are apparently so prone to error? A plausible answer is that most visual illusions involve artificial figures, are far removed from the world around us, and so can be dismissed as tricks played by psychologists with nothing better to do.

There is some validity in the above argument. However, it doesn't account for all illusions. For example, you can show the Müller-Lyer illusion with real three-dimensional objects (DeLucia & Hochberg, 1991). Place three open books in a line so the ones on the left and the right are open to the right and the middle one is open to the left (see Figure 2.20). The spine of the book in the middle should be the same distance from the spines of each of the other two books. However, the distance between the spine of the middle book and that of the book on the right should look longer.

Figure 2.20   The spine of the middle book is closer to the spine of which other book? Now check your answer with a ruler.

TWO VISUAL SYSTEMS: PERCEPTION AND ACTION

We turn now to an alternative explanation of the paradox that visual perception seems very accurate in everyday life but can be error-prone in the laboratory. According to Milner and Goodale (1998, 2008), we have *two* visual systems. There is a vision-for-perception system used to identify objects (e.g., to decide whether we are confronted by a cat or a buffalo). This system is used when we look at visual illusions.

There is also a vision-for-action system used for visually guided action. This system provides accurate information about our position with respect to objects. It is the system we generally use when avoiding a speeding car or grasping an object.

The notion of two partially independent visual systems has received support from studies in cognitive neuroscience (Gazzaniga et al., 2009). There is a "what" or ventral pathway going to the inferotemporal cortex (see Figure 2.21) corresponding to the vision-for-perception system.

There is also a "where" or "how" pathway (the dorsal pathway) going to the parietal cortex (Figure 2.21) corresponding to the vision-for-action system. Note, however, that these two pathways aren't separated neatly and tidily, and there is considerable interchange of information between them (Zanon et al., 2010). Note also that the "where" or "how" pathway has more involvement in object recognition than suggested by the figure (Farivar, 2009).

We can relate Milner and Goodale's (1998, 2008) theoretical approach to visual illusions. Suppose people were presented with three-dimensional versions of a visual illusion such as the Müller-Lyer. It would be expected that the illusion would be present if they were asked which line was longer, because that would involve the vision-for-perception system. However, the illusion should be reduced in size or disappear if people pointed at the end of one of the two figures, because that would involve the vision-for-action system.

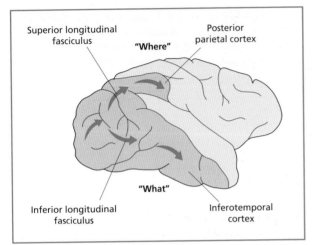

Figure 2.21   The ventral (what) and dorsal (where or how) pathways involved in vision having their origins in primary visual cortex (V1). From Gazzaniga, Ivry, and Mangun (2009). Copyright © 1998 by W. W. Norton & Company, Inc. Used by permission of W. W. Norton & Company, Inc.

Findings

The above predictions have been supported in several studies. Bruno et al. (2008) reviewed 33 studies involving the Müller-Lyer or related illusions in which the observers *pointed* rapidly at one of the figures. The mean illusion effect was 5.5%. In other studies using standard procedures (e.g., verbal estimations of length), the mean illusion effect was 22.4%. Thus, the mean illusion effect was four times greater with the vision-for-perception system than with the vision-for-action system.

The hollow-face illusion is one of the most powerful illusions. In this illusion, a realistic hollow mask looks like a normal face (see Figure 2.22; visit the website: www.richardgregory.org/experiments). In a study by Króliczak et al. (2006), a target (a small magnet) was placed on the face mask or on a normal face. Here are two of the tasks:

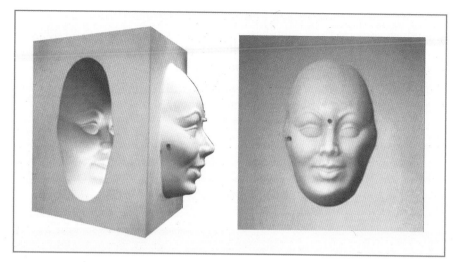

Figure 2.22 Left: normal and hollow faces with small target magnets on the forehead and cheek of the normal face; right: front view of the hollow mask that appears as an illusory face projecting forwards. Reprinted from Króliczak et al. (2006), Copyright © 2006, with permission from Elsevier.

1. Draw the target position (using the vision-for-perception system);
2. Make a fast flicking finger movement to the target (using the vision-for-action system).

There was a strong illusion effect when observers drew the target position. In contrast, observers' performance was very accurate (i.e., illusion-free) when they made a flicking movement. These findings were as predicted theoretically.

There was also a third condition in which observers made a slow pointing finger movement to the target. Performance might have been expected to be accurate in this condition because it involved use of the vision-for-action system. In fact, however, the illusory effect was fairly strong. Why was this? According to Króliczak et al. (2006), actions involve the vision-for-perception system as well as the vision-for-action system when they are preceded by conscious cognitive processes.

More evidence that the vision-for-perception system can influence our actions was shown by Creem and Proffitt (2001). They distinguished between *effective* and *appropriate* grasping. For example, we can grasp a toothbrush effectively by its bristles, but appropriate grasping involves picking it up by the handle. Creem and Proffitt's key assumption was that appropriate grasping involves accessing stored knowledge about the object. As a result, appropriate grasping requires use of the vision-for-perception system.

Creem and Proffitt (2001) tested the above hypothesis by asking people to pick up various objects with handles (e.g., toothbrush; hammer; knife). The handle always pointed away from the participant, and the measure of interest was the percentage of occasions on which the objects were grasped appropriately. Participants' ability to grasp objects appropriately was greatly impaired when they performed a learning task involving retrieving words from long-term memory at the same time. These findings suggest that retrieval of knowledge (using the vision-for-perception system) is necessary for appropriate grasping.

Evaluation

➕ The notion that there are fairly separate vision-for-perception and vision-for-action systems is very influential.

⊕ Findings showing that action-based performance (e.g., pointing; grasping) often reduces or eliminates visual illusory effects are consistent with the existence of two visual systems (Stottinger et al., 2010).

⊖ The two visual systems typically *interact* with each other (Schenk & McIntosh, 2010). However, the emphasis within the theory is on their *separate* contributions to vision and action.

⊖ Actions are influenced by the vision-for-perception system more than was implied by early versions of the theory. Actions are most likely to be influenced by the vision-for-perception system when they aren't automatic but instead are based on conscious cognitive processes (Milner & Goodale, 2008).

Section Summary

• It has been claimed that many visual illusions occur because we treat two-dimensional figures as if they were three-dimensional. However, this doesn't explain why the Müller-Lyer illusion can be found with three-dimensional objects.

Two visual systems: Perception and action

• Much evidence suggests the existence of two partially independent systems specialized for perception and for action. According to Milner and Goodale, the vision-for-perception system is much more susceptible than the vision-for-action system to visual illusions. This prediction has been supported many times. However, the vision-for-perception system influences actions when they are based on conscious cognitive processes. More generally, the two systems often interact with each other rather than functioning separately.

IN SIGHT BUT OUT OF MIND

Have a look around you (go on!). I imagine you have the strong impression of seeing a vivid and detailed picture of the visual scene in front of your eyes. In fact, however, many psychologists argue that we are deluding ourselves!

Suppose you are watching a video in which students are passing a ball to each other. At some point a woman in a gorilla suit walks right into camera shot, looks at the camera, thumps her chest, and then walks off (see Figure 2.23). Altogether she is on the screen for 9 s. I am sure you feel it is absolutely certain that you would spot the woman dressed up as a gorilla almost immediately. Simons and Chabris (1999) carried out an experiment along the lines just described (see the video at www.simonslab.com/videos.html). What percentage of their participants do you think failed to spot the gorilla? Think about your answer before reading on.

It seems probable that practically no one would fail to spot a "gorilla" taking 9 s to stroll across a scene. In fact, the findings were VERY surprising: 50% of observers didn't notice the woman's presence at all!

Simons and Levin (1998) carried out similar research in which people walking across a college campus were asked for directions by a stranger. About 10 or 15 s into the discussion, two men carrying a wooden door passed between the stranger and the participants. While that was happening, the stranger was substituted with a man of different height, build, and voice wearing different clothes. However, half the participants failed to realize their conversational partner had changed! You can see this video on the website given above (The "Door" Study).

At this point, let's consider the terms used to describe the phenomena just discussed. First, there is **inattentional blindness**, the failure to notice an unexpected object appearing in a visual display (e.g., the gorilla in the midst of students). Second, there is **change blindness**, the failure to detect that an object has moved, changed, or disappeared (e.g., one stranger being replaced with a different one).

The notion that we greatly overestimate our ability to detect visual changes was confirmed by Levin et al. (2002). Observers saw various videos involving two people having a conversation in a restaurant. In one video, the plates on their table changed from red to white, and in another a scarf worn by one of them disappeared.

The above videos had previously been used by Levin and Simons (1997), who found that no observers detected any of the changes. Levin et al. asked their participants whether they thought they would have noticed the changes if they hadn't been forewarned about them. Forty-six per cent claimed they would have noticed the change in the color of the plates, and 78% the disappearing scarf. Levin et al. used the term **change blindness blindness** to describe our wildly optimistic beliefs about our ability to detect visual changes.

Change blindness is important in the real world. For example, an Airbus AT320-111 coming in to land at Strasbourg, France in 1992 mysteriously crashed into a mountain a considerable distance short of the runway. The most likely explanation is that the pilot didn't notice an important signal change on the visual display in front of him. Galpin et al. (2009) found that drivers and nondrivers viewing a complex driving-related scene showed much evidence of change blindness for central items that seemed relatively unimportant.

On a more positive note, change blindness is a blessing for magicians. Most magic tricks involve misdirection – the spectators' attention is drawn away from some action crucial to the success of the trick. When this is done skillfully, spectators fail to see how the magician is doing his/her tricks while thinking they have seen everything that is going on.

Movie makers are also grateful for the existence of change blindness. It means we rarely spot visual changes when the same scene has been shot more than once with parts of each shot being combined in the final version. In *Basic Instinct*, there is a famous scene in which Sharon Stone crosses her legs to reveal her lack of underwear. During that scene, the cigarette she was holding suddenly disappears and then reappears.

Figure 2.23 Frame showing a woman in a gorilla suit in the middle of a game of passing the ball. From Simons and Chabris (1999). Figure provided by Daniel Simons. www. Simonslab.com.

In the movie *Diamonds Are Forever*, James Bond tilts his car on two wheels to drive through an alleyway. As he enters the alleyway, the car is balanced on its right wheels, but when it emerges on the other side it is miraculously on its left wheels! You can see more examples at: www.jonhs.com/moviegoofs

WHEN IS CHANGE BLINDNESS FOUND?

The extent to which we show change blindness or inattentional blindness depends on several factors. You can (hopefully!) see the effects of one of these factors if you look at Figure 2.24 and try to spot the difference between the pictures. Rensink et al. (1997) found that observers took an average of 10.4 s to spot the difference between the first pair of pictures but only 2.6 s with the second pair of pictures. This discrepancy occurred because the height of the railing is of marginal interest whereas the position of the helicopter is of central interest.

In studies such as those of Simons and Chabris (1999) and Simons and Levin (1998), observers were not told beforehand to expect a change in the

Figure 2.24   (a) the object that is changed (the railing) undergoes a shift in location comparable to that of the object that is changed (the helicopter) in (b). However, the change is much easier to see in (b) because the changed object is more important. From Rensink et al. (1997). Copyright © 1997 by SAGE. Reprinted by permission of SAGE Publications.

(a) Change in marginal interest (MI)

(b) Change in central interest (CI)

visual display (incidental approach). Observers are much more likely to detect a change when told in advance to expect one (intentional approach). Beck et al. (2007) found that observers detected visual changes 90% of the time using the intentional approach but only 40% using the incidental approach.

Substantial evidence for change blindness can be found even with the intentional approach. Rosielle and Scaggs (2008) asked students to identify what was wrong with a picture of a familiar scene on their college campus (see Figure 2.25 for examples). Nearly all the students (97%) rated the scene as familiar, but only 20% detected the change. Such findings indicate that our long-term memory for complex scenes can be much less impressive than we believe to be the case.

You will remember the surprising finding of Simons and Chabris (1999) that 50% of observers failed to detect a woman dressed as a black gorilla. There were two teams of students in the video (one dressed in white and the other dressed in black), and observers counted the passes of the team of students

Original scene   **Altered scene**

Figure 2.25 Examples of the original and altered versions of the photographs. From Rosielle and Scaggs (2008).

dressed in white. The observers focused on people dressed in white, which led them to ignore the black gorilla.

Simons and Chabris (1999) carried out a further experiment in which observers counted the passes made by either members of the team dressed in white or the one dressed in black. The gorilla's presence was detected by only 42% of observers when the attended team was the one dressed in white. However, the gorilla's presence was detected by 83% of observers when the attended team was dressed in black. What do these findings mean? An unexpected object (i.e., the gorilla) attracts more attention and so is more likely to be detected when it is *similar* to task-relevant stimuli.

Hollingworth and Henderson (2002) studied the role of attention in change blindness. They recorded eye movements while observers looked at a visual scene (e.g., kitchen; living room) for several seconds. It was assumed that the object fixated at any given moment was being attended. There were two kinds of changes that could occur to each visual scene:

- **Type change**, in which an object was replaced by an object from a different category (e.g., a plate was replaced by a bowl).
- **Token change**, in which an object was replaced by an object from the same category (e.g., a plate was replaced by a different plate).

There were two main findings (see Figure 2.26). First, changes were much more likely to be detected when the changed object had received attention (been fixated) before the change occurred. Second, change detection was much better when there was a change in the type of object rather than merely swapping one member of a category for another (token change).

WHAT CAUSES CHANGE BLINDNESS?

It has generally been assumed that change blindness (and its opposite, change detection) depends on attentional processes. Thus, we detect changes when we are attending to an object that changes, and we show change blindness when not attending to that object (Rensink, 2002). This approach receives support from the finding that observers are more likely to detect changes in an object when it is fixated prior to the change (Hollingworth & Henderson, 2002).

The above approach assumes that our visual perception of unattended objects is very incomplete. However, other explanations are possible (Simons & Rensink,

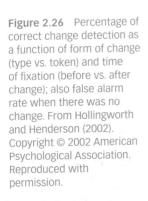

Figure 2.26 Percentage of correct change detection as a function of form of change (type vs. token) and time of fixation (before vs. after change); also false alarm rate when there was no change. From Hollingworth and Henderson (2002). Copyright © 2002 American Psychological Association. Reproduced with permission.

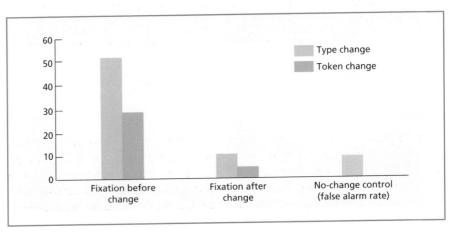

2005). Perhaps we initially form detailed and complete representations but these representations decay rapidly or are overwritten by a subsequent stimulus (Lamme, 2003). That would be consistent with our subjective impression that we briefly have access to reasonably complete information about the visual scene in front of us.

Support was reported by Landman et al. (2003). Observers were presented with an array of eight rectangles (some horizontal and the others vertical), followed 1600 ms later by a second array of eight rectangles. The observers' task was to decide whether any of the rectangles had changed orientation from horizontal to vertical or vice versa.

There was very little change blindness provided the observers' attention was directed to the rectangle that might change within 900 ms of the offset of the first array. Thus, we have access to fairly complete information about a visual scene for almost 1 s provided no other visual stimulus is presented.

In sum, our visual system is designed very efficiently. We have access to fairly detailed information about the current visual scene. However, it is important that what we currently perceive isn't disrupted by what we last perceived. This is achieved by overwriting or replacing the latter with the former. A consequence is that we often exhibit change blindness.

Section Summary

- There is much evidence that most people are very susceptible to inattentional blindness and change blindness. Our optimistic belief about our ability to detect visual changes is known as change blindness blindness.

When is change blindness found?

- Change blindness is less likely to occur when observers expect a change compared to when they aren't forewarned of a change. It also tends to occur when the changed object is relatively unimportant, when the changed object resembles task-relevant stimuli, and when it has been fixated prior to the change.

What causes change blindness?

- Change blindness is due in part to our inability to retain detailed information about a visual scene for more than a very short period of time. It is also due in part to failures of attention. In addition, there is sometimes overwriting or replacing of information about the previous visual representation by the current one.

DOES PERCEPTION REQUIRE CONSCIOUS AWARENESS?

Can we perceive aspects of the visual world without any conscious awareness that we are doing so? In other words, is there such a thing as unconscious perception or **subliminal perception** (i.e., perception occurring even though the stimulus is below the threshold of conscious awareness)? Common sense suggests that the answer is "No." However, there is increasing evidence that the correct answer is "Yes."

Key Term
Subliminal perception: perceptual processing occurring below the level of conscious awareness that can nevertheless influence behavior.

The case for subliminal perception apparently received support from the notorious "research" carried out in 1957 by James Vicary, who was a struggling market researcher. He claimed to have flashed the words HUNGRY? EAT POPCORN and DRINK COCA-COLA for 1/300th of a second (well below the threshold of conscious awareness) numerous times during showings of a movie called *Picnic* at a cinema in Fort Lee, New Jersey. Vicary claimed there was an increase of 18% in the cinema sales of Coca-Cola and a 58% increase in popcorn sales. Alas, Vicary admitted in 1962 that the study was a hoax.

This hasn't stopped advertisers from trying to influence our buying habits via subliminal perception. Wilson Bryan Key (1980) had a very close look at a Howard Johnson's menu. He claimed that the picture of a plate of clams on the menu actually depicted a sex orgy involving several people and a donkey!

In what follows, I consider two main strands of research on subliminal perception. First, I discuss studies on individuals with normal vision presented with stimuli they can't see consciously.

Second, I discuss studies on brain-damaged patients denying conscious awareness of visual stimuli presented to parts of their visual field. In spite of that, they are often able to detect and localize visual stimuli presented to the "blind" region.

PERCEPTION WITHOUT AWARENESS

There are three main ways we can present individuals having intact vision with visual stimuli below the level of conscious awareness. First, we can present stimuli that are very weak or faint. Second, we can present stimuli very briefly. Third, we can use masking – the target stimulus is immediately followed by a masking stimulus that inhibits processing of the target stimulus.

How do we decide whether an observer is consciously aware of a given visual stimulus? Merikle et al. (2001) distinguished two approaches:

1. *Subjective threshold:* This is defined by an individual's failure to report conscious awareness of a stimulus; it is the most obvious measure to use.
2. *Objective threshold:* This is defined by an individual's inability to make an accurate forced-choice decision about a stimulus (e.g., guess at above chance level whether it is a word).

In practice, observers often show "awareness" of a stimulus assessed by the objective threshold even when the stimulus doesn't exceed the subjective threshold. What should we do in such circumstances? Many psychologists argue that the objective threshold is more valid than a reliance on observers' possibly inaccurate or biased reports of their conscious experience. What is clear is that evidence for subliminal or unconscious perception based on the objective threshold is more convincing than evidence based on the subjective threshold.

Findings

Naccache et al. (2002) asked participants to decide rapidly whether a clearly visible target digit was smaller or larger than 5. Unknown to them, an invisible masked digit was presented for 29 ms immediately before the target. The masked digit was congruent with the target (both digits on the same side of 5) or incongruent.

There was no evidence of conscious perception of the masked digits. No participants reported seeing any of them (subjective measure). In addition, their performance when guessing whether the masked digit was below or above 5 was at chance level (objective measure). However, performance with the target digits was faster on congruent than on incongruent trials, indicating that unconscious perceptual processing of the masked digits had occurred.

Jiang et al. (2006) presented pairs of pictures followed by a mask making them invisible to observers (based on the objective threshold). One picture was an intact picture of a nude male or female and the other was a scrambled version. These subliminal pictures influenced participants' attentional processes (see Chapter 3). The attention of heterosexual males was attracted to intact pictures of invisible female nudes, and that of heterosexual females to invisible male nudes. These findings indicate there was some perceptual processing of invisible sexual stimuli.

It is generally assumed that information perceived with awareness can be used to *control* our responses, whereas information perceived without awareness cannot. If so, there should be situations in which perceiving with or without awareness has very different effects on behavior.

Persaud and McLeod (2008) found supporting evidence in a study in which they presented the letter 'b' or 'h' for 10 ms (short interval) or 15 ms (long interval). In the key condition, participants were told to respond with the letter that had *not* been presented. With the longer presentation interval, participants responded correctly with the nonpresented letter on 83% of trials. This suggests there was some conscious awareness of the stimulus in that condition.

With the short presentation interval, however, participants responded correctly on only 43% of trials (significantly below chance). Thus, there was some processing of the stimulus but participants lacked awareness of that processing.

How much visual processing occurs below the level of conscious awareness? In one study (Rees, 2007), activation was assessed in brain areas associated with face processing or with object processing while pictures of invisible faces or houses were presented. The identity of the picture (face vs. house) could be predicted with almost 90% accuracy by studying patterns of brain activation. Thus, even stimuli that can't be perceived consciously can be processed reasonably thoroughly by the visual system.

BLINDSIGHT

Several British soldiers in the First World War blinded by gunshot wounds that had destroyed their primary visual cortex (V1) were treated by a captain in the Royal Army Medical Corps called George Riddoch. These soldiers could perceive motion in those parts of the visual field in which they claimed to be blind (Riddoch, 1917)!

Many years later, Larry Weiskrantz (2004) at the University of Oxford studied a similar phenomenon. He described brain-damaged patients with some visual perception in the absence of any conscious awareness as having **blindsight**, which neatly captures the paradoxical nature of their condition.

Most patients with blindsight have extensive damage to V1. However, their loss of visual awareness in the blind field is probably not due directly to the V1 damage. Damage to V1 has knock-on effects throughout the visual system, leading to greatly reduced activation of subsequent visual processing areas (Silvanto, 2008).

Key Term
Blindsight: an apparently paradoxical condition often produced by brain damage to early visual cortex in which there is behavioral evidence of visual perception in the absence of conscious awareness.

Findings

One of the most thoroughly studied blindsight patients is DB. He began to experience increasingly frequent very severe migraines. As a result, he had a brain operation that destroyed the right half of his primary visual cortex (V1). DB showed some perceptual skills including an ability to detect whether a visual stimulus had been presented to the blind area and to identify its location. However, he reported no conscious experience in his blind field. According to Weiskrantz et al. (1974, p. 721), "When he was shown a video film of his reaching and judging orientation of lines [by presenting it to his intact visual field], he was openly astonished."

Another much-studied blindsight patient is GY. He has extensive damage to V1 in the left hemisphere and a smaller area of damage in the right parietal area caused by a car accident at the age of eight. In a study by Persaud and Cowey (2008), GY was presented with a stimulus in the upper or lower part of his visual field. On some trials (inclusion trials), he was told to report the part of the visual field to which the stimulus had been presented. On other trials (exclusion trials), GY was told to report the *opposite* of the stimulus's actual location (e.g., "Up" when it was in the lower part).

GY tended to respond with the real rather than the opposite location on exclusion trials as well as inclusion trials (see Figure 2.27). This suggests he had access to location information but lacked any conscious awareness of that information. In contrast, healthy individuals showed a large difference in performance on inclusion and exclusion trials (see Figure 2.27) indicating they had conscious access to location information.

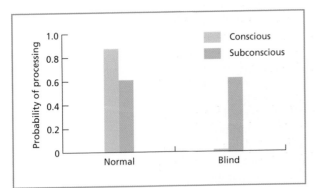

Figure 2.27 Estimated contributions of conscious and subconscious processing to GY's performance in exclusion and inclusion conditions in his normal and blind fields. Reprinted from Persaud and Cowey (2008), Copyright © 2008, with permission from Elsevier.

Some research on patients with blindsight has focused on whether they can discriminate between emotional stimuli presented below the level of conscious awareness. This effect (known as **affective blindsight**) has been obtained in several studies (e.g., Tamietto & de Gelder, 2008), and is discussed in Chapter 12.

Researchers often ask blindsight patients to indicate on a yes/no basis whether they have seen a given stimulus. That opens up the possibility that blindsight patients have some conscious vision but simply set a high threshold for reporting awareness. Overgaard et al. (2008) used a four-point scale of perceptual awareness: "clear image"; "almost clear image"; "weak glimpse"; and "not seen". Their blindsight patient, GR, had to decide whether a triangle, circle, or square had been presented to her blind field.

GR was correct 100% of the time when she had a clear image, 72% of the time when her image was almost clear, 25% of the time when she had a weak glimpse, and 0% of the time when the stimulus wasn't seen. Thus, the use of a sensitive method to assess conscious awareness suggests that degraded conscious vision sometimes underlies blindsight patients' ability to perform at above-chance levels on visual tasks.

Issues

There is much evidence suggesting that blindsight is a genuine phenomenon. However, there are various reasons why it is sometimes hard to interpret the

Key Term

Affective blindsight: the ability to discriminate among different emotional stimuli in spite of the absence of conscious perception.

evidence. First, blindsight patients differ in how much conscious perception they possess (Danckert & Rossetti, 2005). Weiskrantz (2004) used the term blindsight Type 1 to describe patients with no conscious awareness. He used the term blindsight Type 2 to describe those patients with awareness that something was happening. An example of Type 2 blindsight was found in patient EY. He "sensed a definite pinpoint of light," although "it does not actually look like a light. It looks like nothing at all" (Weiskrantz, 1980).

Second, as Cowey (2010, p. 20) pointed out, "Subjects are too seldom asked to describe exactly what they mean when they say they are 'aware'." Blindsight patients may appear to have less conscious perception when the definition of awareness is stringent than when it is lenient (Overgaard et al., 2008).

Section Summary

Unconscious perception

- Conscious awareness of a visual stimulus can be assessed by using a subjective or an objective threshold (the latter is more stringent). There is evidence for unconscious perception using behavioral data and the objective threshold. Studies using brain-imaging data suggest there can be substantial processing of visual stimuli in the absence of conscious awareness.

Blindsight

- Blindsight patients show some ability to indicate the location and movement of visual stimuli they deny seeing. Some of these patients also demonstrate affective blindsight. However, the use of sensitive methods to assess conscious awareness suggests that some blindsight patients have degraded conscious vision in their "blind" area.

AUDITORY PERCEPTION

As mentioned in the Introduction to this chapter, speech perception is easily the most important form of auditory perception. However, other kinds of auditory perception (e.g., music perception) also play a major role in many people's lives. In this section of the chapter, we will mainly consider the processes involved in speech perception. However, we start by comparing speech perception with other forms of auditory perception.

IS SPEECH PERCEPTION SPECIAL?

There has been controversy concerning the relationship between speech perception and auditory perception in general (Cleary & Pisoni, 2001; Peretz & Coltheart, 2003; Todd et al., 2006). One possibility (Trout, 2001) is that humans are born with a special mechanism designed for speech perception only. However, most theorists argue in favor of a general mechanism used to process both speech and nonspeech sounds. Some of the relevant evidence is discussed below.

Categorical perception

Suppose we present listeners with a series of sounds starting with /ba/ and gradually moving towards /da/ and ask them to report what sound they hear. It might be expected the listeners would report a gradual change from perceiving one phoneme to the other. In fact, however, there is an abrupt shift in perception (Liberman et al., 1967). This tendency for speech sounds intermediate between two phonemes to be perceived as one phoneme or the other is known as **categorical perception**.

Further evidence for categorical perception of phonemes was reported by Raizada and Poldrack (2007). Two auditory stimuli were presented at the same time, and listeners decided whether they represented the same phoneme. Differences in brain activation of the two stimuli were strongly amplified when they were on opposite sides of the boundary between two phonemes. This amplification effect probably plays a role in producing categorical perception of phonemes.

The existence of categorical perception doesn't mean we can't distinguish at all between slightly different sounds assigned to the same phoneme category. Listeners decided faster that two sounds represented the same syllable when the sounds were identical than when they were not (Pisoni & Tash, 1974).

At one time, it was claimed that categorical perception didn't occur with nonspeech sounds. If so, that would suggest that speech processing involves a special mechanism. However, there is increasing evidence that this claim is inaccurate. Locke and Kellar (1973) studied the identification of chords by musicians and nonmusicians. Musicians showed much clearer evidence of categorical perception than nonmusicians when categorizing chords as A minor or A major. This finding may help to explain why categorical perception of phonemes is so strong – we are all expert listeners to phonemes.

Categorical perception of phonemes is influenced by context. Ganong (1980) presented listeners with various sounds ranging between a word (e.g., dash) and a nonword (e.g., tash). There was a clear context effect – an ambiguous initial phoneme was more likely to be assigned to a given phoneme category when it produced a word than when it did not. Thus, context expanded the category of the expected phoneme. Context also influences categorical perception of musical chords (McMurray et al., 2008) via top-down processes.

There is reasonable evidence that listeners make some use of the speech production system when engaged in speech perception. Möttönen and Watkins (2009) wondered whether the speech production system is relevant to categorical perception of phonemes. They applied transcranial magnetic stimulation (TMS; see Glossary) to the motor cortex to inhibit processes associated with lip movements. This led to impaired categorical perception of speech sounds involving lips in their articulation. Thus, speech perception depends in part on motor processes. This probably represents an important difference from the processing of nonspeech sounds.

Cognitive neuroscience

There is considerable overlap in the brain areas associated with the processing of speech and nonspeech sounds. Husain et al. (2006) found that various speech and nonspeech sounds activated similar regions in the primary and nonprimary areas of the temporal cortex, intraparietal cortex, and frontal lobe. In addition, there were only relatively minor differences in patterns of brain activity when speech and nonspeech sounds were processed.

Clear evidence that somewhat different brain areas are involved in speech and music processing comes from studies on brain-damaged individuals. Some of them have intact speech perception but impaired music perception, whereas others have intact music perception but impaired speech perception (Peretz & Coltheart, 2003).

| Key Term

Categorical perception: the finding that when a sound is intermediate between two **phonemes**, the listener typically perceives one or other of the phonemes.

Summary

Most evidence suggests that several forms of auditory perception (including speech perception) involve the same general mechanisms. For example, there is evidence of categorical perception for speech and music sounds, and in both cases categorical perception is influenced by top-down processes. In addition, similar patterns of brain activity occur when speech and nonspeech sounds are processed.

There are also some differences in the processes involved in speech perception and other forms of auditory perception. The processes involved in speech perception are often more complex than those involved in processing nonspeech sounds, and so more brain areas are activated during speech perception (Obleser et al., 2006). Another difference is that motor processes are probably more important during speech perception than during auditory perception generally.

SPEECH PERCEPTION

The take-home message of this section will be that speech perception is much more complex than it may appear. Why do you think that is? Consider the problems you have experienced if you have tried to understand foreigners speaking in a language you studied at school. If your experience is anything like mine, what you hear is someone who seems to be speaking incredibly rapidly without pausing for breath.

Struggling to understand foreign speakers reveals two problems listeners have to contend with all the time. First, language is typically spoken at about 10 phonemes (basic speech sounds conveying meaning) per second, so we have to process it very rapidly. Amazingly, we can understand speech artificially speeded up to 50–60 sounds or phonemes per second (Werker & Tees, 1992).

Second, there is the **segmentation problem**. This is the difficulty of separating out (or distinguishing) words from the pattern of speech sounds. This problem arises because speech typically consists of a continuously changing pattern of sound with few periods of silence. This can make it hard to know when one word ends and the next word begins.

Listeners also have to face the problem of **coarticulation**. This refers to the fact that how a speaker produces a given phoneme depends in part on the phonemes preceding and following it. For example, the /b/ phonemes in "bill," "bull," and "bell" are all slightly different acoustically (Harley, 2008). While coarticulation can cause problems, it tells us something about the following phoneme.

Finally, Mattys and Liss (2008) pointed out that listeners in everyday life often try to understand degraded speech. For example, other people may be talking at the same time and/or there may be distracting sounds (e.g., noise of traffic; noise of aircraft). As yet, we don't know much about how we minimize distraction because listeners in the laboratory are rarely confronted by this problem.

Segmentation problem

How do listeners manage to work out where one word ends and the next starts? Various factors are involved. First, certain sequences of speech sounds (e.g., <m, r> are never found together within English words. Such sequences suggest a likely boundary between words (Dumay et al., 2002).

Second, segmentation is influenced by the possible-word constraints in English. For example, a stretch of speech lacking a vowel isn't a possible word. Norris et al. (1997) found that listeners found it hard to identify the word "apple" in "fapple" because the /f/ couldn't possibly be an English word. In

---

Key Terms

Segmentation problem: the listener's problem of dividing the almost continuous sounds of speech into separate **phonemes** and words.

Coarticulation: the finding that the production of a **phoneme** is influenced by the production of the previous sound and by preparations for the next sound; it provides a useful cue to listeners.

contrast, listeners easily detected the word "apple" in "vuffapple" because "vuff" could conceivably be an English word.

Third, there is stress. In the English language, the initial syllable of most nouns and verbs is stressed. When listeners heard strings of words without the stress on the first syllable presented faintly, they often misheard them (Cutler & Butterfield, 1992). For example, "conduct ascents uphill" was often misperceived as the meaningless "A duck descends some pill."

The fact that stress information is misleading for words in which the initial syllable isn't stressed suggests it has limited value in deciding where one word ends and the next starts. Word context is important. Mattys et al. (2005) found that lexical cues (e.g., providing information about syntax) were more useful than stress in facilitating word segmentation in a no-noise condition. However, stress was more useful than lexical cues in noise.

McGurk effect

Deaf people make much use of visual information in the form of lip-reading to assist them in understanding speech. What is less well-known is that people whose hearing is entirely intact also use lip-reading (Rosenblum, 2008).

McGurk and MacDonald (1976) prepared a videotape of someone saying "ba" repeatedly. The sound channel then changed so there was a voice saying "ga" in synchronization with lip movements still indicating "ba." Listeners heard "da," which is a blending of the visual and auditory information. This combining of visual and auditory information when the two sources of information are in conflict is the **McGurk effect**. It is a robust effect and has been found even with a female face and a male voice (Green et al., 1991).

The McGurk effect is influenced by top-down processes based on listeners' expectations. More listeners show the McGurk effect when the crucial word (based on blending the discrepant visual and auditory cues) is consistent with the meaning of the rest of the sentence than when it was not.

Context effects

When listeners try to identify sounds or words, they often make use of contextual information to assist them in that task (see discussion of categorical perception). Consider the following study by Warren and Warren (1970). Listeners heard a sentence in which a small portion had been removed and replaced with a meaningless sound. The sentences used were as follows (the asterisk indicates a deleted portion of the sentence):

- It was found that the *eel was on the axle.
- It was found that the *eel was on the shoe.
- It was found that the *eel was on the table.
- It was found that the *eel was on the orange.

Listeners' perception of the crucial element in the sentence (i.e., "*eel") was influenced by sentence context. Those listening to the first sentence heard "wheel," those listening to the second sentence heard "heel," and those exposed to the third and fourth sentences heard "meal" and "peel," respectively. The auditory stimulus ("*eel") was always the same, so all that differed was the contextual information. This is the **phonemic restoration effect**.

Various explanations of the phonemic restoration effect have been offered (e.g., Grossberg, 2003; Warren, 2006). One plausible explanation is that contextual information is used by top-down processes to create expectations about what we are likely to hear. These expectations cause listeners to interpret "*eel" in different ways depending on the sentence context.

Everyone agrees that context influences our perception of spoken words. However, *when* in processing these influences occur is less clear. The traditional view assumes that contextual information is processed *after* information concerning the meanings of words within a sentence (Hagoort & van Berkum, 2007).

Some researchers have assessed the validity of the traditional view using event-related potentials (ERPs; see Glossary) or "brain waves." This technique permits very precise assessment of the timing of different processes, which is important when assessing the point in time at which context has its effect. The N400 component is of particular importance in research on sentence comprehension. It is a negative wave with a peak at about 400 ms. A large N400 in sentence processing typically indicates there is a mismatch between the meaning of the word currently being processed and its context.

Evidence against the traditional view was reported by Nieuwland and van Berkum (2006) using ERPs. Here is an example of the materials they used:

A woman saw a dancing peanut who had a big smile on his face. The peanut was singing about a girl he had just met. And judging from the song, the peanut was totally crazy about her. The woman thought it was really cute to see the peanut singing and dancing like that. The peanut was salted/in love, and by the sound of it, this was definitely mutual.

"Salted," which was appropriate in terms of word meanings but inappropriate within the story context, was used in the material presented to some listeners, and "in love," which was appropriate in the story context but inappropriate in terms of word meanings, in the material presented to others. The key finding was that the N400 was greater for "salted" than for "in love". Thus, contextual information can have a very rapid impact on sentence processing.

Hagoort and van Berkum (2007) discussed an unpublished experiment of theirs in which participants listened to sentences. Some sentences included a word inconsistent with the apparent characteristics of the speaker (e.g., someone with an upper-class accent saying, "I have a large tattoo on my back"). There was a large N400 to the inconsistent word ("tattoo"). As Hagoort and van Berkum (2007, p. 806) concluded, "By revealing an immediate impact of what listeners infer about the speaker, the present results add a distinctly social dimension to the mechanisms of online language interpretation."

In sum, contextual information influences perception of spoken sounds and words. It used to be assumed that the effects of context occurred relatively late in speech perception. However, research using ERPs has provided strong evidence that contextual information has a rapid influence on speech perception.

Motor theory

Let's return to the issue of how listeners perceive words accurately even though the speech signal provides variable information. One influential approach is based on the assumption that listeners effectively *mimic* the articulatory movements of the speaker. The motor signal thus produced is claimed to provide much less variable or inconsistent information about what the speaker is saying than the speech signal itself. Thus, the motor system we use to produce speech is used to assist speech perception. This motor theory was initially put forward by Liberman et al. (1967). Various other versions have been suggested (Galantucci et al., 2006).

Support for motor theory was reported by Dorman et al. (1979). A tape was made of the sentence "Please say shop," and a 50 ms period of silence was inserted between "say" and "shop." As a result, the sentence was misheard as "Please say chop." Our speech musculature forces us to pause between "say" and "chop" but not between "say" and "shop." Thus, the evidence from internal articulation would favor the wrong interpretation of the last word in the sentence.

In a study by Fadiga et al. (2002), Italian participants listened to Italian words. Some of the words (e.g., "terra") required strong tongue movements when pronounced, whereas others (e.g., "baffo") did not. The key finding was that there was greater activation of the listeners' tongue muscles when presented with words such as "terra."

According to the motor theory, listeners would find it harder to perceive speech if parts of the motor system were disrupted by repetitive transcranial magnetic stimulation (rTMS; see Glossary). Meister et al. (2007) applied rTMS to the left premotor cortex. This impaired performance on a listening task requiring language processes.

The motor theory of speech perception is supported by several kinds of evidence. However, it doesn't account for all the findings. For example, some brain-damaged patients whose motor speech system has been almost destroyed nevertheless have an essentially intact ability to perceive spoken words (Harley, 2008). Another puzzling finding from the perspective of motor theory is that 6- to 8-month infants perform reasonably well on syllable detection tasks even though they have extremely limited expertise in producing speech (Polka et al., 2008).

In sum, the evidence suggests that listeners often mimic the speaker's articulatory movements when trying to understand speech. However, this is only one strategy among many, and speech perception is possible in the absence of such mimicking.

Section Summary

Is speech perception special?

- There has been controversy as to whether speech perception depends on a special mechanism or on more general mechanisms common to all auditory perception. The finding that categorical perception is found in the processing of speech and music stimuli is consistent with the notion of a general mechanism, as is the similarity in patterns of brain activity associated with speech and nonspeech processing. However, motor processes are probably more important in speech perception.

Speech perception

- Listeners engaged in speech perception contend with degraded speech, the segmentation problem, and coarticulation. The McGurk effect shows that speech perception depends in part on visual information (i.e., lip-reading). The phonemic restoration effect shows the importance of context in speech perception. Contextual information is often used early in processing to help listeners to identify spoken words. Some of the speech production system can assist speech perception. However, that system is not essential for speech perception to occur.

Essay Questions

1. "Face recognition involves different processes from object recognition." Discuss.
2. Describe and discuss the similarities and differences between visual perception and visual imagery.
3. What factors determine whether or not we experience change blindness?
4. What problems do listeners experience when trying to understand speech? How do they overcome these problems?

Further Reading

- Boloix, E. (2007). The representation of visual scenes: New insight from change blindness studies. *Année Psychologique*, *107*, 459–487. Research and theory on change blindness are discussed at length in this interesting article.
- Cowey, A. (2010). The blindsight saga. *Experimental Brain Research*, *200*, 3–24. Alan Cowey provides an excellent overview of theory and research on blindsight.
- Dror, I. E., & Mnookin, J. L. (2010). The use of technology in human expert domains: Challenges and risks arising from the use of automated fingerprint identification systems in forensic science. *Law, Probability and Risk*, *9*, 47–67. This article indicates clearly the limitations associated with current systems of fingerprint identification.
- Ganis, G., Thompson, W. L., & Kosslyn, S. M. (2009). Visual mental imagery: More than "seeing with the mind's eye". In J. R. Brockmole (Ed.), *The visual world in memory* (pp. 215–249). New York, NY: Psychology Press. The major contemporary approach to visual imagery is discussed at length in this chapter.
- Hagoort, P., & van Berkum, J. (2007). Beyond the sentence given. *Philosophical Transactions of the Royal Society B*, *362*, 801–811. This article provides comprehensive coverage of the authors' outstanding research on the processing of heard words in sentences.
- Harley, T. A. (2008). *The psychology of language: From data to theory* (3rd ed.). Hove, UK: Psychology Press. Trevor Harley discusses in detail the processes involved in recognizing auditory words.
- Mather, G. (2009). *Foundations of sensation and perception* (2nd ed.). New York, NY: Psychology Press. Several chapters in this textbook (especially Chapters 5 and 9) address important issues in visual and auditory perception.
- McKone, E., Kanwisher, N., & Duchaine, B. C. (2007). Can generic expertise explain special processing for faces? *Trends in Cognitive Sciences*, *11*, 8–15. Three experts present an excellent account of our understanding of the processes involved in face recognition.
- Milner, A. D., & Goodale, M. A. (2008). Two visual systems re-viewed. *Neuropsychologia*, *46*, 774–785. David Milner and Melvyn Goodale discuss and evaluate their very influential theory based on the notion that there are two visual systems.
- Peissig, J. J., & Tarr, M. J. (2007). Visual object recognition: Do we know more now than we did 20 years ago? *Annual Review of Psychology*, *58*, 75–96. Thankfully, the answer to the question posed by the authors is positive! They provide a good overview of developments in our understanding of object recognition in recent decades.

Chapter 3

Contents

Attention and consciousness

3

INTRODUCTION

Attention is absolutely invaluable in everyday life. We use attention to avoid being hit by cars as we cross the road, to search for missing objects, and to perform two tasks at the same time. However, attention generally refers to selectivity of processing, as was emphasized by the American psychologist William James (1890, pp. 403–404) many years ago:

> Attention is ... the taking into possession of the mind, in clear and vivid form, of one out of what seem several simultaneously possible objects or trains of thought. Focalization, concentration, of consciousness are of its essence.

Learning Objectives

After studying Chapter 3, you should be able to:

- Explain how visual and auditory attention differ from visual and auditory perception.
- Explain how bottleneck theories attempt to account for people's limited attentional resources.
- Answer the question posed by the author – "spotlight, zoom lens, or donut?" – and explain which is the best analogy for human attentional processes.
- Define cross-modal attention, and describe the kinds of illusion that cross-modal attention makes possible.
- Explain how disorders of attention inform us about how attentional processes work in the brain.
- Compare and contrast goal-directed (top-down) and stimulus-driven (bottom-up) attentional systems.
- Compare and contrast controlled and automatic processes.
- Identify conditions under which multitasking and task-switching are least costly in terms of cognitive resources.

James (1890) distinguished between "active" and "passive" modes of attention. Attention is active when controlled in a top-down way by the individual's goals or expectations. It is passive when controlled in a bottom-up way by external stimuli (e.g., loud noise). This distinction remains important (Yantis, 2008).

There is another important distinction between focused and divided attention. **Focused attention** (or selective attention) is studied by presenting people with two or more stimulus inputs at the same time and instructing them to respond to only one. Work on focused or selective attention tells us how effectively we can select certain inputs rather than others. It also allows us to study the nature of the selection process and the fate of unattended stimuli.

One way we use focused attention in everyday life is when we search the environment for a given object. For example, we may look out of a window trying to see where our cat is or we may look at a bookshelf for a particular book. This involves visual search and focused or selective attention. Visual search generally involves memory as well as focused attention, because we want to avoid re-attending to stimuli already rejected as nontargets. Geyer et al. (2007) studied eye movements on a visual search task. They found that observers rarely fixated previously inspected stimuli.

Divided attention is also studied by presenting at least two stimulus inputs at the same time. However, the instructions indicate that individuals must attend (and respond) to *all* stimulus inputs. Divided attention is also known as multitasking, a skill that is increasingly important in today's 24/7 world. Studies of divided attention or multitasking provide useful information about an individual's processing limitations. They also tell us about attentional mechanisms and their capacity.

SELECTIVE AUDITORY ATTENTION

Many years ago, the British scientist Colin Cherry became fascinated by the "cocktail party" problem – how can we follow just one conversation when several people are talking at once? Cherry (1953) found that this ability involved using physical differences (e.g., sex of speaker; voice intensity; speaker location) to maintain attention to a chosen auditory message. When Cherry presented two messages in the same voice to both ears at once (thus eliminating these physical differences), listeners found it hard to separate out the two messages on the basis of meaning differences alone.

Cherry (1953) also used the shadowing task. **Shadowing** involves people repeating back out loud (or shadowing) the auditory message presented to one ear while a second auditory message is played to the other ear. Very little information seemed to be extracted from the second or nonattended message. Listeners seldom noticed when that message was spoken in a foreign language or reversed (backwards) speech. In contrast, physical changes (e.g., a pure tone) were nearly always detected. The conclusion that unattended information receives practically no processing was supported by Moray (1959). He found there was very little memory for unattended words presented 35 times each.

WHERE IS THE BOTTLENECK?

How can we explain our surprisingly limited ability to extract information from two auditory messages presented at the same time? Many psychologists

---

Key Terms

Focused attention: a situation in which individuals try to attend to only one source of information while ignoring other stimuli; also known as selective attention.

Divided attention: a situation in which two tasks are performed at the same time; also known as **multitasking**.

Shadowing: repeating word for word one auditory message as it is presented while a second auditory message is also presented.

(Donald Broadbent, 1958; Anne Treisman, 1960; J. Anthony Deutsch and Diana Deutsch, 1963) argued we have a processing bottleneck. Just as a bottleneck in the road (e.g., where it is especially narrow) can cause traffic congestion, so a bottleneck in the processing system can seriously limit our ability to process two or more simultaneous inputs.

Where is the bottleneck located? Several answers were suggested. At one extreme was Broadbent (1958). He argued there is a filter (bottleneck) *early* in processing that allows information from one input or message through it on the basis of its physical characteristics. The other input remains briefly in a sensory buffer and is rejected unless attended to rapidly.

Treisman (1964) argued that the location of the bottleneck was more *flexible* than Broadbent had suggested. She proposed that listeners start with processing based on physical cues, syllable pattern, and specific words and move on to processes based on grammatical structure and meaning. If there is insufficient processing capacity to permit full stimulus analysis, later processes are omitted.

At the other extreme from Broadbent (1958) were Deutsch and Deutsch (1963). They argued that *all* stimuli are fully analyzed, with the most important or relevant stimulus determining the response. This theory places the bottleneck in processing much nearer the response end of the processing system than does Broadbent's theory.

Most evidence indicates that unattended stimuli are *not* fully analyzed. Treisman and Riley (1969) asked participants to shadow (repeat back aloud) one of two auditory messages. They were told to stop shadowing and to tap when they detected a target in either message. According to Deutsch and Deutsch (1963), there is complete perceptual analysis of all stimuli. As a result, there should have been no differences in detection rates between the two messages. In fact, many more target words were detected on the shadowed message.

Coch et al. (2005) asked listeners to attend to one of two auditory messages. Their task was to detect targets presented on the attended or unattended message. Event-related potentials (ERPs; see Glossary) were recorded to provide a measure of processing activity. ERPs 100 ms after target presentation were greater when the probe was presented on the attended message than on the unattended one. This suggests that there was more processing of attended than of unattended targets.

Suppose listeners try to detect target tones presented against a background of complex masking tones. Gutschalk et al. (2008) found that initial activation in the auditory cortex was very similar for detected and undetected target tones. However, a subsequent pattern of activation in auditory cortex 50–250 ms after onset of the target tone was present only for detected sounds. Thus, successful selective auditory attention is associated with more thorough processing.

Broadbent's (1958) ideas about selective auditory attention were influenced by studies in which two simultaneous auditory inputs were presented, one to each ear. On this dichotic listening task, three digits were presented to one ear at the same time as three different digits were presented to the other ear. Listeners reported all the digits. Most recalled the digits ear by ear rather than pair by pair. Thus, if 496 were presented to one ear and 852 to the other ear, recall would be 496852 rather than 489562. This suggested that the digits on one ear (e.g., 562) were stored briefly while those on the other ear (e.g., 496) were processed.

The above findings are consistent with the notion that listeners select auditory stimuli for processing on the basis of their physical features (i.e., ear of arrival). In fact, however, listeners can exhibit more *flexibility*. Gray and Wedderburn (1960) used a version of the dichotic task in which "Who 6 there?" might be presented to one ear as "4 goes 1" was presented to the other ear. The preferred order of report was *not* ear by ear. Instead it was determined by meaning (e.g., "Who goes there?" followed by "4 6 1"). These findings are inconsistent with Broadbent's emphasis on selection by physical features.

We have seen that listeners report very little about the unattended message in the shadowing task. This provides support for Broadbent's (1958) assumption that there is an early bottleneck in processing. However, there is sometimes reasonable awareness of what is on the unattended message. Most studies used listeners with very little experience of shadowing messages, so that nearly all their available processing resources were allocated to shadowing. In one study (Underwood, 1974), naïve listeners detected only 8% of the digits on the nonshadowed message. In contrast, an experienced researcher in the area (Neville Moray) detected 67%. His expertise meant that he didn't need to allocate substantial processing resources to the shadowing task.

In most early work on the shadowing task, the two messages were rather similar (i.e., auditorily presented verbal messages). This high similarity produced interference and made it harder to process both inputs. There is less evidence of a bottleneck when one message is in the auditory modality and the other in the visual modality. In one study (Kunar et al., 2008), listeners heard words over a telephone and shadowed each word. At the same time, they performed a visual task involving multiple object tracking. The shadowing task didn't interfere with the object-tracking task, indicating that two dissimilar inputs can be processed more fully than assumed by Broadbent.

RECENT DEVELOPMENTS

Several theories of selective auditory attention were put forward about 50 years ago. Unsurprisingly, these theories were oversimplified. We now know that the auditory system makes use of very sophisticated processes. For example, in a study by Dean et al. (2005), listeners were exposed to continuous wide-band noise whose characteristics changed every 50 ms. The firing of neurons in the midbrain changed rapidly to maximize the precision with which the sound environment was represented.

Our ability to segregate one auditory message out of many depends on top-down processes as well as bottom-up ones determined directly by the auditory input. The importance of top-down processes is indicated by the existence of extensive descending pathways from the auditory cortex to brain areas involved in early auditory processing (Robinson & McAlpine, 2009). These processes may serve to enhance the processing of important stimuli at the expense of less important ones.

Kurt et al. (2008) focused on processes within the auditory system of relevance to understanding how listeners cope in cocktail-party situations. They found evidence for a "winner-take-all" procedure in which processing of one sound (the winner) suppressed the brain activity of all the other sounds (the losers).

With respect to the cocktail-party problem, the implication of Kurt et al.'s (2008) finding is that inhibitory processes reduce the brain activity associated with voices the listener wants to ignore. These inhibitory processes are more effective when there are clear-cut physical differences between the to-be-attended auditory input and the others. For example, it is easier to inhibit the input from children's voices when listening to a man than when listening to a particular child.

Section Summary

- It is much easier to separate out two auditory messages on the basis of physical differences than differences in meaning. It has been argued that a bottleneck occurring early or late in processing limits our ability to process two simultaneous auditory messages. Such a bottleneck doesn't seem to operate during early processing. There is less evidence of a bottleneck when two simultaneous messages are in different modalities.

Recent developments
- Top-down processes within the auditory system enhance the processing of important stimuli. For example, inhibitory processes reduce the brain activity associated with irrelevant auditory stimuli. This helps to explain how listeners cope at cocktail parties.

SELECTIVE VISUAL ATTENTION

Over the past 30 years or so, researchers have increasingly studied visual rather than auditory attention. Why is this? One reason is that vision is probably our most important sense modality, with more of the cortex devoted to it than to any other sense. Another reason is that it is generally easier to control precisely the presentation times of visual than of auditory stimuli.

SPOTLIGHT, ZOOM LENS, OR DONUT?

Have a look around the room in which you are sitting and pay attention to any objects that seem interesting. Now answer the following question: Is your visual attention like a spotlight? A spotlight illuminates a relatively small area, little can be seen outside its beam, and it can be redirected flexibly to focus on any given object. It has been argued that the same is true of visual attention (e.g., Posner, 1980).

Other psychologists (e.g., Eriksen & St. James, 1986) compared visual attention to a zoom lens. They argued that we can increase or decrease the area of focal attention at will, just as a zoom lens can be moved in or out to alter the visual area it covers. This certainly makes sense. For example, when driving a car it is mostly desirable to attend to as much of the visual field as possible to anticipate danger. However, when we spot a potential hazard, we focus on it to avoid having a crash.

Support for the zoom-lens theory was reported by Müller et al. (2003). Observers initially saw an array of four squares and were cued to focus their attention on one given square, two given squares, or all four squares. After that, four objects were presented (one in each square), and observers decided whether a target object (e.g., a white circle) was present in one of the cued squares.

Figure 3.1 (a) Shaded areas indicate the cued locations and the near and far locations are not cued. (b) Probability of target detection at valid (left or right) and invalid (near or far) locations. Based on information in Awh and Pashler (2000).

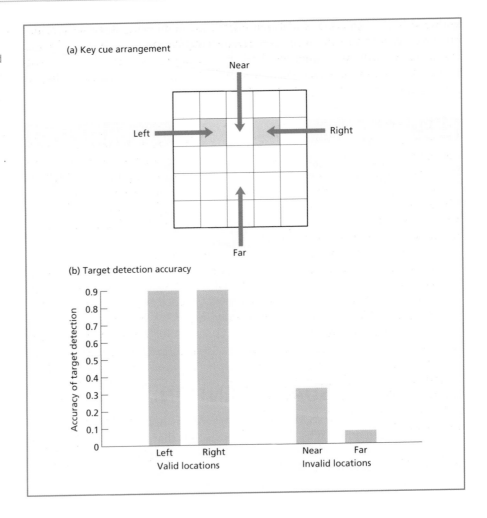

(a) Key cue arrangement

Near

Left   Right

Far

(b) Target detection accuracy

Accuracy of target detection

Left   Right   Near   Far
Valid locations   Invalid locations

According to the zoom-lens theory, we would expect targets to be detected fastest in the Müller et al. (2003) study when the attended region was small (i.e., only one square). Detection times should be slowest when the attended region included all four squares. Both these findings were obtained.

The zoom-lens theory sounds plausible. However, we can use visual attention even more flexibly than assumed by that theory. Suppose you were asked to report the identity of two digits that would probably be presented to locations a little way apart (see Figure 3.1; Awh & Pashler, 2000). Suppose also that on some trials one digit was presented in the space between the two cued locations. According to zoom-lens theory, the area of maximal attention should include the two cued locations *and* the space in between. As a result, detection of the digit presented in the middle should have been very good. In fact, it was poor.

Awh and Pashler's (2000) findings show **split attention**, in which attention is directed to two regions of space not adjacent to each other. This suggests that attention can resemble multiple spotlights. Additional evidence for multiple spotlights was reported by Morawetz et al. (2007). Stimuli were presented to five locations at the same time. One location was in the center of the visual field and the other four were in the four corners. When the observers were told

Key Term

Split attention: allocation of attention to two (or more) nonadjacent regions of visual space.

to attend to the upper-left and bottom-right locations only, there were peaks of brain activation in brain areas corresponding to these locations. Of most interest here, there was much less brain activation in the area between those locations including the center of the visual field. Thus, attention can be shaped like a donut with nothing in the middle.

WHAT HAPPENS TO UNATTENDED STIMULI?

As we would expect, unattended visual stimuli are processed less thoroughly than attended ones. Martinez et al. (1999) compared event-related potentials (ERPs; see Glossary) to attended and unattended visual displays. The ERPs to attended visual stimuli were comparable to those to unattended visual stimuli 50–55 ms after stimulus onset. After that, however, the ERPs to attended stimuli were greater than those to unattended stimuli. Thus, attention influences all but the very early stages of processing.

We can find out more about the fate of unattended visual stimuli by considering brain-damaged patients. Of particular interest are patients with **neglect**. Most of these patients have damage to the right hemisphere (often caused by stroke) and little awareness of visual stimuli presented to the left side of the visual field. This occurs because of the nature of the visual system – information from the left side of the visual field proceeds to the right hemisphere of the brain. When neglect patients draw an object or copy a drawing, they typically leave out most of the details from the left side of it (see Figure 3.2).

Patients with neglect typically fail to attend to stimuli presented to the left side of the visual field and have no conscious awareness of them (Danckert & Ferber, 2006; Chokron et al., 2008). However, such stimuli receive some processing. Vuilleumier et al. (2002) presented two pictures simultaneously, one to the left visual field and the other to the right visual field. Neglect patients couldn't report the picture presented to the left visual field. After that phase

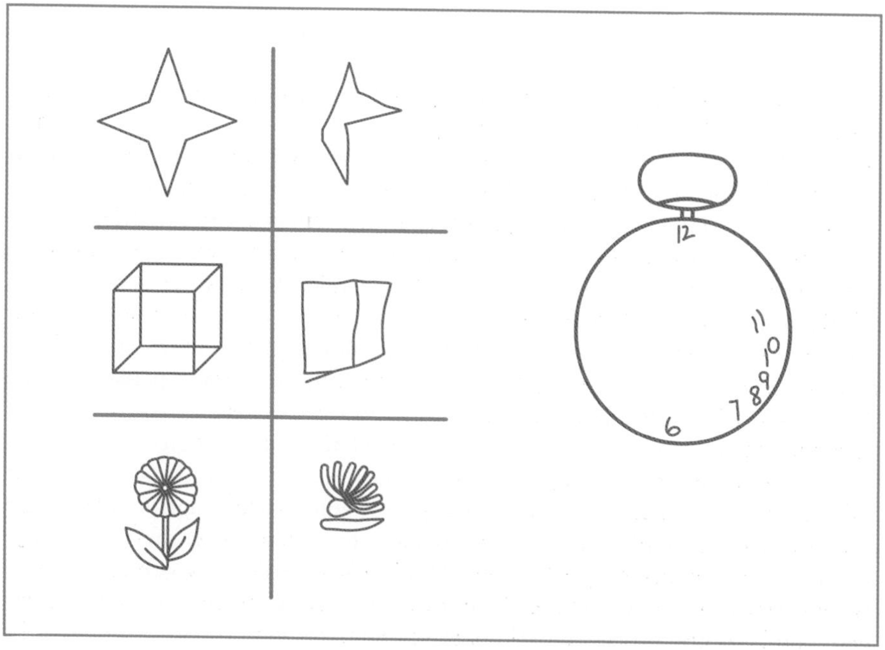

> **Key Term**
>
> **Neglect:**
> a disorder of visual attention in which stimuli or parts of stimuli presented to the side opposite the brain damage are undetected and not responded to; the condition resembles **extinction** but is more severe.

Figure 3.2 Left is a copying task in which a patient with unilateral neglect distorted or ignored the left side of the figures to be copied (shown on the left). Right is a clock-drawing task in which the patient was given a clock face and told to insert the numbers into it. Reprinted from Danckert and Ferber (2006), Copyright © 2006, with permission from Elsevier.

of the experiment, the patients identified degraded pictures. They performed better on old pictures that had been presented to the left visual field than on new pictures. Thus, the old pictures had received some processing during the first phase of the experiment.

Vuilleumier et al. (2008) assessed brain activity to see whether neglect patients processed task-irrelevant checkerboard stimuli. When the overall attentional load was low, neglect patients showed increased brain activity to these stimuli even when they were presented to the left visual field. Thus, visual stimuli that weren't consciously perceived nevertheless received some processing.

In sum, unattended visual stimuli are typically processed to some extent. For example, neglect patients generally are unaware of stimuli presented to the left visual field. However, memory tests (Vuilleumier et al., 2002) and patterns of brain activity (Vuilleumier et al., 2008) indicate that these stimuli are processed.

Distraction effects

In an ideal world, we might be immune from distraction. However, as we all know to our cost, it is often hard to avoid attending to (and processing) stimuli irrelevant to our current task. What factors determine how distracted we are by task-irrelevant stimuli?

One factor is anxiety – individuals with anxious personalities are more distractible than those with nonanxious personalities (Eysenck et al., 2007). Consider a study by Calvo and Eysenck (1996) in which individuals high and low in test anxiety (susceptibility to anxiety in test situations) were compared. The participants' task was to read a text for understanding so they could answer questions on a subsequent comprehension task. The participants read the text without interference or an unrelated story was presented over headphones during reading (distraction condition). The comprehension performance of the high-anxious participants was impaired by distraction, whereas distraction had no effect on the low-anxious ones.

It seems reasonable to assume that our attention is captured more by salient or distinctive distractors than by those lacking salience or distinctiveness. However, that isn't the whole story. Consider a study by Folk et al. (1992) in which they used apparently salient distractors (having an abrupt onset) and less salient distractors (defined by color).

When the observers looked for abrupt-onset targets, abrupt-onset distractors captured attention but color distractors did not. In contrast, when the observers looked for color targets, color distractors captured attention but abrupt-onset distractors did not. Thus, distraction effects were determined by the *relevance* of the distractors to the current task rather than by salience.

In the real world, we are often distracted by stimuli irrelevant to our current task. For example, more than 10% of drivers hospitalized after car accidents reported they had been distracted by irrelevant stimuli such as a person outside the car or an insect inside it (McEvoy et al., 2007).

Sophie Forster and Nilli Lavie (2008) argued that the extent to which we are distracted by totally irrelevant stimuli depends on the demands of the current task. Tasks vary in terms of perceptual load: some tasks (high load) require nearly all our perceptual capacity whereas others (low load) do not. Forster and Lavie predicted that people would be less susceptible to distraction while performing a high-load task than a low-load one – a high-load task leaves little spare capacity for processing distracting stimuli. If you are a car driver, you will probably agree you are more likely to be distracted while driving along an empty highway than when weaving in and out of heavy traffic.

Forster and Lavie (2008) presented six letters in a circle and participants decided which target letter (X or N) was present. The five nontarget letters resembled the target letter more closely in shape in the high-load condition than in the low-load condition. On some trials, a picture of a cartoon character (e.g., Mickey Mouse; Superman; Spongebob Squarepants) was presented as a distractor. These distractors interfered with task performance only under low-load conditions.

So far we have focused on distraction by *external* stimuli. However, we can also be distracted by *internal* stimuli (e.g., task-irrelevant thoughts or "mind wandering"). Participants had significantly fewer task-irrelevant thoughts while performing a high-load task than a low-load task (Forster & Lavie, 2009).

In sum, the extent to which attention is diverted to task-irrelevant stimuli depends on several factors. Anxious individuals are more easily distracted than nonanxious ones, distractors that are task-relevant are more disruptive than those that are not, and distraction is greater when the ongoing task is a low-load one. Finally, task-irrelevant stimuli close in space to task stimuli are more distracting than those further away (Khetrapal, 2010).

CROSS-MODAL EFFECTS

So far we have considered processes involved in visual attention when we are presented *only* with visual stimuli. In the real world, however, we very often encounter visual and auditory stimuli at the same time or visual and tactile stimuli.

What happens in such circumstances? One possibility is that attentional processes in each sensory modality (e.g., vision; hearing) operate *independently* of those in all other modalities. In fact, that is incorrect. We typically combine or integrate information from different sense modalities at the same time – this is **cross-modal attention**.

Molholm et al. (2007) asked participants to attend only to the visual or the auditory features of an object. There was clear evidence of cross-modal attention – object features in the task-irrelevant modality were typically processed. This was especially so when the task required attending to an object's visual features, suggesting that visual attention influences auditory processing more than auditory attention influences visual processing.

Ventriloquist illusion

What happens when there is a *conflict* between simultaneous visual and auditory stimuli? We will focus on the **ventriloquist illusion**. In this illusion, which anyone who has been to the movies or watched TV will have experienced, sounds are misperceived as coming from their apparent visual source. Ventriloquists try to speak without moving their lips while at the same time manipulating the mouth movements of a dummy. It seems as if the dummy rather than the ventriloquist is speaking.

Something similar happens at the movies. We look at the actors and actresses on the screen and see their lips moving. The sounds of their voices are actually coming from loudspeakers to the side of the screen, but we hear those voices coming from their mouths.

Certain conditions need to be satisfied for the ventriloquist illusion to occur (Recanzone & Sutter, 2008). First, the visual and auditory stimuli must occur

Key Terms

Cross-modal attention: the coordination of attention across two or more sense modalities (e.g., vision and hearing).

Ventriloquist illusion: the mistaken perception that sounds are coming from their apparent visual source, as in ventriloquism.

close together in time. Second, the sound must match *expectations* raised by the visual stimulus (e.g., high-pitched sound apparently coming from a small object). Third, the sources of the visual and auditory stimuli should be close together in space.

Why does vision capture sound in the ventriloquist illusion? The main reason is that the visual modality typically provides more precise information about spatial location. However, when visual stimuli are severely blurred and poorly localized, sound captures vision (Alais & Burr, 2004). Thus, we combine visual and auditory information effectively attaching more weight to the more informative sense modality.

Rubber hand, body swap, and Barbie doll illusions

In the ventriloquist illusion, people mistakenly attach too much importance to visual information when it conflicts with auditory information. There are several other illusions that depend on an over-reliance on visual information. Below we will briefly consider some illusions that depend on *integrating* information from the visual and tactile (touch) modalities.

One such illusion is the **rubber hand illusion** (Hohwy & Paton, 2010). In this illusion, the participant sees a rubber hand that appears to extend from his/her arm while their real hand is hidden from view. Then the rubber hand and the real hand are both stroked at the same time. Most participants perceive that the rubber hand is their own hand. This illusion occurs because we place more reliance on vision than on tactile sensations.

The body swap illusion, which also depends on integrating information from vision and touch, is more dramatic. What happens here is that the participant and the experimenter squeeze each other's hands repeatedly. The participant wears a specially designed helmet equipped with two CCTV cameras so that he/she sees what is happening from the viewpoint of the experimenter (Petkova & Ehrsson, 2008).

What do participants experience in this situation? The participants perceive that the stimulation caused by squeezing hands originates in the experimenter's hand rather than their own! This is the **body swap illusion**.

Petkova and Ehrsson (2008) explored this illusion further by moving a knife close to the hand of the participant or the experimenter. The participants showed a greater emotional response when the knife was close to the experimenter's hand than when it was close to their own hand.

Why does the body swap illusion occur? Of major importance, we have all spent a lifetime seeing the world from the first-person perspective. We also place special emphasis on vision as a reliable source of information. As a result, we can even experience ourselves in someone else's body when viewing the world from their viewpoint.

Van der Hoort et al. (2011) extended the body swap illusion. Participants equipped with head-mounted displays connected to CCTV cameras saw the environment from the viewpoint of a doll. When the participant's body and the doll's body were touched simultaneously, the participant experienced the doll's body as his/her own. The doll varied in size in different conditions. When the doll was small, other objects were perceived as larger and further away than when the doll was large. This is the **body size effect**. In one of their experiments, van der Hoort et al. used a Barbie doll (see Figure 3.3), so the body size effect could also be described as the Barbie doll illusion.

| Key Terms

Rubber hand illusion: the misperception that a rubber hand is one's own; it occurs when the visible rubber hand is touched at the same time as the individual's own hidden hand.

Body swap illusion: the mistaken perception that part or all of someone else's body is one's own; it occurs when, for example, shaking hands with someone else while seeing what is happening from the viewpoint of the other person.

Body size effect: an extension of the **body swap illusion** in which the size of the body mistakenly perceived to be one's own influences the perceived size of objects in the environment.

Why does the body size effect occur? As with the body swap illusion, it depends in large measure on our lifelong experience of seeing everything from the perspective of our own body combined with our general reliance on the visual modality. Note that this illusion is not solely based on visual information – it is only when visual information from the perspective of the doll is combined with the appropriate touch information that the effect is found.

Conclusions

In sum, we generally regard vision as providing us with valid information about the environment. The extent of our reliance on the visual modality can be tested by setting up situations in which the visual input provides misleading information. When that is done, people often continue to rely on visual information and this leads to various illusions. This reliance on visual information can lead people to experience another person's body (or even a doll's body) as their own when visual information is combined with touch information.

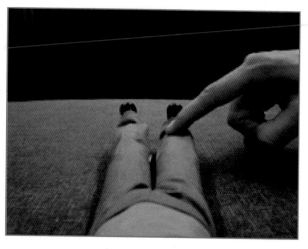

Figure 3.3   This shows what participants in the Barbie doll experiment could see. From the viewpoint of a small doll, objects such as a hand look much larger than when seen from the viewpoint of a large doll. This exemplifies the body size effect. From Van der Hoort et al. (2011). Public Library of Science. With kind permission from the author.

Section Summary

Spotlight, zoom lens, or donut?

- Visual attention has been compared to a spotlight, but it is more similar to a zoom lens. However, visual attention is more flexible than a spotlight or a zoom lens. The existence of split attention means that attention can be directed to two nonadjacent regions of space.

What happens to unattended stimuli?

- There is reduced processing of unattended visual stimuli compared to attended ones in healthy individuals. Neglect patients show some processing of stimuli of which they have no conscious awareness. Task-irrelevant stimuli resembling task-relevant stimuli are most likely to capture attention. Anxious individuals are more likely than nonanxious ones to attend to distracting stimuli. People are less susceptible to distraction while performing tasks high in perceptual load.

Cross-modal attention: Ventriloquist illusion

- In cross-modal attention, attentional processes are coordinated across two or more sensory modalities. In the ventriloquist illusion, sounds are misperceived as coming from their apparent visual source. Vision captures sound because the visual modality typically provides more precise information about spatial locations. Over-reliance on visual information also plays a major role in explaining various illusions involving vision and touch (rubber hand illusion; body swap illusion; Barbie doll illusion).

DISORDERS OF VISUAL ATTENTION

We can learn much about attentional processes by studying brain-damaged individuals suffering from various attentional disorders. We will consider two of the main attentional disorders: neglect and extinction (neglect was discussed briefly earlier in the chapter).

According to Driver and Vuilleumier (2001, p. 40), "Neglect patients often behave as if half of their world no longer exists. In daily life, they may be oblivious to objects and people on the neglected side of the room, eat from only one side of their plate … and make-up or shave only one side of their face." The attentional problems of neglect patients can be seen clearly when they copy drawings of objects. They typically leave out most of the details from the left side of such drawings.

Extinction is often found in patients suffering from neglect. **Extinction** involves the inability to detect a visual stimulus on the side opposite to the brain damage (contralesional side) when a second visual stimulus is present on the same side as the brain damage (ipsilesional side). Extinction is a serious condition because we are typically confronted by multiple stimuli at the same time in everyday life.

It is generally assumed that extinction depends on a *competition* mechanism (Marzi et al., 2001): Stimuli presented on the contralesional side compete unsuccessfully for attention with those presented on the other side. Evidence that competition is important was reported by Marzi et al. (1996). They worked out how much attention patients allocated to contralesional stimuli when presented on their own. Those patients having the poorest ability to attend to contralesional stimuli under these conditions generally also showed the most severe extinction.

EXPLAINING NEGLECT: TWO ATTENTIONAL SYSTEMS

How can we explain neglect? Before answering that question we need to discuss the important distinction between two attentional systems (Corbetta et al., 2008; Corbetta & Shulman, 2002). First, there is a goal-directed attentional system influenced by expectations, knowledge, and current intentions. This system makes use of top-down processes.

Second, there is a stimulus-driven attentional system which uses bottom-up processes. This system is used when an unexpected and potentially important stimulus occurs (e.g., flames appearing under the door of your room). This system has a "circuit-breaking" function, meaning that visual attention is redirected from its current focus.

Bartolomeo and Chokron (2002) argued that neglect patients have suffered damage to the stimulus-driven system, but their goal-directed system is reasonably intact. Evidence that the attentional performance of neglect patients improves when they can use the goal-directed system was reported by Smania et al. (1998). They compared the time taken to detect stimuli when the side of the visual field to which they were presented was predictable (permitting use of the goal-directed system) and when it was random (*not* permitting use of that system). Neglect patients responded faster in both the attended and unattended (neglect) fields when the side to which stimuli would be presented was predictable. Thus, they made some use of the goal-directed system.

Information from the two attentional systems must be *combined* somewhere in the brain to determine which stimulus will receive attention. The posterior

Key Term

Extinction:
a disorder of visual attention in which a stimulus presented to the side opposite the brain damage is not detected when another stimulus is presented at the same time to the same side as the brain damage.

parietal cortex (an area typically damaged in neglect patients) is where this happens (Bays et al., 2010). The stimulus producing most activation in this area from the goal-directed and stimulus-driven systems is the focus of attention.

Neglect patients fail to detect contralesional stimuli because activation in the posterior parietal cortex is insufficient to capture attention. This could be due to deficits in either the goal-directed or stimulus-driven system. Bays et al. (2010) recorded neglect patients' eye movements when they were searching for target stimuli. The patients had comparable deficits in both attentional systems. This explains why their ability to detect contralesional stimuli is so poor.

REDUCING NEGLECT

There have been various attempts to reduce the attentional problems of patients suffering from neglect. One approach has involved training patients to make more use of top-down control by providing detailed and explicit information about the locations of stimuli. This approach has had limited success (Parton et al., 2004) because neglect patients have deficits in the goal-directed attentional system (Bays et al., 2010).

When neglect patients in the dark are asked to point straight ahead, they typically point several degrees off to the right. Rossetti et al. (1998) wondered whether it would be useful to correct this error by having neglect patients wear prisms shifting the visual field 10 degrees to the right. When wearing prisms, patients in the dark pointed almost directly ahead. They also included more detail on the left side of their drawings of a daisy for some time after prism removal. Indeed, prism adaptation is effective for several weeks after prism removal (Chokron et al., 2007).

Why does prism adaptation have such beneficial effects? It makes it easier for neglect patients to use top-down processes to shift their attention voluntarily leftwards (Nijboer et al., 2008). This voluntary attentional shift leftwards compensates for patients' habitual rightward bias.

Section Summary

- Neglect involves a lack of awareness of contralesional stimuli. Extinction is similar except that this lack of awareness occurs mostly in the presence of an ipsilesional stimulus. Extinction depends on a competition mechanism – stimuli in the contralesional field compete unsuccessfully with those in the ipsilateral field.

Explaining neglect: Two attentional systems

- We have goal-directed and stimulus-driven attentional systems. Information from these two systems is combined in posterior parietal cortex (an area typically damaged in neglect patients). Both attentional systems show a deficit in neglect patients.

Reducing neglect

- The symptoms of neglect can be reduced somewhat by training designed to increase patients' use of the goal-directed attentional system. Prism adaptation improves patients' ability to shift their attention leftwards voluntarily.

Key Term

Face-in-the-crowd effect:
the finding that threatening (especially angry) faces can be detected more rapidly among other faces than faces with other expressions.

VISUAL SEARCH

We spend much of our time searching for various objects. For example, we look at the mess on our desk for a crucial piece of paper or try to spot a friend in a large group. The processes involved in such activities have been examined in studies on visual search in which a specified target must be detected as rapidly as possible.

It can be very important to detect angry faces, because someone who is angry may threaten or attack us. This suggests we might be able to detect faces with an angry expression more easily than faces with other emotional expressions. Precisely this was found by Hansen and Hansen (1988), a finding known as the **face-in-the-crowd effect**. Hansen and Hansen argued that this "pop-out" effect may occur because we detect angry expressions in a fairly automatic way not requiring attention. This effect has been replicated using fairly naturalistic crowd scenes (Pinkham et al., 2010).

The emotional state of the observer is also important in visual search. For example, Juth et al. (2005) found that observers detected angry schematic faces faster than happy ones, and this speeded detection was greater among anxious individuals.

There are various reasons why emotional faces are detected faster than non-emotional ones (see Frischen et al., 2008 for a review). Calvo and Marrero (2009) found that happy faces were detected faster than angry or sad ones. Observers detected happy faces rapidly because the teeth were visible rather than because of the positive emotion.

Suppose you want to attract the attention of a friend sitting across the room at a party. You could try waving your hand or arms on the assumption that moving objects are especially easy to detect. Royden et al. (2001) found that observers rapidly detected a moving target among stationary distractors. It took much longer to detect a stationary target among moving distractors.

In the Real World 3.1: *Security checks*

Airport security checks have become more thorough in the years since 9/11. When your luggage is X-rayed, an airport security screener sits by the X-ray machine searching for illegal and dangerous items (see Figure 3.4). How effective is this type of visual search? Training ensures that it is reasonably effective. However, mistakes do occur. Israel is well known for the thoroughness of its security checks. Nevertheless, on November 17, 2002, a man slipped through security at Ben Gurion airport in Tel Aviv with a pocketknife. He then tried to storm the cockpit of El Al flight 581 en route to Istanbul.

There are two major reasons why it is hard for airport security screeners to detect dangerous items. First, security screeners are looking for a wide range of different objects including knives, guns, and improvised explosive devices. This poses special problems. In one study (Menneer et al., 2009), observers detected two categories of objects: metal threats and improvised explosive devices. Some observers looked for both categories of object on each trial (dual-target search), whereas others looked for only a single category (single-target search). The ability to detect target objects was significantly worse with dual-target search than with single-target search.

A major problem with dual-target search in the experiment above was that the two target

Figure 3.4 See if you can spot the dangerous weapon. It is located a little above the center of the picture. Its blade and shaft are dark blue and the handle is orange. From McCarley et al. (2004). Reproduced with permission from Blackwell Publishing Ltd.

categories didn't share any obvious features (e.g., color; shape). When the two categories shared a feature (color), target detection was comparable in the dual-target and single-target conditions (Menneer et al., 2009). Finding a match between stored representations of targets and the stimuli presented is easier for security screeners when there is reasonable overlap between the stored representations for different target categories.

Second, illegal and dangerous items are (thankfully!) present in only a minute fraction of passengers' luggage. The rarity of targets may make it hard for airport security screeners to detect them. Wolfe et al. (2007) addressed that issue. Observers looked at X-ray images of packed bags and the targets were weapons (knives or guns). When targets appeared on 50% of trials, 80% were detected. When targets appeared on 2% of the trials, the detection rate was only 54%.

Why was performance so poor when targets were rare? It was *not* due to a lack of attention. Instead it was due to excessive caution about reporting a target because each target was so unexpected.

What can be done to improve the performance of security screeners? First, sophisticated training schemes have been set up. Koller et al. (2009) studied airport security screeners who had been doing the job for an average of 3 years. Some received a computer-based training system (X-Ray Tutor). This system starts with threat items presented in easy views and moves on progressively to threat items presented in harder views with part of their shape obscured. Performance feedback was provided on each trial.

Training produced a substantial improvement in detection performance: more so with improvised explosive devices than guns or knives. It requires more training to detect improvised explosive devices because they are less familiar and have more variable shapes than guns or knives. Training improves the ability to recognize targets. However, it doesn't reduce the number of eye movements before target fixation (McCarley et al., 2004).

Second, security screening could take account of Menneer et al.'s (2009) findings. Security screeners could specialize in searching for categories of threat items sharing features. However, that would necessitate having two or more screeners inspect each bag, which would increase costs.

Third, security screening at airports already takes account of the impaired performance with rare targets in a simple way. The number of threat targets is increased artificially by including some "test bags" containing such items.

FEATURE INTEGRATION THEORY

What determines how long it takes to find ordinary, nonthreatening targets? One important factor was identified by Treisman and Gelade (1980) (see Research Activity 3.1).

In Treisman and Gelade's (1980) research, observers detected a target in a visual display of between one and 30 items. The target was defined by a single

Research Activity 3.1: *Single features vs. combinations of features*

Below are two arrays consisting of 30 items each. With Array A, your task is to find the red item as rapidly as possible. With Array B, your task is to find the red letter S as rapidly as possible.

ARRAY A	ARRAY B
S	T
S	S
T	T
S	S
T	T
S	T
S	S
T	T
T	S
S	S
T	S
S	T
S	T
T	S
S	T
T	T
T	S
S	T
T	T
S	S
S	S
T	S
T	T
T	S
S	T
T	S
S	S
T	T
S	T
T	S

What you probably found was that you detected the target item much faster with Array A than with Array B. Why is it so much easier to find the targets in Array A than Array B? The answer to that question can be found by returning to the main text.

feature (a blue letter or an S) or by a combination or conjunction of features (a green letter T). When the target was a green letter T, all nontargets shared one feature with it (they were the brown letter T or the green letter X).

The findings are shown in Figure 3.5. When the target was defined by a single feature, observers detected the target about as quickly regardless of the number of distractors (as with Array A). In contrast, observers found it much harder when the target was defined by a *combination* (or conjunction) of two features. In this condition, performance was considerably slower when there were many distractors than when there were few or none (as in Array B). It also took much longer to decide that a target wasn't present than that it was present – you have to inspect *all* the items to decide that a target isn't present, but not to decide that one is present.

Why is visual search so much faster when the target is defined by a single feature? According to Treisman and Gelade's (1980) feature integration theory, targets defined by a single feature "pop out" effortlessly regardless of the number of distractors. This suggests we can use parallel processing (processing several stimuli at once) with such targets. In contrast, we need to process targets defined by a combination of features one by one using time-consuming serial processing.

How do we integrate the features with targets defined by a combination of features? According to the theory, focused attention provides the "glue" allowing us to form unitary objects from the available features. In the absence of focused attention, features from different objects may be combined at random, thus producing an **illusory conjunction**. Friedman-Hill et al. (1995) studied a brain-damaged patient who had problems focusing his attention accurately on object locations. As predicted, he produced many illusory conjunctions in which the shape of one stimulus was combined with the color of another.

Limitations and theoretical developments

Feature integration theory has been highly influential (Quinlan, 2003). However, the approach is limited. Of major importance, the speed of visual search doesn't depend only on

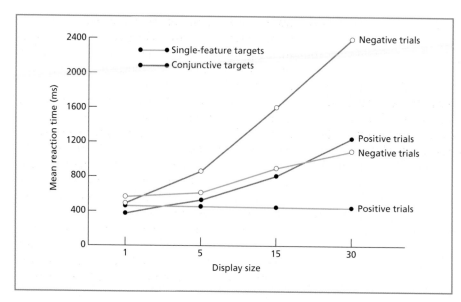

Figure 3.5 Performance speed on a detection task as a function of target definition (conjunctive vs. single feature), display size, and presence (positive trials) or absence (negative trials) of a target. Adapted from Treisman and Gelade (1980).

the target characteristics emphasized by Treisman and Gelade (1980). Duncan and Humphreys (1989, 1992) identified two additional factors. First, there is *similarity* among the distractors. Search is faster when the distractors are very similar to each other (Humphreys et al., 1985).

Second, there is the similarity between the target and the distractors. The number of distractors has a large effect on time to detect targets defined by a single feature when targets *resemble* distractors (Duncan & Humphreys, 1989). Visual search for targets defined by more than one feature is typically limited to those distractors sharing at least one of the target's features. For example, if looking for a blue circle in a display containing blue triangles, red circles, and red triangles, you would ignore red triangles.

Wolfe (e.g., 2007) explained the above findings. According to him, the initial processing of basic features (e.g., color) produces an activation map, with every item in the visual display having its own level of activation. Suppose someone is searching for red, horizontal objects. Attention is then directed towards items on the basis of their level of activation starting with those most activated. This assumption explains why search times are longer when some distractors share one or more features with targets (e.g., Duncan & Humphreys, 1989).

Wolfe's approach is a useful development of the original version of feature integration theory. A central problem with the initial feature integration theory was that targets in large displays are typically detected faster than predicted. The activation-map notion shows how visual search can be made more efficient by ignoring stimuli not sharing any features with the target.

How do we know whether processing on a visual search task is parallel or serial? We can address this issue by using multiple targets. Suppose *all* the stimuli are targets. If processing is serial (one item at a time), the first item analyzed will *always* be a target, and so target-detection times shouldn't depend on the number of items in the display. If processing is parallel, observers could take in information from *all* the targets simultaneously. The more targets there are, the more information is available. As a result, target-detection time should *decrease* as the number of targets increases.

Key Term

Illusory conjunction: mistakenly combining features from two different stimuli to perceive an object that isn't present.

Thornton and Gilden (2007) used a combination of single-target and multiple-target trials with 29 different visual tasks. The pattern suggestive of parallel processing was found with search tasks in which targets and distractors only differed along a single feature dimension (e.g., color; size; orientation). The pattern suggestive of serial processing was found with complex visual tasks involving the detection of a specific direction of rotation (e.g., pinwheels rotating clockwise).

What conclusions can we draw? First, some visual search tasks involve parallel search whereas others involve serial search. Second, Thornton and Gilden (2007) found that 72% of the tasks involved parallel processing and only 28% serial processing. Thus, parallel processing models account for more of the findings on visual search. Third, the relatively few tasks involving serial processing were especially complex and had the longest average target-detection times.

TOP-DOWN PROCESSES

In most research, the target is equally likely to appear anywhere within the visual display and so search is essentially *random*. This is very different from the typical state of affairs in the real world. Suppose you are outside in the garden looking for your cat. Your visual search would be *selective*, ignoring the sky and focusing mostly on the ground (and perhaps the trees). Thus, your search would involve top-down processes based on your knowledge of where cats are most likely to be found.

Ehinger et al. (2009) studied top-down processes in visual search. They obtained eye fixations of observers searching for a person in numerous real-world outdoor scenes. Observers typically fixated the regions of each scene most likely to be relevant (e.g., sidewalks) and ignored irrelevant regions (e.g., sky; trees) (see Figure 3.6). Observers also fixated locations very different from neighboring regions, and areas containing visual features characteristic of a human figure.

There is another way in which top-down processes influence visual search. Bird and car experts searched for car and bird photographs among photographs of real objects (Hershler & Hochstein, 2009). Experts exhibited better visual search performance when searching for targets relevant to their expertise. This occurred because experts scanned a larger region of visual space during each eye fixation when searching for expert-relevant targets.

Figure 3.6 The first three eye fixations made by observers searching for pedestrians. As can be seen, the great majority of their fixations were on regions in which pedestrians would most likely be found. Observers' fixations were much more similar in the left-hand photo than in the right-hand one, because there are fewer likely regions in the left-hand one. From Ehinger et al. (2009).

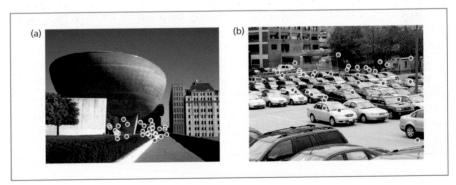

Evaluation

➕ Feature integration theory showed that the processes involved in visual search depend on the nature and complexity of the target.

➕ Research has indicated that a problem faced by security screeners is that the rarity of dangerous targets (e.g., bombs) makes them excessively cautious about reporting such targets.

➕ The factors allowing us to detect emotional faces (e.g., angry ones) rapidly have been identified in research on the face-in-the-crowd effect.

➖ Feature integration theory omitted several important factors in visual search such as the similarity among distractors and the similarity between the target and the distractors.

➖ In most research on visual search, the location of the target is random. This is very different from the real world, in which we can typically predict to some extent where a target (e.g., missing cat) is likely to be found.

Section Summary

• Angry faces are often detected more readily than faces with other emotional expressions: the face-in-the-crowd effect. This is especially the case with anxious observers. Moving objects are easier to detect than stationary ones.

Security checks

• It is harder for airport security screeners to detect dangerous objects if such objects are presented only rarely and the screeners are searching for several types of object. Training (including feedback) improves the ability to recognize target objects but doesn't improve the effectiveness of scanning. Increasing the number of threat targets artificially by using "test bags" can improve the effectiveness of security screening.

Feature integration theory

• Observers generally find it easier to detect targets defined by a single feature than those defined by a combination of two features. The similarity among the distractors and the similarity between the target and the distractors also influence the speed of visual search. Most visual search tasks involve parallel processing. However, a minority of tasks (especially complex ones) involve serial processing.

Top-down processes

• In the real world, top-down processes influence visual search and make it selective. Our environmental knowledge allows us to search for targets where they are most likely to be found. Experts' visual search is faster for targets related to their area of expertise than for other targets.

MULTITASKING

In common with most people, your life is probably becoming busier and busier. In our hectic 24/7 lives, there is an increased tendency for people to try to do two things at once. Examples include holding a conversation on a cell or mobile phone while driving and chatting with friends or while watching television. A survey in 2003 by ComPsych revealed that 54% of workers read emails while on the phone and 11% write to-do lists during meetings.

What we are talking about here is **multitasking**, which involves performing two or more tasks during the same period of time. If you are one of those people that engage in multitasking most of the time, you should perhaps take heed of a study by Ophir et al. (2009). They used a questionnaire to identify individuals who engage in high and low levels of multitasking. These two groups were given various tasks. On one task, an array of rectangles was presented twice and participants decided whether the target rectangle had changed orientation. This was done with or without distraction. Distraction only adversely affected the performance of the high multitaskers. The same group was also at a disadvantage when they had to switch between classifying numbers and letters.

What do these findings mean? According to Ophir et al. (2009), those who attend to several media simultaneously develop "breadth-based cognitive control." In other words, they aren't *selective* or discriminating in their allocation of attention. That makes it hard for them to avoid being distracted and to switch attention efficiently. In contrast, low multitaskers are more likely to have top-down attentional control. Note that we can't be sure that high levels of multitasking are responsible for unselective attention, because all that has been found is an *association* between those two measures.

There may be some disadvantages in being a low multitasker. Such individuals may be so focused on the immediate task that they ignore other potentially useful information (Lin, 2009). This may make them less creative and adaptive in real life.

The central issue discussed in this section is the effectiveness (or otherwise!) of our attempts to juggle two or more tasks. The fact that most of us often engage in multitasking suggests that we believe ourselves capable of performing two tasks at once. We multitask because we think it will save us precious time compared to the traditional approach of doing one thing at a time. If that isn't the case, we are simply wasting time and incurring higher stress levels by continuing to engage in multitasking.

There is a common belief that women are better than men at multitasking. This belief may owe something to the fact that women engage in more multitasking than men. Floro and Miles (2001) studied two-adult Australian households. Women involved in child care were much more likely than men to multitask (e.g., doing household work at the same time).

There are gender differences in the corpus callosum (involved in the transmission of information from one brain hemisphere to the other). The density of axons or nerve fibers in the corpus callosum is greater on average in women than in men (Highley et al., 1999). This might make it easier for women to multitask successfully. However, Rubinstein et al. (2001) found no gender differences in multitasking performance in a series of experiments in which participants switched rapidly between different tasks.

When performing two tasks at the same time, we might process information from only one task at a time (serial processing). Alternatively,

---

| Key Term

Multitasking:
performing two or more tasks at the same time by switching rapidly between them.

we might process information from both tasks simultaneously (parallel processing). What are the advantages and disadvantages of each form of processing? Lehle et al. (2009) trained people to engage in either serial or parallel processing when performing two tasks together. Those using serial processing performed better than those using parallel processing. However, they found the tasks more effortful.

In the Real World 3.2: *Can we think and drive?*

In everyday life, an issue of great importance is whether the ability to drive a car safely is impaired when the driver uses a cell or mobile phone. More than 40 countries have passed laws restricting the use of handheld cell phones by drivers (although hands-free phones are sometimes allowed). These restrictions have led millions of irate motorists to complain that their civil liberties have been infringed.

What does the evidence show? Redelmeier and Tibshirani (1997) studied the cell-phone records of 699 drivers who had been involved in a car accident. The likelihood of an accident was 4.3 times greater when drivers used a cell phone (whether handheld or hands-free). However, Kolko (2009) found that the introduction of laws against the use of hands-free cell phones only reduced traffic fatalities when the weather was bad or the roads were wet.

Many experimental studies have considered the effects of using cell phones on simulated driving performance. Caird et al. (2008) reviewed the findings from 33 studies. Reaction times to events (e.g., onset of brake lights on the car in front) increased by 250 ms compared to no-phone control conditions. The figure was similar whether drivers were using handheld or hands-free cell phones, and was larger when drivers were talking rather than listening.

The slowing of 250 ms may sound trivial. However, it translates into travelling an extra 18 feet (5.5 m) before stopping for a motorist doing 50 mph (80 kph). This could mean the difference between stopping just short of a child in the road and killing that child.

Caird et al. (2008) found that drivers had little awareness of the negative impact of using cell phones – they didn't slow down or keep a greater distance behind the car in front. The drivers in these studies knew they were being observed and so probably tried to perform as well as possible. This suggests that the adverse effects of using cell phones may well be even greater in real life.

Use of cell phones is dangerous because it has adverse effects on attention. Drivers using hands-free cell phones were less likely than drivers not using cell phones to attend closely to the brake lights of the car in front or to objects such as pedestrians or advertising hoardings (Strayer & Drews, 2007).

There are a few exceptions to the general rule that it isn't possible to combine using a cell phone and driving. Watson and Strayer (2010) had participants perform a simulated driving task on its own or while performing a complex working memory task presented over a cell phone. Of 200 participants, there were five whose driving performance was unaffected by the additional task. The high level of performance of these "supertaskers" on both tasks suggests that they found them easy and less requiring of attention than the other participants did.

Is it as dangerous for drivers to converse with their passenger as it for them to converse on a cell phone? Drews et al. (2008) found that conversations using a cell phone were associated with more driving errors. Drivers were better able to converse with a passenger and drive safely because their conversations became less complex as the difficulty of the driving conditions increased.

In sum, it is surprisingly hard to perform two tasks at once even when they are very different (verbal vs. visual processing). This suggests that performing two tasks together can overload some limited-capacity resource such as attention (see main text).

The adverse effects of cell-phone use are *not* limited to drivers. As you may have noticed, people using a cell phone while walking along often seem fairly oblivious to their surroundings. Hyman et al. (2009) carried out an amusing study in which students walking across Western Washington University's Red Square were exposed to a unicycling clown. Of those walking on their own, 51% noticed the clown, compared to only 25% of those using cell phones. Cell-phone use even affected the apparently very simple task of walking – students using cell phones walked more slowly, weaved about more, and changed direction more often than other walkers. Thus, cell-phone use is so demanding of processing resources that it disrupts our perception of the environment and our walking ability.

PRACTICE AND DUAL-TASK PERFORMANCE

Everyone knows the saying, "Practice makes perfect." Evidence apparently supporting this saying was reported by Spelke et al. (1976). Two students (Diane and John) received 5 hours' training a week for 3 months on various tasks. Their first task was to read short stories for comprehension while writing down words to dictation. Initially they found it very hard to combine these tasks, and their reading speed and handwriting both suffered severely. After 6 weeks of training, however, Diane and John could read as rapidly and with as much comprehension when taking dictation as when only reading. In addition, the quality of their handwriting had improved.

Spelke et al. (1976) were still not satisfied with the students' performance. For example, Diane and John could recall only 35 out of the thousands of words they had written down at dictation. Even when 20 successive dictated words came from the same category (e.g., four-footed animals), the students were unaware of that. With further training, however, they could write down the names of the categories to which the dictated words belonged while maintaining normal reading speed and comprehension.

We have seen that practice can have a dramatic effect on people's ability to perform two tasks at the same time. It has often been assumed that this happens because practice allows some processing activities to become automatic. Let's consider the classic research by Shiffrin and Schneider (1977) and Schneider and Shiffrin (1977) using an approach developed and extended by Hill and Schneider (2006). They distinguished between controlled and automatic processes:

- Controlled processes are of limited capacity, require attention, and can be used flexibly in changing conditions; serial processing is involved.
- Automatic processes have no capacity limitations, don't require attention, and are very hard to modify once learned; parallel processing is involved.

Shiffrin and Schneider (1977) used a task in which participants memorized up to four letters (the memory set) and were then shown a visual display containing up to four letters. Their task was to decide rapidly whether one of the letters in the visual display was the same as any of the letters in the memory set. The crucial manipulation was the type of mapping used:

1. *Consistent mapping:* Only consonants were used as members of the memory set, and only numbers were used as distractors in the visual display (or vice versa). Example: H B K D (memory set) followed by 4 3 B 7 (visual display) requires a "Yes" response.
2. *Varied mapping:* A mixture of numbers and consonants formed the memory set and provided distractors in the visual display. Example: H 4 B 3 (memory set) followed by 2 J 7 C (visual display) requires a "No" response.

What do you think happened? You may have guessed correctly that consistent mapping led to faster performance than varied mapping. However, the actual difference may be even greater than you thought (see Figure 3.7). According to Shiffrin and Schneider (1977), the participants performed well with consistent mapping because they used automatic processes operating at the same time (parallel processing). These automatic processes have evolved through years of practice in distinguishing between numbers and letters.

In contrast, performance with varied mapping required controlled processes of limited capacity and requiring attention. In this condition, participants compared each item in the memory set with every item in the visual display one at a time (serial processing) until a match was found or every comparison had been made.

Stronger evidence that automatic processes develop with practice was provided in another experiment by Shiffrin and Schneider (1977). They used consistent mapping with the consonants B to L forming one set and the consonants Q to Z forming the other set. As before, items from only one set were always used in the construction of the memory set and the distractors in the visual display were all selected from the other set. For example, if "G" was in the memory set, that was the only consonant between B and L that could possibly appear in the visual display. There was a dramatic improvement in performance speed over 2100 trials, apparently reflecting the development of automatic processes.

So far it has appeared that automatic processes are more useful than controlled ones. However, automatic processes suffer from the serious limitation that they are *inflexible* whereas controlled processes are not. Shiffrin and Schneider (1977) showed this in the second part of the experiment discussed above. The initial 2100 trials with one consistent mapping were followed by 2100 trials with the reverse consistent mapping. Thus, the items in the memory set were now always drawn from the consonants Q to Z if they had previously been drawn from the set B to L. It took nearly 1000 trials before performance recovered to the level at the very start of the experiment!

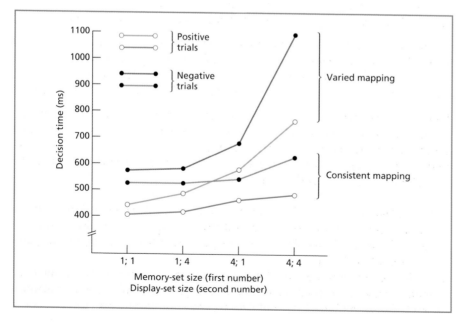

Figure 3.7 Response times on a decision task as a function of memory-set size, display-set size, and consistent versus varied mapping. Data from Shiffrin and Schneider (1977).

DOES PRACTICE MAKE PERFECT?

We have seen that practice can produce very large improvements in performance. However, there are typically *some* interference effects in dual-task performance even after substantial amounts of practice. For example, look back at Figure 3.7. If performance were totally automatic in the consistent mapping condition, response speed should have been unaffected by the number of items in the memory set and the visual display. In fact, however, performance became slower as the number of items increased.

Some theorists (e.g., Levy et al., 2006) argue that we will *always* find evidence of interference in dual-task performance if sensitive techniques are used. One such technique involves two presented stimuli (e.g., two lights) each associated with a different response (e.g., pressing different buttons). The participants must respond to each stimulus as rapidly as possible. When the second stimulus is presented very shortly after the first, there is generally a marked slowing of the response to the second stimulus. This is the **psychological refractory period (PRP) effect**.

The PRP effect does *not* occur simply because people aren't used to responding to two immediately successive stimuli. Pashler (1993) found that the effect was still observable after more than 10,000 practice trials. However, there are occasional reports that some people fail to show the PRP effect. For example, Schumacher et al. (2001) found that almost half his participants showed a very small PRP effect after more than 2000 trials of practice. However, the two tasks were both very simple.

Clear evidence for an absence of a PRP effect was reported by Greenwald (2003) using extremely simple tasks. One task involved vocal responses to auditory stimuli: saying "A" or "B" in response to hearing those letter names. The other task involved moving a joystick to the left to an arrow pointing left and to the right to a right-pointing arrow. There was no PRP effect. Why was that? Both tasks used by Greenwald had a very *direct* relationship between stimuli and responses (e.g., saying "A" when you hear "A"), which minimized the involvement of attentional processes.

How can we explain the various findings in this area? The starting point is to reject the assumption made by Shiffrin and Schneider (1977) that there is a clear-cut distinction between automatic and controlled processes. A more plausible perspective was provided by Moors and de Houwer (2006). They identified four key features of automaticity:

1. Unconscious: lack of conscious awareness of the process
2. Efficient: using very little attentional capacity
3. Fast
4. Goal-unrelated: uninfluenced by the individual's current goals.

| Key Term |

Psychological refractory period (PRP) effect: the slowing of the response to the second of two stimuli when they are presented close together in time.

None of these four features is all-or-none. For example, a process can be fairly fast or slow, and it can be moderately efficient or inefficient. The evidence also indicates that the four features of automaticity aren't always found together. Thus, there is no firm dividing line between automaticity and nonautomaticity or controlled processing.

What predictions follow from the above approach? Two tasks should be performed together reasonably well if both possess in reasonable measure the four features of automaticity. Conversely, multitasking should be very poor if the two tasks lack most of those features. The evidence reviewed by Moors and de Houwer (2006) is consistent with those predictions.

Section Summary

- Individuals who engage in much multitasking find it hard to allocate their attention selectively and are distractible. It has proved hard to obtain evidence of gender differences in multitasking.

Can we think and drive?

- Cell phones (handheld or hands-free) generally impair driving performance, especially in adverse driving conditions. Impaired attentional control and limited processing capacity are responsible. There are a few "supertaskers" with a high overall level of performance whose driving is unaffected by using a cell phone.

Practice and dual-task performance

- Dual-task performance often improves substantially with practice. There is evidence that this happens because some processing activities become relatively automatic through practice. However, automatic processes suffer from the limitation that they are inflexible and hard to alter.

Does practice make perfect?

- There is nearly always some evidence of interference in dual-task performance even after extensive practice. However, that isn't the case when there are very direct relationships between stimuli and responses. Most findings on dual-task performance can be explained by assuming that processes vary in the extent to which they are automatic. The major features of automaticity are as follows: unconscious; efficient; fast; and goal-unrelated.

CONSCIOUSNESS

The topic of consciousness is one of the most fascinating in the whole of cognitive psychology. There has recently been a substantial increase in research on consciousness (much of it involving brain imaging), the fruits of which will be discussed here. Before doing so, we must consider what is meant by "consciousness." It can be defined as: "The normal mental condition of the waking state of humans, characterized by the experience of perceptions, thoughts, feelings, awareness of the external world, and often in humans ... self-awareness" (Colman, 2001, p. 160).

Steven Pinker (1997) argued we need to consider three issues when trying to understand consciousness:

1. *Sentience:* This is our subjective experience or awareness, which is only available to the individual having the experience.
2. *Access to information:* This relates to our ability to report the content of our subjective experience without being able to report on the processes producing that experience.
3. *Self-knowledge:* This is our ability to have conscious awareness of ourselves.

There are various ways to assess conscious awareness. With respect to visual consciousness, much use has been made of behavioral measures (see Chapter 2). We can ask people to provide verbal reports of their visual experience, or to make a yes/no decision concerning the presence of a target object.

With some brain-damaged patients, this is hard to do. For example, consider patients with locked-in syndrome, who generally possess full conscious awareness but are almost totally paralyzed. The most famous case of locked-in syndrome was Jean-Dominique Bauby, who was a French journalist. Amazingly, he managed to write a book about himself solely by blinking his left eyelid to choose the next letter in the text (Bauby, 1997). Bauby's book was called *The Diving Bell and the Butterfly*, and it was later turned into a successful movie.

It is possible to gain a deeper understanding of consciousness by identifying its major neural correlates. This involves obtaining behavioral measures of conscious awareness, and then relating them to the associated patterns of brain activity. It is sometimes impossible to obtain behavioral measures of consciousness. It can then be very useful to obtain brain-imaging data (see In the Real World 3.3).

In the Real World 3.3: *The vegetative state*

Some unfortunate patients with severe brain damage are in a vegetative state. The vegetative state (see Glossary) is defined by an apparent lack of awareness and a failure to respond to all external stimuli. The behavioral evidence obtained from patients in that state strongly suggests they totally lack conscious awareness.

Owen et al. (2006) studied a 23-year-old woman who was in the vegetative state as a result of a very serious road accident in July 2005. This woman showed no behavioral responsiveness to stimulation. She was asked to imagine playing a game of tennis or visiting the rooms of her house starting from the front door. These two tasks were associated with different patterns of brain activity. For example, activation in the supplementary motor area was found only when she imagined playing tennis. Of key importance, the patterns of brain activity were very similar to those shown by healthy participants.

Owen et al. (2006) also presented the patient with sentences containing ambiguous words (italicized) (e.g., "The *creak* came from a *beam* in the ceiling"). She showed greater brain activation in areas involved in processing meaning with ambiguous than with unambiguous words. Thus, brain activity probably provided a more valid assessment of the presence of conscious experience than did behavioral measures. Coleman et al. (2009) studied 41 brain-damaged patients, many of whom were in the vegetative state. None showed any signs of consciousness when behavioral measures were used. However, functional magnetic resonance imaging (fMRI; see Glossary) revealed that two patients in the vegetative state showed evidence of speech comprehension. Of interest, the amount of speech processing indicated by fMRI was strongly associated with the amount of behavioral recovery 6 months later. Thus, brain imaging can sometimes provide a more sensitive measure of conscious awareness than behavioral measures.

In sum, the findings from patients in the vegetative state are dramatic. Until recently, it had always been assumed that such patients lacked all conscious awareness of themselves and of the environment around them. This assumption has been seriously challenged by the brain-imaging findings strongly suggesting that some patients in the vegetative state have a limited form of awareness.

ATTENTION AND CONSCIOUSNESS

What is the relationship between consciousness and attention? It seems reasonable to assume they are closely related. Baars (1997) invited us to consider sentences such as, "We look in order to see," or "We listen in order to hear." He argued that looking or listening involves using attention to select an event, whereas seeing or hearing involves conscious awareness of the selected event. Thus, attention is like choosing a television channel and consciousness resembles the picture on the screen.

There is often a close relationship between attention and consciousness. However, that isn't always the case (Koch & Tsuchiya, 2007; Lamme, 2003). For example, attention can influence behavior in the absence of consciousness. Jiang et al. (2006) presented pictures of male and female nudes that were invisible to the participants. In spite of their invisibility, these pictures influenced participants' attentional processes. Heterosexual males attended to invisible female nudes, whereas heterosexual females attended to invisible male nudes. Gay males had a tendency to attend to the location of nude males, and gay/bisexual females' attentional preferences were between those of heterosexual males and females.

We have just seen that there can be attention in the absence of consciousness. It is also possible to have consciousness in the absence of attention. This was shown in a study by Landman et al. (2003) discussed in Chapter 2. The limited capacity of attention means that we can attend to only approximately three or four items. However, Landman et al. found that people could maintain approximately seven visually presented items in conscious awareness for almost 1 s. Thus, we can be consciously aware of more information than is currently being attended to.

Evidence that attention and consciousness aren't necessarily closely linked was reported by van Boxtel et al. (2010). Observers were shown gratings and given the task of reporting the duration of their afterimage (persisting sensory experience following the offset of the stimulus). The amount of attention available to process the gratings was manipulated, as was the visibility of the gratings (to vary conscious awareness of them).

Consciously seeing the grating *increased* afterimage duration, whereas attention to the grating *decreased* afterimage duration. Thus, the cognitive processes associated with attention and consciousness can differ substantially.

In sum, what we are consciously aware of is generally determined by focused attention. However, conscious awareness without attention is possible, as is attention in the absence of conscious awareness. Sometimes the effects of attention and consciousness are very different (van Boxtel et al., 2010).

CONTROLLING ACTIONS: FREE WILL

What controls our actions? It feels as if we form a conscious intention (e.g., "I think I'll get myself a coffee"), which is then followed by us finding ourselves in a café drinking a cup of coffee. In other words, our actions are driven by conscious intentions or **free will**. This view has been challenged by several theorists. Daniel Wegner (2003) argued that what we have is the *illusion* of conscious or free will. Our actions are actually caused by unconscious processes. However, we draw the mistaken inference that our actions are determined by our conscious intentions.

If Wegner is right, we should make mistakes such as assuming we didn't cause something to happen even though we did. Support for this prediction comes from the unlikely source of the spiritualist movement that swept through

Key Term
Free will: the notion that we freely or voluntarily choose what to do from a number of possibilities; this notion has been challenged by those who claim that nonconscious processes determine our actions.

nineteenth-century Europe. Advocates of spiritualism believed that spirits of the dead could convey messages and even move tables. Several people would sit around a table with their hands resting on the top and pressing down on it. After a while, the table would start to vibrate and eventually it would move. The sitters firmly believed they hadn't caused the table to move and that spirits were responsible.

The sitters' beliefs were refuted by the English scientist Michael Faraday. He constructed a table with two tops divided by ball bearings but the sitters thought it was just an ordinary table. Faraday stuck pieces of paper onto the *upper* table-top, and asked the sitters to put their hands on the piece of card in front of them. The key finding was that the upper table-top moved *before* the lower table-top. Thus, the sitters were moving the table rather than the table (possibly via spirits) moving their fingers. That means that sitters' conscious experience that their actions didn't cause the table to move was mistaken.

What causes us to assume (sometimes mistakenly) that our conscious thoughts have caused our actions? According to Wegner (2003), three principles are involved. First, we regard our thoughts as causing our actions when they occur just beforehand (priority principle). Second, thoughts *consistent* with the actions that follow are more likely to be regarded as being causally responsible than inconsistent ones (consistency principle). Third, thoughts not accompanied by obvious alternative causes of action are more likely to be perceived as causing those actions (exclusivity principle). These ideas have been developed by White (2009).

Evidence that these principles are important was reported by Wegner and Wheatley (1999). They used a 20 cm square board mounted onto a computer mouse. There were two participants at a time, both of whom placed their fingers on the board. When they moved the board, this caused a cursor to move over a screen showing numerous pictures of small objects. Every 30 s or so, the participants were told to stop the cursor and indicate the extent to which they had consciously intended the cursor to stop where it did.

Both participants wore headphones. One participant was genuine, but the other was a confederate working for the experimenter. The genuine participant thought they were both hearing different words through the headphones. In fact, however, the confederate was actually receiving instructions to make certain movements. On some trials, the confederate was told to stop on a given object (e.g., cat), and the genuine participant heard the word "cat" 30 s before, 5 s before, 1 s before, or 1 s after the confederate stopped the cursor.

Genuine participants wrongly believed they had caused the cursor to stop where it did when they heard the name of the object on which it stopped 1 or 5 s before the stop. Thus, the participants mistakenly inferred that their conscious intention had caused the action when it had not. This mistaken belief can be explained by the principles of priority, consistency, and exclusivity.

Wegner and other researchers have carried out several similar studies to that of Wegner and Wheatley (1999) in recent years, and have generally obtained similar findings (Nahmias, 2005). There are some limitations with these studies. First, the findings are often not especially strong (Nahmias, 2005). For example, only just over 60% of participants in the study by Wegner and Wheatley (1999) believed their conscious intention caused the cursor to stop even when all three principles applied.

Second, most studies have involved very artificial-set-ups designed to make it hard for participants to realize their conscious intentions hadn't caused certain actions. By analogy, no one would say visual perception is hopelessly fallible because we make mistakes when identifying objects in a thick fog!

Inside the brain

Cognitive neuroscience findings apparently casting doubt on the notion that our conscious intentions determine our actions were reported by Benjamin Libet et al. (1983). Participants were asked to bend their wrist and fingers at a time of their choosing. The time at which they were consciously aware of the intention to perform the movement and the moment at which the hand muscles were activated were recorded. In addition, they recorded the readiness potential in the brain – this is thought to reflect pre-planning of a bodily movement.

What did Libet et al. (1983) find? The readiness potential occurred 350 ms *before* participants reported conscious awareness of the intention to bend the wrist and fingers. In addition, conscious awareness preceded the actual hand movement by about 200 ms. Thus, some preparation of a forthcoming action occurs *before* the individual is consciously aware of what he/she is going to do.

On some trials, participants were told to veto the action they had decided to make. Libet et al. (1983) claimed that the decision to veto an action was based on a conscious intention in contrast to the position with performed actions. We may not have free will but perhaps we have free won't!

Several studies have used variations on Libet's experimental approach. Most of the findings were consistent with those of Libet et al. (1983; Banks & Pockett, 2007). However, it is hard to know exactly *when* participants have conscious awareness of their intention. Banks and Isham (2009) used conditions in which participants had their hand in full view or saw it in a delayed video image. The reported decision time was 44 ms later in the latter condition. Thus, the reported time of conscious decisions can be influenced by what happens *after* the decision.

Stronger evidence was reported by Soon et al. (2008). They focused on activation in brain areas (e.g., prefrontal cortex) associated with decision processes. Participants decided whether to make a response with their left or right index finger. Soon et al.'s findings were dramatic. The decision that participants were going to make could be predicted from brain activity in parts of the prefrontal and parietal cortex up to 7 s before they were consciously aware of their decision! In addition, activity in motor areas 5 s before conscious awareness of participants' decisions predicted the timing of their responses.

Intentional action typically depends on three different decisions: deciding *what* action to produce; deciding *when* to produce it; and deciding *whether* to produce it. This led Brass and Haggard (2008) to propose the what, when, and whether (WWW) model of intentional action, in which different brain areas are involved in the three different decisions. The study by Soon et al. (2008) suggested that the prefrontal and parietal cortex is involved in *what* decisions and motor areas in *when* decisions.

What can we conclude from the various findings? According to John-Dylan Haynes (one of the researchers in the Soon et al., 2008, study), "Your decisions are strongly prepared by brain activity. By the time consciousness kicks in, most of the work has already been done."

On the face of it, it looks as if we often make decisions without being consciously aware of having done so. That led Greene and Cohen (2004) to doubt whether we should hold individuals personally responsible for their actions – "I didn't do it, it was my brain!"

There are various reasons for disagreeing with the above viewpoint. First, it is based on the misleading assumption that an individual's personal identity and his/her brain are completely separate (Kaliski, 2009).

Second, research has focused on *what* and *when* decisions regarding the performance of *trivial* actions. Such research may be of little relevance to real-life situations in which we decide whether to perform some significant action. We probably make most use of our sense of personal responsibility when making *whether* decisions. Suppose a violent criminal wields a knife in his left hand to murder someone at three o'clock in the afternoon. The *whether* decision was probably preceded by a conscious intention even if the *what* (left hand or right hand?) and *when* (now or later?) decisions were not.

Evaluation

⊕ There is evidence (e.g., Soon et al., 2008) that some decisions are largely prepared by brain activity occurring before there is conscious awareness of having made a decision.

⊕ Our reliance on the priority, consistency, and exclusivity principles can lead us to believe mistakenly that our conscious thoughts have caused our actions.

⊖ Much of the research is rather artificial and may not be of direct relevance to everyday decision making.

⊖ Decisions about what action to produce and when to produce it may be mostly prepared within the brain prior to conscious awareness. However, it is less clear that the same is true of decisions concerning whether to perform an action.

IS CONSCIOUSNESS UNITARY?

Most people believe they have a single, unitary consciousness, although a few are in two minds on the issue. However, consider **split-brain patients**. In most of these patients, the corpus callosum (the major connection between the two hemispheres) has been cut surgically to contain severe epileptic seizures within one hemisphere.

It is sometimes believed that split-brain patients have great difficulty in functioning effectively in everyday life. This is *not* the case. Indeed, it wasn't realized initially that cutting the corpus callosum caused any problems for split-brain patients. The reason is that they ensure that environmental information reaches both hemispheres by moving their eyes around. Impaired performance in split-brain patients is produced by presenting visual stimuli briefly to only one hemisphere so the information is not available to the other hemisphere.

Do split-brain patients have two consciousnesses, one in each hemisphere? Contrasting answers to this question have been offered. Roger Sperry (1913–1994), who won the Nobel prize for his influential work on split-brain patients, claimed that these patients *do* have two consciousnesses.

In contrast, Gazzaniga et al. (2009) argued that split-brain patients have only a *single* conscious system. This system is based in the left hemisphere, and is known as the interpreter. It "seeks explanations for internal and external

Key Term

Split-brain patients: patients in whom most of the direct links between the two hemispheres have been severed; as a result, they can experience problems in coordinating their processing and behavior.

events in order to produce appropriate response behaviors" (Gazzaniga et al., 2009, p. 465). A major reason why the left hemisphere is likely to be dominant is that language abilities in the great majority of people are centered in that hemisphere.

We start by considering the self-reports of split-brain patients very shortly after an operation to cut through the corpus callosum. None of them has ever reported feeling that their experience of themselves has changed dramatically because they now have two selves or consciousnesses (Colvin & Gazzaniga, 2007).

The fact that the right hemisphere of most split-brain patients has limited ability to process language makes it hard to know whether it possesses its own consciousness. However, Gazzaniga and LeDoux (1978) found a split-brain patient, Paul S, who had reasonably good right-hemisphere language abilities. The left hand is connected to the right hemisphere, and Paul S showed limited evidence of consciousness in his right hemisphere by responding correctly to questions using his left hand. For example, he could spell out his own name, that of his girlfriend, and his current mood.

In a further study (Gazzaniga, 1992), Paul S was presented with a chicken claw to his left hemisphere and a snow scene to his right hemisphere. When asked to select relevant pictures from an array, he chose a picture of a chicken with his right hand (connected to the left hemisphere) and he chose a shovel with his left hand (connected to the right hemisphere).

The above findings may suggest that Paul S had a separate consciousness in each hemisphere. However, here is how he explained his choices: "Oh, that's simple. The chicken claw goes with the chicken, and you need a shovel to clean out the chicken shed" (Gazzaniga, 1992, p. 124). Thus, Paul S's left hemisphere was *interpreting* behavior initiated by the right hemisphere with no clear evidence the right hemisphere was contributing much to the interpretation.

Other research has provided more evidence that split-brain patients may have two consciousnesses. Baynes and Gazzaniga (2000) discussed the case of VJ. Her writing is controlled by the right hemisphere, whereas her speech is controlled by the left hemisphere. VJ was the first split-brain patient to have been visibly upset by the independent control of her right and left hands. For example, she was discomfited when she observed her left hand (controlled by the right hemisphere) writing fluently to stimuli that couldn't be seen by the left hemisphere.

Uddin et al. (2005) pointed out that the ability to recognize one's own face probably indicates reasonable self-awareness. They presented NG, a 70-year-old split-brain patient, with pictures representing different percentages of her own face and an unfamiliar face. She recognized her own face equally well whether it was presented to her left or right hemisphere. Her self-recognition performance was only slightly worse than that of healthy individuals, suggesting the existence of some basic self-awareness in both hemispheres.

In sum, research on split-brain patients hasn't fully resolved the issue of whether it is possible to have two separate consciousnesses. The commonest view is that the left hemisphere in split-brain patients plays the dominant role in consciousness. An interpreter or self-supervisory system providing coherent interpretations of events is located in that hemisphere.

In contrast, the right hemisphere engages in various low-level processing activities (e.g., basic self-awareness; Uddin et al., 2005). However, it probably lacks its own consciousness. It could be very disruptive if each hemisphere had its own consciousness because of potential conflicts between them.

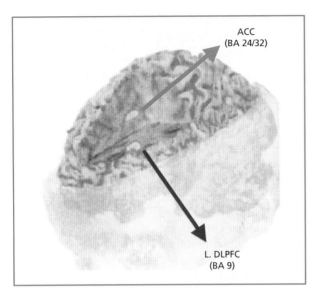

Figure 3.8 The anterior cingulate cortex (ACC) and the dorsolateral prefrontal cortex (DLPFC), regions that are strongly associated with consciousness. Adapted from MacDonald et al. (2000). Reproduced with permission of AAAS.

BRAIN AND CONSCIOUSNESS

We have seen that cognitive neuroscience has helped to shed much light on various aspects of consciousness. It has also proved very useful in addressing the following important question: What are the differences between processing accompanied or unaccompanied by conscious awareness?

We will consider briefly global workspace theory (e.g., Baars & Franklin, 2007). Three of its central assumptions are as follows:

1. The early stages of information processing involve many special-purpose processors carrying out specialized functions (e.g., color processing; motion processing) in relative isolation from each other. These processors are located in numerous brain areas and are generally not associated with conscious awareness.

2. Consciousness is associated with *integrating* information from several special-purpose processors. As a result, "Conscious contents evoke widespread brain activation" (Baars & Franklin, 2007, p. 956). Think about your own conscious awareness of the visual environment. You are rarely consciously aware of an object without also being aware of its color, distance from you, and so on.

3. Even though consciousness can be associated with activation in numerous brain areas, two areas are especially likely to be activated: parts of the prefrontal cortex and the anterior cingulate (see Figure 3.8)

Findings

There is experimental support for all the above assumptions. For example, Dehaene et al. (2001) tested the notion that unconscious processing is limited mainly to special-purpose processors. In one condition, words were presented on their own and could be perceived consciously. The other condition involved **masking** – a second stimulus (mask) disrupts the processing of a first stimulus presented very shortly beforehand. The words couldn't be perceived consciously in the masking condition.

There was widespread activation in the visual cortex, parietal cortex, and prefrontal cortex when the words were consciously perceived. In contrast, activation was largely confined to the visual cortex in the masking condition, and there was no detectable activation in the parietal or prefrontal areas.

Lamy et al. (2009) obtained evidence relevant to the second assumption. They asked participants to indicate the location of a target stimulus and to report on their subjective awareness of its presence. They used event-related potentials (ERPs; see Glossary) to compare brain activity on trials on which there was or wasn't conscious awareness of the target stimulus.

What Lamy et al. (2009) found can be seen in Figure 3.9. As you can see, the amplitude of early ERP components was unaffected by whether or not there was conscious awareness. However, conscious awareness was associated with a late

Key Term

Masking:
suppression of the processing of stimulus (e.g., visual; auditory) by presenting a second stimulus (the masking stimulus) very soon afterwards.

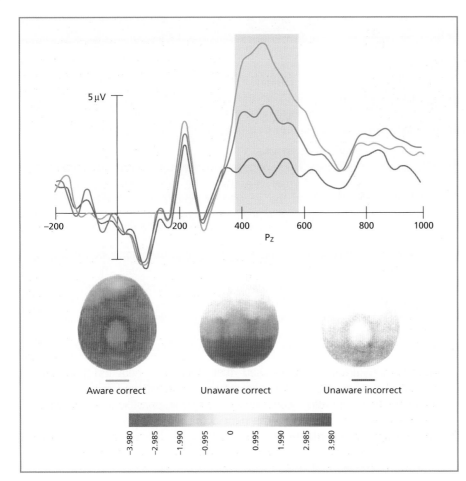

Figure 3.9 Event-related potential (ERP) waveforms in the aware-correct, unaware-correct, and unaware-incorrect conditions. The greatest differences among the conditions occurred for the P3 component (shown in light gray). In the bottom part of the figure, the extent of brain positivity in the three conditions is shown in red. From Lamy et al. (2009). © 2009 by the Massachusetts Institute of Technology.

wave of activation (P3) between 400 ms and 600 ms after stimulus onset spread widely across the brain. This can be regarded as the "signature" of conscious awareness. However, there is an issue about causality with these findings – did this brain activity *precede* and influence conscious awareness or did it occur merely as a *result* of conscious awareness?

We turn now to the third assumption. Eriksson et al. (2006) presented auditory stimuli (sounds of objects) and visual stimuli (pictures of objects) under masked conditions so they were hard to perceive consciously. They compared brain activation on trials on which the stimulus was identified (conscious perception) with those when it wasn't identified (lack of conscious perception). The key finding was that activation in the lateral prefrontal cortex and the anterior cingulate was associated with both auditory and visual conscious awareness.

Stronger evidence that the prefrontal cortex is important for conscious awareness might be obtained by studying patients with damage to that area. Precisely that was done by Del Cul et al. (2009). On each trial, a digit was followed rapidly by a masking stimulus, and participants indicated whether they had seen the masked number. The masking stimulus had to be delayed longer for brain-damaged patients than for healthy controls for the digit to be consciously perceived. Thus, damage to prefrontal cortex makes it harder to achieve conscious perception.

Section Summary

The vegetative state

- Behavioral evidence from patients in the vegetative state strongly suggests that they have no conscious awareness. However, brain-imaging research indicates that a few vegetative state patients have some ability to comprehend speech and may thus have limited conscious awareness.

Attention and consciousness

- There are often close links between focused attention and conscious awareness, with the former preceding the latter. However, attention can influence behavior in the absence of consciousness, and conscious awareness can exist in the absence of attention.

Controlling actions: Free will

- People sometimes have the mistaken belief that their conscious thoughts have caused their actions. The decision someone will make can be predicted on the basis of their brain activity several seconds before they are consciously aware of having made a decision. However, such research has focused on *what* and *when* decisions concerning different actions and has ignored the more important *whether* decisions.

Is consciousness unitary?

- It has sometimes been claimed that split-brain patients have two consciousnesses, one in each hemisphere. However, the left hemisphere plays the dominant role in consciousness and is responsible for interpreting internal and external events. The right hemisphere seems to be involved mostly in low-level processing.

Brain and consciousness

- The early stages of information processing involve specialized processors that aren't associated with conscious awareness. Consciousness is associated with the subsequent integration of information from these processors. Consciousness is especially associated with activation in parts of the prefrontal cortex and the anterior cingulate. Damage to the prefrontal cortex makes it harder to achieve conscious perception.

Essay Questions

1. How do we manage to attend to one auditory message in the presence of other, distracting auditory messages?
2. It has been claimed that visual attention resembles a spotlight or a zoom lens. How valid are these claims?
3. What has been discovered about visual search? What advice can psychologists give to those involved in airport security checks?
4. Does practice make perfect? If not, why not?
5. How desirable is it to prohibit the use of cell phones by drivers?
6. How has brain-imaging research increased our understanding of human consciousness?

Further Reading

- Chokron, S., Bartolomeo, P., & Sieroff, E. (2008). Unilateral spatial neglect: 30 years of research, discoveries, hope, and (especially) questions. *Revue Neurologique*, *164*, S134–S142. This paper provides an excellent account of research on neglect and the relevance of such research to our understanding of attentional processes.
- Moors, A., & De Houwer, J. (2006). Automaticity: A theoretical and conceptual analysis. *Psychological Bulletin*, *132*, 297–326. The main issues and controversies surrounding the topic of automaticity are discussed at length in this excellent article.
- Rayner, K. (2009). Eye movements and attention in reading, scene perception, and visual search. *Quarterly Journal of Experimental Psychology*, *62*, 1457–1506. Keith Rayner discusses in detail the role of attentional processes in several important activities such as reading and visual search.
- Salvucci, D. D., & Taatgen, N. A. (2011). *The multitasking mind*. New York, NY: Oxford University Press. The authors put forward a theory of multitasking and consider how we can overcome the disadvantages associated with multitasking.
- Styles, E. A. (2006). The psychology of attention (2nd ed.). Hove, UK: Psychology Press. The second edition of this textbook by Elizabeth Styles provides thorough coverage of most of the topics discussed in this chapter.
- Velmans, M., & Schneider, S. (2007). *The Blackwell companion to consciousness*. Malden, MA: Blackwell. This book edited by Max Velmans and Susan Schneider consists of 55 chapters by leading experts in the field of consciousness.

Chapter 4

Contents

Short-term and working memory

4

INTRODUCTION

How important is memory? Imagine if we were without it. We would be unable to talk, read, or write, because we would remember nothing about language. We would have extremely limited personalities because we would have no recollection of the events of our lives and thus no sense of self. In sum, we would have the same lack of knowledge as newborn babies.

We use memory for numerous purposes throughout every single day of our lives. It allows us to keep track of conversations, to answer questions in examinations, to make sense of what we read, to recognize people's faces, and to understand what we read in books and on television.

The wonders of human memory are discussed in this chapter and the following two. At the most general level, this chapter is concerned with short-term

---

Learning Objectives

After studying Chapter 4, you should be able to:

- Define, compare, and contrast short-term memory and working memory.
- Explain what is meant by the "seven, plus or minus two" capacity of short-term memory.
- Explain how the recency effect informs us of the capacity and duration of short-term memory.
- Provide examples of how working memory capacity is measured.
- Describe the unitary-store approach to short-term memory.
- Describe the components of Baddeley's working memory model, and explain how working memory processes happen according to this model.
- Discuss the implications of having higher or lower working memory capacity.

memory, whereas Chapters 5 and 6 deal with long-term memory. In Chapter 5, the emphasis is on how we can make sense of the incredible richness of human memory. Our memory ranges from detailed personal memories of previous holidays to knowledge of how to ride a bicycle or play the piano. In Chapter 6, we consider the main ways in which we use long-term memory in everyday life.

Let's return to the content of this chapter. In everyday language, the term "short-term memory" refers to our memory over a period up to several hours or days after learning. In contrast, psychologists use the term to refer to memory over a much shorter period (a few seconds). For example, we might use short-term memory to briefly remember the number needed to open a combination lock or to make a phone call. Short-term memory can be contrasted with long-term memory, which refers to memory over periods of time ranging between several seconds and a lifetime.

The bearded Viennese psychoanalyst Sigmund Freud (1925/1961) provided an apt analogy for short-term and long-term memory. He argued that memory is like a "mystic writing pad" consisting of a celluloid on top of a hard slab. When you write on the celluloid it leaves a clear record on the celluloid and a faint record on the slab. When you pull the pad most of the way out of its container, the record on the celluloid disappears leaving only the one on the slab. In this analogy, the celluloid is short-term memory and the hard slab is long-term memory.

In the early part of the chapter, we focus on the traditional approach to short-term memory. It was regarded as a *store* that could hold a limited amount of information, for example, while we dial someone's phone number. Within that approach, it is important to establish the capacity of short-term memory, its duration, and its relationship to long-term memory.

Later in the chapter, we consider the contemporary approach based on working memory. The basic idea is that in our everyday lives we use short-term memory even when what we are doing isn't *explicitly* a memory task. For example, suppose you have to write an essay in psychology. When thinking what to write in the next sentence you need to keep in mind what you have just written, which requires short-term memory. The term "working memory" describes a system that combines processing (e.g., what will I write next?) with short-term storage (e.g., what have I just written?).

SHORT-TERM MEMORY

Suppose we think of short-term memory as a store or box that holds information briefly. The most obvious question is the following: how many items of information can we keep in the box? Another question is, "How long does information stay in short-term memory?" Below we consider answers to those questions.

CAPACITY

John Jacobs (1887) was the first person to use an experimental approach to measure the capacity of short-term memory. He presented participants with a random sequence of digits or letters, after which they repeated the items back in the same order. **Memory span** was the longest sequence of items recalled accurately at least 50% of the time. Digit span was greater than letter span (9.3 vs. 7.3 items, respectively).

> **| Key Term**
>
> **Memory span:**
> the number of items (e.g., digits; words) that an individual can recall immediately in the correct order; it is used as a measure of the capacity of short-term memory.

Note that memory span involves presenting items in a *random* order. Performance would obviously be much higher if the items formed a meaningful sequence such as PSYCHOLOGY or EXPERIMENT. George Miller (1956) took account of the above point. He argued that the capacity of short-term memory is "seven, plus or minus two." This is the case whether the units are numbers, letters, or words. He claimed that we should focus on **chunks** (integrated pieces of information). What forms a chunk depends on your personal experience. For example, "IBM" is *one* chunk for those familiar with the company name International Business Machines but *three* chunks for everyone else.

The capacity of short-term memory has been estimated at about seven chunks. However, Herb Simon (1974) found that the span in chunks was less with larger chunks than with smaller ones. He studied memory span for words, two-word phrases, and eight-word phrases, arguing that each phrase formed a chunk. The number of chunks recalled fell from six or seven with unrelated words to four with two-word phrases and three with eight-word phrases.

Other factors are also involved in span measures. For example, the time taken to pronounce each word on a list influences the number of words that can be recalled in the correct order (see Research Activity 4.1). Pronunciation

> **Key Terms**
>
> **Chunks:**
> stored units formed from integrating smaller pieces of information.

Research Activity 4.1: *Word length and recall*

Write each of the words below on a separate piece of card and make two piles, one for each list. Then ask a friend to present five words from List A at one word per second, after which you try to recall the words in the correct order. After that, do the same with List B. Next present six words from List A, and then six from List B. Work out the maximum number of words you can remember correctly in order from each list.

LIST A	LIST B
cult	advantage
dare	behavior
fate	circumstance
guess	defiance
hint	fantasy
mood	interim
oath	misery
plea	narrowness
rush	occasion
truce	protocol
verb	ridicule
zeal	upheaval

The words are taken from a paper by Mueller et al. (2003). Their participants had an average span of 6.72 with List A words and of 5.09 with List B words. *Why* was there this difference? The words in List A took an average of 418 ms on average to say compared to 672 ms for those on the right. Thus, the number of items that can be stored in short-term memory depends in part on the time required to pronounce each one.

Key Term

Rehearsal:
subvocal reiteration of verbal material (e.g., words); often used in the attempt to increase the amount of information that can be remembered.

Recall:
retrieving information from long-term memory in the presence or absence of cues.

Recency effect:
the tendency in free recall for the last few items (typically two or three) to be much more likely to be recalled than those from the middle of the list; this effect has been used to measure the capacity of short-term memory.

time explains some cross-cultural differences in digit span. Chinese Mandarin speakers have much greater digit span than English speakers (Chen et al., 2009). This difference probably depends mainly on the fact that digits in spoken Mandarin take significantly less time to say than digits in spoken English.

Cowan (2000) argued that the capacity of short-term memory is often exaggerated. For example, people may recall some of the information from long-term memory rather than short-term memory. They may also engage in **rehearsal** (saying the items over to themselves silently) to increase **recall**.

When the above factors are largely eliminated, the capacity of short-term memory is about four chunks. Cowan et al. (2005) used the running memory task – a series of digits ended at an unpredictable point, with the participants' task being to recall the items from the end of the list. The digits were presented very rapidly to prevent rehearsal, and the mean number of items recalled was 3.87.

Chen and Cowan (2009) presented participants with chunks, some of which were single words and others word pairs they had learned previously. Rehearsal of these chunks was prevented by articulatory suppression (saying "the" repeatedly). The key finding was that the participants could only recall about three chunks in the absence of rehearsal.

RECENCY EFFECT

There is another way to work out the capacity of short-term memory. Suppose we present a list of unrelated words and then ask our participants to provide free recall (producing as many words as possible in any order). The **recency effect** refers to the finding that the last few items in a list are usually much better remembered in immediate recall than those from the middle of the list. Counting backwards for 10 s between the end of list presentation and start of recall mainly reduces memory performance for the last two or three items (Glanzer & Cunitz, 1966; see Figure 4.1). These items are in the short-term store at the end of list presentation and so especially vulnerable (Farrell, 2010).

Figure 4.1 Free recall as a function of serial position and duration of the interpolated task. Adapted from Glanzer and Cunitz (1966).

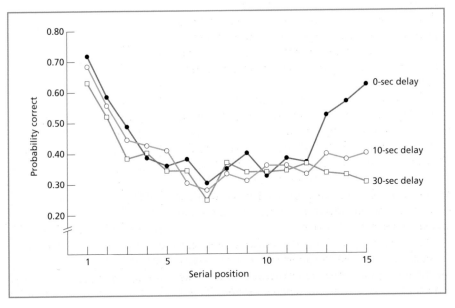

Support for the notion that the recency effect consists of items in short-term memory comes from research on patients with amnesia (see Chapter 5). This is a condition involving severe impairment of long-term memory but not of short-term memory. As predicted, amnesic patients have as large a recency effect as healthy individuals in spite of having poor long-term memory for the rest of the items (Carlesimo et al., 1996).

Summary and conclusions

The capacity of short-term memory is very limited. The estimates based on span measures are somewhat higher than those based on the recency effect. Why is that? Participants performing a span task are trying to maximize the number of items held in short-term memory. In contrast, participants given a free recall task use various strategies to maximize the total number of items recalled, including some from long-term memory. Thus there is less emphasis on using the total capacity of short-term memory.

DURATION

In a classic study, Peterson and Peterson (1959) studied the duration of short-term memory. Participants remembered a three-consonant item (e.g., XRQ) while counting backwards by threes followed by recall of the consonants in the correct order. Memory performance reduced to about 50% after 6 s and forgetting was almost complete after 18 s (see Figure 4.2).

Why is forgetting so rapid? There are two main classes of explanation (Jonides et al., 2008). First, there may be *decay* over time caused by various physiological processes. Second, there may be *interference* from items on previous trials and/or interference from the task (i.e., counting backwards) during the retention interval.

Evidence that much forgetting from short-term memory is due to interference was reported by Keppel and Underwood (1962) using the Peterson–Peterson task. There was only minimal forgetting on the very first trial, with forgetting increasing steadily over the following three or four trials. These findings suggested that forgetting of any letter sequence was due to interference from previous letter sequences. This is proactive interference (see Chapter 5).

Nairne et al. (1999) argued that the rate of forgetting observed by Peterson and Peterson (1959) was especially rapid for two reasons. First, they used all the consonants repeatedly. This may have caused considerable interference as suggested by Keppel and Underwood's (1962) findings. Second, the memory task was difficult because participants had to remember the items *and* the presentation order.

Nairne et al. (1999) presented different words on each trial to reduce interference, and tested memory *only* for order information. There was remarkably little forgetting even over 96 s. These

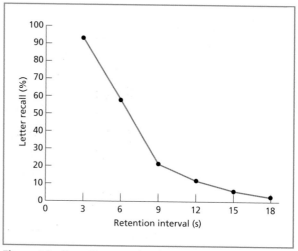

Figure 4.2 Forgetting over time in short-term memory. Data from Peterson and Peterson (1959).

findings suggest that forgetting in short-term memory is due to interference rather than decay.

Berman et al. (2009) also found that interference is more important than decay. Short-term memory performance on any given trial was disrupted by words presented on the previous trial. Suppose this disruption effect occurred because the words from the previous trial hadn't decayed sufficiently. If so, disruption would have been greatly reduced by *increasing* the interval of time between trials from 1 s to 13 s. In fact, increasing the intertrial interval had *no* effect on performance. However, the disruption effect was largely eliminated when interference from previous trials was reduced.

In sum, there is surprisingly little evidence that information in short-term memory is forgotten because it decays. Rather, such forgetting is due mostly to interference, much of it proactive interference.

SHORT-TERM VS. LONG-TERM MEMORY

Most theorists have assumed that there is a very important distinction between short-term and long-term memory. For example, there are enormous differences in capacity: a few items for short-term memory vs. essentially unlimited capacity for long-term memory. There are also massive differences in duration: a few seconds for short-term memory vs. periods of time up to several decades for long-term memory.

Atkinson and Shiffrin (1968) incorporated short-term and long-term stores in their influential multistore model (see Figure 1.2 in Chapter 1). They assumed that stimulation from the environment is initially received by the sensory stores. These stores are modality-specific, meaning there is a separate one for each sensory modality. When we see a stimulus in the environment, information about it is held briefly in the visual sensory store (iconic store). When we hear a stimulus, information about it is held briefly in the auditory sensory store (echoic store).

Some fraction of the information in the sensory stores is attended to and processed further within the short-term store. This store has very limited capacity, as we have seen. Some information processed in the short-term store is transferred to the long-term store, which has essentially unlimited capacity. Long-term storage of information often depends on rehearsal. It was assumed that there is a direct relationship between the amount of rehearsal in the short-term store and the strength of the stored memory trace.

Findings

Strangely, some of the most convincing evidence that short-term and long-term memory are separate in healthy individuals comes from research on brain-damaged patients. Suppose there are separate short-term and long-term memory systems located in different brain regions. If so, some brain-damaged patients should have impaired long-term memory but intact short-term memory. Others should have impaired short-term memory but intact long-term memory.

Patients suffering from amnesia have enormous problems with some kinds of long-term memory, although not all (see Chapter 5). For present purposes, note that the overwhelming majority have essentially intact short-term memory. In a review of 147 amnesic patients, Spiers et al. (2001) concluded that *none* had a significant problem with short-term memory.

A few brain-damaged patients have impaired short-term memory but intact long-term memory. For example, consider KF, who suffered brain damage after a motorcycle accident. He had no problem with long-term learning and recall, but his digit span was greatly impaired (Shallice & Warrington, 1970). It turned out that KF's problems with short-term memory were less widespread than initially assumed. His forgetting of visual stimuli and of meaningful sounds (e.g., telephones ringing) was much less than his forgetting of auditorily presented letters, words, and digits (Shallice & Warrington, 1974). Nevertheless, KF's problems with short-term memory contrasted sharply with his good long-term memory.

Evaluation

- The distinction among three kinds of memory store (sensory stores; short-term store; and long-term store) is supported by the evidence.

- The three kinds of store differ from each other in several ways. For example, short-term memory has very limited capacity and short temporal duration, whereas long-term memory has essentially unlimited capacity and some information lasts a lifetime.

- The evidence from brain-damaged patients supports the notion that short-term memory and long-term memory involve different brain areas (see Chapter 5).

- The conceptions of short-term memory and long-term memory are *oversimplified*. As we will see shortly, Baddeley and Hitch's (1974) working memory model replaced the concept of a single short-term store with a working memory system consisting of three different components (later raised to four). In similar fashion, Atkinson and Shiffrin's (1968) notion of a *single* long-term memory system has been discarded because the evidence indicates that there are several long-term memory systems (see Chapter 5).

- Atkinson and Shiffrin (1968) argued that information is in short-term memory *before* long-term memory. In fact, the information processed in short-term memory *must* have already made contact with information in long-term memory (Logie, 1999). For example, we can only rehearse "IBM" as a single chunk in short-term memory by using relevant information stored in long-term memory. Thus, processing in short-term memory occurs *after* long-term memory has been accessed.

- Atkinson and Shiffrin (1968) assumed that rehearsal is of central importance when we store information in long-term memory. We do sometimes use rehearsal to promote effective learning. However, it is not involved in establishing most of our long-term memories.

UNITARY-STORE APPROACH

In recent years, various theorists (e.g., Jonides et al., 2008) have argued that the entire multistore approach is misguided and should be replaced by a unitary-store model. The basic assumption in this model is that short-term memory is simply that fraction of long-term memory activated at any given moment. Thus, whereas Atkinson and Shiffrin (1968) emphasized the *differences* between short-term and long-term memory, advocates of the unitary-store approach emphasize the *similarities*.

Processing within short-term memory is often heavily influenced by information from long-term memory. Evidence that semantic [meaning] information from long-term memory affects processing in short-term memory was reported by Ruchkin et al. (1999). Words and pseudowords sounding very similar to words were presented aurally, and were followed by serial recall. If participants had processed only information about the sounds of the stimuli in short-term memory, brain activity would have been very similar for words and pseudowords. In fact, there was much more brain activity associated with words than with pseudowords. This suggests that semantic information from long-term memory was processed when words were presented.

According to the unitary-store model, short-term and long-term memory are closely connected. If so, it is hard to explain why amnesic patients have essentially intact short-term memory in spite of having severe problems with long-term memory. According to Jonides et al. (2008), amnesic patients *would* show impaired short-term memory if the memory task were sufficiently complex.

Shrager et al. (2008) tested the above prediction using various tasks in which memory was assessed after a short retention interval. Amnesic patients were significantly impaired compared to healthy controls on some tasks but not on others. However, the memory tasks on which amnesic patients performed poorly involved long-term memory as well as short-term memory. Shrager et al. concluded that short-term memory processes are intact in amnesic patients. They only show impaired performance on so-called "short-term memory tasks" when those tasks actually depend substantially on long-term memory.

There are many interactions between short-term and long-term memory. However, it is simplistic to argue that short-term memory is *only* activated long-term memory (Baddeley, 2007). For example, people can generate novel visual images to stimuli in short-term memory (Logie & van der Meulen, 2009). This clearly goes well beyond activating memory traces in long-term memory.

Section Summary

Capacity
- Span measures suggest that the capacity of short-term memory is about seven chunks, but is somewhat lower with words having long pronunciation times. When attempts are made to eliminate the effects of rehearsal and long-term memory on short-term memory, its capacity is only three or four chunks. In similar fashion, the capacity of short-term memory based on the recency effect is two or three items.

Duration
- Information in short-term memory is generally forgotten within a few seconds. This is mostly due to interference (much of it proactive interference) rather than decay.

> **Short-term memory vs. long-term memory**
> - Evidence from brain-damaged patients suggests that there are separate short-term and long-term memory systems. In Atkinson and Shiffrin's influential multistore model, information is in short-term memory before long-term memory and rehearsal in short-term memory strongly influences long-term memory. Both of these assumptions are oversimplifications.
>
> **Unitary-store approach**
> - According to unitary-store theorists, the information in short-term memory is that fraction of long-term memory currently activated. One problem with this theory is that amnesic patients have intact short-term memory in spite of having very poor long-term memory. Another problem is that we can manipulate information in short-term memory in complex ways involving far more than the mere activation of information in long-term memory.

WORKING MEMORY

Is short-term memory useful in everyday life? Textbook writers (including me earlier in the chapter!) sometimes answer the question by pointing out that it allows us to remember a telephone number for the few seconds required to dial it. However, that is no longer of much relevance – nearly everyone has a cell or mobile phone that stores all the phone numbers needed regularly.

In 1974, two British psychologists (Alan Baddeley and Graham Hitch) came up with a convincing answer to the above question. They argued that we generally use short-term memory when engaged in the performance of complex tasks. With such tasks, you have to carry out various processes to complete the task. However, you also have to store briefly information about the outcome of early processes in short-term memory as you move on to later processes.

Suppose you were given the addition problem 13 + 18 + 24. You would probably add 13 and 18 and keep the answer (31) in short-term memory. You would then add 24 to 31 and produce the correct answer of 55.

Baddeley and Hitch (1974) argued that we should replace the notion of short-term memory with that of working memory. **Working memory** refers to a system combining processing and short-term memory functions. Baddeley and Hitch's crucial insight was that short-term memory is essential in the performance of numerous tasks that aren't explicitly memory tasks.

Think back to Atkinson and Shiffrin's (1968) theory of memory, in which the importance of verbal rehearsal in short-term memory was emphasized. Baddeley and Hitch (1974) accepted that verbal rehearsal is important. However, they argued that other kinds of information can also be stored in short-term memory. For example, suppose you are driving along focusing on steering the car, avoiding pedestrians, and keeping a safe distance behind the car in front. In addition, you may be storing relevant visual and spatial information (e.g., width of the road; the distance of the car behind you). Thus, short-term (or working) memory involves spatial and visual processes as well as verbal ones.

Key Term
Working memory: a system that can store information briefly while other information is processed.

WORKING MEMORY MODEL

Baddeley and Hitch (1974) proposed the original version of the working memory model. We will focus on the most recent version consisting of four components (see Figure 4.3):

- **Central executive:** This is a limited capacity processing system acting as an attentional controller. It is the "boss" of the working memory system and controls what happens within the other components. It can process information from any sensory modality (e.g., visual, auditory) but has no storage capacity.
- **Phonological loop:** This is involved in the processing and brief storage of phonological (speech-based) information.
- **Visuo-spatial sketchpad:** This is involved in the processing and brief storage of visual and spatial information.
- **Episodic buffer:** This is a storage system that can hold information from the phonological loop, the visuo-spatial sketchpad, and long-term memory.

You are probably thinking that the working memory model seems rather complicated. However, the basic ideas are straightforward. When we carry out a task, we can use verbal processing (phonological loop), visual processing, or spatial processing (visuo-spatial sketchpad). Performing the task successfully requires that we attend to relevant information and use verbal, visual, and spatial processes effectively (central executive). During the performance of a task, we often need a general storage system combining and integrating information from the other components and from long-term memory (episodic buffer).

It is assumed that all four components of working memory have limited capacity. It is also assumed that each component can function fairly independently of the others. These two assumptions allow us to predict whether or not two tasks can be performed successfully at the same time:

- If two tasks use the *same* component of working memory, they can't be performed successfully together. This is because that component's limited capacity will be exceeded.
- If two tasks involve *different* components, it should be possible to perform them as well together as separately.

Figure 4.3 The Baddeley (2000) version of the four components of the working memory system, including the connections among them. Fluid systems involve processing whereas crystallized systems involve stored knowledge.

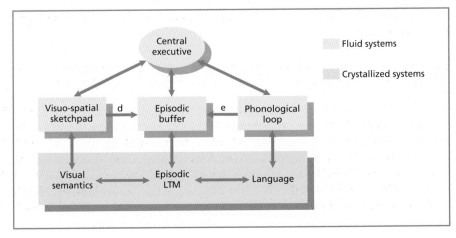

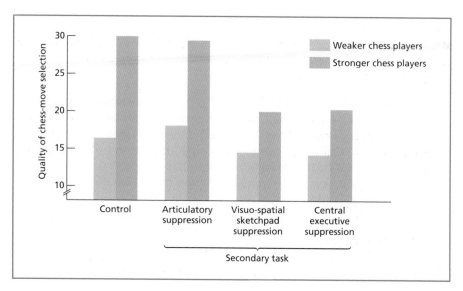

Figure 4.4 Effects of secondary tasks on quality of chess-move selection in stronger and weaker players. Adapted from Robbins et al. (1996).

We can see how this works in practice by considering which components of working memory are involved in playing chess. Robbins et al. (1996) asked weaker and stronger players to select moves from various chess positions. The chess players carried out this chess task while performing one of the following secondary tasks:

- *Random number generation:* This task involves trying to produce a random series of digits and requires the central executive.
- *Pressing keys on a keypad in a clockwise pattern:* This task involves the visuo-spatial sketchpad.
- *Rapid repetition of the word "see-saw":* This involves the phonological loop.

The findings of Robbins et al. (1996) are shown in Figure 4.4. The quality of the chess moves selected was reduced when the secondary task involved the central executive or the visuo-spatial sketchpad. In contrast, rapid word repetition didn't reduce the quality of chess moves, meaning the phonological loop wasn't involved in selecting chess moves. The effects of the various secondary tasks on the quality of the chess moves selected were similar for weaker and stronger players. This suggests both groups used the working memory system similarly when choosing moves.

In the Real World 4.1: *Simultaneous interpreting*

Millions of people around the world have jobs (e.g., air traffic controller; Nolan, 2010) that place considerable demands on working memory. One such job is that of simultaneous interpreter or translator. As we might expect, those inexperienced in simultaneous interpreting find it exceptionally demanding (Christoffels et al., 2006).

What makes simultaneous translation so demanding? Simultaneous interpreters have at the same time to comprehend what is said in one language, translate from that language into a second language, and speak in that second language. Other demanding aspects of simultaneous interpretation are less obvious (Albir & Alves, 2009). For example, the interpreter's background knowledge is generally weaker than the speaker's. In addition, he/she has to start translating the auditory message without knowing in detail what the speaker will say next.

Most skills required for simultaneous translation involve the central executive. Attentional control is a major function of the central executive, and attentional control is needed to switch attention appropriately among cognitive processes involved in simultaneous translation.

Simultaneous interpreters generally show "translation asymmetry" – they find it harder to translate from their dominant language into their weaker language than the other way around. Rinne et al. (2000) found that simultaneous interpreting mostly involved the left hemisphere, especially parts of the prefrontal cortex associated with semantic processing and verbal working memory. Of most importance, there was more brain activation when the interpreters translated into their weaker language, suggesting that this imposes high demands on working memory.

It is not always advantageous to use one's dominant language, especially if the switch from a weaker language is unexpected. Philipp et al. (2007) gave individuals fluent in German, English, and French the task of naming digits. Naming times were much longer immediately after they shifted from one of their nondominant languages (English or French) into their dominant language (German). Before the shift, participants had to inhibit their dominant language, and it took time to overcome this inhibition when shifting. Language switching involves several brain areas associated with cognitive control (e.g., inhibitory processes), and such control involves the central executive (Abutalebi & Green, 2008).

Do simultaneous interpreters have superior working memory to other people? This issue was addressed by Christoffels et al. (2006) in a study of bilingual individuals whose native language was Dutch and whose second language was English. Some were simultaneous interpreters with an average of 16 years of experience whereas others were teachers of English.

Christoffels et al. (2006) used various tasks to assess working memory capacity. One was a reading-span task in which participants read sentences and then recalled the last word in each sentence. There was also a speaking-span task in which participants were presented with several words and then produced aloud a sentence for each word they remembered. These tasks were performed in both Dutch and English. The interpreters performed better than the teachers on both tasks and in both languages. These findings suggest that excellent working memory ability is a real advantage if you want to be a successful interpreter. However, it is possible in addition that becoming an interpreter helps to develop working memory abilities.

When we listen to a speaker, we can use the phonological loop to store some of the information briefly and so make comprehension easier. In contrast, simultaneous interpreters generally talk almost continuously. As a result, they have little or no access to the phonological loop to aid comprehension. The ability to overcome this problem is important in simultaneous interpretation.

Christoffels (2006) asked participants to listen to stories while saying the Dutch words for *dog*, *cat*, and *mouse* repeatedly. High levels of subsequent recall for the stories were associated with good simultaneous interpreting performance. Thus, the ability to understand spoken language without using the phonological loop is advantageous for simultaneous interpreting.

In sum, several findings indicate that simultaneous translation relies heavily on the working memory system. For example, simultaneous translators have greater working memory capacity than other people. The central executive is of special importance for simultaneous translation – relevant functions include attentional switching, inhibitory processes, and performing various cognitive processes at the same time. It is much less clear that the phonological loop or visuo-spatial sketchpad plays an important role in simultaneous translation.

PHONOLOGICAL LOOP

Suppose we test people's memory span by presenting visually a series of words and requesting recall in the order the words were presented. Do you think they would use the phonological loop on this task? So far as most people are concerned, the answer is "Yes." We consider two kinds of supporting evidence below.

First, there is the **phonological similarity effect**. This effect is found when a short list of visually presented words is recalled immediately in the correct order. Recall performance is worse when the words are phonologically similar (i.e., having similar sounds) than when they are phonologically dissimilar. For example, FEE, HE, KNEE, LEE, ME, and SHE form a list of phonologically similar words, whereas BAY, HOE, IT, ODD, SHY, and UP form a list of phonologically dissimilar words.

Larsen et al. (2000) found using those lists that the ability to recall the words in order was 25% worse with the phonologically similar list. This phonological similarity effect occurred because the participants used speech-based rehearsal processes within the phonological loop. However, subsequent research showed that the phonological similarity effect doesn't *only* involve the phonological loop – semantic processes also play a part (Acheson et al., 2010).

Second, there is the **word-length effect**. This is the finding that word span (number of words recalled immediately in the correct order) is greater for short words than for long ones. As we saw earlier (Chen et al., 2009; Mueller et al., 2003), word span is greater when the time taken to pronounce the words is relatively short than when it is relatively long. This suggests that the capacity of the phonological loop is limited in terms of temporal duration, like a tape loop (Baddeley, 2007).

What use is the phonological loop in everyday life? We have seen it is useful for remembering a series of unrelated words in the correct order. However, that isn't a skill we need very often. One way to obtain an answer is to study brain-damaged individuals with a very impaired phonological loop. This was done by Baddeley et al. (1988). They tested a patient, PV, who had a digit span of only two items but good long-term memory. Somewhat surprisingly, PV coped very well with everyday life, including running a shop and raising a family.

Baddeley et al. (1988) wondered whether the phonological loop is useful when learning language. PV (a native Italian speaker) performed as well as healthy participants when learning to associate pairs of unrelated words in Italian. However, her performance was dramatically inferior to that of healthy controls when learning to associate Russian words with their Italian translations. Indeed, she showed no learning at all over 10 trials!

The notion that the phonological loop is useful when learning new words received additional support from Papagno et al. (1991). Native Italian speakers learned pairs of Italian words and pairs of Italian–Russian words. Articulatory suppression (repeating an irrelevant sound to reduce use of the phonological loop) greatly slowed down the learning of foreign vocabulary. However, it had little effect on the learning of pairs of Italian words. Thus, the negative effects of articulatory suppression on learning were limited to new words.

Key Terms

Phonological similarity effect:
the finding that immediate recall of word lists in the correct order is impaired when the words sound similar to each other.

Word-length effect:
fewer long words than short ones can be recalled immediately after presentation in the correct order.

Andersson (2010) studied language comprehension in Swedish children. Phonological loop processes predicted the children's comprehension performance when reading a text in their foreign language (English) but not in their native language (Swedish). Why was this the case? An efficient phonological loop is more important when reading in a foreign language because of the greater difficulty in working out how to pronounce the words.

VISUO-SPATIAL SKETCHPAD

The visuo-spatial sketchpad is used for the temporary storage and manipulation of visual patterns and spatial movement. In essence, visual processing involves remembering *what* and spatial processing involves remembering *where*. The visuo-spatial sketchpad is very useful in everyday life – we use it to find the route when moving from one place to another (Logie & Della Sala, 2005) or when watching television (Toms et al., 1994).

We also use the visuo-spatial sketch pad when playing computer games. Logie et al. (1989) studied performance on a complex computer game called *Space Fortress* which involves maneuvering a space ship around a computer screen. Performance on *Space Fortress* was severely impaired early in training when participants had to perform an additional visuo-spatial task at the same time, but less so thereafter. Thus, the visuo-spatial sketchpad was used throughout training on *Space Fortress*, but its involvement decreased with practice.

What is the capacity of the visuo-spatial sketchpad? It can hold about four items (Vogel et al., 2001; Xu & Chun, 2009). Vogel et al. (2001) presented a display of between 3 and 12 objects. After 900 ms, a second display (identical to the first or with one object changed) was presented. Participants' ability to decide whether the two displays were identical was almost perfect with four objects. Performance declined progressively as the number of items in the display increased above four.

A single system?

The $64,000 question concerning the visuo-spatial sketchpad is as follows: Are visual and spatial processing combined in a *single* system? Much evidence indicates that there are important differences between them. For example, blind people are generally good at using spatial information to move around even though they can't engage in visual processing. Indeed, Fortin et al. (2008) actually found that blind individuals were *better* than sighted ones at learning routes through human-size mazes.

Blind individuals probably performed so well in the study by Fortin et al. (2008) because of their extensive practice in spatial processing. Support for that interpretation comes from another finding reported by Fortin et al. – the hippocampus was larger in the blind than the sighted participants. The relevance of this is that the hippocampus is involved in spatial processing.

Convincing evidence that the visuo-spatial sketchpad consists of *separate* spatial and visual components was reported by Klauer and Zhao (2004). There were two main tasks. One was a spatial task (memory for dot locations) and the other a visual task (memory for Chinese characters). Sometimes the main task was performed with a color discrimination task to provide visual interference. At other times, it was performed with a movement discrimination task to provide spatial interference.

What would we predict if there were separate spatial and visual components? First, the spatial interference task should disrupt performance more on the spatial main task than on the visual main task. Second, the visual interference task should disrupt performance more on the visual main task than on the spatial main task. Both of these predictions were confirmed (see Figure 4.5).

Cognitive neuroscience

Studies in cognitive neuroscience indicate that visual and spatial processing involve different brain regions. Smith and Jonides (1997) carried out an ingenious study in which two visual stimuli were presented together followed by a probe stimulus. Participants decided whether the probe was in the same location as one of the initial stimuli (spatial task) or had the same form (visual task). Even though the stimuli were identical in the two tasks, there were clear differences in patterns of brain activation. There was more activity in the *right* hemisphere during the spatial task than the visual task. However, there was more activity in the *left* hemisphere during the visual task than the spatial one.

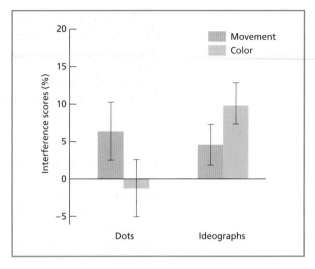

Figure 4.5 Amount of interference on a spatial task (dots) and a visual task (Chinese ideographs) as a function of secondary task (spatial: movement vs. visual: color discrimination). From Klauer and Zhao (2004), Copyright © 2000 American Psychological Association. Reproduced with permission.

Zimmer (2008) reviewed findings on the brain areas associated with visual and spatial processing. Areas within the occipital and temporal lobes were activated during visual imagery tasks. In contrast, areas within the parietal cortex (especially the intraparietal sulcus) were activated during spatial imagery tasks (there is further discussion of the brain areas associated with different kinds of imagery in Chapter 2).

Gender differences

Males often outperform females on tasks involving spatial processing. Liu et al. (2008) carried out a meta-analysis (see Glossary) based on 113 studies in which males and females were given training in spatial skills. Training typically improved spatial skills but failed to eliminate the gender gap.

What causes the gender difference? Terlecki and Newcombe (2005) argued it is due to a "digital divide" – males have more spatial experience than females because they spend far more time playing video games. The video-game performance of females improved with practice as much as that of males, suggesting that there may be little or no gender difference in natural spatial ability. However, males outperformed females in spatial skills long before the advent of video games (Liu et al., 2008).

Support for Terlecki and Newcombe's (2005) conclusion was provided by Spence et al. (2009). Male and female participants who had rarely if ever played video games were initially matched for spatial skills. After that, they received training in playing a first-person shooter video game called *Medal of Honor: Pacific Assault*. The key finding was that the male and female participants benefited equally from practice and reached the same level of performance.

CENTRAL EXECUTIVE

The central executive (which resembles an attentional system) is the most important and versatile component of the working memory system. It is involved in processes such as planning and coordination, but it doesn't store information. The central executive is also involved in inhibitory processes that prevent our attention to a task being distracted by irrelevant stimuli such as the sound of a television (Miyake et al., 2000; Friedman & Miyake, 2004). Every time we engage in any complex cognitive activity such as reading a text or solving a problem we make extensive use of the central executive. It is also used extensively when we are engaged in writing text (see Chapter 9).

Parts of the prefrontal cortex are much involved in the functions of the central executive. Mottaghy (2006) reviewed studies using repetitive transcranial magnetic stimulation (rTMS; see Glossary) to disrupt activity within the dorsolateral prefrontal cortex. Performance on many complex cognitive tasks was impaired by this manipulation, indicating that dorsolateral prefrontal cortex is of importance in central executive functioning. However, it is *not* the only area involved. Patients with damage to the prefrontal cortex don't always show executive deficits, and some patients with no damage to prefrontal cortex nevertheless have executive deficits (Andrés, 2003).

We can gain some understanding of the importance of the central executive in our everyday lives by studying brain-damaged patients whose central executive is impaired. Such individuals suffer from **dysexecutive syndrome** (Baddeley, 2007), which involves problems with planning, organizing, monitoring behavior, and initiating behavior. Patients with dysexecutive syndrome typically have damage within the prefrontal cortex, but some have damage to posterior (mainly parietal) regions (Andrés, 2003). Unsurprisingly, sufferers from dysexecutive syndrome have great problems in holding down a job and functioning adequately in everyday life (Chamberlain, 2003).

The notion of a dysexecutive syndrome implies that brain damage to the frontal lobes typically impairs *all* central executive functions. That is often the case with patients having widespread damage to the frontal lobes, but is *not* true of patients with more specific brain damage. Stuss and Alexander (2007) argued that there are *three* major executive processes based in different parts of the frontal lobes:

- *Task setting:* This involves relatively simple planning as when starting to learn to drive a car.
- *Monitoring:* This involves checking that the current task is being performed adequately.
- *Energization:* This involves sustained attention or concentration.

Key Term

Dysexecutive syndrome: a condition in which damage to the frontal lobes causes impaired functioning of the **central executive** involving deficits in organizing and planning behavior.

Many patients with specific brain damage have problems largely limited to one of the above processes. Problems with task setting were associated with damage to the left lateral frontal region, problems with monitoring with damage to the right lateral frontal region, and problems with energization with damage to the superior medial region of the frontal cortex.

In sum, the central executive consists of various functions, three of which are task setting, monitoring, and energization. Note, however, that many complex cognitive tasks require all three functions at different stages of task performance.

EPISODIC BUFFER

As we have seen, the central executive plays a major role in the processing of many different kinds of information. However, it doesn't possess any storage capacity. That led Baddeley (2000) to add a fourth component to his theory. The episodic buffer (see Glossary) is a limited-capacity storage system used to store briefly information from the phonological loop, the visuo-spatial sketchpad, and long-term memory (Repovš & Baddeley, 2006).

According to Baddeley (2007), the complexities of integrating several different kinds of information mean there are close links between the episodic buffer and the central executive. If so, we would expect to find prefrontal activation on tasks involving the episodic buffer. This is because the prefrontal cortex is typically activated during tasks requiring the central executive.

The usefulness of the episodic buffer can be seen in a study by Baddeley and Wilson (2002) on immediate recall of prose. It used to be argued that good immediate prose recall involves the ability to store relevant information in long-term memory. According to this position, amnesic patients with very impaired long-term memory should have very poor immediate prose recall.

In contrast, Baddeley and Wilson argued that the ability to show good immediate recall of prose depends on two factors: (1) the capacity of the episodic buffer; and (2) an efficiently functioning central executive creating and maintaining information in the buffer. It follows that even severely amnesic patients should have good immediate prose recall provided their central executive is efficient. As predicted, immediate prose recall was much better in amnesics having little deficit in executive functioning than in those with a severe executive deficit.

Darling and Havelka (2010) asked participants to recall random digits in the correct order. The digits were presented visually all to the same location, or arranged along a horizontal line, or on a keypad resembling the layout on a cell or mobile phone. It was assumed that performance would be best in the keypad condition. In that condition, visual information (digits) and spatial information based on the familiar keypad layout could be integrated in the episodic buffer. As predicted, serial recall was best in the keypad condition.

In sum, the episodic buffer helps to provide the "glue" to integrate information within working memory. As such, it fulfills a very valuable function. As yet, however, we lack a detailed account of how this integration process works.

Section Summary

Working memory model
- According to Baddeley, the working memory system consists of a central executive, phonological loop, visuo-spatial sketchpad, and episodic buffer. All these components have limited capacity but can function fairly independently of each other.

Simultaneous interpreting
- Simultaneous interpreting makes substantial demands on working memory because it involves several different processes in rapid succession. Switching from one language to another requires inhibitory control processes, and it is more demanding to translate from the dominant language into the weaker

one. Simultaneous interpreters tend to have greater working memory capacity than other people.

Phonological loop

- The involvement of the phonological loop in short-term memory is shown by the phonological similarity and word-length effects. The phonological loop is very useful when learning and comprehending a foreign language. Baddeley argued that the phonological similarity effect only depends on the phonological loop, but in fact it involves semantic processing as well (Acheson et al., 2010).

Visuo-spatial sketchpad

- The visuo-spatial sketchpad is used when moving from one place to another and when playing computer games. It consists of separate visual and spatial components involving different brain areas. The common finding that males have slightly better spatial skills than females may be due mostly to the much greater amount of time males devote to video games.

Central executive

- The central executive is an attention-like system used with numerous complex cognitive tasks. Patients with dysexecutive syndrome have extensive damage to the prefrontal cortex and other areas. This causes severely impaired central executive functioning and major disruptions to their everyday lives. Task setting, monitoring, and energization are three of the main functions of the central executive.

Episodic buffer

- The episodic buffer is used to integrate and to store briefly information from long-term memory and the other working memory components. It is an important component of the working memory system. However, its workings remain somewhat unclear.

WORKING MEMORY CAPACITY

So far we have focused on the theoretical approach to working memory pioneered by Baddeley and Hitch (1974). Of central importance within that approach is the notion that the working memory system consists of four somewhat separate components. Other theorists have focused more on individual differences in working memory capacity (e.g., Barrett et al., 2004), and have argued that such individual differences influence processing and performance on numerous cognitive tasks. In essence, it is assumed that working memory is used when we need to store some information briefly while processing other information. Some individuals are better able to combine processing and storage and so have high working memory capacity.

How can we assess working memory capacity? The most used method was devised by Daneman and Carpenter (1980). People read several sentences for comprehension (processing task) and then recall the final word of each sentence (storage task). The largest number of sentences from which an individual can recall the final words more than 50% of the time is his/her **reading span**. An individual's reading span is taken as a measure of his/her working memory capacity.

Daneman and Carpenter assumed the processes used in comprehending the sentences require a smaller proportion of the available working memory capacity of those with a large capacity. As a result, they have more capacity available for retaining the last words of the sentences.

Various other ways of assessing working memory capacity have been devised. Turner and Engle (1989) presented participants with a series of items such as "IS $(4 \times 2) - 3 = 5$? TABLE." They had to answer each arithmetical question and remember the last word. Performance on this task allowed Turner and Engle to calculate the **operation span**, which is the maximum number of items for which the participants could recall the last words.

Individuals high in working memory capacity perform most tasks better than those of low capacity. For example, we will see in Chapter 8 that high working memory capacity is associated with superior language comprehension skills. Since the ability to process and store information at the same time is important in everyday life, we might assume that individuals high in working memory capacity should tend to have high intelligence. We turn to this issue next.

How strong is the relationship between working memory capacity and general intelligence? Conway et al. (2003) reviewed the relevant research. The typical correlation or association between working memory capacity and general intelligence was moderately high (about +0.6). Thus, individuals with greater working memory capacity are generally more intelligent than those with smaller capacity.

There are various types of intelligence. For example, there is fluid intelligence, which involves a rapid understanding of novel relationships. There is also crystallized intelligence, which depends on knowledge and expertise and can be assessed by vocabulary tests. Unsworth (2010) found that working memory was more strongly related to fluid intelligence than to crystallized intelligence. Why are working memory capacity and crystallized intelligence weakly related? Crystallized intelligence involves acquired knowledge whereas working memory involves various cognitive processes and temporary information storage.

What remains unclear is the causality issue. We don't really know whether having high working memory capacity causes a high level of intelligence or whether a high level of intelligence produces high working memory capacity.

ATTENTIONAL CONTROL

Why is there a strong association between working memory capacity and intelligence (especially fluid intelligence)? An important reason is that individuals high in working memory capacity have superior attentional control to those of low capacity (Barrett et al., 2004). As a consequence, they are less susceptible to distraction.

Several studies have focused on working memory capacity and distractibility. Poole and Kane (2009) used a visual search task in which participants searched for a target stimulus. Individuals high in working memory capacity *only* detected

Key Terms

Reading span:
the greatest number of sentences read for comprehension for which an individual can recall all the final words more than 50% of the time.

Operation span:
the maximum number of items (arithmetical questions + words) for which an individual can recall all the last words.

targets faster than those low in working memory capacity when distractors were present.

Sorqvist (2010) wondered whether working memory capacity was related to distractibility with everyday distractors. Recall of a prose passage was more adversely affected by the sounds of planes flying past one by one among those low in working memory capacity than among high-capacity individuals.

Other research has considered attentional processes more generally. When people perform a sustained attention task, they occasionally have slow reaction times due to lapses of attention. Individual differences in working memory capacity had no effect on relatively fast reaction times. However, those of high capacity had significantly fewer lapses of attention (Unsworth et al., 2010a).

Bleckley et al. (2003) focused on the allocation of attention. Individuals low in working memory capacity consistently allocated their attention as a spotlight in a fairly inflexible way. In contrast, those high in working memory capacity showed more flexible allocation of attention.

We have considered research suggesting that a key advantage of individuals high in working memory capacity is that they have superior attentional control. If that hypothesis is correct, they should outperform those of low capacity even on simple tasks undemanding of processing resources.

The above prediction was tested by Unsworth et al. (2004) using the prosaccade and antisaccade tasks. The prosaccade task involves making an eye movement in the direction of a cue, whereas the antisaccade task involves making an eye movement in the *opposite* direction to the cue. Only the antisaccade task imposes demands on attentional control. There were no differences between the two groups on the prosaccade task. However, on the antisaccade task, high-capacity individuals performed better than low-capacity ones – they made eye movements in the correct direction faster and also made fewer errors. Thus, high-capacity individuals have superior attentional control.

There is a causality issue with the findings we have discussed. It is arguable whether high working memory capacity depends on high attentional control, or whether the causality operates in the opposite direction.

DUAL-COMPONENT MODEL

The discovery that individuals high and low in working memory capacity differ in attentional control doesn't exclude the possibility that there are other important differences between the two groups. Unsworth and Spillers (2010) put forward a dual-component model of working memory capacity. Attentional control was one component and long-term memory was the other. Long-term memory is likely to be important because measures of working memory capacity involve the retrieval of information from long-term memory. In addition, individuals high in working memory capacity have superior long-term memory to those of low capacity (Unsworth et al., 2010b).

In their study, Unsworth and Spillers (2010) obtained several measures of attentional control, long-term memory, and fluid intelligence. What did they find? Attentional control and long-term memory were both moderately strongly associated with working memory capacity, with the contribution of long-term memory being somewhat greater. In addition, individual differences in fluid intelligence were associated with attentional control, long-term memory, and working memory capacity.

Evaluation

⊕ Individual differences in working memory capacity are important. For example, they predict language comprehension ability (see Chapter 8).

⊕ Much has been discovered about the differences between those high and low in working memory capacity. The former have higher fluid intelligence, better attentional control, and superior long-term memory than the latter.

⊕ The dual-component model provides a coherent account of individual differences in working memory capacity.

⊖ Attentional control can involve inhibiting the processing of distractors, sustaining attention on the current task, and focusing on task-relevant stimuli. As yet, it is unclear which of these processes is most associated with working memory capacity.

⊖ Individual differences in working memory capacity don't depend only on attentional control and long-term memory (Unsworth & Spillers, 2010). Thus, additional factors (hitherto unidentified) must be involved.

Section Summary

• Measures of working memory capacity require processing and brief storage of information. High scorers have superior language comprehension skills. They also have higher intelligence (especially fluid intelligence), but the direction of causality between working memory capacity and intelligence is unclear.

Attentional control

• Individuals high in working memory capacity have superior resistance to distraction, fewer lapses of attention, and more flexible allocation of attention than low-capacity individuals. They exhibit superior attentional control even on undemanding tasks. It is unclear whether working memory capacity partly determines attentional control, or whether at least some of the causality is in the opposite direction.

Dual-component model

• According to the dual-component model, individual differences in working memory capacity depend on attentional control and long-term memory. Both components are important, with long-term memory more so than attentional control.

Evaluation

- It has been established that individuals high and low in working memory capacity differ in intelligence (especially fluid intelligence), attentional control, and long-term memory. Future research will probably identify additional differences between high- and low-capacity individuals.

Essay Questions

1. How can we assess the capacity of short-term memory?
2. Describe the theoretical approach to working memory proposed by Baddeley.
3. In what ways is the central executive the most important component of the working memory system?
4. How separate are visual and spatial processes within the visuo-spatial sketchpad?
5. What are some of the main cognitive differences between individuals high and low in working memory capacity?

Further Reading

- Baddeley, A., Eysenck, M. W., & Anderson, M. C. (2009). *Memory*. New York, NY: Psychology Press. Chapters 2 and 3 of this textbook provide detailed coverage of short-term memory and working memory.
- Cowan, N. (2005). *Working memory capacity.* Hove, UK: Psychology Press. The various theoretical perspectives on working memory capacity are discussed at length by Nelson Cowan.
- Jonides, J., Lewis, R. L., Nee, D. E., Lustig, C. A., Berman, M. G., & Moore, K. S. (2008). The mind and brain of short-term memory. *Annual Review of Psychology*, *59*, 193–224. The authors discuss short-term memory at length, and compare the multistore and unitary-store models.
- Repovš, G., & Baddeley, A. (2006). The multi-component model of working memory: Explorations in experimental cognitive psychology. *Neuroscience*, *139*, 5–21. This paper provides an overview of the working memory model and relevant research.
- Unsworth, N., & Spillers, G. J. (2010). Working memory capacity: Attention control, secondary memory, or both? A direct test of the dual-component model. *Journal of Memory and Language*, *62*, 392–406. Nash Unsworth and Gregory Spillers put forward a theoretical model to account for individual differences in working memory capacity.

Chapter 5

Contents

Learning and long-term memory

5

INTRODUCTION

Learning and memory are two of the most important topics within cognitive psychology. Why is that the case? If we were unable to learn, we wouldn't have any information available to remember. In the absence of both learning and memory, our lives would be devoid of meaning. The devastating effects associated with the progressive destruction of the human memory system can be seen in patients suffering from Alzheimer's disease.

Learning and memory are closely connected. Learning involves the accumulation of knowledge or skills and would be impossible in the absence

---

Learning Objectives

After studying Chapter 5, you should be able to:

- Define long-term memory (contrasted with short-term memory).
- Discuss theories of how information passes back and forth between short-term and long-term memory.
- Define, compare, and contrast declarative memory and nondeclarative (implicit) memory.
- Define, compare, and contrast episodic memory and semantic memory.
- Define, compare, and contrast recognition and recall.
- Explain how the levels-of-processing theory accounts for long-term memory encoding and retrieval.
- Discuss what recommendations encoding specificity theorists would make to improve memory retrieval.
- Describe anterograde amnesia, and indicate how the study of amnesic patients has increased our understanding of long-term memory.
- Explain how proactive and retroactive interference affect forgetting.
- Explain the importance of consolidation.

of memory. In similar fashion, memory would be impossible in the absence of learning, because we can only remember things learned previously.

CHAPTER STRUCTURE

This chapter starts by considering two major approaches to learning. First, I discuss the levels-of-processing approach. This is based on the assumption that what we remember depends very much on the nature of the processing occurring at the time of learning. As we will see, that approach has proved successful. However, it has relatively little to say about implicit learning (learning occurring in the absence of conscious awareness of what is being learned). Major differences between implicit learning and explicit learning (learning involving conscious awareness) are discussed.

As we saw in Chapter 4, Atkinson and Shiffrin (1968) argued there is a *single* long-term memory store. However, that seems improbable. Just think about it. We all have an amazing variety of information stored in long-term memory. For example, long-term memory can contain details of our last summer holiday, the fact that Paris is the capital of France, information about how to ride a bicycle or play the piano, and so on. That makes it important to identify the main types of long-term memory, and to discuss the characteristics of each one. This is done taking account of the important evidence obtained from amnesic patients.

Finally, we discuss forgetting, and our reduced ability to remember information with increases in the length of time since learning. Several factors contributing to memory failures are discussed.

LEVELS OF PROCESSING

What determines how well we remember information over the long term? A very influential answer was proposed by Fergus Craik and Robert Lockhart (1972). They argued in their levels-of-processing approach that what is crucial is how we process that information during learning. There are various levels of processing ranging from shallow or physical analysis of a stimulus (e.g., detecting specific letters in words) to deep or semantic analysis. The greater the extent to which *meaning* is processed, the deeper the level of processing.

Craik and Lockhart's (1972) main theoretical assumptions were as follows:

- The level or depth of processing of a stimulus has a large effect on its memorability.
- Deeper levels of analysis produce more elaborate, longer lasting, and stronger memory traces than shallow levels of analysis.

Craik and Lockhart (1972) disagreed with Atkinson and Shiffrin's (1968) assumption that rehearsal always improves long-term memory. They argued that rehearsal that consists simply of repeating previous analyses (maintenance rehearsal) doesn't enhance long-term memory. In fact, this is not strictly correct. Maintenance rehearsal typically has a beneficial effect (but a rather small one) on long-term memory (Glenberg et al., 1977).

Numerous studies support the main assumptions of the levels-of-processing approach. Craik and Tulving (1975) compared recognition performance as a function of the task performed at learning:

- *Shallow grapheme task:* Decide whether each word is in uppercase or lowercase letters.
- *Intermediate phoneme task:* Decide whether each word rhymes with a target word.
- *Deep semantic:* Decide whether each word fits a sentence containing a blank.

Depth of processing had impressive effects on memory performance, which was three tines higher with deep than with shallow processing.

Craik and Tulving (1975) argued that *elaboration* of processing (i.e., the amount of processing of a given kind) is important as well as processing depth. They used the deep semantic task discussed above and varied elaboration by using simple sentence frames (e.g., "She cooked the ___") and complex ones (e.g., "The great bird swooped down and carried off the struggling ___"). Cued recall was twice as high for words accompanying complex sentences, showing that memory is better following more elaborate processing.

Long-term memory depends on the kind of elaboration as well as the amount. Bransford et al. (1979) presented minimally elaborated similes (e.g., "A mosquito is like a doctor because they both draw blood") or multiply elaborated similes (e.g., "A mosquito is like a raccoon because they both have heads, legs, jaws"). Recall was much better for the minimally elaborated similes because they were much more distinctive (see below).

We are especially likely to remember information if we relate it to ourselves, perhaps because this encourages deep processing. In the initial study, Rogers et al. (1977) found that asking participants to decide whether words applied to themselves led to better recall than having them process words in terms of their meaning. This is known as the **self-reference effect**. Symons and Johnson (1997) combined the findings from 129 studies on the self-reference effect in a meta-analysis (see Glossary). On average, long-term memory was better when learning occurred under self-reference conditions than any others.

Various factors contribute to the self-reference effect. Organization is especially important – the to-be-remembered information can all be related to the self-concept. Indeed, self-reference was associated with poorer recall than typical semantic processing if it failed to encourage organization (Klein & Kihlstrom, 1986).

DISTINCTIVENESS

Another factor important in determining long-term memory is distinctiveness (Hunt, 2006). **Distinctiveness** means that a memory trace differs from other memory traces because it was processed differently at the time of learning (as in Research Activity 5.1). There is much evidence that distinctive memories are generally better remembered than nondistinctive ones (see Research Activity 5.1).

Key Terms

Self-reference effect: enhanced long-term memory for information if it is related to the self at the time of learning.

Distinctiveness: this characterizes memory traces that are distinct or different from other memory traces stored in long-term memory; it leads to enhanced memory.

Research Activity 5.1: *Distinctiveness and long-term memory*

Below is a list of 45 words with five words belonging to each of nine categories:

CHAIR	CAT	TANK
PIANO	ELEPHANT	KNIFE
CLOCK	GIRAFFE	POISON
TELEPHONE	MOUSE	WHIP
CUSHION	TIGER	SCREWDRIVER
APPLE	BICYCLE	DRESS
GRAPEFRUIT	TRACTOR	MITTENS
COCONUT	TRAIN	SWEATER
PEACH	CART	SHOES
BLUEBERRY	SLED	PYJAMAS
CARROTS	MICHAEL	DONNA
LETTUCE	DANIEL	PAULA
ASPARAGUS	JOHN	BETH
ONION	RICHARD	SUSAN
POTATO	GEORGE	ANNE

Ask a friend of yours to consider the list words category by category. Their task is to write down one thing common to all five words within a category (Condition 1). Once completed, let your friend see everything they wrote down and ask them to recall as many of the list words as possible.

Ask another friend to consider the list words category by category. Within each category, one thing known about that word that is not true of any other word presented in that category should be written down (Condition 2). After that, your friend should be presented with what they wrote down, and asked to recall as many words as possible.

This task is based closely on an experiment reported by Hunt and Smith (1996). They found that recall was far higher in Condition 2 than in Condition 1 (97% correct vs. 59%). The reason is that the instructions in Condition 2 lead to much more distinctive or unique memory traces than those in Condition 1 because each word is processed differently from the others. Other research has generally found that distinctive memories are well remembered in tests of explicit memory (conscious recollection). However, Smith and Hunt (2000) reported that distinctiveness had no effect on implicit memory (no conscious recollection). Thus distinctiveness doesn't *always* enhance long-term memory.

Are the effects of distinctiveness separate from those of processing depth? There is much evidence that they can be. For example, Eysenck and Eysenck (1980) studied long-term memory for distinctive memory traces receiving only shallow processing. They used nouns that aren't pronounced in line with the rules of pronunciation (e.g., comb has a silent "b"; yacht has a silent "ch"). In one condition, participants said these nouns in a distinctive way by pronouncing them in line with their spelling (e.g., pronouncing the "b" in comb and the "ch" in yacht). Thus, the processing was shallow (i.e., phonemic) but the memory traces were distinctive. As predicted, recognition memory was as good in this condition as in a deep processing condition involving processing the meanings of the nouns.

Additional evidence was reported by Kirchhoff et al. (2005). Some words (e.g., onyx; abyss) are high in orthographic distinctiveness because the pattern of letters is unusual. Kirchhoff et al. (2005) found that orthographic distinctiveness and deep or semantic processing made separate contributions to enhancing long-term memory.

Why are distinctive memories so well remembered? Later in the chapter, we will see that much forgetting is due to interference – our long-term memory for what we have learned can be distorted or interfered with by information we learned beforehand or afterwards. That is especially so when the other information is very *similar* to what we are trying to remember. Distinctive memory traces may be easy to remember because they are *dissimilar* to other memory traces and so are less liable to interference (Eysenck, 1979).

LIMITATIONS

So far we have emphasized the importance of what happens at the time of learning. However, memory depends very much on the *relevance* of our stored information to the requirements of the memory test. Consider a study by Morris et al. (1977). Participants answered semantic or shallow (rhyme) questions for lists of words. Memory was tested in one of two ways:

1. Standard recognition test on which participants selected list words and avoided nonlist words;
2. Rhyming recognition test on which participants selected words that rhymed with list words; the words themselves were not presented. For example, if the word FABLE appeared on the test and TABLE was a list word, participants should have selected it.

With the standard recognition test, there was the typical superiority of deep over shallow processing (see Figure 5.1). More interestingly, the *opposite* result was reported with the rhyme test. This disproves the notion that deep processing always enhances long-term memory. Morris et al. (1977) explained these findings in terms of **transfer-appropriate processing**. Whether what we have learned leads to good performance on a subsequent memory test depends on the *relevance* of that information (and its associated processing) to the memory test. For example, storing semantic information is irrelevant when the memory test requires the identification of words rhyming with list words. What is required for this kind of test is shallow rhyme information.

We turn now to another limitation of the levels-of-processing approach. The research discussed so far mainly involved explicit memory (conscious recollection). The effects of depth of processing are typically much less with implicit memory (memory not involving conscious recollection). For example, Challis et al. (1996) used various tests of explicit and implicit memory. One test of implicit memory was the word-fragment task. Participants were originally presented with a list of words. Later they were asked to complete word fragments (e.g., c _ pp _ _) with the first word coming to mind. Implicit memory was assessed by the tendency to complete these word fragments with list words.

The findings of Challis et al. (1996) were clear-cut. There was a strong effect of processing depth

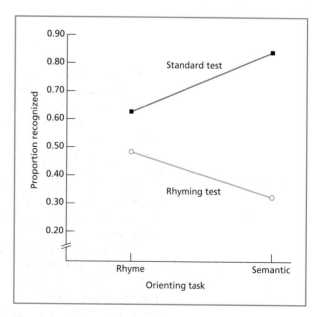

Figure 5.1 Mean proportion of words recognized as a function of orienting task (semantic or rhyme) and of the type of recognition task (standard or rhyming). Data are from Morris et al. (1977), and are from positive trials only.

on performance of all the explicit memory tests (e.g., recognition memory; free recall), with performance generally being best in the self-reference condition. In contrast, there was no effect of processing depth on the word-fragment task.

In sum, the levels-of-processing approach has deservedly been very influential (Roediger, 2008). However, some issues remain unclear. For example, the relative importance of depth, elaboration, and distinctiveness in enhancing long-term memory hasn't been established. In addition, it isn't known why processing depth has much less effect in implicit memory than in explicit memory.

Section Summary

Introduction
- According to levels-of-processing theory, deep or semantic processing enhances long-term memory. Deep processing generally improves long-term memory, especially if learners process words in relation to themselves. However, long-term memory also depends on the elaboration of processing.

Distinctiveness
- Long-term memory is mostly greater for distinctive memory traces than for nondistinctive ones. The effects of distinctiveness are often separate from those of processing depth. The beneficial effects of distinctiveness are often less in implicit than in explicit memory.

Limitations
- Long-term memory depends on the relevance of stored information to the requirements of the memory test as well as on processing depth. The effects of processing depth are typically much less on implicit memory than on explicit memory. The reasons why this is so haven't been discovered.

IMPLICIT LEARNING

Key Terms

Testing effect:
the finding that long-term memory is enhanced when some of the learning period is devoted to retrieving the to-be-remembered information.

Implicit learning:
a form of learning producing long-term memory in which there is no conscious awareness of what has been learned.

Do you think you could learn something without being aware of what you had learned? On the face of it, it sounds improbable. Think about your knowledge of psychology. You can easily bring some of that information to mind, and you have a strong conscious awareness of having learned it. Even if you did acquire information without any conscious awareness, it might seem somewhat pointless and wasteful – if we don't realize we have learned something, it seems unlikely we are going to make much use of it.

Learning occurring in the absence of conscious awareness of what has been learned is known as **implicit learning**. Implicit learning can be contrasted with explicit learning, which involves conscious awareness of what has been learned. You probably possess several skills that are hard to describe. For example, it is notoriously difficult to verbalize what we know about riding a bicycle. Indeed,

In the Real World 5.1: *The testing effect*

Answer this question taken from research by Karpicke et al. (2009). Imagine you are reading a textbook for an upcoming exam. After you have read the chapter one time, would you rather:

A. Go back and restudy either the entire chapter or certain parts of the chapter?
B. Try to recall material from the chapter (without the possibility of restudying the material)?
C. Use some other study technique?

Karpicke et al. found that 57% of their students gave answer A, 21% gave answer C, and only 18% gave answer B. What is interesting about this pattern of responses is that the least frequent answer (B) is actually the correct one in terms of its effectiveness in promoting good long-term memory!

The available research provides convincing evidence for the **testing effect**: Long-term retention of material is better when memory is tested during the time of learning. Bangert-Drowns et al. (1991) reviewed the findings from 35 classroom studies. A significant testing effect was found in 83% of these studies, and the magnitude of the effect tended to increase as the number of testing occasions went up.

Roediger and Karpicke (2006) carried out a thorough study on the testing effect. Students read a prose passage covering a general scientific topic and memorized it in one of three conditions:

1. *Repeated study:* The passage was read four times and there was no test.
2. *Single test:* The passage was read three times and then students recalled as much as possible from it.
3. *Repeated test:* The passage was read once and then students recalled as much as possible on three occasions.

Finally, memory for the passage was tested after 5 min or 1 week.

The findings are shown in Figure 5.2. Repeated study was the most effective strategy when the final test was given 5 minutes after learning. However, there was a dramatic reversal in the findings when

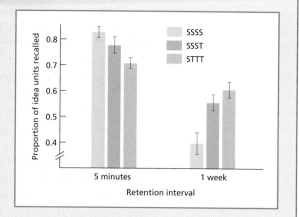

Figure 5.2 Memory performance as a function of learning conditions (S, study; T, test) and retention interval (5 min vs. 1 week). From Roediger and Karpicke (2006). Copyright © Blackwell Publishing. Reproduced with permission.

the final test occurred after 1 week. There was a very strong testing effect – average recall was 50% higher in the repeated test condition than the repeated study condition! That could make the difference between doing very well on an examination and failing it.

Students in the repeated study condition predicted they would recall more of the prose passage than did those in the repeated test condition. This helps to explain why many students mistakenly devote little or no time to testing themselves when preparing themselves for an examination.

How can we explain the findings? Many people feel reassured if they find it easy to retrieve material they have been learning. However, only effortful or demanding retrieval improves long-term memory (Bjork & Bjork, 1992). For example, Metcalfe and Kornell (2007) studied the learning of foreign vocabulary (e.g., house – maison). During learning the French word was presented at the same time as the English word or there was a short delay. Subsequent long-term memory was much better when there was a short delay, because it allowed the participants to engage in effortful retrieval.

the verbal descriptions most people give of how to ride a bicycle are inaccurate and would lead anyone following them to fall off pretty quickly!

There are close links between implicit learning and implicit memory (memory not depending on conscious recollection). Research on implicit memory is discussed later in the chapter.

ASSESSING IMPLICIT LEARNING

The most commonly used implicit learning task involves serial reaction time. On each trial, a stimulus appears at one of several locations on a computer screen. Participants respond as rapidly as possible with the response key corresponding to its location. There is a complex repeating sequence over trials, but participants aren't told this.

Towards the end of the experiment, there is typically a block of trials conforming to a novel sequence, but this information isn't given to the participants. Participants speed up during the course of the experiment but respond much more slowly during the novel sequence (see Shanks, 2005, for a review). When questioned, participants usually show no conscious awareness there was a repeating sequence or pattern in the stimuli presented to them.

How can we show that people's learning is implicit? It is necessary (but not sufficient) for them to deny conscious awareness of what they have learned. It is not sufficient because of what Shanks and St. John (1994) called the "retrospective problem." That problem occurs when people are consciously aware of what they are learning at the time but have forgotten about it by the time they are asked about their conscious awareness at the end of the experiment.

Shanks and St. John (1994) suggested two criteria that need to be met to show implicit learning:

1. *Information criterion:* The information participants are asked to provide on the awareness test must be the information responsible for the improved level of performance.
2. *Sensitivity criterion:* The test of awareness must be sensitive to all of the relevant knowledge acquired by learners. People may be consciously aware of more task-relevant knowledge than appears on an insensitive awareness test, which may lead us to underestimate their consciously accessible knowledge.

It has often been argued that the serial reaction time task involves only implicit learning. However, there is increasing evidence that healthy participants often have some conscious awareness of what they have learned on this task. Consider a study by Wilkinson and Shanks (2004) on the serial reaction time task. The participants showed clear evidence of sequence learning. This was followed by a test of explicit learning. Participants were either told to guess the next location in the sequence (inclusion condition) or to avoid guessing the next location (exclusion condition).

If sequence knowledge is wholly implicit and unavailable to consciousness, then performance shouldn't have differed in the inclusion and exclusion conditions. In fact, however, participants' predictions were significantly better in the inclusion than the exclusion condition, indicating the existence of some conscious knowledge. Thus, some conscious or explicit knowledge was acquired in addition to implicit learning.

SYSTEMS IN IMPLICIT AND EXPLICIT LEARNING

How do the systems involved in implicit learning differ from those involved in explicit learning? Reber (1993) identified five major differences:

1. *Robustness:* Implicit systems are relatively unaffected by disorders (e.g., amnesia) affecting explicit systems.
2. *Age independence:* Implicit learning is less influenced by age or developmental level.
3. *Low variability:* There are smaller individual differences in implicit learning than in explicit learning.
4. *IQ independence:* Performance on implicit tasks is less affected by IQ than is performance on explicit tasks.
5. *Commonality of process:* Implicit systems are common to most species whereas explicit systems are not.

Relatively little research is of direct relevance to the third or fifth differences identified by Reber (1993). As a result, we will focus on the other three differences.

There is much evidence supporting the first difference identified by Reber (1993). As is discussed fully later in the chapter, amnesic patients have severe problems with explicit memory but their implicit learning and memory are often essentially intact.

Howard and Howard (1992) obtained evidence supporting the second difference above. Young and older adults performed an implicit learning task (serial reaction time). An asterisk appeared in one of four positions on a screen, and participants pressed the corresponding key as soon as possible. Both groups of participants showed comparable learning of the repeating sequence. There was also a test of explicit learning on which participants predicted where the asterisk would appear next. The younger group performed significantly better than the older group on this task.

Evidence supporting the fourth difference was reported by Gebauer and Mackintosh (2007). They used various implicit learning tasks (e.g., serial reaction time) given with standard implicit instructions or with explicit instructions indicating that rules were to be discovered. Intelligence was positively associated with performance when explicit instructions were given but not when implicit instructions were used.

BRAIN DAMAGE

It is often assumed that implicit learning (but not explicit learning) depends substantially on the striatum and other parts of the basal ganglia (e.g., Foerde & Poldrack, 2009). The striatum is located in the upper part of the brainstem and the inferior part of the cerebral hemispheres (see Figure 5.3). If so, then patients with damage to the basal ganglia should have impaired implicit learning but intact explicit learning. Patients with Parkinson's disease (the symptoms of which include limb tremor and muscle rigidity) have damage to the basal ganglia, and so should have poor implicit learning. Strong supporting evidence

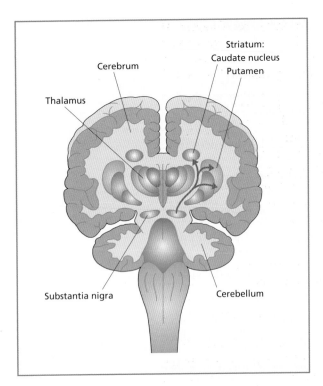

Figure 5.3 The striatum (which includes the caudate nucleus and the putamen) is of central importance in implicit learning.

was reported by Brown et al. (2003). They studied patients with Parkinson's disease who had received surgical treatment that disrupted the output of the basal ganglia to the frontal cortex. These patients showed no implicit learning at all on the serial reaction time task.

Consistent impairment on the serial reaction time task by patients with Parkinson's disease was also reported by Wilkinson and Jahanshahi (2007). In addition, they obtained convincing evidence that patients' learning was implicit (i.e., lacked conscious awareness). The patients performed at chance level when trying to recognize old sequences. Furthermore, their task knowledge wasn't under conscious control. This was shown by their inability to suppress the expression of what they had learned when instructed to do so.

The prediction that patients with Parkinson's disease should have intact explicit learning has generally not been supported. These patients generally have impaired explicit learning, especially when the learning is fairly complex (see Vingerhoets et al., 2005 for a review). That suggests that the basal ganglia may play a part in explicit learning, although smaller than their role in implicit learning.

If explicit learning (but not implicit learning) depends substantially on the medial temporal lobes including the hippocampus, then patients with damage to that area should have impaired explicit learning but intact implicit learning. Amnesic patients typically have damage to that area (Aggleton, 2008). Meulemans and Van der Linden (2003) found that amnesic patients showed as much implicit learning as healthy controls on an artificial grammar learning task. They also used a test of explicit learning in which participants wrote down 10 letter strings they regarded as grammatical. The amnesics' performance was much worse than that of healthy controls on this test.

Vandenberghe et al. (2006) used the serial reaction time task. The amnesic patients showed less learning than healthy controls on this task. However, all their learning was implicit with no indication of explicit learning.

In sum, there is evidence that rather different brain regions underlie implicit and explicit learning. More specifically, the basal ganglia are more important in implicit learning than in explicit learning. In contrast, the medial temporal lobes are more essential in explicit than implicit learning. The findings from brain-damaged patients are reasonably consistent with the notion that there is an important distinction between implicit and explicit learning.

BRAIN IMAGING

Different areas of the brain should be activated during implicit and explicit learning if they are genuinely different. Conscious awareness is associated with activation in many brain regions. The main ones are the dorsolateral prefrontal cortex and the anterior cingulate (Dehaene et al., 2006; see Chapter 3). Accordingly, these areas should be more active during explicit than implicit learning. In contrast, the findings from brain-damaged patients discussed above suggest that the striatum should be activated more during implicit than explicit learning.

There is some support for the above predictions. Aizenstein et al. (2004) found there was greater activation in the prefrontal cortex and anterior cingulate during explicit rather than implicit learning. Orban et al. (2010) found that implicit learning on the serial reaction time task was associated with activity in part of the striatum. However, what has typically been found is that several brain areas are activated on implicit and explicit learning tasks. These brain areas are often common to both kinds of tasks, and include the striatum, the dorsolateral prefrontal cortex, the supplementary motor area, and the premotor cortex (see Wilkinson et al., 2009, for a review).

How can we explain the above findings? We need to distinguish clearly between the explicit and implicit components of learning. That is precisely what Destrebecqz et al. (2005) did with the serial reaction time task. Activation in the striatum was associated with the implicit component of learning. In contrast, the medial prefrontal cortex and anterior cingulate were associated with the explicit component.

In sum, brain-imaging studies have produced somewhat inconsistent findings. However, the findings of such studies are in line with those on brain-damaged patients when researchers distinguish carefully between implicit and explicit aspects of learning.

CONCLUSIONS

The issue of whether implicit learning exists has been considered in three somewhat separate strands of research. One strand involves behavioral studies on healthy participants, another strand involves behavioral studies on brain-damaged patients, and the third strand involves brain-imaging studies on healthy individuals. Evidence from all three research strands provides some support for the notion that there are major differences between implicit and explicit learning. However, definitive evidence has proved elusive.

What conclusions can we draw from the available research? It is too often assumed that finding that explicit learning plays some part in explaining performance on a given task means that *no* implicit learning occurred. It is likely that the extent to which learners are consciously aware of what they are learning varies from individual to individual and from task to task. Perhaps we have greatest conscious awareness when the representations of what we have learned are stable, distinctive, and strong, and least when those representations are unstable, nondistinctive, and weak (Kelly, 2003). All kinds of intermediate position are also possible.

Sun et al. (2009) argued that learning nearly always involves implicit and explicit aspects, and that the balance between these two types of learning changes over time. On some tasks, there is initial implicit learning based on the performance of successful actions followed by explicit learning of the rules apparently explaining why those actions are successful. On other tasks, learners start with explicit rules and then engage in implicit learning based on observing their actions directed by those rules.

What is needed in future research? If learning on the great majority of tasks is partly explicit and partly implicit, then it is important to find ways of distinguishing clearly between these two forms of learning. When this is done, clear-cut differences in the brain regions associated with explicit and implicit learning have been found (Destrebecqz et al., 2005).

Section Summary

Assessing implicit learning

• It has been argued that implicit learning differs from explicit learning in that it is more robust, less affected by age and IQ, and less variable. It is necessary to satisfy the information and sensitivity criteria to show the existence of implicit learning.

Brain damage

• Patients with damage to the striatum generally show greater impairment of implicit than explicit learning. Patients with damage to the medial temporal lobes (including the hippocampus) typically suffer greater reductions in explicit than implicit learning. These findings suggest that there is an important distinction between implicit and explicit learning.

Brain imaging

• Brain-imaging studies have produced rather inconsistent findings. However, such studies have tended to identify the same brain areas underlying implicit and explicit learning as are identified by research on brain-damaged patients.

Conclusions

• Behavioral studies with healthy and brain-damaged individuals and brain-imaging studies with healthy individuals provide some support for a distinction between implicit and explicit learning. It is likely that learning on many tasks is a mixture of implicit and explicit, with implicit learning predominating when learned representations are unstable, nondistinctive, and weak.

LONG-TERM MEMORY SYSTEMS

As I mentioned earlier, we all have a huge variety of information stored in long-term memory. This information includes knowledge about the world, about our personal experiences throughout our lifetime, how to read books, how to perform various skills, and so on. There is general agreement that there are several different long-term memory systems. In what follows, we will consider the number and nature of these memory systems.

DECLARATIVE VS. NONDECLARATIVE MEMORY

The most important distinction between different types of long-term memory is that between declarative memory and nondeclarative memory.

Declarative memory involves conscious recollection of events and facts – it refers to memories that can be "declared" or described. Declarative memory is sometimes referred to as explicit memory, defined as memory that "requires conscious recollection of previous experiences" (Graf & Schacter, 1985, p. 501). Declarative memory is what you use when you remember someone's name when you see them, when you remember some fact in psychology, or when you remember how to get to your friend's house.

In contrast, **nondeclarative memory** does *not* involve conscious recollection, and is sometimes referred to as implicit memory. Typically, we obtain evidence of nondeclarative memory by observing changes in behavior. For example, consider the following anecdote from Edouard Claparède (1873–1940) reported by him in 1911. He studied a female patient who suffered from amnesia due to chronic alcoholism. She couldn't recognize doctors and nurses she had seen virtually every day over a period of several years, indicating that her declarative memory was extremely poor.

One day Claparède hid a pin in his hand before shaking hands with the patient. The following day she was very sensibly reluctant to shake hands with him. However, she felt very embarrassed because she couldn't explain her reluctance. Her behavior indicated the presence of nondeclarative memory of what had happened the previous day even though she had no conscious recollection of it.

Declarative memory

How many types of declarative or explicit memory are there? First, there is episodic memory. This is the memory system we use when we remember that the word "chair" appeared in the last list we learned, that we had cereal for breakfast, and that we went to the movies yesterday.

Second, there is semantic memory. This is the memory system we use when remembering facts and information, such as the name of the current President of the United States, the number of planets in the solar system, or the meaning of the word "psychology." More generally, semantic memory consists of our knowledge of language and of the world.

Third, there is autobiographical memory. We use autobiographical memory when we remember personal experiences of importance in our lives. For example, we might think about our first boyfriend/girlfriend or the best holiday of our lives. It is similar to episodic memory, but differs in that episodic memory tends to be concerned with relatively trivial experiences. In spite of its importance, autobiographical memory is not discussed in this chapter. Since it is such an important aspect of everyday memory, it is dealt with at length in the next chapter (Chapter 6).

Nondeclarative memory

There are various varieties of nondeclarative memory. First, much nondeclarative memory involves priming. **Priming** is what happens when there is enhanced (e.g., faster) processing of a stimulus because the same (or a similar) stimulus was presented previously. Suppose you are presented with words that are shown very briefly so that it is hard to identify them. Suppose also that some of these words were presented previously on a list of words you learned. The typical finding is that briefly presented words are more likely to be identified if the same words appeared on the list (Tulving & Schacter, 1990). This finding

Key Terms

Declarative memory: also known as explicit memory, this is memory that involves conscious recollection of information; see **nondeclarative memory**.

Nondeclarative memory: also known as implicit memory, this is memory that doesn't involve conscious recollection of information; see **declarative memory**.

Priming: this is a form of **nondeclarative memory** involving facilitated processing of (and response to) a target stimulus because the same or a related stimulus was presented previously.

Research Activity 5.2: *Implicit or nondeclarative memory*

A droodle is a combination of a doodle and a riddle. Several droodles are shown below (see Figure 5.4). Your task is to guess what is shown in each one. Record the time taken to identify each droodle.

You probably found it relatively difficult to identify at least some of the droodles. However, it is likely that if you looked at them at some point in the future you would almost instantly recognize them. This facilitated processing represents a priming effect based on nondeclarative or implicit memory, although declarative or explicit memory might also be involved.

Many droodles permit more than one possible interpretation. However, likely answers are as follows. The first picture is a Mexican wearing a hat and riding a bicycle. The second picture is a woman gardening, the third picture is a trombone player in a phone booth, and the fourth picture shows a bear climbing up the far side of the tree.

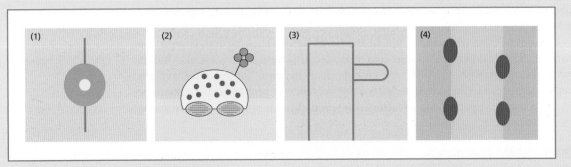

Figure 5.4 Droodles from www.sticksite.com/droodles/index.html

occurs even though most people are unaware that their ability to perceive the flashed words has been influenced by the study list. Thus, the list words act as primes that enhance perceptual identification.

Second, there is another form of nondeclarative memory known as **procedural** memory or skill learning (Foerde & Poldrack, 2009). Examples of skill learning are word processing, playing a musical instrument, and playing a sport. Research on implicit learning (discussed earlier) is of direct relevance. The tasks used to study implicit learning (e.g., serial reaction time) provide an assessment of procedural memory.

EPISODIC MEMORY

We use **episodic memory** to remember past events that have happened to us. Episodic memories generally fulfill what are known as the www criteria – they contain information about *what* happened, *where* it happened, and *when* it happened. You might expect that the episodic memory system would work like a video recorder, providing us with accurate and detailed information about past events. That is *not* the case. As Schacter and Addis (2007, p. 773) pointed out, "Episodic memory is … a fundamentally constructive, rather than reproductive process that is prone to various kinds of errors and illusions."

Many people bemoan the limitations of their own memory system and regard it as rather defective. In fact, however, forgetting can be very useful (Schacter, 1999). For example, suppose you remembered the dates and times

---

Key Terms

Procedural memory: this is a form of **nondeclarative memory** involving learned skills and concerned with "knowing how."

Episodic memory: a form of **declarative memory** concerned with personal experiences or episodes occurring in a given place at a given time; see **semantic memory**.

of your classes from last year. That information might make it harder for you to remember the dates and times of classes this semester. Much of the time we only need to remember the current situation rather than what used to be the case (Schacter, 1999).

We generally want to access the gist or essence of our past experiences but don't want to remember the trivial details. Consider the Russian Shereshevskii (also discussed in Chapter 6). He was first discovered when working as a journalist. His editor was amazed that he could remember complex briefing instructions without taking any notes.

Shereshevskii had a truly amazing memory, and could recall events from the distant past in great detail (Luria, 1968). He was sometimes so overwhelmed by specific images he couldn't see the forest for the trees, as when trying to make sense of a prose passage: "Each word calls up images, they collide with one another, and the result is chaos. I can't make anything out of this." The take-home message is that it is a good idea to forget information irrelevant to your current life and activities.

There are two other reasons why our episodic memory system is prone to error (Schacter & Addis, 2007). First, it would require an incredible amount of processing to produce a semipermanent record of all our experiences, because we experience thousands of events every single day.

Second, imagining possible future events and scenarios is important to us for various reasons (e.g., forming plans for the future). Some of the constructive processes involved in episodic memory are also used to imagine the future. As a result, individuals with very poor episodic memory (e.g., amnesic patients) should also have impaired ability to imagine future events.

Hassabis et al. (2007) asked amnesic patients and healthy controls to imagine future events (e.g., "Imagine you are lying on a white sandy beach in a beautiful tropical bay"). The amnesic patients produced imaginary experiences consisting of isolated fragments of information lacking the richness and spatial coherence of the experiences imagined by the controls.

Addis et al. (2007) compared brain activity when individuals generated past and future events and then elaborated on them. There was considerable overlap in patterns of brain activity. The areas activated during elaboration of past and future events included the left anterior temporal cortex (associated with conceptual and semantic information about one's life) and the left frontopolar cortex (associated with self-referential processing). However, there was more activation in several brain areas (e.g., the right frontopolar cortex) during the generation of future than of past events. Thus, more intensive constructive processes are required to imagine future events than to retrieve past events.

As we have seen, the generation of future events depends mainly on episodic memory. However, we may also use our knowledge of the world when imagining future events. Thus, it is likely that semantic memory is also involved (Szpunar, 2010).

Recognition memory

We can assess episodic memory by using a test of recognition memory. Participants are presented with a word list followed by a memory test. On this test is a mixture of words from the list and new words, and the participants' task is to decide which ones were presented previously. **Recognition memory** can occur in two rather different ways: It may involve familiarity or recollection.

Key Term
Recognition memory: deciding whether a given stimulus was encountered previously in a particular context (e.g., the previous list).

Recollection involves the ability to retrieve contextual information as well as familiarity.

We can clarify the distinction between familiarity and recollection with the following anecdote. Several years ago I walked past a man in Wimbledon, the part of London in which I live. I was immediately confident I recognized him. However, I simply couldn't think of the situation in which I had seen him previously. After some thought (this is the kind of thing academic psychologists think about!), I realized the man was a ticket-office clerk at Wimbledon railway station. Initial recognition based purely on familiarity was replaced by recognition based on recollection.

The simplest way of distinguishing between familiarity and recollection is the remember/know task (Tulving, 1985). On this task, participants indicate whether their positive recognition decisions were based on recollection of contextual information (remember responses) or solely on familiarity (know responses).

Recollection is a more complex and attention-demanding process than familiarity. There have been several studies in which participants' attention during a recognition test was distracted by irrelevant stimuli. Such distraction typically disrupts recollection more than familiarity (see Yonelinas, 2002 for a review). In similar fashion, distraction at the time of learning also adversely affects recollection more than familiarity (Yonelinas, 2002).

The binding together of information about stimuli ("what" information) and the context in which they were seen ("where" information) is needed for recollection but not for familiarity (Diana et al., 2007). Where in the brain does this binding occur? According to Diana et al., the hippocampus is of crucial importance. It follows that patients with damage to the hippocampus should have severely impaired recollection but less impaired familiarity judgments.

Skinner and Fernandes (2007) reviewed studies of amnesic patients with and without damage in the medial temporal lobes (including the hippocampus). The findings are shown in Figure 5.5. As you can see, both brain-damaged groups had comparable levels of recognition performance on measures of familiarity. As predicted, patients with medial temporal lobe and hippocampal damage performed much worse than the other brain-damaged group on measures of recollection. These findings suggest that recollection involves different processes from judgments of familiarity. They are consistent with the notion that the hippocampus is of central importance to recollection.

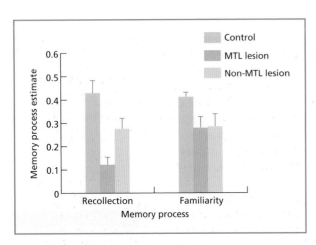

Figure 5.5 Mean recollection and familiarity estimates for healthy controls, patients with medial temporal lobe (MTL) lesions or brain damage, and patients with non-MTL lesions. Reprinted from Skinner and Fernandes (2007), Copyright © 2007, with permission from Elsevier.

SEMANTIC MEMORY

What is the capital of France? How many months are there in a year? Who is the current President of the United States? Do rats have wings? Is umplitude an English word?

I am sure you found all those questions relatively easy to answer, and that you answered them quickly. This is possible because we all possess an enormous store of general knowledge that we take for granted. Our organized general knowledge about the world is stored in **semantic memory**. Note that there is extensive coverage of the information stored in semantic memory in Chapter 7.

There are similarities between episodic and semantic memory. Suppose you remember meeting your friend yesterday afternoon at Starbuck's. That involves episodic memory, because you are remembering an event at a given time in a given place. However, semantic memory is also involved – some of what you remember depends on your general knowledge about coffee shops, what coffee tastes like, and so on.

Tulving (2002, p. 5) clarified the relationship between episodic and semantic memory: "Episodic memory ... shares many features with semantic memory, out of which it grew ... but also possesses features that semantic memory does not ... Episodic memory is a recently evolved, late-developing, and early-deteriorating past-oriented memory system, more vulnerable than other memory systems to neuronal dysfunction."

We can test the notion that episodic memory is more vulnerable than semantic memory by studying patients suffering from amnesia, a condition involving extensive impairment of long-term memory. As will be discussed more fully later, amnesic patients generally have greater problems with episodic than with semantic memory (Spiers et al., 2001).

Brain-imaging research also reveals important differences between semantic and episodic memory. In a review, Wheeler et al. (1997) reported that the left prefrontal cortex was more active during episodic than semantic encoding. What about brain activation during retrieval? Wheeler et al. reported that the right prefrontal cortex was more active during episodic memory retrieval than during semantic memory retrieval. Subsequent research has confirmed that the pattern of brain activation differs between semantic and episodic memory. However, it also indicates that these two types of memory depend on *interacting* memory systems (Prince et al., 2007).

Schemas

Much of the information stored in semantic memory is in the form of **schemas**. Schemas are organized packets of knowledge about the world, events, and people. For example, try to imagine what is involved in a typical bank robbery. You may well have imagined the robbers were male, with masks over their faces, and that they were carrying guns. These features are found in most people's bank-robbery schema (Tuckey & Brewer, 2003a; see Chapter 6).

The ways in which information is stored in semantic memory are discussed at length in Chapter 7. Here we will focus on memory distortions caused by our schematic knowledge.

Bartlett (1932) argued that our memory for stories is affected not only by the presented story but also by the participant's store of relevant schematic knowledge. Bartlett had the ingenious idea of presenting people with stories producing a *conflict* between what was presented to them and their prior knowledge. Suppose people read a story taken from a different culture. Their prior knowledge might produce distortions in the remembered version of the story, making it more conventional and acceptable from their own cultural background.

> **Key Terms**
>
> **Semantic memory:**
> a form of **nondeclarative memory** consisting of general knowledge about the world, concepts, language, and so on; see **episodic memory**.
>
> **Schemas:**
> organized knowledge of various kinds (e.g., about the world; typical sequences of events) stored in long-term memory; schemas facilitate perception and language comprehension, and allow us to form expectations (e.g., of likely events in a restaurant).

Bartlett (1932) carried out several studies in which English students read and recalled stories taken from the North American Indian culture. As he predicted, most recall errors conformed to the readers' cultural expectations. He used the term **rationalization** for this type of error.

According to Bartlett (1932), memory for the precise information presented is forgotten over time, whereas memory for the underlying schemas is not. Thus, there should be more rationalization errors (which depend on schematic knowledge) at longer retention intervals.

The above prediction was supported by Sulin and Dooling (1974). Some participants were presented with a story about Gerald Martin: "Gerald Martin strove to undermine the existing government to satisfy his political ambitions … He became a ruthless, uncontrollable dictator. The ultimate effect of his rule was the downfall of his country" (Sulin & Dooling, 1974, p. 256). Other participants received the same story but the main actor was called Adolf Hitler. These participants were much more likely than those in the other group to believe incorrectly they had read the sentence: "He hated the Jews particularly and so persecuted them." Their schematic knowledge about Hitler distorted their memory more at a long than at a short retention interval (see Figure 8.6).

Bartlett (1932) assumed that distortions in what we remember about stories occur mainly because of schema-driven processes at the time of *retrieval*. Supporting evidence was reported by Anderson and Pichert (1978). Participants read a story from the perspective of a burglar or of someone interested in buying a home. After they had recalled the story, they shifted to the alternative perspective (from burglar to home buyer or vice versa) before recalling the story again. On the second recall, participants recalled more information important only to the second perspective or schema than they had done on the first recall.

How can we explain Anderson and Pichert's (1978) findings? Changing the perspective produced a shift in the schematic knowledge accessed by the participants (e.g., from burglar-relevant knowledge to home-buyer-relevant knowledge). Accessing different schematic knowledge enhanced recall, thus providing support for the notion of schema-driven retrieval.

Brewer and Treyens (1981) pointed out that much of the information we remember during the course of our everyday lives is acquired incidentally rather than deliberately. Accordingly, they decided to see whether people would show schema-driven memory errors in incidental memory in a naturalistic situation. They asked participants to spend about 35 s in a room designed to look like a graduate student's office before the experiment proper took place (see Figure 5.6). The room contained a mixture of schema-consistent objects you would expect to find in a graduate student's office (e.g., desk, calendar, eraser, pencils) and schema-inconsistent objects (e.g., a skull, a toy top). Some schema-consistent objects (e.g., books) were omitted.

Figure 5.6 The "graduate student's" room used by Brewer and Treyens (1981) in their experiment. Copyright © 1981 Elsevier. Photo reproduced with kind permission of Professor Brewer.

Schematic knowledge had both positive and negative influences on subsequent unexpected recall and recognition tests. First, objects not present in the room but "recognized" with high confidence were nearly always schema-consistent (e.g., books; filing cabinet). This is clear evidence for schemas leading to errors in memory. Second, participants recalled more schema-consistent than schema-inconsistent objects for objects that were present *and* those that weren't. In a similar study, Lampinen et al. (2001) found that far more schema-consistent objects that hadn't been present were falsely recalled 48 h after presentation. Thus, the impact of schematic knowledge can increase over time.

NONDECLARATIVE MEMORY

The essence of nondeclarative memory is that it doesn't involve conscious recollection but instead reveals itself through behavior. As we saw earlier, two major kinds of nondeclarative memory are priming (facilitated processing of repeated stimuli) and skill learning or procedural memory. There are important differences between these forms of nondeclarative memory. Priming often occurs rapidly whereas procedural memory or skill learning is typically slow and gradual (Knowlton & Foerde, 2008). In addition, priming involves learning tied to specific stimuli, whereas skill learning generalizes to other stimuli. For example, it wouldn't be much use if you learned how to hit backhands at tennis very well, but could only do so provided that the ball came towards you from a given direction at a given speed!

We will start with priming. First, there is perceptual priming. This occurs when repeated presentation of a stimulus leads to faster or more accurate processing of its perceptual features. Tulving et al. (1982) looked at perceptual priming. Their participants learned a list of multi-syllable and relatively rare words (e.g., toboggan). One hour or one week later, they were simply asked to fill in the blanks in word fragments to make a word (e.g., _ O_ O_GA_). The solutions to half the fragments were previously learned list words, but the participants weren't told this. Perceptual priming was shown by the finding that the participants completed more of the fragments correctly when the solutions matched list words.

Second, there is conceptual priming. This occurs when repeated presentation of a stimulus leads to faster or more accurate processing of its *meaning*. Have a look back at Figure 5.4. I imagine you interpreted the pictures much more easily this time than before – this is conceptual priming.

What processes are involved in priming? One popular view is based on the notion of perceptual fluency: repeated presentation of a stimulus means it can be processed more efficiently using fewer resources. If so, priming should be associated with reduced levels of brain activity. Much evidence supports this prediction (Poldrack & Gabrieli, 2001).

The precise brain regions showing reduced activation vary depending on whether perceptual or conceptual priming is involved. Early visual areas in the occipital lobe at the back of the brain often show reduced activity with perceptual priming (Schacter et al., 2007). Voss et al. (2008) presented participants with pictures of famous (e.g., Madonna; Harrison Ford; Richard Gere) and nonfamous faces. The participants had to decide whether each face was famous or nonfamous. Conceptual priming was associated with reduced activity in the left prefrontal cortex.

Research Activity 5.3: *Perceptual priming and implicit memory*

This Research Activity should be carried out with a friend. Read Passage A and then turn your mind to something else for a few minutes. Finally, have a look at the word fragments below. Try to fill in the missing letters to form complete words. Simply write down the first appropriate word that comes to mind. Then ask a friend to read Passage B, to do something else for a few minutes, and then to fill in the missing letters to form complete words.

Passage A
Tom was a bashful young man who had recently arrived in the country. Every day he left his house and headed for his office. There he had a cup of coffee every morning, using a spoon to stir the sugar in. Occasionally, he would consult an almanac. After work, he walked to the station through a meadow. When the sun was shining, he would see his shadow as he walked.

Passage B
Lucy is much affected by climate, having a preference for the summer. She likes to wear a purple skirt as she goes to work in a large factory. On the way to work, she passes a zoo. Her favorite animals in the zoo are a giraffe and a spider. When Lucy returns home in the evening, she likes to play the violin while letting her cigarette burn in the ashtray.

Word fragments

al _ _ n _ c	_ _ ht _ ay
b _ sh _ u _	_ l _ m _ te
_ _ u _ t _ y	f _ _ t _ ry
of _ _ c _	_ urp _ _
_ p _ on	su _ m _ _
_ h _ do _	_ io _ _ n
h _ us _	_ _ r _ f _ e
_ e _ d _ w	_ p _ d _ r

The word fragments in the left column can all form words contained in Passage A. Those in the right column can all form words from Passage B. Perceptual priming should mean that you performed better on the left column whereas your friend performed better on the right column.

We turn now to procedural memory or skill learning. It has sometimes been argued that skill learning and priming depend on the same mechanism (Gupta & Cohen, 2002). However, skill learning is typically much more general and flexible than priming, which suggests that the underlying mechanisms differ. If the mechanisms differ, then individuals who perform well on skill learning won't necessarily perform well on priming tasks, and vice versa. Schwartz and Hashtroudi (1991) investigated this issue using a word-identification task to assess priming and an inverted-text reading task to assess skill learning. There was no relationship between performance on the two tasks.

Much research on implicit learning (discussed earlier in the chapter) involves procedural memory. Many of the tasks used to study procedural memory (e.g., serial reaction time task) require learning far removed from that occurring in everyday life. What happens when more realistic tasks are used? Anderson et al. (2007) studied car driving in two patients with severe amnesia. The findings suggested that the patients had reasonably intact procedural memory. Their steering, speed control, safety errors, and driving with distraction were all comparable to healthy controls. Since amnesic patients have very poor declarative memory, these findings strengthen the argument that procedural and declarative memory are very different.

Section Summary

Declarative vs. nondeclarative memory

- Declarative or explicit memory involves conscious or deliberate retrieval of events and facts. Nondeclarative or implicit memory doesn't involve conscious or deliberate retrieval. Episodic, semantic, and autobiographical memory are all forms of declarative memory. Priming is a form of nondeclarative memory in which there is more efficient processing of a repeated stimulus. Another form of nondeclarative memory is skill learning or procedural memory.

Episodic memory

- Episodic memories generally contain information about what happened, where it happened, and when it happened. Episodic memory is constructive rather than reproductive and allows us to imagine possible future events. Recognition memory can be based on recollection or on familiarity. Recollection (but not familiarity) depends on binding together stimulus and contextual information within the hippocampus at the time of learning.

Semantic memory

- General knowledge is stored in semantic memory. Much of the information in semantic memory is in the forms of schemas (packets of knowledge). Schematic knowledge (e.g., stereotypes) often causes systematic distortions in long-term memory, especially at long retention intervals. However, schematic knowledge can assist in the retrieval of schema-consistent information.

Nondeclarative memory

- Priming can be perceptual (enhanced processing of perceptual features) or conceptual (enhancing processing of meaning). Priming involves learning tied to specific stimuli, whereas skill learning or procedural memory generalizes to other stimuli. Priming is associated with enhanced processing efficiency and reduced brain activation.

AMNESIA

This section is concerned with **amnesia**, which is a condition caused by brain damage in which there are severe problems with long-term memory. Amnesia is most often caused by closed head injury, and another common cause is chronic alcohol abuse.

Key Term

Amnesia:
a condition caused by brain damage in which there are serious impairments of long-term memory (especially **declarative memory**).

In this chapter, I have referred from time to time to findings from amnesic patients. Some of the findings involve **retrograde amnesia** (impaired memory for events occurring *before* the onset of amnesia).

However, most research on amnesia has focused on **anterograde amnesia** – this is a reduced ability to remember information learned *after* the onset of amnesia. In view of the important role that patients with anterograde amnesia have played in increasing our understanding of long-term memory, I will be discussing findings from such patients in detail.

Why have amnesic patients contributed so much to our understanding of long-term memory? The study of amnesics (and other brain-damaged patients with memory problems) provides a good test-bed for theories of healthy memory. For example, strong evidence for the distinction between short-term and long-term memory comes from studies on amnesic patients (see Chapter 4). In essence, some patients have severely impaired long-term memory but intact short-term memory, and other patients have the opposite pattern.

Patients with anterograde amnesia vary in the precise brain areas that are damaged. However, there is typically damage to an integrated brain system including the hippocampus, the medial temporal lobes, and the medial diencephalon (Aggleton, 2008; see Figure 5.7). The hippocampal formation and the medial temporal lobes are also important in retrograde amnesia (Moscovitch et al., 2006).

We can see the devastating effects of anterograde amnesia by considering the case of Clive Wearing. On March 26, 1985 he developed encephalitis (infection of the brain). The hippocampus is a part of the brain of central importance in long-term memory, and the encephalitis destroyed most of it. As a result, Clive Wearing can remember practically nothing of his daily activities and can't even remember the names of his children from his first marriage.

When Clive Wearing became aware that something was terribly wrong with him, he wept almost nonstop for over a month. One of his favorite questions was, "What's it like to have one long night lasting ... how long? It's like being dead."

If you are a movie fan you may have mistaken ideas about amnesia (Baxendale, 2004). In the movies, serious head injuries typically cause characters to forget the past while still being fully able to engage in new learning. In the

Figure 5.7 Damage to a number of regions in the medial temporal lobes and surrounding structures can produce an amnesic syndrome (marked with an asterisk). From Parkin (2001).

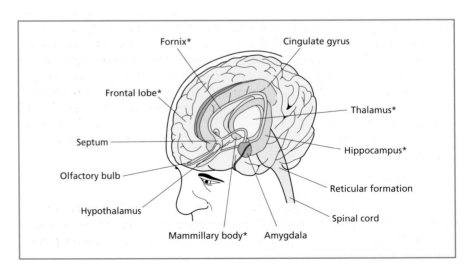

real world, however, new learning is generally greatly impaired. In the movies, amnesic individuals often suffer a profound loss of identity or their personality changes completely. In fact, such personality shifts are extremely rare. Most bizarrely, the rule of thumb in the movies is that the best cure for amnesia caused by severe head injury is to suffer another massive blow to the head!

Amnesic patients have severe impairments of long-term memory. However, these impairments are only found with certain forms of long-term memory. The traditional viewpoint (e.g., Nadel & Moscovitch, 1997) is that amnesic patients have substantial problems with declarative memory involving conscious recollection. However, their nondeclarative memory (not involving conscious recollection) is essentially intact. As we will see, there is only partial support for these predictions.

WHAT REMAINS INTACT?

Earlier in the chapter, we considered amnesics' performance on tasks involving implicit learning. The findings were somewhat mixed. However, their performance is sometimes comparable to that of healthy individuals (e.g., Meulemans & Van der Linden, 2003).

Spiers et al. (2001) reviewed 147 cases of anterograde amnesia, most of whom had severe problems with several aspects of long-term memory. However, nondeclarative memory was essentially intact in these patients: "None of the cases was reported to ... be impaired on tasks which involved learning skills or habits, priming, simple classical conditioning and simple category learning" (Spiers et al., 2001, p. 359).

Hamann and Squire (1997) studied an amnesic patient, EP, who seemed to have no explicit memory at all. For example, on a test of recognition memory he was correct on only 52% of trials (chance = 50%) compared to 65% for other amnesic patients and 81% for healthy controls. However, his performance on priming tasks (involving nondeclarative memory) was good. EP was given the task of trying to identify briefly presented words and pseudowords. He found it easier to identify those that had been presented previously than those that hadn't. His performance on this priming task was as good as that of healthy controls.

There has been some research in which amnesics' procedural memory on everyday tasks has been considered. We have already discussed a study (Anderson et al., 2007) in which the car driving performance of amnesics was comparable to healthy controls. Cavaco et al. (2004) used five skill-learning tasks requiring skills similar to those needed in the real world. For example, there was a weaving task and a control stick task requiring movements similar to those involved in operating machinery. Amnesic patients showed comparable rates of learning to those of healthy individuals on all five tasks in spite of having impaired declarative memory for the tasks assessed by recall and recognition tests.

WHAT IS IMPAIRED?

The review by Spiers et al. (2001) suggested that amnesic patients had no problems with nondeclarative memory. However, they had severe problems with declarative memory, with the ability to form episodic memories being impaired in all cases.

Why is amnesics' episodic memory so poor? An important reason is that amnesics' newly formed episodic memories are very fragile. Dewar et al. (2010) found that 90% of their amnesics recalled nothing of a story presented only 10 min earlier if they performed a tone-detection task during the retention interval. However, recall performance was much better if the patients spent the interval quietly in a darkened, empty room. Thus, amnesic patients *can* form new episodic memories, but such memories are very easily disrupted.

Spiers et al. (2001) found in their review that many amnesic patients had only modest problems with the formation of new semantic memories. However, some amnesic patients have a poor ability to form new semantic memories. McCarthy et al. (2005) studied an amnesic patient, RFR. He was good at recognizing the faces of newly famous people and recalling their names. However, he was generally unable to provide additional information about these celebrities. For example, he didn't know how or why he recognized a picture of Bill Clinton. RFR also had only a limited ability to acquire new word meanings.

The evidence assembled by Spiers et al. (2001) suggested that episodic memory is generally more vulnerable than semantic memory to the effects of brain damage. If so, we might be able to discover amnesic patients with very poor episodic memory but intact semantic memory. Vargha-Khadem et al. (1997) did precisely that. They studied Beth and Jon, both of whom had suffered damage to the hippocampus at an early age before they had had the chance to develop semantic memories. Both these patients had very poor episodic memory for the day's activities, television programs, and telephone conversations. In spite of this, Beth and Jon both attended ordinary schools and their levels of speech and language development and their factual knowledge were within the normal range.

Vargha-Khadem et al. (2002) carried out a follow-up study on Jon at the age of 20. His semantic memory continued to be much better than his episodic memory. Brandt et al. (2006) also studied Jon as an adult. They obtained evidence suggesting that Jon's apparent recall of information from episodic memory actually involved the use of semantic memory. Thus, Jon's episodic memory may be even worse than previously assumed.

In spite of patients such as Beth and Jon, many amnesic patients have severe problems with semantic memory as well as episodic memory. Why is that so if semantic memory and episodic memory form fairly separate memory systems? There are two main answers. First, the two memory systems don't function entirely independently of each other. For example, suppose you think of an episodic memory of a sunlit beach on holiday. You need to use semantic memory to understand what is meant by words such as *beach* and *holiday*.

Second, the brain areas involved in the formation of new episodic and semantic memories are very close to each other. Episodic memory (especially recollection) depends heavily on the hippocampus (Diana et al., 2007; Vargha-Khadem et al., 1997). In contrast, semantic memory involves brain areas adjacent to the hippocampus (Vargha-Khadem et al., 1997). Thus, brain damage sufficient to impair episodic memory will typically also impair semantic memory.

WHAT IS THE PROBLEM?

Findings such as those discussed above suggest that amnesics have a problem with declarative memory (explicit memory) but not with nondeclarative memory (implicit memory) (e.g., Nadel & Moscovitch, 1997). That viewpoint has proved very successful, and seems to account for most findings.

However, an alternative theoretical approach has attracted increasing interest (e.g., Reder et al., 2009). According to this approach, amnesic patients find it hard to form *associations* between two concepts or pieces of information (the binding hypothesis). This is required more often with explicit memory. As we will see, there is much to recommend this new approach.

Suppose we consider amnesics' performance on a procedural memory task that involves forming associations. Amnesics should perform poorly according to the binding hypothesis but should not perform poorly according to the traditional viewpoint. Relevant findings were reported by Ryan et al. (2000). Amnesic patients and healthy individuals were presented with color images of real-world scenes in three conditions:

1. *Novel scenes:* The scene hadn't been presented before.
2. *Repeated old scenes:* An identical scene had been presented before.
3. *Manipulated old scenes:* The scene had been presented before, but the positions of some objects had been altered.

The participants' eye fixations were recorded. The key measure was the proportion of eye fixations in the critical region (i.e., the part of the scene that had been altered in the manipulated condition). The healthy controls had more eye movements in the critical region in the manipulated condition than in the other two conditions (see Figure 5.8). This was because they had implicit memory for the relations among the objects in the original scene. In contrast, the amnesic patients didn't devote more fixations to the critical region in the manipulated condition. This was because they lacked implicit memory for the original object relations. These findings support the binding hypothesis.

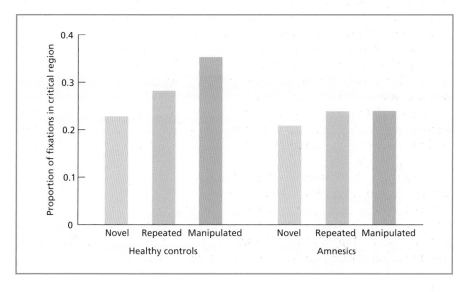

Figure 5.8 Proportion of eye fixations in the critical region in healthy controls and amnesic patients as a function of condition (novel, repeated, manipulated). Data from Ryan et al. (2000).

Suppose we consider amnesics' performance on an explicit memory task that doesn't require forming associations. According to the traditional viewpoint, their performance should be poor. In contrast, amnesics' performance should be normal according to the binding hypothesis. Relevant research was reported by Huppert and Piercy (1976). Large numbers of pictures were presented on Day 1 and on Day 2. Some of those presented on Day 2 had been presented on Day 1 and others had not. Participants were then presented with numerous pictures and indicated whether they had ever seen them before. No prior binding of picture and temporal context was necessary to make such familiarity judgments. The amnesic patients and healthy controls performed comparably well on this task, as predicted by the binding hypothesis.

Huppert and Piercy (1976) also used a recognition-memory test on which participants decided which pictures had been presented on Day 2. Successful performance on this task required binding of picture and temporal context at the time of learning. Healthy controls performed much better than amnesic patients on this task. Thus, amnesic patients were at a great disadvantage when binding was necessary for good memory performance, precisely as predicted by the binding hypothesis.

More support for the binding hypothesis comes from the review of recognition-memory studies by Skinner and Fernandes (2007) discussed earlier. Memory performance was assessed by recollection (for which binding was required) or by familiarity (for which binding wasn't essential). As predicted by the binding hypothesis, amnesic patients with damage to the hippocampus performed much worse on recollection tests than on familiarity tests.

CONCLUSIONS

Declarative memory tasks generally require the formation of associations and nondeclarative memory tasks often do not. As a result, the findings from most studies are consistent with the traditional viewpoint *and* with the binding hypothesis. However, when the two theoretical positions make different predictions, the findings tend to support the binding hypothesis. When associations need to be formed, amnesic patients perform poorly even on implicit memory tasks (e.g., Ryan et al., 2000). When associations don't need to be formed, amnesic patients perform well even on explicit memory tasks (e.g., Huppert & Piercy, 1976).

Section Summary

- The study of patients with amnesia has provided a good test-bed for theories of memory. Most research has focused on anterograde amnesia, in which there is very poor memory for most information acquired after the onset of the amnesia.

What remains intact?
- Amnesic patients typically have an essentially intact ability to acquire numerous new skills including weaving and operating machinery. They also show intact performance on priming tasks. It has been argued that amnesic patients have intact nondeclarative memory.

> **What is impaired?**
> - The greatest impairment in amnesic patients is in the formation of new episodic memories. In addition, they often have problems in forming new semantic memories. Thus, amnesic patients seem to have problems with declarative memory.
>
> **What is the problem?**
> - According to the binding hypothesis, amnesics' crucial problem lies in the formation of associations between two concepts or pieces of information. In support, amnesics' declarative memory is often good when associations don't have to be formed. In addition, their nondeclarative memory is poor when associations need to be formed.

FORGETTING

So far in this chapter we have focused mainly on what we remember. However, most of us feel that we have a really poor memory, which can be embarrassing. Many years ago, the British Royal family toured South America. As they left by plane from one airport, a member of the crowd waving them off enthusiastically realized with a sinking feeling he should have been on the plane rather than the tarmac!

Some evidence that our memories can be poor for important information comes from the study of passwords. In one study (Brown et al., 2004), 31% of American students admitted to having forgotten one or more passwords. Almost half of these students increased the memorability of their passwords by using their own name in password construction – this may not be the ideal way to have a secure password! However, as we would expect, passwords that are meaningful and familiar are best remembered (Ostojic & Phillips, 2009).

What should we do with our passwords? Brown et al. suggested keeping a record of your passwords in a place to which only you have access (e.g., a safe deposit box). Of course, you then need to remember where you have put your passwords!

Winograd and Soloway (1986) provided some guidance here. Students found it harder to remember where objects had been hidden when the locations were unlikely (e.g., hiding jewelry in the oven) than when they were likely (e.g., hiding a thermometer in the medicine chest).

The rate of forgetting is generally fastest shortly after learning and decreases progressively as time goes by. This was first shown by the German psychologist Hermann Ebbinghaus (1885/1913). He carried out extensive studies with himself as the only participant (not a practice to be recommended!). His basic approach involved learning lists of nonsense syllables having little or no meaning. At various intervals of time after learning a list, he relearned it. He assessed how much was still remembered by the reduction in the number of trials during relearning compared to original learning (the savings method). Forgetting was very rapid over the first hour after learning but slowed down considerably after that (see Figure 5.9).

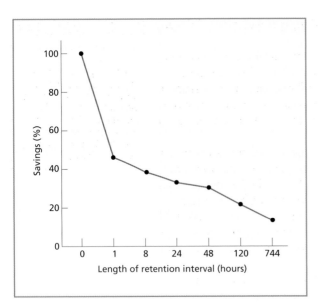

Figure 5.9 Forgetting over time as indexed by reduced savings during relearning. Data from Ebbinghaus (1885/1913).

We have assumed so far that forgetting is something to be avoided. However, that is often *not* the case (Schacter, 1999). Our world is dynamic and there are frequent changes in the information useful to us. For example, it is not useful to remember where you parked your car yesterday, what your schedule of lectures was last semester, or where your friends used to live. What you want to do is to *update* your memory of such information and forget what was previously the case. Fortunately, our memory system is reasonably efficient at doing precisely that.

FORGETTING FROM IMPLICIT MEMORY

In what follows, the main focus is on forgetting from explicit memory (involving conscious recollection). However, we will also consider forgetting from implicit memory (not involving conscious recollection).

Implicit memory is often better than explicit memory. You may be very skillful at carrying out numerous tasks on your computer. However, if someone asks you what you need to do to perform one of those tasks, you may find it hard to use conscious processes to put it into words. In my career, I have typed about 6 million words using touch-typing. However, I have very little conscious awareness of where each letter is – if you asked me where a given letter is on the keyboard, I would probably move the appropriate finger before knowing the answer! This is an example of good implicit memory combined with poor explicit memory.

Experimental evidence that implicit memory can be much better than explicit memory was reported by Mitchell (2006). Participants were given the implicit memory task of identifying pictures from fragments having seen some of them in an experiment 17 years previously. They did significantly better with the pictures seen before, thus providing strong evidence for implicit memory after all those years! However, there was rather little explicit memory for the experiment 17 years earlier. Indeed, one-third of the participants had no conscious recollection at all of having taken part in it!

Some of the main theories of forgetting are discussed below. An alternative approach to forgetting focuses on "recovered memories." These are traumatic memories (e.g., of sexual abuse) that had apparently been forgotten for many years but are then remembered. This approach is discussed in Chapter 6.

CONTEXT EFFECTS

When we store away information about an event, we typically also store away information about the context in which that event was experienced. As a result, long-term memory is generally better when the context at retrieval is the same as that at the time of learning. More generally, memory is better when the information available at the time of retrieval matches (is the same as) that contained in the memory trace. That is the **encoding specificity principle** put forward by Endel Tulving (e.g., 1979).

Duncan Godden and Alan Baddeley showed the importance of context in a study on deep-sea divers (Godden & Baddeley, 1975). Divers listened to 40 words on the beach or under 10 feet of water. They were then tested on their ability to recall these words in the same environment or the other one. Recall was considerably better when the environment was the same at test as at learning than when it was different (Figure 5.10).

So far we have considered the importance of context in the form of the *external* environment. However, the *internal* environment is also important. Christopher Miles and Elinor Hardman (1998) wondered whether our internal cardiovascular state might influence how much we can remember. Participants learned a list of words while resting at their ease on an exercise bicycle or while pedaling the bicycle vigorously to raise their heart rate to over 120 beats per minute. Word recall was 20% higher when participants were in the same cardiovascular state at retrieval as at learning.

Marian and Kaushanskaya (2007) studied bilingual Mandarin–English speakers. They were asked questions such as "Name a statue of someone standing with a raised arm while looking into the distance" in English or in Mandarin. There was a language-dependency effect – participants were more likely to respond "Statue of Liberty" when asked in English but "Statue of Mao" if asked in Mandarin. Thus, the language context influences the information we retrieve.

| Key Term

Encoding specificity principle:
the notion that retrieval depends on the *overlap* between the information available at retrieval and the information within the memory trace; memory is best when the overlap is high.

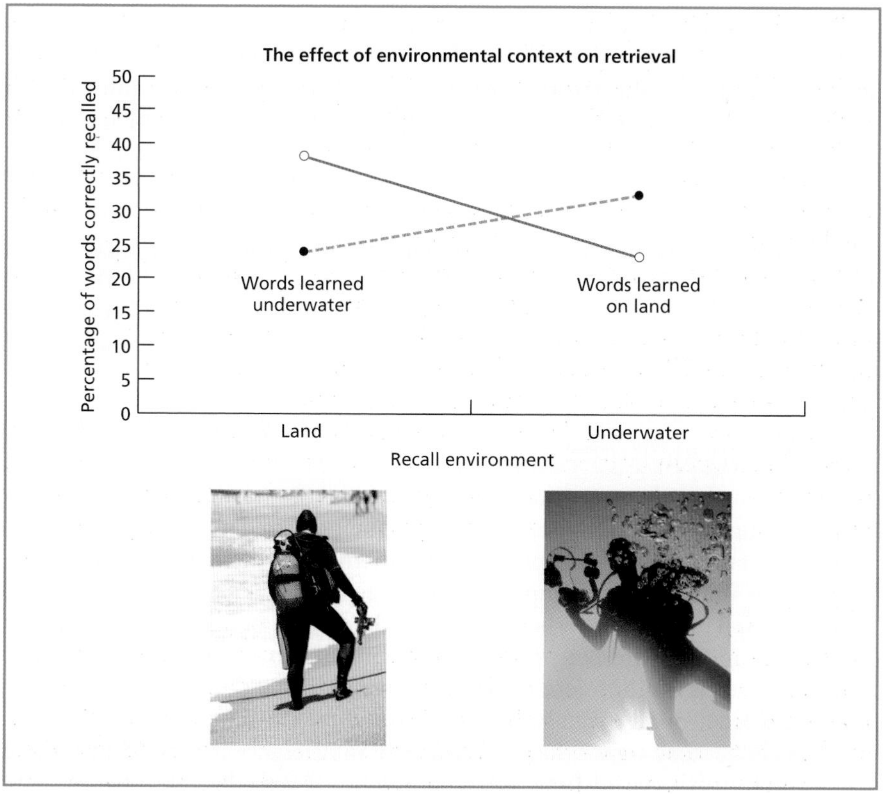

Figure 5.10 Words learned and tested in the same environment are better recalled than those items for which the environmental context varied between study and test. Data from Godden and Baddeley (1975).

Recognition memory is generally better than recall. For example, we may be unable to recall an acquaintance's name, but if someone mentions their name we instantly recognize it. However, it follows from the encoding specificity principle that recall could be better than recognition memory. This should happen when the information in the recall cue overlaps more than the information in the recognition cue with the information stored in memory.

Muter (1978) tested the above prediction. Participants were presented with people's names (e.g., DOYLE; THOMAS) and told to circle those they "recognized as a person who was famous before 1950." They were then given recall cues in the form of brief descriptions plus first names of the famous people whose surnames had appeared on the recognition test (e.g., author of the Sherlock Holmes stories: Sir Arthur Conan _____; Welsh poet: Dylan _____). Participants recognized only 29% of the names but recalled 42% of them.

The notion of encoding specificity implies that retrieval occurs fairly automatically. However, that isn't always the case. Herron and Wilding (2006) found that active processes can be involved in retrieval. People found it easier to recollect episodic memories relating to when and where an event occurred when they adopted the appropriate mental set or frame of mind beforehand.

In sum, memory (and forgetting) depends on contextual information. Several different kinds of context (e.g., external cues; internal states; linguistic context) influence memory performance. However, retrieval sometimes goes way beyond encoding specificity. For example, consider the question, "What did you do 10 days ago?" I am reasonably confident that you found yourself using a fairly complex strategy to produce the answer, and didn't simply match retrieval information with memory-trace information.

There is another issue about the context-dependent approach. What matters is not only the informational overlap between retrieval information and stored information. What is also important is the extent to which retrieval information allows us to discriminate the correct responses from the incorrect ones (Eysenck, 1979). Consider the following thought experiment (Nairne, 2002). Participants read aloud this word list: write, right, rite, rite, write, right. They then try to recall the word in the third position. We increase the informational overlap for some participants by providing them with the sound of the item in the third position. This increased informational overlap is totally unhelpful because it doesn't allow participants to discriminate the correct spelling of the sound from the wrong ones.

INTERFERENCE EFFECTS

If any of your female acquaintances are married, you may have found yourself remembering their maiden name rather than their married name. Their previous name interferes with (or disrupts) your ability to recall their current name. The notion that interference is important in forgetting goes back to the German psychologist Hugo Münsterberg (1863–1916). Men had pocket watches in those days, and Münsterberg kept his watch in one particular pocket. When he started to keep it in a different pocket for reasons lost in the mists of history, he often fumbled around in confusion when asked for the time.

The above story shows the key features of interference theory. Münsterberg had learned an association between the stimulus, "What's the time, Hugo?", and the response of removing the watch from his pocket. Subsequently the stimulus remained the same but a different response was now associated with it.

Münsterberg's memory problem is an example of **proactive interference**, in which previous learning disrupts later learning and memory. This type of interference has often been shown in studies on paired-associate learning (see Figure 5.11). Participants initially learn pairs of words on List 1 (e.g., Cat–Dirt). They then learn different pairs of words on List 2 (e.g., Cat–Tree). Finally, they are given the first word (e.g., Cat–???) and asked to recall the word paired with it on the second list. Memory performance tends to be poor because of interference from the initial associate (e.g., Dirt).

Most research on proactive interference has involved explicit memory. However, proactive interference occurs with implicit memory as well. Lustig and Hasher (2001) used a word-fragment completion task (e.g., A _ L _ _ GY), on which participants wrote down the first appropriate word coming to mind. Participants previously exposed to words almost fitting the fragments (e.g., ANALOGY) showed evidence of proactive interference.

What causes proactive interference? Jacoby et al. (2001) argued there is competition between two responses: the correct one and the incorrect one. As a result, there are two potential reasons why proactive interference occurs: (1) the incorrect response is very strong; or (2) the correct response is very weak. Jacoby et al. found that proactive interference was due much more to the strength of the incorrect response than to the weakness of the correct response.

There is also **retroactive interference**, in which later learning disrupts memory for previous learning. This has also often been studied using paired-associate learning (see Figure 5.11). In general terms, both proactive and retroactive interference are maximal when two different responses have been associated with the same stimulus (e.g., Cat–Tree and Cat–Dirt) (Underwood & Postman, 1960).

> **Key Terms**
>
> **Proactive interference:** disruption of memory by previous learning (often of similar material); see **retroactive interference**.
>
> **Retroactive interference:** disruption of memory for what was learned originally by other learning or processing during the retention interval; see **proactive interference**.

	Proactive interference		
Group	*Learn*	*Learn*	*Test*
Experimental	A–B (e.g., Cat–Dirt)	A–C (e.g., Cat–Tree)	A–C (e.g., Cat–Tree)
Control	–	A–C (e.g., Cat–Tree)	A–C (e.g., Cat–Tree)

	Retroactive interference		
Group	*Learn*	*Learn*	*Test*
Experimental	A–B (e.g., Cat–Tree)	A–C (e.g., Cat–Dirt)	A–B (e.g., Cat–Tree)
Control	A–B (e.g., Cat–Tree)	–	A–B (e.g., Cat–Tree)

Note: for both proactive and retroactive interference, the experimental group exhibits interference. On the test, only the first word is supplied, and the participants must provide the second word.

Figure 5.11 Methods of testing for proactive and retroactive interference.

Here is an everyday example of retroactive interference. Suppose you became skillful in carrying out a range of tasks on one computer. After that, you become an expert at performing the same tasks on a different computer with different software. If you went back to your first computer, you might discover that you kept doing things that were correct with the second computer even though they were wrong with this computer.

Isurin and McDonald (2001) argued that retroactive interference explains why people forget some of their first language when acquiring a second one. Bilingual participants fluent in two languages were first presented with various pictures and the corresponding words in Russian or Hebrew. Some were then presented with the same pictures and the corresponding words in the other language. Finally, they were tested for recall of the words in the first language. There was substantial retroactive interference – recall of the first-language words became progressively worse the more learning trials there were with the second-language words.

Lustig et al. (2004) argued that retroactive interference in paired-associate learning might occur for two reasons: (1) The correct response is hard to retrieve; or (2) the incorrect response is highly accessible. For example, if participants learn "bed–sheet" on List 1 and "bed–linen" on List 2, they may fail to produce "sheet" on the final test because its strength is weak or because the word "linen" is very strong. Lustig et al. found that retroactive interference was due mainly to the strength of the incorrect response.

Retroactive interference is generally greatest when the new learning resembles previous learning. However, there is some retroactive interference when people expend mental effort during the retention interval even though no new learning is required (Dewar et al., 2007). In Dewar et al.'s experiment, participants learned a list of words and were then exposed to various tasks during the retention interval before list memory was assessed. There was significant retroactive interference even when the intervening task involved detecting differences between pictures or detecting tones. Dewar et al. (2007) concluded that retroactive interference can occur in two ways:

1. Expenditure of mental effort during the retention interval.
2. Learning of material similar to the original learning material.

CONSOLIDATION

We have considered several factors that play important roles in forgetting. However, we haven't directly addressed the issue of why the rate of forgetting is greatest shortly after learning. The answer may be **consolidation** (Wixted, 2004). Consolidation is a physiological process lasting for a long time (possibly years) that fixes information in long-term memory. A key assumption of consolidation theory is that recently formed memories that are still being consolidated are especially vulnerable to interference and forgetting. In other words, "New memories are clear but fragile and old ones are faded but robust" (Wixted, 2004, p. 265).

According to some versions of consolidation theory (e.g., Eichenbaum, 2001), the process of consolidation involves two major phases. The first phase occurs over a period of hours and centers on the hippocampus. The second

> **Key Term**
>
> **Consolidation:**
> a physiological process involved in establishing long-term memories; this process lasts several hours or more, and newly formed memories that are still being consolidated are fragile.

phase applies only to episodic and semantic memories. It takes place over a period of time ranging from days to years and involves interactions between the hippocampal region and the neocortex.

Evidence for consolidation theory comes from the study of brain-damaged patients with retrograde amnesia, in which there is impaired memory for events occurring before the onset of the amnesia. Many of these patients have suffered damage to the hippocampus as the result of an accident. Since the hippocampus is of central importance in the first phase of consolidation, the most recently formed memories should be the ones most impaired in these patients. This pattern has been found in numerous patients with retrograde amnesia (Manns et al., 2003).

According to consolidation theory, newly formed memories should be more susceptible to retroactive interference from subsequent learning than older ones. The predicted findings have been obtained even when the interfering material is dissimilar to the material learned originally. In such cases, there is often more retroactive interference when it is presented *early* in the retention interval (Wixted, 2004).

Finally, consider the effects of alcohol on memory. Individuals who drink excessive amounts of alcohol sometimes suffer from "blackout." This is an almost total loss of memory for all events occurring while they were conscious but very drunk. These blackouts indicate a failure to consolidate memories formed while intoxicated.

An interesting finding is that memories formed shortly *before* alcohol consumption are often better remembered than those formed by individuals who don't subsequently drink alcohol (Bruce & Pihl, 1997). Alcohol probably prevents the formation of new memories that would interfere with the consolidation process of the memories formed just before alcohol consumption. Thus, alcohol protects previously formed memories from disruption.

Evaluation

⊕ Consolidation theory explains why the rate of forgetting decreases over time.

⊕ Consolidation theory successfully predicts that retrograde amnesia is greater for recently formed memories and that retroactive interference effects are greatest shortly after learning.

⊕ The theory identifies the brain areas most associated with consolidation.

⊖ Forgetting involves several factors other than consolidation. For example, forgetting is greater when there is little informational overlap between the memory trace and the retrieval environment (encoding specificity principle).

⊖ Consolidation theory deemphasizes the role of *cognitive* processes in forgetting.

⊖ As we will see in the next section, consolidation processes are more complex than was implied by early versions of consolidation theory.

Section Summary

Introduction

- The rate of forgetting is generally fastest shortly after learning and then decreases progressively. Forgetting occurs in both explicit and implicit memory tasks. Recall and recognition are two of the most used measures of explicit memory.

Context effects

- According to the encoding specificity principle, memory is generally better when the context at retrieval matches that at learning. This context can involve the external environment or internal physiological or emotional state. As predicted by the encoding specificity principle, recall is sometimes better than recognition memory.

Interference effects

- What we have learned can be forgotten due to previous similar learning (proactive interference) or learning during the retention interval (retroactive interference). Both forms of interference are greatest when the same stimulus is associated with two responses. Proactive and retroactive interference are due more to the strength of incorrect responses than the weakness of correct ones.

Consolidation

- Consolidation is a physiological process involved in the storage of memories. Recently formed memories that are still being consolidated are especially vulnerable to forgetting. Consolidation theory explains why retrograde amnesia is generally greater for recently formed memories. However, its focus is physiological and psychological and cognitive processes are deemphasized.

MISREMEMBERING

We saw earlier that it is often useful for us to update our information (e.g., about our lecture schedule) and at the same time to forget previously relevant information. What is involved in this updating process? As discussed above, learning leads to a consolidation process in which memory traces are initially very fragile but become decreasingly so over time.

Several theorists (e.g., Hardt et al., 2010) have put forward a more complex version of consolidation theory. According to them, *reactivation* of a memory trace that has already been consolidated puts it back into a fragile state. This leads to **reconsolidation** (a new consolidation process), with the fragility of the memory trace allowing it to be updated and altered.

Reconsolidation is very useful if we want to update our knowledge because what we learned previously is no longer relevant. However, it can cause us to misremember if we subsequently want to recall the information we learned originally. This is how it happens. We learn some information at Time 1. At

Key Term

Reconsolidation: this is a new **consolidation** process that occurs when a previously formed memory trace is reactivated; it allows that memory trace to be updated.

Time 2, we learn additional information. If the memory traces based on the information learned at Time 1 are activated at Time 2, those Time 1 memory traces immediately become fragile. As a result, some information learned at Time 2 will mistakenly become incorporated into the memory traces of the Time 1 information and cause misremembering.

An early study showing the importance of reconsolidation was by Walker et al. (2003). They used a finger-tapping task in which participants remembered a given sequence of responses. Two conditions were very similar in that one sequence was learned initially and then a second sequence was learned 24 hours later. The only difference was that in one condition the participants briefly rehearsed the first sequence before learning the second one.

According to reconsolidation theory, brief rehearsal should have made the memory traces of the first sequence fragile and thus produced errors in memory. That is precisely what happened – long-term memory for the first sequence was much worse when it was briefly rehearsed.

Walker et al. (2003) found that reconsolidation played an important role in motor memory. Hupbach et al. (2007, 2008) showed that reconsolidation is also important in memory for a set of objects. In one condition, participants' memory traces of their Time 1 learning were reactivated by reminding them of that learning just before the new learning at Time 2 (e.g., "Can you describe the general procedure of what you did on Monday?").

When participants were later asked to recall the Time 1 information, they misremembered some of the Time 2 information as having been learned at Time 1. There was much less such misremembering when participants were *not* reminded of their Time 1 learning prior to Time 2 learning. This was because the Time 1 memory traces were less likely to be reactivated in this condition.

Perhaps the misremembering observed by Hupbach et al. (2007, 2008) was due to *confusion* about when information had been learned rather than to reconsolidation. This issue was addressed by Hupbach et al. (2009). Their findings indicated that misremembering was due much more to reconsolidation than to confusion.

HINDSIGHT BIAS

Several findings in the memory literature can be explained in terms of reconsolidation. For example, consider hindsight bias. **Hindsight bias** occurs when someone provided with accurate information about the outcome of an event mistakenly recalls that they knew it all along. For example, suppose you were asked "How high is the Eiffel tower?", and estimated its height at 650 feet. You are then told its actual height is 1063 feet (324 m). You would show hindsight bias if you subsequently claimed you had always known it was about 1000 feet high.

Hindsight bias depends on various cognitive and motivational factors (see Guilbault et al., 2004, for a review). However, memory distortions play an important role. According to Hardt et al. (2010), providing the correct information about an event (e.g., Eiffel tower is 1063 feet) *reactivates* the relevant memory trace (e.g., Eiffel tower is 650 feet) and can cause it to become altered. In other words, hindsight bias occurs partly as a result of memory alterations caused by reconsolidation.

Key Terms
Hindsight bias: the tendency for people to exaggerate how accurately they would have predicted some event in advance after they know what actually happened.

If hindsight bias depends on basic physiological processes involved in reconsolidation, it should be hard to eliminate. That is precisely what Pohl and Hell (1996) found in a study using difficult general knowledge questions. Some participants were warned in advance about hindsight bias, but this failed to reduce the size of the bias. Other participants were given individual feedback about the errors in their recall, but this also failed to reduce hindsight bias when they were tested again.

POST-EVENT MISINFORMATION EFFECT

Reconsolidation also helps to explain the post-event misinformation effect (see Glossary). This effect (discussed more fully in Chapter 6) occurs when eyewitness memory for an incident is distorted by misleading information presented afterwards. For example, Loftus and Zanni (1975) showed people a short video of a car accident. Afterwards, some eyewitnesses were asked, "Did you see the broken headlight?" In fact, there was no broken headlight even though the question implied there was. This misleading question led several eyewitnesses to claim mistakenly they had seen a broken headlight.

According to the reconsolidation account, the presentation of misleading information causes reactivation of the memory traces of the original incident. This makes those memory traces fragile and can lead to some of the misleading information being incorporated into the memory traces. This provides a potential explanation of the post-event misinformation effect, although other factors are also involved (see Chapter 6).

Eyewitnesses rarely mistakenly recall details from the original incident as having been present in the post-event information (Mitchell et al., 2003). This probably happens because updating involving reconsolidation doesn't apply to the memory traces based on post-event information.

Section Summary

- Reactivation of a memory trace that has already been consolidated makes it fragile again and leads to reconsolidation. Reconsolidation processes can cause misremembering.

Hindsight bias

- Hindsight bias occurs when someone mistakenly believes they knew something all along when given the correct answer. Hindsight bias may be very hard to eliminate because it depends in part on reconsolidation processes.

Post-event misinformation effect

- The post-event misinformation effect occurs when misleading information provided after an event causes distortions in an eyewitness's memory for that event. Speculatively, reconsolidation processes may be partly responsible.

Essay Questions

1. What are some of the main factors involved in effective learning of information?
2. "Implicit learning is very different from explicit learning." Discuss.
3. Discuss some of the main forms of long-term memory.
4. What can amnesics remember? What can't they remember?
5. Why do we forget?

Further Reading

- Baddeley, A., Eysenck, M. W., & Anderson, M. C. (2009). *Memory*. New York: Psychology Press. This introductory textbook discusses at length all the main areas within memory research.
- Della Sala, S. (2010). *Forgetting*. New York: Psychology Press. The major contemporary approaches to understanding forgetting are discussed in this edited book.
- Foerde, K., & Poldrack, R. A. (2009). Procedural learning in humans. In L. R. Squire (Ed.), *The new encyclopedia of neuroscience* (Vol. 7, pp. 1083–1091). Oxford, UK: Academic Press. This chapter provides a thorough overview of theory and research on procedural learning and memory.
- Reder, L. M., Park, H., & Kieffaber, P. D. (2009). Memory systems do not divide on consciousness: Reinterpreting memory in terms of activation and binding. *Psychological Bulletin*, *135*, 23–49. The distinction between explicit/declarative and implicit/nondeclarative memory systems is discussed in light of the evidence and an alternative theoretical perspective is proposed.

Chapter 6

Contents

Everyday memory

6

INTRODUCTION

Over the past 30 years, there has been a rapid increase in research on everyday memory. The study of everyday memory is concerned with the ways we use memory in our daily lives. Everyday memory differs in some important ways from the kinds of memory traditionally studied in the laboratory and discussed in Chapters 4 and 5. Much of everyday memory relates to our goals and motivations (Cohen, 2008). We can see this most clearly with prospective memory (remembering to carry out intended actions). Most of our intended actions are designed to assist us in achieving our current goals. For example, I often form the intention to track down an article or book needed for me to achieve the goal of completing a chapter in one of my textbooks.

Learning in most everyday memory research is *incidental* (i.e., not deliberate), with individuals learning information relevant to their goals or interests. In most traditional memory research, however, learning is *intentional*. What individuals learn is determined largely by the instructions they are given.

We turn now to probably the most crucial difference between memory as traditionally studied and memory in everyday life. Participants in traditional memory studies are generally motivated to be as *accurate* as possible in their memory performance. There are occasions in everyday life when we strive for maximal accuracy in our recall (e.g., during an examination; remembering a

---

Learning Objectives

After studying Chapter 6, you should be able to:

- Explain which features of human memory are illustrated by schema theories.
- Define repressed memories, false memories, recovered memories, and flashbulb memories, and explain how autobiographical memory is not always perfect.
- Explain how the cognitive interview addresses limitations of natural eyewitness testimony.
- Define, compare, and contrast prospective and retrospective memory.
- Describe how various mnemonic devices are intended to take advantage of how the long-term memory system works.

shopping list). However, everyday remembering mostly occurs in social settings and is intended for communication purposes. Our goals are often to be agreeable, to sound impressive, or to entertain rather than to be totally accurate.

Relevant research was reported by Marsh and Tversky (2004). Students recorded information about their retelling of personal memories to other people over a period of one month. The students admitted that 42% of these retellings were inaccurate. In addition, one-third of the retellings they classified as accurate nevertheless contained distortions.

The key issue is whether saying is believing – if what you say is deliberately distorted, does this change your memory and make it less accurate? Very often the answer is "Yes." Dudukovic et al. (2004) asked participants to read a story and then retell it three times accurately (as in traditional memory research) or entertainingly (as in the real world). Not surprisingly, entertaining retellings contained more emotion but fewer concrete details than accurate retellings. The participants were asked subsequently to recall the story accurately. Those who had previously provided entertaining retellings recalled fewer story events, fewer details, and were less accurate than those who had provided accurate retellings. Thus, the goals we have in remembering can distort our long-term memory even after those goals have changed (Marsh, 2007).

It isn't *always* the case that saying is believing. The goals we have when communicating determine whether our subsequent memories will be distorted. If a speaker says inaccurate things to his/her audience merely to be polite or to obtain money, then there is no distortion effect in memory (Echterhoff et al., 2008). Thus, saying is *not* believing when what you say is motivated by external influences such as the chance to gain some money.

CHAPTER STRUCTURE

In this chapter, we will consider four of the most important topics in everyday memory. First there is autobiographical memory, which is concerned with personal memories about our own lives. It is extremely important because our sense of who we are depends on having an intact autobiographical memory. Much of what it is to be human is lost if someone suffers brain damage that eliminates most (or all) of their personal memories.

Second, we turn to one of the most important applications of memory research in the real world: eyewitness testimony. In thousands of court cases, the defendant was judged guilty or innocent mostly based on eyewitness evidence. As a result, it is vital to know the accuracy (or otherwise) of eyewitnesses' memories of a crime.

Third, we discuss the factors determining whether we remember to carry out intended actions such as buying something at the shops or meeting a friend. This is prospective memory, which is really important in everyday life. Anyone who rarely does what he/she has promised to do (e.g., meet up with friends) is unlikely to succeed socially or at work!

Fourth, most people fervently wish their memory was better. There are numerous popular books full of suggestions as to how to improve your memory. Towards the end of this chapter, I focus on those memory strategies for which there is clear evidence of their effectiveness, showing how they can be used in everyday life. I also consider briefly the strategies used by memory experts to achieve incredible memory feats.

Section Summary

- Learning in everyday life is often incidental and the information learned is relevant to the individual's goals or interests. Most everyday remembering is intended for communication purposes rather than strict accuracy. Our goals in everyday remembering can distort the accuracy of subsequent long-term memory.

Chapter structure

- This chapter deals with four major topics in everyday memory: autobiographical memory, eyewitness testimony, prospective memory, and memory strategies designed to enhance long-term memory.

AUTOBIOGRAPHICAL MEMORY

We have hundreds of thousands of memories relating to an endless variety of things. However, those relating to the experiences we have had and to people important to us have special significance and form our **autobiographical memory** (memory for the events of one's own life). *Why* are our autobiographical memories of consuming interest to us? They relate to our major life goals, to our most powerful emotions, and to our personal meanings.

> **Key Term**
>
> **Autobiographical memory:**
> a form of **declarative memory** involving memory for personal events across the lifespan.

Research Activity 6.1: *Autobiographical memories and personality*

Recall an event in your life that caused you to experience *happiness*. Write down a brief description of the event as you now remember it. Then do the same for each of the following emotions in turn: *anger*; *pride*; *fear*; *relief*; and *sadness*.

Now go back over your descriptions. Some of your memories may be communal (involving your relationships with other people). They may relate to love and friendship and to the emotions that others caused you to experience. Other memories may be agentic (involving themes of independence, achievement, and personal power). In other words, these are memories in which the associated emotional states are due to *personal* success and failure rather than your relationships with others.

Woike et al. (1999) carried out a very similar study. They argued that our personality influences the kinds of emotional autobiographical memories we recall. They distinguished between two types of personality:

1. *Agentic personality type*, with an emphasis on independence, achievement, and personal power.
2. *Communal personality type*, with an emphasis on interdependence and similarity to others.

Woike et al. (1999) found that students with an agentic personality recalled more autobiographical memories concerned with agency (e.g., success, absence of failure, failure). In contrast, those with a communal personality recalled more memories concerned with communion (e.g., love, friendship, betrayal of trust). When you look back at the autobiographical memories you wrote down, do you feel they reveal your personality?

HOW GOOD IS AUTOBIOGRAPHICAL MEMORY?

If your autobiographical memory is like mine, you probably find you often forget past experiences, even ones that seemed important and emotional at the time. However, that is not true of everyone. Elizabeth Parker, Larry Cahill, and James McGaugh (2006) reported the fascinating case of AJ, a woman born in 1965. She has an incredible ability to recall detailed information about almost day of her life over the past several decades. Parker et al. coined the term **hyperthymestic syndrome** (formed from two Greek words meaning "remembering" and "more than normal") to describe this ability. In 2008, "AJ" published a book (*The Woman Who Can't Forget*) about her life under her real name of Jill Price.

You might think it would be a huge advantage to have access to incredibly detailed information about your own autobiographical memory. However, that isn't how Jill Price sees it: "Most have called it a gift, but I call it a burden. I run my entire life through my head every day and it drives me crazy!!!" (Parker et al., 2006, p. 35). Strangely, her memory generally is very ordinary. For example, her ability to recall lists of words is about average and she finds it very hard to remember which locks fit each of the five keys on her keyring.

What are the secrets of her outstanding autobiographical memory? First, she has obsessional tendencies, and spends most of her time thinking about herself and her past. Second, she has poor inhibitory processes and so finds it much harder than most people to switch her personal memories off. Third, Jill Price makes the passage of time seem more concrete by representing it in spatial form (e.g., drawing January in the 11 o'clock position on a circle and working counterclockwise from there). This linkage of time and space is often associated with very good memory (Simner et al., 2009). Fourth, areas of the temporal lobe that store events and dates are larger in Jill Price's brain than most other people's (Cahill et al.; unpublished).

Most people have good autobiographical memories for certain things. Bahrick et al. (1975) made use of photographs from high-school yearbooks dating back many years. Ex-students showed remarkably little forgetting of information about their former classmates at retention intervals up to 25 years. Performance was 90% for recognizing a name as being that of a classmate, for recognizing a classmate's photograph, and for matching a classmate's name to his/her school photograph. Performance remained very high on the last two tests even after almost 50 years, but performance on the name recognition task declined.

Bahrick et al. (2008) asked American ex-college students to recall their academic grades. Distortions in recall occurred shortly after graduation but thereafter remained fairly constant over retention intervals up to 54 years. As you might guess, the great majority of distortions involved inflating the actual grade.

Bahrick (1984) used the term "permastore" to refer to very long-term stable memories. This term was derived from permafrost, the permanently frozen subsoil found in Polar regions. It seems probable that the contents of the permastore consist mainly of information that was very well learned in the first place.

| Key Term |

Hyperthymestic syndrome:
an exceptional ability to remember the events of one's own life; in other words, outstanding **autobiographical memory**.

AUTOBIOGRAPHICAL MEMORY SYSTEM

Conway and Pleydell-Pearce (2000) put forward a theory of autobiographical memory (developed by Conway, 2005). They argued that we possess a self-memory system having two major components, as follows.

1. *Autobiographical knowledge base* containing personal information at three levels of specificity:
   - *Lifetime periods:* These generally cover substantial periods of time defined by major ongoing situations (e.g., time at high school).
   - *General events:* These include repeated events (e.g., visits to a sports club) and single events (e.g., a holiday in California). General events are often related to each other as well as to lifetime periods.
   - *Event-specific knowledge:* This knowledge consists of images, feelings, and other details relating to general events, and spanning time periods from seconds to hours. Knowledge about a specific event is usually organized in the correct temporal order.
2. *Working self:* This is concerned with the self, what it may become in the future, and with the individual's current set of goals. The goals of the working self will influence the kinds of memories stored within the autobiographical knowledge base. They also partly determine which autobiographical memories we recall.

Conway and Pleydell-Pearce (2000) argued that autobiographical memories can be accessed through generative (voluntary) retrieval or direct (involuntary) retrieval. We use generative retrieval when we deliberately construct autobiographical memories by combining the resources of the working self with information contained in the autobiographical knowledge. In contrast, direct retrieval doesn't involve the working self. Autobiographical memories produced by direct retrieval are triggered by specific cues (e.g., hearing the word "gambling" on the radio may produce direct retrieval of a trip to Las Vegas). Generative retrieval is more effortful and involves more active involvement by the rememberer than does direct retrieval.

Conway (2005) argued that we want our autobiographical memories to exhibit *coherence* (consistency with our current goals and beliefs). However, we also often want our autobiographical memories to exhibit *correspondence* (being accurate). In the battle between coherence and correspondence, coherence tends to win over time.

Findings

Studies of brain-damaged patients support the notion that there are three types of autobiographical knowledge. Of particular importance are cases of retrograde amnesia involving widespread forgetting of events preceding the brain injury (see Chapter 5). Many patients have great difficulty in recalling event-specific knowledge, but their ability to recall general events and lifetime periods is less impaired (Conway & Pleydell-Pearce, 2000). Rosenbaum et al. (2005) studied an amnesic patient, KC, who has no episodic memories involving event-specific knowledge. However, he can access some general autobiographical knowledge about his life.

According to the theory of Conway and Pleydell-Pearce (2000), our generative retrieval of autobiographical memories is influenced by the goals of the working self. As a result, such autobiographical memories should reflect success or failure with respect to our current goals. As we saw earlier, Woike et al. (1999) found that most autobiographical memories recalled in response to emotional cues were consistent with people's major goals.

Berntsen (1998) compared the memories produced by voluntary retrieval (i.e., elicited by cues) and by involuntary retrieval (i.e., coming to mind with no attempt to recall them). More of the latter memories were of specific events (89% vs. 63%, respectively). Berntsen and Hall (2004) repeated these findings. In addition, the cues most associated with direct or involuntary retrieval of autobiographical memories were specific ones, such as being in the same place as the original event (61% of cases) or being in the same place engaged in the same activity (25% of cases).

Berntsen (2010) summarized the differences between involuntary and voluntary memories. Involuntary memories are less relevant to our sense of identity than voluntary ones. They are also associated with more emotional reactions when retrieved.

Why do we have involuntary autobiographical memories? Such memories provide us with a sense of personal continuity over time (Rasmussen & Berntsen, 2009). If we retrieve involuntary memories in a novel situation, the information we retrieve may prove useful in deciding how to respond in that situation.

Evaluation

⊕ The theoretical approach of Conway and Pleydell-Pearce (2000) and Conway (2005) is a comprehensive one.

⊕ Several of the theory's assumptions (e.g., the hierarchical structure of autobiographical memory; the intimate relationship between autobiographical memory and the self; the importance of goals in autobiographical memory) are well supported by the evidence.

⊖ The ways in which the working self interacts with the autobiographical knowledge base to produce recall of specific autobiographical memories are not well understood.

⊖ Autobiographical memories vary in the extent to which they contain episodic information (e.g., contextual details) and semantic information (e.g., schema-based information). However, this issue isn't fully addressed within the theory.

FLASHBULB MEMORIES

Many people think they have a really poor memory and are always forgetting things. In spite of this pessimism, most people feel they have excellent memory for dramatic world events (e.g., the terrorist attacks on America carried out on September 11, 2001: 9/11). Such memories are known as **flashbulb memories**.

According to Roger Brown and James Kulik (1977), flashbulb memories are much more accurate and long-lasting than other memories. They argued that dramatic events activate a special neural mechanism if the events are

Key Term

Flashbulb memories: vivid and detailed memories of dramatic and significant events.

surprising and have real consequences for the individual. This mechanism "prints" the details of such events permanently in the memory system. Details are often stored away about the person who supplied the information, the place where the news was heard, the ongoing event when the news was heard, the individual's own emotional state, the emotional state of others, and the consequences of the event for the individual.

Here is an example of a flashbulb memory showing most of the above features. I was in the Psychology Department at Royal Holloway in the University of London on September 11, 2001. I went down to the office of Rosemary Westley (the Departmental Superintendent) to ask her something, and she gave me the terrible news of the attack on the Word Trade Center in New York. The news made both of us feel very emotional about the victims and about the terrorists responsible for the appalling loss of life.

Our flashbulb memories are often less accurate than we imagine. Kathy Pezdek (2003) asked American students the following questions about 9/11: (1) "On September 11, did you see the videotape on television of the first plane striking the first tower?"; (2) "Was the Pentagon struck before the first tower collapsed?" With the first question, 73% said "Yes." This is incorrect – there was videotape of the *second* tower being hit. With the second question, 39% incorrectly answered "No" (the Pentagon was struck at 9:41 and the first tower collapsed at 10:28). People's strong emotional reactions to learning of the terrorist attacks of 9/11 were especially poorly remembered (Hirst et al., 2009).

Jennifer Talarico and David Rubin (2003) obtained evidence that there is nothing very special about flashbulb memories. They assessed students' memories for the events of September 11 one day afterwards. At the same time, they assessed students' memory for a very recent everyday event. The students were tested again 7, 42, or 224 days later.

Talarico and Rubin (2003) came up with two key findings (see Figure 6.1). First, the reported vividness of flashbulb memories remained very high over the entire 32-week period. Second, flashbulb memories showed no more consistency or lack of change than did everyday memories. Thus, there was a major discrepancy between people's beliefs in the strength of their flashbulb memories and the actual accuracy of those memories.

Why do we mistakenly believe our flashbulb memories are accurate? Winningham et al. (2000) studied participants' memories of the unexpected acquittal of O. J. Simpson on a murder charge. These memories changed considerably in the first few days after hearing the news but then remained consistent. We may subsequently forget that our memories of dramatic world events are constructed over a period of time rather than being fully formed initially.

We may also underestimate the impact of other people on our flashbulb memories. For example, it was found in one study (Coman et al., 2009) that memories for 9/11 could be altered by a single conversation several years later.

In sum, flashbulb memories probably depend on the same underlying processes as ordinary autobiographical memories. Flashbulb memories are similar to other autobiographical memories in terms of accuracy, consistency, and longevity (Talarico & Rubin, 2009). However, the events relating to flashbulb memories tend to have greater distinctiveness and significance than

Figure 6.1   (a) Vividness ratings and (b) consistency of memory as a function of type of memory (flashbulb vs. everyday) and length of retention interval. Data from Talarico and Rubin (2003).

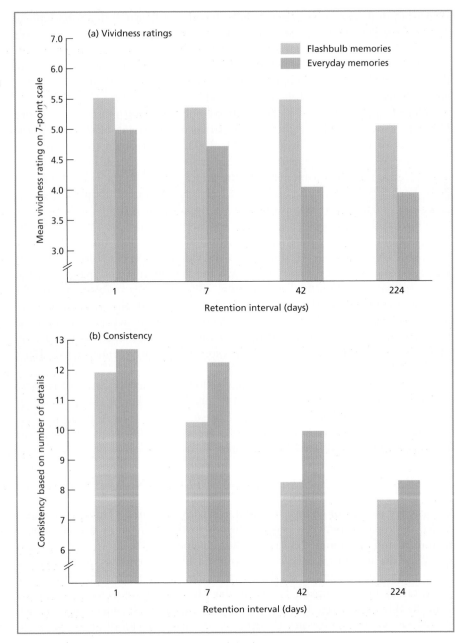

ordinary autobiographical events, which would make them more memorable. In the words of Talarico and Rubin (2009, p. 79), "Flashbulb memories result from ordinary memory processes and extraordinary event characteristics."

RECOVERED MEMORIES

We turn now to one of the most famous ideas put forward by the bearded Austrian psychologist Sigmund Freud. He claimed that very threatening or traumatic memories often can't gain access to conscious awareness, using the term **repression** to refer to this phenomenon. These traumatic memories remain stored in long-term memory over many years, and some may be recovered a long time after they were formed.

In recent years, there has been much controversy concerning **recovered memories**. These are traumatic memories (typically of childhood sexual abuse) that were forgotten

In the Real World 6.1: *Recovered memories*

Elke Geraerts et al. (2007) wondered whether the genuineness of recovered memories depends on the *context* in which they were recovered. They divided adults who had suffered childhood sexual abuse into three groups:

1. Those whose recovered memories had been recalled inside therapy (suggestive therapy group);
2. Those whose recovered memories had been recalled outside therapy (spontaneous recovery group);
3. Those who had continuous memories of abuse (continuous memory group).

Geraerts et al. (2007) discovered how many of these memories had corroborating evidence (e.g., the perpetrator had confessed) to provide a rough assessment of validity. There was corroborating evidence for 45% of the individuals in the continuous memory group, for 37% of those who had recalled memories outside therapy, and for 0% of those who had recalled memories inside therapy.

The above findings suggest that recovered memories fall into two categories. First, many recalled inside therapy are likely to be false memories produced by patients under the therapist's influence. Second, most recalled spontaneously outside therapy are likely to be genuine.

Geraerts et al. (2009) used a memory task known to produce false memories – people given lists of semantically related words often falsely "recognize" other semantically related words not actually presented. Women in the suggestive therapy group produced more false memories than those in the spontaneous recovery or continuous

memory groups. This suggests they may be prone to memory errors.

How can we explain spontaneous recovered memories produced outside therapy? One explanation involves repression of traumatic memories. However, that is unlikely. Only 8% of individuals reporting recovered memories of childhood sexual abuse recall having experienced them as traumatic (Clancy & McNally, 2005/2006). They generally recalled them as confusing or uncomfortable.

An alternative explanation is that spontaneous recovered memories involve similar mechanisms to other memories. For example, we sometimes forget our previous recollections of events. Geraerts et al. (2009) found that abused women often forgot they had previously recalled certain autobiographical events in the laboratory. This was more common among those in the spontaneous recovery group than those in the suggestive therapy or continuous memory groups.

Some spontaneous memories may not have been retrieved previously due to a lack of relevant retrieval cues. Several women reporting spontaneous recovered memories indicated that these memories had been triggered by cues such as seeing a movie about childhood sexual abuse or returning to the scene of the abuse (Clancy & McNally, 2005/2006).

In sum, there is more support for the false memory explanation than for the repression explanation (McNally & Geraerts, 2009). Many recovered memories (especially those recalled spontaneously) are genuine. Spontaneous recovered memories can probably be explained by simple mechanisms (e.g., forgetting that these memories have been recalled previously; a previous lack of powerful retrieval cues).

for many years but are suddenly remembered in adult life. It is possible to explain these recovered memories in terms of the repression of traumatic events. However, Loftus and Davis (2006) claimed that many of these so-called recovered memories are **false memories** – they refer to events and experiences that never actually happened.

Some claimed recovered memories are undoubtedly false. For example, some people "remember" having being abducted by space aliens (Clancy et al., 2002)! Lief and Fetkewicz (1995) found that 80% of adult patients who admitted reporting false recovered memories had therapists who made direct suggestions that they had been the victims of childhood sexual abuse. This suggests that recovered memories recalled *inside* therapy may be more likely to be false than those recalled *outside* therapy.

It is hard to obtain clear-cut evidence for two main reasons. First, there are generally no independent witnesses of the alleged sexual abuse. Second, we can't be sure that adults claiming to have recovered memories had no conscious recollection of childhood sexual abuse during the years of adolescence.

WHAT DO OLDER PEOPLE REMEMBER?

Suppose we ask older people around the age of 70 to recall personal memories from their life. From which parts of their lives would most memories come? Perhaps surprisingly, older people are not especially likely to recall distant childhood memories. Instead, they show a **reminiscence bump** – this is the tendency to recall numerous memories from adolescence and early adulthood.

Conway et al. (2005) asked older people from America, China, Japan, England, and Bangladesh to recall autobiographical memories. There was a reminiscence bump in all five cultures (see Figure 6.2). Interestingly, the Chinese were more likely than others to recall events with a social or group orientation. This probably occurred because they have a collectivistic culture in which the emphasis is on group cohesion. In contrast, the Americans were more likely to recall events oriented to the individual – America is an individualistic culture with an emphasis on personal responsibility and achievement.

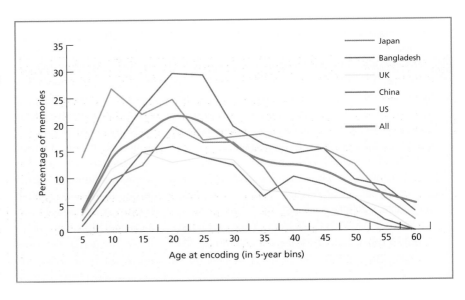

Figure 6.2 Lifespan retrieval curves from five countries. From Conway et al. (2005). Reprinted with permission from SAGE publications.

How can we explain the reminiscence bump? Rubin et al. (1998) argued that early adulthood is a period during which many important novel events occur, and that novel events are easier to remember. However, there wasn't much support for this theory in an Internet-based study on nearly 3500 people by Janssen and Murre (2008). The events recalled from early adulthood weren't especially novel, nor were they strongly emotional. It may simply be that memory processes function better in adolescence and early adulthood than in childhood or middle age.

Berntsen and Rubin (2002) found that older individuals showed a reminiscence bump for *positive* memories but not for *negative* ones. How can we interpret this finding? One interpretation is based on the notion of a **life script**, which consists of cultural expectations concerning the major life events in a typical person's life (Rubin et al., 2009). Examples of such events are falling in love, marriage, and having children. Most of these events are emotionally positive and generally occur between the ages of 15 and 30. As predicted, the major life events individuals recalled from their own lives had clear similarities to those included in their life script.

Glück and Bluck (2007) adopted a similar viewpoint. They argued that the reminiscence bump consists mostly of autobiographical memories associated with a real sense of development and progress in our lives. Such memories are typically positive and involve a high level of perceived control. Glück and Bluck (2007) tested these ideas on individuals aged between 50 and 90 who recalled personally important autobiographical memories. A reminiscence bump was present *only* for memories that were positive and involved high perceived control (see Figure 6.3).

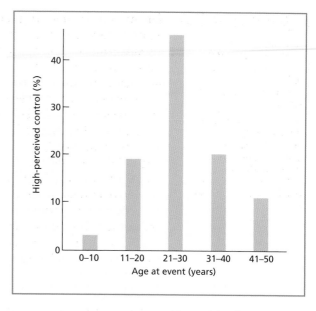

Figure 6.3 The presence of a strong reminiscence bump for positive events with high perceived control recalled by adults between 50 and 90 years of age. From Glück and Bluck (2007). Copyright © The Psychonomic Society. Reproduced with permission.

Section Summary

- Our most important autobiographical memories reflect our life goals and personality. Individuals with an agentic personality regard memories concerned with personal achievement as important, whereas those with a communal personality emphasize memories concerned with love and friendship.

How good are our autobiographical memories?

- Most people have excellent retention of information about their school classmates even several decades later because this information was very well learned. A few obsessional individuals have an exceptional ability to recall detailed information about their lives.

Key Term

Life script:
the typical major life events for individuals living within a given society; sample life events are getting married and having children.

Autobiographical memory system
- The self-memory system consists of hierarchically organized knowledge and the working self. Autobiographical memories can be accessed through voluntary or involuntary retrieval. Voluntary retrieval is influenced by the working self's goals, whereas involuntary retrieval is influenced by specific cues. Involuntary autobiographical memories enhance our sense of personal continuity in life.

Flashbulb memories
- Many people believe their flashbulb memories for dramatic events are more accurate than is actually the case. They underestimate the changes that occur to such memories over the first few days after the event and the impact of discussions about the event with other people.

Recovered memories
- People sometimes claim to have recovered memories of traumatic events that had been forgotten for many years. Traumatic memories recalled spontaneously are likely to be genuine. However, those recalled inside therapy are likely to be false memories produced by patients under the therapist's influence. These patients tend to be rather suggestible.

What do older people remember?
- Older people recall numerous personal memories from adolescence and early adulthood (the reminiscence bump). There is a much clearer reminiscence bump for positive than for negative memories. These positive memories often relate to events associated with a real sense of personal development and progress forming part of the life script (major life events based on cultural expectations).

EYEWITNESS TESTIMONY

Occasionally the accuracy (or otherwise) of an individual's memory is of enormous importance. Suppose you are the only eyewitness to a very serious crime in which someone is killed. Subsequently the person you identify as the murderer on a lineup is found guilty even though there is no other strong evidence. Such cases (and there are large numbers every year) raise the following question: Is it safe to rely on eyewitness testimony?

The introduction of DNA tests has made it easier to answer the above question. These tests can often help to establish whether the person convicted of a crime was actually the culprit. Note, however, that such tests can only indicate that a given individual was present at the scene of the crime, *not* that he/she committed the crime.

In the United States, about 200 people have been shown to be innocent by DNA tests. More than 75% were found guilty on the basis of mistaken eyewitness identification. In early 2008, DNA testing led to the release of Charles Chatman, who spent nearly 20 years in prison in Dallas County,

Texas. He was 20 years old when a young woman who had been raped picked him out from a lineup. As a result of her eyewitness testimony, Chatman was sentenced to 99 years in prison. On his last night in prison, Chatman said to the press: "I'm bitter, I'm angry. But I'm not angry or bitter to the point where I want to hurt anyone or get revenge."

POST-EVENT MISINFORMATION EFFECT

Why do you think eyewitnesses often make mistakes when recalling a crime they have observed? Perhaps the most obvious explanation is that eyewitnesses often fail to pay attention to the crime and to the criminal (or criminals). After all, the crime they observe typically occurs suddenly and unexpectedly. However, Elizabeth Loftus and John Palmer in 1974 argued it is *not* only what happens at the time of the crime that matters. According to them, eyewitness memories are fragile and can – surprisingly easily – be distorted by what happens *after* observing the crime. As we will see, misleading information provided after an event can produce distorted memories – the post-event misinformation effect.

In their well-known study (Loftus & Palmer, 1974), eyewitnesses were shown a film of a multiple-car accident. After viewing the film, they described what had happened and then answered specific questions. Some were asked, "About how fast were the cars going when they hit each other?" Others were asked the same question but with the word "hit" replaced by "collided," "bumped," "contacted," or "smashed into."

What did Loftus and Palmer (1974) find? Speed estimates were higher (40.8 mph) when the word "smashed" was used, lower with "collided" (39.3), and lower still with "bumped" (38.1) and "hit" (34). One week later, all the eyewitnesses were asked, "Did you see any broken glass?" In fact, there was no broken glass. However, 32% of those previously asked about speed using the verb "smashed" said they had seen broken glass. In contrast, only 14% of eyewitnesses who had been asked using the verb "hit" said they had seen broken glass. Thus, our memory for events is so fragile it can be distorted by changing ONE word in one question!

How worried should we be that eyewitnesses' memory can be systematically distorted by information presented after they observe a crime? In fact, most research has focused on distortions for peripheral or minor details (e.g., presence of broken glass) rather than central features. In one study (Dalton & Daneman, 2006), eyewitnesses watched a video clip of an action sequence and were then presented with misinformation about central and peripheral features. Memory distortions were much more common following misinformation about peripheral features than following misinformation about central ones. However, eyewitnesses showed some susceptibility to misinformation even about central features.

How does misleading post-event information distort what eyewitnesses report? One possibility is **source misattribution** (Johnson et al., 1993). The basic idea is that a memory probe (e.g., a question) activates memory traces overlapping with it in terms of information. Any memory probe may activate memories from various sources. The individual decides on the *source* of any activated memory on the basis of the information it contains. Source misattribution is likely when the memories from two sources resemble each other.

Key Terms

Post-event misinformation effect: the distorting effect on eyewitness memory of misleading information provided after the crime or other event.

Source misattribution: errors in long-term memory that occur when the rememberer is mistaken about the source or origin of a retrieved memory.

Evidence of source misattribution was reported by Allen and Lindsay (1998). They presented two narrative slide shows describing two events with different people in different settings. However, some details in the two events were similar (e.g., a can of Pepsi vs. a can of Coke). When eyewitnesses recalled the first event, some details from the second event were mistakenly recalled.

Several other factors contribute to the post-event misinformation effect (Wright & Loftus, 2008). First, misinformation is likely to be accepted when related information from the original event wasn't stored in memory. Second, post-event information and information from the original event are often combined in memory. Third, how a study is conducted may bias eyewitnesses towards reporting the misinformation rather than information from the original event.

REMEMBERING FACES

Information about the culprit's face is very often the most important information that eyewitnesses may or may not remember. We will consider factors determining whether culprits' faces are remembered (see also Chapter 2). In several countries, there has been a dramatic increase in the number of closed-circuit television (CCTV) cameras. How easy is it to identify someone from CCTV images? Burton et al. (1999) considered this question. They presented people with a target face taken from a CCTV video together with an array of 10 high-quality photographs (see Figure 6.4).

The participants' task in the Burton et al. (1999) study was to select the matching face or to decide the target face wasn't present in the array. When the target face was present, it was selected only 65% of the time. When it wasn't present, 35% of the participants nevertheless claimed that a face in the array matched the target face!

Eyewitnesses sometimes remember a face but fail to remember the precise circumstances in which they saw it. In one study (Ross et al., 1994), eyewitnesses observed an event in which there was a bystander as well as the culprit. Eyewitnesses were three times more likely to select the bystander than someone else they hadn't seen before from a line-up including the bystander but not the culprit. This is known as **unconscious transference** – a face is correctly recognized as having been that of someone seen before but incorrectly judged to be responsible for a crime. Ross et al. found that there was no unconscious transference effect when eyewitnesses were informed before seeing the line-up that the bystander and the culprit were not the same person.

Same-race faces are recognized better than cross-race faces – the **cross-race effect**. For example, Behrman and Davey (2001) found from an analysis of 271 actual criminal cases that the suspect was much more likely to be identified when he/she was of the same race as the eyewitness rather than a different race (60% vs. 45%, respectively).

How can we explain the cross-race effect? Expertise is a factor. Eyewitnesses having the most experience with members of another race often show a smaller cross-race effect than others (see review by Shriver et al., 2008). Alternatively, we may process the faces of individuals belonging to groups with which we identify (our ingroup) more thoroughly than those of individuals belonging to groups with which we don't identify (outgroups).

Key Terms

Unconscious transference: the tendency of eyewitnesses to misidentify a familiar (but innocent) face as belonging to the person responsible for a crime.

Cross-race effect: the finding that recognition memory for same-race faces is more accurate than for other-race faces.

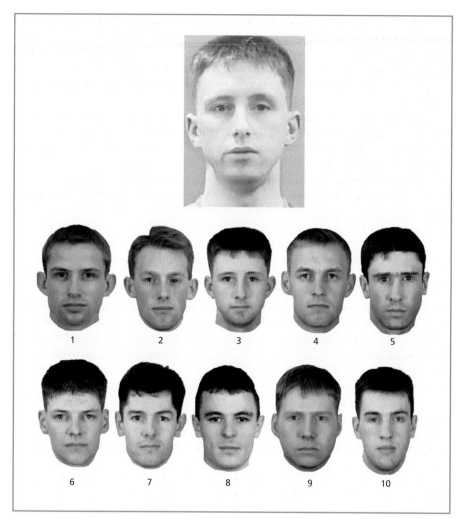

Figure 6.4 Example of full-face neutral target with an array used in the experiments. You may wish to attempt the task of establishing whether or not the target is present in this array and which one it is. The studio and video images used are from the Home Office Police Information Technology Organisation. Target is number 3. From Bruce et al. (1999), Copyright © 1999 American Psychological Association. Reprinted with permission.

Shriver et al. (2008) showed the importance of ingroup identification in a study among middle-class white students at the University of Miami. They saw photographs of college-aged males in impoverished contexts (e.g., dilapidated housing; rundown public spaces) or in wealthy contexts (e.g., large suburban homes; golf courses). They then received a test of recognition memory.

What did Shriver et al. (2008) find? There was the usual cross-race effect when white and black faces had been seen in wealthy contexts. However, the cross-race effect disappeared when white and black faces had been seen in impoverished contexts. The reason was that the white faces weren't regarded as belonging to the students' ingroup.

CONFIRMATION BIAS

Eyewitness testimony can be distorted via **confirmation bias**, i.e., event memory is influenced by the observer's expectations. In one study (Lindholm & Christianson, 1998), Swedish and immigrant students saw a videotaped simulated robbery in which the perpetrator seriously wounded a cashier with

> **Key Term**
>
> **Confirmation bias:** distortions of memory caused by the influence of expectations concerning what is likely to have happened.

a knife. After watching the video, participants were shown color photographs of eight men (four Swedes and four immigrants). Both Swedish and immigrant participants were twice as likely to select an innocent immigrant as an innocent Swede. Immigrants are overrepresented in Swedish crime statistics, and this influenced participants' expectations concerning the likely ethnicity of the criminal.

Bartlett (1932) argued that we possess numerous schemas (packets of knowledge – see Glossary) stored in long-term memory. These schemas lead us to form certain expectations and can distort our memory by causing us to reconstruct an event's details based on "what must have been true" (see Chapter 5). Most people's bank-robbery schema includes information that robbers are typically male, wear disguises and dark clothes, and have a getaway car with a driver (Tuckey & Brewer, 2003a). Tuckey and Brewer showed eyewitnesses a video of a simulated bank robbery followed by a memory test. As predicted by Bartlett's theory, eyewitnesses recalled information relevant to the bank-robbery schema better than irrelevant information (e.g., the color of the getaway car).

Tuckey and Brewer (2003b) focused on eyewitnesses' memory for ambiguous information. Some eyewitnesses saw a robber's head covered by a balaclava (ski mask) so the robber's gender was ambiguous. As predicted, eyewitnesses mostly interpreted the ambiguous information as being consistent with their bank-robbery schema. Thus, their recall was systematically distorted by including information from their bank-robbery schema even when it didn't correspond to what they had observed.

VIOLENCE AND ANXIETY

What are the effects of anxiety and violence on the accuracy of eyewitness memory? There is evidence for **weapon focus** – eyewitnesses attend to the criminal's weapon, which reduces their memory for other information. In one study, Loftus et al. (1987) asked participants to watch one of two sequences: (1) a person pointing a gun at a cashier and receiving some cash; (2) a person handing a check to the cashier and receiving some cash. The participants looked more at the gun than at the check. As predicted, memory for details unrelated to the gun/check was poorer in the weapon condition.

Pickel (2009) pointed out that people often attend to stimuli that are *unexpected* in a current situation (inconsistent with their schema of that situation). This impairs their memory for other stimuli. This led her to argue that the weapon focus effect will be greater when the presence of a weapon is very unexpected. As predicted, there was a stronger weapon focus effect when a criminal carrying a folding knife was female, because it is more unexpected to see a woman with a knife. Also as predicted, the weapon focus effect was greater when a criminal with a knitting needle was male rather than female.

What are the effects of stress and anxiety on eyewitness memory? In one study, students received an inoculation and had their pulse taken 2 minutes later (Peters, 1988). Two groups were formed: (1) those whose heart rate was much higher during inoculation than 2 minutes later (high reactive); and (2) those whose heart rate was similar on the two occasions (low reactive). Identification accuracy for the inoculating nurse was 31% for the high-reactive group and 59% for the low-reactive group. Thus, participants regarding the inoculation

| Key Term |

Weapon focus:
the finding that eyewitnesses pay so much attention to some crucial aspect of the situation (e.g., the weapon) that they ignore other details.

as stressful and anxiety-provoking showed much worse memory than those regarding it as innocuous.

Deffenbacher et al. (2004) combined the findings from several studies in a meta-analysis (see Glossary). On average, culprits' faces were identified 54% of the time in low-anxiety or low-stress conditions versus 42% for high-anxiety or high-stress conditions. The average proportion of details recalled correctly was 64% in low-stress conditions and 52% in high-stress conditions. Thus, stress and anxiety generally impair eyewitness memory.

FROM LABORATORY TO COURTROOM

Can we apply findings from laboratory studies to real-life crimes and eyewitnesses? There are several differences. First, eyewitnesses are much more likely to be the victims in real life than in the laboratory. Second, it is much less stressful to watch a video of a violent crime than to experience it in real life. Third, in laboratory research the consequences of an eyewitness making a mistake are trivial. However, they can literally be a matter of life or death in an American court of law.

In spite of these differences, there are important similarities. Ihlebaek et al. (2003) used a staged robbery involving two robbers armed with handguns. In the live condition, eyewitnesses were ordered repeatedly to "Stay down." A video taken during the live condition was presented to eyewitnesses in the video condition. Participants in both conditions exaggerated the duration of the event, and they showed similar patterns in terms of what was well and poorly remembered. However, eyewitnesses in the video condition recalled more information.

In a study by Pozzulo et al. (2008), eyewitnesses observed a staged theft live or via video. Identification accuracy of the culprit was comparable in the two conditions. However, eyewitnesses in the live condition reported more stress and arousal.

Tollestrup et al. (1994) analyzed police records concerning the identifications by eyewitnesses to crimes involving fraud and robbery. Factors found to be important in laboratory studies (e.g., weapon focus; retention interval) were also important in real-life crimes.

In sum, artificial laboratory conditions typically don't distort the findings. If anything, the errors in eyewitness memory obtained under laboratory conditions *underestimate* memory deficiencies for real-life events. Overall, laboratory research provides evidence of genuine relevance to the legal system.

COGNITIVE INTERVIEW

The cognitive interview (Geiselman & Fisher, 1997) is very effective at eliciting information from eyewitnesses. It is based on four general retrieval rules:

1. Mental reinstatement of the environment and any personal contact experienced during the crime.
2. Encouraging the reporting of every detail, including apparently minor ones.
3. Describing the incident in several different orders.
4. Reporting the incident from different viewpoints, including those of other eyewitnesses.

Köhnken et al. (1999) found across over 50 studies that the cognitive interview led to the recall of 41% more correct details than standard police interviews. However, the cognitive interview also produced slightly more errors on average than a standard interview.

The cognitive interview is effective because it is based on our knowledge of human memory. The first two rules above are based on the encoding specificity principle (Tulving, 1979; see Chapter 5). According to this principle, recall depends on the overlap or match between the context in which an event is witnessed and the context at recall. The third and fourth rules are based on the assumption that memory traces are complex and contain several kinds of information. As a result, information about a crime can be retrieved using different retrieval routes.

Perfect et al. (2008) compared recall when eyewitnesses closed their eyes or kept them open. Eyewitnesses recalled more visual and auditory details with no increase in false recall when their eyes were closed. This approach was effective because it reduced distraction from the immediate environment.

The cognitive interview involves several factors, some of which are more important than others. For example, it isn't essential for eyewitnesses to recall in different orders and from various perspectives. Ginet and Verkampt (2007) omitted those factors from the cognitive interview. They still found that 17% more details of a road accident were recalled with the cognitive interview than with a standard interview.

The cognitive interview has some limitations. First, it is less effective at enhancing recall when used at longer retention intervals (Geiselman & Fisher, 1997). Second, the cognitive interview increases the amount of *incorrect* information recalled by eyewitnesses, and this can lead detectives to misinterpret the evidence. Third, the cognitive interview doesn't reduce the adverse effects of misleading information provided after witnessing an incident (the post-event misinformation effect) (Centofanti & Reece, 2006).

Section Summary

- Eyewitness testimony is very important. Sometimes it leads to innocent individuals being wrongly imprisoned, as is indicated by DNA evidence.

Post-event misinformation effect
- Misleading information provided after an event can distort eyewitnesses' memory, especially for minor details. The post-event misinformation effect is sometimes due to source misattribution when memories from two sources resemble each other. Misinformation is likely to be accepted when related information wasn't stored at the time of the original event.

Remembering faces
- Face recognition is often poor, especially when the culprit is of a different race or ingroup to the eyewitness. Even when eyewitnesses recognize a face, they may misremember the circumstances in which they saw it originally.

Confirmation bias
- Eyewitnesses' memory can be distorted by their expectations based on schemas stored in long-term memory. For example, eyewitnesses tend to interpret ambiguous information about a bank robbery as being consistent with their bank-robbery schema (e.g., bank robbers are male).

Violence and anxiety
- When the criminal has a weapon, eyewitnesses attend to it (especially when it is unexpected in the context). Weapon focus leads to reduced memory for other information. Stress and anxiety impair memory for culprits' faces and details of the crime scene.

Cognitive interview
- The assumption that recall depends on the overlap between the recall context and that during an incident is central to the cognitive interview. The cognitive interview has proved very effective. However, the precise reasons remain unclear and it increases false memories.

PROSPECTIVE MEMORY

Think of occasions on which your memory has let you down. Perhaps you remember your mind going blank in the middle of an examination or forgetting someone's name when introducing two people to each other. These are failures of **retrospective memory**, which is concerned with remembering events, words, and so on from the past.

There is an important distinction between retrospective memory and prospective memory. **Prospective memory** involves remembering to carry out intended actions without being instructed to do so. In essence, it is remembering to remember. Failures of prospective memory (absentmindedness when action is required) can be as frustrating and embarrassing as failures of retrospective memory. For example, think of occasions you completely forgot you had arranged to meet a friend.

How else do prospective and retrospective memory differ other than in their respective emphasis on the future or the past? Retrospective memory generally involves remembering *what* we know about something and is often high in information content. In contrast, prospective memory typically focuses on *when* to do something, and has low information content (Baddeley et al., 2009). Another difference is that prospective memory is generally more directly related to our plans, motives, and goals than is retrospective memory. Finally, as Moscovitch (2008, p. 309) pointed out, "Research on prospective memory is about the only major enterprise in memory research in which the problem is not memory itself, but the uses to which memory is put."

We shouldn't exaggerate the differences between prospective and retrospective memory. For example, both types of memory involve responding in light of what has been learned previously. A questionnaire-based study revealed the existence of a general memory factor including both prospective and retrospective memory (Crawford et al., 2003).

| Key Terms |

Retrospective memory: memory for events, words, people, and so on encountered or experienced in the past; see **prospective memory**.

Prospective memory: remembering to carry out some intended action in the absence of any explicit reminder to do so; see **retrospective memory**.

Remembering often involves a mixture of prospective and retrospective memory. For example, suppose you agree to buy various supermarket goods for yourself and the friends with whom you share an apartment. Two things need to happen. First, you must remember your intention to go to the supermarket (prospective memory). Even if you remember to go to the supermarket, you then have to remember precisely what you had agreed to buy (retrospective memory).

Age has similar effects on prospective and retrospective memory. Retrospective memory declines with age (Baddeley et al., 2009) and so does prospective memory. Uttl (2008) carried out a meta-analysis combining the findings from many studies and found a steady age-related decline in prospective memory. This decline was especially great when there were large demands on processing resources. These age effects on prospective memory were confirmed by Maylor and Logie (2010) in an Internet study with over 300,000 participants. Prospective memory performance was best among teenagers, and there was a steady decline through the twenties, thirties, and forties.

In the Real World 6.2: *Airplane crashes*

More than 50% of fatal accidents involving aircraft are due to pilot error. Dismukes and Nowinski (2007) studied reports submitted to the Aviation Safety Reporting System (ARAS) relating to incidents and accidents. They uncovered 75 reports in which memory failure was important. In 74 cases, there was a failure of prospective memory, with only one case involving retrospective memory!

Why were there practically no failures of retrospective memory? The main reason is that airline pilots receive lengthy and demanding training. As a result, they have excellent knowledge and memory of all the operations needed to fly a plane.

Here is a concrete example of an airplane crash due to a failure of prospective memory. On August 31, 1988, a Boeing 727 (Flight 1141) was held in a long line awaiting departure from Dallas–Fort Worth airport. The air traffic controller unexpectedly told the crew to move up past the other airplanes to the runway. This caused the crew to forget to set the wing flaps and leading edge slats to 15° (a failure of prospective memory). As a result, the plane crashed a few thousand feet beyond the end of the runway, leading to several deaths.

Pilots often suffer from failures of prospective memory due to interruptions. Latorella (1998) found that commercial pilots interrupted while flying a simulator made 53% more errors than those who weren't interrupted. Of course, interruptions occur frequently in most workplaces. However, such failures can have far more serious consequences for pilots than for most other workers (Loukopoulos et al., 2009).

How can we reduce the negative effects of interruptions on prospective memory? Some answers were provided by Dodhia and Dismukes (2009). Participants answered blocks of questions, each containing different types of question (e.g., math; vocabulary). If an interrupting block of questions was presented before they completed one block, they were told to return to the interrupted block after completing the interrupting block.

When the interruption was followed immediately by the interrupting block, only 48% of the participants resumed the interrupted block afterwards (see Figure 6.5). In another condition, 63% of participants who spent 4 s staring at a blank screen after being interrupted returned to the interrupted block. In a further condition, there was a pause of 10 s between the end of the interrupting block and the start of the next block. In this condition, 88% of the participants resumed the interrupted task.

What do the above findings mean? They indicate that it is important for people to have a few seconds in which to form a new plan when an unexpected interruption changes the situation. It is also important to have a few seconds at the end of an interruption to recall the intention of returning to the interrupted task. The take-home message is as follows: When interrupted, pause briefly while you develop a new plan to carry out all your intended actions.

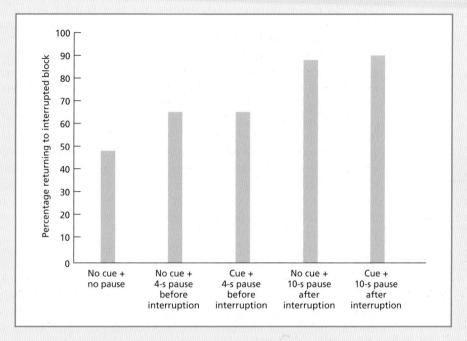

Figure 6.5   Percentages of participants returning to an interrupted task as a function of cuing and pause duration before or after interruption. Data from Dodhia and Dismukes (2009).

TYPES OF PROSPECTIVE MEMORY

Prospective memory (whether event-based or time-based) consists of five stages (Ellis & Cohen, 2008):

1. *Encoding:* The individual stores away information about *what* action needs to be performed, *when* the action needs to be performed, and the *intention* to act.
2. *Retention:* The stored information has to be retained over a period of time.
3. *Retrieval:* When a suitable opportunity presents itself, the intention has to be retrieved from long-term memory.
4. *Execution:* When the intention is retrieved, it needs to be acted upon.
5. *Evaluation:* The outcome of the preceding stages is evaluated. If prospective memory has failed, there is replanning.

Even though they both involve the five stages outlined above, we can distinguish between time-based and event-based prospective memory. **Time-based prospective memory** involves remembering to perform a given action at a given time (e.g., arriving at a café at 8.00 pm). In contrast, **event-based prospective memory** involves remembering to perform an action in the right circumstances (e.g., passing on a message when you see someone).

Sellen et al. (1997) equipped participants with badges containing buttons. They were told to press their button at prespecified times (time-based task) or when in a prespecified place (event-based task). Prospective memory was better on the event-based task than on the time-based task (52% vs. 33%, respectively). This was so even though participants given the event-based task spent less time thinking about it.

Kim and Mayhorn (2008) compared time-based and event-based prospective memory in naturalistic situations and the laboratory over a one-week period. Event-based memory was superior to time-based memory. There was also a general tendency for prospective memory to be better under naturalistic conditions, perhaps because participants were more motivated to remember intentions under such conditions.

How similar are the strategies used during the retention interval on event-based and time-based tasks? Time-based tasks more often lack external cues to perform the required action than do event-based tasks, and thus are often harder. As a result, we might predict that people performing time-based tasks would be more likely to use deliberate self-initiated processes to rehearse intended actions.

Lia Kvavilashvili and Laura Fisher (2007) tested the above hypothesis, but found the strategies were remarkably similar for both tasks. Participants made a phone call at a given time after an interval of one week (time-based task) or as soon as they received a certain text message (event-based task) that arrived after one week. There were nine rehearsals on average over the week with the time-based task and seven with the event-based task. About 50% of the rehearsals with both tasks occurred automatically (i.e., the task simply popped into the participant's mind).

Hicks et al. (2005) argued that the notion that event-based tasks are easy and time-based ones are hard is oversimplified. What also matters is whether the target is well or poorly specified. Consider two event-based tasks. One is well specified (detect the words *nice* and *hit*) and the other is poorly specified (detect animal names). Hicks et al. found for both event-based and time-based tasks that more processing resources were required when the target was poorly specified.

MONITORING

Tap your forehead 3–5 s after reading this sentence. That is an unusual request. However, I will explain the reason for asking you to do this in a moment.

What happened on the above prospective memory task? I imagine you *monitored* (paid attention to) the passing of time to maximize the chance that you tapped your forehead at the right time. Monitoring is central to the preparatory attentional and memory processes (PAM) theory (Smith, 2003; Smith & Bayen, 2005). According to this theory, a monitoring process starts when an individual forms an intention and is maintained until the required action is performed. Monitoring is demanding because it involves capacity-consuming processes such as those involved in attention.

Smith (2003) tested the above hypothesis. Participants decided as rapidly as possible whether letter strings formed words (lexical decision task). This task was performed on its own or at the same time as a prospective memory task – pressing a button whenever a target word was presented. The key findings related to performance on trials on which a target word was *not* presented. Lexical decision was much slower for participants performing the prospective memory task than those not doing it (1061 ms vs. 726 ms). Thus, the monitoring associated with a prospective memory task can utilize processing resources and so impair performance on another task.

Smith et al. (2007) considered the effects of a very simple prospective memory task (pressing the key "P" on a keyboard whenever a pink stimulus was presented). This task had a disruptive effect on performance speed of the central task carried out at the same time. Thus, monitoring and/or attentional processes can be involved even with apparently very undemanding prospective memory tasks.

However, the notion that we *always* engage in monitoring when trying to remember to perform some action in the future seems implausible. For example, if you have the intention of going to the movies this evening, it is unlikely you are going to monitor that intention throughout the entire day. Evidence suggesting that monitoring is infrequent was reported by Reese and Cherry (2002) in a prospective memory study. Participants were interrupted at various points during the main task and asked what they were thinking about. Only 2% of the time did they report thinking about the prospective memory task.

Processing on prospective memory tasks is flexible and depends on the precise conditions. For example, consider the following study by Scullin et al. (2010). Participants were given a lexical decision task in which they decided rapidly whether each letter string formed a word. At the same time, they performed a prospective memory task which involved pressing a button whenever a target item was detected. In one condition, the target was the word *generous*, and in another condition it was initial letter *g*.

The prospective memory task didn't slow down performance on the lexical decision task with the word target but did with the letter target. Thus, participants didn't engage in monitoring with the word target but did with the letter target. Why was this? The lexical decision task required participants to process the letter strings as words. This made it easy for participants to respond to the word target even in the absence of monitoring. In contrast, the processing on the lexical decision task didn't focus attention on the first letter of each string. As a result, participants needed to monitor the first letter with the initial-letter target.

The findings of Scullin et al. (2010) are as predicted by multiprocess theory (Einstein & McDaniel, 2005). According to this theory, monitoring is needed on prospective memory tasks when the ongoing task doesn't direct attention to the target. In contrast, spontaneous retrieval (and an absence of monitoring) occurs when the ongoing task *directs attention* to the target. Thus, the processes we use on prospective memory tasks vary between fairly demanding ones (e.g., monitoring) and those imposing very few demands (e.g., relatively automatic ones).

IMPROVING PROSPECTIVE MEMORY

The simplest way of improving your prospective memory is to use external memory aids (objects or devices designed to assist memory). There is an enormous number of such memory aids. Examples include diaries, calendars, knotted handkerchiefs, shopping lists, sticky notes, smartphones, and alarm clocks (Herrmann et al., 2006). For example, if I have to take some books or papers into work the next day, I typically put them on top of the desk in my study to ensure that I remember them.

Another way of improving your prospective memory is to take steps to prevent unexpected interruptions from causing you to forget to carry out an intended action. Such interruptions often mean your original plan can't be implemented as anticipated. As a result, it is necessary to take a few seconds to produce a new action plan.

It is especially important to think of the *context* in which an intended action is likely to be carried out when you form the intention. Consider a study by Cook et al. (2005), in which participants were told to make a response after between 6 and 7 minutes had elapsed. In one condition, participants expected this time window to occur during the third phase of the experiment when they were engaged in a specified task. When this expectation about the context in which the intended action was to be performed was true, 71% of the participants performed the prospective memory task correctly. This compared to only 48% in the control condition who had no expectation.

The above findings suggest that prospective memory is good when there is a *match* between the information stored initially and that available at the time the intended action should be produced. Matching of stored information and that available at the time of retrieval is also important in retrospective memory and is incorporated into the encoding specificity principle (see Glossary and Chapter 5).

Hannon and Daneman (2007) considered performance on the prospective memory task of pressing a key whenever they saw the name of any of four categories or members of any category (target items). They argued that three factors influence performance. First, there is the initial encoding of information about the targets and a plan for performing the intended action. Second, there is the retrieval of information about the targets when the response needs to be made. Third, there is the match between the encoding information and the retrieved information. Prospective memory performance depended far more on the extent of the match than on the other two factors.

Section Summary

Introduction
- Prospective memory involves remembering to carry out actions without being instructed to do so. It relates to our plans and goals. Prospective memory focuses on when to do something, whereas retrospective memory focuses on remembering what we know.

Airplane crashes
- Many airplane crashes involve failures of prospective memory. These failures often occur as a result of interruptions. Prospective memory failures can be reduced by forming a new plan after an unexpected interruption has changed the situation.

> **Types of prospective memory**
> * Event-based prospective memory is often better than time-based prospective memory. In addition, it is also often less demanding because more external cues are available. However, the demands of a prospective memory task depend on how well specified the target is as well as on the type of task.
>
> **Monitoring**
> * Monitoring and/or attentional processes are often involved even with apparently very undemanding prospective memory tasks. However, there is an absence of monitoring when the ongoing task directs attention to the target on the prospective memory task.
>
> **Improving prospective memory**
> * Prospective memory can be improved by using external memory aids. It can also be improved by ensuring that contextual information stored at the time an intention is formed matches that likely to be available when the intended action should be performed.

MEMORY EXPERTISE

Those of us with only average memory ability often envy those who have exceptional memories and feel we might learn something from them. However, there can be disadvantages in having an amazing memory. For example, Shereshevskii (often known as S) could almost effortlessly commit to memory lists of more than 100 digits, long strings of nonsense syllables, or poetry in unknown languages (Luria, 1968).

Why was S's memory so outstanding? He made extensive use of **synesthesia**, which is the capacity for a stimulus in one sense modality to evoke an image in another. S found it very hard to forget anything, which meant his memory was cluttered up with all sorts of information he didn't want to recall. As a result, many people thought he was disorganized and unintelligent. He eventually solved his inability to forget by imagining the information he didn't want to remember on a blackboard and then imagining himself rubbing it out!

A little later, we will consider a few individuals with exceptional memories. We will focus on the strategies they use to attain exceptional levels of memory performance. Before that, we will discuss some of the memory strategies we can all use to improve our memory.

MNEMONICS

Every self-help book designed to improve your memory provides many examples of effective mnemonic techniques (e.g., McPherson, 2004). Indeed, there are more such techniques than you can shake a stick at. Here we will focus on a few of the most important mnemonic techniques, assessing their strengths and limitations.

> **Key Term**
>
> **Synesthesia:**
> a sensory experience in which a stimulus in one sense modality (e.g., hearing) evokes an image in a second sense modality (e.g., vision).

Visual imagery: Method of loci and pegword technique

Mnemonics are techniques used to improve memory. Some of the most effective mnemonics involve visual imagery. For example, there is the **method of loci**. What happens is that the to-be-remembered items of information are associated with well-known locations (e.g., places along a walk) (see Research Activity 6.2).

Research Activity 6.2: *Method of loci*

Think of 10 locations in your home, choosing them so that the sequence of moving from one to the next is obvious; for example, from front door to entrance hall to kitchen to bedroom. Check that you can imagine moving through your 10 locations in a consistent order without difficulty. Now think of 10 items and imagine them in those locations. If your first item is a *pipe*, you might imagine it poking out of the letterbox in your front door with great clouds of smoke billowing into the street. If the second item is a *cabbage*, you might imagine your hall obstructed by an enormous cabbage, and so on. When it comes to recall, walk mentally the route around your house.

Now try to create similarly striking images associating your 10 chosen locations with the words below:

shirt
eagle
paperclip
rose
camera
mushroom
crocodile
handkerchief
sausage
mayor

The same set of locations can be used repeatedly as long as only the most recent item in a given location is remembered.

Try to recall the 10 items listed two paragraphs ago. No, don't look! Rely on the images you created.

The method of loci is often remarkably effective. Bower (1973) compared recall of five lists of 20 nouns each for groups using (or not using) the method of loci. The former group recalled 72% of the nouns against only 28% for the latter group. Kondo et al. (2004) confirmed that the method of loci enhances memory. It was associated with greater brain activation than participants' customary learning techniques, suggesting it involves more complex and elaborate processes.

The effectiveness of the method of loci depends on which locations are used. Massen et al. (2009) found that the method of loci led to better recall when based on a route to work

Key Terms

Mnemonics:
these consist of numerous methods or systems that learners can use to enhance their long-term memory for information.

Method of loci:
a memory technique in which the items that are to be remembered are associated with various locations that are well known to the learner.

rather than a route in the participant's house. An individual's route to work is generally more constant than the ways they move around their own house, and is thus easier to use.

The method of loci is limited in that it is hard to recall any given item without working your way through the list until you come to it. Another apparent limitation occurs when the method of loci is used with several lists of items. If the same locations are used with each list, there is a danger of proactive interference (previous learning disrupting the learning and memory of subsequent lists). In fact, however, there is little or no proactive interference using the method of loci provided the words on successive lists are dissimilar (Massen & Vaterrodt-Plünnecke, 2006).

It is often argued that the method of loci isn't useful when people learn material in the real world. De Beni et al. (1997) addressed this issue. They presented a 2000-word text orally or in written form to students who used the method of loci or rehearsed parts of the text. Memory was tested shortly after presentation and 1 week later.

The method of loci led to much better recall than rehearsal at both retention intervals with oral presentation of the material. Thus, it was very effective when there was a lecture-style presentation. In contrast, there was *no* effect of learning method when the text was presented in written form. Similar findings were reported by De Beni and Moè (2003). The method of loci was ineffective with written presentation because the visual nature of the presentation interfered with the use of visual imagery associated with the method of loci.

The pegword system resembles the method of loci in that it relies on visual imagery and allows you to remember sequences of 10 unrelated items. First of all you memorize 10 pegwords. As each pegword rhymes with a number from one to ten, this is relatively easy. Try it for yourself:

One = bun Two = shoe Three = tree Four = door Five = hive Six = sticks Seven = heaven Eight = gate Nine = wine Ten = hen

Having mastered this, you are ready to memorize 10 unrelated words. Suppose these are as follows: battleship, pig, chair, sheep, castle, rug, grass, beach, milkmaid, binoculars. Take the first pegword (bun) and form an image of a bun interacting with a battleship (e.g., a battleship sailing into an enormous floating bun). Now take the second pegword (shoe) and imagine it interacting with a pig (e.g., a large shoe with a pig sitting in it). Work through the rest of the items forming a suitable interactive image in each case.

The pegword technique is very effective. Morris and Reid (1970) found it doubled the number of words recalled. Other research indicates it is as effective as the method of loci (Wang & Thomas, 2000). However, the technique has some limitations. First, it requires extensive training. Second, it is easier to use with concrete than with abstract material. For example, it isn't easy to form interactive images involving abstract concepts (e.g., *morality*; *insincerity*). Third, there are doubts about its applicability to real life, since we rarely need to remember a sequence of several unrelated items.

Visual imagery: Remembering names

Most people have problems remembering names. When being introduced to someone new, we tend to look at them and make whatever initial remarks are appropriate, with the result that their name "goes in one ear and out the other." It can be socially embarrassing if you have to admit you have completely forgotten someone's name.

One way of remembering people's names is based on a visual imagery mnemonic. You start by searching for an imageable substitute for the person's name (e.g., Eysenck becomes "ice sink"). Then some prominent feature of the person's face is selected, and the image is linked with that feature. For example, the nose might be regarded as a tap over the sink. Brief training in this method improved recall of names to faces by almost 80% under laboratory conditions (Morris et al., 1978). This finding is consistent with much evidence that long-term memory is better for information previously processed in a distinctive fashion (Eysenck, 1979).

The imagery mnemonic for learning names works well in the peace and quiet of the laboratory. In real-life social situations, however, it may be hard to form good imagery mnemonics. Morris et al. (2005) invited university students to attend a party having received instructions about learning the names of the other students there. One group was trained to use the imagery mnemonic. A second group was told to try to retrieve the names at increasing intervals after first hearing them (expanded retrieval practice). There was also a control group simply told to learn people's names. Between 24 and 72 hours after the party, the students were shown photographs of the students who had been at the party and wrote their names underneath.

Students in the expanded retrieval practice condition recalled 50% more names than those in the control group. The imagery mnemonic was even less effective than no specific memorizing strategy. Thus, it is important to combine use of the visual imagery mnemonic with repeated attempts to recall the name.

Verbal techniques

There are several verbal mnemonics (see Baddeley et al., 2009). One of the most effective is the story method. It is used to remember a series of unrelated words in the correct order by linking them together within the context of a story. Note that the story method often involves the use of visual imagery as well as producing sentences. Suppose we apply the story method to the 10 words used to illustrate use of the pegword technique:

In the kitchen of the battleship, there was a pig that sat in a chair. There was also a sheep that had previously lived in a castle. In port, the sailors took a rug and sat on the grass close to the beach. While there, they saw a milkmaid watching them through her binoculars.

Bower and Clark (1969) showed that the story method can be very effective. They gave participants the task of recalling 12 lists of 10 words each in the correct order when given the first word of each list as a cue. Those who had formed narrative stories recalled 93% of the words compared to only 13% for those who didn't do so.

The story method is limited in that it requires fairly extensive training – it took me a few minutes to form the story given above! Another limitation is that you generally have to work your way through the list if you want to find a given item (e.g., the seventh one).

Why do mnemonic techniques work?

The success of mnemonic techniques owes much to the fact that they allow us to use our knowledge (e.g., about familiar walks). However, detailed knowledge isn't always enough. Suppose we asked taxi drivers and students to recall lists of streets in the city in which they lived. You might imagine that the taxi drivers (with their superb knowledge of the spatial layout of the city's streets) would always outperform the students. That is *not* the case. Kalakoski and Saariluoma (2001) asked Helsinki taxi drivers and students to recall lists of 15 Helsinki street names in the order presented. The taxi drivers did much better than the students when the streets formed a continuous route through the city. However, their advantage disappeared when nonadjacent street names taken from all over Helsinki were presented in a random order.

What can we conclude from the study by Kalakoski and Saariluoma (2001)? What is crucial is *organization* – the taxi drivers couldn't use their special knowledge effectively to organize the to-be-remembered information when the street names were random.

Why are techniques such as the method of loci, the pegword method, and the story method so effective? According to Ericsson (1988), there are three requirements to achieve very high memory skills:

1. *Meaningful encoding:* The information should be processed meaningfully, relating it to pre-existing knowledge. This is clearly the case when you use known locations (method of loci) or the number sequence (pegword method), or when taxi drivers use their knowledge of their own town or city. This is the encoding principle.
2. *Retrieval structure:* Cues should be stored with the information to aid subsequent retrieval. The connected series of locations or the number sequence provide an immediately accessible retrieval structure, as does the knowledge of spatial layout possessed by taxi drivers. This is the retrieval structure principle.
3. *Speed-up:* Extensive practice allows the processes involved in encoding and retrieval to function faster and faster. The importance of extensive practice can be seen in the generally superior memory for street names shown by taxi drivers compared to students in Kalakoski and Saariluoma's (2001) study. This is the speed-up principle.

We can see the above principles at work in a study by Ericsson and Chase (1982) on somebody called "SF." He was paid to practice the digit-span task for 1 hour a day for 2 years. The digit span (the number of random digits that can be repeated back in the correct order) is typically about 6 or 7 items. SF eventually attained a span of 80 items!

How did SF do it? He reached a digit span of 18 items by using his extensive knowledge of running times (encoding and retrieval principles). For example, if the first few digits were "3594" he would note this was Bannister's time for the first sub-four-minute mile, and so he would store these digits away as a single chunk or unit. He then increased his digit span to 80 items by organizing

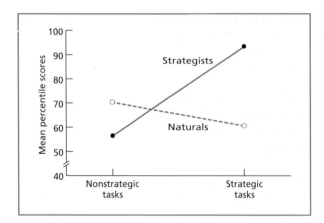

Figure 6.6 Memory performance strategists and naturals on strategic and nonstrategic tasks. Data from Wilding and Valentine (1994).

those chunks into a hierarchical structure and by extensive practice (the speed-up principle). Sadly, his outstanding digit span didn't generalize to other memory tasks – SF had only average letter and word spans.

INDIVIDUALS WITH EXCEPTIONAL MEMORY

Why are some people's memories far better than those of the rest of us? Are they "naturally" gifted, or have they simply devoted much time to developing effective mnemonic techniques? To answer this question, John Wilding and Liz Valentine (1994) tested contestants at the World Memory Championships and audience members with outstanding memory abilities. They classified their participants into two groups:

1. *Strategists:* those who reported frequent use of memory strategies.
2. *Naturals:* those who claimed naturally superior memory ability from early childhood, and who had a close relative with excellent memory ability.

Both groups were given two kinds of memory task. There were strategic tasks (e.g., associating names with faces) that are susceptible to the use of memory strategies. There were also nonstrategic tasks (e.g., recognition of snow crystals) that don't lend themselves to memory strategies. The participants' performance was compared to that of a control group of individuals with average memory.

What Wilding and Valentine (1994) found is shown in Figure 6.6. The 50th percentile represents the average score in the control group, and so both groups did better than that on both kinds of memory task. However, the most impressive memory performance (surpassing more than 90% of the population) was obtained by strategists on strategic tasks. Thus, an excellent memory is due more to training than to natural ability.

Several individuals with exceptional memory have been studied in recent years. Most of them share two characteristics. First, they have devoted much time to developing effective memory strategies. Second, their general memory ability is surprisingly average.

Chao Lu set a new world record on November 20, 2005 when he recited pi to 67,890 digits. He averaged 1.28 digits per second and took a total of 24 hours and 4 minutes. His main memory strategy involved grouping digits into pairs, forming a visual image, and then turning these images into words. For example, the sequence 21148 became "At a volcano *cave*, *crocodile* ate one piece of *rose*, and found a *gourd*." In spite of his outstanding performance, Chao Lu's visual digit span was only average. This was probably because he had insufficient time to use his usual memory strategies.

PI recited pi to over 64,000 digits at the age of 22 (Raz et al., 2009). He used a modified form of the method of loci to learn this digit sequence, considering the digits two at a time. Sometimes he converted two-digit groups to words based on the similarity of their pronunciations. At other times he generated images resembling the physical characteristics of the digits (e.g., 10 looks like a putter and a hole and led to the word *golf*). Then PI produced stories based on his earlier processing. Surprisingly, PI's visual memory for neutral faces and common events was very poor.

An important reason why PI was so successful is that his working memory abilities exceed those of 99% of the population. As part of their study, Raz et al. (2009) assessed brain activity while PI recited the first 540 digits of pi in the laboratory. Areas within the prefrontal cortex associated with working memory and attentional control were activated.

Thompson et al. (1991) argued that Rajan Mahadevan was an exception to the general rule that individuals with exceptional memory are made rather than born. For several years, Rajan held the world record for memorizing the highest number of digits of pi (31,811). He had a digit span of 59 for visually presented digits and 63 for heard digits. Thompson et al. claimed that Rajan divided digit strings into groups of 10 to 15 digits during learning (several times more than other memory experts) because his basic memory capacity was far greater than that of other people.

Ericsson et al (2004) disagreed with Thompson et al. (1991). They found that Rajan's initial symbol span using various symbols (e.g., ?, @, *) was only six, which is about average for college students. In addition, his memory for word lists and stories was only average. These findings cast much doubt on the notion that Rajan has an innately superior memory capacity.

In sum, individuals such as Chao Lu and PI have a three-stage approach to memorizing huge numbers of digits. First, adjacent digits are formed into small groups or chunks. Second, a visual image or word is used to represent each chunk. Third, language is used to combine and integrate the information from successive chunks. Tomoyari, an individual with exceptional memory who recited the first 40,000 digits of pi in 1987, used a similar learning strategy (Takahashi et al., 2006). As you might imagine, all of these memorists devoted thousands of hours to the seemingly impossible task of being able to recite tens of thousands of digits of pi.

Section Summary

Mnemonics
- The method of loci is very effective. It can be used with orally presented lectures as well as word lists, but is ineffective with written texts. The pegword technique is also effective, but requires extensive training. Forming distinctive images can enhance face–name associations provided that sufficient time is available to do so. The story method is an effective verbal technique, but it requires extensive training. Most mnemonic techniques involve meaningful encoding, retrieval structure, and extensive practice.

Individuals with exceptional memory

• Some individuals have dramatically better memories than most people. The reason is typically that they have devoted considerable time to developing effective memory strategies. This is indicated by the fact that most of them have only average performance on memory tasks ill-suited to their memory strategies. Individuals with exceptional memory learning huge numbers of digits often form visual images of grouped digits, and then use language to combine successive groups.

Essay Questions

1. Why are some autobiographical memories much easier to recall than others?
2. "Eyewitness testimony is generally inaccurate and prone to error." Discuss.
3. What factors determine whether or not we remember to perform intended actions?
4. Describe some of the main mnemonic techniques. How useful are they in everyday life?

Further Reading

- Baddeley, A., Eysenck, M. W., & Anderson, M. C. (2009). *Memory*. New York, NY: Psychology Press. This memory textbook contains detailed accounts of most of the topics discussed in this chapter.
- Ellis, J. A., & Cohen, G. (2008). Memory for intentions, actions, and plans. In G. Cohen & M. Conway (Eds.), *Memory in the real world* (3rd ed., pp. 141–172). Hove, UK: Psychology Press. Judi Ellis and Gillian Cohen discuss a wide range of issues relating to prospective memory in this chapter.
- Hunt, R. R., & Worthen, J. B. (2010). *Mnemonology: Mnemonics for the 21st century*. New York, NY: Psychology Press. Reed Hunt and James Worthen identify the underlying cognitive processes responsible for numerous successful mnemonic techniques.
- Lindsay, R. C. L., Ross, D. F., Read, J. D., & Toglia, M. P. (Eds.). (2006). *The handbook of eyewitness psychology: Volume II: Memory for people*. Mahwah, NJ: Lawrence Erlbaum Associates. This edited book contains contributions from the world's leading experts on eyewitness memory for people.
- Loukopoulos, L. D., Dismukes, R. K., & Barshi, I. (2009). *The multitasking myth: Handling complexity in real-world operations*. Burlington, VT: Ashgate. This book deals with the main reasons for pilot error, including an emphasis on problems with prospective memory.
- Morris, P. E., & Fritz, C. O. (2006). How to ... improve your memory. *The Psychologist, 19*, 608–611. Peter Morris and Catherine Fritz discuss several ways of improving your memory based on solid experimental evidence.
- Williams, H. L., Conway, M. A., & Cohen, G. (2008). Autobiographical memory. In G. Cohen and M. Conway (Eds.), *Memory in the real world* (3rd ed., pp. 21–90). Hove, UK: Psychology Press. An extensive review of research on autobiographical memory including Martin Conway's theoretical approach.

Chapter 7

Contents

General knowledge

7

INTRODUCTION

We all possess huge amounts of general knowledge about words and about the world in which we live. You probably know the meanings of at least 20,000 words, you know the name of the current President of the United States, that London is the capital of England, and so on. This general knowledge is stored in semantic memory (discussed in Chapter 5).

It is almost impossible to exaggerate the importance of this general knowledge in our everyday lives. For example, your ability to perceive the animal in front of you as a dog or a cat depends on relating sensory information to relevant knowledge in semantic memory.

General knowledge is also important when memorizing information. For example, consider the task of learning a categorized word list consisting of, say, four words belonging to each of six categories (e.g., four-footed animals; girls' names). Subsequent recall is much higher when the words are presented in their categories rather than in random order (Shuell, 1969). This is because it is

---

Learning Objectives

After studying Chapter 7, you should be able to:

- Define concepts and categories, and explain their importance to human cognition.
- Describe the hierarchical levels by which concepts may be categorized.
- Compare and contrast the prototype approach, the exemplar approach, and the knowledge-based approach to conceptual categorization.
- Explain the spreading activation theory of semantic memory.
- Define schemas and scripts, and discuss how they are helpful to human functioning but also their shortcomings.
- Apply knowledge of top-down and bottom-up processing to explain the boundary extension phenomenon.
- Discuss how stereotypes are assessed implicitly and explicitly, and how they might affect human cognition and behavior.

much easier to use category knowledge to organize the material during learning and retrieval when the words are presented category by category.

General knowledge is also vital when it comes to making sense of what you read. Consider the following: *Tom was driving along when a tire on his car blew. He arrived home very late.* You would use your general knowledge to work out that the blown tire forced Tom to stop immediately, and he didn't have a spare tire readily available to replace it.

A substantial amount of our general knowledge relates to individual words or concepts. For example, we know that cats are smallish animals having four legs, fur, a tail, and so on. However, knowledge of the meanings of numerous words and concepts would be totally insufficient to allow us to interact successfully with the world around us.

We also need to store schemas (well-integrated packets of information; see Glossary) in semantic memory. For example, we have a *house* schema. This schema typically contains the following information: a house is a building (generally rectangular) with several rooms in which people live; it is usually made of bricks, stone, or wood.

FURTHER FUNCTIONS OF CONCEPTS

Look around you and describe to yourself what you can see. In my own case, I am word processing in my study at home. I can see a lamp, a desk, a printer, a computer, several books, a few photographs, and trees out in the garden.

You may be thinking, "So what?" This would involve missing an important point. You understood my description even though it wasn't very detailed and specific. For example, I didn't point out that the lamp is made of metal and is adjustable, nor did I indicate that the desk is made of light brown wood with a black top. This suggests we generally focus on the essentials of objects or concepts and don't clutter our minds with irrelevant details.

Why is so much of our knowledge of the world stored in the form of concepts? The single most important reason is that concepts provide a very *efficient* way of representing our knowledge of the world and the objects in it. Concepts allow us to focus on the *similarities* among objects that resemble each other but aren't identical.

Another function of concepts is that they permit us to make accurate *predictions* about objects in the world (Heit, 1992). For example if we categorize an animal as a cat, we can predict it is unlikely to do us any harm. In contrast, if we categorize an animal as a lion, we can predict that it may be dangerous and so take avoiding action.

A further function of concepts is *communication*. When we have conversations with other people, we constantly use concepts to convey information about ourselves and the world as we understand it.

What would it be like to be unable to categorize your experience? The South American writer Jorge-Luis Borges (1964, pp. 93–94) answered this question when he described the experiences of a fictional man called Funes who found himself in that situation:

Funes remembered not only every leaf of every tree of every wood, but also every one of the times he had perceived or imagined it … Not only was it difficult for him to comprehend that the symbol dog embraces so many unlike individuals of diverse size and form; it bothered him that the dog at three fourteen (seen from the side) should have the same name as the dog at three fifteen (seen from the front). His own face in the mirror, his own hands, surprised him every time he saw them.

Contrary to what is often believed, deciding whether an object belongs to a category is often very unclear and open to debate. Consider the concept of a *planet*, which has historically been defined as a large body circling a sun. That definition came under pressure a few years ago. Pluto is regarded as a planet, but it is smaller and its orbit is less circular than those of other objects in our solar system.

There are numerous other cases where category membership is unclear. McCloskey and Glucksberg (1978) asked 30 people tricky questions such as, "Is a stroke a disease?" and "Is a pumpkin a fruit?" They found that 16 said a stroke is a disease and 14 said it wasn't. A pumpkin was regarded as a fruit by 16 people but not as a fruit by the remainder. More surprisingly, when McCloskey and Glucksberg tested the same people a month later, 11 had changed their minds about *stroke* being a disease, and eight had altered their opinion about *pumpkin* being a fruit!

There are considerable individual differences in beliefs about the nature of category membership. Some individuals believe that category membership should be all-or-none whereas others have more flexible beliefs (Simmons & Hampton, 2006). The former individuals are more likely to argue that category membership is a matter of fact rather than of opinion.

A final point needs to be made here. Concepts are often thought of as fixed and inflexible. In fact, how we represent a concept *changes* as a function of the context in which it appears (Barsalou, 2008). For example, when we read the word *frog* in isolation, the phrase "eaten by humans" probably remains inactive in our memory system. However, "eaten by humans" *becomes* active when reading about frogs in a French restaurant. Thus, concepts are unstable or flexible to the extent that the precise concept information activated varies from situation to situation.

In the Real World 7.1: *Semantic dementia*

It is generally accepted that the general knowledge stored in semantic memory plays a major role in everyday life. This can be demonstrated most clearly by considering individuals lacking such knowledge. Precisely that was done by the Colombian novelist Gabriel García Márquez in his novel *One Hundred Years of Solitude*. The inhabitants of Macondo are struck by the insomnia plague. This gradually causes them to lose information about the meanings and functions of the objects around them, thereby producing a state of despair.

Here is how the central character (José Arcadio Buerdia) responds to this desperate situation:

The sign that he hung on the neck of the cow was an exemplary proof of the way in which the inhabitants of Macondo were prepared to fight against loss of memory: This is the cow. She must be milked every morning so that she will produce milk, and the milk must be boiled in order to be mixed with coffee to make coffee and milk.

The fictional account provided by Gabriel García Márquez is amazingly similar to the real-life experiences of brain-damaged patients suffering from semantic dementia (Rascovsky et al., 2009). **Semantic dementia** is a condition in which there is widespread loss of knowledge about the meanings of concepts and words (Patterson et al., 2007). It always involves damage to the anterior temporal lobes but other areas are relatively spared initially. As we will see, patients with semantic dementia show substantial loss of meaning across all sensory modalities.

Patients with semantic dementia have problems categorizing objects from pictures, especially when the categorization is relatively difficult. They can categorize pictures at a very general level (e.g., animal; nonliving) better than at an intermediate (e.g., dog; cat) or specific level (e.g., Labrador; collie) (Rogers & Patterson, 2007). Thus, patients find it hard to assign detailed meaning to visual objects.

Patients with semantic dementia perform poorly when asked to draw objects (see Figure 7.1; Rascovsky et al., 2009). The patient GW omitted important features from his drawings – his fish lacks fins, one of his birds lacks wings, and the elephant lacks a trunk. These drawings indicate that GW has very limited access to information concerning object meanings.

Patients with semantic dementia also have problems in the auditory modality. They can't identify objects when listening to their characteristic sounds (e.g., a phone ringing; a dog barking; Patterson et al., 2007).

Patients with semantic dementia are also poor at identifying flavors when tasting jelly beans with various flavors such as coffee, coconut, and vanilla (Piwnica-Worms et al., 2010). A 67-year-old female patient (CMR) was found to have reduced empathy (the ability to understand others' feelings). She was also poor at identifying facial emotions (Calabria et al., 2009). These findings indicate the widespread nature of the loss of meaning experienced by patients with semantic dementia.

What is spared in semantic dementia? Strikingly, patients in the early stages of the disease seem to have almost intact autobiographical memory and episodic memory (concerned with personal experiences) for the preceding 12 months (Matuszewski et al., 2009). This allows them to remember day-to-day events, to honor appointments, and to function in their everyday lives until the disease becomes more severe (Rascovsky et al., 2009). Patients are often good at jigsaw puzzles (which require visuo-spatial abilities) and spend much of their time solving them (Green & Patterson, 2009).

Finally, some aspects of language are spared initially (Kertesz et al., 2010). Patients make very few errors of pronunciation and their speech is grammatical. However, they make subtle grammatical errors (e.g., "That's made me cried a lot": Meteyard & Patterson, 2009). In addition, their speech is often not very meaningful (e.g., frequent use of general, uninformative words such as "thing" and "stuff").

The problems experienced by patients with semantic dementia have various negative consequences. They often exhibit behavioral changes such as lowered emotional mood states, rigid patterns of behavior, and mild obsessions (Green & Patterson, 2009).

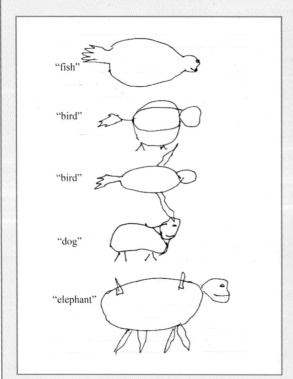

Figure 7.1 Drawings of animals by patient GW show major semantic deficits. Important distinguishing features are missing: the fish lacks fins, the first bird lacks wings, and the elephant has no trunk. From Rascovsky et al. (2009) by permission of Oxford University Press.

Patients with semantic dementia are often especially concerned about the gradual loss of autobiographical memory. One patient (RB) kept a list of where he had lived over the preceding 32 years. He carried this list around with him the whole time to help to preserve his sense of self. He also recorded familiar names together with information on location or occupation (e.g., "Virgil and Lois = were in Yukon").

In sum, the progressive erosion of semantic memory in patients with semantic dementia causes a very wide-ranging loss of meaning. This can lead to behavioral abnormalities and loss of a sense of personal identity. From a theoretical perspective, it is important that early-stage patients can show reasonably intact autobiographical and episodic memory, pronunciation of words, knowledge of grammar, and visuo-spatial processing. The pattern of findings shows clearly those aspects of cognition more or less reliant on semantic memory.

CHAPTER ORGANIZATION

In the rest of this chapter, we will start by considering our knowledge of words and concepts. The emphasis will be on the functions of concepts and how they are organized in semantic memory. After that, the focus switches to our schematic knowledge. We will consider the uses to which we put such knowledge and the impact it has on our behavior.

In what follows, I will sometimes refer to concepts and at other times to categories. A **concept** is a mental representation that represents a category of objects, whereas a **category** is a set or class of objects that belongs together. There is much overlap between concepts and categories. However, the focus is more on the nature of the information stored in memory when we consider concepts than when we consider categories.

Key Terms

Concept:
a mental representation representing a **category** of objects; stored in long-term memory.

Category:
a set or class of objects that belong together (e.g., articles of furniture; four-footed animals).

Section Summary

- The general knowledge we have stored in semantic memory has a huge impact on our everyday lives. Much of this knowledge relates to individual words and concepts. More general information is in the form of schemas or packets of well-organized information.

Further functions of concepts

- Concepts provide an efficient way of representing our knowledge about the world. They allow us to make predictions about the world and to communicate our knowledge and experience to others.

Semantic dementia

- Brain-damaged patients with semantic dementia suffer a widespread loss of their conceptual knowledge, which seriously disrupts their everyday lives. However, patients in the early stages of semantic dementia have reasonably intact autobiographical and episodic memory, and are often good at jigsaw puzzles.

> **Chapter organization**
> • The next part of the chapter is concerned with the functions of concepts and their organization in semantic memory. After that, the focus switches to broader, schema-based knowledge within semantic memory.

CONCEPT ORGANIZATION IN SEMANTIC MEMORY

In this section, we focus on the ways in which the information stored within semantic memory is organized. There is much evidence that semantic memory is highly organized or structured. For example, it takes about one second to decide that a *sparrow* is a *bird* or to think of a *fruit* starting with *p*.

In view of its complexities, it is unsurprising that several rather different theories of the organization of semantic memory have been proposed. In what follows, we consider some of these theoretical approaches in light of the relevant data. These data have been obtained from healthy and brain-damaged patients, and have included behavioral and brain-imaging data.

HIERARCHIES OF CONCEPTS

Many concepts are organized into hierarchies. Rosch et al. (1976) identified three levels within such hierarchies. There are superordinate categories at the top, basic-level categories in the middle, and subordinate categories at the bottom. For example, *furniture* is a superordinate category, *chair* is a basic-level category, and *easy chair* is a subordinate category.

Which level in the hierarchy is used most often in everyday life? We often talk about superordinate categories (e.g., "That furniture is expensive"), and about subordinate concepts (e.g., "my new Cadillac"). However, we typically deal with objects at the intermediate, basic level (e.g., whether there are enough chairs and desks in the office).

Rosch et al. (1976) asked people to list all the attributes of concepts at each level in the hierarchy. Very few attributes were listed for the superordinate categories because the categories were abstract. Many attributes were listed for the categories at the other two levels. However, very similar attributes were listed for different categories at the lowest level.

Thus, basic-level categories are generally the most useful – they have the best balance between informativeness and distinctiveness. Informativeness is missing at the highest level of the hierarchy and distinctiveness is missing at the lowest level.

Rosch et al. (1976) asked participants to name pictures of objects. Basic-level names were used 1595 times in the course of the experiment. In contrast, subordinate names were used only 14 times, and superordinate names just once.

Basic-level categories possess other special properties not shared by categories at other levels. First, it is the most general level at which people use similar motor movements for interacting with category members. For example, all chairs can be sat on in roughly the same way and this differs markedly from how we interact with tables.

Second, the basic level is the one usually acquired first by young children. Bourdais and Pecheux (2009) studied categorization in 13- and 16-month-old infants. These infants found categorization easiest at the basic level and hardest at the superordinate level.

In spite of the evidence just discussed, we don't *always* prefer basic-level categories. For example, we would expect a botanist to refer to the various different kinds of plants in a garden rather than simply describing them all as plants!

Tanaka and Taylor (1991) studied the concepts of birdwatchers and dog experts shown pictures of birds and dogs. Both groups used subordinate names much more often in their expert domain than in their novice domain. More specifically, bird experts used subordinate names 74% of the time with birds, dog experts used subordinate names 40% of the time with dogs, and the two groups used subordinate names only 24% of the time in their novice domain. These differences occurred because the participants had substantially more knowledge about subordinate categories in their area of expertise than in their novice domain.

There is one type of object for which most of us generally use subordinate categories rather than basic-level ones – faces! For example, photographs of famous individuals can be categorized at the subordinate level (e.g., Barack Obama) rather than at the basic level (i.e., human face) (Anaki & Bentin, 2009). This reflects the knowledge and expertise we have in recognizing individual faces because it is such an important ability in our everyday lives.

Finally, it is important to consider cultural differences. Nearly all the research on humans' use of categories has involved participants representing very few cultures. More specifically, the participants who are tested typically come from Western, educated, industrialized, and democratic (WEIRD) societies (Henrich et al., 2010).

Some research (Coley et al., 1997; Medin & Atran, 2004) has compared categorization in members of the Itza culture in Guatemala and American undergraduates. The Itza were more likely than the Americans to categorize plants, animals, and birds at the subordinate level. This probably reflects their closer contact with the natural environment.

SPREADING ACTIVATION THEORY

Allan Collins and Elizabeth Loftus (1975) argued that semantic memory is organized on the basis of semantic relatedness or semantic distance. Semantic relatedness can be measured by asking people to decide how closely related pairs of words are. Alternatively, people can list as many members as they can of a given category. Those members produced most often are regarded as most closely related to the category.

You can see parts of the organization of semantic memory assumed by Collins and Loftus (1975) in Figure 7.2. An important feature is that the length of the links between two concepts indicates the degree of semantic relatedness between them. Thus, for example, *red* is more closely related to *orange* than it is to *sunsets*.

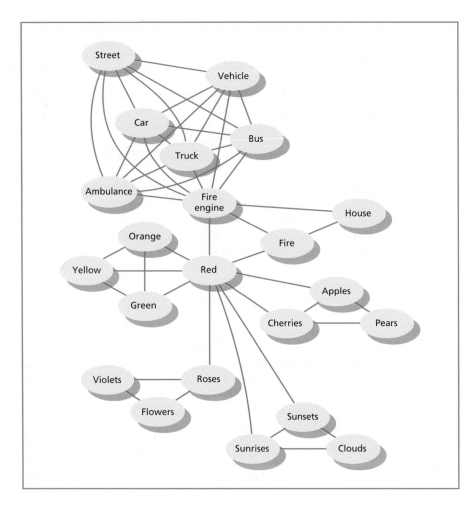

Collins and Loftus (1975) emphasized the notion of spreading activation (see Glossary). Whenever a person sees, hears, or thinks about a concept, the appropriate node in semantic memory is activated. This causes activation to spread strongly to closely related concepts and weakly to those more distantly related. For example, activation would pass strongly and rapidly from *robin* to *bird* in the sentence, "A robin is a bird," because *robin* and *bird* are closely related semantically.

Findings

There is experimental support for the theory. For example, the members of most categories vary considerably in terms of how typical or representative they are of the category to which they belong. Rosch and Mervis (1975) found that oranges, apples, bananas, and peaches were rated as much more typical fruits than olives, tomatoes, coconuts, and dates (see Table 7.1).

Rips et al. (1973) discovered that the time taken to decide that a category member was a fruit was much less for typical fruits than for atypical ones. This is known as the **typicality effect**. It can be explained by the theory if we assume that typical category members are closer semantically to the category label than are atypical ones.

> **Key Term**
>
> **Typicality effect:**
> the finding that the time taken to decide that a category member belongs to a **category** is less for more typical than for less typical members.

Table 7.1   Typicality of items belonging to six categories. Reprinted from Rosch and Mervis (1975). Copyright © 1975, with permission from Elsevier.

Typicality	Furniture	Fruit	Vehicle	Weapons	Clothing	Vegetables
1	Chair	Orange	Car	Gun	Pants	Peas
2	Sofa	Apple	Truck	Knife	Shirt	Carrots
3	Table	Banana	Bus	Sword	Dress	String beans
4	Dresser	Peach	Motorcycle	Bomb	Skirt	Spinach
5	Desk	Pear	Train	Hand grenade	Jacket	Broccoli
6	Bed	Apricot	Trolley	Spear	Coat	Asparagus
7	Bookcase	Plum	Bicycle	Cannon	Sweater	Corn
8	Footstool	Grape	Aeroplane	Bow and arrow	Underpants	Cauliflower
9	Lamp	Strawberry	Boat	Club	Socks	Brussels sprouts
10	Piano	Grapefruit	Tractor	Tank	Pyjamas	Lettuce
11	Cushion	Pineapple	Cart	Tear gas	Bathing suit	Beets
12	Mirror	Blueberry	Wheelchair	Whip	Shoes	Tomato
13	Rug	Lemon	Tank	Ice pick	Vest	Lima beans
14	Radio	Watermelon	Raft	Fists	Tie	Eggplant
15	Stove	Honeydew	Sled	Rocket	Mittens	Onion
16	Clock	Pomegranate	Horse	Poison	Hat	Potato
17	Picture	Date	Blimp	Scissors	Apron	Yam
18	Closet	Coconut	Skates	Words	Purse	Mushroom
19	Vase	Tomato	Wheelbarrow	Foot	Wristwatch	Pumpkin
20	Telephone	Olive	Elevator	Screwdriver	Necklace	Rice

Other predictions of the theory have been tested. Meyer and Schvaneveldt (1976) asked participants to decide as rapidly as possible whether a letter string formed a word (lexical decision task). In the key condition, a target word (e.g., *butter*) was immediately preceded by a semantically related word (e.g., *bread*) or by an unrelated word (e.g., *nurse*). According to the theory, activation should have spread from the first word to the target word only when they were semantically related. This activation should have made it easier to identify the second word. As predicted, there was a facilitation (or semantic priming) effect only for semantically related words.

McNamara (1992) used the same basic approach as Meyer and Schvaneveldt (1976). Suppose the first word was *red*. This was sometimes followed by a word one link away (e.g., *roses*) and sometimes by a word two links away (e.g., *flowers*). More activation should spread from the activated word to words one link away than to those two links away, and so the facilitation effect should have been greater in the former case. That is precisely what McNamara (1992) found.

Jones (2010) studied mediated priming on a lexical decision task. What happens here is that the initial word is only *indirectly* related to the target word on the lexical decision task (e.g., *spoon – soup – can*). In the example, the semantic relationship between *spoon* and *can* is mediated by the word *soup*.

According to spreading activation theory, mediated priming should occur through automatic activation of the link between *spoon* and *soup* and that between *soup* and *can*. In fact, a mediated priming effect was only found when participants could use strategic processing – there was *no* effect when they could use only automatic processing.

Limitations

What are the limitations of spreading activation theory? The theory is of very little relevance to the processing of meaning within semantic memory. Consider the two following sentences: "A cat is a mammal" and "A cat is not a mammal." Their meanings are very different, but the semantic activation from *cat* to *mammal* is probably similar.

More generally, the take-home message is that the theory is rather narrow in scope – the notion of semantic activation only sheds light on some of the processing involving semantic memory. In addition, the theory has little to say on the precise information about concepts that is stored in long-term memory.

ORGANIZATION WITHIN THE BRAIN

It seems to be assumed within spreading activation theory that our knowledge of any given object or concept is stored in *one* location in the brain. It could be argued that research on patients with semantic dementia (discussed earlier in the chapter) is consistent with the same assumption.

However, that isn't the whole story so far as brain-damaged patients are concerned. Many of them don't have the very general impairment of semantic memory shown by patients with semantic dementia. Instead, they have category-specific deficits, in which the loss of semantic knowledge is *specific* to certain categories of objects.

The most common pattern shown by patients with category-specific deficits is that their ability to identify objects from pictures is worse for living things (e.g., animals) than nonliving things (e.g., man-made objects). There are *four* times as many patients with a greater impairment for living than for nonliving things than the opposite pattern (Martin & Caramazza, 2003).

The areas of brain damage are different in the two groups (Gainotti, 2000). Nearly all patients with a selective impairment for knowledge of living things have damage to the anterior, medial, and inferior parts of the temporal lobes. In contrast, those with greater impairment for nonliving things have damage in fronto-parietal areas extending further back in the brain than the areas damaged in the other group.

Farah and McClelland (1991) argued that much of our information about living and nonliving things consists of two kinds of properties. First, there are perceptual/sensory properties (e.g., what an object looks like), which are especially important with living things.

Second, there are functional properties (e.g., what an object is used for), which are especially important with nonliving things. The functional properties of objects are stored in different parts of the brain from sensory properties (Lee et al., 2002).

Cree and McRae (2003) argued that we should divide sensory properties into visual (including color), auditory, taste, and tactile ones. For example, there are similarities among fruits, vegetables, and foods because sensory features associated with taste are important to all three categories. We should also divide functional features into entity behaviors (what a thing does) and functional information (what humans use it for). Cree and McRae found that the evidence from brain-damaged patients with category-specific deficits supported these divisions of sensory and functional properties.

According to Cree and McRae (2003), the brain is organized so that any given type of property (e.g., color; motion) is stored in a given region of the brain. There is reasonable evidence for that assumption. Martin and Chao (2001) reviewed brain-imaging findings indicating that category knowledge about color, motion, and shape is processed in different brain regions.

Cappla (2008) also considered brain-imaging research on semantic memory. The brain areas activated during semantic memory tasks depended on stimulus modality (visual vs. auditory), concept type (concrete vs. abstract; natural kinds vs. artifacts), and the type of object properties accessed (visual vs. action). Overall, the findings suggest that semantic memory consists of a widely distributed network of brain areas.

Section Summary

Hierarchies of concepts

- There are hierarchies of concepts consisting of superordinate, basic-level, and subordinate categories. Basic-level categories are generally the most useful because they combine informativeness with distinctiveness. However, experts make extensive use of subordinate categories, and we all categorize faces much more at the subordinate level than at the basic level.

Spreading activation theory

- Collins and Loftus (1975) argued that concepts in semantic memory are organized in terms of semantic relatedness or distance. Activation of a word or concept causes activation to spread to related words or concepts. The typicality and semantic priming effects support the theory. However, activation doesn't always spread in the automatic fashion assumed by the theory. The theory is somewhat narrow in focus and has little to say about the processing of meaning in semantic memory.

Organization within the brain

- Many patients have category-specific deficits that differ depending on the brain areas damaged. These deficits can involve specific sensory properties (e.g., visual; auditory) or specific functional properties (e.g., what a thing does). Brain-imaging research confirms that concept information in semantic memory is widely distributed within the brain.

ORGANIZATION OF CONCEPTS

In this section, we consider in detail various theoretical approaches to concept organization. First, we will be discussing the prototype and exemplar approaches. Both approaches are designed to account for the major categories of concepts and the nature of category membership. After that, we turn to the role of knowledge and experience in influencing the organization of concepts. For example, our knowledge of a concept often includes information about the causal relations among its features or the appropriate action to take with respect to it.

PROTOTYPE APPROACH

The prototype approach (Hampton, 2007, 2010; Rosch & Mervis, 1975) has been very influential. According to this approach, each category has a prototype, which is a central description or conceptual core representing the category.

What does a prototype look like? The most popular view is that it is a set of characteristic attributes or features in which some attributes are weighted more than others. We can assess prototypes by asking people to indicate those attributes typical of a category. For example, the characteristic or typical attributes of *fruit* might include: contains seeds, grows above ground, is edible, is sweet, and is round.

Various phenomena led to the development of prototype theory (Hampton, 2010). For example, as we saw earlier, the borders of many categories are unclear. That makes sense if we decide whether an object is a category member on the basis of its resemblance to the category prototype.

Another relevant phenomenon is found when people are asked to list features of a category. What generally happens is that they list features true only of a majority of category members (Hampton, 2010). In other words, their descriptions correspond reasonably well to that category's prototype.

Fehr (2004) considered whether there is a prototype for friendship intimacy for same-sex friendships. She found evidence that there was. Women and men agreed that self-disclosure, emotional support, and loyalty are all typical features of *friendship intimacy* and so contribute heavily to the prototype. Shared activities and practical support are less prototypical features. As might be expected, women attached more importance than men to the key features of self-disclosure, emotional support, and loyalty.

Within the prototype approach, an object is a member of a category if there is a good match between its attributes or features and those of the prototype. It follows that members of a category share some attributes or features with other category members: These are known as family resemblances.

Why are family resemblances important? According to the prototype approach, category members having the highest family resemblance scores come closer than other category members to representing the category's prototype. Thus, category members with high resemblance scores are "better" or more typical category members than those having low family resemblance scores.

Why is it useful for us to form prototypes for the categories we have stored in long-term memory? We have seen that the boundaries of many categories are rather vague and hard to establish. In addition, these boundaries can change when we discover new information, as when a child finds out that *tomato* is technically a fruit rather than a vegetable. Thus, what is generally most consistent and unchanging about a category or concept is its conceptual core, which is in essence what a prototype is.

Findings

Impressive evidence of the importance of family resemblances within categories was reported by Rosch and Mervis (1975). They used six categories with 20 members varying in typicality representing each category (see Table 7.1). The participants' task was to list the attributes of category members.

Most of the attributes of any given category member were shared by at least some of the other members of the same category. This information was used to calculate family resemblance scores for each member. For example, suppose a category member had two attributes, one possessed by 16 category members and the other possessed by 14 category members. That would give a family resemblance score of 16 + 14 = 30.

Rosch and Mervis's (1975) key finding was that typical category members had much higher family resemblance scores than atypical category members. The correlation between typicality and family resemblance ranged between +.84 (for vegetables) and +.94 (for weapons).

Rosch and Mervis (1975) also considered the numbers of attributes shared by the five most typical and those shared by the five least typical members of each category. We will discuss the findings from the vehicle category, but similar results were obtained with the other categories. The five most typical members of the vehicle category (*car*, *truck*, *bus*, *motorcycle*, and *train*) had 36 attributes in common (e.g., wheels, engine, driver). In contrast, the five least typical members (*horse*, *blimp*, *skates*, *wheelbarrow*, and *elevator*) had only two attributes in common.

Most versions of prototype theory assume that family resemblances are very important in determining typicality. However, that isn't the case with some goal-derived categories. These are categories in which all category members satisfy a given goal (e.g., birthday presents that make the recipient happy).

Barsalou (1985) found that family resemblance scores didn't predict typicality scores for members of goal-derived categories. What is going on here? Typical members of goal-derived categories are those best satisfying the goal (e.g., providing pleasure to someone celebrating his/her birthday) rather than sharing attributes with other category members.

The prediction from prototype theory that prototypes represent a central tendency within a category sometimes fails when applied to experts. Lynch et al. (2000) asked tree experts and novices to provide goodness-of-example ratings for trees.

According to prototype theory, we would expect that trees of average height should be rated as the best examples. In fact, experts identified very tall, non-weedlike trees as the best examples of trees. In other words, their ratings were determined by the extent to which any given tree corresponded to an *ideal* tree rather than by its *typicality* or representativeness.

The findings from the novices in the study by Lynch et al. (2000) differed considerably from those of the experts, but also failed to support prototype theory. For novices, the most important factor determining goodness-of-example ratings was their familiarity with the trees. As a result, *maple* and *oak* emerged as the best examples of trees and *ginko* and *catalpa* were among the worst.

There are other ways in which prototype theories are oversimplified. For example, biological concepts (e.g., crab; grape) differ in important ways from artifact concepts (e.g., church; taxi). According to Hampton et al. (2009), biological concepts have a much tighter causal structure than artifact (manmade) concepts. As a result, a missing typical feature from a biological concept influences categorization more than does a missing typical feature from an artifact concept.

Below is an example of the information provided to some participants in the Hampton et al. (2009) study:

1. A creature with legs and claws that looks and acts like a crab.
2. The scientists found that the structure of its eyes was identical to that typically found only in crabs.
3. They found that the creature had offspring that looked and acted just like lobsters.

The participants' task was to decide whether the creature was a *crab*. The discrepant information in (3) greatly reduced their confidence that it was a crab. In contrast, one piece of discrepant information had much less impact with artifacts or manmade objects. Prototype theory doesn't provide a clear account of this difference between biological and artifact concepts.

Evaluation

+ The prototype approach provides a reasonable account of the typicality ratings found with the members of many categories.

+ It is plausible that summary descriptions (prototypes or conceptual cores) of most categories are stored in long-term memory.

− Prototype approaches are more applicable to some kinds of concepts than to others. For example, some abstract concepts don't seem to have prototypes (Hampton, 1981) and family resemblances fail to predict typicality ratings for the members of goal-derived categories (Barsalou, 1985).

− Concepts are more complex than assumed by the prototype approach. For example, the approach doesn't provide a coherent explanation of effects due to expertise (Lynch et al., 2000) or the differences between biological and artifact concepts (Hampton et al., 2009).

EXEMPLAR APPROACH

The exemplar approach is a major alternative to prototype theories (e.g., Rips & Collins, 1993). Instead of there being some abstract description (central prototype), the assumption is one of a memory system storing large numbers of specific examples or exemplars. Thus, for example, instead of having a prototype for *bird* that is a list of all the characteristic features of category members (e.g., has-wings; flies; etc.), we just have a store of all the instances of birds encountered in the past. Many effects attributed to prototypes can be dealt with by this kind of account depending on which instances come to mind in a specific context.

Before proceeding, it is worth mentioning that the prototype and exemplar approaches may differ less than appears to be the case. Rogers and McClelland (2005) put forward a model showing that a *single* associative learning process could produce many of the concept-related findings predicted by prototype and exemplar theories.

Findings

Much evidence supporting prototype theories can also be explained by exemplar theories. For example, consider the faster categorization judgments for some category members than for others. When asked, "Is a robin a bird?", you can answer much faster than when asked, "Is a penguin a bird?" Given that you have encountered many robins in the past, there are likely to be more stored instances of robins than penguins. Therefore, a robin instance will be retrieved from memory much faster than a penguin instance, thus giving rise to the difference in judgment times.

According to the exemplar approach, an important factor influencing a category member's typicality is the *frequency* with which it has been encountered. Evidence of this was reported by Laura Novick (2003). The typicality of *airplane* as a vehicle was assessed before 9/11 and then at various times after the terrorist attack.

The huge publicity generated by 9/11 caused an increase in the rated typicality of *airplane* 5 hours and 1 month after the terrorist attack. However, its typicality returned to its pre-attack level 4.5 months after the attack. In similar fashion, it is assumed that a robin is a more typical instance of a bird than a penguin because there are many more stored instances of *robins* than of *penguins*.

However, there are other important determinants of typicality. With members of ordinary concrete categories (e.g., vehicles), typicality was predicted by family resemblance as well as by frequency (Barsalou, 1985).

The members of some categories are much more *variable* than others. For example, most rulers are 12 inches in length and so vary little in size. However, most pizzas in the United States are also 12 inches in size, but they can vary between about 2 and 30 inches. Exemplar theories preserve the variability of instances in a category, whereas a prototype is a kind of average over the instances of a category and usually excludes such variability information.

Rips and Collins (1993) asked participants whether a new object 19 inches in size was a pizza or a ruler. If they used prototypes, there should have been a 50–50 split between pizza and ruler given that the prototype average is 12 inches for each. However, if information about size variability was used (as predicted by exemplar-based theories), then participants should mostly have said the object was a pizza. The findings supported the exemplar approach.

Storms et al. (2000) compared the exemplar approach with the prototype approach for common categories such as *furniture*, *fruit*, and *birds*. Participants were given various tasks such as rating the typicality of exemplars of each category and then deciding rapidly whether individual words were members of the category. Performance on all four tasks was predicted reasonably well by the prototype and exemplar approaches. However, the predictions of the exemplar-based approach were consistently more accurate than those of the prototype approach.

The exemplar approach generally works less well with simple concepts than with complex ones. Smith and Minda (2000) considered data from several studies. There was less support for exemplar theories when relatively simple concepts were learned than when complex ones were learned. Why is this? According to Feldman (2003), simple concepts are learned by extracting their common regularities (e.g., all even numbers are divisible by 2). In contrast, it isn't possible to learn more complex concepts in that way (because they lack common regularities) and so we rely on exemplars.

Feldman (2003) found that exemplar theories greatly underestimated how much easier people find it to learn simple concepts than complex ones. This is because such theories fail to appreciate the key role of common regularities or generalizations in the acquisition of simple concepts.

Evaluation

⊕ When attempts have been made to contrast the predictions of exemplar models with those of prototype models, exemplar models have generally outperformed prototype models (Storms et al., 2000).

⊕ Exemplar models provide explanations for concepts' typicality ratings, the effects of typicality on categorization time, and effects due to the variability of instances within a category.

⊖ Exemplar models tend to be less successful when applied to the learning of simple concepts than very complex ones (Feldman, 2003; Smith & Minda, 2000).

⊖ Most exemplar models assume that every instance of a category we encounter is stored in memory. On that assumption, it is hard to see how we prevent information (and storage) overload.

⊖ Exemplar models are narrow in scope. Simply ask yourself the question, "Is all my knowledge of any given concept provided by the dozens or hundreds of examples of that concept stored in long-term memory?" Hopefully, you agree that the answer must be, "No!"

KNOWLEDGE-BASED APPROACH

The theories discussed so far fail to provide a full account of the knowledge we have about many concepts. In addition to knowledge of a concept's features (emphasized within prototype theories), we also generally have some understanding of the *relations* among the features. For example, *dangerous* and *sharp* are two features of the concept of an axe. These two features are related in that many people argue that axes are dangerous precisely because they are sharp (Heussen & Hampton, 2007).

Causal relations are especially important. For example, we know a car has a motor, needs fuel, and is self-propelled. However, an object might have all these features and still not be a good example of a car. Consider an object in which the motor ran on clockwork and only caused the windshield wipers to move, the fuel was only used to warm the passengers, and the object moved when the wind caught its sails (Hampton, 2010).

The above object differs considerably from the cars with which we are familiar. With such cars, fuel drives the motor, and the motor causes the car to move. In other words, the features are *causally* related to each other.

We can see the importance of causal relations among features in a study by Ahn et al. (2000). Participants were told that members of a given category tend to have three features (e.g., blurred vision; headaches; insomnia). They were also told that blurred vision causes headaches and that headaches cause insomnia. Then participants indicated the likelihood that an item belonged to the category if one feature was absent.

The rated likelihood of membership was lowest when the initial cause (i.e., blurred vision) was absent and highest when the final effect (i.e., insomnia) was missing. Thus, people believe that if the cause is missing, it is unlikely that an item is a member of the category.

Additional evidence that causal relations are important was reported by Rehder and Kim (2009). They presented participants with information such as the following:

> *Kehoe ants' underlying feature (blood high in iron sulfate) caused its first observable feature (hyperactive immune system) but not its second (thick blood).*

Thus, *hyperactive immune system* was of greater causal significance than was *thick blood*.

On a subsequent categorization task, the presence of the feature *hyperactive immune system* was regarded as stronger evidence that a creature was a Kehoe ant than was the presence of *thick blood*. In similar fashion, the absence of the feature *hyperactive immune system* reduced the likelihood of classification as a Kehoe ant more than the absence of *thick blood*. Thus, an observable feature causally related to an underlying feature is more diagnostic than one that is not.

In sum, the features of a concept are generally *not* totally independent of each other. It is commonly the case that many of the features are causally related, and these causal relations have a powerful influence over categorization.

Section Summary

Prototype approach

- A prototype is a conceptual core consisting of characteristic features. Prototype theories assume that family resemblances are very important in determining typicality, but that isn't the case with goal-derived categories. Some abstract concepts don't seem to have prototypes. The prototype approach is oversimplified in that it doesn't account for some of the effects of expertise or major differences between biological and artifact categories.

Exemplar approach

- The exemplar approach assumes we store large numbers of specific examples of categories. Typicality ratings are assumed to reflect the underlying pattern of category instances. The predictions of the exemplar approach are often more accurate than those of the prototype approach. The exemplar approach is narrow in scope and apparently assumes huge storage capacity for category exemplars.

Knowledge-based approach

- Causal relations among a concept's features are important. Those features causally related to other features determine categorization judgments to a greater extent than do other features. It is clear that a concept's features generally aren't entirely independent of each other.

USING CONCEPTS

The theories discussed in this chapter have shed much light on the nature of concepts. However, such theories (including both prototype and exemplar theories) are rather remote from the realities of everyday life. Why that is the case was expressed forcefully by Lawrence Barsalou (2003, p. 536) in this description of typical theoretical assumptions:

> *The conceptual system is a **detached database**. As categories are encountered in the world, their invariant properties are extracted and stored in descriptions much like an encyclopaedia. The result is a database of generalised categorical knowledge that is relatively detached from the goals of specific agents. (emphasis in original)*

With the above kind of conceptual system, concepts are *amodal*. This means that they are stored in the form of abstract symbols. Concepts are also relatively *stable*: Any given individual uses the same representation of a concept on different occasions. In addition, different people generally have fairly similar representations of a concept.

According to Barsalou (e.g., 2003, 2008), all the above theoretical assumptions about concepts are incorrect. In everyday life, we generally do *not* process concepts in isolation. Instead, we process them in various different settings, and the nature of that processing is influenced by the current context or setting. More generally, the representation of any given concept will vary from situation to situation depending on the individual's current goals and the major characteristics of the situation.

Barsalou (2009) illustrated the differences between his situated simulation theory and previous theories by considering the concept of a *bicycle*. Traditionally, it was assumed that a fairly complete abstract representation of the concept would be activated in all situations. This representation might correspond approximately to the *Chambers Dictionary* definition: "a vehicle with two wheels one directly in front of the other, driven by pedals."

According to Barsalou (2009), those aspects of the *bicycle* concept that are activated depend on the individual's current goals. For example, information about the tires is especially likely to be activated if you want to repair your bicycle, whereas the height of the saddle is important if you want to ride it.

It follows from Barsalou's position that we need to focus on connections among the conceptual system, the perceptual system, and the motor or action system. Research Activity 7.1 provides an example of the links between conceptual processing and perception. Below we consider links between conceptual processing and motor processing or action.

FINDINGS

It makes sense that our processing of concepts referring to objects that we can see or hear should have a perceptual quality (Wu & Barsalou, 2009). On the face of it, this notion seems less useful when applied to abstract concepts such as "truth," "freedom," and "invention."

However, Barsalou and Wiemer-Hastings (2005) reported evidence suggesting that even abstract concepts are associated with some perceptual

Research Activity 7.1: *Concept activation and the perceptual system*

This Research Activity (based on research reported by Wu and Barsalou, 2009) is best done with a friend. Take each of the words in List A in turn and write down as many properties as you can of each one. Then ask your friend to do the same task for the noun phrases in List B.

List A	List B
Lawn	Rolled-up lawn
Watermelon	Half watermelon
Car	Comfortable car

If you compare the two sets of properties, you will probably find some interesting differences. You probably focused on *external* properties of the concepts (e.g., plant; blades; rind; green and yellow; bonnet; trunk) and omitted some of their *internal* properties (e.g., dirt; soil; pips; red; heater; radio). In contrast, your friend may have shown the opposite pattern, focusing more on internal properties and less on external ones.

What is the meaning of the above finding (first reported by Wu & Barsalou, 2009)? It indicates that our processing of concepts often has a *perceptual* quality about it. It is harder to think of object properties that wouldn't be visible if you were actually looking at the object itself.

Wu and Barsalou (2009) discovered that participants often wrote down properties referring to the background situation rather than the object itself. Indeed, between 25% and 50% of the total properties produced related to the background situation.

You may have found something similar. For example, *lawn* may have led you to write down properties such as *picnic* or *you play on it*, and *car* to write down *highway* or *holiday*. In our everyday lives, we typically perceive objects in a particular situation or context, and this aspect of perception is also found when we process concepts.

properties. Participants indicated the characteristic properties of various abstract concepts. Many properties referred to settings or events associated with the concept (e.g., scientists working in a laboratory for "invention") and others referred to relevant mental states. Thus, much of the knowledge we have of abstract concepts is relatively concrete.

Chaigneau et al. (2009) obtained evidence that situational information is important in object categorization. Observers were shown novel objects presented in isolation or with situational information. Accurate object categorization was much better when full situational information was provided than when it was absent. These findings support Barsalou's contention that stored conceptual representations of objects include situational information.

There are many objects in our environment to which we generally respond with a particular kind of gesture. For example, we poke a doorbell, we hold pliers with an open grasp, and we hold a mug with a closed grasp. When we process a concept such as one of the above, do we access our knowledge of the relevant gesture?

Bub et al. (2008) addressed the above issue. Participants learned to make specific gestures to various color cues (e.g., red = poke; blue = open grasp). After that, words were presented in these colors, but participants were told to continue to make the *learned* gestures to the color.

There were two kinds of trial. On congruent trials, the same gesture was relevant to the word *and* to the color. For example, when the stimulus was *doorbell* in red, word and color both suggested the poke gesture. There were also incongruent trials, in which a different gesture was relevant to the word and the color. For example, when the stimulus was *pliers* in red, the word suggested an open grasp whereas the color suggested a poke gesture.

What did Bub et al. (2008) find? The key result was that participants took longer to make the appropriate gesture to the color on incongruent trials than on congruent ones. Thus, words referring to concepts led participants to access relevant gestural knowledge even when it impaired performance.

Other evidence supports the view that the motor system is activated when we process concepts. Hauk et al. (2004) used as their starting point the finding that tongue, finger, and foot movements produce different patterns of activation along the motor strip in the brain. When they presented participants with words such as "lick," "pick," and "kick," these verbs activated parts of the motor strip overlapping with (or very close to) the corresponding part of the motor strip. Thus, for example, *lick* activated areas associated with tongue movements.

Paulus et al. (2009) wondered whether the motor system plays an important role in the acquisition of many object concepts. Observers saw novel objects associated with the action of smelling or the action of hearing. There was significant interference with concept acquisition when observers had to squeeze a ball at the time of learning. Thus, concept learning was slowed down when motor processing of the object was disrupted by an ongoing motor task.

In sum, the ways we use conceptual knowledge in everyday life often involve the perceptual and motor systems. This potentially assists in explaining why concepts show variability and instability from one situation to another. In other words, the precise meaning we assign to a concept depends on the situation and on the perceptual and motor processes engaged by the current task.

Evaluation

⊕ The ways in which we actually use conceptual knowledge in everyday life are closely related to the perceptual and motor systems.

⊕ The variability of concept representations across situations is as predicted by the theory.

⊖ There may be less of a difference between situated simulation theory and traditional theories than Barsalou argues. The contextually appropriate conceptual representations emphasized by Barsalou may well contain the stable conceptual core emphasized traditionally (Mazzone & Lalumera, 2010). Thus, both theoretical approaches may be partly correct.

⊖ Much remains to be discovered about how conceptual representations are influenced by perceptual and motor processes.

Section Summary

• Traditional theories assume that concepts consist of general, abstract representations. According to Barsalou's situated simulation theory, the representation of a concept is variable and depends on the situation and the individual's goals. Barsalou argues that the perceptual and motor systems are both closely connected to the conceptual system.

Findings
- Concept processing often has a perceptual quality, and situational information frequently forms part of the representation of concepts. When people process a concept to which they generally respond with a particular gesture, they access their knowledge of that gesture. Brain-imaging findings suggest the motor system is activated when we process concepts.

Evaluation
- The perceptual and motor systems contribute substantially to concept processing. The influence of situations and goals on concept representations is consistent with the existence of a stable core to those representations.

SCHEMAS

So far in this chapter we have focused on knowledge stored in the form of concepts. However, much of our knowledge of the world is broader in scope than that. More specifically, we possess schemas (see Glossary), which are organized packets of knowledge about the world, events, or people.

Bower et al. (1979) focused on a type of schema known as scripts. **Scripts** are used to store information about typical events. They asked people to list 20 actions or events that usually occur when one is eating in a restaurant.

In spite of the varied restaurant experiences of their participants, there was much agreement on the actions associated with the restaurant script. At least 73% mentioned sitting down, looking at the menu, ordering, eating, paying the bill, and leaving. In addition, at least 48% included entering the restaurant, giving the reservation name, ordering drinks, discussing the menu, talking, eating a salad or soup, ordering dessert, eating dessert, and leaving a tip.

Cosentino et al. (2006) assessed whether some brain-damaged patients had special problems with script memory by presenting them with short texts. Some of these texts contained sequencing or script errors (e.g., dropping fish in a bucket *before* casting the fishing line). Other texts contained semantic or meaning errors (e.g., placing a flower on the hook in a story about fishing).

Healthy controls and patients with semantic dementia (discussed earlier) both detected as many sequencing errors as semantic ones (see Figure 7.3). The findings were very different in patients with fronto-temporal dementia, which differs from semantic dementia in that it includes damage to the prefrontal cortex. These patients failed to detect twice as many sequencing errors as semantic ones. Thus, the prefrontal cortex (used for complex cognitive processing) is more important in using script-based knowledge than in accessing knowledge about individual concepts.

Schematic knowledge is useful for four main reasons. First, schemas allow us to form *expectations*. In a restaurant, for example, we expect to be shown to a table, to be given a menu, to order food, and so on. If any one of these expectations is violated, we usually take action. For example, if no menu is produced, we catch the eye of the waiter or waitress. Schemas help to make the world more predictable, because our expectations are generally confirmed.

Second, schemas help to prevent cognitive overload. For example, consider **stereotypes** (schemas involving simplified generalizations about various

Key Terms

Scripts:
knowledge in the form of *schemas* of the typical actions associated with certain events (e.g., restaurant meals; football games).

Stereotypes:
schemas incorporating oversimplified generalizations (often negative) about certain groups.

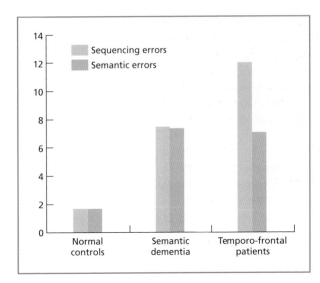

Figure 7.3 Semantic and sequencing errors made by patients with semantic dementia, temporo-frontal patients, and normal controls. The units on the *y*-axis are the mean number of errors in each condition. Data from Cosentino et al. (2006).

groups). When we meet someone for the first time, we often use stereotypical information (e.g., about their sex, age, and ethnicity) to assist us to form an impression of that person. It is simpler (but potentially very misleading) to use such information rather than to engage in detailed cognitive processing of his/her behavior (Macrae & Bodenhausen, 2000).

Evidence that schemas reduce cognitive processing was reported by Macrae et al. (1994). The participants performed two tasks at the same time. One task involved forming impressions of imaginary people when given their names and personality traits, and the other was a comprehension task. Participants who were able to use stereotypical information on the impression formation task performed better on both tasks than those not provided with that information. Thus, stereotypes reduced processing demands and led to enhanced performance.

Third, schemas play an important role in reading and listening because they allow us to fill in the gaps in what we read or hear and so enhance our understanding (see Chapter 8). More specifically, they provide the basis for us to draw inferences as we read or listen.

Fourth, schematic knowledge can assist us when we perceive visual scenes. Palmer (1975) presented a picture of a scene (e.g., a kitchen) followed by the very brief presentation of the picture of an object. The object was appropriate to the context (e.g., loaf) or inappropriate (e.g., mailbox). There was a further condition in which no contextual scene was presented initially.

The probability of identifying the object was greatest when it was appropriate to the context, with activation of schematic knowledge of the scene facilitating visual perception. Performance was worst when the context was inappropriate because activated schematic knowledge was unrelated to the object subsequently presented.

Below we consider research on schemas. In spite of the great usefulness of schematic knowledge, we will see it can cause various errors in memory and perception.

MEMORY AND PERCEPTION ERRORS

There is much research showing that what we remember can be distorted because we sometimes rely too much on our schematic knowledge. There is a full discussion of this research in Chapter 5. Here we will just discuss a single example. In a study by Brewer and Treyens (1981), participants spent half a minute in a room that looked like a graduate student's office (see Figure 5.6). Afterwards, many of them falsely remembered that objects consistent with their schema of such an office (e.g., books; filing cabinet) had been present.

We have seen that schematic knowledge can cause memory errors for relatively complex texts and visual scenes. More surprisingly, memory distortions can be triggered by schematic knowledge even when observers are presented with relatively simple visual information.

Suppose you are shown pictures of familiar objects (e.g., squirrel; balloon; eye) and are asked to describe a function for each one. Some objects are presented in their complete form but others are incomplete. You are then given an unexpected memory test.

Do you think you would remember whether any given object had been presented in its complete or incomplete form? The participants recognized most of the objects. However, they tended to falsely remember seeing complete versions of pictures presented in an incomplete form (Foley et al., 2007).

These findings suggest that we use schematic information to complete the objects. More specifically, Foley et al. (2007) argued that people generate visual images of the presented objects and these images are reactivated at testing. As predicted, there was less evidence of false remembering when the objects didn't resemble the images of them that easily come to mind.

In related research, observers searched for targets in complex scenes (Foley et al., 2002). Observers tended to remember having seen the whole of the target even when in fact it had been partly obscured by other objects.

Boundary extension

Suppose you observe the photograph of a scene for 250 ms. This view is then briefly disrupted for 42 ms, followed by the identical view, a more close-up view, or a wider-angle view of the same scene. Note the very brief delay between the presentations of the two photographs.

When the second photograph was the same as the first one, it tended to be rated as closer up than the original (Intraub & Dickinson, 2008). In other words, observers remembered the first photograph as more extensive than was actually the case. This is known as **boundary extension**.

What causes boundary extension? At the most general level, top-down processes combine with sensory information to give us a full and coherent representation of the scene in front of us.

More specifically, our perceptual schemas allow us to form expectations concerning the visual world outside the boundaries of the scene we are observing (Intraub et al., 1998). Sometimes we can't discriminate between the part of our mental representation of a scene derived from the sensory input and the part based on the relevant perceptual schema (Intraub, 2010).

Does boundary extension occur relatively automatically or does it depend on focused attention? Intraub et al. (2008) addressed this issue. Participants viewed photographs and sometimes performed an attentionally demanding task at the same time. There was greater boundary extension when focused attention was directed to another task. Thus, boundary extension can occur automatically and doesn't necessarily require focused attention.

In sum, schematic knowledge can produce various errors in perception and memory. However, it is worth remembering (as pointed out initially) that schematic knowledge generally facilitates our ability to make sense of our environment and to act appropriately.

STEREOTYPES

This section is concerned with the ways in which stereotypes (simplified generalizations about groups) influence our thinking and behavior. Start with Research Activity 7.2.

> **Key Term**
>
> **Boundary extension:** the finding that internal representations of visual scenes are more complete and extensive than the actual scene; dependent on perceptual **schemas** and expectations.

Research Activity 7.2: *Effects produced by stereotypes*

Read the following passage from Reynolds et al. (2006), and answer the question at the end of it:

A man and his son were away for a trip. They were driving along the highway when they had a terrible accident. The man was killed outright but the son was alive, although badly injured. The son was rushed to the hospital and was to have an emergency operation. On entering the operating theater, the surgeon looked at the boy, and said, "I can't do this operation. This is my son." How can this be?

If you found the problem difficult, you are in good company. We tend to have a stereotypical view that surgeons are men. However, some surgeons are female, and the surgeon in the passage above was the boy's mother! Thus, stereotypical information can interfere with problem solving.

The problem shows us that stereotypes (generalizations about groups) can influence our thinking and behavior. Kreiner et al. (2008) showed that stereotypes can influence our understanding of what we read. Participants read sentences such as the following while their eye movements were recorded:

1. Naturally the manicurist fell in love while reminding herself of the romantic letters.
2. Naturally the manicurist fell in love while reminding himself of the romantic letters.

Most participants fixated longer on the pronoun (herself/himself) when it was inconsistent with their stereotypical expectation (i.e., that manicurists are female) than when it was consistent.

In sum, schematic information in the form of stereotypes has been shown to influence performance on various cognitive activities including problem solving and language comprehension. More specifically, performance is impaired when there is a conflict between an individual's expectation based on his/her stereotypes and the information presented on the task.

Assessing stereotypes: Explicit vs. implicit measures

How can we assess an individual's stereotypes? Historically, this was mostly done by questionnaires. For example, McCauley and Stitt (1978) asked participants questions such as, "What percentage of Turks are efficient?" or "What percentage of people in the world are efficient?" The answers allowed the researchers to measure stereotypes for the inhabitants of many different countries.

The greatest problem with most questionnaire measures is social desirability bias – individuals may pretend their stereotypes of other groups are less negative than is actually the case. Individuals' questionnaire responses assess *explicit* stereotypes (those under conscious control). An alternative approach is designed to assess *implicit* stereotypes, i.e., those for which the individual lacks conscious awareness. Below we consider explicit and implicit gender stereotypes.

There are several gender stereotypes. For example, it is often thought that men are more competitive than women, and that women are warmer and more caring than men (Eagly, 2001). It is also believed by many that males are better suited than females to science whereas females are better suited than males to the liberal arts (Nosek et al., 2005).

Nosek et al. (2005) assessed implicit gender stereotypes by using a version of the Implicit Association Test (IAT). Words belonging to each of the following four categories were presented: male (e.g., he, boy); female (e.g., she, girl);

science (e.g., physics, chemistry); and liberal arts (e.g., arts; history). The task was to categorize each word as rapidly as possible.

In the first condition, one response key was pressed for male and science items and a second response key was pressed for female and liberal arts items. In the second condition, one response key was used for male and liberal arts items and the other was used for female and science items.

What do you think Nosek et al. (2005) found? Individuals with implicit gender stereotypes should have found the first condition easier because it involves associating male and science items and associating female and liberal arts items.

As predicted, performance was faster and more accurate in the first than the second condition. There was a modest positive association between implicit gender stereotypes as assessed by the IAT and explicit gender stereotypes. This finding has been obtained several times (e.g., Nosek & Hansen, 2008), and suggests that the two types of stereotype are based in part on the same information.

Nosek et al. (2009) carried out a very large Internet-based study using the same IAT as that used by Nosek et al. (2005). (You can do it yourself by accessing https://implicit.harvard.edu.) Nosek et al. obtained data from about 300,000 individuals in 34 countries and ranked them in terms of the extent of implicit gender stereotypes.

Their key finding was that sex differences in 8th-grade science performance favoring males were much greater in countries high in national *implicit* gender stereotyping. There are probably two factors at work here: Gender stereotyping adversely affects female science performance, and sex differences in science performance increase gender stereotyping. Interestingly, national levels of *explicit* gender stereotyping (based on self-report data) were almost unrelated to sex differences in science performance.

Measures of implicit stereotypes can sometimes provide a more valid assessment than measures of explicit stereotypes of the stereotypical information an individual has stored in memory. For example, Cunningham et al. (2001) discovered a modest tendency for American students having implicit racial stereotypes to have explicit ones as well. Of more interest, there was greater evidence of racial prejudice with the implicit measures than with the explicit ones.

In sum, various methods can be used to identify the stereotypical information that individuals have stored in memory. Implicit measures of stereotypes are sometimes more revealing than explicit measures, and often predict behavior well. It is often assumed that the processes underlying performance on the IAT and other implicit measures are relatively "automatic" and don't involve conscious awareness. However, effects on the IAT can sometimes be controlled consciously (De Houwer et al., 2009), and so that assumption may be oversimplified.

Stereotype stability: Context effects

Most of the research discussed so far has been based on the assumption that an individual's stereotypes are relatively stable and invariant over time. That assumption may sound reasonable but is actually incorrect. Garcia-Marques et al. (2006) asked participants to select five traits out of 43 that best described various groups (e.g., gypsies; gays). The same participants then repeated the task 2 weeks later. To their surprise, Garcia-Marques et al. found considerable instability over that time period, especially for less typical traits.

Stereotypes are unstable and changeable over time for several reasons. One is that they are much influenced by context. The impact of context on stereotype activation was shown clearly by Casper et al. (2010). Suppose you were presented with the word *Italian*. The stereotype of Italians includes the notion that they are romantic. Accordingly, it might be expected that you would then be able to decide rapidly that the letter string *romantic* was a word because *Italian* activates the attributes of the Italian stereotype.

The expected finding was obtained when the contextual picture accompanying *Italian* was of a rose. However, decision making was slower and there was no evidence of stereotype activation when the word *Italian* was accompanied by a picture of an expensive car. *What* do these findings mean? They suggest that appropriate contextual information is needed for stereotype activation. Thus, stereotypes are much more *flexible* than was assumed historically.

Section Summary

Introduction
- Schematic knowledge is stored in semantic memory. Such knowledge allows us to form expectations, to prevent cognitive overload, to draw inferences, and to perceive visual scenes accurately.

Memory and perception errors
- Schematic knowledge can produce systematic distortions in long-term retrieval of information. It can also lead people to falsely remember incomplete objects as having been complete. In addition, schematic knowledge can lead to boundary extension, in which the view in a photograph is remembered as more extensive than it was.

Stereotypes
- Stereotypical information that conflicts with task information can interfere with problem solving and language comprehension. Stereotypes can be assessed by explicit or implicit measures. Girls perform worse at science relative to boys in countries with a high level of implicit gender stereotyping. Stereotypes are less stable than usually imagined. This is partly because stereotype activation depends on contextual information.

Essay Questions

1. What are the consequences of brain damage that cause memory for words and concepts to be lost?
2. What are the main assumptions of the prototype and exemplar approaches to concepts? In what ways are these approaches limited?
3. Discuss some of the ways in which the conceptual system is linked to the perceptual and motor systems.
4. What is schematic knowledge? How useful is such knowledge in everyday life?

Further Reading

- Baddeley, A., Eysenck, M. W., & Anderson, M. C. (2009). *Memory*. New York, NY: Psychology Press. Chapter 6 in this textbook is devoted to semantic memory and stored knowledge.
- Barsalou, L.W. (2008). Grounded cognition. *Annual Review of Psychology*, *59*, 617–645. Lawrence Barsalou discusses his influential approach based on the assumption that there are close links among the perceptual, motor, and conceptual systems.
- Hampton, J. A. (2010). Concepts in human adults. In D. Mareschal, P. Quinn, & S.E.G. Lea (Eds.), *The making of human concepts* (pp. 293–311). Oxford, UK: Oxford University Press. James Hampton provides a useful overview of theory and research on concepts.
- Patterson, K., Nestor, P. J., & Rogers, T. T. (2007). Where do you know what you know? The representation of semantic knowledge in the human brain. *Nature Reviews Neuroscience*, *8*, 976–987. The ways in which our conceptual knowledge is stored in the brain are identified in this important review article.

Contents

Understanding language 8

INTRODUCTION

Our lives would be remarkably limited without language. Our social interactions rely very heavily on language, and a good command of language is vital for all students. As the English writer Samuel Johnson said, language is "the dress of thought." The main reason we are much more knowledgeable than people of previous generations is that knowledge is passed from one generation to the next via language.

What is language? According to the *Dictionary of Psychology* (Colman, 2001), language is "a conventional system of communicative sounds and sometimes (though not necessarily) written symbols." The crucial word here is "communicative," because the primary function of language is to *communicate*.

However, language also fulfills other functions. Crystal (1997) identified *eight* functions of language, of which communication was one. In addition,

---

Learning Objectives

After studying Chapter 8, you should be able to:

- Apply knowledge of top-down and bottom-up processes to the process of speech perception.
- Define parsing, and discuss models that account for how sentence parsing occurs.
- Define, compare, and contrast bridging/backward inferences and elaborative/forward inferences.
- Describe how eye-tracking is used in order to investigate reading comprehension processes.
- Discuss the evidence for phonological activation during reading.
- Explain how the dual-route model accounts for word reading in English, and also discuss the limitations of the model.
- Describe the two different types of dyslexia, and discuss how they shed light on how word reading processes occur in the human brain.
- Discuss the role of gestures in speech comprehension.

we use language for thinking, to record information, to express emotion (e.g., "I love you"), to pretend to be animals (e.g., "Woof! Woof!"), to express identity with a group (e.g., singing in church), and so on.

IS LANGUAGE INNATE?

Young children acquire language with breathtaking speed. From the age of about 16 months onwards, they often acquire 10 or more new words every day. By the age of 5, children have mastered most of the grammatical rules of their native language. They do this even though most parents have a rather limited (or no) ability to express their knowledge of those rules.

How can we explain the rapidity with which young children master language? Noam Chomsky (1965) argued that the linguistic input to which children are exposed is too limited to provide an answer on its own. He claimed that humans possess a language acquisition device consisting of innate knowledge of grammatical structure.

Chomsky (1986) later replaced the notion of a language acquisition device with the idea of a Universal Grammar common to all languages. It consists of various **linguistic universals**, which are features common to nearly every language. Examples of linguistic universals are the distinction between nouns and verbs, and word order. In English, the typical word order is subject–verb–object (e.g., "The man kicked the ball").

Greenberg (1963) studied numerous languages around the world. The English order was the norm in 35% of those languages, with a further 44% using the subject–object–verb order. Overall, the subject preceded the object in 98% of those languages. This makes much sense. The subject is the word or phrase that a sentence is about, whereas the object is the person or thing acted upon by the verb. The central importance of the subject within the sentence means it is entirely appropriate for it to precede the object.

According to Chomsky, children's learning of language doesn't depend solely on the language acquisition device. Children also require some exposure to (and experience with) the language environment provided by their parents and other people to develop language. Such experience determines *which* specific language any given child will learn.

Chomsky's views have been very influential. However, there is much skepticism about their correctness (Christiansen & Chater, 2008). There are two main reasons for this skepticism. First, the linguistic input to which young children are exposed is much richer than Chomsky believed (Reali & Christiansen, 2005). It is also relatively easy for children to understand. Mothers and other adults use child-directed speech when speaking to young children. **Child-directed speech** involves very short, simple sentences, a slow rate of speaking, use of a restricted vocabulary, and extra stress on key words.

Second, the world's languages differ much more from each other than assumed by Chomsky. It is true that the main European languages are all very similar in many ways. However, large differences appear when all the world's 6000 to 8000 languages are considered. Evans and Levinson (2009, p. 429) did precisely that and concluded as follows: "There are vanishingly few universals of language in the direct sense that all languages exhibit them. Instead, diversity can be found at almost every level of linguistic organization."

Key Terms

Linguistic universals: according to Chomsky, the features (e.g., word order) that are common to virtually all languages; there is controversy concerning the existence of such features.

Child-directed speech: very short and simple utterances based on a limited vocabulary; designed to make it easy for young children to understand what is being communicated.

Bickerton (1984) was influenced by Chomsky's views and put forward the language bioprogram hypothesis. According to this hypothesis, children will create a grammar even if they aren't exposed to a proper language during their early years.

Some of the strongest support for Bickerton's hypothesis comes from the study of pidgin languages. These are new, primitive languages created when two or more groups of people having different native languages are in contact. Pinker (1984) discussed research on laborers from China, Japan, Korea, Puerto Rico, Portugal, and the Philippines who were taken to the sugar plantations of Hawaii 100 years ago. These laborers developed a very simple pidgin language that lacked most grammatical structure. Here is an example: "Me cape buy, me check make," which means "He bought my coffee; he made me out a check." The offspring of these laborers developed Hawaiian Creole, which is a proper language and fully grammatical.

We don't know how much the development of Hawaiian Creole depended on the laborers' prior exposure to language. Clearer evidence that language can develop in groups with practically no exposure to a developed language was reported by Senghas et al. (2004). They studied deaf Nicaraguan children at special schools. Attempts (mostly unsuccessful) were made to teach them Spanish. However, these deaf children developed a new system of gestures that expanded into a basic sign language passed on to successive groups of children who joined the school. Since Nicaraguan Sign Language bore very little relation to Spanish or to the gestures made by hearing children, it is a genuinely new language owing remarkably little to other languages.

What do the above findings mean? They certainly suggest that humans have a strong innate *motivation* to acquire language (including grammatical rules) and to communicate with others. However, the findings don't provide strong support for the notion of a language acquisition device. Overall, as we have seen, the evidence for a language acquisition device is very weak.

LANGUAGE CHAPTERS

There are four main language skills: reading; speech perception; speaking; and writing. It is perhaps natural to assume that any given individual will have generally strong or weak language skills. That assumption may often be correct with respect to first-language acquisition, but is very frequently not so with second-language acquisition. For example, I spent 10 years at school learning French, and I have spent numerous summer holidays there. I can just about read newspapers and easy novels in French, and I can write coherent (if somewhat ungrammatical) French. However, like many British people, I find it agonizingly difficult to understand rapid spoken French, and my ability to speak French is poor.

It is convenient to divide the four main language skills into two groups. In the first group we have reading and speech perception. These skills are concerned with *comprehension* of language presented in the visual and auditory modalities, respectively. Reading and speech perception are the skills discussed in this chapter.

In the second group are speaking and writing. These skills are concerned with the *production* of language in the auditory and visual modalities, respectively. We will defer a discussion of these two language skills until Chapter 9.

Section Summary

Is language innate?

- Chomsky argued that children acquire language rapidly because they have a language acquisition device or a Universal Grammar. He underestimated the importance of environmental factors (e.g., child-directed speech), and there is very little evidence of a Universal Grammar. What is inherited is a strong motivation to acquire language and to communicate.

Language chapters

- This chapter is concerned with language comprehension in the form of reading or listening to speech. The next chapter deals with language production in the form of speech or writing.

READING: BASIC PROCESSES

It is important to study reading because adults without effective reading skills are at a great disadvantage, especially in Western cultures. That means that we need to understand the processes involved in reading to help poor readers. Reading involves several perceptual and other cognitive processes as well as a good knowledge of language and of grammar. Thus, reading can be regarded as visually guided thinking.

In the Real World 8.1: *Learning to read English*

Children learning to read in the English language face more of a challenge than those learning to read in most other languages. Indeed, it takes them about *three* years to reach a level of mastery of reading aloud that children learning other languages attain in *one* year (Seymour et al., 2003).

Why is English so difficult? Most languages (e.g., Spanish) are characterized by a *consistent* relationship between spelling and sound. As a result, it is easy to predict how an unfamiliar word should be pronounced, and there are few (or no) irregular words. In contrast, there are numerous irregular or exception words in English including some of the most common words in the language (e.g., "some"; "was").

Children learning most languages are taught primarily by the **phonics approach**. This approach is also much used by children learning English (Share, 2008). The main emphasis is on teaching children how to form connections between letters or groups of letters and the sounds of spoken English. It also involves learning to blend the sounds of letters together to pronounce unknown words.

When the phonics approach is used to teach children to read in English, the emphasis is often on pronouncing words letter by letter. David Share (2008) argued that a major advantage of this approach is that it ensures that children attend to the order and identity of letters when reading. As a result, this approach should improve readers' ability to recognize words and to spell them correctly.

Suppose we ask children to engage in silent reading of words and nonwords while repeatedly saying something meaningless. This would largely prevent them processing the sounds of the words and nonwords they are reading, and so should disrupt their ability to learn word spellings. Precisely this was found by de Jong et al. (2009) with 7- and 8-year-old children. Their findings suggest that phonological recoding of words occurs during silent reading and is important when learning word spellings.

The phonics approach has been criticized for being too narrow (e.g., Goodman, 1986), because it focuses mostly on allowing readers to pronounce words accurately. In fact, however, readers' main goal is to understand the meaning of what they read, which is the emphasis of the **whole-language approach**. According to Ken Goodman (1986, p. 39), who is a leading advocate of this approach, "Developing readers must be encouraged to predict and guess as they try to make sense of print." A reader may recognize a given word by taking account of the relevant sentence context. For example, in the sentence, "The captured soldier pleaded for _____," we might guess that the missing word is "mercy."

There is much overlap between the whole-language approach and the whole-word approach. According to the whole-word approach (which used to be called the "look-and-say" approach), readers should focus on relating the entire word to its meaning. In so doing, they shouldn't focus on the way it sounds.

Evidence that semantic knowledge (information about word meanings) is important in learning to read was reported by Nation and Cocksey (2009). They used very consistent words (consisting of letter patterns pronounced the same in all words in which they appear) and exception words having very unusual spelling–sound relationships. The exception words are harder to read.

Those children with good semantic knowledge of words had significantly greater reading accuracy than those with poor semantic knowledge. This was especially the case with the exception words that couldn't be read accurately by relying solely on phonics.

There is good evidence that the phonics approach is useful in teaching children to read in almost every language (Share, 2008). So far as English is concerned, Ehri et al. (2001) reported a meta-analysis (see Glossary) combining the findings from many studies. Phonics instruction led to fairly large improvements in word reading, text comprehension, and spelling. Overall, phonics instruction was more beneficial than whole-word or whole-language instruction in enhancing reading abilities.

The ability to decode or identify individual words is very important when learning to read. However, other skills are also involved. According to the Simple View of Reading (e.g., Kendeou et al., 2009), children's reading comprehension is determined by their *listening* comprehension skills as well as their word decoding skills. Kendeou et al. found that both of these skills contributed to children's reading comprehension.

In sum, several kinds of information need to be acquired by young children learning to read in English. First, they must learn the connections between the letters in words and sounds. Second, they must learn to use context to assist in identifying individual words. Third, they must learn to relate words to their meanings.

IT'S IN THE EYES

How can we understand the processes involved in reading? One useful (and unobtrusive) method is to record eye movements during reading. The reader wears a piece of equipment (Figure 8.1) allowing precise assessment of *where* the eyes fixate and *when* they move.

Our eyes seem to move smoothly across the page when we read. In fact, they actually move in rapid jerks (saccades), as you can see if you look closely at someone reading. Once a saccade is initiated, its direction can't be changed. There are fairly frequent regressions in which the eyes move backwards in the text, accounting for about 10% of all saccades. Saccades take 20–30 ms to complete, and are separated by fixations lasting 200–250 ms. The length of each saccade is about eight letters or spaces. Information is extracted from the text only during each fixation and not during the intervening saccades.

Key Terms

Whole-language approach:
a method of teaching young children to read in which the emphasis is on understanding the meaning of text; it includes using sentence context to guess the identity of unknown words.

Saccades:
rapid eye movements that are separated by eye fixations lasting about 250 ms.

Figure 8.1 An eye tracker that records and stores information about an observer's eye fixations. Photo supplied by SR Research Ltd.

Readers typically fixate about 80% of content words (nouns, verbs, and adjectives) but only 20% of function words (articles, conjunctions, and pronouns). Words not fixated tend to be common, short, or predictable. In contrast, words fixated for longer than average are generally rare words or words that are unpredictable in the sentence context.

How does the reading system function to produce these effects? A simple view would be that readers fixate on a word until they have processed it adequately, after which they immediately fixate the next word until it has been adequately processed. Alas, there are *two* major problems with this view. First, it takes 85–200 ms to execute an eye-movement program. If readers operated according to the simple view described above, they would waste time waiting for their eyes to move to the next word. Second, it is hard to see how readers could skip words – they wouldn't know anything about the next word until they had fixated it.

The E-Z Reader model (Pollatsek et al., 2006) provides an elegant solution to the above problems. A crucial assumption is that the next eye movement is programmed after only *part* of the processing of the currently fixated word has occurred. This assumption greatly reduces the time between completion of processing on the current word and eye movement to the next word.

Any spare time is used to start processing the next word. It is harder and more time-consuming to process rare words than common ones, and there is typically less spare time available with rare words. As a result, the fixation time on a word is longer when it is preceded by a rare word. If the processing of the next word is completed rapidly enough (e.g., it is highly predictable in the sentence context), it is skipped.

According to the model, readers can attend to two words (the currently fixated one and the next word) during a single fixation. However, it is a *serial* processing model (i.e., at any given moment only *one* word is processed).

The major assumptions of the model have all received support (see Reichle et al., 2003, for a review). However, nearly all the research has focused on the English language, and the reading strategies used by readers of English may not be universal. Rayner et al. (2007) studied eye movements in Chinese readers reading Chinese text. Chinese differs from English in that it is written without spaces between successive characters and consists of words mostly made up of two characters. In spite of that, the pattern of eye movements was similar to that previously found for readers of English.

The assumption that words are processed serially (one at a time) has been criticized. It has been suggested (Engbert et al., 2005) that there is parallel processing – the processing of the word currently fixated is influenced by the previous word and the next one. That makes sense given that the perceptual span (the letters and spaces we can perceive in one fixation) is about 18 letters.

Finding that characteristics of the next word influence the fixation duration on the current word would provide evidence for parallel processing. The findings are mixed (see Rayner et al., 2007 for a review), but Barber et al. (2010) reported supporting evidence. However, most of the effects were fairly small and suggest that any parallel processing is limited in scope.

Evaluation

➕ There is reasonable evidence indicating the existence of close connections between eye movements and cognitive processes during reading.

➕ The assumptions of the model have all received support from research.

➖ The model focuses mainly on early and basic processes in reading rather than on higher-level processes (e.g., those involved in integrating information across words).

➖ The assumption that processing during reading is always serial seems to be incorrect, although the extent of parallel processing is typically modest.

SOUND AS WELL AS VISION?

We have seen that young children learning to read are often taught explicitly to pronounce each word out loud. That suggests that **phonology** (the sounds of words) is important at early stages of learning to read. However, it is easy to think of reading in adults as being predominantly a *visual* skill. After all, the information presented to a reader is visual in nature, and we are generally not aware of sounding out words as we read. However, adults often resort to inner speech when reading a demanding text.

Does phonology influence the reading process in adults? Evidence that the answer is "Yes" was reported by van Orden (1987). Participants made many more errors when asked questions such as "Is it part of a person's face? KNOWS" than when asked "Is it part of a person's face? SNOBS." "KNOWS" is a homophone (word having one pronunciation but two spellings) and is homophonic with "NOSE," which is part of the face. The participants made errors because they engaged in phonological processing of the words.

We now move on to the notion of phonological neighborhood. Two words are phonological neighbors if they differ in only one phoneme (e.g., "gate" has "bait" and "get" as neighbors). If phonology is used in visual word recognition, then words with many phonological neighbors should have an advantage. Yates (2005) found support for this assumption using various tasks involving word processing. The number of phonological neighbors also influences word processing within sentences (Yates et al., 2008).

Another approach is based on priming (see Glossary), in which a prime word or other stimulus is presented very shortly before the target word. The prime word is related to the target word (e.g., in spelling, meaning, or sound). What is of interest is to see the effects of the prime on processing of (and response to) the target word. With masked priming, the prime is followed rapidly by a second masking stimulus so it can't be perceived consciously.

Rastle and Brysbaert (2006) considered the effects of masked priming in several meta-analyses (combining the findings from many studies). For example,

Key Term

Phonology:
the sounds of words; of importance in reading.

the target word (e.g., "clip") can be preceded by a phonologically identical nonword prime (e.g., "klip") or a phonologically different nonword prime (e.g., "plip"). Target words were processed faster on various tasks (e.g., reading time) when preceded by phonologically identical primes. Thus, phonological processing occurred rapidly and automatically.

We have seen that phonological processing often plays an important role when one is identifying words in reading. However, words can be read *without* the involvement of phonological processing. Suppose we used a proofreading task that involved detecting spelling mistakes and other *visual* errors. On such a task, phonological processing might be less important than on an ordinary reading task.

Jared et al. (1999) used a proofreading task, and found the use of phonology depended on the nature of the words and participants' reading ability. Eye-movement data suggested that phonology was used in accessing the meaning of low-frequency words (those only rarely encountered) but not high-frequency ones. In addition, poor readers were more likely than good ones to access phonology.

In sum, there is clear evidence that adults (as well as children) typically engage in phonological as well as visual processing when reading. This phonological processing occurs rapidly and doesn't require conscious awareness. However, phonological processing may not occur if the task is strongly visual (e.g., proofreading) and the material is easy (e.g., common words).

TWO ROUTES IN READING

Reading aloud familiar words seems about as easy a task as you can imagine. That is also so with most **nonwords** (strings of letters that are typically pronounceable – examples are "cruss" and "trin"). I would be surprised if you had any difficulty at all in reading out the following words and nonwords:

CAT   FOG   COMB   PINT   MANTINESS   FASS

Key Terms

Nonwords:
letter strings that do not form words but are nevertheless pronounceable.

Internal lexicon:
information about the sounds, spellings, and meanings of words stored in long-term memory; it functions as a dictionary.

Graphemes:
basic units of written language; a word consists of one or more graphemes.

Phonemes:
these are the basic units of sound; words consists of one or more phonemes.

Close inspection of what you have just done reveals some hidden complexities. For example, how do you know the *b* in *comb* is silent, and that *pint* doesn't rhyme with *hint*? Presumably you have specific information about how to pronounce these words stored in long-term memory. However, that can't explain your ability to pronounce nonwords such as *mantiness* and *fass*.

According to Coltheart et al. (2001), we use *two* routes when reading aloud (Figure 8.2). There is a *direct* route (Routes 2 and 3 in the figure), in which we access information about the meaning and sound of the word in an **internal lexicon** or dictionary. There is also an *indirect* route (Route 1 in the figure), in which we convert the **graphemes** (basic units of written language) into **phonemes** (basic units of sound) by using various rules.

Coltheart et al. (2001) assumed that we use both routes when reading aloud. However, naming visually presented words typically depends mostly on the direct rather than the indirect route, because the former route generally operates faster.

Coltheart et al. (2001) distinguished between regular and irregular words. Regular words are ones in which the pronunciation is predictable from the letters (e.g., *tint*; *punt*). Irregular words are ones in which the pronunciation is *not* predictable from the letters (e.g., "island"; "yacht"). According to Coltheart et al., we *must* use the direct route with irregular words because we

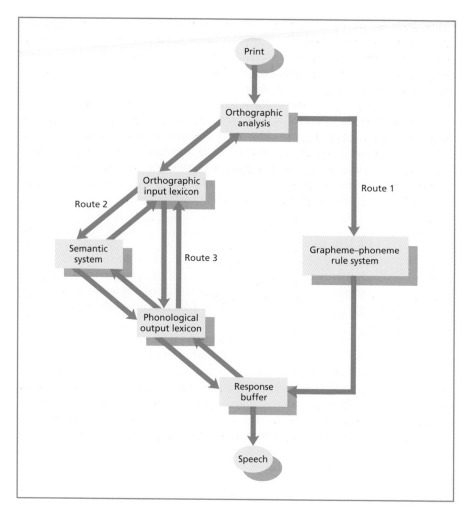

Figure 8.2 Basic architecture of the dual-route cascade model. Route 1 is the indirect route in reading and Routes 2 and 3 together form the direct route. Adapted from Coltheart et al. (2001).

would mispronounce them if we relied on the indirect route. In contrast, we can't use the direct route with unfamiliar words or with nonwords, because we don't possess any information about them in our internal lexicon.

We would expect the two routes in reading identified by Coltheart et al. (2001) to involve processes in different brain areas. This issue was addressed by Seghier et al. (2008). As predicted, different brain areas were associated with the reading of irregular words (direct route) and nonwords (indirect route).

Brain-damaged patients

Suppose we could find brain-damaged patients who relied almost exclusively on the indirect route in reading and so made little use of the internal lexicon. Since they could use rules to convert letters into sounds, they would be able to pronounce regular words and nonwords accurately. However, they should struggle with irregular words.

The precise pattern described above has been observed in some patients. A male patient, KT, read 100% of nonwords accurately as well as 81% of regular words. However, he was successful with only 41% of irregular words

(McCarthy & Warrington, 1984). Patients (like KT) who can read regular words but not irregular words are said to suffer from **surface dyslexia**.

Suppose we could find brain-damaged patients who relied almost exclusively on the direct route. They would be able to pronounce familiar words (whether regular or irregular). However, they would struggle with nonwords about which there is no information in the internal lexicon.

Caccappolo-van Vliet et al. (2004) studied two patients conforming to the above pattern. IB was a 77-year-old woman who had worked as a secretary, and MO was a 48-year-old male accountant. Their performance on reading regular and irregular words exceeded 90% compared to under 60% with nonwords. Patients (like IB and MO) who can read familiar words but not unfamiliar words and nonwords have **phonological dyslexia**.

Limitations of the dual-route model

Several theorists (e.g., Perry et al., 2007; Plaut et al., 1996) have argued that the speed with which words can be read aloud depends on *consistency*. Consistent words have letter patterns that are always pronounced the same in all words in which they appear and are predicted to be faster to name than inconsistent words.

In contrast, the focus in the dual-route model is on *regularity* (the extent to which a word's pronunciation is predictable from its spelling). The prediction from this model is that regular words should be named faster than irregular ones. In fact, the evidence indicates that the time taken to pronounce words depends more on their consistency than on their regularity (Glushko, 1979).

Nonwords can also be consistent or inconsistent. For example, the word body "–ust" is very consistent because it is always pronounced in the same way in monosyllabic words, and so the nonword "nust" is consistent. In contrast, the word body "-ave" is inconsistent because it is pronounced in different ways in different words (e.g., "save" and "have"), and so the nonword "mave" is inconsistent.

According to the dual-route model, nonwords are pronounced using spelling–sound pronunciation rules. As a result, there should be no difference between consistent and inconsistent nonwords. In fact, however, inconsistent nonwords take longer to pronounce than consistent ones (Glushko, 1979; Zevin & Seidenberg, 2006). According to the dual-route model, the pronunciation rules should generate only *one* pronunciation for each nonword. However, Zevin and Seidenberg found that the pronunciations of inconsistent nonwords were rather variable.

What do the above findings show us? They suggest that the reading of nonwords isn't as neat and tidy as implied by the dual-route model. More specifically, the model claims that nonwords are processed *only* via the indirect route based on rules that translate letters into sounds. However, the evidence suggests the direct route is also involved, because the time taken to pronounce nonwords depends in part on consistency.

In sum, the processes involved in reading words and nonwords are more *flexible* than assumed by the dual-route model. According to the connectionist approach put forward by Plaut et al. (1996) and Harm and Seidenberg (2001), it is a matter of "all hands to the pump." All the relevant knowledge we possess about word sounds, word spellings, and word meanings is used at the same

| Key Terms |

Surface dyslexia: a condition in which brain-damaged patients have difficulty in accessing words in their internal lexicon or dictionary; this causes difficulties in reading irregular words aloud.

Phonological dyslexia: a condition in which brain-damaged patients have difficulty in phonological processing; this causes them to find it hard to pronounce unfamiliar words and **nonwords** (but not familiar words) when reading aloud.

time whether we are reading words or nonwords. This approach has received more experimental support than has the dual-route model.

Focus on English

Nearly all the research on reading aloud has focused on the *English* language. Does that matter? Many researchers argue that it does and that what is true of learning to read aloud in English is sometimes not the case with other languages (Share, 2008; Zhou et al., 2009).

As discussed earlier, the spelling–sound complexities in English are greater than in most other major languages. Seymour et al. (2003) studied children from 14 countries reading words and nonwords in their native language. On average, these children could read aloud 87% of familiar, high-frequency words. However, children reading in English scored an average of only 34%, which was substantially lower than the figure for any other country. English-speaking children were also at a huge disadvantage when reading nonwords. The average accuracy of reading nonwords across all the countries was 82%, but it was only 29% in English.

What are the implications of the above findings? One of the aims of the dual-route model was to shed light on how we pronounce irregular words. This is clearly important with respect to English, which has numerous irregular words. However, this aim has somewhat less relevance to most other languages, which have relatively few irregular words. In spite of that, the dual-route model has been applied successfully to other languages. For example, Havelka and Rastle (2005) used the model to explain reading aloud in Serbian.

Section Summary

Learning to read English

- It is especially hard to learn to read English because there are numerous irregular or exception words. Children often learn to read using the phonics approach. This approach focuses on teaching readers to pronounce words accurately. In contrast, the whole-language and whole-word approaches focus more on understanding the meanings of words. In addition to word-decoding skills, listening comprehension skills are important in learning to read.

It's in the eyes

- Readers move their eyes in rapid jerks or saccades about four times per second. The next eye movement is programmed after only partial processing of the currently fixated word. The E-Z Reader model assumes that reading involves only serial processing, but parallel processing is sometimes used.

Sound as well as vision?

- Phonological processing is generally important in adult reading. For example, words are processed faster when preceded by an unseen phonologically identical prime than one that is not phonologically identical. This suggests that phonological processing can occur rapidly and automatically. Phonological processing is less important on reading tasks (e.g., proofreading) that require detailed visual processing.

Two routes in reading

- According to the dual-route model, two routes can be used when reading words aloud. The direct route involves accessing information about each word's meaning and sound in an internal lexicon. The indirect route involves converting letters into sounds. Patients with surface dyslexia use mostly the indirect route, whereas those with phonological dyslexia use mostly the direct route. In fact, the processes involved in reading are more flexible than assumed by the dual-route model. That model is relevant to reading in all languages, but is especially so with the English language.

SPEECH PERCEPTION: BASIC PROCESSES

Most of us are very good at understanding what other people are saying to us even when they speak in a strange dialect and/or ungrammatically. In our everyday lives, we take our ability to understand the speech of others for granted. Indeed, in view of the enormous experience we have all had in using the English language and in listening to other people, speech perception seems very easy and straightforward.

In fact, speech perception is actually much more complex than it appears to be. The main reasons for this complexity are discussed at length in Chapter 2, and will only be mentioned briefly here.

First, language is spoken very rapidly, at a rate of about 10 phonemes (basic speech sounds) per second. Second, speech typically consists of a continuously changing pattern of sound with few periods of silence, making it hard to decide when one word ends and the next begins. Third, the way any given phoneme (basic unit of sound) is pronounced depends in part on the phonemes preceding and following it. Thus, listeners have to adjust to variations in pronunciation. Fourth, much of the time when we listen to someone speaking there is background noise from other people, traffic, and so on. This issue is discussed in the next section.

It used to be assumed that listeners' interpretation of speech proceeds at the same rate as information contained in the speech signal reaches the auditory cortex. If this assumption were correct, it would greatly limit the time available for speech perception. In fact, listeners can integrate information over a longer period of time than previously assumed (Dahan, 2010). More specifically, listeners generally form initial hypotheses about the words they are hearing. However, they can use later-arriving information to modify those initial hypotheses if necessary. Such flexibility makes it easier for listeners to achieve accurate speech perception.

How do we recognize sounds and spoken words? That is a central question in research on speech perception. Several theories have been proposed to answer it. The motor theory (Liberman et al., 1967) was discussed in Chapter 2. It is assumed in this theory that listeners mimic or copy the speaker's articulatory movements, and that this provides less variable information than the speech signal itself.

The evidence indicates that motor processes sometimes facilitate speech perception, but it can occur in their absence (see Chapter 2). We will shortly be discussing a more influential approach to speech perception – this is the TRACE model.

REALISTIC LISTENING CONDITIONS

Most research on speech perception has involved idealized conditions (Mattys et al., 2009). Listeners are presented with a single, carefully recorded speech signal to which they give their undivided attention. Contrast such listening conditions with those typically found in our everyday lives. We often try to understand what one person is saying while other people are also talking or some of our attention is focused on something else.

Mattys et al. (2009) studied the effects of *imperfect* listening conditions on speech perception. They identified two major ways in which the identification of a spoken word can be made more difficult:

1. *Energetic masking:* Distracting sounds can cause the audibility of the spoken word to be degraded due to blending of their acoustic signals. Here the problem affects bottom-up processing.
2. *Informational masking:* Performing a second task at the same time as trying to identify a spoken word creates cognitive load and makes it harder to use stored knowledge about words (e.g., their meanings). Here the problem affects top-down processing.

The task used by Mattys et al. (2009) involved presenting a phrase (e.g., *mile doption*; *mild option*) and asking participants to decide the identity of a word in the phrase (e.g., *mild* or *mile*). They reported several important findings.

First, energetic masking impaired performance on the word-identification task. Second, informational masking also impaired task performance. These two findings indicate that bottom-up and top-down processes are both important in recognition of spoken words. Third, energetic masking led listeners to place more reliance on salient or conspicuous acoustic detail, whereas informational masking led them to rely more on their knowledge of words and word meanings.

What are the implications of these findings? It has generally been assumed that adverse listening conditions don't affect the processes used by listeners involved in speech perception. However, this assumption is inconsistent with Mattys et al.'s (2009) findings. In fact, listeners respond to adverse listening conditions by altering the balance between bottom-up and top-down processes. Thus, the precise nature of the alteration depends on whether energetic or informational masking is involved.

TRACE MODEL

McClelland and Elman (1986) and McClelland (1991) put forward a network model of speech perception based on connectionist principles (see Chapter 1). A key assumption of the model is that bottom-up and top-down processes

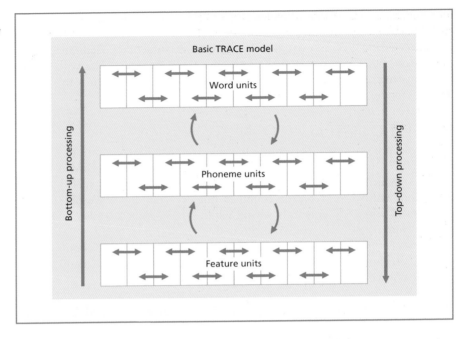

interact flexibly in spoken word recognition. It is assumed there are processing units or nodes at three different levels: features (e.g., voicing; manner of production); phonemes (basic units of sound); and words (see Figure 8.3). There are facilitatory connections between levels, so that processing at one level can influence processing at another level.

A distinctive feature of the TRACE model is its emphasis on the importance of top-down processes (e.g., context effects). There is increasing evidence that context effects can have an almost immediate effect on speech perception (see Hagoort & van Berkum, 2007 for a review). This supports the notion that top-down processes are important. This research is discussed fully in Chapter 2.

Findings

Suppose we ask listeners to detect target phonemes or sounds presented in words and nonwords. According to the TRACE model, performance should be better in the word condition (this is the word superiority effect). Why is that? In that condition, there would be top-down activation from the word level to the phoneme level that would facilitate phoneme detection.

Mirman et al. (2008) tested the above prediction. Listeners detected a target phoneme (/t/ or /k/) in words and nonwords. Words were presented on 80% or 20% of the trials. The argument was that attention to (and activation at) the word level would be greater when most of the auditory stimuli were words. This should increase the word superiority effect.

What did Mirman et al. (2008) find? First, the predicted word superiority effect was found in most conditions (see Figure 8.4). Second, the magnitude of this effect was greater when 80% of the auditory stimuli were words than when only 20% were. These findings provide strong evidence for the involvement of top-down processes in speech perception.

Ganong (1980) presented listeners with various sounds ranging between a word (e.g., *dash*) and a nonword (e.g., *tash*). There was a context effect – an ambiguous initial phoneme was more likely to be perceived as forming a word rather than a nonword. This effect is known as the lexical identification shift. According to the TRACE model, this effect occurs because there is top-down activation from the word level.

The model attaches too much importance to top-down processing. McQueen (1991) presented ambiguous phonemes at the end of auditory stimuli. Each ambiguous phoneme could be perceived as completing a word or a nonword. According to the model, top-down effects from the word level should have produced a preference for perceiving the phonemes as completing words. This prediction was confirmed *only* when the stimulus was degraded. It follows from the model that the effect (i.e., the lexical identification shift) should be greater when the stimulus is degraded and so less bottom-up information is available. However, the absence of an effect when the stimulus wasn't degraded is inconsistent with the model.

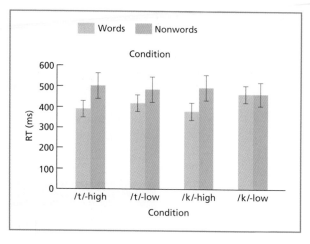

Figure 8.4   Mean reaction times for recognition of /t/ and /k/ phonemes in words and nonwords when words were presented on a high (80%) or low (20%) proportion of trials. From Mirman et al. (2008). Reprinted with permission of the Cognitive Science Society Inc. and John Wiley & Sons.

Imagine you are listening to spoken words. Would you activate the *spellings* of those words? It seems unlikely that orthography (information about word spellings) is involved in speech perception, and there is no allowance for its involvement in the TRACE model.

In fact, however, orthography *does* play a role in speech perception. Perre and Ziegler (2008) gave listeners a **lexical decision task** (deciding whether auditory stimuli were words or nonwords). The words varied in the consistency between their phonology or sounds and their orthography or spelling. This should be irrelevant if orthography isn't involved in speech perception. In fact, listeners performed the lexical decision task more slowly when the words were inconsistent than when they were inconsistent. This happened because the phonological representations of words contain orthographic information (Perre et al., 2010).

Evaluation

⊕ The TRACE model provides reasonable accounts of phenomena such as the lexical identification shift and the word superiority effect in phoneme monitoring.

⊕ A significant strength of the TRACE model is its assumption that bottom-up and top-down processes both contribute to spoken word recognition, combined with explicit assumptions about the processes involved.

⊕ The TRACE model emphasizes the role of top-down processes. This allows it to account for effects when bottom-up processes are insufficient to deal with limited stimulus information (e.g., McQueen, 1991).

Key Term

Lexical decision task: strings of letters are presented, and the task is to decide as rapidly as possible whether each string is a word or a nonword.

- The model exaggerates the importance of top-down processes to speech perception when the auditory stimulus isn't degraded (e.g., McQueen, 1991).

- The model ignores some factors influencing auditory word recognition. For example, it fails to predict that orthographic information plays a significant role in speech perception (Perre et al., 2010; Perre & Ziegler, 2008).

Section Summary

- Speech perception is complex because of the speed of spoken language, the variable nature of the stimulus input, and the presence of background noise. Speech perception is facilitated by listeners' ability to modify their initial hypotheses about the stimulus input in light of subsequent information.

Realistic listening conditions
- Speech perception can be made more difficult in two ways: (1) by adding distracting sounds; (2) by requiring listeners to perform a second task at the same time. Speech perception is impaired by both of these manipulations. However, the two manipulations have very different effects on the precise processing used by listeners.

TRACE model
- According to the TRACE model, there are processing units at the level of features, phonemes, and words. The model's emphasis on top-down processes allows it to account for the word superiority effect and lexical identification shift. The model exaggerates the importance of top-down processes, and ignores the role played by orthographic information in speech perception.

UNDERSTANDING SENTENCES

When we read (or listen to) a sentence, our central goal is typically to understand it. Achieving this goal involves using various processes and kinds of information. Here we will consider only some of the relevant factors. First, whether we are reading or listening to a sentence, we need to identify its syntactical (grammatical) structure. Second, it can be demanding to understand a sentence fully, and there is some evidence that processing often falls short of that needed for complete understanding.

PARSING

Key Term
Parsing: identifying the grammatical structure of sentences that are read or heard.

As indicated already, it is important for readers and listeners to identify language's syntactical (grammatical) structure. This is known technically as **parsing**. What exactly is grammar? It is concerned with how words are combined within a sentence.

Most of the time, it seems as if parsing or assigning grammatical structure to sentences is fairly easy. However, numerous sentences (e.g., "They are flying planes"; "They are cooking apples") pose problems because their grammatical structure is ambiguous. Other examples of ambiguous sentences are "Kids make nutritious snacks" and "Local high school dropouts cut in half" (Matlin, 2009).

How do we go about making sense of sentences? Everyone agrees that we use syntactic or grammatical information plus semantic information about the meanings of the individual words. However, there has been controversy concerning the details. Some theorists (e.g., Frazier & Rayner, 1982) argue that *only* syntactic information is used initially, with semantic information being used at a later stage.

Other theorists (e.g., MacDonald et al., 1994; Van Gompel et al., 2005) argue that it is much more a question of, "All hands to the pump." In other words, we use *all* sources of information (syntactic, semantic, and world knowledge) from the outset to influence the initial interpretation of a sentence.

According to MacDonald et al.'s (1994) constraint-based theory, competing analyses of the current sentence are activated at the same time and are ranked according to activation strength. The syntactic structure receiving most support from the various sources of information is highly activated, with other syntactic structures being less activated. Readers become confused when reading ambiguous sentences if the correct syntactic structure is less activated than one or more incorrect structures.

According to MacDonald et al.'s (1994) theory, one factor influencing the assignment of syntactic structure to a sentence is verb bias. Many verbs can occur within various syntactic structures, but are found more often in some syntactic structures than others. Readers will tend to assume initially that the more common syntactic structure is correct: this is **verb bias**.

Here is an example of verb bias. The verb "read" is most often followed by a direct object (e.g., "The ghost read the book during the plane journey"). However, it can also be used with a sentence complement (e.g., "The ghost read the book had been burned") (Harley, 2008). Readers resolved ambiguities and identified the correct syntactic structure more rapidly when the sentence structure was consistent with the verb bias (Garnsey et al., 1997). This finding is *not* predicted by the garden-path model, according to which verb bias should not influence the initial identification of syntactic structure.

Boland and Blodgett (2001) used noun/verb homographs (e.g., duck, train) – words that can be used as a noun or a verb. For example, if you read a sentence that started, "She saw her duck and ...", you would not know whether the word "duck" was being used as a noun ("... and chickens near the barn") or a verb "... and stumble near the barn").

According to the constraint-based approach, readers should initially construct a syntactic structure in which the homograph is used as its more common part of speech (e.g., "duck" is mostly a verb and "train" is mostly a noun). As predicted, readers rapidly experienced problems (revealed by eye movements) when noun/verb homographs were used in their *less* common form.

Other studies discussed previously provide additional support for constraint-based theory. For example, there is evidence (e.g., Spivey et al., 2002; Tanenhaus et al., 1995) indicating that prior context (which provides

Key Term
Verb bias: the finding that some verbs occur more often within one particular syntactic or grammatical structure than within others.

relevant information about meaning) influences sentence processing at an early stage.

Syntax vs. meaning

Nearly all theories of parsing and of sentence processing have an important limitation. Such theories are based on the assumption that the representations that we form of sentences are "complete, detailed, and accurate" (Ferreira et al., 2002, p. 11), in part because we successfully work out their syntactic or grammatical structure.

There is increasing evidence that the above assumption is unduly optimistic. Ferreira (2003) presented sentences auditorily, and found that her listeners' sentence representations were often inaccurate. A sentence such as, "The mouse was eaten by the cheese," was sometimes misinterpreted as meaning the mouse ate the cheese. The sentence, "The man was visited by the woman" was sometimes mistakenly interpreted to mean the man visited the woman.

Why are people so prone to error when processing sentences (especially passive ones)? According to Ferreira (2003), we use heuristics or rules of thumb to simplify the task of understanding sentences. A very common heuristic (the NVN or noun–verb–noun strategy) is to assume that the subject of a sentence is the agent of some action, whereas the object of the sentence is the recipient or theme. We use this heuristic because a substantial majority of English sentences conform to this pattern.

Christianson et al. (2010) made a similar point. They argued that listeners in the study by Ferreira (2003) faced a conflict between the syntactic structure of the passive sentences and their semantic knowledge of what is typically the case in the real world. Sometimes that conflict is resolved by favoring semantic knowledge and relatively ignoring syntactic information.

Christianson et al. (2010) tested their viewpoint in the following way. Some listeners heard plausible passive sentences such as, "The fish was caught by the angler," and then had to describe an unrelated line drawing. Listeners tended to produce passive sentences in their description. In other words, they were influenced by the syntactic structure of the original sentence.

Other listeners heard implausible passive sentences such as, "The angler was caught by the fish." These listeners tended NOT to produce passive sentences in their descriptions of the line drawings. Thus, they paid relatively little attention to the syntactic structure of the original sentence.

The findings discussed so far are consistent with a broader viewpoint. According to this viewpoint, our typical comprehension goal is to produce "good enough" representations that will suffice for current purposes (Swets et al., 2008, p. 211). As a result, our sentence processing will often be deficient.

It follows from the good-enough approach of Swets et al. (2008) that readers should only process sentences thoroughly if there is a good reason to do so. As predicted, participants read sentences (especially syntactically ambiguous ones) more slowly when anticipating detailed comprehension questions than when expecting superficial comprehension questions (Swets et al.; see Figure 8.5). Indeed, ambiguous sentences were read *more* rapidly than non-ambiguous ones when superficial questions were asked. However, this ambiguity advantage disappeared when more challenging comprehension questions were anticipated.

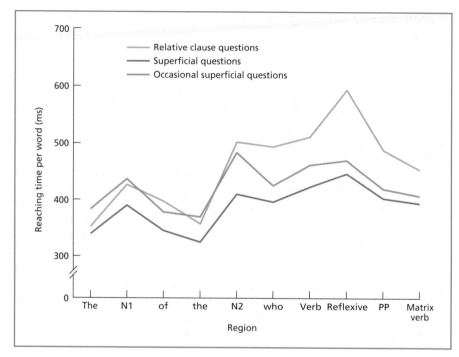

Figure 8.5 Sentence reading times as a function of the way in which comprehension was assessed: detailed (relative clause) questions; superficial questions on all trials; or occasional superficial questions. Sample sentence: The maid of the princess who scratched herself in public was terribly humiliated. From Swets et al. (2008). Copyright © The Psychonomic Society. Reproduced with permission.

EXTRACTING MEANING

When we listen to someone speaking, the words they use may be insufficient on their own to permit us to work out the speaker's intended meaning. More specifically, there is often a discrepancy between the speaker's *literal* and the *intended* meaning, and listeners need to focus on extracting the intended meaning.

There are frequently two ways in which listeners are assisted in the task of deciding on the speaker's intended meaning. First, they often find it easier to understand what the speaker means if they focus on the common ground (mutual knowledge and beliefs) they share with the speaker. The same is true to a lesser extent of readers trying to understand a writer's intended meaning.

Second, when we are listening to a sentence, we can often obtain useful information from the speaker's accompanying gestures. The ways in which these factors influence sentence comprehension are discussed below.

Pragmatics

Pragmatics is concerned with practical language and comprehension, especially those aspects going beyond the speaker's literal meaning by taking account of the social context. Thus, pragmatics deals with *intended* rather than *literal* meaning as expressed by speakers and understood by listeners. Cases in which the intended meaning is not the same as the literal meaning include irony, sarcasm, and understatement. For example, we assume that someone who says, "The weather's really great!" when it has been raining nonstop for several days actually thinks the weather is terrible.

> **Key Term**
>
> **Pragmatics:**
> in sentence comprehension, using the social context and other information to work out the intended meaning of what is said.

Listeners typically try to work out the speaker's intentions from what he/she has just said. Consider the following example (Holtgraves, 1998, p. 25):

Ken: Did Paula agree to go out with you?
Bob: She's not my type.

Holtgraves found that most people interpreted Bob's reply as meaning that Paula hadn't agreed to go with him, but he wanted to save face.

Suppose Bob gave an indirect reply that didn't seem to involve face saving (e.g., "She's my type"). Listeners took almost 50% longer to comprehend such indirect replies than to comprehend typical indirect replies (e.g., "She's not my type"). This was because it was hard to understand the speaker's motivation with indirect replies.

How rapidly do listeners understand the speaker's intention? Holtgraves (2008a) explored this issue. Participants read or listened to part of a conversation (e.g., Bob says to Andy, "I definitely will do it tomorrow"). This was followed by a single word (e.g., "promise"), with participants deciding rapidly whether the word captured the speaker's/writer's intention.

Holtgraves' (2008a) key finding was that participants recognized the speaker's/writer's intention rapidly and automatically. The speaker's intention is also well-remembered (Holtgraves, 2008b). This suggests that listeners regard it as especially important to focus on the speaker's intention or intentions.

Listeners often have to go beyond a speaker's literal meaning. For example, there is the use of **metaphor**, in which a word is said to mean something it only resembles. For example, someone who is always cheerful may be described as a ray of sunshine.

Walter Kintsch (2000) put forward a model of metaphor understanding consisting of two components:

1. *The latent semantic analysis component:* This represents the meanings of thousands of words based on their relations or associations with other words.
2. *The construction–integration component:* This uses information from the first component to form interpretations of statements. Consider a statement such as "Lawyers are sharks," which consists of an argument (lawyers) and a predicate or assertion (sharks). This component *selects* predicate features relevant to the argument and *inhibits* irrelevant predicate features.

According to Kintsch's model, our understanding of metaphors depends on our ability to *inhibit* semantic properties of the predicate irrelevant to the argument. Individuals high in working memory capacity (the ability to combine processing and storage; discussed later) are better than those low in such capacity at inhibiting distracting information (see Chiappe & Chiappe, 2007, for a review). As predicted, Chiappe and Chiappe found that individuals with high working memory capacity interpreted metaphors faster and more accurately than those with low working memory capacity.

The nonreversibility of metaphors is an important phenomenon (Chiappe & Chiappe, 2007). For example, "My surgeon is a butcher" has a very different meaning from "My butcher is a surgeon." According to Kintsch's model,

| Key Term

Metaphor:
an expression in which something or someone is said to mean something it only resembles; for example, someone who is very brave may be described as a "lion in battle."

only those features of the predicate (second noun) *relevant to the argument* (first noun) are selected. Thus, changing the argument changes the features selected.

Suppose we present a metaphor such as, "My lawyer was a shark." According to the model, it should take longer to understand that metaphor when literal properties of sharks (e.g., "has fins"; "can swim") *irrelevant* to its metaphorical meaning have recently been activated. As predicted, the above metaphor took longer to understand when preceded by a sentence emphasizing the literal meaning of "shark" (e.g., "Sharks can swim") (McGlone & Manfredi, 2001).

Common ground

Even when listeners identify correctly every word the speaker says, they sometimes fail to understand fully the meaning of what is being said. What is important here is the **common ground** (the shared knowledge and beliefs between speaker and listener). Suppose you overhear a conversation between two people who know each other very well. You probably find it very hard to understand what is being said because you lack the common ground shared by those involved in the conversation.

It seems reasonable to assume that listeners strive to work out the common ground existing between them and the speaker. However, that can be very effortful. According to Keysar et al. (2000), listeners often use a rapid and non-effortful rule of thumb known as the **egocentric heuristic**. This involves listeners interpreting what they hear based on their own knowledge rather than on knowledge shared with the speaker.

Keysar et al. (2000) obtained evidence consistent with use of the egocentric heuristic. For example, consider what happened when the listener could see *three* candles of different sizes but the speaker could see only *two*. The task was to move the small candle. If the listener used common ground information, he/she would move the smaller of the two candles the speaker could see. However, if the listener used the egocentric heuristic, he/she would initially consider the candle the speaker couldn't see. In fact, listeners' initial eye movements were often directed to the candle only they could see, and they reached for that object on 20% of trials.

Subsequent research suggested that listeners generally make use of the common ground. Suppose a speaker and a listener have agreed to use a given term (e.g., "the multicolored objects") to refer to a target stimulus, thus establishing common ground. Subsequently, the same speaker or a different (new) speaker uses the same term to describe the target stimulus. Listeners fixated the target more rapidly when the speaker was the same than when the speaker was different. This happened because common ground had been established with the original speaker but not with the new one.

Which listeners are most likely to ignore the common ground? This question was addressed by Brown-Schmidt (2009). Listeners who had deficient inhibitory control were more likely to interpret what the speaker said inappropriately and less likely to make use of common-ground information.

Gestures

We all spend much of our time listening to other people speaking (e.g., a friend sitting next to you; a politician giving a speech on television). They often make

> **Key Terms**
>
> **Common ground:**
> the shared knowledge and beliefs possessed by a speaker and a listener; its use assists communication.
>
> **Egocentric heuristic:**
> a rule of thumb in which listeners rely solely on their own knowledge when interpreting what speakers are saying rather than on the **common ground** between them; it can inhibit effective communication.

hand gestures while they speak. *Why* do they do this? There are two major possibilities. First, speakers may find that using gestures makes it easier for them to communicate what they want to say.

Second, speakers may use gestures for the benefit of their listener(s) in the hope that the gestures will provide useful additional information. There is evidence supporting both possibilities (e.g., Bavelas et al., 2008; Jacobs & Garnham, 2007; see Chapter 9).

How useful are hand gestures to listeners? Kelly et al. (1999) presented participants with videotapes of various scenarios. In one scenario, Adam and Bill need burgers in a hurry because Bill has forgotten to buy them. Adam says, "You better go get the burgers," to which Bill replies, "But the store is clear across town." For some participants, the last sentence was accompanied by Bill pointing at Adam's bike. Not surprisingly, participants were more likely to realize that Bill wanted Adam to collect the burgers by using his bike when Bill made an appropriate hand gesture.

Kelly et al. (2010b) presented a gesture briefly (e.g., chopping vegetables; washing dishes) followed by a target (speech and gesture together). The speech and gesture were *congruent* (e.g., both referring to chopping) or *incongruent* (e.g., saying "chop" combined with a twisting gesture). The task was to decide whether either part of the target was related to the gesture presented initially.

Performance was better when the speech and gesture presented together were congruent than when they were incongruent. Thus, speech and gesture were both easy to understand when they conveyed the same information. There was a substantial increase in the error rate when speech and gesture were incongruent. These findings indicate that language comprehension depends on an integrated system combining information from gestures and from speech.

Kelly et al. (2010a) presented participants with brief videos consisting of a word and a gesture. The gender of the speaker and the gesturer was the same or different and the content of the speech and the gesture was congruent or incongruent. For example, a gesture indicating "Stir" is incongruent with the word "Cut." Participants indicated whether the person speaking was male or female.

The key finding was that participants performed the task more slowly when the gesture was incongruent with the word than when it was congruent. Thus, listeners use gestural information in an automatic way even when it isn't required for the current task.

Speakers can communicate meaning in nonverbal ways by body movements as well as hand gestures. We would expect professional actors to be especially good at doing this. Noice and Noice (2007) found that nonactors could accurately work out actors' intended goal-directed meaning on the basis of their body and hand movements without knowledge of the situation or the accompanying dialog.

In sum, listeners make much use of the gestural information provided by speakers, and integrate it with speech information. Indeed, they do so automatically regardless of its relevance to the current task. Body movements can also communicate meaning.

Section Summary

Parsing

- The majority of the evidence suggests that most or all sources of information (syntactic, semantic, world knowledge) are used from the outset during sentenced comprehension. When there is a conflict between the syntactic structure of a sentence and listeners' knowledge of the world, they often favor semantic knowledge at the expense of syntactic structure. More generally, listeners (and readers) are often content with "good enough" representations that are inaccurate.

Extracting meaning

- Listeners often recognize speakers' intended meaning by focusing on their goals. Those of high cognitive ability are faster and more accurate than those of low ability at understanding metaphors, in part because they are better able to inhibit features irrelevant to the argument. When it is effortful to use the common ground, listeners sometimes interpret what they hear based on their own knowledge using the egocentric heuristic. Speech and gesture form an integrated system in language comprehension. Listeners use gestural information automatically even when it is irrelevant to their current task. Speakers can also use body movements to communicate their intended meaning.

UNDERSTANDING DISCOURSE

So far we have focused on the processes involved in understanding individual words and sentences. In real life, however, we are generally presented with **discourse** (written text or speech at least several sentences in length). The processes involved in making sense of discourse overlap considerably with those involved in making sense of individual sentences. However, processing discourse is more complex. For example, if we are reading a story, we need to integrate information across many sentences to make coherent sense of what we are reading.

If someone asks us to describe a story or book we have read recently, we discuss the major events and themes and omit the minor details. Thus, our description is highly *selective*. This selectivity depends on the meaning extracted from the story while reading it and on selective processes at the time of retrieval.

Gomulicki (1956) showed how selectively stories are comprehended and remembered. One group of participants wrote a précis (a summary) of a story visible in front of them, and a second group recalled the story from memory. A third group was given each précis and recall, and found it very hard to tell them apart. Thus, story memory resembles a précis in that people focus on important information.

In what follows, some of the main processes involved in discourse comprehension are discussed. It is very important to make coherent sense of

Key Term

Discourse:
connected language that is a minimum of several sentences in length; it includes written text and connected speech.

discourse. As a result, we often draw inferences as we read a text. We may also try to construct a mental model describing the situation referred to in the text.

DRAWING INFERENCES

When reading or listening to someone, our understanding often goes beyond what is written or said. In other words, we draw **inferences** to fill in the gaps in the information presented. If a writer or speaker spelled everything out in such detail that there was no need to draw any inferences, you would probably be bored to tears!

Here is an example of inference drawing taken from Rumelhart and Ortony (1977):

1. Mary heard the ice-cream van coming.
2. She remembered the pocket money.
3. She rushed into the house.

You probably made various inferences while reading the story. For example, Mary wanted to buy some ice-cream; buying ice-cream costs money; Mary had some pocket money in the house; and Mary had only a limited amount of time to get hold of some money before the ice-cream van appeared. Note that none of these inferences is stated *explicitly*.

We can draw a distinction between bridging and elaborative inferences. Bridging inferences establish coherence between the current part of the text and the preceding text, and so are also known as *backward* inferences. Elaborative inferences embellish or add details to the text by making use of our world knowledge. They are sometimes known as *forward* inferences because they often involve anticipating what will come next in the text.

Which elaborative inferences are drawn?

Everyone agrees that various elaborative inferences are made while we read text or listen to speech. However, there has been much controversy concerning the number and nature of the elaborative inferences typically drawn. According to the constructionist approach (e.g., Bransford et al., 1972; Kaup et al., 2007; Zwaan & Madden, 2004), readers typically construct a relatively complete mental model (see Glossary) of the situation and events referred to in the text. According to this approach, numerous elaborative inferences are typically drawn while reading a text.

The constructionist position has come under attack. McKoon and Ratcliff (1992) challenged it with their minimalist hypothesis. According to this hypothesis, readers automatically draw only two kinds of inference. First, there are inferences that make coherent sense of the parts of a text currently being processed. Second, there are inferences based on information that is readily available. Other inferences may be drawn if directly relevant to the reader's goals in reading a text.

The extent to which elaborative inferences are drawn depends very much on the reader's goals. Calvo et al. (2006) instructed some participants to read sentences for comprehension whereas others were explicitly told to anticipate what might happen next. Participants in the latter condition drew more elaborative inferences than those in the former condition. Even when

Key Term
Inferences: in sentence comprehension, going beyond what is said or written to make more complete sense of the speaker's or writer's intended meaning.

participants reading for comprehension drew elaborative inferences, they did so more slowly that those in the anticipation condition.

Individual differences have been ignored in most of the research. As we will see in the next section, individuals differ considerably in terms of the inferences they draw (e.g., Calvo, 2001; Murray & Burke, 2003). The existence of such individual differences points to a limitation of the minimalist and constructionist approaches.

INDIVIDUAL DIFFERENCES: WORKING MEMORY CAPACITY

There are considerable individual differences in almost all complex cognitive activities. Accordingly, theories based on the assumption that everyone comprehends text in the same way are unlikely to be correct. Murray and Burke (2003) considered inference drawing in participants with high, moderate, or low reading skill. They were tested on predictive inferences (e.g., inferring "break" when presented with a sentence such as "The angry husband threw the fragile vase against the wall").

All three groups showed some evidence of drawing predictive inferences. However, these inferences were only drawn automatically by participants with high reading skill.

Just and Carpenter (e.g., 1992) assumed there are individual differences in the capacity of working memory, a system used for both storage and processing (see Chapter 4). Storage and processing demands during language comprehension can be heavy, and working memory has strictly limited capacity. As a result, individuals high in working memory capacity (see Glossary) should perform better on comprehension tasks than those low in such capacity.

The essence of working memory is that it combines processing and temporary storage of information. There are two main ways in which working memory capacity has been assessed (see Chapter 4 for a more complete account). Reading span is the largest number of sentences read for comprehension from which the final words can be recalled (see Glossary). Operation span (see Glossary) is similar except that individuals are presented with arithmetical questions followed by words, and they have to remember all the words. Individuals with large reading and operation spans are said to have high working memory capacity.

How well do reading span and operation span predict comprehension performance? This issue was addressed by Daneman and Merikle (1996) in a meta-analysis (see Glossary) of 77 studies. There were two key findings. First, measures of working memory capacity (e.g., reading span; operation span) predicted comprehension performance better than did measures of storage capacity (e.g., digit span; word span).

Second, comprehension performance was predicted as well by operation span as by reading span. This is of importance because operation span and language comprehension involve different kinds of material (i.e., arithmetical questions vs. sentences).

Calvo (2001) considered the role of individual differences in working memory capacity. Target sentences (e.g., "The pupil studied for an hour approximately") followed a relevant sentence (predicting sentence) or an irrelevant sentence (control sentence). Individuals with high working memory capacity spent less time on integrating information from the target sentence when it followed a predicting sentence, whereas those with low working memory capacity did not. Thus, high-capacity individuals rapidly drew elaborative inferences when the predicting sentence was presented but low-capacity individuals did not.

Working memory capacity is related to the ability to inhibit or suppress unwanted information (Barrett et al., 2004). Sanchez and Wiley (2006) considered the role of working memory capacity in the ability to inhibit irrelevant processing. They studied the seductive details effect, which is exemplified in the tendency for text comprehension to be reduced if accompanied by irrelevant illustrations. Individuals low in working memory capacity showed a greater seductive details effect on text comprehension. In addition, they looked at the irrelevant illustrations more often and for longer periods of time.

Prat et al. (2007) reported a brain-imaging study in which individuals low and high in working memory capacity read sentences of varying complexity for comprehension. Those high in working memory capacity were generally faster and more accurate in their comprehension performance. In addition, the brain-imaging evidence revealed *three* important differences between those low and high in working memory capacity:

1. *Efficiency:* High-capacity individuals were more efficient. They had less activation in various brain areas, suggesting that their planning abilities were more efficient than those of low-capacity individuals.
2. *Adaptability:* The effects of word frequency on brain activation were greater in high-capacity individuals in several brain areas, suggesting that they were more responsive to differences between words.
3. *Synchronization:* High-capacity individuals had greater synchronization of brain activation across several brain regions. This suggests that their comprehension processes were more coordinated and organized.

These findings help to identify the reasons why individuals high in working memory capacity have superior comprehension ability to those low in working memory capacity. They process sentences in more adaptable and coordinated ways that are associated with greater efficiency.

Evaluation

+ Just and Carpenter's (1992) theoretical approach emphasizes that there are substantial individual differences in language comprehension.

+ These individual differences apply to specific processes such as those involved in drawing elaborative inferences (Calvo, 2001) and inhibiting unwanted information (Sanchez & Wiley, 2006).

+ The cognitive neuroscience approach (e.g., Prat et al., 2007) offers the prospect of clarifying the processing differences between low- and high-capacity individuals.

− Individuals high in working memory capacity tend to be more intelligent than those low in such capacity (Just & Carpenter, 1992; see Chapter 4). Some differences between low- and high-capacity individuals may reflect intelligence rather than simply working memory capacity.

The cognitive processing of low- and high-capacity individuals differs in several ways (Baddeley, 2007). We have focused on differences in attentional control and ability to inhibit irrelevant information. However, high-capacity individuals also have larger vocabularies than low-capacity individuals (Chiappe & Chiappe, 2007). As a result, it is often hard to know precisely *why* high-capacity individuals' comprehension performance surpasses that of low-capacity individuals.

SCHEMA THEORIES

Our processing of stories or other texts involves relating the information in the text to relevant structured knowledge stored in long-term memory. What we process in stories, how we process story information, and what we remember from stories we have read all depend in part on such stored information. We will start by considering theories emphasizing the importance of schemas. Schemas are well-integrated packets of knowledge about the world, events, people, and actions (see Glossary, and Chapters 5 and 7).

The schemas stored in long-term memory include scripts that deal with knowledge about events and consequences of events. In many cases, different people's schemas resemble each other. For example, most people's restaurant schema includes actions such as ordering, eating, and paying the bill (Bower et al., 1979).

Frames are another type of schema. Frames are knowledge structures relating to some aspect of the world (e.g., building). They consist of fixed structural

Research Activity 8.1: *Story comprehension*

Read the following passage taken from Bransford and Johnson (1972, p. 722) and try to make sense of it:

The procedure is quite simple. First, you arrange items into different groups. Of course one pile may be sufficient depending on how much there is to do. If you have to go somewhere else due to lack of facilities, that is the next step; otherwise, you are pretty well set. It is important not to overdo things. That is, it is better to do too few things at once than too many. In the short run this may not seem important, but complications from doing too much can easily arise. A mistake can be expensive as well. The manipulation of the appropriate mechanisms should be self-explanatory, and we need not dwell on it here. Soon, however, it will become just another fact of life. It is difficult to foresee any end to the necessity for this task in the immediate future, but then one never can tell.

I imagine you found it very difficult to make much sense of the passage. The reason is that you lacked the relevant schema. In fact, the title of the passage is "Washing clothes." Now reread the passage, which should be much easier to understand armed with that schematic information.

In their study, Bransford and Johnson (1972) found that participants hearing the passage in the absence of a title rated it as incomprehensible and recalled an average of only 2.8 idea units. In contrast, those supplied beforehand with the title "Washing clothes" found it easy to understand and recalled 5.8 idea units on average. Relevant schema knowledge helped *comprehension* rather than simply acting as a retrieval cue. We know this because participants receiving the title *after* hearing the passage but *before* recall produced only 2.6 idea units on average.

information (e.g., has floor and walls) and slots for variable information (e.g., materials from which the building is constructed).

Why are schemas important? First, they contain much of the information needed to understand what we hear and read. Second, schemas allow us to form *expectations* (e.g., of the sequence of events in a restaurant). They make the world relatively predictable because our expectations are generally confirmed.

Bartlett's theory

As is discussed more fully in Chapter 5, Bartlett (1932) argued that our memory for discourse is strongly influenced by the reader's or listener's relevant schematic knowledge. How can we show that this is the case? Suppose we present our participants with discourse that activates schematic knowledge. Some of the schematic knowledge that is activated is likely to go beyond the information actually presented in the discourse itself. As a result, participants' attempts to remember the discourse will be inaccurate because they will include some of this schematic knowledge.

Bartlett (1932) argued that our memory for the information presented in discourse shows fairly rapid forgetting, but that our schematic knowledge shows little or no forgetting over time. That led him to predict that the tendency for schematic knowledge to produce distortions in discourse memory would increase over time.

There have been numerous attempts to test Bartlett's theory (see Chapter 5), most of which have provided support for it. Here we will briefly consider one such attempt. Sulin and Dooling (1974) presented their participants with a story about a ruthless dictator. Some of the participants were informed that this ruthless dictator was called Gerald Martin, whereas others were told that his name was Adolf Hitler. The basic idea was that those participants told the story was about Adolf Hitler would activate their schematic knowledge of him. That would lead them to believe mistakenly that information they possessed about Hitler had been presented in the story. This tendency should increase at longer retention intervals.

What did Sulin and Dooling (1974) find? There was only a strong tendency to falsely recognize information relevant to the Hitler schema but not presented in the story among participants told the story was about Hitler tested at the long retention interval (see Figure 8.6). These findings indicate that our memory for discourse depends in part on our schematic knowledge.

EVENT-INDEXING MODEL

Zwaan and Radvansky (1998) argued that readers construct situation models to describe the situation laid out in stories. There are frequent changes to the situation model as the situation develops and changes. According to Zwaan and Radvansky's event-indexing model, readers

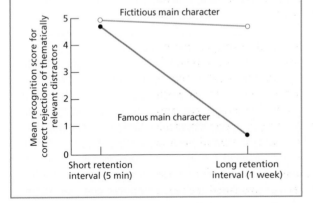

Figure 8.6   Correct rejection of a thematically relevant distractor as a function of main actor: fictitious main character = Gerald Martin; famous main character = Adolf Hitler. Data from Sulin and Dooling (1974).

monitor five aspects of the situation to decide whether their situation model needs to change:

1. *The protagonist:* the central character or actor in the present event compared to the previous one.
2. *Temporality:* the relationship between the times at which the present and previous events occurred.
3. *Causality:* the causal relationship of the current event to the previous one.
4. *Spatiality:* the relationship between the spatial setting of the current event and a previous event.
5. *Intentionality:* the relationship between the character's goals and the present event.

According to the model, it takes readers some time to adjust to changes in any of the five aspects by *updating* their situation model. As predicted, reading speed decreased by 35% when one of the aspects changed compared to when there was no change (Rinck & Weber, 2003). Reading speed slowed down even more when there were two or more changes.

Some evidence indicates that readers don't *always* construct a situation model. Zwaan and van Oostendorp (1993) gave readers part of an edited mystery novel describing the details of a murder scene including the locations of the body and various clues. Most readers didn't form a situational or spatial model when they read normally, something of which a legion of detective story writers since Agatha Christie have taken advantage. However, a spatial model was formed (at the cost of a substantial increase in reading time) when the initial instructions emphasized the importance of constructing a spatial representation.

The findings of Zwaan and Oostendorp (1993) suggest that limited processing capacity may often restrict the formation of situation models. If that is so, the ability to form situation models should improve with practice. Brunyé and Taylor (2008a) presented readers with descriptions of various routes. Spatial models were formed faster and more accurately with practice. Further research indicated that the attention-like central executive (see Glossary) and the visuo-spatial sketchpad (see Glossary) are both involved in the formation of spatial models (Brunyé & Taylor, 2008b).

When we read a description of characters in a story, we form personality models based on our impressions of them. Since we regard most people's personalities as relatively permanent and unchanging, we might expect readers to be reluctant to change their personality model when presented with information refuting their previous assessment of a given character. Rapp and Kendeou (2009) found that this was the case even though readers noticed that the new information was discrepant with previous information about the character.

When readers update their situation model, what happens to the information that is now outdated? Zwaan and Madden (2004) distinguished between two views. One is the *here-and-now view,* in which current information is more available than outdated information. The other is the *resonance view,* according to which new information in a text resonates with all the old text-related information stored in memory.

O'Brien et al. (2010) obtained support for the resonance view. Some participants were presented with a passage in which it was decided that a given tree wouldn't be cut down. After that, however, the tree was struck by lightning and had to be cut down. Then came the following sentence: "All that remained of the tree was the stump." The participants were slow to understand the sentence because they accessed outdated information (i.e., the decision not to cut down the tree). Thus, outdated information can disrupt text comprehension even when inconsistent with the current situation model.

Evaluation

+ Readers often construct situation models when reading a text.

+ The event-indexing model identifies key processes involved in creating and updating situation models.

+ It is assumed correctly that the formation of situation models can be both cognitively demanding and time-consuming.

− The model is of direct relevance to narrative texts consisting of sequences of events but not to explanatory texts such as textbooks (McNamara & Magliano, 2009).

− The model doesn't take sufficient account of the effects of the reader's goals on comprehension processes (McNamara & Magliano, 2009). For example, readers are more likely to form a strong situation model when a story is described as a newspaper report than when described as literary (Zwaan, 1994). Those reading a novel may focus on the text itself (e.g., the wording; stylistic devices). In contrast, those reading a newspaper article want to update their representation of a real-world situation.

EXPERIENTIAL-SIMULATIONS APPROACH

We have seen that people very often construct situation models when reading a text. Advocates of the experiential-simulations approach (Kaup et al., 2007; Zwaan et al., 2002) have specified more precisely the information contained in situation models. According to them, such models contain many *perceptual* details that would be present if the described situation were actually perceived (Kaup et al., 2007; Zwaan et al., 2002).

Support for the above approach was reported by Zwaan et al. (2002). Participants read sentences such as the following: "The ranger saw an eagle in the sky" or "The ranger saw an eagle in the nest." They were then presented with a picture, and decided rapidly whether the object in the picture had been mentioned in the sentence. When the picture was of the same object, it could be a *match* for the implied shape of the object (e.g., an eagle with outstretched wings after "in the sky" sentence) or a *mismatch* (e.g., an eagle with folded wings after the "in the sky" sentence). Participants responded much faster when the object's shape in the picture matched that implied by the sentence, suggesting that people construct a perceptual simulation of the situation described by sentences.

What happens when people are presented with negated sentences such as, "There was no eagle in the sky" or "There was no eagle in the nest?" Do they continue to create experiential simulations in the same way as when presented with sentences describing what is the case? Kaup et al. (2007) found that the processing of negative sentences involved very similar initial experiential simulations to those produced by corresponding affirmative sentences.

What happens when we read sentences exhorting us to make (or refrain from making) a motor response? Zwaan (2009) argued that we produce motor simulations when comprehending such sentences just as we produce perceptual simulations when reading about the visual world.

Supporting evidence was reported by Tomasino et al. (2010). There was significantly less activation in the premotor and motor areas of the brain when participants read negative imperatives (e.g., "Don't write") than when they read positive imperatives (e.g., "Do grasp"). These findings suggest that the experiential-simulations approach should be extended to cover *motor* simulations as well as *perceptual* ones.

Section Summary

Drawing inferences

- According to the constructionist approach, readers typically draw numerous inferences. According to the minimalist hypothesis, relatively few inferences are drawn automatically. However, other inferences may be drawn if they are directly relevant to the reader's goals. Most of the evidence favors the minimalist hypothesis.

Individual differences: Working memory capacity

- Individuals high in working memory capacity have superior comprehension performance to those with low capacity. They draw elaborative inferences more rapidly and find it easier to inhibit irrelevant processing. Their sentence processing is generally more efficient and coordinated.

Schema theories

- We use scripts (stored schemas about events and the consequences of events) when processing discourse. Scripts can enhance the comprehension and retrieval of discourse. However, schematic knowledge can lead to errors in memory, especially at longer retention intervals.

Event-indexing model

- According to the event-indexing model, readers construct situation models that are modified as the situation develops and changes. However, outdated information can slow down comprehension processes. The extent to which readers construct situation models depends on the reader's goals, the type of text (narrative vs. explanatory), and the amount of effort needed for model construction.

Experiential-simulations approach

- According to the experiential-simulations approach, readers form perceptual simulations of the events described in text. Readers may also form motor simulations of the actions described in text.

Essay Questions

1. How do children learn to read English?
2. Evaluate the evidence that two routes are used in reading aloud.
3. Describe and evaluate the TRACE model of spoken word recognition.
4. What sources of information do listeners use to make sense of what speakers are saying?
5. How is language comprehension influenced by individual differences in working memory capacity?
6. Discuss theoretical approaches that emphasize the role of situation models in discourse processing.

Further Reading

- Evans, N., & Levinson, S. C. (2009). The myth of language universals: Language diversity and its importance for cognitive science. *Behavioral and Brain Sciences, 32*, 429–448. This article indicates the numerous differences that exist among the world's languages. These differences highlight the limitations in most research, which has focused on English and other major European languages.
- Harley, T. A. (2008). *The psychology of language: From data to theory* (3rd ed.). Hove, UK: Psychology Press. Several chapters (e.g., 6, 7, and 9) of this excellent textbook by Trevor Harley contain detailed information about the processes involved in recognizing visual and auditory words.
- McNamara, D. S., & Magliano, J. (2009). Toward a comprehensive model of comprehension. *Psychology of Learning and Motivation: Advances in Research and Theory, 51*, 297–384. The authors describe and evaluate several of the leading models of discourse comprehension.
- Perry, C., Ziegler, J. C., & Zorzi, M. (2007). Nested incremental modeling in the development of computational theories: The CDP+ model of reading aloud. *Psychological Review, 114*, 273–315. A synthesis of various major theoretical approaches to reading aloud is provided in this article.
- Swets, B., Desmet, T., Clifton, C., & Ferreira, F. (2008). Underspecification of syntactic ambiguities: Evidence from self-paced reading. *Memory & Cognition, 36*, 201–216. The central thrust of this article is that readers are often satisfied with limited (and sometimes inaccurate) sentence processing.
- Zwaan, R. A. (2009). Mental simulation in language comprehension and social cognition. *European Journal of Social Psychology, 39*, 1142–1150. The author discusses the role of situation models in language comprehension.

Chapter 9

Contents

Language production

INTRODUCTION

We all spend much of our time using language to communicate with others. We talk to friends and acquaintances in person and on the phone, we send emails and texts. We can also use language to communicate with ourselves – most students spend time taking notes on lectures and reading assignments.

There are two main forms of language production: speaking and writing. Nearly all of us spend more time engaged in speaking than in writing. However, most students and professional people spend several hours a week writing and word processing.

Speaking and writing are both goal-directed activities having *communication* as their main goal. People speak and write to impart information, to be friendly, and so on. Perhaps most importantly, we speak and write to *influence* other people (Guerin, 2003). Thus, motivational and social factors need to be considered in addition to purely linguistic ones. We will be discussing various motivational and social factors in this chapter.

There has been much more research on reading and speech comprehension than on speech production and writing. Why is that the case? One important

Learning Objectives

After studying Chapter 9, you should be able to:

- Discuss the similarities and differences between speaking (oral production) and writing (written production).
- Name and describe the four Gricean maxims.
- Discuss the role of gestures in language production.
- Discuss the verbal cues to differentiate between lying and truth telling.
- Explain what the tip-of-the-tongue state, Spoonerisms, Freudian slips, and other speech errors tell us about how speech production happens.
- Explain what the studies of use of prosodic cues tell us about how speech production works.
- List and describe the three kinds of knowledge relevant to the planning stage of writing.
- Apply knowledge of Baddeley's working memory model components to the process of writing.

reason is that it is more difficult to carry out research on language production than on language comprehension. We can *control* the material to be comprehended, but it is harder to constrain an individual's production of language.

SIMILARITIES

What are the similarities between speaking and writing? Most importantly, both involve deciding on the overall message to be communicated. At this stage, the actual words to be spoken or written aren't considered. This is followed by the production of language, which often proceeds on a clause-by-clause basis.

Evidence that speaking and writing can be similar comes in a study by Hartley et al. (2003). They studied an individual (Eric Sotto) who dictated word-processed academic letters using a voice-recognition system or simply word processed them. Eric Sotto had much less experience of dictating word-processed letters than word processing them. In spite of that, the letters he produced by speaking didn't differ in readability or in typographical and grammatical errors from those that were word processed. However, there were fewer long sentences when dictation was used.

DIFFERENCES

What are the differences between speaking and writing? First, speakers generally have much less time than writers to plan their language production. As a result, speaking is more spontaneous than writing. This helps to explain why spoken language is generally shorter and less complex than written language (Cleland & Pickering, 2006).

Second, speakers generally know precisely who is receiving their messages. In contrast, writers often do not, especially if they are writing a book that may be read (if they are lucky!) by thousands of people.

Third, speakers have the advantage over writers that they generally receive moment-by-moment feedback from the listener or listeners (e.g., expressions of bewilderment). This allows them to adapt what they say to suit the listeners' needs. The fact that writers don't receive immediate feedback means they must write clearly – this slows down the communication rate.

Fourth, writers usually have direct access to what they have produced so far, whereas speakers do not. However, Olive and Piolat (2002) found no difference in the quality of the texts produced by writers having (or not having) access to visual feedback of what they had written.

What are the consequences of the above differences between speaking and writing? Spoken language is often informal and simple in structure, with information being communicated rapidly. Written language is more formal and has a more complex structure. Writers need to write clearly because they don't receive immediate feedback, and this slows down the rate at which they write.

Section Summary

Similarities
- Speaking and writing are both goal-directed activities having communication as their main goal. With speaking and writing, there is an initial stage at which the overall message is decided on, followed by the production of language.

> **Differences**
> * Speakers generally have much less time than writers to plan their language production. Speakers are more likely than writers to know exactly who will receive their message. Speakers generally receive instant feedback from their listener(s), whereas writers rarely receive rapid feedback from their readers. Speakers differ from writers in not having direct access to what they have produced so far.

SPEECH PRODUCTION: COMMUNICATION

As already indicated, the most important goal that speakers have is to communicate with other people. On the face of it (by the sound of it?), speech production is an easy task. It generally seems almost effortless when we chat with friends or acquaintances about the topics of the day. Indeed, we frequently seem to speak without much preparation or planning. We typically speak at three words a second (almost 200 words a minute), and this rapid speech rate fits the notion that speaking is very undemanding of processing resources.

The reality is often very different from the account of speech production in the previous paragraph. In fact, speakers often resort to various strategies to reduce processing demands. One example is **preformulation** – this involves reducing processing costs by producing phrases used before. About 70% of our speech consists of word combinations we use repeatedly (Altenberg, 1990).

Preformulation is especially common among groups of people (e.g., auctioneers; sports commentators) who need to speak very rapidly. Speaking quickly leads them to repeat many expressions (e.g., "They're off and racing now"; "They're on their way") (Kuiper, 1996).

Another strategy we use to make speech production easier is underspecification, which involves using simplified expressions. Smith (2000) illustrated underspecification: "Wash and core six cooking apples. Put them in an oven." In the second sentence, the word "them" underspecifies the phrase "six cooking apples."

Sometimes speech production takes the form of monolog, in which one person talks to another person. Most of the time, however, it involves dialog or conversation. It could be argued that speech production is harder in interactive dialog than in monolog because speakers have to adjust what they say to fit what the previous speaker just said. However, the opposite is generally the case. Speakers often copy phrases and even sentences they heard when the other person was speaking (Pickering & Garrod, 2004). Thus, the other person's words serve as a prime or prompt. As a result, dialog is often much more repetitive than monolog.

There is another way in which monolog is harder than dialog. Speakers delivering a monolog have to generate their own ideas. In contrast, speakers within a dialog typically make extensive use of the ideas communicated by the other person.

Another way in which speakers make use of what they have just heard the other person say is via syntactic priming. **Syntactic priming** occurs when a previously experienced syntactic structure influences current processing. Here

> **Key Terms**
>
> **Preformulation:** the production by speakers of phrases used frequently before; it is done to reduce the demands of speech production.
>
> **Syntactic priming:** the tendency for the sentences produced by speakers to have the same syntactic structure as sentences they have heard or read shortly beforehand.

is a concrete example. If you have just heard a passive sentence (e.g., "The man was bitten by the dog"), this increases the chances you will produce a passive sentence yourself. This occurs even when you are talking about a different topic. Syntactic priming often occurs in the absence of conscious awareness of copying a previous syntactic structure (Pickering & Ferreira, 2008).

Evidence of syntactic priming was reported by Cleland and Pickering (2003). A confederate of the experimenter described a picture to participants using an adjective–noun order (e.g., "the red sheep") or a noun–relative-clause order (e.g., "the sheep that's red"). Participants used the syntactic structure they had heard even when the words in the two sentences were very different.

Why is syntactic priming so common in speech? The main reason is that the processing demands on speech production are reduced when a heard syntactic structure is copied.

PRINCIPLES OF COMMUNICATION

For most people (unless there is something seriously wrong with them), speech nearly always occurs as conversation in a social context. Grice (1967) argued that the key to successful communication is the Cooperative Principle, according to which speakers and listeners must try to be cooperative.

In addition to the Cooperative Principle, Grice (1967) proposed four maxims (general principles) the speaker should heed:

- *Maxim of quantity:* The speaker should be as informative as necessary, but not more so.
- *Maxim of quality:* The speaker should be truthful.
- *Maxim of relation:* The speaker should say things relevant to the situation.
- *Maxim of manner:* The speaker should make his/her contribution easy to understand.

What needs to be said (maxim of quantity) depends on what the speaker wishes to describe (the referent). It is also necessary to know the object (or objects) from which the referent must be distinguished. It is sufficient to say, "The boy is good at soccer" if the other players are all men, but not if some of them are also boys. In the latter case, it is necessary to be more specific (e.g., "The boy with red hair is good at soccer").

Those involved in a conversation typically exhibit cooperation in terms of smooth switches between speakers. Two people talking at once occurs less than 5% of the time, and there is typically a gap of under 500 ms between the end of one speaker's turn and the start of the next speaker's turn (Ervin-Tripp, 1979).

Why are the switches between speakers so smooth? Sacks et al. (1974) found that those involved in a conversation follow certain rules. For example, when the speaker gazes at the listener, this is often an invitation to the listener to become the speaker. If the speaker wishes to continue speaking, he/she can indicate this by hand gestures or filling pauses with meaningless sounds (e.g., "Errrrrr").

Brennan (1990) argued that one common way a conversation moves from one speaker to another is via an *adjacency pair*. What the first speaker says provides a strong invitation to the listener to take up the conversation. A question followed by an answer is a very common example of an adjacency pair. If the first speaker completes what he/she intended to say without producing the first part of an adjacency pair, then the next turn goes to the listener who speaks first.

Speakers are only moderately successful at adhering to the maxim of quantity (being only as informative as necessary). Suppose a speaker wants a listener to put an apple in a box. If only one apple is present, it follows from the maxim of quantity that speakers should say something like, "Put the apple in the box." In fact, about one-third of the time, speakers produced an unnecessarily detailed sentence (e.g., "Put the apple on the towel in the box") (Engelhardt et al., 2006). Speakers often find it cognitively demanding to work out that listeners don't need the additional information and then to delete it while preparing their utterance.

Research Activity 9.1: *Maxim of quantity*

Have a look at the two displays shown in Figure 9.1. Describe the object labeled 3 in display (a) so a listener would know which object lablled you are describing, and then do the same thing for the object in display (b).

When the participants in a study by Ferreira et al. (2005) were given this task, they performed poorly on display (a). You have to say something like "the baseball bat" to discriminate between the top object and the bat that is a flying mammal. However, about one-third of participants simply said, "bat," and so failed to adhere to the maxim of quantity. With display (b), over 95% of participants correctly said something like "the larger bat" to discriminate it from the smaller bat that is in the display. Thus, they adhered to the maxim of quantity.

Why is performance so poor with display (a)? The problem is that there is no similarity between the two bats in terms of visual shape or meaning. The only similarity is at the phonological or sound level, and that only becomes apparent late in processing when the speaker is about to name the object.

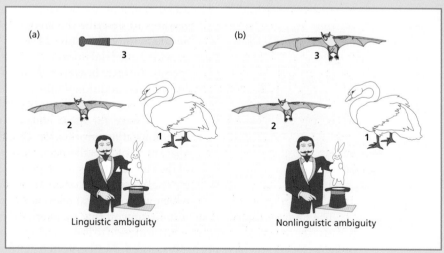

Figure 9.1 Sample displays in which the object labeled 3 had to be named so as to discriminate it from the other objects. In (a), there is linguistic ambiguity (baseball bat vs. mammal bat); in (b), there is nonlinguistic ambiguity (large vs. small bat). Performance was much worse with linguistic than with nonlinguistic ambiguity. Adapted from Ferreira et al. (2005). Copyright © 2005, with permission from Elsevier.

ENHUNICATION COMMUNICATION

There are several ways other than those already discussed in which speakers can make it easier for listeners to understand what they are saying. In this section, we will consider three such ways: gestures; discourse markers; and prosodic cues.

Gestures

When two people converse, the speaker generally makes various gestures coordinated in timing and meaning with the words being spoken. These gestures serve a communicative function by increasing listeners' ability to make sense of the speaker's message (see Chapter 8).

Evidence that many gestures produced by speakers are designed to assist in communication was reported by Mol et al. (2009). They asked speakers to describe an animated cartoon to a video camera. In one condition, the speakers were told the camera was being used as a web cam and that another participant would be watching and listening to them. In another condition, they were told the information would be sent to an artificial audiovisual summarizer but not to another person. There were six times as many gestures per 100 words when the speakers thought they were communicating to another person.

Jacobs and Garnham (2007) showed that speakers can be very responsive to the listener's *needs*. Speakers described comic strips to listeners. When the listener was attentive and couldn't see the comic strips, speakers made plentiful gestures. When the listener was inattentive and could see the comic strips, speakers made far fewer gestures.

We have seen that speakers adjust their gestures to take account of the listener's needs. However, speakers can *underestimate* the value of gestures as a means of communication. Gerwing and Allison (2009) asked pairs of participants to use words and gestures to describe the layout of an apartment. Speakers thought only 25% of their gestures provided essential information missing from their speech. In fact, however, 97% of their gestures contributed additional information.

Gerwing and Allison (2009) found that gestures were far more effective than words at communicating information about features of the apartment such as the sizes, shapes, and locations of the various rooms (see Figure 9.2). Gestures are especially useful for conveying spatial information, which was of central relevance to the task.

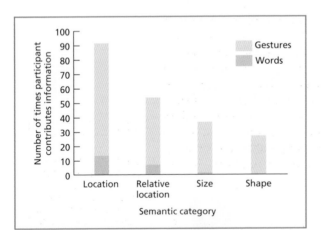

Figure 9.2 The number of times participants conveyed information about location, relative location, size, and shape by gestures and by words. From Gerwing and Allison (2009). Copyright © 2009 John Benjamins Publishing Company.

The findings discussed so far may suggest that speakers use gestures mainly because they provide useful *visual* information to listeners. In fact, that is only part of the story. As you have probably noticed, speakers often gesture during phone conversations even though their gestures aren't visible to the listener. However, they make fewer gestures when using the phone than when talking face to face (Bavelas et al., 2008). In addition, the gestures are larger and more expressive in the face-to-face condition.

Why do speakers make *any* gestures when on the phone? Presumably they find that using gestures makes it easier for them to communicate what they want to say. Frick-Horbury and Guttentag (1998) presented the definitions of 50 relatively uncommon words, and participants tried to think which words were being defined. Here is an example: "a one-sided drum with loose metallic disks in the side that is played by shaking." The answer is "tambourine."

Some participants in the study by Frick-Horbury and Guttentag (1998) held a rod with both hands, which limited their ability to make gestures. They produced an average of only 19 words. In contrast, participants whose hands were free produced an average of 24 words. Thus, gestures may help us to retrieve words we want to say.

Discourse markers

In spontaneous conversational speech we use several discourse markers (e.g., "well"; "you know"; "oh"; "but anyway"). **Discourse markers** are spoken words or phrases that help the process of communication in spite of having little direct relevance to what the speaker is saying (Bolden, 2009).

Four frequent discourse markers are as follows: "oh," "um," "you know," and "like." *Why* do you think speakers use these expressions? Most people argue that "oh" and "um" indicate the speaker is experiencing problems in deciding what to say next (Fox Tree, 2007). In contrast, they think that *you know* is used to check for understanding and to connect with the listener(s), but are unsure of the significance of *like*.

Analyses of spoken language indicate that people's interpretations of *oh*, *um*, and *you know* are basically accurate (Fox Tree, 2007). The word *like* is often used to indicate a discrepancy between what someone says and what they mean.

Bolden (2006) considered which of the discourse markers "oh" and "so" speakers use when moving on to a new conversational topic. The word "oh" was used 98.5% of the time when the new topic directly concerned the *speaker*, whereas "so" was used 96% of the time when it was of most relevance to the *listener*. You almost certainly do the same, but probably without realizing.

Context influences our use of discourse markers. The discourse markers "oh" and "well" are used more often in casual conversations than in interviews, whereas "you know," "like," "yeah," and "I mean" are used equally often in both situations (Fuller, 2003). These differences may occur because speakers need to respond more to what the other person has said in conversations than in interviews. The avoidance of "like" in interviews is a good idea. Overuse of the word "like" reduces the chances of job interviewees being hired (Russell et al., 2008).

Prosodic cues

Prosodic cues include rhythm, stress, and intonation. They make it easier for listeners to understand what speakers are trying to say (see Chapter 9). However, speakers often fail to provide prosodic cues even when they are needed. Keysar and Henly (2002) asked participants to read ambiguous sentences to convey a specific meaning, with listeners deciding which meaning was intended. The speakers did *not* use prosodic cues (or used them ineffectively), because the listeners only guessed correctly 61% of the time. Speakers made limited use of prosodic cues because they overestimated the listener's understanding of the intended meaning.

Key Terms

Discourse markers: words or phrases used by a speaker (e.g., "oh"; "so") that assist communication even though they are only of indirect relevance to his/her message.

Prosodic cues: various aspects of speech (e.g., rhythm; stress) used by speakers to assist communication; used most often by speakers when what they are saying is somewhat ambiguous.

Snedeker and Trueswell (2003) argued that prosodic cues are much more likely to be provided when the context fails to clarify the meaning of an ambiguous sentence. Speakers said ambiguous sentences (e.g., "Tap the frog with the flower": You either use the flower to tap the frog or you tap the frog that has the flower). They provided many more prosodic cues when the context failed to disambiguate the sentence.

Suppose we discover in some situation that speakers generally produce prosodic cues that resolve syntactic ambiguities. Does that necessarily mean that speakers are responsive to the needs of their listener(s)? According to Kraljic and Brennan (2005), it doesn't. Speakers producing spontaneous sentences made extensive use of prosodic cues, and listeners successfully used these cues to disambiguate what they heard.

The above findings suggest that speakers are responsive to listeners' needs. However, Kraljic and Brennan (2005) found that speakers provided prosodic cues regardless of whether the listener needed them. Thus, speakers' use of prosodic cues did *not* indicate any particular responsiveness to their listener.

COMMON GROUND

It is often assumed that speakers try to ensure that their message is understood. According to Clark (e.g., Clark & Krych, 2004), speakers and listeners typically work together to maximize common ground. This consists of mutual beliefs, expectations, and knowledge. In other words, speakers and listeners try to get "on the same wavelength."

Speakers typically make various assumptions about the listener to establish common ground. There are *global* assumptions (e.g., the listener's preferred language; the listener's general knowledge; shared personal experiences). There are also *local* assumptions relating to what the listener knows or is attending to at any given moment. Speakers are more likely to make incorrect local assumptions than global ones because the local assumptions keep changing (Arnold, 2008).

In spite of the problems, speakers and listeners frequently achieve common ground fairly effortlessly. As we saw earlier, speakers often copy phrases and even sentences they heard when the other person was speaking (Pickering & Garrod, 2004). Thus, the other person's words serve as a prime or prompt.

Problems with use of common ground

It is cognitively demanding to keep focusing on precisely what the listener knows, and this limits the influence of common ground on speakers' utterances. Speakers often produce utterances that are easy for them to say rather than easy for their listener(s) to understand. For example, speakers often produce ambiguous sentences even though such sentences pose special difficulties for listeners (Ferreira, 2008).

According to Horton and Keysar (1996), speakers often plan their utterances *without* considering the listener's perspective and common ground. However, these plans are then monitored and corrected to take account of the common ground.

Horton and Keysar (1996) asked participants to describe moving objects so the listener could identify them. There was a shared-context condition in which the participants knew the listener could see the same additional objects that they could see. There was also a non-shared-context condition in which the participants knew the listener could *not* see the other objects. The object descriptions had to be produced rapidly (speeded condition) or slowly (unspeeded condition).

If the participants used the common ground, they should have utilized contextual information in their descriptions only in the shared-context condition. That is what happened in the unspeeded condition. However, those in the speeded condition included contextual information in their descriptions regardless of its appropriateness. In that condition, there was insufficient time for the cognitively demanding monitoring process to operate.

The study by Horton and Keysar (1996) was limited in that the listeners did not speak. Common ground can be achieved much more easily in a situation involving interaction and dialog (Clark & Krych, 2004). There were pairs of participants, with one being a director who instructed the other member (the builder) how to construct Lego models. Errors were made on 39% of trials when no interaction was possible compared to only 5% when the participants could interact.

Clark and Krych (2004) also found that directors often very rapidly altered what they said to maximize the common ground between themselves and the builders in the interactive condition. For example, when Ken (one of the builders) held a block over the right location while Jane (one of the directors) was speaking, she instantly interrupted herself to say, "Yes": "and put it on the right hand half of the – yes – of the green rectangle."

Bard et al. (2007) identified two possible strategies speakers might take with respect to the common ground:

1. *Shared responsibility:* The speaker may expect the listener to volunteer information if he/she notices a problem with the common ground.
2. *Cognitive overload:* The speaker may try to keep track of the listener's knowledge as well as his/her own, but generally finds that this requires excessive cognitive processing.

Bard et al. (2007) asked speakers to describe the route on a map so another person (the experimenter's confederate) could reproduce it. Each speaker had access to two kinds of information indicating the confederate was having difficulties in reproducing the route:

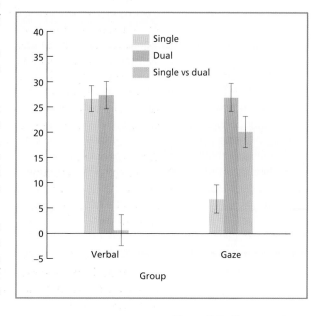

Figure 9.3 The percentage of the speaker's utterances directing the confederate back to the route when the confederate signaled a problem. This signaling occurred only verbally or only via gaze (single conditions) or both verbally and via gaze (dual condition). From Bard et al. (2007). Copyright © 2007, with permission from Elsevier.

1. The confederate said he/she had a problem.
2. The confederate's fake eye movements were focused away from the correct route.

What would we expect to find? According to the shared responsibility account, the speaker should pay more attention to what the confederate said than to his/her direction of gaze. This is because only the former involves the confederate volunteering information. According to the cognitive overload account, the speaker should focus more on the gaze feedback than on what the confederate said, because it is easier to process gaze information. In fact, speakers took much more account of what the confederate *said* (see Figure 9.3).

Evaluation

➕ Communication is most effective when speakers take full account of listeners' knowledge and the common ground. However, this is often too cognitively demanding.

➕ In practice, speakers make more use of the common ground when time is not limited, when interaction is possible between speakers and listeners, and when listeners state that they have a problem.

➖ Most research is artificial in that speakers and listeners don't know each other beforehand. It is more demanding to keep track of the other person's knowledge in such situations than when two long-term friends converse.

➖ In the laboratory, common ground generally relates to information presented in visual displays. In everyday life, the common ground typically refers to past events or knowledge of mutual acquaintances as well as information directly available.

In the Real World 9.1: *Lying and truth-telling*

Most speakers try to communicate their thoughts to one or more listeners. However, speakers often communicate indirectly and inadvertently. For example, listeners can sometimes extract cues about the honesty of a speaker by paying careful attention to what he/she is saying. However, most people are very poor at detecting deception (Bond & DePaulo, 2008) even though people lie in 27% of their face-to-face interactions and 37% of their phone calls (Hancock, 2007).

We would expect trained experts (e.g., detectives) to detect lying much more accurately than we can. However, criminal justice practitioners are typically surprisingly poor at deciding accurately which suspects are lying and which are telling the truth (King & Dunn, 2010). In what follows, we will consider why we are so poor at detecting lying.

Verbal vs. nonverbal behavior

Most people believe (mistakenly) that liars can be detected more easily through their nonverbal behavior than what they say. Even trained police officers typically pay more attention to suspects' nonverbal behavior than to their verbal behavior, arguing that it is harder for liars to control their nonverbal behavior (Vrij, 2008).

Aspects of nonverbal behavior thought to be associated with lying are restless movements, lack of eye contact, a guilty expression, and evidence of stress in the voice. Voice stress was studied by Harnsberger et al. (2009). They analyzed acoustic information extracted from the speech signal, but were unable to distinguish between lying and truth-telling. However, liars often use fewer illustrators (controllable hand and arm gestures) and press their lips together more often than truth-tellers (DePaulo et al., 2003).

Liars can generally be distinguished from truth-tellers more effectively through verbal than through nonverbal behavior. Mann et al. (2008) used interviews with suspects. Some police officers saw and heard the interviews, whereas others only saw the interviews or only heard them.

The police officers' ability to identify liars and truth-tellers was worst in the visual-only condition, indicating the importance of hearing what suspects had to say. In the visual-only condition, the police exhibited a lie bias – they used their mistaken stereotypical views about nonverbal cues to lying to identify several truth-tellers as liars.

Verbal cues

How can we use the content of someone's speech to decide whether they are lying or telling the truth?

Newman et al. (2003) found that judges were very poor (52% correct) at deciding whether someone was lying or telling the truth. In fact, however, deceptive communicators used fewer first-person singular pronouns (e.g., "I") and fewer exclusive words (e.g., "but"; "except"; "without"). Thus, liars distanced themselves from their lies and presented a simple account.

The most-used technique is criteria-based content analysis (Steller & Köhnken, 1989), which uses 19 criteria to distinguish between lying and truth-telling. This technique is moderately effective. For example, Blandón-Gitlin et al. (2009) compared adults' true and false accounts of recent events and also of childhood events. The truthful accounts differed from the false ones with respect to various criteria: they were more logical and coherent and also contained more details.

Criteria-based content analysis has various limitations. First, several of the criteria are of little value in identifying lying (Vrij, 2008). Second, there are no clear decision rules for categorizing a spoken account as lying or truth-telling. Third, liars are less likely to be detected by criteria-based content analysis if they have received "coaching" and know how what they say is going to be assessed.

Porter and ten Brinke (2010) reviewed the literature on detection of lying. A large number of pauses, a slow speech rate, vague descriptions, repeated details, and a lack of reproduced conversation are all associated with lying. Thus, the information used by liars is less detailed (e.g., less perceptual and spatial information).

Blandón-Gitlin et al. (2009) found that their participants found it harder to reconstruct fictitious events than genuine ones. If lying is more cognitively demanding than truth-telling, then liars might find it harder to camouflage their lying if their cognitive load were increased. Vrij et al. (2008) did precisely this by asking people to recall an event in reverse order or while performing another task. Police officers were more successful at detecting lying in these cognitive-load conditions than under standard conditions.

In sum, there are various ways in which speech production by liars describing events differs from that of truth-tellers. Liars generally speak more slowly, with many pauses. They are also more likely to distance themselves from their lies and to produce simple accounts lacking perceptual and spatial detail. Finally, lying is generally more demanding than telling the truth.

The take-home message is that speakers often focus mainly on their own knowledge rather than their listener's. Presumably they do this to make life easier for themselves. However, speakers do attend when the listener says something is amiss. Most speakers try to communicate their thoughts to one or more listeners. However, speakers often communicate indirectly and inadvertently. For example, listeners can sometimes extract cues about the honesty of a speaker by paying careful attention to what he/she is saying. However, most people are very poor at detecting deception (Bond & DePaulo, 2008), in part because they focus excessively on the speaker's nonverbal behavior.

We would expect trained experts (e.g., detectives) to detect lying much more accurately than we can. However, criminal justice practitioners are typically surprisingly poor at deciding accurately which suspects are lying and which are telling the truth (King & Dunn, 2010). In what follows, we will consider why we are so poor at detecting lying.

Section Summary

- Speakers reduce the processing demands on them by using preformulation and underspecification. Speech production in the context of dialog is facilitated by copying part of what the other person has said and by syntactic priming.

Principles of communication
- According to the Cooperative Principle, speakers and listeners must try to be cooperative. Speakers sometimes fail to adhere to the maxim of quantity by providing more or less information than necessary to listeners.

Enhancing communication
- Gestures make it easier for speakers to express their message and also facilitate the listener's task, especially when spatial information is being communicated. Discourse markers are used when the speaker is experiencing problems or to connect with the listener. Speakers use prosodic cues such as rhythm, stress, and intonation to make the listener's task easier. However, they are often fairly unresponsive to the listener's needs.

Common ground
- Speakers and listeners work together to maximize common ground (e.g., mutual beliefs and knowledge). Speakers often find it too demanding to keep track of the common ground, and expect the listener to volunteer information if he/she notices a problem with communication.

Lying and truth-telling
- Liars can generally be detected from truth-tellers more effectively through verbal than through nonverbal behavior. The accounts provided by liars are often vaguer and less detailed than those of truth-tellers. Lying is easier to detect when liars provide their accounts under cognitive load.

STAGES OF SPEECH PRODUCTION

Several levels or stages of processing are involved in speech production. We initially decide what we want to say and finish up by producing a sentence or other utterance. Gary Dell (1986) argued that four levels are involved (see Figure 9.4). Initial planning of the message to be communicated is considered at the semantic level. At the syntactic level, the grammatical structure of the words in the planned utterance is decided. At the morphological level, the **morphemes** (basic units of meaning) are worked out. At the phonological level, the phonemes or basic units of sound within the sentence (see Glossary) are added.

Figure 9.4 implies that the processes involved in speech and word production proceed neatly and tidily from the semantic level through the syntactic and morphological levels down to the phonological level. It is certainly true that speakers typically have some idea of what they want to say (semantic level) before working out the words they are going to say. However, as we will see, processes at the different levels frequently *interact* with each other.

TIP-OF-THE-TONGUE STATE

Sometimes we find it hard to move from one level to another. For example, we have all had the experience of having a concept or idea in mind while searching

Key Term
Morphemes: the basic units of meaning; words consist of one or more morphemes.

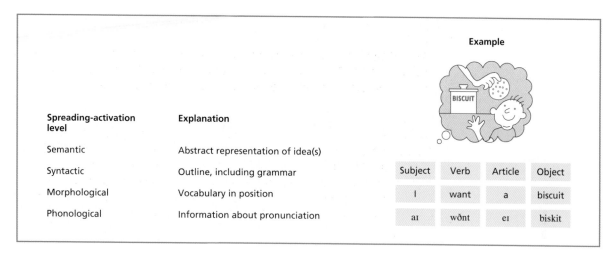

Spreading-activation level	Explanation		Example		
Semantic	Abstract representation of idea(s)				
Syntactic	Outline, including grammar	Subject	Verb	Article	Object
Morphological	Vocabulary in position	I	want	a	biscuit
Phonological	Information about pronunciation	aɪ	wɒnt	eɪ	bɪskɪt

Figure 9.4 The sentence "I want a biscuit" broken down into spreading-activation levels.

in vain for the right word to describe it. This frustrating situation defines the **tip-of-the-tongue state**. Don't despair when you are in the tip-of-the-tongue state. Individuals in that state often guess the first letter of the word correctly as well as the number of syllables (Brown & McNeill, 1966). Indeed, they fairly frequently produce the word itself if they spend a few minutes struggling to retrieve it.

The tip-of-the-tongue state happens when semantic processing is successful but phonological processing is unsuccessful (i.e., we cannot produce the sound of the word). As would be expected, we mostly experience the tip-of-the-tongue state with relatively rare words.

Evidence that problems with accessing phonological information underlie the tip-of-the-tongue state was reported by Harley and Bown (1998). Words sounding unlike nearly all other words (e.g., apron; vineyard) were much more susceptible to the tip-of-the-tongue state than words sounding like several others (e.g., litter; pawn). The unusual phonological forms of words susceptible to the tip-of-the-tongue state make them hard to retrieve.

What can be done to assist individuals in the tip-of-the-tongue state to produce the sought word? One approach is to present them with words sharing the first syllable with the correct word. This has been shown to be effective (Abrams, 2008).

Bilinguals (individuals fluent in two languages) experience the tip-of-the-tongue state more often than monolinguals (individuals fluent in only one language). Why is this? One possibility is that bilinguals' attempts to find a word in one language are disrupted by *interference* from the phonological representations of words in their other language.

In fact, the above explanation doesn't account for all the findings. Bilinguals fluent in American Sign Language and English had more tip-of-the-tongue states than monolinguals when searching for English words (Pyers et al., 2009). This couldn't be due to phonological interference because there is no phonological overlap between English and American Sign Language.

How can we explain the overall tendency for bilinguals to experience the tip-of-the-tongue state more than monolinguals? The most likely explanation is

Key Term

Tip-of-the-tongue state: the frustration experienced by speakers when they have an idea or concept in mind but can't find the appropriate word to express it.

that bilinguals use many words (in either of their two languages) somewhat less frequently than monolinguals. As a result, the connections between meaning and phonological form are less well established.

SPEECH PLANNING

To what extent do speakers plan their utterances in advance? One possibility is that planning occurs at the level of the **phrase** (a group of words expressing a single idea). Another possibility is that it occurs at the level of the **clause** (a part of a sentence containing a subject and a verb).

Planning at the phrase level was reported by Martin et al. (2004). Participants produced sentences to describe moving pictures. The sentences had a simple initial phrase (e.g., "The ball moves above the tree and the finger") or they had a complex initial phrase (e.g., "The ball and the tree move above the finger"). Speakers took longer to start speaking when using complex initial phrases than when using simple ones, indicating they were planning the initial phrase before speaking. Similar findings were reported by Martin et al. (2010).

The phrase is often important in speakers' advance planning. However, there are two main reasons why there is no simple answer to the question of how much speakers plan in advance:

1. Planning can occur at four different levels (refer back to Figure 9.4). There is often more advance planning at the higher levels of planning (e.g., message planning at the semantic level) than at lower levels (e.g., the sounds of individual words).
2. The amount of planning can vary considerably depending on various factors (e.g., time available for planning; sentence complexity).

We will consider these two factors in turn.

Planning level

Some support for the notion that the extent of forward planning by speakers varies at different processing levels comes from the study of speech errors (discussed more fully in the next section). Here we will consider two types of speech error: word-exchange errors and sound-exchange errors. Word-exchange errors involve two words changing places. The words exchanged typically come from the same clause but are often some way apart in the sentence (e.g., "My chair seems empty without my room"). The finding that a word (e.g., "chair") can be spoken much earlier than was intended suggests some aspects of planning can be extensive. It may be that the general syntactic structure of an utterance is planned clause-by-clause (Harley, 2008).

Sound-exchange errors (also known as spoonerisms – discussed later) involve two sounds exchanging places (e.g., "She fainted the pence" instead of "She painted the fence"). Such errors typically occur over *short* distances within the sentence (Harley, 2008). This suggests that the sounds of words to be spoken are only planned shortly in advance.

Experimental support for the notion that phonological planning (involving the sounds of words) is less extensive than planning at other stages was reported by Meyer (1996). Speakers produced sentences based on pairs of objects (e.g.,

"The arrow is next to the bag"). At the same time, they heard an auditory distractor related in sound or meaning to the first or second noun.

Meyer (1996) found there was an effect on the time to start speaking when the distractor was related in sound to the first noun but not the second one. Thus, speakers only retrieve the sound of the *first* noun before starting to speak. In contrast, the time taken to start speaking was longer when the distractor was related in meaning to *either* the first *or* the second noun. This indicates that the meanings of the words to be spoken were planned prior to speaking.

Flexibility in planning

The amount of planning preceding speech is *flexible* and depends on processing demands experienced by speakers. Consider a study by Ferreira and Swets (2002). Participants answered mathematical problems varying in difficulty level. The time taken to start speaking and the length of time spent speaking were recorded. If there was complete planning before speaking, the time taken to start speaking would be longer for more difficult problems than for easier ones, but the time spent speaking wouldn't vary. In contrast, if people started speaking before planning their responses, the time taken to start speaking might be the same for all problems. However, speech duration should be longer with harder problems.

What did Ferreira and Swets (2002) find? Task difficulty affected the time taken to start speaking but *not* the time spent speaking. Thus, participants planned their responses fully before speaking. However, the findings differed when participants had to start producing their answers to mathematical problems very rapidly. In these circumstances, some planning occurred before speaking, with additional planning occurring during speaking. Thus, speakers do as much prior planning as possible in the time available before starting to speak.

Wagner et al. (2010) identified several factors determining the extent of grammatical advance planning. First, individuals who spoke relatively slowly tended to engage in more planning than those who spoke rapidly. Second, speakers engaged in more planning before producing simple sentences (e.g., "The frog is next to the mug") than more complex ones ("The blue frog is next to the blue mug"). Third, there was more planning when speakers were operating under a low cognitive load than when they were burdened with a high cognitive load (e.g., remembering digits for a few seconds).

How can we account for the flexibility of speakers' advance planning? They are faced with a tradeoff between avoiding errors and cognitive demands. If they focus on avoiding errors, the cognitive demands on them will be substantial. On the other hand, if they try to minimize cognitive demands, they will make many errors while speaking. In practice, speakers mostly engage in extensive planning when such planning is not very cognitively demanding (e.g., the sentence to be produced is simple; there is no additional task).

SPEECH ERRORS

Most of the time, people produce speech that is accurate and coherent. However, we are all prone to error. It has been estimated that the average person makes a speech error once every 500 sentences (Vigliocco & Hartsuiker, 2002). In spite of their rarity, speech errors are important. Why is this? In essence, we can use information about the relative frequencies of different kinds of speech error to shed light on the processes underlying speech production.

Why do we make speech errors? There are many reasons. However, the single most important one (discussed more fully later) was identified by Gary Dell (1986). He emphasized the notion of **spreading activation**: Activation or energy spreads from an activated node (e.g., word) to related nodes or words.

According to Dell (1986) and Dell et al. (2008), the processes involved in speech production occur in parallel (at the same time). When we plan an utterance, this leads to activation of several of the sounds and words in the intended sentence before we speak. The crucial assumption is that speech errors occur whenever an incorrect item is more activated than the correct one.

Suppose we intend to say, "You have wasted the whole term." This may lead activation of all the words in the sentence during the planning process. As a result, we may say something like, "You have tasted the whole worm."

Activation typically extends to words related in meaning to those in the intended sentence. For example, you may intend to say, "Give me a spoon." However, activation of the word "spoon" may lead to activation of the related word "fork," leading you to say, "Give me a fork."

Lexical bias effect

Our speech errors are *not* random in nature. For example, our phonological speech errors generally form words rather than nonwords: the **lexical bias effect**. Informal evidence of this effect was reported by the Reverend William Archibald Spooner. He gave his name to the **spoonerism**, which occurs when the initial letter or letters of two or more words are switched mistakenly. Spooner is credited with several memorable spoonerisms (e.g., "You have hissed all my mystery lectures"; "The Lord is a shoving leopard to his flock"). Alas, most of the Rev. Spooner's gems were the result of much painstaking effort.

The most used way of studying the lexical bias effect was introduced by Baars et al. (1975). They presented word pairs in rapid succession, and the participants had to say both words in a pair rapidly. With some word pairs, swapping the first letters produced two new words (e.g., "deep cot" could become "keep dot"). This wasn't the case with other word pairs (e.g., "deed cop" could become "keed dop"). The key finding was that people made many more slips consisting of words than of nonwords.

The lexical bias effect can be related to the **Freudian slip**, a motivated error in speech revealing the speaker's true desires. Freud being Freud, he emphasized speech errors related to sex. This led Motley (1980) to carry out the following study. Male participants said out loud pairs of items such as "goxi furl" and "bine foddy." The experimenter was a male or a female "who was by design attractive, personable, very provocatively attired, and seductive in behavior" (Motley, 1980, p. 140).

Motley (1980) counted the number of sex-related spoonerisms (e.g., turning "goxi furl" into "foxy girl"; turning "bine foddy" into "fine body") that were produced. As predicted there were more such spoonerisms when the passions of the male participants were inflamed by the female experimenter.

Why does the lexical bias effect occur? Two main explanations have been suggested. First, Dell (1986) and Dell et al. (2008) argued that speakers generally produce the sounds most highly activated at any given moment.

Key Terms

Spreading activation: the notion that activation of a word or node within the brain causes some activation to spread to several related words or nodes.

Lexical bias effect: the tendency for speech errors to form words rather than nonwords; see **spoonerism**.

Spoonerism: a speech error in which the initial letter or letters of two words (typically close together) are mistakenly switched, an example of **lexical bias**.

Freudian slip: a speech-production error that reveals the speaker's (often unconscious) sexual or other desires.

These sounds are typically the correct ones. However, occasionally they are not because several phonemes (sounds) and words may all be activated at the same time. Activation at the word level helps to explain the lexical bias effect. For example, seeing "deep cot" may activate the words "keep" and "dot," and this extra activation can produce an error. In contrast, seeing "deed cop" does *not* activate "keed" or "dop" and so speakers are unlikely to produce these nonwords.

Second, we may *monitor* our own internal speech before speaking out loud to eliminate any nonwords (Hartsuiker et al., 2005; Levelt et al., 1999). In other words, the monitoring system asks the question, "Is this a word?"

Both explanations possess some validity (Nooteboom & Quené, 2008). Evidence that we engage in self-monitoring of our internal speech was reported by Nooteboom and Quené (2008). They used the technique introduced by Baars et al. (1975) that was discussed earlier. Participants frequently started to produce a spoonerism but then stopped themselves and produced the correct words. For example, they would see "BARN DOOR" and say, "D ... BARN DOOR."

Mixed-error effect

We have seen that Dell (e.g., 1986) argues that several different kinds of information are activated at the same time when someone is preparing to speak. All that activation is responsible for many (or even most) speech errors. Consider, for example, the **mixed-error effect**, which occurs when an incorrect word is both semantically and phonemically related to the correct word.

Dell (1986) quoted the example of someone saying "Let's stop" instead of "Let's start," where the word "stop" is both semantically and phonemically related to the correct word (i.e., "start"). The existence of this effect suggests that the various levels of processing *interact* flexibly with each other. More specifically, the mixed-error effect suggests that semantic and phonological factors can both influence word selection at the same time.

Ferreira and Griffin (2003) provided evidence of the mixed-error effect. In their key condition, participants were presented with an incomplete sentence such as, "I thought that there would still be some cookies left, but there were ..." followed by picture naming (e.g., of a priest). Participants often produced the wrong word "none." This was due to the semantic similarity between *priest* and *nun* combined with the phonological identity of *nun* and *none*.

Other speech errors

We will briefly mention some other speech errors. First, there are semantic substitution errors, in which the correct word is replaced by a word of similar meaning. For example, we say "Where is my tennis bat?" instead of "Where is my tennis racket?" In 99% of cases, nouns substitute for nouns and verbs substitute for verbs (Hotopf, 1980). An explanation of semantic substitution errors is discussed shortly.

Second, there are *number-agreement errors*, in which singular verbs are mistakenly used with plural subjects or vice versa. For example, consider the two sentence fragments, "The family of mice ..." and "The family of rats ...". Strictly speaking, the verb should be singular in both cases. However, many people use a plural verb with such sentences because family is a collective noun. This tendency was greater when the noun closest to the verb was more

> **Key Term**
>
> **Mixed-error effect:**
> a type of speech error where the incorrect word is related in terms of both meaning and sound to the correct one.

obviously plural (e.g., *rats* ends in –s, which is a strong predictor of a plural noun) (Haskell & MacDonald, 2003).

Why do we make number-agreement errors? One reason is that we often have insufficient processing resources to avoid such errors. McDonald (2008) asked participants to decide whether various sentences were grammatically correct. This was done with or without an externally imposed cognitive load. Participants with this load found it especially difficult to make accurate decisions concerning subject–verb agreement.

SPREADING ACTIVATION

As we saw earlier, Dell (1986) argued that several kinds of information are activated at the same time when we are planning an utterance. As a result, we are prone to error when an incorrect item is more activated than the correct one. A potential problem with Dell's spreading-activation approach is that it seems to predict that we would make more speech errors than is actually the case. For example, the theory predicts too many errors in situations in which two or more words are activated simultaneously (e.g., Glaser, 1992).

How can chaos be avoided? Dell et al. (2008) argued that through learning we possess a "syntactic traffic cop." It monitors what we intend to say and inhibits any words not belonging to the appropriate syntactical or grammatical category. This syntactic traffic cop explains why we nearly always replace a noun with a noun and a verb with a verb when we make mistakes when speaking.

We might expect that some patients have suffered damage to the syntactic traffic cop and so should make numerous syntactic errors. Supporting evidence was reported by Berndt et al. (1997) in a study on patients with **aphasia** (impaired language abilities due to brain damage). The patients named pictures and videos of objects (noun targets) and actions (verb targets).

The errors made by some of the patients nearly always involved words belonging to the correct syntactic category. The errors made by other patients were almost randomly distributed across nouns and verbs. It could be argued that the latter patients had an impaired syntactic traffic cop.

Individual differences

There are large individual differences in the number and nature of errors made when speaking. Dell et al. (1997) made an important contribution to understanding why these individual differences exist. They argued that most speech errors belong to two categories:

1. *Anticipatory:* Sounds or words are spoken ahead of their time (e.g., "cuff of coffee" instead of "cup of coffee"). These errors mainly reflect inefficient planning.
2. *Perseveratory:* Sounds or words are spoken later than they should have been (e.g., "beef needle" instead of "beef noodle"). These errors reflect failure to monitor what one is about to say (planning failure).

According to Dell et al. (1997), expert speakers plan ahead more than non-expert ones, and so have increased activation of *future* sounds and words. As a result, a high proportion of the speech errors of expert speakers should

> **Key Term**
>
> **Aphasia:**
> a condition due to brain damage in which the patient has severely impaired language abilities.

be anticipatory. In contrast, non-expert speakers should have relatively few anticipatory errors.

Dell et al. (1997) assessed the effects of practice on the anticipatory proportion (the proportion of total errors [anticipation + perseveration] that is anticipatory). In one study, participants were given extensive practice at saying several tongue twisters (e.g., five frantic fat frogs; thirty-three throbbing thumbs). As expected, the number of errors decreased as a function of practice. However, the anticipatory proportion *increased* from .37 early in practice to .59 at the end of practice, in line with prediction.

Dell et al. (1997) argued that speech errors are most likely when the speaker hasn't formed a coherent speech plan. In such circumstances, there will be relatively few anticipatory errors, and so the anticipatory proportion will be low. Thus, the anticipatory proportion should decrease as the overall error rate (anticipatory + perseverative) increases.

Dell et al. (1997) worked out the overall error rate and the anticipatory proportion for several sets of published data. The anticipatory proportion decreased from about .75 with low overall error rates to about .40 with high overall error rates (see Figure 9.5).

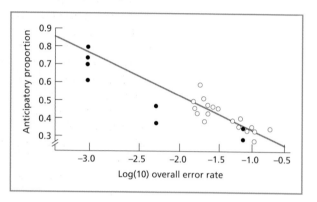

Vousden and Maylor (2006) tested the theory by assessing speech errors in 8-year-olds, 11-year-olds, and young adults who said tongue twisters aloud at a slow or fast rate. There were two main findings. First, the anticipatory proportion increased as a function of age. This is predicted by the theory, because older children and young adults have had more practice at producing language.

Second, fast speech produced a higher error rate than slow speech and also resulted in a lower anticipatory proportion. This is in agreement with the prediction that a higher overall error rate should be associated with a reduced anticipatory proportion.

Figure 9.5 The relationship between overall error rate and the anticipatory proportion. Filled circles come from studies reported by Dell et al. (1997) and unfilled circles come from other studies. Adapted from Dell et al. (1997).

Facilitation effects

According to Dell's spreading-activation theory, information about several words is often processed at the same time. This can produce facilitation effects. Support for this prediction was reported by Meyer and Damian (2007). Participants named target pictures while ignoring simultaneously presented distractor pictures. The names of the objects in the two pictures were phonologically related (e.g., dog – doll; ball – wall) or unrelated.

Meyer and Damian (2007) found that the naming of target pictures was *faster* when accompanied by phonologically related distractors. This finding indicates that the phonological representations of the distractors were activated at the same time as those of target names.

A facilitation effect is *not* always found. In one study (Janssen et al., 2008), English speakers were presented with colored objects (e.g., *red rake*) and named the color or the object. When the phonological representations of color and object were related (as in the *red rake* example), there was a facilitation effect when the *object* was named. In English, color adjectives are typically processed before object names, and so both words were activated before the object was named. In contrast, there was no facilitation effect when the object color was named, because there was little or no activation of the object name.

The above findings suggest the extent of phonological activation depends on word order – phonological activation is often limited to those words essential for the current task. Janssen et al. (2008) obtained further support for this account by carrying out the same experiment on French speakers. In French, the adjective typically *follows* the noun. For example, the French for *red rake* is *rateau rouge*. Accordingly, we would expect the findings to be exactly the opposite of those in English. That is what Janssen et al. found. Thus, activation can be constrained by word order and can be less extensive than assumed by Dell (1986).

In sum, Dell's theoretical approach provides a plausible explanation of many speech errors (e.g., the mixed-error effect; lexical bias effect; semantic substitution errors). It also provides an explanation for the interesting finding that the proportion of speech errors that is anticipatory increases as a function of practice and increasing expertise. Finally, Dell's theoretical approach can account for some facilitation effects. However, it seems that the number of speech errors is often less than would be expected by Dell. In addition, facilitation effects are less extensive than his theory would predict.

Section Summary

Stages of speech production

- Speech production involves several levels or stages of processing: message planning level; syntactic level; morphological level; and phonological level. The tip-of-the-tongue state occurs when semantic processing is successful but phonological processing is unsuccessful.

Speech planning

- There is often more advance planning at the semantic and syntactic levels than at the level of speech sounds. The extent of speakers' advance planning is relatively greater when speakers speak slowly, when they aren't performing an additional task at the same time, and when simple sentences are planned. Much of the flexibility in advance planning occurs because there is a tradeoff between avoiding errors in speech and the cognitive load on speakers.

Speech errors

- Speech errors occur when an incorrect item is more activated than the correct one. Our phonological speech errors generally form words rather than nonwords, in part because we monitor our internal speech before speaking out loud. The mixed-error effect, in which an incorrect spoken word is semantically and phonologically related to the correct word, indicates that several kinds of information are activated at the same time. Number-agreement errors are frequent because it is often cognitively demanding to prevent them.

> **Spreading activation**
> • Dell's spreading-activation theory seems to predict too many speech errors when several words are activated at the same time. We may have a "syntactic traffic cop" that inhibits words not belonging to the appropriate syntactic category. The proportion of speech errors that is anticipatory rather than perseveratory increases as a function of expertise and practice. Dell's theory predicts phonological facilitation effects which are sometimes (but not always) found.

WRITING

The main function of writing is to communicate with other people. We send text messages to make social arrangements or express our feelings, students write essays to fulfill course requirements, and so on.

Writing involves the retrieval and organization of information stored in long-term memory. In also involves complex thought processes; indeed, it is basically a form of thinking (e.g., Kellogg, 1994; Oatley & Djikic, 2008). Thus, although writing is an important topic in its own right (no pun intended!), it is *not* separate from other cognitive activities.

Most expert writers also possess excellent reading skills (Harley, 2008). However, the study of brain-damaged patients has indicated that there are some exceptions. For example, consider the case of Howard Engel, the Canadian mystery writer who suffered a stroke. As a result, he found reading incredibly difficult. In spite of that, he has continued to write books. One of these (*The man who forgot how to read*) was published in 2007 and contains an account of his experiences.

KEY PROCESSES

Hayes and Flower (1986) identified three key writing processes:

1. The *planning process:* this involves producing ideas and organizing them into a writing plan to satisfy the writer's goals.
2. The *sentence-generation process:* this involves turning the writing plan into the actual writing of sentences.
3. The *revision process:* this involves evaluating what has been written. Its focus ranges between individual words and the overall structural coherence of the writing.

The "natural" sequence of the three processes is planning, sentence generation, and revision. However, writers often deviate from this sequence if, for example, they spot a problem with what they are writing before producing a complete draft.

Findings

We can identify the processes involved in writing by using **directed retrospection.** Writers stop at various times during the writing process and categorize what

> **Key Term**
>
> **Directed retrospection:** a technique used in writing research in which writers categorize the process(es) in which they have just been engaged.

In the Real World 9.2: *Expressive writing*

What you write (especially if it is about a personally significant topic) can communicate much about you to other people. For example, suppose we compare the poetry of poets who subsequently committed suicide and those who did not. Those who committed suicide used more first-person singular words (e.g., I; me; my) than poets in the nonsuicide group (Stirman & Pennebaker, 2001). However, they used fewer first-person plural words (e.g., we; us; our) than nonsuicidal poets in the later stages of their lives. Thus, the poetry of suicidal poets reveals less social integration than that of nonsuicidal poets.

There are interesting effects of psychiatric status and gender on what people write. For example, psychiatric outpatients focus less than nonclinical controls on positive future events. Such patients used fewer words relating to optimism, energy, the future, and communication in their writing than nonclinical controls (Junghaenel et al., 2008).

Newman et al. (2008) compared the writings of men and women in a database consisting of over 14,000 text files. Women used more words relating to social and psychological processes than men. In contrast, men used more words dealing with object properties and impersonal topics. Thus, what we write can reveal the kind of person we are.

It is generally agreed that writing on personally relevant topics can communicate to others much about what you are like as a person. Intriguingly, there is also evidence that the psychological well-being of individuals can be improved by writing about their negative emotional experiences. Thus, one goal of writing may be to help us to free our minds of unwanted thoughts.

Supporting evidence has come using a technique pioneered by James Pennebaker. It involves **expressive writing** – individuals reveal their deepest thoughts and feelings about a topic of personal significance to them on a few occasions spread out over several days.

We can see the beneficial effects of expressive writing in a study on dating couples (Slatcher & Pennebaker, 2006). One person in each couple wrote about his/her intimate thoughts and feelings about the relationship or about daily activities on each of three consecutive days.

Three months later, those who engaged in expressive writing were more likely to be in the same relationship than those who wrote about daily activities – the figures were 77% and 52%, respectively. Couples in the expressive writing group showed an increase in the number of positive emotion words they included in their instant messages to their partner in the days after expressive writing.

Expressive writing can also improve physical health. Weinman et al. (2008) created a small wound in participants who subsequently wrote about a traumatic event (expressive writing) or about time management. The wounds of those who had engaged in expressive writing had healed better 14 and 21 days after the wound was inflicted.

Beneficial effects of expressive writing have been found in numerous studies. Joanne Frattaroli (2006) carried out a meta-analysis (see Glossary) combining findings from 146 studies. There were relatively small (but significant) positive effects of expressive writing on psychological health, physiological functioning, reported health, and general functioning.

Why does expressive writing have these beneficial effects? For many individuals, expressive writing allows them to make sense of their negative life experiences. Only those benefiting most from expressive writing showed a subsequent increase in the use of causation words (e.g., because; cause; effect) and insight words (e.g., consider; know) (Pennebaker, 1993).

Another factor is exposure – repeated exposure to negative thoughts and feelings reduces their impact. The beneficial effects of exposure can be seen in the finding that individuals who have several fairly lengthy expressive writing sessions generally show the greatest positive effects (Frattaroli, 2006).

Key Term

Expressive writing:
writing in a heartfelt way on a topic of deep personal significance to the writer; it has beneficial effects on emotional states and health.

they were just doing (e.g., planning, sentence generation, revision). Kellogg (1994) discussed studies involving directed retrospection. On average, writers devoted about 30% of their time to planning, 50% to sentence generation, and 20% to revision.

Levy and Ransdell (1995) analyzed writing processes systematically. As well as asking people to verbalize what they were doing, Levy and Ransdell obtained video recordings as those people wrote essays on computers. The participants spent less time engaged in planning during the course of the study. Initially they devoted 40% of their time to planning, but this reduced to 30% later.

One of Levy and Ransdell's (1995) most surprising findings was that the length of time spent on each process before moving on to another process was often very short. In the case of text generation, the median time was 7.5 s, and it was only 2.5 s for planning, reviewing, and revising. These findings suggest the various processes involved in writing are heavily interdependent and much less separate than we might imagine. Levy and Ransdell also found that writers who shifted rapidly among the various writing processes tended to produce the best-quality texts.

Levy and Ransdell (1995) reported a final interesting finding – writers were only partially aware of how they allocated time. Most *overestimated* the time spent on reviewing and revising, and *underestimated* the time spent on generating text. The writers estimated they spent just over 30% of their time reviewing and revising, but actually devoted only 20% of their time to them!

Kellogg (1988) considered the effects of producing an outline (focus on the main themes) on subsequent letter writing. Producers of outlines spent more time in sentence generation than no-outline participants, but less time in planning and reviewing or revising. Producing an outline increased the quality of the letter. Why was this? Producers of outlines didn't have to devote so much time to planning, which is the hardest process in writing.

Planning

Writing depends heavily on the writer's knowledge. Alexander et al. (1991) identified three kinds of relevant knowledge:

1. *Conceptual knowledge:* information about concepts and schemas stored in long-term memory.
2. *Socio-cultural knowledge:* information about the social background or context.
3. *Metacognitive knowledge:* knowledge about what one knows.

Hayes and Flower (1986) identified strategic knowledge as important. This concerns ways of organizing the goals and subgoals of writing to construct a coherent writing plan. Good writers use strategic knowledge flexibly to change the structure of the writing plan if problems arise.

Sentence generation

Kaufer et al. (1986) found that essays were always at least eight times longer than outlines or writing plans. The technique of asking writers to think aloud permitted Kaufer et al. to explore the process of sentence generation. Expert and average writers accepted about 75% of the sentence parts they verbalized. The length of the average sentence part was 11.2 words for the expert writers compared to 7.3 words for the average writers. Thus, good writers use larger units or "building blocks."

Revision

Revision is a key process in writing. Expert writers devote more of their writing time to revision than non-expert ones (Hayes & Flower, 1986). Of importance, expert writers focus more on the coherence and structure of the arguments expressed. Faigley and Witte (1983) found that 34% of revisions by experienced adult writers involved a change of meaning compared to only 12% of the revisions by inexperienced college writers.

WRITING EXPERTISE

Why are some writers more skillful than others? As with any complex cognitive skill, extensive and deliberate practice over a prolonged period of time is very important (see Chapter 10). Practice can help to provide writers with additional relevant knowledge, the ability to write faster (e.g., using word processing), and so on. We will see shortly that the working memory system (see Chapter 4) plays a key role in writing. All components of working memory have limited capacity, and writing demands on these components decrease with practice. That would provide experienced writers with spare processing capacity to enhance the quality of their writing.

Individual differences in writing ability probably depend mostly on planning and revision processes. Bereiter and Scardamalia (1987) argued that two major strategies are used in the planning stage:

1. a knowledge-telling strategy
2. a knowledge-transforming strategy.

The knowledge-telling strategy involves writers simply writing down everything they know about a topic with minimal planning. The text already generated provides retrieval cues for generating the rest of the text. In the words of a 12-year-old child who used the knowledge-telling strategy (Bereiter & Scardamalia, 1987, p. 9), "I have a whole bunch of ideas and write them down until my supply of ideas is exhausted." With increasing writing expertise, most adolescents shift from the knowledge-telling strategy to the knowledge-transforming strategy. This involves use of a *rhetorical problem space* and a content problem space. Rhetorical problems relate to the achievement of the goals of the writing task (e.g., "Can I strengthen the argument?"), whereas content problems relate to the specific information to be written down (e.g., "The case of Smith vs. Jones strengthens the argument"). There should be movement of information in both directions between the content space and the rhetorical space. This happens more often with skilled writers.

Bereiter et al. (1988) argued that knowledge-transforming strategists would be more likely than knowledge-telling strategists to produce high-level main points capturing important themes. Children and adults wrote an essay. Those producing a high-level main point used on average 4.75 different knowledge-transforming processes during planning. In contrast, those producing a low-level main point used only 0.23 knowledge-transforming processes on average.

Successful use of the planning process also depends on the writer's relevant knowledge. Adults possessing much knowledge or relatively little on a topic were compared by Hayes and Flower (1986). The experts produced more goals and subgoals, and so constructed a more complex overall writing plan. In addition, the experts' various goals were much more interconnected.

Expert writers also differ from non-expert ones in their ability to use the revision process. Hayes et al. (1985) found that expert writers detected 60% more problems in a text than non-experts. The expert writers correctly identified the nature of the problem in 74% of cases against only 42% for the non-expert writers. Levy and Ransdell (1995) found that writers who produced the best essays spent 40% more of their time reviewing and revising them than those producing the essays of poorest quality. Revisions made towards the end of the writing session were especially important.

Knowledge-crafting: Focus on the reader

Kellogg (2008) argued that really expert writers attain the knowledge-crafting stage (see Figure 9.6). This is an advance on the knowledge-transforming stage: "In … knowledge-crafting, the writer is able to hold in mind the author's ideas, the words of the text itself, and the imagined reader's interpretation

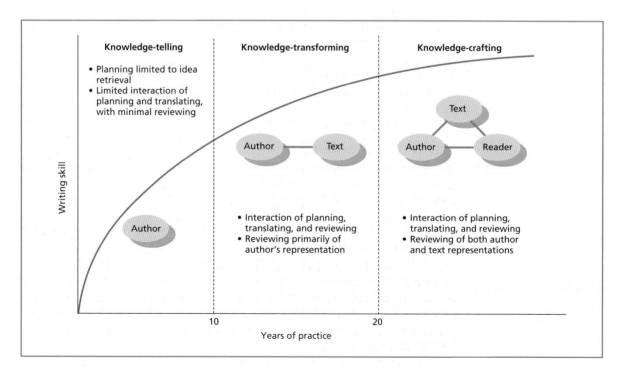

Figure 9.6 Kellogg's three-stage theory of the development of writing skill. From Kellogg (2008). Reprinted with permission of *Journal of Writing Research*.

of the text" (Kellogg, 2008, p. 5). The distinctive feature of the knowledge-crafting stage is its focus on the reader's needs.

It is important to consider the reader because of the **knowledge effect** – the tendency to assume that other people share the knowledge we possess. Hayes and Bajzek (2008) found that individuals familiar with technical terms greatly overestimated the knowledge other people would have of these terms (this is a failing that may have afflicted the author of this book!). Hayes and Bajzek discovered that providing feedback to improve writers' predictions of the knowledge possessed by others made their texts more understandable.

Instructing writers explicitly to consider the reader's needs often produces beneficial results. The revisions made to a text by students aged 11 or 15 were improved by the instruction to "read as the reader" (Holliway & McCutcheon, 2004). However, *feedback* from readers is especially effective. Schriver (1984) asked students to read an imperfect text and predict the comprehension problems another reader would have. Then the students read a reader's verbal account produced while he/she tried to understand that text. After the students had been given various texts plus readers' accounts, they became better at predicting the problems readers would have.

Sato and Matsushima (2006) found the quality of text writing by 15-year-old students wasn't improved by instructing them to attend to potential readers, perhaps because the instructions were insufficiently detailed. However, feedback from the readers about the comprehension problems they encountered was effective, and the benefits transferred to subsequent writing.

In sum, nonexpert writers typically focus on producing text they find easy to understand without paying much attention to the problems other readers might encounter with it. In contrast, expert writers engage in knowledge-crafting: they focus explicitly on the needs of their potential readers. Expert writers writing on topics on which they possess considerable knowledge are liable to overestimate the amount of relevant knowledge possessed by their readers. Most writing problems (including the knowledge effect) can be reduced by providing writers with detailed feedback from readers.

WORKING MEMORY

You have probably found that writing is often difficult and effortful. This is because it involves complex cognitive processes such as attention, thinking, and memory. It has been argued (e.g., Kellogg, 2001a) that writing depends heavily on the working memory system (discussed at length in Chapter 4). Its key component is the central executive, an attention-like system involved in organizing and coordinating cognitive activities.

Other components of the working memory system are the visuo-spatial sketchpad (involved in visual and spatial processing) and the phonological loop (involved in verbal rehearsal). Every component has limited capacity. Writing can involve all these working memory components (Olive, 2004).

Findings

According to Kellogg's working memory theory, all the main processes involved in writing depend on the central executive component of working memory. As a consequence, writing quality is likely to suffer if *any* writing process is made

> **Key Term**
>
> **Knowledge effect:** the tendency of writers to assume (often mistakenly) that those reading what they have written possess the same knowledge.

more difficult. As predicted, the quality of the written texts was lower when the text had to be written in capital letters rather than normal handwriting (Olive & Kellogg, 2002).

How can we assess the involvement of the central executive in writing? One way is to measure reaction times to auditory probes (sounds) presented in isolation (control condition) or while participants are engaged in writing. If writing uses much of the available capacity of working memory (especially the central executive), then reaction times should be longer in the writing condition.

Olive and Kellogg (2002) used this probe technique to assess the involvement of the central executive in the following conditions:

1. *Transcription:* A prepared text was simply copied, so no planning was required.
2. *Composition:* A text had to be composed, i.e., the writer had to plan and produce a coherent text. There was a pause in writing when the auditory signal was presented.
3. *Composition + transcription:* A text had to be composed, and the participant continued writing when the auditory signal was presented.

Olive and Kellogg (2002) found composition was more demanding than transcription, because composition involves planning and sentence generation. In addition, composition + transcription was more demanding than composition on its own. Thus, writers can apparently engage in higher-level processes (e.g., planning) *and* lower-level processes (writing words) at the same time.

Additional evidence that two processes can occur at the same time was reported by Olive et al. (2009). In one condition, participants wrote a narrative or an essay in their normal handwriting. They often engaged in translating or sentence generation while actually writing, and sometimes combined actual writing with planning or revising. In another condition, participants were required to write in an unfamiliar handwriting that was relatively effortful. In this condition, they were less likely to combine writing processes with actual writing, presumably because using an unfamiliar handwriting was cognitively demanding.

Kellogg (2001a) assumed that writers with much relevant knowledge about an essay topic would have large amounts of well-organized information stored in long-term memory. This knowledge should reduce the effort involved in writing an essay. He asked students with varying degrees of relevant knowledge to write an essay about baseball, and used the probe technique to assess processing demands. As predicted, processing demands were lower in those students with the most background knowledge.

Kellogg (2001b) used the probe technique to assess the processing demands of planning, translating (sentence generating), and reviewing (revising) during the production of texts in longhand or on a word processor. It was assumed that students would find use of a word processor more demanding than writing in longhand because of their lesser familiarity with word processing.

Kellogg (2001b) obtained three main findings. First, probe reaction times were slowed down considerably during planning, translating, and reviewing, indicating that all three writing processes are very demanding. Second, reviewing or revising was more demanding than planning and translating. Third, word processing was more demanding than writing in longhand.

Roussey and Piolat (2008) used the probe technique, and found that reviewing or revising was more demanding of processing resources than comprehension. This was more so for participants low in working memory capacity (see Glossary and Chapter 4), suggesting that text reviewing or revising is especially demanding for such individuals. Other studies (e.g., Olive et al., 2009) have confirmed that revising is the most demanding writing process. These studies also suggested that translating or sentence generation may be less demanding than planning.

Why is reviewing/revising so demanding? Text reviewing or revision involves language comprehension processes plus additional processes (e.g., problem solving and decision making).

Vanderberg and Swanson (2007) assessed the involvement of the central executive in writing. They considered writing performance at the *general* (e.g., planning, sentence generation, revision) and *specific* (e.g., grammar, punctuation) levels. Individuals with the most effective central executive functioning had the best writing performance at both levels. In addition, high levels of central executive functioning were associated with good performance on the various stages of writing (planning; translation; revision).

In sum, *all* the major writing processes are cognitively demanding, and make use of the central executive component of the working memory system. This is especially the case with respect to the revision process. We turn now to two other components of this system: the phonological loop and visuo-spatial sketchpad.

Phonological loop

Chenoweth and Hayes (2003) investigated the role of the phonological loop in writing. Participants performed the task of typing sentences to describe cartoons on its own or while repeating a syllable continuously. Syllable repetition uses the phonological loop and is known as articulatory suppression. Articulatory suppression caused writers to produce shorter sequences of words in rapid succession, suggesting that it suppressed their "inner voice."

It could be argued that the reason why articulatory suppression impaired writing performance was that the writing task was a fairly complex one. Hayes and Chenoweth (2006) asked their participants to transcribe or copy texts from one computer window to another. In spite of the apparent simplicity of this writing task, participants transcribed more slowly and made more errors when the task was accompanied by articulatory suppression. These findings suggest that the phonological loop is often important in writing.

Visuo-spatial sketchpad

The involvement of the visuo-spatial sketchpad in writing was assessed by Levy and Ransdell (2001). A visuo-spatial task (detecting when two consecutive characters were in the same place or similar in color) increased writers' initial planning time.

Kellogg et al. (2007) asked students to write descriptions of concrete (e.g., house; pencil) and abstract (e.g., freedom; duty) nouns while performing a detection task. The writing task slowed detection times for visual stimuli *only* when concrete words were being described. Thus, the visuo-spatial sketchpad is more involved when writers are thinking about concrete nouns than abstract ones.

Evaluation

⊕ The main writing processes are very demanding or effortful and make substantial demands on working memory (especially the central executive). The demands on the central executive are especially great during revision or reviewing (Kellogg, 2001b; Roussey & Piolat, 2008).

⊕ Individuals with good central executive functioning have good planning, translation, and revision processes (Vanderberg & Swanson, 2007).

⊕ The phonological loop and the visuo-spatial sketchpad are both involved in the writing process. However, the involvement of the visuo-spatial sketchpad depends on the type of text being produced (Kellogg et al., 2007).

⊖ Writing performance doesn't *necessarily* depend on the involvement of the phonological loop. Some patients with a severely impaired phonological loop nevertheless have essentially normal written language (Gathercole & Baddeley, 1993).

⊖ Kellogg's theoretical approach doesn't indicate clearly *why* planning and sentence generation are so demanding. We need a more fine-grain analysis of writers' strategies during the planning process.

⊖ The theory focuses on the effects of writing processes on working memory. However, working memory limitations probably influence *how* we allocate our limited resources during writing. For example, we may shift rapidly from one writing process to another when our processing capacity is in danger of being exceeded.

WORD PROCESSING

There has been a substantial increase in the use of word processors in recent years. Most evidence suggests that this has had beneficial effects. Goldberg et al. (2003) carried out meta-analyses (combining findings from many studies) to compare writing performance when students used word processors or wrote in longhand.

Those who used word processors were more involved in their writing than those who wrote in longhand and produced longer essays. Those essays were of higher quality, especially among students who found writing a struggle. One reason why word processing leads to enhanced writing quality is that word-processed essays tend to be better organized than those written in longhand (Whithaus et al., 2008). One reason for this is that it is much easier to change the organization or structure of a word-processed essay than one written in longhand.

Some students don't seem to benefit from word processing their essays. Indeed, Russell (1999) found that students with below-average typing skills did *worse* when word processing than when writing in longhand. This was presumably because much of their attention was devoted to typing the individual letters rather than focusing on what they were writing.

Kellogg and Mueller (1993) compared text produced by word processor and by writing in longhand. There were only small differences in writing quality or the speed at which text was produced. However, use of the probe technique indicated that word processing involved more effortful planning and revision (but not sentence generation) than writing in longhand. Those using word processors were much less likely than those writing in longhand to make notes (12% vs. 69%, respectively), which may explain the findings.

In sum, we would not expect word processing to have a dramatic impact on writing quality. Factors such as access to relevant knowledge, skill at generating sentences, and ability to revise text effectively are essential to high-quality writing no matter how produced. However, the balance of advantage clearly lies with word processing compared to writing in longhand. This is comforting news to me – I have word processed all the books I have written in the past 25 years!

Section Summary

Expressive writing

- Psychiatric status and gender both have predictable effects on what people write. Expressive writing can enhance psychological wellbeing, physical health, and general functioning. The opportunity to make sense of negative life experiences and the reduction in negative emotions as a result of repeated exposure explain the beneficial effects of expressive writing.

Key processes

- Writing involves planning, sentence generation, and revision. Writers often shift rapidly among these processes, with most time being devoted to sentence generation or translation. Good writers use larger units or "building blocks" than other writers and devote a greater proportion of their time to revision.

Writing expertise

- Good writers adopt a knowledge-transforming strategy and are better than poor writers at detecting problems during the revision process. Expert writers attain the knowledge-crafting stage, in which the focus is on the reader's needs.

Working memory

- All the main processes involved in writing rely on the central executive, with revision imposing the greatest demands on it. This is because revision involves language comprehension, problem solving, and decision making. Individuals with the most effective central executive functioning excel at planning, translation, and revision. The ability to produce relatively large sequences of words when writing depends in part on the phonological loop. The visuo-spatial sketchpad is more involved when writers' thinking is concrete rather than abstract.

Word processing

- Relevant knowledge and general writing skills are essential whether essays are word-processed or written by hand. In spite of that, word-processed essays are often better organized and longer than those written by hand. However, the opposite tends to be the case with students having below-average typing skills.

Essay Questions

1. How do speakers assist listeners to understand what they are saying?
2. How can we tell whether someone is lying?
3. To what extent do speakers plan what they are going to say?
4. Describe some of the main speech errors. Why do we make these errors?
5. Describe and discuss the most important writing processes.
6. Discuss how the working memory system is involved in writing.

Further Reading

- Boelte, J., Goldrick, M., & Zwitserlood, P. (2009). *Language production: Sublexical, lexical, and supralexical information*. New York, NY: Psychology Press. Many key issues in language production are addressed fully by leading experts in the area.
- Eysenck, M. W., & Keane, M. T. (2010). *Cognitive psychology: A student's handbook* (6th ed.). New York, NY: Psychology Press. Chapter 11 of this textbook is devoted to the psychology of speech production and writing.
- Gaskell, G. (Ed.). (2007). *Oxford handbook of psycholinguistics*. Oxford, UK: Oxford University Press. Part IV of this useful handbook contains chapters by leading experts on major topics in language production.
- Harley, T. A. (2008). *The psychology of language: From data to theory* (3rd ed.). Hove, UK: Psychology Press. Trevor Harley discusses the main issues in speech production in Chapters 13 and 14 of his excellent textbook.
- Olive, T. (2004). Working memory in writing: Empirical evidence from the dual-task technique. *European Psychologist, 9,* 32–42. This article focuses on the role played by the working memory system in writing.

Chapter 10

Contents

Problem solving

10

INTRODUCTION

Life presents us with plenty of problems, although thankfully the great majority are fairly trivial ones. We have the problem of working out how to mend our bicycle, how to get hold of a crucial reference for an essay that needs to be handed in on Friday, how to analyze the data from last week's laboratory exercise or practical, and so on.

What do we mean by problem solving? There are three main aspects:

1. It is purposeful (i.e., goal-directed).
2. It involves deliberate or controlled processes and so isn't totally reliant on automatic processes.
3. A problem exists only when the person trying to solve it lacks the relevant knowledge to produce an immediate solution. Thus, a mathematical calculation may be a problem for most of us but not for a professional mathematician.

There are important differences among problems. **Well-defined problems** are ones in which all aspects of the problem are clearly specified, including the initial state or situation, the range of possible moves or strategies, and the goal or solution. The goal is well specified in the sense that it is clear when the goal has been reached. For example, a maze is a well-defined problem in which reaching the center is the goal.

Ill-defined problems are underspecified. Suppose you set yourself the goal of becoming happier. There are potentially endless strategies you could adopt, and it is very hard to know which ones would be more or less effective. Happiness is a somewhat slippery notion, so how are you going to decide whether you have solved the problem of becoming happier?

Most everyday problems are ill-defined. However, psychologists have focused mainly on well-defined problems. Why is this? One important reason is that well-defined problems have a best strategy for their solution. This makes it easy to identify the errors and deficiencies in the strategies adopted by human problem solvers.

It is also important to distinguish between knowledge-rich and knowledge-lean problems. **Knowledge-rich problems** can only be solved by those having much relevant specific knowledge. In contrast, **knowledge-lean problems** don't require such knowledge because most of the information needed to solve the problem is contained in the initial problem statement.

Most research on problem solving has involved knowledge-lean problems, in part because this minimizes individual differences in relevant knowledge. However, knowledge-rich problems are very important in the real world. For example, there are the problems faced by scientists when trying to make scientific discoveries. More generally, experts spend most of their working lives dealing with knowledge-rich problems. Expertise is discussed towards the end of the chapter.

MONTY HALL PROBLEM

In the Real World 10.1: *Monty Hall problem*

We can discuss key issues in solving well-defined problems by considering the notorious Monty Hall problem. It formed a prominent part in Monty Hall's television show:

> Suppose you're on a game show and you're given the choice of three doors. Behind one door is a car, behind the others, goats. You pick a door, say, Number 1. The host, who knows what is behind the doors, now opens one of the two remaining doors, say Number 3. The door he opens must have a goat behind it. If both remaining doors have goats behind them, he chooses one randomly. He then says to you, "Do you want to switch to door Number 2?" Is it to your advantage to switch your choice?

If you stayed with your first choice, you are in good company. About 85% of people make that decision (Burns & Wieth, 2004), as did most of those on the TV program. Unfortunately, it is wrong! It seems as if either choice has a 50% chance of being correct. In fact, however, there is a two-thirds chance of being correct if you switch your choice.

Marilyn vos Savant (who was claimed to have the highest IQ in the world: 228) published this problem and its solution in *Parade* magazine in 1990. This triggered thousands of indignant letters from readers (including nearly 1000 with PhDs) disagreeing with the correct answer. Even Paul Erdös, one of the greatest twentieth-century mathematicians, initially rejected the correct answer.

It is likely that you furiously disagree with the correct answer, namely, that you should switch your choice. If so, perhaps Research Activity 10.1 will persuade you.

Research Activity 10.1: *Monty Hall problem*

This activity is based on the Wikipedia entry for the Monty Hall problem. Take three cards from a pack of playing cards: ace of spades (car); two of hearts (goat); and two of diamonds (goat). Shuffle the cards and place one card face down in front of you (this is equivalent to door Number 1). Then look at the two remaining cards and discard a red two. If the card that is face down is the ace, you would have won by not switching. If the remaining card in your hand is the ace, you would have won by switching.

Perform this procedure 30 times. On average, you should find that you have won 20 times by switching but only 10 times by not switching. If you remain unconvinced that the correct answer is that you should switch, consider this analysis of the problem by Krauss and Wang (2003). They pointed out that there are only three possible arrangements with the Monty Hall problem (see Figure 10.1). With Arrangements 1 and 2, your first choice was incorrect, and so Monty Hall opens the only remaining door with a goat behind it. As a result, switching is certain to succeed. With Arrangement 3, your first choice was correct and you would win by refusing to switch. Thus, switching succeeds with two out of three arrangements (1 and 2) and fails only with Arrangement 3, producing a two-thirds chance that switching will succeed.

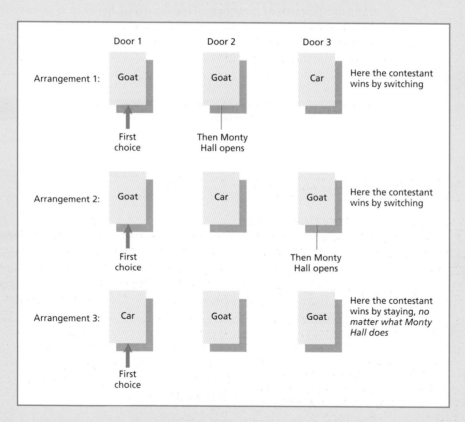

Figure 10.1 Explanation of the solution to the Monty Hall problem: In two out of three possible car–goat arrangements, the contestant would win by switching; therefore she should switch. From Krauss and Wang, 2003. Copyright © 2003 American Psychological Association. Reproduced with permission.

Why do most people find the Monty Hall problem so hard? First, we typically use a heuristic or rule of thumb known as the uniformity fallacy (Falk & Lann, 2008). This fallacy involves assuming that all the available options are equally likely whether they are or not.

Second, the Monty Hall problem places substantial demands on the central executive (an attention-like component of working memory: See Chapter 4). Participants were much less likely to solve the Monty Hall problem if they performed a demanding task involving the central executive at the same time (8% vs. 22%; De Neys & Verschueren, 2006).

Third, most people find it hard to think about causality and mistakenly believe that the host's actions are random. Burns and Wieth (2004) made the causal structure of the problem clearer. There are three boxers, one of whom was so good he was certain to win any bout. You select one boxer and then the other two boxers fight each other. The winner of this bout then fights the boxer you selected initially, and you win if you choose the winner of this second bout. You decide whether you want to stay with your initial choice or switch to the winner of the first bout. With this version of the problem, 51% correctly decided to switch versus only 15% with the standard three-door problem. This occurred because it is easy to see that the boxer who won the first bout did so because of skill rather than any random factors.

Section Summary

- Problems can be well-defined or ill-defined and knowledge-lean or knowledge-rich. Much laboratory research has focused on well-defined, knowledge-lean problems, but expertise research involves knowledge-rich problems.

Monty Hall problem
- The great majority of people produce the wrong answer to the Monty Hall problem. Why is it so difficult? First, it requires a complex understanding of causality. Second, it places substantial demands on the attention-like central executive. Third, it requires avoiding the uniformity fallacy (assuming all available options are equally likely).

HOW USEFUL IS PAST EXPERIENCE?

Common sense indicates that our ability to solve a problem is much better if we have relevant past experience with similar problems than if we do not. Indeed, the main reason adults can solve problems much faster than children (and can solve a wider range of problems) is their enormous relevant past experience. Is past experience *always* useful? The answer is a resounding "No!"

FUNCTIONAL FIXEDNESS

Duncker (1945) obtained evidence of **functional fixedness**. This is observed when we fail to solve problems because we assume from past experience that any given object has only a limited number of uses. Duncker gave participants a candle, a match box containing matches, some tacks, and several other objects (see Figure 10.2).

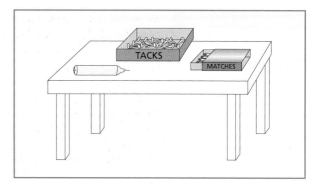

The participants' task was to attach the candle to a wall by a table so it didn't drip onto the table below. Most participants tried to nail the candle directly to the wall or to glue it to the wall by melting it. Only a few came up with the correct answer, which is to use the inside of the match box as a candle holder and then to nail it to the wall with the tacks.

Figure 10.2 Some of the materials provided for participants instructed to mount a candle on a vertical wall in the study by Duncker (1945).

According to Duncker (1945), his participants "fixated" on the box's function as a container rather than as a platform. This account was supported by the finding that more correct solutions were produced when the match box was empty (rather than full) at the start of the experiment. Having the match box empty made it seem less like a container.

There are other ways of improving performance on Duncker's candle problem. Frank and Ramscar (2003) used a condition in which "candle," "book of matches," and "box of tacks" were underlined. The percentage of solutions in this condition was more than double the success rate when no words were underlined.

Why did the simple addition of underlining a few words produce such a large improvement in performance? The underlinings led participants to attend more to the objects underlined, and thus focus more directly on the key objects involved in problem solution.

Duncker (1945) showed that problem-solving performance could be impaired by functional fixedness caused by accumulated past experience with the crucial object in the problem. However, adverse effects of functional fixedness can be found even when individuals have only very limited experience with an object.

Ye et al. (2009) asked people to decide whether each of nine objects could be used for a given function (e.g., packable-with – usable as packing material to pack an egg in a box). Immediately afterwards, they decided whether the same objects could be used for a different function (e.g., play catch-with over a distance of 15 feet). Some objects (e.g., ski cap; pillow) could be used for both functions. Deciding that one of these objects possessed the first function significantly reduced the probability of detecting that it also possessed the second function.

More striking evidence that functional fixedness is hard to avoid was reported by Chrysikou and Weisberg (2005). Participants designed various objects (e.g., a disposable, spill-proof coffee cup). In one condition, they were shown a picture of an inadequate coffee cup with the accompanying description explicitly stating various problems with it. Nevertheless, the participants' designs consistently included elements of the example coffee cup identified

Key Term

Functional fixedness: the inflexible focus on the usual function or functions of an object in problem solving.

| Key Term |

Mental set:
a readiness to think or
act in a given way, often
because this has been
shown to be successful in
the past.

as problematic. The take-home message is that the ideas we encounter often constrain our subsequent thinking, a theme continued in the section on insight.

MENTAL SET

Suppose participants in an experiment are presented with a series of problems, all of which can be solved using the same strategy. This leads them to develop a **mental set** – a tendency to approach problems in a way that proved successful in the past. Forming a mental set is of value because successive problems can be solved faster and with fewer processing demands (Cherubini & Mazzocco, 2004).

What happens when the expectation that a current problem can be solved using the old strategy is incorrect? That was the question posed in classic research by Luchins (1942) and Luchins and Luchins (1959) using water-jar problems.

One of the problems used by Luchins was as follows: Jar A can hold 28 quarts of water, Jar B 76 quarts, and Jar C 3 quarts (see Figure 10.3). The task is to end up with exactly 25 quarts in one of the jars. The solution isn't difficult, as I'm sure you will agree. Jar A is filled, and then Jar C is filled from it, leaving 25 quarts in Jar A. Not surprisingly, 95% of participants who had previously been given similar problems solved it. Other participants were trained on a series of problems all having the same complex three-jar solution. Of these participants, only 36% managed to solve this very simple problem!

How can we explain the poor performance on the simple problem of those participants trained on complex problems? People often maintain a mental set even when it prevents a problem being solved. In the words of Luchins (1942, p. 1), "The successive, repetitious use of the same method mechanized many of the subjects – blinded them to the possibility of a more direct and simple procedure."

More dramatic evidence of how mental set can prevent us from thinking clearly was reported by Levine (1971). Participants were presented with a series of cards each bearing the letters A and B, with instructions to work out the hypothesis the experimenter had in mind. On each trial, the participant said "A" or "B" and the experimenter indicated whether this was correct. For the first few problems, the solution involved a position sequence (e.g., the letter on the left was correct on the first trial, the letter on the right on the second trial, and so on).

After several problems involving position sequences, participants were given a very simple problem not involving a position sequence: "A" was always correct and "B" was always incorrect. About 80% of university students failed to solve this problem within 100 trials! They assumed the answer must be some kind of position sequence, and there are almost endless possible position sequences.

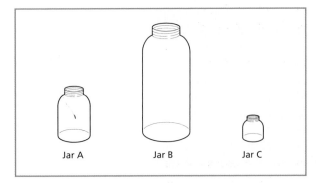

Jar A   Jar B   Jar C

Figure 10.3 One of the water-jar problems used by Luchins (1942) and Luchins and Luchins (1959): Jar A holds 28 quarts, Jar B holds 76 quarts, and Jar C holds 3 quarts.

It is understandable that people given a series of unfamiliar problems make extensive use of a mental set. However, it seems likely that experts given a problem in their area of expertise would be relatively immune from its damaging effects. In fact, this is *not* the case. Bilalić et al. (2008a) presented expert chess players with a chess problem and told them to find the shortest way to win. The problem could be solved in five moves using a familiar strategy but in only three moves using a less familiar solution. Only 50% of the International Masters and 0% of the Candidate Masters found the shorter solution.

Bilalić et al. (2008b) carried out a similar study designed to clarify why expert chess players often failed to find the shorter solution. After these players had found the familiar solution, they reported they were looking hard for a better one. However, their eye movements revealed they were still looking at features of the chessboard position related to the familiar solution. Thus, the direction of attention remained partly under the control of the processes responsible for the initial solution.

Section Summary

Functional fixedness

- Past experience can disrupt current problem solving due to functional fixedness, in which the focus is on a limited number of uses of an object. More generally, the ideas we encounter can constrain our subsequent thinking.

Mental set

- Problem solvers often develop a mental set (a tendency to use a strategy that proved successful in the past). This can disrupt performance when the current problem can't be solved using the old strategy. Experts are adversely affected by mental set, even when they are deliberately trying to prevent such effects. One reason for this is that their attentional processes are still partly influenced by mental set.

DOES INSIGHT EXIST?

We all spend lots of time working slowly but surely through problems until we reach the solution – what we might call "grind-out-the-answer" problems. For example, solving a complicated multiplication problem involves several processing operations that must be performed in the correct sequence.

Do you believe that most problems involve moving slowly towards the solution? If you do, then you are in for a shock! There are many problems in which the solution depends on **insight** or "aha" experience involving a sudden transformation of the problem.

Key Term

Insight:
the experience of suddenly realizing how to solve a problem.

Research Activity 10.2: *Rebus problems*

You may be familiar with **rebus problems** which contain verbal and visual cues to a familiar phrase. For example, "a **front**" is a bold front and "PUNISHMENT" is capital punishment. It is often assumed that solving such problems involves insight.

The following rebus problems are taken from MacGregor and Cunningham (2009). They are divided into those depending on *one* principle for their solution and those that depend on *two* principles. See how many you can solve (answers

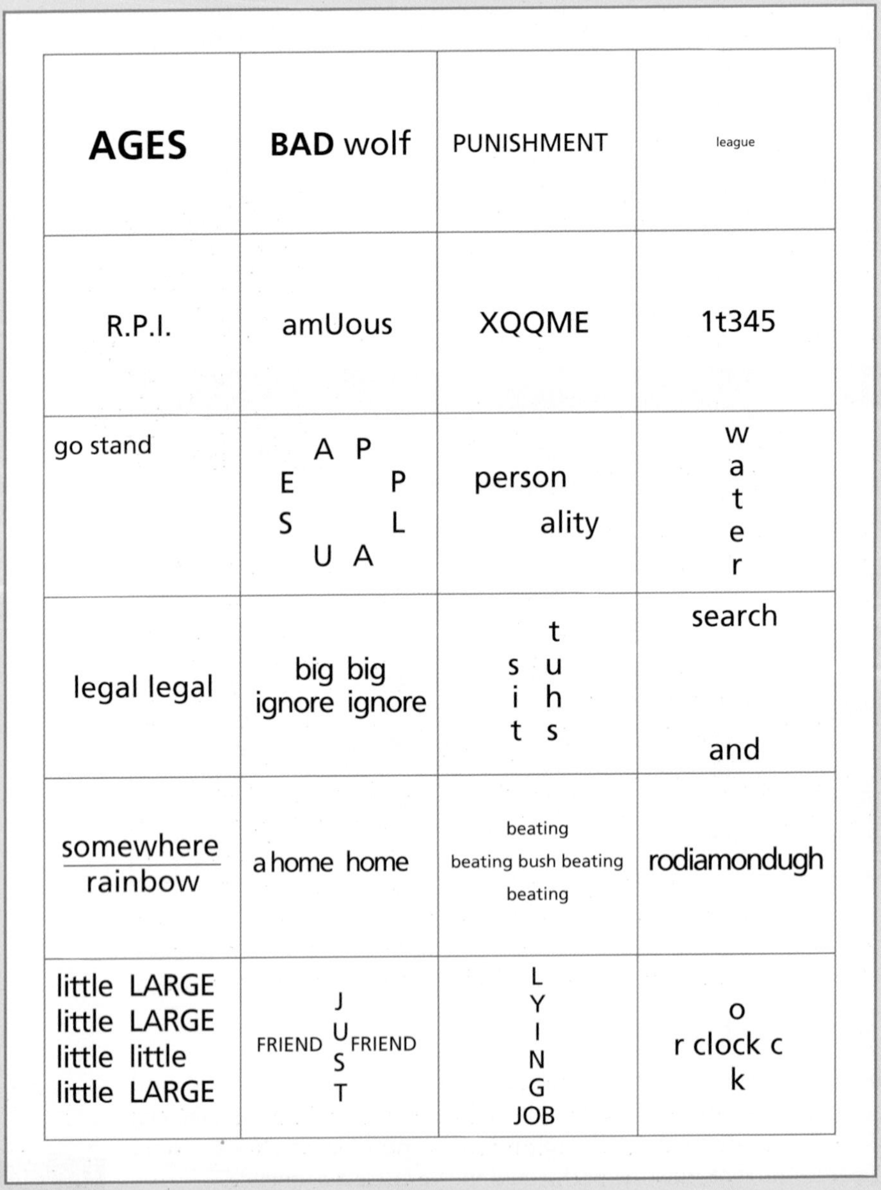

AGES	**BAD** wolf	PUNISHMENT	league
R.P.I.	amUous	XQQME	1t345
go stand	A P E P S L U A	person ality	w a t e r
legal legal	big big ignore ignore	t s u i h t s	search and
somewhere rainbow	a home home	beating beating bush beating beating	rodiamondugh
little LARGE little LARGE little little little LARGE	J FRIEND $\overset{U}{\underset{S}{}}$ FRIEND T	L Y I N G JOB	o r clock c k

Figure 10.4 Rebus puzzles. The puzzles in the first, third, and fifth rows require one principle or restructuring to be used for their solution. In contrast, those in the second, fourth, and sixth rows require two principles or restructurings to be used. From MacGregor and Cunningham (2009) http://docs.lib.purdue.edu/jps/vol2/iss2/7.

are in the Appendix at the back of the book) and how long it takes to solve each rebus. See also whether thinking of each answer is associated with insight or an "aha" experience.

Most people take longer to solve rebus problems that depend on two principles than on one (MacGregor & Cunningham, 2008, 2009). Why is that? Two-principle rebus problems require two separate insights for their solution whereas one-principle problems require only one.

MacGregor and Cunningham (2008) argued that insight is often involved in solving rebus problems. Those who performed best on rebus problems generally had high self-rated insight and also performed well on other kinds of insight problems.

The mutilated checkerboard (or draughtboard) problem (see Figure 10.5) is an example of an insight problem. The board is initially covered by 32 dominoes occupying two squares each. Then two squares from diagonally opposite corners are removed. Can the remaining 62 be filled by 31 dominoes? Think what your answer is before reading on.

Nearly everyone given this problem starts by mentally covering squares with dominoes (Kaplan & Simon, 1990). Alas, this strategy is not terribly effective because there are 758,148 possible permutations of the dominoes!

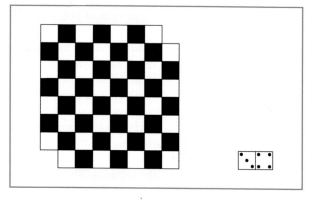

Figure 10.5 The mutilated checkerboard problem.

Since very few people solve the mutilated checkerboard problem without assistance, I'll assume you are in that large majority (my apologies if you aren't!). If I tell you something you already know, the chances are much greater you will rapidly solve the problem. Remember that each domino covers one white and one black square. If that clue doesn't do the trick, think about the colors of the two squares that have been removed – they must have been the *same* color. Thus, the 31 dominoes *can't* cover the mutilated board.

The take-home message from the mutilated checkerboard problem is that how we think about a problem (the problem representation) is often of great importance in problem solving. Many psychologists (e.g., Ohlsson, 1992) argue that what happens with many problems is that we initially construct one or more problem representations. Eventually we form the correct problem representation, which involves a sudden restructuring of the problem (known as insight). Later we will consider a theoretical approach based on changing representations.

INSIGHT VS. NON-INSIGHT PROBLEMS

Different processes are involved in solving insight and non-insight (or analytic) problems. Metcalfe and Wiebe (1987) considered various insight and non-insight problems. An example of the former is as follows: You have black and brown socks in your drawer in a ratio of 4 to 5. How many socks do you need to take out to ensure you have a pair the same color? The answer is 3 – the ratio of the two sock colors is irrelevant. An example of a non-insight problem was one of Luchins' water-jar problems discussed earlier.

Metcalfe and Wiebe (1987) found that there was a progressive increase in "warmth" (closeness to solution) during non-insight problems. This is as expected since they involve a sequence of processes. In contrast, the warmth ratings during insight problems remained at the same low level until suddenly increasing dramatically just before the solution was reached.

Brain-imaging findings also indicate that there are important differences in the processing of insight and non-insight problems. Bowden et al. (2005) used remote associate problems. Three words were presented (e.g., "fence"; "card"; "master"), and participants thought of a word (e.g., "post") that would go with each one to form compound words. The participants indicated whether their answers involved insight (i.e., sudden awareness).

Bowden et al. (2005) found that the anterior superior temporal gyrus (ridge) was activated only when solutions involved insight. In their second experiment, event-related potentials (ERPs; see Glossary) were recorded. There was a burst of high-frequency brain activity one-third of a second before the participants indicated they had achieved an insightful solution. This brain activity was centered on the right anterior superior temporal gyrus. According to Bowden et al., this area is vital to insight because it is involved in processing general semantic (meaning) relationships.

Bowden and Beeman (1998) had previously found that the right hemisphere plays an important role in insight. Participants were presented with problems similar to those used by Bowden et al. (2005). Before solving each problem, they were shown the solution word or an unrelated word and decided whether it provided the solution. The word was presented to the left or right hemisphere. Participants responded much faster when the word was presented to the right hemisphere.

Why is insight more associated with the right than the left hemisphere? Integration of weakly active and distant associations occurs mostly in the right hemisphere (Bowden & Jung-Beeman, 2007). These processing activities are very relevant for producing insight. In contrast, strong activation of closely connected associations occurs mostly in the left hemisphere.

Insightful solutions to problems seem to "pop into the mind" in a relatively automatic and effortless way. In contrast, deliberate processes involving working memory seem to be required to solve analytic or non-insight problems. Lavric et al. (2000) considered the effects of counting auditory stimuli (requiring the involvement of working memory) on various problems. The counting task impaired performance on analytic problems but not on insight ones, suggesting that working memory is more important for analytic problems than insight ones. In similar fashion, Fleck (2008) found that individual differences in working memory capacity predicted performance on analytic problems but not on insight ones.

While our subjective experience tells us that insight occurs suddenly and unexpectedly, the same isn't true of the underlying processes. Consider a study by Novick and Sherman (2003). Expert anagram solvers often solved five-letter anagrams in an insightful way within 2–3 s having not been consciously aware of making progress until the answer "popped out."

These experts were presented with strings of five letters that could (or could not) be rearranged to form words. Even when these letter strings were presented very briefly (for 469 or 953 ms), the experts were reasonably good at deciding whether they were anagrams. Thus, *partial* information was available to the experts at times much shorter than those needed to produce pop-out or insight solutions.

Sheth et al. (2009) presented their participants with brainteaser and verbal puzzles while taking EEG records. Insight solutions were *preceded* by increased involvement of various brain areas, including those associated with recombining different representations. Thus, processing of direct relevance to the production of insightful solutions is occurring even though problem solvers aren't consciously aware of this processing.

REPRESENTATIONAL CHANGE THEORY

What factors facilitate insight? This question was addressed by Ohlsson (1992) in his representational change theory. When trying to solve a problem, we often encounter a block or impasse where we have represented the problem wrongly – think back to the mutilated checkerboard problem. We need to change the problem representation for insight to occur. This can occur in three ways:

1. *Constraint relaxation*: Inhibitions on what is regarded as permissible are removed.
2. *Re-encoding*: Some aspect of the problem representation is reinterpreted (this is what is needed with the mutilated checkerboard problem).
3. *Elaboration*: New problem information is added to the representation.

We can see the importance of constraint relaxation in a study by Bulbrook (1932). Participants were presented with a string of beads. Most of the string consisted of two small white beads alternating with one larger yellow bead, except in the middle, where there were 5 white beads together. The task was to produce a regular pattern without unstringing or restringing the beads. To solve the problem it was necessary to realize it was permissible to use a pair of pliers to break some of the beads. Even though pliers were readily available, 43% of the participants failed to solve the problem.

More evidence that insight can involve relaxing constraints we have needlessly imposed on ourselves was reported by Knoblich et al. (1999). They used sticks to present mathematical problems involving Roman numerals. Each problem presented had an incorrect solution, and the task was to move *one* stick to turn it into a true statement. For example VI = VII + I (6 = 7 + 1) becomes true by turning it into VII = VI + I (7 = 6 + 1).

What is the correct answer to the following problem: IV = III − I (4 = 3 − 1)? If you are like the participants in the study by Knoblich et al. (1999), you probably found this problem harder than the previous one. The correct answer is IV − III = I (4 − 3 = 1). Our experience of arithmetic tells us that many operations change the values (numbers) in an equation (as in our first example). In contrast, relatively few operations change the operators (i.e., plus, minus, and equal signs) as in our second example. Thus, insight on problems of the second type requires us to relax the normal constraints of arithmetic.

What happens when successive problems require the same or a different kind of insight? Öllinger et al. (2008) answered this question using arithmetic problems similar to those of Knoblich et al. (1999). There was facilitation when the *same* kind of insight (e.g., constraint relaxation) was involved over a number of problems. However, there was interference and a slowing of solution times when an insight problem required a different kind of insight from the previous problems.

Reverberi et al. (2005) argued that the lateral frontal cortex is the part of the brain involved in imposing constraints on individuals' processing when they are confronted by an insight problem. Thus, patients with damage to that brain area should *not* impose artificial constraints when solving insight problems, and so might perform better than healthy individuals. That is exactly what they found. Brain-damaged patients solved 82% of the hardest match-stick arithmetic problems compared to only 43% of healthy controls.

Enhancing insight

We have seen that many people struggle to solve insight problems. Performance can be improved by providing training to avoid (or overcome) the difficulties caused by incorrect representations of the problem. Cunningham and MacGregor (2008) found that such training enhanced performance on insight problems presented in an artificial format but not on those that were more realistic. The reason was that participants' performance on realistic problems was at a relatively high level even in the absence of training.

The use of subtle cues can also improve performance on insight problems. Thomas and Lleras (2009) gave participants Duncker's radiation problem (discussed later in connection with research by Gick and Holyoak, 1980). Some participants were given an additional task that led them to shift their attention in a pattern relevant to solving the candle problem. This increased the chance of them showing insight even though they were unaware of any relationship between their shifts in attention and the candle problem.

It has often been found that individuals perform better on insight problems when in a positive mood rather than a neutral or negative mood (see Subramaniam et al., 2009, for a review). Subramaniam et al. found that positive mood was associated with increased brain activity in the anterior cingulate cortex immediately prior to problem presentation. This brain area is associated with conflict resolution, suggesting that a positive mood allows people to approach insight problems more flexibly.

Finally, Slepian et al. (2010) came up with a very simple way of increasing insight. They noted that a *light bulb* is often used as an image representing insight. They wondered whether an illuminating light bulb would activate concepts associated with insight and thereby enhance insight problem solving through a process of priming (see Glossary). Many more of the participants exposed to the illuminating light bulb solved a complex insight problem than those not exposed to it (44% vs. 22%, respectively).

INCUBATION

Much research on problem solving has involved introducing a period of time away from an unsolved problem. This is known as **incubation**. In order to assess the effects of incubation on problem solution, there is generally a control condition in which participants work continuously on the problem.

Sio and Ormerod (2009) carried out a meta-analysis (see Glossary) of 117 incubation studies, and reported three main findings. First, there was a fairly small (but highly significant) overall incubation effect, with positive effects being reported in 85 of the studies.

Second, there was a stronger incubation effect with creative problems having multiple solutions than with linguistic and verbal problems having a single solution. Incubation often leads to a widening of the search for knowledge,

Key Term
Incubation: requiring participants to put a problem aside for some time to observe the effects on the subsequent likelihood of solving it; incubation generally enhances problem solving.

and this may well be more useful with multiple-solution problems than with single-solution ones.

Third, the effects were greater when there was a relatively long preparation time prior to incubation. This may have occurred because an impasse or block in thinking is more likely to develop when the preparation time is long.

Simon (1966) argued that incubation involves a special type of forgetting. What tends to be forgotten over time is control information relating to the strategies tried by the problem solver. This forgetting makes it easier for problem solvers to adopt a new approach after the incubation period. This approach was supported by Vul and Pashler's (2007) findings. Misleading information was either presented or not presented at the start of each problem. There was an incubation effect only when the break allowed misleading information to be forgotten.

It is often claimed that "sleeping on a problem" can be a very effective form of incubation. For example, August Kekulé's dreams led to the discovery of a simple structure for benzene. Wagner et al. (2004) tested the value of sleep in a study in which participants performed a complex mathematical task and were retested several hours later. The mathematical problems were designed so they could be solved in a much simpler way than the one used initially by nearly all the participants. Of those who slept between training and testing, 59% found the short cut, compared to only 25% of those who did not.

Section Summary

- Insight involves a sudden transformation of a problem to provide the solution. In this transformation, one problem representation is replaced by another one, resulting in an "aha" experience.

Insight vs. non-insight problems

- There is a sudden increase in perceived closeness to solution with insight problems but a more gradual increase with non-insight ones. A brain region in the temporal lobe is activated only when solutions involve insight. Individual differences in working memory capacity predict performance on noninsight problems better than on insight ones.

Representational change theory

- According to representational change theory, changing the problem representation in insight problems can occur through constraint relaxation, re-encoding, or elaboration. Patients with damage to the lateral frontal cortex (involved in imposing constraints on processing) perform better than healthy controls on insight problems.

Enhancing insight

- Insight can be enhanced in various ways. These include training to overcome the difficulties caused by incorrect problem representations, using subtle cues, inducing a positive mood state, and presenting an illuminating light bulb.

Incubation

- Incubation generally enhances problem solving, especially when there is a long preparation time and the problem has multiple solutions. Incubation seems to work via forgetting of the problem solver's unsuccessful strategies.

PROBLEM-SOLVING STRATEGIES

A major landmark in research on problem solving was the publication in 1972 of a book entitled *Human Problem Solving* by Allen Newell and Herb Simon. Their central insight was that the strategies we use when tackling complex problems take account of our limited ability to process and store information. Newell and Simon assumed we have very limited short-term memory capacity and that complex information processing is typically serial (one process at a time). These assumptions were included in their General Problem Solver (a computer program designed to solve well-defined problems).

How do we cope with our limited processing capacity? According to Newell and Simon (1972), we rely heavily on heuristics or rules of thumb. Heuristics have the advantage they don't require extensive information processing. However, they have the disadvantage they may not lead to problem solution.

MEANS–ENDS ANALYSIS

The most important heuristic identified by Newell and Simon (1972) is **means–ends analysis**:

- Note the difference between the current state of the problem and the goal state.
- Form a subgoal to reduce the difference between the current and goal states.
- Select a mental operator that permits attainment of the subgoal.

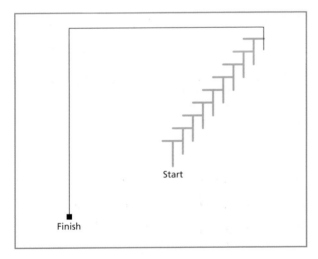

Figure 10.6 The maze used in the study by Sweller and Levine (1982). Adapted from Sweller and Levine (1982).

Means–ends analysis is generally very useful and assists people in their attempts to solve problems. However, Sweller and Levine (1982) found that people used that heuristic even when it wasn't useful. Participants were given the maze shown in Figure 10.6, but most of it wasn't visible to them. All participants could see where they were in the problem. Some could also see the goal state (goal-information group), whereas others could not (no-goal-information group).

Use of means–ends analysis requires knowledge of the location of the goal, so only the goal-information group could have used that heuristic. However, the problem was designed so means–ends analysis wouldn't be useful – every correct move involves turning *away* from the goal. Participants in this group performed very poorly – only 10% solved the problem in 298 moves! In contrast, participants in the no-goal-information group solved the problem in an average of only 38 moves. Thus, people are so attached to means–ends analysis they use it even when it prevents them from discovering the problem structure.

HILL CLIMBING

Another important heuristic is hill climbing. **Hill climbing** involves changing the present state within the problem into one closer to the goal. It is a simpler strategy than means–ends analysis, and is mostly used when the problem solver has no clear understanding of the structure of a problem.

The hill-climbing heuristic involves a focus on short-term goals. As a result, it often fails to lead to problem solution (Robertson, 2001). Someone using this heuristic is like a climber who wants to reach the highest mountain peak in the area. He/she uses the strategy of always moving upwards. This strategy may work. However, it is likely the climber will find himself/herself trapped on a hill separated by several valleys from the highest peak.

Key Term

Progress monitoring: this is a heuristic used in problem solving in which insufficiently rapid progress towards solution leads to the adoption of a different strategy.

PROGRESS MONITORING

MacGregor et al. (2001) argued that individuals engaged in problem solving make use of a heuristic known as **progress monitoring**. This involves assessing their rate of progress towards the goal. If progress is too slow to solve the problem within the maximum number of moves allowed, a different strategy is adopted.

Evidence of progress monitoring was reported by MacGregor et al. (2001). Participants were given the nine-dot problem (see Figure 10.7(a)), in which you have to draw four straight lines connecting all nine dots without lifting your pen off the paper.

The solution is shown in Figure 10.7(b). The key conditions are shown in Figure 10.7(c) and (d). It is often assumed that people fail to solve the problem because they mistakenly assume the lines must stay within the square. As a result, we might expect participants given (c) to perform better than those given (d). However, individuals given (c) can cover more dots with the next two lines than those given (d) while remaining within the square. Thus, they are less likely to decide to shift to a superior strategy. The take-home message is that if the strategy you are using can't allow you to solve a problem, the sooner you realize that the better.

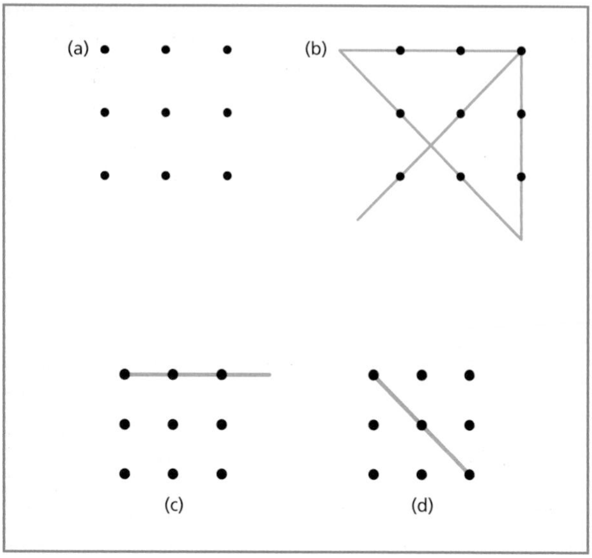

Figure 10.7 The nine-dot problem (a) and its solution (b); two variants of the nine-dot problem (c, d) presented in MacGregor et al. (2001). Copyright © 2001 by the American Psychological Association. Reprinted with permission.

PLANNING

Newell and Simon (1972) assumed that most problem solvers engage in only a modest amount of planning because they have limited short-term memory capacity. An alternative assumption is that planning incurs costs in time and effort, and is often unnecessary because simple heuristics suffice. Evidence favoring the latter possibility was reported by Delaney et al. (2004), who used water-jar problems in which the task was to finish up with specified amounts of water in each of three water jars. Some participants were told to generate the complete solution before making any moves, whereas others (control group) were free to adopt whatever strategy they wanted.

The control participants showed little evidence of planning. However, the key finding was that those in the planning group showed very clear evidence of being able to plan. They solved the problem in far fewer moves than control participants. Thus, we have a greater ability to plan than is usually assumed, but often choose not to plan unless it is essential.

As would be expected, the amount of forward planning is strongly influenced by the level of expertise. Charness (1981) presented chess players with various chess positions and asked them to think aloud as they planned what to do. A move in chess is defined as a turn by each player, and a ply is a half-move (i.e., one player has a turn). Expert chess players worked out the implications of possible moves about three plies further ahead in the game than did non-expert ones.

USING ANALOGIES

One way to solve problems is by making use of analogies or similarities between the current problem and problems solved in the past. The history of science is full of examples of successful **analogical problem solving**. For example, the New Zealand physicist Ernest Rutherford used a solar system analogy to understand the structure of the atom. He argued that electrons revolve around the nucleus as the planets revolve around the sun.

In order for people to make successful use of a previous problem to solve a current one, they must detect *similarities* between the two problems. According to Chen (2002), there are three main types of similarity between problems:

1. *Superficial similarity:* Solution-irrelevant details (e.g., specific objects) are common to the two problems.
2. *Structural similarity:* Causal relations among some of the main components are shared by the two problems.
3. *Procedural similarity:* Procedures or actions for turning the solution principle into concrete operations are common to the two problems.

Findings

Suppose you are given a problem to solve. How likely is it you would make use of a relevant analogy to solve it? Some findings are discouraging. Gick and Holyoak (1980) used a problem in which a patient with a malignant stomach tumor can only be saved by a special kind of ray. However, a ray strong enough to destroy the tumor will also destroy the healthy tissue, whereas a ray that won't harm healthy tissue will be too weak to destroy the tumor.

If you are puzzled as to the correct answer, here is an analogy to help you. A general wants to capture a fortress but the roads leading to it are mined, making it too dangerous for the entire army to march along any one of them. However, the mines were set so that small bodies of men could pass over them safely. The general solved the problem by having his army converge at the same time on the fortress by walking along several different roads. Gick and Holyoak (1980) found that 80% of people solved the radiation problem when informed that this story (which they had encountered previously) was relevant. However, only 40% did so when *not* informed of the story's relevance.

The above findings indicate that having a relevant analogy stored in long-term memory is no guarantee it will be used. The main reason was that there

| Key Term

Analogical problem solving:
a type of problem solving based on detecting analogies or similarities between the current problem and problems solved in the past.

were few superficial similarities between the story and the problem. Keane (1987) found that participants were much more likely to recall spontaneously a previous story with superficial similarities to the radiation problem (a story about a surgeon using rays on a cancer) than one lacking such similarities (the general-and-fortress story).

We have seen that people focus on superficial rather than structural similarities between problems when given a possible analogy before the current problem. In everyday life, however, people generally produce their own analogies rather than being given them. When molecular biologists and immunologists generate hypotheses, the analogies they use involve structural similarities rather than superficial ones (Dunbar & Blanchette, 2001). Expertise is not needed to generate analogies based on structural similarities, as Bearman et al. (2007) discovered with management novices analyzing a business case.

Research Activity 10.3: *Weigh-the-elephant problem*

Consider the weigh-the-elephant problem (studied by Chen, 2002). In this problem, a boy has to weigh an elephant, but his scales only weigh objects up to 200 pounds. How did he solve the problem? See if you can work this out before looking at the answer.

You need to use smaller objects to balance the weight of the elephant, after which you weigh the smaller objects separately on the scale. For example, you could put the elephant into a boat (perhaps easier said than done!) and mark the water level on the boat. After the elephant has been removed from the boat, put smaller objects into it until the water level is the same. Finally, weigh the objects one by one and work out the total weight.

Most participants in the study by Chen (2002) found it hard. He wondered what kinds of analogy would best enhance problem solving. Participants were presented with an analogy having both structural and procedural similarity with the weigh-the-elephant problem or an analogy having only structural similarity. Participants in the second condition performed worse. They realized the value of finding objects of equivalent weight to the elephant. However, they couldn't find the right procedures or actions to solve the problem (e.g., putting the small objects in a boat), which are the key to the solution.

Analogical problem solving involves the working memory system (Cho et al., 2007; see Chapter 4). In one study (Morrison et al., 2001), participants received verbal analogies (e.g., BLACK: WHITE :: NOISY: QUIET) and picture-based analogies involving cartoon characters. These analogies were solved on their own or while participants performed a secondary task.

What did Morrison et al. (2001) find? First, performance on verbal and pictorial analogies was impaired when the secondary task involved the central executive (an attention-like system). Thus, solving analogies requires the central executive. Second, performance on verbal analogies was impaired when the secondary task involved the phonological loop (a verbal rehearsal system). This occurred because both tasks involved the phonological loop. Third, performance on pictorial analogies suffered when the additional task involved the visuo-spatial sketchpad (a system for processing and briefly storing visual and spatial information). This occurred because both tasks involved the visuo-spatial sketchpad.

How can we improve analogical problem solving? Kurtz and Lowenstein (2007) argued that we find it easier to grasp the underlying structure of a problem if we compare it *directly* with another problem sharing the same structure. Gick and Holyoak (1980) used Duncker's radiation problem in which a patient with a malignant stomach tumor can only be saved by a special kind of ray. All participants initially received the problem about the general and the fortress. The control group then received the radiation problem. An experimental group considered similarities between the radiation problem and an analogous problem. Performance on the radiation problem was much better in the experimental group than in the control group. Thus, directly comparing the structure of two analogous problems greatly improves analogical problem solving.

CROSS-CULTURAL DIFFERENCES

Most research on problem-solving strategies has been carried out in the United States and United Kingdom; other cultures may use rather different strategies. Güss and Wiley (2007) asked students in the United States and India to indicate how often they used various problem-solving strategies. The Indian students were most likely to indicate use of means–ends analysis and free production (generating several ideas) and the American students were most likely to report using the analogy strategy. However, the cross-cultural differences were small.

Güss et al. (2010) studied problem-solving behavior in microworlds. Microworlds are realistic computer-based tasks in which the participant is assigned a role and makes decisions in a changing situation. One microworld they used was WINFIRE, in which the commanding officer of a fire brigade had to minimize the damage caused by fires. The performance of students from five countries (Brazil, Germany, India, the Philippines, and United States) was compared.

Güss et al. (2010) argued that most non-Western cultures (e.g., Brazil; India; the Philippines) are *high-context* cultures, meaning that people's behavior is strongly influenced by the immediate social and physical context. In contrast, Germany and the United States are *low-context* cultures in which people's behavior is less influenced by the immediate context and more by perceptions of personal control. This leads them to engage in more planning.

There were two main findings:

1. Those in high-context cultures gathered more information than those in low-context cultures about the microworld situation. This is consistent with their greater emphasis on responding to the immediate situation. Even though they gathered much information, those in high-context cultures failed to use this information to enhance planning.
2. Those in low-context cultures (especially Germany) engaged in more planning than those in high-context cultures. This may have occurred because perceived ability to control situations is greater among those in low-context cultures.

Most research on problem solving has been carried in low-context cultures. Given the differences in strategies used by problem solvers in low-context and high-context cultures, it is important for future research to adopt a more crosscultural approach.

Section Summary

- According to Newell and Simon (1972), humans have very limited short-term memory capacity and complex information processing is serial. When solving problems, we make extensive use of heuristics or rules of thumb.

Means–ends analysis

- Means–ends analysis is a heuristic that involves forming a subgoal designed to reduce the difference between the current and goal states. It is used even when counterproductive.

Hill climbing

- This heuristic is simpler than means–ends analysis. It is generally used when the problem solver has no clear understanding of problem structure and is of limited usefulness.

Progress monitoring

- Progress monitoring involves assessing the rate of progress towards the goal. If progress is too slow to solve the problem within the maximum number of moves permitted, the problem solver adopts a different strategy.

Planning

- Problem solvers often engage in only a modest amount of planning, because it is cognitively demanding. However, they can plan effectively if required to do so. There is greater forward planning by experts than by non-experts.

Using analogies

- Individuals solving a current problem can use analogies based on a previous problem sharing superficial, structural, or procedural similarities with it. In the laboratory, people often focus on superficial similarities. However, they often use structural similarities when producing their own analogies. Analogical problem solving involves the working memory system, especially the central executive. Understanding the underlying structure of problems enhances analogical problem solving.

Cross-cultural differences

- Cultures can be divided into high-context (behavior strongly influenced by the immediate context) and low-context (behavior influenced by perceptions of personal control). Individuals in low-context cultures plan more than those in high-context cultures, whereas those in high-context cultures gather more information about the problem situation.

HYPOTHESIS TESTING AND SCIENCE

Hypothesis testing is an important type of problem solving. The way to solve many problems is to form a hypothesis (potential explanation) and then to test it. If that hypothesis proves to be incorrect, another hypothesis is formed. This continues until the problem is solved. Studying hypothesis testing may tell us much about the processes involved in scientific research and discovery.

Karl Popper (1968) argued it is important to discriminate between confirmation and falsification with respect to the testing of hypotheses. Most people show **confirmation bias**, which involves the attempt to obtain evidence confirming the correctness of one's hypothesis. In contrast, falsification involves the attempt to falsify hypotheses by experimental tests.

According to Popper (1968), it is impossible to achieve confirmation via hypothesis testing. Even if all the evidence accumulated so far supports a hypothesis, *future* evidence may disprove it. As the philosopher Bertrand Russell pointed out, a turkey might form the hypothesis, "Each day I am fed," because this hypothesis has been confirmed every day of its life. However, the generalization provides no *certainty* that the turkey will be fed tomorrow. Indeed, if tomorrow is Thanksgiving, it is likely to be proved false. Popper concluded that falsification was a more useful strategy than confirmation.

Peter Wason (1960) devised a hypothesis-testing task to see whether people focus on confirmation or on falsification. Participants were told that three numbers (2–4–6) conformed to a simple relational rule. They generated sets of three numbers and provided reasons for each choice. After each choice, the experimenter indicated whether the set of numbers conformed to the rule. The rule was, "Three numbers in ascending order of magnitude." The rule sounds easy. However, it took most participants a long time to discover it. Only 21% were correct with their first attempt and 28% never discovered the rule at all.

Why was performance so poor on the 2–4–6 problem? According to Wason (1960), most people show confirmation bias (see Glossary), which involves a greater focus on evidence apparently confirming one's hypothesis than on disconfirming evidence. For example, participants whose original hypothesis or rule was that the second number is twice the first and the third is three times the first number often generated sets of numbers consistent with that hypothesis (e.g., 6–12–18; 50–100–150). Wason argued that confirmation bias and failure to try hypothesis disconfirmation prevented participants from replacing their initial hypothesis (which was too narrow and specific) with the correct general rule.

What can be done to improve performance on the 2–4–6 task? Cowley and Byrne (2005) argued that people show confirmation bias because they are attached to their own initial hypothesis and are loath to abandon it. However, they might be much more willing to try to falsify the same hypothesis if told it was someone else's. This prediction was confirmed by Cowley and Byrne: 62% of participants abandoned the other person's hypothesis compared to only 25% who abandoned their own hypothesis.

The 2–4–6 task is unusual in that the correct rule is much more *general* than any of the initial hypotheses participants are likely to form. Thus, when participants generate sets of numbers fitting their specific hypothesis, those numbers are also almost bound to fit the rule as well. This prevents them

Key Terms

Confirmation bias: the tendency in **hypothesis testing** for people to focus excessively on evidence that apparently supports their own hypothesis while ignoring the search for disconfirming evidence.

Hypothesis testing: an approach to problem solving based on forming a hypothesis or tentative explanation which is then subjected to one or more tests.

from discovering the correct rule. Cherubini et al. (2005) encouraged their participants to form more general hypotheses by initially giving them sets of numbers such as 6–8–10 and 9–14–15. This greatly increased the probability that their first hypothesis would be correct.

In the real world, people engaged in hypothesis testing often produce diagrams or graphs to assist them. Vallée-Tourangeau and Payton (2008) provided half their participants with a diagrammatic representation of each

In the Real World 10.2: *Scientific hypothesis testing*

So far we have focused on laboratory research. However, Popper's (1968) approach is of direct relevance to scientific research in the real world. It follows from his analysis that scientists should focus on falsification. However, much of the evidence suggests that many scientists seek confirmatory rather than disconfirmatory evidence when testing their hypotheses! More precisely, some research groups focus on confirmation whereas others attach more importance to disconfirmation (Tweney & Chitwood, 1995).

Dunbar (1993) gave his participants the hard task of providing an explanation for the ways genes are controlled by other genes using a computer-based molecular genetics laboratory. The difficulty of this task can be seen in the fact that the scientists solving this problem in real life were awarded the Nobel prize! In the experiment, participants were led to focus on the hypothesis that the gene control was by *activation* whereas it was actually by *inhibition*.

Dunbar (1993) found that those participants who simply tried to find data consistent with their activation hypothesis failed to solve the problem. In contrast, the 20% of participants who solved the problem set themselves the goal of explaining the discrepant findings. According to the participants' own reports, most started with the general hypothesis that activation was the key controlling process. They then applied this hypothesis focusing on one gene after another as the potential activator. Only when all the various specific activation hypotheses had been disconfirmed did some participants focus on explaining the data not fitting the general activation hypothesis.

The issue of whether real scientists focus on confirmation or disconfirmation was considered by Gorman (1995) in an analysis of Alexander Graham Bell's research on the development of the telephone. Bell showed evidence of confirmation bias in that he continued to focus on undulating current and electromagnets even after he and others had obtained good results with liquid devices. Fuselsang et al. (2004) studied professional scientists working on issues in molecular biology relating to how genes control and promote replication in bacteria, parasites, and viruses. Of 417 experimental results, over half (223) were inconsistent with the scientists' predictions. The scientists responded to 88% of these inconsistent findings by blaming problems on their method (e.g., wrong incubation temperature). In only 12% of cases did the scientists modify their theories to accommodate the inconsistent findings.

About two-thirds of the inconsistent findings were followed up, generally by changing the methods used. In 55% of cases, the inconsistent findings were replicated. The scientists' reactions were very different this time – in 61% of cases, the scientists changed their theoretical assumptions.

How defensible was the scientists' behavior in the study by Fuselsang et al. (2004)? Note that almost half of the inconsistent findings weren't replicated when a second study was carried out. Thus, it was reasonable for the scientists to avoid prematurely accepting findings that might be inaccurate.

In sum, falsification is a less straightforward matter than assumed by Popper. It is often most useful to adopt the following strategy: "Confirm early, disconfirm late" (Thagard, 2005). Established theories should be falsifiable. However, it is often more beneficial for scientists to seek confirmatory evidence during the development of a new theory.

set of numbers they generated. This had a large effect – the success rate on the problem was 44% compared to only 21% for those participants tested under standard conditions. The provision of an external representation led participants to be less constrained in their selection of hypotheses.

An individual's level of expertise may also influence his/her tendency to show confirmation bias. Cowley and Byrne (2005) found that chess masters often thought of sequences of moves falsifying their current hypothesis or plan during a game. In contrast, non-expert chess players were more likely to confirm their current hypothesis even though it would lead to negative consequences.

SCIENTIFIC DISCOVERY

It is now time to broaden our discussion of scientific research to discuss the main processes involved in scientific discovery. Klahr and Dunbar (1988) argued that there is a dual-space search: One space contains the experimental possibilities in the situation and the other contains possible hypotheses. In searching the hypothesis space, the initial state is some knowledge of the domain or specific area, and the goal state is a hypothesis accounting for that knowledge in a more concise, universal form. Hypothesis generation in this space may involve various mechanisms (e.g., memory search; analogical mapping; reminding).

Search in the experiment space is directed towards experiments that will discriminate between rival hypotheses and yield interpretable outcomes. On the basis of **protocol analysis** (analysis of participants' verbalizations while performing the task), Klahr and Dunbar (1988) distinguished two groups of participants:

1. Theorists who prefer to search the space of hypotheses.
2. Experimenters who prefer to search the space of experiments.

Klahr and Dunbar's (1988) analysis has been influential. However, there are doubts about the use of protocol analysis. Feldon (2010) asked psychologists varying in their research expertise to explain their problem-solving processes while engaged in simulated design of an experiment followed by data analysis. Most of these explanations were inaccurate, especially when they involved abstract cognitive processes such as mental modeling.

Subsequent theorists have extended Klahr and Dunbar's ideas. Thagard (1998) argued that the number of search spaces varies across scientific problems. He used as an example the discovery of the bacterial origins of stomach ulcers. The scientists involved in this discovery made use of *three* search spaces: experiment space, hypothesis space, and instrumentation space.

Schunn and Klahr (1996) went one better as a result of research in a complex microworld laboratory. They identified *four* problem spaces in science: In addition to an experiment space and a hypothesis space, there was also a paradigm space and a representation space. The paradigm space is an offshoot of the experiment space and consists of various classes of experiment. The data-representation space is an offshoot of the hypothesis space and consists of ways of representing phenomena.

Strong vs. weak methods

A popular view is that a few "great" individuals (e.g., Newton; Einstein) are responsible for nearly all the major creative achievements in science. The creative and intellectual abilities of these individuals stretch far beyond those of the mass of humanity (otherwise known as *us*). The essence of this view is "the belief that scientific discovery is the result of genius, inspiration, and sudden insight" (Trickett & Trafton, 2007, p. 868). As we will see, this view is largely incorrect.

Klahr and Simon (2001) focused on the processes used by scientists in the various problem spaces described above. They distinguished between two kinds of method used by scientists:

1. *Strong methods:* These methods are acquired through a lengthy process of acquiring huge amounts of detailed domain-specific knowledge (knowledge in a specific area) about scientific phenomena, theories, procedures, experimental paradigms, and so on. Such methods are often sufficient to solve relatively simple scientific problems, but are insufficient to permit creative scientific discoveries.
2. *Weak methods:* These methods are very general and can be applied to almost any scientific problem. Indeed, they are so general they are also used in most everyday problem solving. Some of the main weak methods were discussed earlier in the chapter. They include trial and error, hill climbing, means–ends analysis, planning, and use of analogies.

Numerous studies have considered the weak methods used by scientists. Kulkarni and Simon (1988) found much evidence that scientists make extensive use of the **unusualness heuristic** or rule of thumb. This involves focusing on unusual or unexpected findings and then using these findings to guide the search through the space of hypotheses and the space of experiments.

Zelko et al. (2010) asked leading scientists in several countries to identify the strategies they used in their research. Every researcher had a main heuristic or rule of thumb that he/she used much of the time. The heuristics included the following: challenge conventional wisdom; adopt a step-by-step approach; carry out numerous experiments on a trial-and-error basis.

Trickett and Trafton (2007) argued that scientists make much use of "what if" reasoning, in which they work out what would happen in certain imaginary circumstances. A famous example of such reasoning involves Albert Einstein. At the age of 16, he imagined himself pursuing a beam of light, which led eventually to his theory of relativity. "What if" reasoning is attractive because it can be used even when we possess only partial knowledge and it doesn't require an experiment.

In their research, Trickett and Trafton (2007) studied experts in various science subjects thinking aloud when interpreting recently acquired data in their area of expertise. Their key finding was that these experts made much use of "what if" reasoning, especially when the data were unexpected.

Scientists often make use of inductive reasoning, in which generalizations are formed on the basis of a set of observations. This approach is limited, because future observations might differ from those found so far and thus disprove the generalization. Induction by generalization is very common in

Key Term

Unusualness heuristic: a rule of thumb used by scientists in which the emphasis is on unusual or unexpected findings that may lead to the development of new hypotheses and lines of experimentation.

science (Thagard, 1998). For example, consider the approach taken by the scientists Marshall and Warren, who were awarded the Nobel prize in 2005. They discovered that nearly all patients with gastric enteritis had the bacterium *Helicobacter pylori* in their stomachs. This led them to hypothesize that this bacterium was the cause of many stomach ulcers.

Earlier we discussed a study by Dunbar (1993) in which participants tried to work out how certain genes are controlled by other genes. There were very clear similarities between the participants' approach and that taken by the Nobel-prize winning scientists (Monod and Jacob) who carried out the original research. For example, Monod and Jacob resembled the participants in finding it hard to appreciate that the gene control involved inhibition rather than activation. It seems that the scientists couldn't solve this problem by using strong methods based on their expertise. As a result, they were reduced to using weak methods (e.g., heuristics) similar to those used by the participants.

Evaluation

⊕ The processes involved in scientific discovery have been shown to be less mysterious than is often assumed.

⊕ Scientists entering the unknown often rely on the same weak methods that most of us use to cope with our daily problems.

⊕ Several heuristics used by scientists (e.g., unusualness heuristic; challenging conventional wisdom; adopting a step-by-step approach) have been identified.

⊖ Klahr and Simon's (2001) approach has been deservedly influential, but it is more descriptive than explanatory. They identified several weak methods used by scientists. However, we can't predict beforehand *which* of these methods will be used by a given scientist confronting a particular problem.

⊖ Klahr and Simon's approach is also not very explicit about how scientists combine their scientific knowledge incorporated in strong methods with the range of weak methods at their disposal.

Section Summary

• People often show confirmation bias in the laboratory when performing hypothesis-testing tasks in which the correct hypothesis is very general. However, this is much less the case when they are encouraged to form more general hypotheses at the outset. Diagrams or graphs can enhance performance on hypothesis-testing tasks. Experts (e.g., chess masters) show less confirmation bias than non-experts.

Scientific hypothesis testing
- Scientists often focus on confirmation rather than falsification when engaged in scientific hypothesis testing. This occurs partly because it can be very hard to decide whether experimental findings genuinely falsify a hypothesis. The best strategy is often to confirm early on but to disconfirm or falsify thereafter.

Scientific discovery
- Scientists engaged in scientific discovery search through hypothesis space and experiment space, and perhaps paradigm space and representation space as well. Scientists possess strong methods based on their expertise, but these are typically insufficient to produce creative discoveries. Scientists very often use weak methods that are very general and can be applied to almost any scientific problem. Examples are the unusualness heuristic, "what if" reasoning, and a step-by-step approach.

EXPERTISE

So far we have mostly discussed studies in which the time available for learning has been short, the tasks involved relatively limited, and previous specific knowledge not required. In the real world, however, individuals often spend several years acquiring knowledge and skills in a given area (e.g., psychology; law). The end point of such long-term learning is the development of expertise. Expertise is "highly skilled, competent performance in one or more task domains [areas]" (Sternberg & Ben-Zeev, 2001, p. 365).

The development of expertise resembles problem solving in that experts are very efficient at solving numerous problems in their area of expertise. However, as mentioned in the Introduction, most research on problem solving involves "knowledge-lean" problems requiring no special training or knowledge for their solution. In contrast, studies on expertise have typically used "knowledge-rich" problems requiring much knowledge beyond that presented in the problem itself.

CHESS-PLAYING EXPERTISE

There are various reasons why it is valuable to study chess-playing expertise (Gobet et al., 2004). First, we can measure chess players' level of skill very precisely based on their results against other players. Second, expert chess players develop cognitive skills (e.g., pattern recognition; selective search) that are useful in many other areas of expertise. Third, chess experts have a remarkable memory for chess positions in the same way that experts in other fields have excellent memory for information relevant to their particular expertise.

Key Term
Expertise: a very high level of thinking and performance in a given domain (e.g., chess) achieved from many years of practice.

In the Real World 10.3: *Cab drivers*

London, England is famous for its cab or taxi drivers with their distinctive black cabs. It is very hard to obtain a license to drive these cabs. It involves acquiring "The Knowledge" – detailed knowledge of the 25,000 streets within six miles of Charing Cross and of the locations of thousands of hospitals, Tube stations, pubs, and restaurants. Unsurprisingly, it takes about three years to acquire all this information.

How do cab drivers manage to develop this extraordinary knowledge and expertise? A high level of intelligence is certainly not essential, because the average IQ of London cab drivers is around the average in the population.

There is much evidence that a part of the brain known as the hippocampus is important. When cab drivers navigated their way around a virtual London in the laboratory, parts of the hippocampus and the occipital or visual cortex were activated (Woollett et al., 2009).

Maguire et al. (2006) tested a patient, TT. He had acquired The Knowledge 40 years earlier, but had recently suffered extensive hippocampal damage. TT still possessed a good knowledge of London landmarks and their spatial relationships. However, his navigation skills had deteriorated considerably. He relied excessively on main roads, and became lost when driving from one place to another using minor roads.

Does acquisition of The Knowledge have a direct effect on the hippocampus? The answer appears to be "Yes." Experienced London cab drivers have a greater volume of gray matter in the *posterior* hippocampus than novice drivers or other control groups (see Woollett et al., 2009, for a review). Older full-time cab drivers had greater gray matter volume in the posterior hippocampus than those of the same age who had already retired (Woollett et al., 2009).

Children's brains exhibit plasticity, meaning that their form can be altered by extensive experience. For example, there were significant changes in motor and auditory brain areas in 6-year-old children who received 15 months of instrumental musical training (Hyde et al., 2009). In addition, those children with the greatest brain changes showed the greatest improvements in musical skills. The findings with London cab drivers suggest the *adult* brain also has considerable plasticity, meaning that its form can be altered through extensive experience.

Figure 10.8 A London black cab. Photo by David Iliff. http://creativecommons.org/licenses/by-sa/3.0/deed.en

Are there any disadvantages in acquiring huge amounts of spatial knowledge about the streets of London? Cab drivers performed poorly on tasks requiring them to learn and remember *new* word–word or object–place associations. However, they performed well on tests of their memory for the *past* (e.g., autobiographical information) (Woollett & Maguire, 2009).

Woollett and Maguire (2009) also found that London cab drivers had a smaller volume of gray matter in the *anterior* hippocampus than other people (Woollett et al., 2009). This is relevant because the anterior hippocampus is important for processing novel stimuli and encoding information. What may be happening is that the very extensive involvement of the hippocampus in learning The Knowledge impairs the ability to acquire new information.

Why are some people much better than others at playing chess? The obvious answer is that they have devoted far more time to *practice* – it takes about 10,000 hours of practice to become a grandmaster. All this practice improves chess-playing ability in several ways. Of special importance, expert chess players have much more detailed information about chess positions stored in long-term memory than non-experts. According to Gobet (Gobet & Waters, 2003; Gobet & Chass, 2009), much of this information is in the form of templates. **Templates** are abstract structures containing information relating to about 10 pieces. Each template focuses on a particular *pattern* involving about 10 pieces, with flexibility in terms of the pieces and their locations.

Gobet and Waters (2003) claimed that expert chess players possess much more template-based information than non-experts. They can use this information to remember chess positions. As a result, experts' memory for chess positions should be much better than that of non-experts, even though they don't differ in general memory ability (De Groot, 1965). This prediction was supported by Gobet and Clarkson (2004). Expert players recalled chess board positions much better than beginners. Both groups recalled on average from two templates, but the maximum template size was much larger for the expert players (13–15 pieces vs. 6 for beginners).

Gobet and Waters (2003) assumed that outstanding chess players owe their excellence mostly to their superior template-based knowledge of chess positions rather than their use of slow, strategy-based processes. They also assumed that experts' knowledge can be accessed rapidly, which allows them to narrow down the possible moves they need to consider. If these assumptions are correct, the performance of outstanding players should remain very high when they make their moves under severe time pressure.

Burns (2004) tested the above prediction. He used information about expert chess players' performance in normal competitive games and in blitz chess, in which the entire game has to be completed in five minutes. This is less than 5% of the time available in normal chess. The key finding was that performance in blitz chess was highly associated or correlated with that in normal chess. This suggests that individual differences in chess-playing ability depend highly on template knowledge.

We mustn't draw the conclusion that slow search processes are irrelevant. Burns (2004) also found that the same players playing chess under normal and blitz conditions made superior moves in the former condition. Van Harreveld et al. (2007) considered the effects of reducing the time available for chess moves. Skill differences between players were less predictive of game outcome as the time available decreased. This suggests that slow processes are more important for strong players than for weak ones.

General intelligence is another factor that helps to explain individual differences in chess-playing ability. Grabner et al. (2007) found that adult tournament players with high general intelligence had higher chess rankings than those of lower intelligence. However, chess rankings were predicted better by the amount of practice.

MEDICAL EXPERTISE

The ability of doctors to make rapid and accurate diagnoses is very important when considered in the context of 50,000 deaths per year in the United States

> **Key Term**
>
> **Templates:**
> organized abstract structures including information about several chess pieces; these structures (which are larger for chess experts) are useful when players decide on their next move.

being due to medical error. Of course, medical experts with many years of training behind them generally make better decisions than novice doctors.

How does the problem solving of medical experts differ from that of novice doctors? We can approach this question by considering the distinction between explicit reasoning and implicit reasoning (Engel, 2008). Explicit reasoning is fairly slow, deliberate, and is associated with conscious awareness. In contrast, implicit reasoning is fast, automatic, and isn't associated with conscious awareness.

It is often assumed that medical novices engage mainly in explicit reasoning, whereas medical experts engage mainly in implicit reasoning. However, matters are more complex than that. Medical experts in *technical* specialties such as surgery or anesthesiology are less likely to use fast, automatic processes than those in *visual* specialties such as pathology, radiology, or dermatology. Even when medical experts start with fast, automatic processes, they generally cross-check their diagnoses with slow, deliberate processes (McLaughlin et al., 2008).

Krupinsky et al. (2006) recorded eye movements while medical students, pathology residents, and fully trained pathologists examined slides relating to breast biopsy cases. The fully trained pathologists spent the least time examining each slide (4.5 s vs. 7.1 s for residents and 11.9 s for students). Greater experience was associated with extracting more information from the initial fixation. Experts relied heavily on global impression (implicit reasoning). In contrast, novices attended to several different parts of each slide in turn (explicit reasoning).

Kundel et al. (2007) presented difficult mammograms showing (or not showing) breast cancer to doctors experienced in mammography. The average time to fixate a cancer was only 1.13 s. The most expert doctors typically fixated almost immediately on the cancer, suggesting they were using fast, automatic processes. In contrast, the least expert doctors relied on a slower, step-by-step search process.

Can providing additional information to medical experts *reduce* the accuracy of their problem solving? Evidence that it can was reported by Kulatunga-Moruzi et al. (2004) in a study on diagnosing skin lesions. In one condition, participants were only shown case photographs. In another condition, they were initially given a detailed verbal description followed by the relevant case photograph. There were three groups of participants differing in their level of expertise.

The obvious prediction is that all groups should have produced more accurate diagnoses when given verbal descriptions as well as case photographs. That was, indeed, what was found with the least expert group. In striking contrast, the more expert groups performed better when *not* given the verbal descriptions. Experts diagnose skin lesions by rapidly searching for a stored pattern closely resembling the case photograph (a visual strategy). The verbal descriptions had the effect of interfering with their ability to use that strategy effectively.

DELIBERATE PRACTICE

We have seen that prolonged practice is essential for anyone who aspires to become an expert chess player, and the same is true for every type of expertise.

That is a useful starting point. However, what we really need is a theory in which the details of what is involved in *effective* practice are spelled out. Precisely that was done by Ericsson and Ward (2007), who emphasized the importance of deliberate practice. **Deliberate practice** has four aspects:

1. The task is at an appropriate level of difficulty (not too easy or too hard).
2. The learner is given informative feedback about his/her performance.
3. The learner has adequate chances to repeat the task.
4. The learner has the chance to correct his/her errors.

A major prediction of this theoretical approach is that the acquisition of expertise depends more on the amount of deliberate practice than simply on the number of hours devoted to practice. Another prediction (and much more controversial) is that deliberate practice is essentially *all* that is needed to develop expert performance. Innate talent or ability is assumed to be of little or no relevance to the development of expertise.

Findings

Charness et al. (2005) assessed the importance of deliberate practice among tournament-rated chess players. Time spent on serious study alone (deliberate practice), tournament play, and formal instruction all predicted chess-playing performance. However, as predicted, serious deliberate practice was the strongest predictor. Grandmasters had spent an average of 5000 hours on deliberate practice during their first 10 years of playing chess. This was nearly five times as much as the amount of time spent by intermediate players.

Evidence of the importance of deliberate practice has also been found among tournament-rated Scrabble players. Elite players spent more time than average players on deliberate practice activities (e.g., analysis of their own previous games; solving anagrams) (Tuffiash et al., 2007). However, the two groups didn't differ with respect to other forms of practice (e.g., playing Scrabble for fun; playing in Scrabble tournaments).

We have seen there is an association between amount of deliberate practice and performance level among chess and Scrabble players. However, that doesn't prove that the deliberate practice *caused* the higher level of performance. Perhaps those individuals with the greatest talent choose to spend more time practicing than those with less talent.

Evidence going against the above interpretation was reported by Sloboda et al. (1996), who compared highly successful young musicians with less successful ones. The two groups didn't differ in the amount of practice time taken to reach a given level of performance. This suggests that the advantage possessed by very successful musicians is *not* due to their greater level of natural musical ability.

In spite of Sloboda et al.'s (1996) findings, it is probable that deliberate practice and natural talent are both important. Perhaps a talented person reaches a higher level of expertise than the average person for a given amount of deliberate practice (Simonton, 2008). Evidence for natural talent was reported by Howard (2009). He studied expert chess players in three categories: candidates

Figure 10.8 Mean chess ratings of candidates, noncandidate grandmasters (GMs), and all non-grandmasters as a function of number of games played. From Howard (2009). Copyright © The Psychonomic Society. Reproduced with permission.

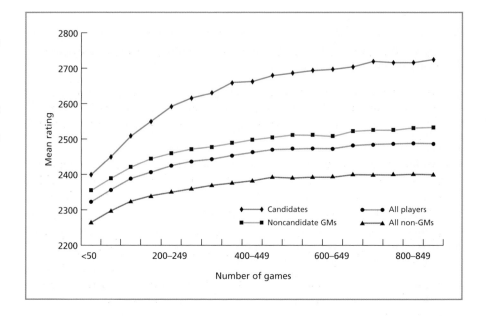

(elite players who have competed for the right to challenge the world champion); noncandidate grandmasters (elite players but less expert than candidates); and nongrandmasters.

The ratings of these three groups as a function of the number of games played are shown in Figure 10.8. There are two points of interest. First, there were clear performance differences among these three groups early on and these differences increased over games. Second, the ratings of players in all groups showed no improvement after they had played about 750 games.

The above findings suggest that it is possible early in their career to identify those who will eventually become top players, suggesting they have very high natural talent. The findings also suggest that there is a ceiling on the performance level that any player can attain based on his/her natural talent.

Howard (2009) found additional evidence of a performance ceiling among five players who had played over 2300 games (representing more than 8000 hours' playing time!). These players showed no improvement at all in performance for the last 1000 (+) games they played. This suggests strongly that there are limits on the beneficial effects of deliberate practice.

There is strong evidence that innate ability or intelligence is important in the development of career-related expertise. Among those in high-complexity jobs (e.g., biologist; city circulation manager), there is a moderately strong association or correlation between work performance and IQ (Gottfredson, 1997). The mean IQ of those in very complex occupations (e.g., accountants; lawyers; doctors) is about 120–130, which is considerably higher than the population mean of 100 (Mackintosh, 1998). There are very few successful individuals in such occupations whose IQ is close to the population average of 100.

Evaluation

⊕ It is indisputable that extensive practice is essential for the development of expertise.

⊕ The main factors making practice effective have been identified. They include using tasks of intermediate difficulty, providing performance feedback, and allowing the learner to repeat the task and to correct his/her mistakes.

⊖ The notion that natural talent is unimportant is unconvincing. As Sternberg and Ben-Zeev (2001, p. 302) argued, "Is one to believe that anyone could become a Mozart if only he or she put in the time? ... or that becoming an Einstein is just a matter of deliberate practice?"

⊖ We need to know more about *why* some individuals decide to devote hundreds or thousands of hours to effortful deliberate practice to achieve very high levels of expertise. Most such individuals probably have considerable natural talent. This natural talent allows them to achieve early success, which then motivates them to continue to engage in very demanding practice.

Section Summary

Cab drivers
• The enormous amount of knowledge about London's streets possessed by London cab drivers increases the volume of parts of the hippocampus. This suggests that there is considerable brain plasticity even in adults. The extensive involvement of the hippocampus in learning about London's streets impairs cab drivers' ability to acquire new information.

Chess-playing expertise
• Chess knowledge is stored in templates, each containing information relating to about 10 pieces. Chess experts possess larger templates than non-experts. In addition, experts make more effective use of slow, strategy-based processes.

Medical expertise
• Medical experts make more use than non-experts of fast, automatic processes when diagnosing, whereas non-experts rely more on slow, deliberate processes. However, experts often cross-check their diagnoses with slow, deliberate processes. Experts' diagnostic performance involves a visual strategy that is disrupted by detailed verbal descriptions.

Deliberate practice
- It has been claimed that deliberate practice is more effective than other forms of practice and that innate talent is irrelevant to the development of expertise. The evidence indicates that deliberate practice is necessary (but not sufficient) for expertise to develop. Natural talent or ability is also needed.

Essay Questions

1. In what circumstances does past experience facilitate or impair problem solving?
2. What is insight? Does it exist?
3. Describe (and evaluate the usefulness of) the main strategies used in problem solving.
4. How do scientists generate and test hypotheses?
5. What is involved in deliberate practice? Is it both necessary and sufficient to achieve expert performance?

Further Reading

- Ericsson, K. A., Charness, N., Hoffman, R. R., & Feltovich, P. J. (Eds.). (2006). *The Cambridge handbook of expertise and expert performance*. Cambridge, UK: Cambridge University Press. Many of the world's leading authorities discuss theories and research on expertise in this edited volume.
- Güss, C. D., Tuason, M. T., & Gerhard, C. (2010). Cross-national comparisons of complex problem-solving strategies in two microworlds. *Cognitive Science, 34*, 489–520. The authors focus on the important (but strangely neglected) topic of cross-cultural differences in problem-solving strategies.
- Sio, U. N., & Ormerod, T. C. (2009). Does incubation enhance problem solving? A meta-analytic review. *Psychological Bulletin, 135*, 94–120. The authors show that there is convincing evidence that problem solving can benefit from incubation.
- Zelko, H., Zammar, G. R., Ferreira, A. P. B., Phadtare, A., Shah, J., & Pietrobon, R. (2010). Selection mechanisms underlying high impact biomedical research – A qualitative analysis and causal model. *Public Library of Science One, 5*, e10535. What is of special interest about this article is that the authors identify individual differences in the problem-solving strategies adopted by leading scientists.

Chapter 11

Contents

Judgment, decision making, and reasoning

INTRODUCTION

Thinking takes many forms. In Chapter 10, we focused on problem solving. In this chapter, we consider three more kinds of thinking: judgment; decision making; and reasoning. All are very important in everyday life. Let's start with judgment. **Judgment** involves deciding on the likelihood of various events using whatever information is available. For example, you might use information about your previous examination performance to work out your chance of succeeding in a forthcoming examination. You also make numerous judgments

---

Learning Objectives
After studying Chapter 11, you should be able to:

- Define, compare, and contrast informal reasoning and deductive reasoning.
- Explain why tasks such as the Wason card selection and the Monty Hall problem illustrate the fact that human decision making and reasoning are not always logical or rational.
- Discuss the experimental evidence that shows how people often ignore base-rate information when making judgments.
- Define, compare, and contrast the representativeness, availability, and recognition heuristics used in judgments and decision making.
- Explain why omission bias, loss-aversion, framing effects, and sunk-cost effects each influence human decision making.
- Define syllogistic reasoning and conditional reasoning, and describe ways these cognitive skills are assessed experimentally.

Key Term
Judgment: this involves an assessment of the likelihood of a given event occurring on the basis of incomplete information; it often forms the initial process in **decision making**.

about your friends and acquaintances, perhaps using knowledge of their past behavior to decide how trustworthy, honest, loyal, and so on they are. What matters in judgment is *accuracy*.

Decision making involves selecting from among several possibilities. You probably had to decide which university to go to, which courses to study, and so on. The factors involved depend on the precise nature of the decision in question. For example, the processes involved in deciding which career path to follow are much more complex and time-consuming than those involved in deciding whether to buy a can of Coca-Cola or Pepsi!

We generally assess the quality of our decisions in terms of their *consequences* – are we happy with our choice of university or courses? However, this isn't always fair. There is the story of a surgeon saying, "The operation was a success. Unfortunately, the patient died!" This may sound like a sick joke. However, a decision can be good based on the information available when it is made even if it seems poor later on.

Judgment often forms part of the decision-making process. For example, when deciding which car to buy, you might make judgments about how much various cars would cost to run, how reliable they would be, and so on. The links between judgment and decision making explain why both are discussed in this chapter.

The second part of this chapter is devoted to reasoning, which involves drawing inferences from the knowledge we possess. Much research on reasoning has involved problems based on logic, although we often don't use logic to solve them. The need for such reasoning is surprisingly common in everyday life. For example, suppose your university library has the following rule: "If you fail to return a book by the due date, you will pay a fine." Nancy returns a book a day late. The conclusion, "Nancy has to pay a fine," follows logically.

There are important differences between decision making and deductive reasoning. We often make decisions in the absence of full information, and the information we have is sometimes ambiguous. When we make a decision, it may be quite some time before we know whether the decision was a good one or not. In contrast, we have all the information needed to draw the appropriate conclusion in deductive reasoning.

Section Summary

- What matters in judgment is accuracy. In contrast, decision quality is generally assessed by its consequences. Judgment often forms part of the decision-making process. Decision making often takes place in the absence of full information, whereas all the information needed to draw the appropriate conclusion is provided in deductive reasoning.

JUDGMENT

In this section, I discuss the main kinds of error occurring when we make judgments. A Research Activity to allow you to see whether you are susceptible to errors in judgment is included. Then there is a discussion of what is known about the factors influencing judgment. Finally, a major theoretical approach designed to explain human judgments is considered.

In the Real World 11.1: *Support theory*

You probably think most people are reasonably good at making accurate judgments in your everyday life. If so, I am probably about to prove you wrong! You almost certainly assume that the probability you will die on your next summer holiday is extremely low. However, it might seem more likely if I asked you the following question: "What is the probability you will die on your next summer holiday from a disease, a car accident, a plane crash, or any other cause?" Obviously, the two different probabilities can't both be right. The take-home message is that an event seems more likely when the various reasons why it might occur are stated *explicitly*.

Mandel (2005) obtained evidence for the above effect in a study carried out during the first week of the 2003 Iraq war. Some people assessed the risk of at least one terrorist attack over the following six months, whereas others assessed the risk of an attack plotted by al-Qaida or not plotted by al-Qaida. The probabilities should be the same in the two conditions. In fact, the mean estimated probability was .30 for a terrorist attack, but it was .48 (.30 for an al-Qaida attack + .18 for a non-al-Qaida attack) in the second condition.

What is going on here? Tversky and Koehler (1994) provided two answers in their support theory. First, explicit descriptions draw attention to aspects of an event that are less obvious in non-explicit descriptions. Second, memory limitations mean people don't remember all the relevant information if it isn't supplied.

We might imagine that experts wouldn't show the above effect, because experts provided with a non-explicit description can presumably fill in the details from their own knowledge. However, Redelmeier et al. (1995) found that expert doctors *did* show the effect. The doctors were given a description of a woman with abdominal pain. Half assessed the probabilities of two specified diagnoses (gastroenteritis and ectopic pregnancy) and of a residual category (everything else). The other half assigned probabilities to *five* specified diagnoses (including gastroenteritis and ectopic pregnancy) and of a residual category (i.e., everything else).

The key comparison was the subjective probability of all diagnoses other than gastroenteritis and ectopic pregnancy. This probability was .50 with the non-explicit description but .69 with the explicit one. Thus, subjective probabilities were higher for explicit descriptions even with experts.

Judgments can also be influenced by emotion. Lerner et al. (2003) carried out an online study immediately after the terrorist attacks of September 11, 2001. The participants focused on aspects of the attacks that made them afraid, angry, or sad. The key finding was that the estimated probability of future terrorist attacks was higher in fearful participants than in sad or angry ones.

BASE RATES

We have seen that people making judgments often ignore base-rate information when it is relevant but use it when it is irrelevant. Here we consider two kinds of situation in which base-rate information is both relevant *and* generally used.

First, Krynski and Tenenbaum (2007) argued that we possess valuable *causal knowledge* allowing us to make accurate judgments using base-rate information in everyday life. For example, suppose a friend has a cough. You know a cough can be caused by a common cold or by lung cancer. You use your base-rate knowledge that far more people have colds than lung cancer to decide your friend is only suffering from a cold. In the laboratory, in contrast, the judgment problems we confront often fail to provide such knowledge.

In one of Krynski and Tenenbaum's (2007) experiments, some participants were given the following judgment task (the false positive

Research Activity 11.1: *Base-rate neglect*

Support theory focuses on judgment errors that depend on whether all the relevant information is presented explicitly. However, judgment errors can occur for other reasons. You can assess your own ability to make correct judgments when all the relevant information is presented explicitly by considering the following problem (Casscells et al., 1978):

If a test to detect a disease whose prevalence [occurrence] is 1/1000 has a false positive rate of 5% [chance of indicating the disease is present when it isn't], what is the chance that a person found to have a positive result actually has the disease, assuming that you know nothing about the person's symptoms or signs?

What is your answer? If you think 95% is the correct answer, you are in good company – that is easily the most common answer. Unfortunately, it is wrong! Casscells et al. (1978) gave the problem to staff and students at Harvard Medical School. Forty-five per cent of them produced the wrong answer of 95% and only 18% produced the correct answer, which is 2%.

Why is 2% correct? The information provided indicates that 999 out of every 1000 do *not* suffer from the disease. The additional fact that the test mistakenly indicates in 5% of cases that someone who is perfectly healthy has the disease means that 50 out of every 1000 people tested would give a misleading positive finding. Thus, 50 times as many people give a false positive as give a true positive result (the one person in 1000 who actually has the disease). Thus, there is only a 2% chance that a person testing positive has the disease.

Most people who get the answer wrong pay insufficient attention to the fact that only one person in 1000 has the disease. The relative frequency with which an event occurs in the population is **base-rate information**. There is considerable evidence that we often fail to take full account of such information when making judgments (Koehler, 1996). This happens when the *relevance* of base-rate information to a judgment task is unclear.

scenario) closely resembling those used previously to show how people neglect base rates:

> *The following statistics are known about women at age 60 who participate in a routine mammogram screening, an X-ray of the breast tissue that detects tumors:*
>
> - *2% of women have breast cancer at the time of screening. Most of them will receive a positive result on the mammogram.*
> - *There is a 6% chance that a woman without breast cancer will receive a positive result on the mammogram.*
>
> *Suppose a women at age 60 gets a positive result during a routine mammogram screening. Without knowing any other symptoms, what are the chances she has breast cancer?*

Key Term

Base-rate information: this is the relative frequency with which an event occurs in the population; it is often ignored (or deemphasized) when individuals make a **judgment**.

The base rate of cancer in the population was often neglected by participants given this task, perhaps because having breast cancer is the *only* cause of positive mammograms explicitly mentioned. Suppose we reworded the problem slightly to indicate there is an alternative cause of positive mammograms. Krynski and Tenenbaum did this by changing the wording of the third paragraph:

> *There is a 6% chance that a woman without breast cancer will have a dense but harmless cyst that looks like a cancerous tumor and causes a positive result on the mammogram.*

Research Activity 11.2: *Base-rate overemphasized*

Are there circumstances in which we *overemphasize* the importance of base-rate information? Consider the following problem (Teigen & Keren, 2007):

Fred travels every day to work on a bus that departs on the hour (i.e., 6:00, 7:00, and 8:00) from the station next to his house.

Based on his long experience, he noticed that, on average, in one out of 10 cases the bus departs before schedule, in eight out of 10 cases it departs 0–10 min late, and in one out of 10 cases it departs more than 10 min late.

Suppose that Fred arrives at the bus stop exactly on time and waits for 10 min *without the bus coming*. What is the probability (chance) that the bus will still arrive?

What is your answer? Teigen and Keren (2007) found the most popular answer (given by 63% of students) was 10%. The second most popular answer (given by 26% of students) was 90%–100%. Only 3% said 50%, which is the correct answer!

Why is 50% correct? According to the base-rate information, there is a 10% chance of the bus being early, 80% chance of it arriving 0–10 min late, and a 10% chance of it arriving more than 10 min late. On this morning, however, it failed to appear in the 0–10 min late time period, so we can eliminate that from consideration. There is an equal probability of the bus being early and more than 10 min late. Since the total probability must come to 100%, the probability that the bus will still arrive is 50% (as is the probability that it was early).

Why do most people rely excessively on the base-rate information (10%/80%/10%) with the above problem? One reason is that the base-rate probabilities are easy to calculate, whereas to move beyond those probabilities involves complex calculations. Another reason is that it is not very obvious why Fred standing *passively* at the bus stop for 10 min has an impact on the probability of the bus arriving more than 10 min late.

Teigen and Keren (2007) used a version of the bus problem in which participants were told there was a 10% chance that a bus from company A would arrive first, an 80% chance that a bus from company B would arrive first, and a 10% chance that a bus from company C would arrive first. On a particular day, however, the company B bus drivers were on strike. When the impact of removing the 80% option was made much more obvious in this way, 82% of participants corrected decided there was a 50% chance that the first bus to arrive would belong to company C.

In sum, the notion that people nearly always underestimate the importance and relevance of base-rate information must be rejected. If base-rate information is easy to calculate, it is sometimes used even when it isn't relevant to a given judgment.

Participants given the benign cyst scenario were far more likely to take full account of the base-rate information than those given the standard false positive scenario (see Figure 11.1). Krynski and Tenenbaum (2007) argued that the reasonably full *causal* knowledge available to participants given the benign cyst scenario allowed them to solve the problem. It also corresponds to real life.

Second, we use base-rate information when strongly *motivated* to do so. Suppose you were asked to put some saliva on a strip of paper. If it turned blue, that would mean you had an enzyme deficiency indicating a health problem. However, there was a 1/10 probability that the test was misleading. Unfortunately, the paper turned blue.

Ditto et al. (1998) gave their participants the above task. Most used the base-rate information (i.e., 1/10 probability of misleading result) to argue that the test was inaccurate. In contrast, participants told the paper turning blue meant they didn't have a health problem perceived the test as accurate – they

Figure 11.1 Percentages of correct responses and various incorrect responses (based on base-rate neglect, odds form, base-rate overuse, and other) with the false-positive and benign cyst scenarios. From Krynski and Tenenbaum (2007), Copyright © 2007, American Psychological Association. Reproduced with permission.

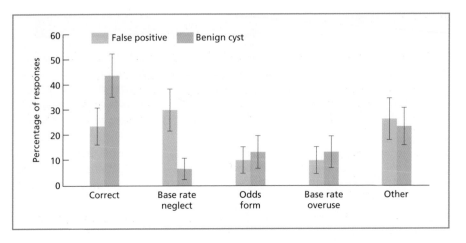

weren't motivated to take account of the base-rate information. In both cases, there is evidence of wishful thinking.

In sum, we frequently make use of base-rate information in our everyday lives when we possess relevant knowledge (e.g., causal knowledge). We also use base-rate information when judgments including such information are more advantageous to us than judgments that ignore it. We also ignore base-rate information when it is disadvantageous to us.

HEURISTICS OR RULES OF THUMB

The most influential psychologists in the area of judgment are the late Amos Tversky and Danny Kahneman (who won the Nobel Prize for Economics). They discovered several interesting **heuristics** or rules of thumb used frequently in everyday life. As we will see, heuristics have the advantage that they require very little cognitive effort (Shah & Oppenheimer, 2008). However, they have the disadvantage that they often produce only approximately correct answers.

Below we consider in some detail the main heuristics used on judgment tasks.

Representativeness heuristic

The **representativeness heuristic** involves deciding an object belongs to a given category because it appears typical or representative of that category (see Research Activity).

Here is a problem from Tversky and Kahneman (1983) for you to consider:

> *Linda is 31 years old, single, outspoken and very bright. She majored in philosophy. As a student, she was deeply concerned with issues of discrimination and social justice, and also participated in anti-nuclear demonstrations.*

Do you think it is more likely that Linda is a bank teller or a feminist bank teller? Most people (including you?) argue that it is more likely that Linda is a feminist bank teller than a bank teller. They do so because they rely on the

Research Activity 11.3: *Representativeness heuristic*

Below is a problem taken from a study by De Neys and Glumicic (2008).

> In a study 1000 people were tested. Among the participants there were 4 men and 996 women. Jo is a randomly chosen participant of this study.
> Jo is 23 years old and is finishing a degree in engineering. On Friday nights, Jo likes to go out cruising with friends while listening to loud music and drinking beer.

What is most likely?

a. Jo is a man
b. Jo is a woman

The great majority of people in the study gave the answer (a) because Jo's behavior is more typical or representative of men than of women. Thus, they used the representativeness heuristic. However, at the same time, they ignored the base-rate information. Jo was selected at *random* from 1000 people, 99.6% of whom were female. Thus, it is very likely that Jo is actually female.

representativeness heuristic – the description sounds more like that of feminist bank teller than of a bank teller.

If your answer agrees with that of most people, I am afraid it is wrong! Every single feminist bank teller must necessarily also be a bank teller. Thus, the probability that Linda is a feminist bank teller *must* be less than the probability that she is a bank teller. The mistaken belief that the conjunction or combination of two events (A and B) is more likely than one of the events on its own is the **conjunction fallacy**.

Many people misunderstand the Linda problem. For example, between 20% and 50% of participants interpret, "Linda is a bank teller," as implying she isn't active in the feminist movement. However, the conjunction fallacy is still found even when almost everything possible is done to ensure that participants don't misinterpret the problem (Sides et al., 2002).

Availability heuristic

The **availability heuristic** involves estimating the frequencies of events on the basis of how easy or hard it is to retrieve relevant information from long-term memory. For example, Lichtenstein et al. (1978) asked people to judge the relative likelihood of different causes of death. Causes of death attracting considerable publicity (e.g., murder) were judged more likely than those that don't (e.g., suicide), even when the opposite was actually the case.

Hertwig et al. (2005) argued that we can interpret Lichtenstein et al.'s (1978) findings in two ways. We can distinguish between two different mechanisms associated with use of the availability heuristic. First, there is the availability-by-recall mechanism: This is based on the number of people that an individual recalls having died from a given risk (e.g., a specific disease). Second, there is the fluency mechanism: This involves judging the number of deaths from a given risk by deciding how easy it would be to bring relevant instances to mind

Key Terms

Conjunction fallacy: the mistaken assumption that the probability of two events occurring in conjunction or combination is greater than one of these events on its own; most famously studied with the Linda problem.

Availability heuristic: a rule of thumb in which the frequency of a given event is estimated (often wrongly) on the basis of how easily relevant information about that event can be accessed in long-term memory.

but without retrieving them. Hertwig et al. found that both mechanisms were used.

We don't always use the availability heuristic. Oppenheimer (2004) presented American participants with pairs of names (one famous, one nonfamous), and asked them to indicate which surname was more common in the United States. For example, one pair consisted of the names "Bush" and "Stevenson" – which name do you think is more common? Here is another one: Which surname is more common: "Clinton" or "Woodall"?

If participants in Oppenheimer's (2004) study had used the availability heuristic, they would have said "Bush" and "Clinton." In fact, however, only 12% said Bush and 30% Clinton. They were correct to avoid these famous names, because the nonfamous name is slightly more common. Why wasn't the availability heuristic used? Participants realized that names such as "Bush" and "Clinton" are very familiar because individuals with those names are famous rather than because the names are common ones.

OUR JUDGMENTS ARE OK!

We have seen that our judgments are often inaccurate because of our reliance on various heuristics or rules of thumb. Such findings led Glymour (2001, p. 8) to ask the question, "If we're so dumb, how come we're so smart?"

Various reasons for our extensive use of heuristics have been suggested. For example, many heuristics or rules of thumb we use are valuable because they rapidly provide approximately correct solutions and avoid the need to think hard (Shah & Oppenheimer, 2008; Todd & Gigerenzer, 2007). Much of the time, being approximately correct is good enough.

Another advantage of heuristics is that they can be used almost regardless of the amount of information we have available. In contrast, complex cognitive strategies are of very limited usefulness when information is sparse.

Gigerenzer & Hoffrage (1999) claimed our judgments are often in error because of the ways in which problems are typically expressed. People find it hard to think in terms of probabilities and percentages, but are better equipped to think in terms of frequencies.

Fast and frugal heuristics

Gigerenzer (e.g., Todd & Gigerenzer, 2007) emphasized the importance of fast and frugal heuristics involving rapid processing of relatively little information. It is assumed we possess an "adaptive toolbox" consisting of several such heuristics.

A key fast and frugal heuristic is the take-the-best heuristic. This is based on "take the best, ignore the rest." Imagine you have to decide whether Herne or Cologne (two German cities) has the larger population. Suppose you start by assuming the most valid cue to city size is that cities whose names you recognize typically have larger populations than those whose names you don't recognize. However, you recognize both names. Then you think of another valid cue to city size, namely, that cities with cathedrals tend to be larger than those without. If you know that Cologne has a cathedral but are unsure about Herne, you produce the answer, "Cologne."

The take-the-best strategy has three components:

1. *Search rule:* Search cues (e.g., name recognition; cathedral) in order of validity.
2. *Stopping rule:* Stop after finding a discriminatory cue (i.e., the cue applies to only one of the possible answers).
3. *Decision rule:* Choose outcome.

The most researched example of the take-the-best strategy is the **recognition heuristic**. This involves using the knowledge that only one of two objects is recognized when making a judgment. In the example above, if you recognize the name "Cologne" but not "Herne," you guess (correctly) that Cologne is the larger city.

Evidence that the recognition heuristic is important was reported by Goldstein and Gigerenzer (2002). American students were presented with pairs of German cities and decided which was larger. When only one city name was recognized, participants used the recognition heuristic 90% of the time.

In another study, Goldstein and Gigerenzer (2002) told American participants that German cities with soccer teams tend to be larger than those without soccer teams. When participants decided whether a recognized city without a soccer team was larger or smaller than an unrecognized city, participants used the recognition heuristic 92% of the time. Thus, as predicted theoretically, they mostly ignored the conflicting information about the absence of a soccer team.

Participants in the above study may have ignored information about the presence or absence of a football team because they felt it wasn't strongly related to city size. Richter and Späth (2006) asked German students to decide which in each pair of American cities was larger. The recognized city was chosen 98% of the time when students were told it had an international airport but only 82% of the time when it did not. The recognition heuristic was sometimes ignored because participants believed that the presence or absence of an international airport was a valid cue to city size.

Goldstein and Gigerenzer (2002) presented American and German students with pairs of American cities and pairs of German cities, and asked them to select the larger city in each pair. The findings were counterintuitive: American and German students performed *less* well on cities in their own country. Students typically recognized both members in the pair with cities in their own country and so couldn't use the recognition heuristic.

The recognition heuristic is less important than claimed by Goldstein and Gigerenzer (2002). Oppenheimer (2003) asked participants to decide whether recognized cities known to be small were larger than unrecognized cities. The small cities were relatively close to Stanford University (where the study took place) and the unrecognized cities were fictitious but sounded plausible (e.g., Las Besas; Rio Del Sol). The recognition heuristic failed to predict the results: The recognized city was judged to be larger on only 37% of trials. Thus, knowledge of city size can override the recognition heuristic.

Is *anything* special about the recognition heuristic? Pachur and Hertwig (2006) argued there is. Retrieving the familiarity information underlying the recognition heuristic occurred more *rapidly* than retrieving any other kind of information about an object. This often gives familiarity information a "competitive edge" over other information and leads to the recognition heuristic being used in many situations.

Evaluation

⊕ People sometimes use fast and frugal heuristics such as the recognition heuristic and the take-the-best strategy to make rapid judgments.

⊕ These heuristics can be surprisingly effective in spite of their simplicity, and it is impressive that individuals with little knowledge can sometimes outperform those with greater knowledge.

⊕ Familiarity or recognition information can be accessed faster and more automatically than other kinds of information. This encourages its widespread use when individuals are under time or cognitive pressure.

⊖ When the decision is important, few people would use fast and frugal heuristics. For example, most women want to consider *all* the relevant evidence before deciding which of two men to marry!

⊖ We often don't know in advance *which* heuristic will be used in a given situation. As a result, the predictive power of this approach is limited.

Natural frequency hypothesis

Gigerenzer and Hoffrage (1999) argued that we encounter examples of any given category at different points in time in everyday life – this is natural sampling. As a result, according to their natural frequency hypothesis, we find it easy to work out the *frequencies* of different kinds of event. However, we have difficulties in dealing with the fractions and percentages used in most laboratory research, which are more abstract than the frequencies of events experienced in everyday life.

It follows from the above hypothesis that performance would improve greatly if problems used natural frequencies (i.e., the *numbers* of individuals belonging to different categories; see below). Note, however, that the frequencies of various events we experience may be distorted. For example, the frequencies of highly intelligent and less intelligent people encountered by most university students are very different from the frequencies in the general population.

It is also important to distinguish between natural frequencies and the word problems actually used in research. In most word problems, participants are simply provided with frequency information and don't have to grapple with the complexities of natural sampling.

Judgment performance is often much better when problems are presented in frequencies rather than probabilities or percentages. For example, Fiedler (1988) used the Linda problem discussed earlier. The standard version was compared to a frequency version in which participants indicated how many of

100 people fitting Linda's description were bank tellers, and how many were bank tellers and active feminists.

Fiedler (1988) found that the percentage of participants showing the conjunction fallacy dropped dramatically with the frequency version. Performance may have been better with the frequency version because people are more used to dealing with frequencies than with probabilities. Alternatively, it may that the frequency version made the problem's structure more obvious.

Hoffrage et al. (2000) gave advanced medical students four realistic diagnostic tasks containing base-rate information in a probability or frequency version. These experts paid little attention to base-rate information in the probability versions. However, they performed much better when given the frequency versions (see Figure 11.2).

Fiedler et al. (2000) tested the theoretical assumption that base rates are taken much more into account when frequencies are sampled. They used the following problem in various forms. There is an 80% probability that a woman with breast cancer will have a positive mammogram compared to a 9.6% probability that a woman without breast cancer will have a positive mammogram. The base rate of cancer in women is 1%. The task is to decide the probability that a woman has breast cancer given a positive mammogram (the correct answer is 7.8%).

Fiedler et al. (2000) didn't give participants the problem in the form described above, because they were interested in people's natural sampling behavior. They provided some participants with index card files organized into the categories of women with breast cancer and those without. They had to select cards, with each selected card indicating whether the woman in question had had a positive mammogram.

Fiedler et al.'s (2000) key finding was that participants' sampling was heavily *biased* towards women with breast cancer. As a result, the participants produced an average estimate of 63% that a woman had breast cancer given a positive mammogram (remember the correct answer is 7.8%).

Why was the participants' sampling so biased? They believed mistakenly that it was more informative to select women with breast cancer than those without.

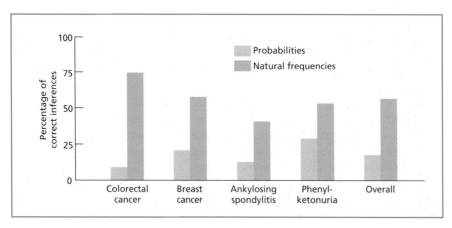

Figure 11.2 Percentage correct inferences by advanced medical students given four realistic diagnostic tasks expressed in probabilities or frequencies. From Hoffrage et al. (2000). Reprinted with permission from AAAS.

Evaluation

+ Use of natural or objective sampling could enhance the accuracy of many of our judgments.

+ Judgments based on frequency information are often superior to those based on probability information.

− There is often a yawning chasm between people's actual sampling behavior and the neat and tidy frequency data provided in laboratory experiments. As Fiedler et al. (2000) found, the samples selected by participants can provide biased and complex information which is very hard to interpret.

− Frequency versions of problems typically make their underlying structure much easier to grasp. Thus, the improved performance found using frequency formats may occur because this makes the problem much simpler rather than because people are naturally equipped to think about frequencies rather than probabilities.

DUAL-PROCESS MODEL

We must beware of assuming that people nearly *always* use heuristics or rules of thumb when making judgments and decisions – reality is more complex. Kahneman and Frederick (e.g., 2005) proposed one such model according to which probability judgments depend on processing within two systems:

- *System 1:* This system is intuitive, automatic, and immediate. More specifically, "The operations of System 1 are typically fast, automatic, effortless, associative, implicit [not open to introspection] and often emotionally charged; they are also difficult to control or modify" (Kahneman, 2003). Most heuristics are produced by this system.
- *System 2:* This system is more analytical, controlled, and rule-governed. According to Kahneman (2003), "The operations of System 2 are slower, serial [one at a time], effortful, more likely to be consciously monitored and deliberately controlled; they are also relatively flexible and potentially rule-governed."

What is the relationship between these two systems? Kahneman and Frederick (2005) argued that System 1 rapidly generates intuitive answers to judgment problems. These intuitive answers are then monitored or evaluated by System 2, which may correct these answers. However, we often make little use of System 2: "People who make a casual intuitive judgment normally know little about how their judgment came about" (Kahneman & Frederick, 2005, p. 274).

Findings

De Neys (2006) tested the dual-process model. Participants were presented with the Linda problem and another very similar conjunction-fallacy problem. Participants who obtained the correct answers (and so presumably used System 2) took almost 40% longer than those who were incorrect (and so presumably using System 1). This is consistent with the assumption that it takes longer to use System 2.

De Neys (2006) also compared performance on the same problems performed on their own or with a demanding secondary task. Participants performed worse on the problems when accompanied by the secondary task (9.5% correct vs. 17%, respectively). This is as predicted because System 2 requires use of cognitively demanding processes.

De Neys and Glumicic (2008) tested the dual-process model in several experiments investigating base-rate neglect. There were *incongruent* problems in which System 1 and System 2 processes would produce different answers. One of the incongruent problems was the one about Jo (see Research Activity 11.3 above). Heuristic processing based on stereotypes (System 1 processing) would produce answer (a), whereas consideration of the base rate (System 2) would produce the correct answer (b).

De Neys and Glumicic (2008) also used *congruent* problems in which the person description and the base-rate information pointed to the same answer. Finally, there were neutral problems in which System 2 processing was needed to obtain the correct answer.

In their first experiment, De Neys and Glumicic (2008) asked participants to think out loud during problem solving. As expected, most participants failed to use base-rate information with incongruent problems. As a result, their performance was much worse with those problems than with congruent ones (under 20% vs. 95%, respectively). Participants doing incongruent problems referred to base-rate information on only 18% of trials, suggesting that they generally ignored such information at the conscious level.

In their second experiment, participants weren't required to think aloud. As before, performance was much worse with incongruent than with congruent problems (22% vs. 97%, respectively). The most interesting findings related to time taken with each type of problem (see Figure 11.3). Participants took longer to

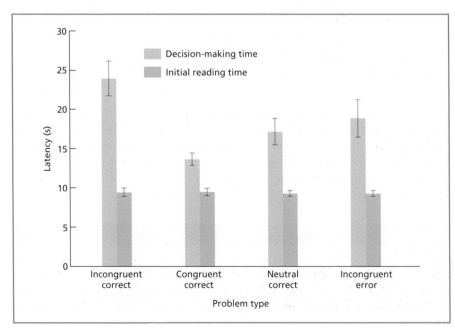

Figure 11.3 Mean times to read and make correct decisions with incongruent, congruent, and neutral problems and incorrect decisions with incongruent problems. Reprinted from De Neys and Glumicic (2008), Copyright © 2008, with permission from Elsevier.

produce answers with incongruent problems than with congruent or neutral ones whether their answers were correct or false. In addition, participants spent longer processing information with incongruent problems than with congruent ones.

What do De Neys and Glumicic's (2008) findings mean? On the face of it, they seem inconsistent. When participants thought aloud, there was little evidence that they considered base-rate information. However, the fact that they took longer to respond with incongruent than with congruent problems indicates that base-rate information influenced their behavior. The most likely explanation is that base-rate information was mostly processed below the level of conscious awareness.

Let's consider in more detail people who make errors on judgment tasks. According to the dual-process model, such people often rely *exclusively* on System 1 or heuristic reasoning. This suggests that people don't know or care about base-rate information. Another possibility (suggested by the findings of De Neys & Glumicic, 2008) is that most people detect a *conflict* between their intuitive, heuristic-based reasoning and base-rate information. In spite of this, however, they fail to *inhibit* the incorrect response based on heuristic reasoning. De Neys et al. (2008) obtained strong support for this alternative explanation.

Evaluation

+ There is reasonable evidence for the existence of two different processing systems corresponding to those assumed within the model.

+ The notion that people's judgments are typically determined by System 1 rather than by System 2 accords with most of the data.

+ The model provides an explanation for individual differences in judgment performance. Individuals making extensive use of System 2 processing perform better than those using only System 1.

− The model is based on the assumption that most people rely almost exclusively on System 1 and so simply ignore base-rate information. In fact, however, most people detect a conflict between their System 1 thinking and base-rate information (De Neys & Glumicic, 2008; De Neys et al., 2008).

− The dual-process model put forward by Kahneman and Frederick (2005) is imprecise. The notion that there are two separate processing systems is oversimplified (Keren & Schul, 2009).

Section Summary

Support theory
- A possible future event seems more likely when reasons it might occur are stated explicitly. This happens because explicit descriptions emphasize

aspects of an event that are less obvious in non-explicit descriptions. In addition, people often fail to remember all the relevant information unless it is supplied.

Base rates
- People often make little or no use of base-rate information when making judgments. In the real world, however, our causal knowledge often allows us to make accurate judgments depending on base-rate information.

Heuristics or rules of thumb
- We often use heuristics (rules of thumb) when making judgments. Examples include the representativeness and availability heuristics. Heuristics allow us to produce approximately accurate judgments very rapidly and fairly effortlessly.

Our judgments are OK!
- Fast and frugal heuristics such as the recognition heuristic often lead to accurate judgments. However, these heuristics are used less often when important decisions have to be made. It has been argued we make more accurate judgments when presented with frequencies rather than fractions or percentages. This typically happens because it makes the underlying problem structure easier to grasp.

Dual-process model
- According to Kahneman and Frederick's dual-process model, probability judgments depend on processing within two systems. One system is intuitive and fast, whereas the other is analytical and slow. We often rely almost exclusively on the intuitive system. This theoretical approach is valuable but deemphasizes the extent to which the analytical system is also involved in judgments.

DECISION MAKING

Life is full of decisions. Which movie will I go to see tonight? Would I prefer to go out with Dick or Harry? What career am I going to pursue after university? Who will I share an apartment with next year?

It is often argued that we are fortunate to live at a time when the choices open to us are greater than at any time in history. However, Barry Schwartz (2004, 2009) disagrees, claiming that an explosion of choice makes decision making more difficult. You can see his point in the following anecdote. He was in a shop called The Gap wanting to buy a pair of jeans. "I told them my size, and they asked if I wanted relaxed fit, easy fit, slim fit, boot cut, button-fly, zipper-fly, acid-washed, or stone-washed. And I said, 'I want the kind that used to be the only kind'" (Schwartz, 2004).

In the Real World 11.2: *Omission bias*

People often must decide whether action or inaction is the better way to respond to a given situation. For example, parents have to decide whether to vaccinate their young child against some disease. There is a clear risk in inaction (i.e., not having the child vaccinated) because the child may then develop the disease and possibly die. There is also a risk in action (i.e., having the child vaccinated) because the vaccine may have dangerous side-effects.

Ritov and Baron (1990) told participants to assume that their child had 10 chances in 10,000 of dying from flu during an epidemic if he/she wasn't vaccinated. The vaccine was certain to prevent the child from catching flu, but had potentially fatal side-effects. Ritov and Baron found that 5 deaths per 10,000 was the average maximum acceptable risk participants were willing to tolerate in order to decide to have their child vaccinated. Thus, people would choose not to have their child vaccinated when the likelihood of the vaccine causing death was much lower than that of the disease against which the vaccine protects!

What was going on in the above study? The participants argued they would feel more responsible for the death of their child if it resulted from their own actions rather than their inaction. This is **omission bias**, in which individuals prefer to risk harm from inaction or omission to the harm resulting from action.

Does omission bias in the laboratory predict omission bias in the real world? Evidence that it does was reported by DiBonaventura and Chapman (2008). They assessed omission bias in university staff under laboratory conditions. They also asked them whether they had accepted a free flu vaccine having possible side-effects. Those showing evidence of omission bias in the laboratory were less likely to have been vaccinated than those who didn't exhibit omission bias.

Omission bias is found in medicine. For example, pulmonologists (experts in treating lung disease) were given scenarios involving evaluation of pulmonary embolism and treatment of septic shock (Aberegg et al., 2005). When these experts were given the option of inaction (i.e., doing nothing), they were less likely to select the best management strategy than when this option was unavailable (40% vs. 59%, respectively). Thus, these medical experts showed strong evidence of omission bias even when making decisions in their own speciality.

We now turn to gamblers in Las Vegas. Since gamblers by definition have chosen to take risks, we might imagine they wouldn't show omission bias. Nothing could be further from the truth. When people play blackjack, we can categorize their mistakes as passive ones (omission bias) or active ones (being too aggressive). Bruce Carlin and David Robinson (2009) found that 80% of gamblers' mistakes were passive ones involving omission bias. Gamblers who showed omission bias lost much more money on average than did those avoiding passive mistakes.

How can we explain omission bias? It is generally assumed that the level of anticipated regret is greater when an unwanted outcome has been caused by an individual's own actions. Support for this assumption was reported by Wroe et al. (2005) in a study on MMR vaccinations, which provide protection against measles, mumps, and rubella. Adverse publicity in the UK suggesting that the vaccination might conceivably lead to autism caused millions of parents to decide not to allow their children to receive it. Many parents argued that the level of anticipated responsibility and regret would potentially be higher if they had their child vaccinated than if they did not.

Not everyone shows omission bias. In one vaccination study (Baron & Ritov, 2004), 58% of the participants showed omission bias but 22% showed the opposite bias: "action bias." Those susceptible to it use the heuristic, "Don't just sit there. Do something!"

There are cross-cultural differences in omission bias. It is found in more educated and less rural Mayan groups but not in less educated, rural Mayans (Abarbanell & Hauser, 2010). In the latter group there are strong social networks, and action is often regarded as fulfilling one's social obligations.

Key Term

Omission bias: a preference for risking harm through inaction compared to risking harm through action; it is shown even when the balance of advantage lies in action rather than inaction.

LOSSES AND GAINS

We all spend much of our time trying to achieve gains (e.g., emotional, financial, at work) while avoiding losses. Thus, we seem to make decisions to maximize the chances of making a gain and minimize the chances of making a loss. For example, suppose someone offered you $200 if a tossed coin came up heads and a loss of $100 if it came up tails. You would jump at the chance (wouldn't you?), given that the bet provides an average expected gain of $50 per toss.

Here are two more decisions. Would you prefer to make a sure gain of $800 or an 85% probability of gaining $1000 and a 15% probability of gaining nothing? Since the expected value of the latter decision is greater than that of the former ($850 vs. $800, respectively), you might well choose the latter alternative. Finally, would you prefer to make a sure loss of $800 or an 85% probability of losing $1000 with a 15% probability of not making any loss? The average expected loss is $800 for the former choice and $850 for the latter one, so you go with the former choice, don't you?

The first problem was taken from Tversky and Shafir (1992) and the other two come from Kahneman and Tversky (1984). In all three cases, most people did *not* make the best choices. Two-thirds of people refused to bet on the toss of a coin. A majority preferred the choice with the smaller expected gain and the choice with the larger expected loss! Kahneman and Tversky accounted for these findings using their prospect theory based on two major assumptions:

1. People identify a reference point generally representing their current state.
2. People are much more sensitive to potential losses than to potential gains; this is **loss aversion**.

Both assumptions are shown in Figure 11.4. The reference point is the point at which the line labeled "losses" and "gains" intersects the line labeled "value." The positive value associated with gains increases relatively slowly as gains become greater. In contrast, the negative value associated with losses increases relatively rapidly as losses become greater.

How does prospect theory account for the findings discussed earlier? If people are much more sensitive to losses than to gains, they should be unwilling to accept bets involving potential losses even though the potential gains outweigh the potential losses. They would also prefer a sure gain to a risky (but potentially greater) gain. Note that prospect theory does *not* predict that people will always seek to avoid risky decisions. If offered the chance of avoiding a loss (even if it means the average expected loss increases from $800 to $850), most people will take that chance because they are concerned to avoid losses.

The television game show *Deal or No Deal* provides a way of testing prospect theory under real-life conditions involving very large potential gains. In the British version, there are 22 boxes each containing a sum of money between 1p ($0.02) and £250,000 ($400,000). Participants initially select one

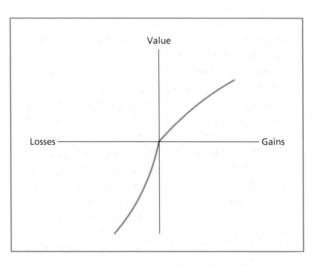

Figure 11.4 A hypothetical value function. From Kahneman and Tversky (1984). Copyright © by the American Psychological Association. Reprinted with permission.

box that will be opened if the game continues to the end. They then choose one box after another.

After every few selections, participants are given the choice between continuing with the game and accepting a cash offer. Towards the end of the game, this decision can become very difficult. For example, Laura Pearce had to decide between a definite cash offer of £44,000 ($70,000) and a 50:50 chance of £3,000 ($4800) or £250,000 ($400,000). What would you do? Laura Pearce took the gamble and won the top prize of £250,000.

Prospect theory has received some support from analyses of contestants' behavior on *Deal or No Deal*. Brooks et al. (2009) found that most contestants were risk-averse, and there was more risk aversion when the stakes were high. In other words, contestants often accepted the cash offer even though on average the rewards would have been greater by continuing. However, males were less risk-aversive than females.

Individual differences (not emphasized within prospect theory) were also important in research by Josephs et al. (1992). They found that individuals high in self-esteem were much more likely to prefer risky gambles than those low in self-esteem. According to Josephs et al., this is because they have a strong self-protective system that helps them to maintain self-esteem when confronted by threat or loss.

Framing effect

Much research has involved the **framing effect,** in which decisions are influenced by irrelevant aspects of the situation. Tversky and Kahneman (1987) used the Asian disease problem. Some participants were told there was likely to be an outbreak of an Asian disease in the United States, and it was likely to kill 600 people. Two programs of actions had been proposed:

- Program A would allow 200 people to be saved.
- Program B would have a one-third probability that all 600 people would be saved and a two-thirds probability that none of the 600 would be saved.

When the issue was expressed in this form, 72% of the participants favored Program A. This was the case even though the two programs (if implemented several times) would on average both lead to the saving of 200 lives.

Other participants in the study by Tversky and Kahneman (1987) were given the same problem, but this time it was negatively framed. They were told that Program A would lead to 400 people dying, whereas Program B carried a 1/3 probability that nobody would die and a 2/3 probability that 600 would die. Even though the numbers of people who would live and die were the same as in the other version of the problem, 78% chose program B.

The above findings can be accounted for in terms of loss aversion. With both versions of the problem, the decision made by most participants was designed to avoid definite losses in terms of deaths.

According to prospect theory, framing effects should only be found when what is at stake has real value for the decision maker. Thus, loss aversion doesn't apply if you don't mind making a loss. Wang et al. (2001) used a life-and-death problem involving 6 billion human lives or 6 billion extraterrestrial lives. There was the usual framing effect when human lives were at stake. However, there was no framing effect when only extraterrestrial lives were involved.

| Key Term

Framing effect:
the finding that decisions are often influenced by aspects of the situation (e.g., precise wording of a problem) that are irrelevant to good decision making.

More importantly, Wang (1996) argued that social and moral factors not considered by prospect theory can influence performance on modified versions of the Asian disease problem. Participants chose between definite survival of two-thirds of the patients (the deterministic option) and a 1/3 probability of all patients surviving and a 2/3 probability of none surviving (the probabilistic option).

In terms of minimizing the number of deaths, the deterministic option is much superior – on average, it leads to the survival of twice as many patients. However, the probabilistic option seems *fairer* in that all patients share the same fate. Participants strongly preferred the deterministic option when the problem related to six *unknown* patients. However, they preferred the probabilistic option when it related to six *close relatives*, because participants were more concerned about fairness in that condition.

How can we eliminate the framing effect? Almashat et al. (2008) obtained a framing effect using various medical scenarios involving cancer treatments. However, this effect disappeared when participants listed the advantages and disadvantages of each option and justified their decision. Thus, the framing effect is eliminated when individuals think carefully about the available options.

Sunk-cost effect

The **sunk-cost effect** is "a greater tendency to continue an endeavor once an investment in money, effort, or time has been made" (Arkes & Ayton, 1999, p. 591). The effect is captured by the expression "throwing good money after bad," and involves loss aversion.

Dawes (1988) discussed a study in which participants were told two people had paid a $100 nonrefundable deposit for a weekend at a resort. On the way there, they both became slightly unwell, and felt they would probably have a more pleasurable time at home than at the resort. Should they drive on or turn back? Many participants argued that the two people should drive on to avoid wasting the $100 – this is the sunk-cost effect. This decision involves extra expenditure (money spent at the resort vs. staying at home) and is less preferred than being at home!

Why did many participants make the apparently poor decision to continue with the trip? They thought it would be hard to explain to themselves and other people why they had wasted $100. The importance of being able to justify one's actions may help to explain why children and several animal species (e.g., blackbirds, mice) are much less affected than adult humans by the sunk-cost effect (Arkes & Ayton, 1999). We are much smarter than other species but they don't feel the need to justify their decisions to other members of the same species.

Emotional factors

Why are we so sensitive to potential losses? According to Shiv et al. (2005), emotions (e.g., anxiety) can make us excessively cautious and risk-averse. That led them to the startling prediction that brain-damaged patients would *outperform* healthy individuals on a gambling task provided the brain damage reduced their emotional experience.

There were three groups of participants in Shiv et al.'s (2005) study. One group consisted of patients with brain damage in areas related to emotion

Key Term

Sunk-cost effect: the finding that individuals who have invested effort, time, or money to little avail tend to invest more resources in the hope of justifying the previous investment; it corresponds to "throwing good money after bad."

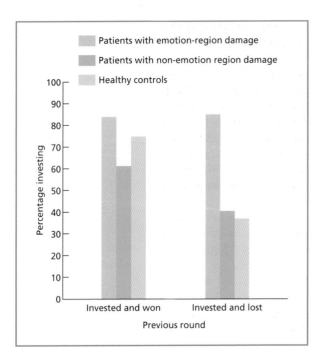

Figure 11.5 Percentage of rounds in which patients with damage to emotion regions of the brain, patients with damage to other regions of the brain, and healthy controls decided to invest $1 having won or lost on the previous round. Data from Shiv et al. (2005).

(amygdala, orbitofrontal cortex, and insular or somatosensory cortex). The other groups consisted of patients with brain damage in areas unrelated to emotion and of healthy controls.

Shiv et al. (2005) initially provided participants with $20. On each of 20 rounds, they decided whether to invest $1. If they did, they lost the $1 if a coin came up heads but won $1.50 if it came up tails. Participants stood to make an average gain of 25 cents per round if they invested compared to simply retaining the $1. Thus, the best strategy to maximize profit was to invest on every single round.

Patients with damage to emotion regions invested in 84% of the rounds compared to only 61% for the other patient group and 58% for the healthy controls. Thus, the patients with restricted emotions performed best. Why was this? Patients with brain damage related to emotion were totally unaffected in their investment decisions by the outcome of the previous round (see Figure 11.5). In contrast, patients with brain damage unrelated to emotion and healthy controls were much less likely to invest following loss on the previous round than following gain.

De Martino et al. (2010) studied loss aversion in two women (SM and AP). Both had suffered severe damage to the amygdala, which is associated with fear. Neither of these women showed evidence of loss aversion. This suggests that loss aversion depends on fear. In the words of De Martino et al. (2010), the amygdala may act as a "cautionary brake."

Talmi et al. (2010) studied the framing effect (discussed earlier) in two female twins with severe damage to the amygdala. The framing effect in these twins was comparable to that found in healthy individuals, suggesting it doesn't depend on the amygdala. Fear may not be a major factor with the framing effect because the participants don't suffer any personal losses.

In sum, emotional factors often play an important role in loss aversion but perhaps not in the framing effect. More specifically, emotional states (especially anxiety) lead individuals to become more loss-averse. This helps to clarify why most individuals are more sensitive to losses than to gains.

Emotions don't *always* impair decision making. Seo and Barrett (2007) found using an Internet-based stock investment simulation that stock investors who experienced more intense feelings had superior decision-making performance to those with less intense feelings. Perhaps the relevant expertise of the participants made it easier for them to prevent their emotional states from biasing their decision making.

SOCIAL CONTEXT

Philip Tetlock (2002) pointed out that participants in most laboratory studies on decision making don't feel accountable to others for the decisions they make. In contrast, our decision making in everyday life is strongly influenced by the social and cultural context in which we live. Of particular importance, we often feel the need to *justify* our decisions to other people, as noted above.

Evidence that the social context is important was reported by Camerer et al. (1997). They examined factors determining how long New York cab drivers decide to work. From a purely economic perspective, the cab driver should work fewer hours when business is slack and longer hours when business is good. In fact, many cab drivers did the opposite. They set themselves a target income for each day and stopped work after reaching it. As a result, they worked unnecessarily long hours when business was poor and missed out on easy money on days when business was good. However, other research suggests that most New York cab drivers work a fairly constant number of hours each day (Farber, 2005).

If the social context is important, accountability should influence decision making. Precisely that was found by Simonson and Staw (1992) in a study on the sunk-cost effect. Some participants were told their decisions would be shared with other students and instructors (high-accountability condition), whereas others were told their decisions would be confidential (low-accountability condition). Participants in the high-accountability condition were more likely to continue with their previously ineffective course of action and thus showed a stronger sunk-cost effect. This occurred because they experienced a greater need to justify their previous decisions.

Accountability pressures can influence the decisions of experts. In a study by Schwartz et al. (2004), medical experts decided on the appropriate treatment for a patient with osteoarthritis. Their decision making was more biased when they were made accountable for their decision by writing an explanation for it and agreeing to be contacted later to discuss it.

In sum, decision making is influenced by social context. That is so in spite of the fact that most relevant research has involved laboratory tasks not making any real demands on social responsibility. There are probably large individual differences in the extent to which people feel the need to justify themselves to others, but little is known about this as yet.

Section Summary

Omission bias

- Omission bias (which involves a preference for risking harm from inaction rather than action) is extremely common and has been found in medical experts and gamblers. It is due to anticipated responsibility and regret. Some individuals use the heuristic, "Don't just sit there. Do something," and show the opposite to omission bias.

Losses and gains

- According to prospect theory, most people show loss aversion – they are much more sensitive to potential losses than to potential gains. The framing effect (in which decisions are influenced by irrelevant aspects of the situation) and the sunk-cost effect (in which good money is thrown after bad) are consistent with the theory. Our sensitivity to potential losses occurs in part because our emotions (especially fear) make us cautious and risk-averse.

Social context
- In the real world, our decision-making is influenced by the social context and by our need to justify our decisions to other people. Decision making sometimes becomes more biased when there is increased accountability for decisions.

COMPLEX DECISION MAKING

So far we have focused mainly on decision making applied to fairly simple problems. In real life, however, we sometimes confront important decisions. For example, medical experts make diagnostic decisions that can literally be a matter of life or death. Other decisions are both important and complex (e.g., Shall I get married? Shall I move to Canada?). How do we deal with such decisions?

The focus in this section is on the strategies we use when making complex decisions. In an ideal world, we would obtain all the relevant information and then make the best decision. Is this true of the real world?

Herb Simon (1957) argued that the answer to the above question is "No." According to him, our decision making typically possesses **bounded rationality** – it is as rational as our processing limitations permit. More specifically, our decision making is "bounded" by constraints in the environment (e.g., information costs) and by constraints in the mind (e.g., limited attention; limited memory). As a result, we produce reasonable solutions to problems by using various heuristics or rules of thumb.

We will consider various influential theories of complex decision making. Most of these theories are based on the assumption that limitations in our information-processing capacity mean that our decisions are only approximately correct.

According to multiattribute utility theory (Wright, 1984), a decision maker should go through the following stages:

1. Identify attributes relevant to the decision;
2. Decide how to weight those attributes;
3. Obtain a total utility (i.e., subjective desirability for each option by summing its weighted attribute values);
4. Select the option with the highest weighted total.

Key Term

Bounded rationality: thinking and decision making are only partially rational because of limited processing resources and complex environments; as a result, **heuristics** are often used.

We can see how multiattribute utility theory works in practice by considering someone deciding which apartment to rent. First, consideration is paid to the relevant attributes (e.g., number of rooms; location; rent per week). Second, the relative utility of each attribute is calculated. Third, the various apartments being considered are compared in terms of their total utility, and the person chooses the one with the highest total utility. In reality, most people's decision making falls short of the thorough processing of information assumed within multiattribute utility theory.

Tversky (1972) put forward elimination-by-aspects theory, which is based on the assumption that humans possess bounded rationality. According to this theory, decision makers eliminate options by considering one relevant attribute after another. For example, someone buying a house may initially consider the attribute of geographical location, eliminating all houses outside a given area. They may then consider the attribute of price, eliminating all properties costing above a certain figure. This process continues attribute by attribute until only one option remains. This is a fairly undemanding strategy. However, it has a major limitation: The *order* in which the attributes are considered can influence the final decision.

Simon (1978) emphasized the importance of **satisficing** (formed from the words satisfy and suffice). The essence of satisficing is that individuals consider various options one at a time and select the first one meeting their minimum requirements.

Alas, satisficing doesn't guarantee that our decisions will be the best ones. However, it is easy to use and is especially valuable when the options become available at different points in time. An example would be the vexed issue of deciding who to marry. Someone using the satisficing heuristic would set a minimum acceptable level, and the first person reaching (or exceeding) that level would be chosen. Of course, if you set the level too low, you may spend many years bitterly regretting having used the satisficing heuristic!

FINDINGS

In one study (Payne, 1976), people decided which apartment to rent on the basis of information about attributes such as rent, cleanliness, noise level, and distance from campus. When there were many apartments to consider, people typically started by using a simple strategy such as elimination-by-aspects and satisficing. When only a few apartments remained in contention, there was often a switch to a more complex strategy corresponding to the assumptions of multiattribute utility theory.

How do women make decisions about men they would like to date? Lenton and Stewart (2008) asked single women to make selections from a real dating website with 4, 24, or 64 potential mates. Unsurprisingly, the women shifted from complex to simple strategies as the number of men on the website increased. The weighted averaging strategy assumed by multiattribute utility theory was used by 81% of the women with four potential mates but by only 41% choosing from 64. The respective figures for the elimination-by-aspects strategy were 39% and 69%, and for the satisficing strategy were 6% and 16%. (The numbers add up to more than 100% because many women used more than one strategy.)

Kathleen Galotti (2002) put forward a theory of decision making based on five phases (see Figure 11.6). The five phases are as follows: setting goals; gathering information; structuring the decision (i.e., listing options + the criteria for deciding among them); making a final choice; and evaluating the decision. As the Figure shows, there is *flexibility* in terms of the order of the phases, and many decision makers return to previous phases if they find it hard to make a decision.

A key phase is that of structuring the decision. Galotti (2007) discussed five studies concerned with important real-life decisions (e.g., students choosing

Key Term
Satisficing: in decision making, a **heuristic** that involves selecting the first option that satisfies the individual's minimum requirements; formed from the words "satisfactory" and "sufficing."

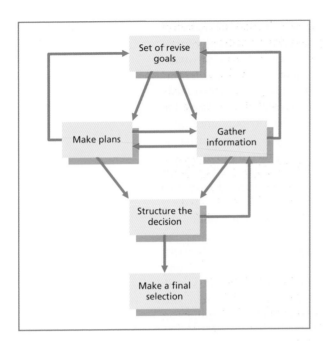

Figure 11.6 The five phases of decision making according to Galotti's theory. Note the flexibility in the ordering of the phases. From Galotti (2002).

a college; college students choosing their main subject). There were several findings:

1. Decision makers constrained the amount of information they considered, focusing on between two and five options (mean = four) at any given time.
2. The number of options under consideration decreased over time.
3. The number of criteria or attributes considered at any given time was between three and nine (mean = six).
4. The number of criteria or attributes being considered didn't decrease over time; sometimes it actually *increased*.

What can we conclude from Galotti's (2007) study? The most striking finding is that people consistently limited the amount of information (options and attributes) they considered. This is inconsistent with multiattribute utility theory but as predicted by Simon's (1957) notion of bounded rationality. In addition, the number of options considered decreased by 18% over a period of several months. A reduction is predicted by Tversky's (1972) elimination-by-aspects theory. However, the actual reduction seems smaller than expected on that theory.

Similar findings to those of Galotti (2007) were reported by Galotti and Tinkelenberg (2009) in a study on parents choosing a first-grade school placement for their child. The parents focused on a restricted number of options (typically three out of the eight (+) potentially available, and they generally considered only about five criteria or attributes at any given time. However, the parents' decision making was *dynamic* over time – over a 6-month period, one-third of the options and over half of the criteria changed on average.

CHANGING PREFERENCES AND FACTS

It was assumed within multiattribute utility theory that a given individual's assessment of the utility or preference (desirability × importance) of any given attribute remains *constant*. In fact, our preferences can easily be changed in ways that are rather irrational.

Simon et al. (2004) asked participants to decide between job offers from two department store chains: "Bonnie's Best" and "Splendor." There were four relevant attributes (salary, holiday package, commute time, and office accommodation). Each job offer was preferable to the other on two attributes and inferior on two attributes.

Participants assessed their preference for each attribute. They were next told that one job was in a much better location than the other, which often tipped the balance in favor of choosing the job in the better location. The participants then assessed their preference for each attribute again. Preferences for desirable attributes of the chosen job increased and preferences for undesirable attributes of that job decreased.

Decisions can even cause people to misremember factual information used during decision making. Advanced nursing students prioritized a male or a female patient for surgery because there were only sufficient resources for one operation (Svenson et al., 2009). After the students had made their decision, their memory for some of the objective facts (e.g., life expectancy without surgery; probability of surviving surgery) was distorted to increase the apparent support for that decision.

Section Summary

- Decision making typically possesses bounded rationality. The elimination-by-aspects theory is based on the assumption of bounded rationality, as is Simon's notion of the satisficing heuristic.

Findings
- People limit the number of options and attributes they consider when making complex real-life decisions. They are more likely to use the elimination-by-aspects or satisficing strategies when the number of options is large than when it is small. There are often dynamic changes in the precise options and criteria under active consideration during decision making.

Changing preferences
- Some aspects of decision making are irrational. For example, our preferences can be changed merely by altering the order in which information is presented to us. After making a decision, we often misremember some of the relevant information so as to increase the apparent support for that decision.

DEDUCTIVE REASONING

Reasoning involves drawing inferences from the knowledge we possess. This is something we do very often in everyday life. For example, I know that Nancy is always punctual on special occasions, and that today's party is a special occasion. This allows me to draw the inference that Nancy will turn up on time.

Our main focus will be on deductive reasoning. **Deductive reasoning** involves drawing conclusions that are definitely valid (or invalid) provided that other statements (**premises**) are assumed to be true. Most deductive-reasoning problems are based on formal logic. However, most people do *not* use traditional logic when presented with a problem in deductive reasoning.

SYLLOGISTIC REASONING

Studies on deductive reasoning often involve syllogisms. A **syllogism** consists of two premises or statements followed by a conclusion. When presented with a syllogism, you have to decide whether the conclusion is valid in light of the premises. The validity (or otherwise) of the conclusion depends *only* on whether it follows logically from the premises. The truth or falsity of the conclusion in

Key Terms

Deductive reasoning: an approach to reasoning in which conclusions can be categorized as valid or invalid given that certain statements or premises are assumed to be true; **conditional reasoning** and syllogistic reasoning are forms of deductive reasoning.

Premises: in **deductive reasoning**, statements that participants are instructed to assume are true.

Syllogism: a type of problem used in studies on **deductive reasoning**; there are two statements or **premises** and a conclusion that may or may not follow logically from the premises.

Research Activity 11.4: *Syllogisms*

Test your powers of deductive reasoning by studying the syllogisms below and deciding which conclusions are valid (these syllogisms are taken from Manktelow, 1999, p. 64). Remember the task involves deciding whether the conclusions follow *logically* from the premises and NOT how sensible the conclusions appear in the real world.

1. *Premises*
   All the athletes are healthy.
   Some healthy people are wealthy.
   Conclusion
   Some of the athletes are wealthy.
2. *Premises*
   All the students are poor.
   No students are stupid.
   Conclusion
   Some poor people are not stupid.
3. *Premises*
   All the men are healthy.
   Some healthy people are women.
   Conclusion
   Some of the men are women.

4. *Premises*
   All the monks are men.
   No monks are women.
   Conclusion
   Some men are not women.

Did you decide that the conclusions to syllogisms 1 and 2 are valid, whereas those to Syllogisms 3 and 4 are invalid? Hopefully, you didn't! In fact, the conclusions to Syllogisms 2 and 4 are valid, whereas those to Syllogisms 1 and 3 are invalid. Syllogisms 1 and 3 have the same structure. However, it is harder to believe that the conclusion of Syllogism 1 is invalid because it is believable. In similar fashion, Syllogisms 2 and 4 have the same structure, but it is harder to decide that the conclusion to Syllogism 4 is valid because it is less believable.

Most people are affected by the believability of syllogism conclusions. **Belief bias** refers to the tendency to accept believable conclusions and to reject unbelievable ones irrespective of their logical validity or invalidity. Evidence concerning the extent of belief bias was reported by Evans et al. (1983; see Figure 11.7). Explanations for belief bias will be discussed shortly.

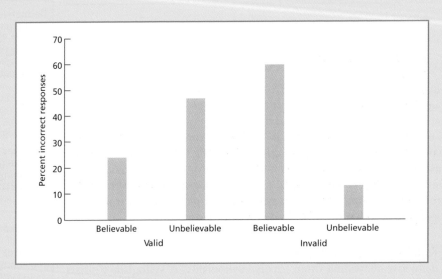

Figure 11.7   Percentage of children performing at a high level on the transfer test (13 or more out of 15) as a function of age (8 vs. 9) and previous relevant training (control vs. experimental). Data from Chen and Klahr (1999).

the real world is irrelevant. Thus, for example, the conclusion of the following syllogism is valid even though it is obviously untrue in the real world:

Premises
Aristotle was a giraffe.
All giraffes have very long necks.

Conclusion
Aristotle had a very long neck.

CONDITIONAL REASONING

Conditional reasoning is a form of deductive reasoning in which people decide on the validity of "If … then" statements. It had its origins in propositional logic, and involves propositions. These are the meanings conveyed by a sentence asserting or denying something, which can thus be true or false.

Note that the meanings of words and propositions in propositional logic differ from those in everyday language. For example, consider the proposition, "It is raining." In propositional logic, this proposition *must* be true or false. In everyday life, on the other hand, there would be uncertainty if it wasn't really raining but it was so misty you could almost call it raining.

Here is another example. In an "If … then" statement, the typical expectation is that the if-part of the statement occurs *before* the then-part (e.g., "If it rains, then I will get wet"). However, our everyday understanding of language can lead to the opposite time order. For example, most people interpret "If the shelf collapsed, then someone put a heavy object on it" as meaning the then-part preceded the if-part (Byrne & Johnson-Laird, 2009).

Differences of meaning between propositional logic and ordinary language are especially great with respect to "if … then." Consider the following, which involves *affirmation of the consequent*:

Premises
If Susan is angry, then I am upset.
I am upset.
Conclusion
Therefore, Susan is angry.

Do you accept the above conclusion as valid? Many people would, but it is *not* valid according to propositional logic. The explanation is as follows: I may be upset for some other reason (e.g., I have lost my credit cards).

Two of the most important rules of inference in conditional reasoning are *modus ponens* and *modus tollens*, both of which are associated with valid conclusions. Here is an example of *modus ponens*:

Premises
If it is raining, then Nancy gets wet.
It is raining.

Conclusion
Nancy gets wet.
Here is an example of *modus tollens*:

Key Terms

Belief bias:
in syllogistic reasoning, mistakenly accepting believable conclusions that are invalid and rejecting unbelievable ones that are valid.

Conditional reasoning: a form of **deductive reasoning** in which an "if … then" statement is followed by a conclusion that is logically valid or invalid.

Premises
If it is raining, then Nancy gets wet.
Nancy does not get wet.

Conclusion
It is not raining.

People consistently perform much better with *modus ponens* than with *modus tollens*. At least part of the reason is that people generally find it harder to deal with negative than with positive information.

Another inference in conditional reasoning is *denial of the antecedent*:

Premises
If it is raining, then Nancy gets wet.
It is not raining.

Conclusion
Therefore, Nancy does not get wet.

Many people argue that the above conclusion is valid, but it is actually invalid. It does not have to be raining for Nancy to get wet. For example, she may have jumped into a swimming pool.

We have seen that people often make mistakes in conditional reasoning. Additional evidence that we have only limited ability to reason logically comes from studies involving the addition of contextual information to a problem. Context (which is irrelevant to the underlying logic) can greatly impair performance on conditional reasoning tasks. Byrne (1989) compared conditional reasoning under standard conditions with a context condition. This additional context is in brackets:

If she has an essay to write, then she will study late in the library.
(If the library stays open, then she will study late in the library)
She has an essay to write.
Therefore, ?

Byrne (1989) found that additional context led to a dramatic reduction in performance with *modus ponens* and *modus tollens*. Thus, we are greatly influenced by contextual information irrelevant to logical reasoning.

De Neys et al. (2005) considered conditional-reasoning performance in individuals high and low in **working memory capacity**, a dimension closely related to intelligence (see Chapter 4). As predicted, the performance of high-capacity individuals was better than that of low-capacity individuals.

Bonnefon et al. (2008) explored individual differences in more detail. Their main focus was on conditional reasoning involving *modus tollens*, denial of the antecedent, and affirmation of the consequent. They argued that there are two processing systems individuals might use to solve conditional reasoning problems. System 1 is rapid and fairly automatic whereas System 2 is slower and more demanding. These two systems (resembling those proposed by Kahneman & Frederick, 2005; see Chapter 10) are discussed in more detail later.

| Key Term

Working memory capacity:
an assessment of how much information can be processed and stored at the same time; individual differences in this capacity are associated with differences in intelligence and attentional control.

Bonnefon et al. (2008) identified four major processing strategies on the basis of participants' performance:

1. *Pragmatic strategy* (System 1): This involves processing the problems as they would be processed informally during a conversation. This strategy was associated with numerous errors.
2. *Semantic strategy* (System 1): This involves making use of background knowledge but not of the form of argument in the problem. This strategy was associated with moderate performance.
3. *Inhibitory strategy* (System 2): This involves inhibiting the impact of the pragmatic strategy and background knowledge on performance. This strategy only worked well with some types of problems.
4. *Generative strategy* (System 2): This involves combining the inhibitory strategy with use of abstract analytic processing. This strategy produced consistently good performance on all problems.

WASON SELECTION TASK

The most studied reasoning task is Wason's selection task, named after the late British psychologist Peter Wason who devised it. You are shown four cards (see Figure 11.8). There is a rule that applies to these cards: "If there is a vowel on one side, then there is an even number on the other side." Decide which cards you need to turn over to decide if the rule is true. If you aren't familiar with this task, think what your answer would be.

The most common answer by far is to select the A and 2 cards. Alas, if you did the same, you got the answer wrong! In fact, you need to see whether any cards *fail* to obey the rule. From this perspective, the 2 card is irrelevant – if there is a vowel on the other side of it, this only tells us the rule *might* be correct. If there is a consonant, we have also discovered nothing about the validity of the rule.

What is the right answer? It involves selecting the A and 7 cards, an answer given by only 5%–10% of university students (Wason, 1968). The 7 is necessary because it would definitely disprove the rule if it had a vowel on the other side.

Figure 11.8 Rule: If there is a vowel on one side of the card, then there is an even number on the other side.

Findings

Why do most people perform poorly on the Wason selection task? One reason is that people find it harder to reason with abstract items (e.g., A; 4) than with concrete ones with which they are more familiar. Wason and Shapiro (1971) used four cards (Manchester, Leeds, car, train) and the rule, "Every time I go to Manchester I travel by car" with British students. The task was to select only those cards needing to be turned over to test the rule. The correct answer (i.e., *Manchester*; *train*) was given by 62% of the participants against only 12% given the standard abstract version of the task.

Another reason for poor performance is **matching bias** (the tendency to select cards matching the items named in the rule regardless of whether they are correct). Ball et al. (2003) used the following problems, with the percentage of participants choosing each card in brackets:

1. Rule: If A then 3
   Cards: A (87%) J (7%) 3 (60%) 7 (3%)
2. Rule: If E then not 5
   Cards: E (83%) L (23%) 2 (13%) 5 (43%)

As you can see, cards matching items in the rule were selected much more often than cards not matching items for both rules. This provides strong evidence for matching bias. Note that selecting the number "3" in Problem 1 is incorrect, whereas selecting the number "5" in Problem 2 is correct.

How can we improve performance on the Wason selection task? A major reason for poor performance is the failure to try to falsify the rule, and so performance should improve if participants are motivated to disprove the rule. This prediction was tested by Dawson et al. (2002). They gave some participants the rule that individuals high in emotional lability experience an early death. There were four cards referring to individuals. One side indicated whether the person was high or low in emotional lability and the other side indicated whether they experienced an early or a late death. What the participants could see on the tops of the cards was as follows: low emotional lability; high emotional lability; early death; late death.

The correct answer was to select the high emotional lability and late death cards. Of participants low in emotional lability (and so having no powerful reason to disprove the rule), only 9% solved the problem. In contrast, of those participants high in emotional lability, 38% solved the problem because they were highly motivated to disprove the rule.

Munro and Stansbury (2009) replicated the above findings. They also discovered that making participants high in emotional lability feel good about themselves reduced their motivation to disprove the rule and impaired their performance.

We can also persuade people to try to disprove the rule by using a deontic rule (e.g., "If there is a p then you *must* do q"). **Deontic rules** are concerned with detection of rule violation (e.g., involving cheating) and so focus participants' attention on the importance of trying to disprove rules.

Sperber and Girotto (2002) gave some participants a deontic version of the selection task. Paolo buys things through the Internet but is concerned he will be cheated. For each order, he fills out a card. On one side of the card, he indicates whether he has received the item ordered, and on the other side he indicates whether he has paid for the items ordered. He places four orders, and what is visible on the four cards is as follows: "item paid for," "item not paid for," "item received," and "item not received."

Which cards does Paolo need to turn over to decide whether he has been cheated? Sperber and Girotto found that 68% of their participants made the correct choices (i.e., "item paid for"; "item not received").

In sum, many participants perform poorly on the Wason selection task because they use simple strategies such as matching bias or trying to confirm the rule. Performance improves greatly when steps are taken to increase participants' focus on the possible falsity of the rule and the need to try to disprove it.

THEORIES OF REASONING

Many theories of deductive reasoning have been put forward over the years (Evans, 2008). In this section, I will consider two of the most important theoretical approaches. First, there is the mental model approach of Johnson-Laird. Second, there is Evans' heuristic-analytic model.

Mental models

Phil Johnson-Laird (e.g., 1983, 2004) assumes that the processes involved in reasoning resemble those involved in language comprehension. So what?, you may be thinking. In fact, this assumption has important implications. First, it implies that when we consider a reasoning problem, we don't immediately switch on cognitive processes specialized for logical thinking. Instead, we use processes closely resembling those you are using to understand this paragraph.

Second, when we read some text or engage in reasoning, we typically focus on what the writer is telling us. We focus on what *is* the case rather than on what is *not* the case. More specifically, we construct a **mental model**, which represents a possible state of affairs in the world. For example, a tossed coin has an infinite number of possible trajectories, but there are only two mental models: heads; tails. Mental models generally represent what is true and ignore what is false – this is known as the **principle of truth**.

Here is a more complex example of a mental model:

Premises
The lamp is on the right of the pad.
The book is on the left of the pad.
The clock is in front of the book.
The vase is in front of the lamp.

Conclusion
The clock is to the left of the vase.

Johnson-Laird (1983) assumed that people use the information contained in the premises (statements assumed to be true) to construct a mental model:

book	pad	lamp
clock		vase

Key Terms
Mental model: used in reasoning, an internal or mental representation of some possible situation or event in the world.
Principle of truth: including what is true but omitting what is false from a mental representation or **mental model**.

The conclusion that the clock is to the left of the vase clearly follows from the mental model. The fact that we can't construct a mental model consistent with the premises but inconsistent with the conclusion indicates that it is valid.

How do we set about constructing mental models? We use the limited processes of working memory (a system combining attentional processes and temporary storage; see Chapter 4). If we can't construct a mental model that falsifies the conclusion, we assume that it is valid. It is demanding to construct mental models. As a result, we follow the **principle of parsimony** (economy): "individuals tend to construct only a single, simple, and typical model" (Jahn et al., 2007, p. 2076).

How can we test the assumption that the limited capacity of working memory is needed to construct mental models? If the assumption is correct, people should find it harder to solve reasoning problems as the number of mental models consistent with the premises increases. This assumption was confirmed by Copeland and Radvansky (2004). Eighty-six per cent of people drew the valid conclusion when the premises only allowed the generation of one mental model. This figure dropped to 39% when two mental models were possible and to 31% with three mental models.

It follows from the theory that syllogistic reasoning should be better in individuals having high working memory capacity than in those with low capacity. That is precisely what Copeland and Radvansky (2004) found.

Jahn et al. (2007) tested the principle of parsimony (the notion that people often construct only a *single* mental model). They presented participants with a series of statements and they decided whether all the statements were consistent with each other. Here is an example:

A table is between the TV and a chair.
The light is on the left of the TV.
The table is next to the light.

Are the above statements all consistent with each other? They are consistent, but many individuals in the study by Jahn et al. (2007) said, "No." What they did was to construct a *single* mental model like this:

light TV table chair
[table can't be next to the light]

If they had ignored the principle of parsimony, they would have constructed an alternative mental model in which the statements were all consistent:

chair table light TV

There are large individual differences in reasoning strategies. Bucciarelli and Johnson-Laird (1999) identified the initial strategies used by people given reasoning problems by videotaping them as they evaluated valid and invalid syllogisms. Some participants initially formed a mental model of the first premise, to which they then added information based on the second premise. Others proceeded in the opposite direction, and still others constructed an initial mental model satisfying the conclusion and then tried to show it was wrong.

| Key Term

Principle of parsimony: in **deductive reasoning**, the tendency to form only one mental model even when additional ones could be constructed.

Evaluation

⊕ Many reasoning errors occur because people use the principle of parsimony (Jahn et al., 2007) and the principle of truth (Johnson-Laird, 2004) when they are inappropriate.

⊕ The notion that reasoning involves similar processes to language comprehension is a powerful one.

⊕ Reasoning performance is constrained by the limitations of working memory.

⊖ It is not very clear how we decide which pieces of information to include in our mental models.

⊖ The theory doesn't fully explain the existence of large individual differences in reasoning strategies.

Heuristic-analytic theory

Jonathan Evans (2006) put forward a theory of reasoning differing from mental model theory in two important ways. First, there is more emphasis on the use of world knowledge and the immediate context in reasoning. Second, there is less emphasis on the use of deductive reasoning. According to Evans' heuristic-analytic theory, human reasoning is based on three principles:

1. *Singularity principle:* Only a *single* mental model is considered at any given time.
2. *Relevance principle:* The most *relevant* (i.e., plausible or probable) mental model based on prior knowledge and the current context is considered.
3. *Satisficing principle:* The current mental model is evaluated and accepted if adequate. Use of this principle often leads people to accept conclusions that might be true but are not necessarily so.

What happens in more detail? First, when someone is presented with a reasoning problem, relatively simple heuristic processes use task features, the current goal, and background knowledge to construct a single hypothetical possibility or mental model. Second, time-consuming and effortful analytic processes may or may not intervene to revise or replace this mental model. These analytic processes are most likely to be used by highly intelligent individuals and when sufficient time is available.

A very useful phenomenon for distinguishing between heuristic and analytic processes is belief bias (discussed earlier; see Glossary and Chapter 12). This bias occurs when a conclusion that is logically valid but not believable is rejected as invalid, or a conclusion that is logically invalid but believable is accepted as valid. The presence or absence of this effect depends on a conflict between heuristic processes based on belief and analytic processes. Belief bias is stronger when only heuristic processes are used than when analytic ones are also used.

The use of analytic processes while reasoning can be reduced by requiring participants to perform a demanding secondary task along with the reasoning task. De Neys (2006) used belief-bias problems involving a conflict between validity and believability of the conclusion and requiring analytic processing for successful reasoning. There were also nonconflict problems that could be solved simply by using heuristic processes. The reasoning problems were presented on their own or at the same time as a secondary task low or high in its demands. As predicted, a demanding secondary task impaired performance on conflict problems but not nonconflict ones.

Evaluation

⊕ There is convincing evidence for the distinction between heuristic and analytic processes, and for the notion that the latter are more effortful than the former (e.g., De Neys, 2006). Phenomena such as belief bias and matching bias indicate the importance of heuristic processes.

⊕ The general notion that the cognitive processes (e.g., heuristic processes; analytic processes) used by individuals to solve reasoning problems resemble those used in numerous other cognitive tasks is very useful.

⊕ The notion that thinking (including reasoning) is based on the singularity, relevance, and satisficing principles has received support. Most of the errors people make on reasoning problems can be explained by their adherence to these principles.

⊕ The theory accounts for some individual differences in performance on reasoning problems. For example, individuals high in working memory capacity or intelligence perform better than those low in working memory capacity or intelligence because they are more likely to use analytic processes.

⊖ It is assumed that there are several analytic processes (Evans, 2006). However, it is not clear how individuals decide *which* ones to use.

⊖ The notion that the processes used on reasoning tasks can be neatly categorized as heuristic or analytic is an oversimplification (Keren & Schul, 2009).

Section Summary

Syllogistic reasoning

• Syllogistic reasoning involves the use of logic. Many people make errors in syllogistic reasoning because of belief bias. This bias involves focusing on the believability of conclusions rather than their logical validity.

Conditional reasoning

• Conditional reasoning involves the use of logic. Many errors are made in conditional reasoning because most people have a limited ability to think logically and because they are influenced by irrelevant contextual information. Individuals high in working memory capacity perform better in conditional reasoning than those of low capacity.

Wason selection task

- Performance is generally very poor on the Wason selection task because participants rely on simple strategies rather than logical reasoning. Far more correct answers are produced when deontic rules are used because such rules increase participants' attention to the possibility that the rule is false. Performance is also improved when participants are personally motivated to disprove the rule.

Mental models

- According to mental model theory, we construct mental models when reasoning. These models represent what is true and ignore what is false, even when what is false is relevant to solving the problem. Often only a single mental model is formed even when there are other possible mental models. It is unclear within the theory how we decide what information to include within a mental model.

Heuristic-analytic theory

- According to heuristic-analytic theory, reasoners use simple heuristic processes to form a mental model. After that, time-consuming analytic processes are sometimes used to revise or replace this mental model. The distinction between heuristic and analytic processes is oversimplified.

INFORMAL REASONING

Most of the research on deductive reasoning we have discussed is fairly narrow and removed from the informal reasoning of everyday life. **Informal reasoning** involves using one's relevant knowledge to argue persuasively in favor of or against some statement. Such reasoning typically has little or nothing to do with logic. We are exposed to numerous informal arguments by our friends and by politicians. You can obtain a clearer idea of the essence of informal reasoning by looking at Research Activity 11.5.

INFORMAL VS. DEDUCTIVE REASONING

Informal reasoning is clearly different from deductive reasoning. People's ability to identify fallacies in informal reasoning is only weakly associated with their deductive reasoning performance (Ricco, 2003). This suggests that rather different cognitive processes can be involved. However, individuals who are good at overcoming belief bias (see Glossary) in deductive reasoning often perform well at detecting informal fallacies (Ricco, 2007).

The *content* of an argument is important in informal reasoning (and in everyday life) but is (at least in principle) irrelevant in formal deductive reasoning. For example, consider the two following superficially similar arguments (Hahn & Oaksford, 2007):

(a) Ghosts exist because no one has proved they do not.
(b) The drug is safe because we have no evidence that it is not.

| Key Term

Informal reasoning:
a form of reasoning that involves arguments based on one's relevant knowledge and experience; it is prone to error and differs from **deductive reasoning** in not being based on logic.

Research Activity 11.5: *Informal reasoning*

Read the arguments below (taken from Ricco, 2007). Decide which of them contain fallacies or errors in reasoning and the nature of those fallacies.

1. The use of soft drugs should be legalized in the United States because a number of our allies in Europe and Asia have legalized them.
2. It's very likely that UFOs (unidentified flying objects) exist because no one has been able to prove that UFOs do not exist.
3. A lack of discipline in adulthood causes students to become criminals in adulthood because it is known that most adult criminals suffered from a lack of discipline in their childhood.
4. We should require every student to study a foreign language because it is important that we provide our students with a quality education.
5. California should have a mandatory seatbelt law because it is needed. Society needs to have laws that require people to wear seatbelts, even if they do not want to wear them.
6. We must stop the movement for a moment of silence in public schools. Because once you allow a moment of silence it soon becomes a moment of teachers leading prayers, and before long, the schools and the government are supporting a specific religion.

In fact, ALL the above arguments are fallacious. Here are the reasons for each argument in turn:
1. Mere fact that others accept or do something is not sufficient reason.
2. Absence of arguments against a claim is not an argument for the claim.
3. Correlation is not necessarily causation.
4. The reason does not appear to have anything to do with the claim.
5. The reason and the claim are the same or too similar.
6. No reasons given as to why one step would lead to another.

The implausibility of ghosts existing means that most people find the second argument much more persuasive than the first.

Another difference between informal reasoning and deductive reasoning is that *contextual factors* are important in informal reasoning. For example, we are more impressed by arguments on a given topic put forward by an expert than the same arguments proposed by a non-expert (Walton, 2010).

Hahn and Oaksford (2007) provided evidence of a different kind of context effect. They used a scenario in which it was argued that a loud noise indicated that there was an approaching thunderstorm. Participants were more convinced by that argument when the scenario took place in a woodland campsite than when it took place near an airport.

Motivational factors

People confronted by deductive-reasoning problems are supposed to be motivated to reason as logically and accurately as possible. What motivates people engaged in informal reasoning? According to Mercier and Sperber (2011), "The function of reasoning is … to devise and evaluate arguments intended to persuade … Skilled arguers are not after the truth but after arguments supporting their views."

It follows from the above hypothesis that people should exhibit **myside bias**. This is the tendency to evaluate propositions from one's own perspective rather than solely on their merits because this confirms us in the rightness of our views.

Stanovich and West (2007) studied myside bias by presenting contentious (but factually correct) propositions such as the following:

1. College students who drink alcohol while in college are more likely to become alcoholic in later life.
2. The gap in salary between men and women generally disappears when they are employed in the same position.

Students were given the task of rating the accuracy of these propositions.

What did Stanovich and West (2007) find? Students who drank alcohol rated the accuracy of proposition (1) lower than those who didn't. Women rated the accuracy of proposition (2) lower than men. In other words, there was strong myside bias.

Earlier in the chapter we discussed belief bias, which involves accepting believable conclusions that are invalid and rejecting unbelievable conclusions that are valid. Belief bias is regarded as indicative of faulty reasoning within the context of laboratory studies on deductive reasoning. In everyday life, however, the situation is very different (Mercier & Sperber, 2011) – we often *deliberately* strive to confirm our own beliefs in the face of the opposing beliefs of others.

The motivation to find support for one's own views sometimes *improves* reasoning performance. We saw earlier in the discussion of the Wason selection task that the personal relevance of the rule can be very important. Dawson et al. (2002) found that individuals who were strongly motivated to disprove the rule (because it implied that they would die young) showed much more accurate reasoning than individuals lacking such motivation.

There is another way in which motivation influences informal reasoning to a greater extent than formal deductive reasoning. In our everyday lives, we are often influenced by the goals or motives of writers, whereas the writer's goals are ignored on traditional deductive-reasoning tasks. This focus on the writer's goals leads us to draw more *inferences* than we would with traditional tasks. For example, suppose someone writes, "If the Kyoto accord is ratified, greenhouse gases will be reduced." You would probably infer that the writer favors reducing greenhouse gases, and so believe the Kyoto accord should be ratified (Thompson et al., 2005).

What are the effects on reasoning when people focus on the writer's perspective or goals? Thompson et al. (2005) addressed this issue. Conditional reasoning was superior when participants focused on the writer's perspective than when they didn't. For example, the logically valid *modus ponens* and *modus tollens* inferences (discussed earlier) were accepted far more often when participants adopted the writer's perspective. Thus, people can reason more logically than appears from their performance on traditional deductive-reasoning tasks.

Conclusions

In principle, there are several important differences between deductive reasoning and informal reasoning. For example, knowledge of the world is supposed to be completely irrelevant in deductive reasoning but very relevant in informal reasoning. However, the differences are much less marked in practice than in principle. For example, the existence of belief bias in deductive-reasoning tasks

Key Term
Myside bias: in informal reasoning, the tendency to evaluate statements in terms of one's own beliefs and behavior rather than on their merits.

means that many people make use of their knowledge of the world even when they have been told not to do so.

There are other ways in which performance on deductive-reasoning tasks resembles that of informal-reasoning tasks more than might have been imagined. Individuals' personal motives often influence informal reasoning but are supposed to be irrelevant of deductive-reasoning tasks. However, personal motivation has been found to influence performance on the Wason selection task (Dawson et al., 2002). Finally, there is much evidence that contextual factors influence informal reasoning (see below). Such factors also influence deductive reasoning (e.g., Byrne, 1989) even though they are strictly irrelevant.

In sum, the processes involved in deductive and informal reasoning resemble each other in many ways. As a result, many findings from studies on informal reasoning are of relevance to research on deductive reasoning. Future research will undoubtedly clarify the similarities and differences between the processing used on the two types of reasoning tasks.

THEORY OF INFORMAL REASONING

Oaksford and Hahn (2004) put forward a theory of informal reasoning (subsequently developed by Hahn & Oaksford, 2007). In this theory, they identified several factors influencing the perceived strength of a conclusion:

1. degree of previous conviction or belief;
2. positive arguments have more impact than negative arguments;
3. strength of the evidence.

Oaksford and Hahn (2004) studied these factors using scenarios such as the following one:

> *Barbara:* Are you taking digesterole for it?
> *Adam:* Yes, why?
> *Barbara:* Well, because I strongly believe that it does have side-effects.
> *Adam:* It does have side-effects.
> *Barbara:* How do you know?
> *Adam:* Because I know of an experiment in which they found side-effects.

The above scenario possesses strong prior belief (i.e., "strongly believe"), a positive belief (i.e., it does have side-effects), and weak evidence (i.e., one experiment). There were several variations of this scenario, some of which involved a weak prior belief, negative belief (i.e., does not have side-effects), or 50 experiments rather than one.

Participants decided how strongly Barbara should now believe the conclusion that the drug has side-effects. As predicted, the conclusion was most strongly supported when there was a strong previous belief, positive arguments were put forward, and the supporting evidence was strong.

Section Summary

Informal vs. deductive reasoning
• The content of an argument is important in informal reasoning but not in deductive reasoning. Contextual factors are also more important in informal

reasoning. With informal reasoning, people are motivated to try to persuade others of their beliefs and views. Such motivation can produce errors (e.g., belief bias; myside bias). However, it can also lead people to reason more logically in some situations. The differences between the processes involved on informal and deductive-reasoning tasks are much less in practice than in principle.

Theory of informal reasoning

- According to Hahn and Oaksford (2007), the perceived strength of a conclusion in informal reasoning depends on three factors: the strength of the evidence, the degree of prior belief, and whether the arguments are positive or negative. The available evidence supports this theory.

ARE HUMANS RATIONAL?

Most people believe that the thinking and reasoning powers of humans are greatly superior to those of any other species. In other words, we regard ourselves as being a rational species.

However, much of the research discussed in this chapter and the previous one apparently indicates that our thinking and reasoning are often inadequate. The message seems to be that most people are simply *not* rational in their thinking. For example, we often ignore important base-rate information when making judgments, we use heuristics inappropriately, and about 90% of people produce the wrong answer on the standard Wason selection task. In addition, we are very prone to belief bias in syllogistic reasoning, making many errors when valid conclusions are unbelievable or invalid ones are believable.

The pessimistic conclusion that most humans are irrational and illogical has been challenged by many psychologists. Evans (2002) pointed out that participants' understanding of a reasoning problem may differ from the experimenter's. In traditional logic, for example, "If a, then b" is valid except in the case of "a" and "not b." However, the word "if" is ambiguous in natural language, with "If a, then b" meaning "If and only if a, then b." Here is an example. If someone says to you, "If you mow the lawn, I will give you five dollars," you are likely to interpret it to imply, "If you don't mow the lawn, I won't give you five dollars" (Geis & Zwicky, 1971). However, this interpretation isn't consistent with traditional logic.

The goals most people have when engaged in informal reasoning in everyday life differ from those they are supposed to have when performing deductive-reasoning tasks in the laboratory. In everyday life, we generally want to persuade ourselves and other people of the correctness of our beliefs rather than to establish the truth. The opposite is supposed to be the case with deductive reasoning. In fact, the approach that most people take on deductive-reasoning tasks resembles the one they have found to be fairly successful in everyday life when engaged in informal reasoning.

In sum, the poor performance shown by most people on judgment and deductive-reasoning tasks may reflect mainly the artificial nature of laboratory tasks. Of central importance is that we spend much of our time trying to argue persuasively rather than to arrive at the truth (Mercier & Sperber, 2011). This motive often works well in everyday life but is ill-suited to most laboratory tasks on judgment or deductive reasoning.

INTELLIGENCE AND RATIONALITY

Even though *average* performance on most judgment and reasoning tasks is relatively poor, it is still possible that some individuals perform consistently well and exhibit rationality. For example, we might expect that high levels of performance would be achieved by those of high intelligence. In fact, that is only partially true (see Stanovich et al., 2011 for a review). Individuals with high IQs are better than those with low IQs at avoiding belief bias in syllogistic reasoning (Macpherson & Stanovich, 2007) and at producing correct responses on the Wason selection task (Stanovich et al., 2011). However, most of these differences are not large.

There are several other tasks on which individual differences in intelligence are essentially irrelevant. For example, there is scarcely any effect of IQ on myside bias (Macpherson & Stanovich, 2007), the framing effect (Stanovich & West, 2007), and omission bias (Stanovich et al., 2011). Part of the reason may be that motivational and emotional factors have an important influence on these biases.

Stanovich (2009, p. 35) used the term **dysrationalia** to refer to "the inability to think and behave rationally despite having adequate intelligence." Why does dysrationalia occur? According to Stanovich, there are two main factors. First, most people (including those with high IQs) tend to be cognitive misers, meaning that they prefer to solve problems with fast, easy strategies (e.g., heuristics) rather than more accurate but more effortful strategies. Second, most people (again including those with high IQs) sometimes lack the specific knowledge (e.g., about probability or logic) needed to solve a given problem.

Key Term

Dysrationalia: the failure of reasonably intelligent individuals to think and reason in a rational fashion.

Section Summary

- The performance of many people on reasoning problems suggests that their reasoning is often inadequate. However, the artificiality of many of the problems used means that human performance on many reasoning problems may underestimate our ability to think rationally. People spend much of their time trying to argue persuasively rather than to seek out the truth, and this motive can lead to errors in tasks on judgment and deductive reasoning.

Intelligence and rationality

- Highly intelligent individuals perform better than those of less intelligence on some judgment and reasoning tasks. However, there is often no relationship between IQ and performance (e.g., framing effect; omission bias). Intelligent individuals may fail to perform well because of a lack of motivation (cognitive miserliness) or a lack of the specific knowledge required for success.

Essay Questions

1. Why do people use heuristics when making judgments? How effective are such heuristics?
2. Describe and evaluate research showing that most people are more sensitive to potential losses than to potential gains.
3. How do people make complex decisions in everyday life?
4. Compare and contrast the mental models and heuristic-analytic approaches to reasoning.
5. What are some of the main features of informal reasoning?
6. How rational is human thinking and reasoning?

Further Reading

- Evans, J. S. T. (2008). Dual-processing accounts of reasoning, judgment, and social cognition. *Annual Review of Psychology, 59*, 255–278. This chapter by Jonathan Evans gives a succinct account of several dual-processing approaches.
- Johnson-Laird, P. N. (2006). *How we reason*. Oxford, UK: Oxford University Press. Phil Johnson-Laird provides a comprehensive account of reasoning with an emphasis on his mental model theory.
- Mercier, H., & Sperber, D. (2011). Why do humans reason? Arguments for an argumentative theory. *Behavioral and Brain Sciences, 34*, 57–74. In this paper, Mercier and Sperber discuss the motives underlying informal reasoning. It provides insights into the reasons why reasoning often appears biased.
- Newell, B. R., Lagnado, D. A., & Shanks, D. R. (2007). *Straight ahead: The psychology of decision making*. Hove, UK: Psychology Press. This book gives an excellent overview of our current understanding of decision making.
- Shah, A. K., & Oppenheimer, D. M. (2008). Heuristics made easy: An effort-reduction framework. *Psychological Bulletin, 134*, 207–222. The authors make a persuasive case that effort reduction is of central importance with heuristics or rules of thumb.
- Stanovich, K. (2010). *Rationality and the reflective mind*. Oxford: Oxford University Press. Keith Stanovich discusses human rationality at length, including an analysis of the role of intelligence in thinking and reasoning.
- Weber, E. U., & Johnson, E. J. (2009). Mindful judgment and decision making. *Annual Review of Psychology, 60*, 53–85. This paper provides a good overview of recent developments within the fields of judgment and decision making.

Chapter 12

Contents

Cognition and emotion

12

INTRODUCTION

Historically, cognitive psychology was strongly influenced by the computer analogy or metaphor, as can be seen in the emphasis on information-processing models. That approach doesn't lend itself readily to an examination of the relationship between cognition and emotion (especially the effects of emotion on cognition). This is so because it is hard to think of computers as having emotional states.

Most cognitive psychologists ignore the effects of emotion on cognition by trying to ensure their participants are in a relatively neutral emotional state. However, there has been a rapid increase in the number of cognitive psychologists working in the area of cognition and emotion. Examples can be found in research on everyday memory (Chapter 6) and decision making (Chapter 11).

At the most general level, two major issues are central to research on cognition and emotion. First, what are the effects of cognitive processes on our emotional experience? Second, what are the effects of emotion on cognition? For example, what are the consequences of feeling anxious for learning and memory?

Learning Objectives

After studying Chapter 12, you should be able to:

- Discuss the importance of the amygdala in relation to cognition and emotion.
- Discuss how cognition influences emotion, as well as how emotion influences cognition.
- Explain the process model of emotion regulation, specifically how attentional deployment (e.g., distraction, cognitive reappraisal) works.
- Define mood-state-dependent memory, and discuss its implications for how memories are encoded and retrieved.
- Explain how various emotions (e.g., anxiety, sadness, anger) influence human judgment and decision-making processes (e.g., risk aversion; risk taking; optimistic judgments).
- Explain how anxiety is related to attentional and interpretive biases.

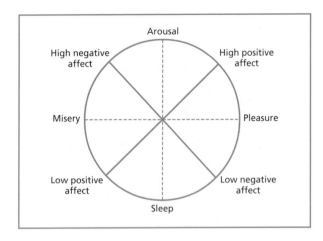

Figure 12.1 The two-dimensional framework for emotion showing the dimensions of pleasure–misery and arousal–sleep (Barrett & Russell, 1998) and the dimensions of positive affect and negative affect (Watson & Tellegen, 1985). Based on Barrett and Russell (1998).

There has been some controversy concerning the structure of emotions. There are two main schools of thought (Fox, 2008). Some theorists (e.g., Izard, 2007) argue we should adopt a *categorical* approach, according to which there are several distinct emotions such as happiness, anger, fear, disgust, and sadness.

The above approach seems to fit our conscious experience. However, other theorists prefer a *dimensional* approach. Barrett and Russell (1998) argued for two uncorrelated dimensions of misery–pleasure and arousal–sleep. In contrast, Watson and Tellegen (1985) favored two uncorrelated dimensions of positive affect and negative affect. In spite of the apparent differences between these two approaches, they refer to the same basic two-dimensional space (see Figure 12.1).

Most emotional states can be fitted within that two-dimensional space. Emotions such as happy and excited fall in the top-right quadrant; contented, relaxed, and calm are in the bottom-right quadrant; depressed and bored are in the bottom-left quadrant; and stressed and tense are in the top-left quadrant.

Watson and Clark (1992) argued that most emotions can be incorporated into a hierarchical structure (see Figure 12.2). Negative Affect and Positive Affect are at the higher level of the hierarchy and more specific emotions are at the lower level.

Watson and Clark (1992) obtained evidence to support their assumptions. Consider, for example, the four negative emotions of fear, sadness, hostility, and guilt. Self-report data showed that these four emotions are distinguishable from each other. In addition, however, these emotions should all contribute to the higher-order negative affect dimension. As predicted, the measures of fear, sadness, hostility, and guilt are all associated or correlated moderately with each other.

A distinction is generally drawn between emotions and moods. *How* do they differ? First, emotions typically last for less time than moods. Second, moods are less intense than emotions and often fail to attract our attention. Third, emotions are generally caused by a specific event (e.g., being shouted at), whereas the reason for being in a given mood is often unclear. However, emotions can create moods and moods can turn into emotions. Thus, there is no sharp distinction between emotions and moods.

Section Summary

- The structure of emotions has been addressed by categorical and dimensional approaches. The two approaches can be reconciled by a hierarchical model with two independent dimensions at the higher level and several specific emotions at the lower level. Emotions differ from moods in being more intense and shorter lasting, and they are triggered by a specific event.

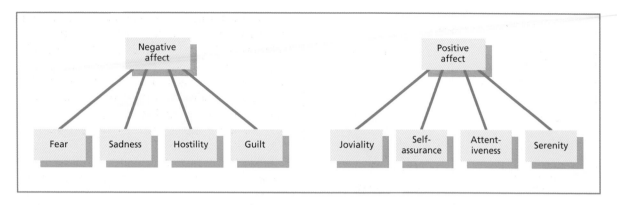

Figure 12.2   A two-level hierarchical model of emotion. Based on Watson and Clark (1992).

HOW DOES COGNITION INFLUENCE EMOTION?

Cognitive processes clearly influence *when* we experience emotional states and *what* particular emotional state we experience in any given situation. For example, suppose you are walking along and someone knocks into you. If you interpret their action as *deliberate*, you would probably experience anger. However, if you interpret their action as *accidental*, you would probably experience much less emotion. In what follows, we consider how cognitive processes influence our emotional states.

COGNITIVE PROCESSES AND THE BRAIN

How do the workings of the cognitive system influence emotional experience? At the most general level, there are two major possibilities. First, the presentation of an aversive stimulus (e.g., photograph of a mutilated body) or a positive stimulus (e.g., photograph of a scene at a party) might produce emotion through low-level bottom-up processes (see Glossary) involving attention and perception.

Second, emotion might be generated through high-level top-down processes (see Glossary) involving stored emotional knowledge. For example, thinking about some future threatening event (e.g., an important examination) can create a state of high anxiety.

Emotional experience typically depends on both bottom-up and top-down processes (Scherer et al., 2001). Ochsner et al. (2009) used brain imaging to explore these two kinds of processes. In the bottom-up condition, participants were presented with aversive photographs and told to view the images and respond naturally to them. In the top-down condition, participants were told to interpret neutral photographs as if they were aversive.

What did Ochsner et al. (2009) find? The brain areas activated in the bottom-up condition included those in the occipital, temporal, and parietal lobes associated with visual perceptual processing. In addition, and most importantly, there was strong activation of the amygdala. The **amygdala** is buried in the front part of the temporal lobe (see Figure 12.3), and is associated

Key Term

Amygdala:
a part of the brain that is strongly associated with several emotions but especially fear or anxiety; it is buried deep within the temporal lobe.

Figure 12.3 Image of the amygdala, a structure that forms part of the limbic system and that is activated in many emotional states. From Ward (2010).

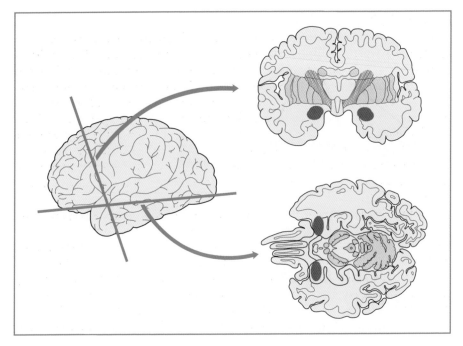

with several emotions (especially fear). The level of self-reported negative affect was associated most strongly with activity in the amygdala.

Ochsner et al. (2009) found that the brain areas activated in the top-down condition differed somewhat from those activated in the bottom-up condition. Top-down processing involved the dorsolateral prefrontal cortex and medial prefrontal cortex, areas associated with high-level cognitive processes. The anterior cingulate and amygdala were also activated. The level of self-reported negative affect was associated most with activation of the medial prefrontal cortex, an area involved in producing cognitive representations of stimulus meaning.

The above findings might suggest that some brain regions (e.g., prefrontal cortex) engage only in cognitive processing whereas other brain regions (e.g., amygdala) are mainly involved in affective processing. This would be an oversimplification. In fact, emotional experience depends on the activation of several brain areas organized into complex networks (Pessoa, 2008).

We have seen that the amygdala plays a role in emotional experience with both bottom-up and top-down processing. The role of the amygdala in emotion was explored in a direct fashion by Calder et al. (1996) and by Scott et al. (1997) in studies on a woman, DR. She had an operation for epilepsy that had caused extensive damage to the amygdala.

When DR described the emotions revealed by various emotional expressions in other people, she was particularly poor at identifying fearful expressions. In another experiment, DR listened to neutral words spoken in various emotional tones and tried to identify the relevant emotion. She was very poor at identifying fear and anger. These findings confirm the importance of the amygdala in emotion.

APPRAISAL APPROACH

Many theorists have argued for the importance of appraisal in determining which emotion we experience in any given situation (Smith & Lazarus, 1993). What is appraisal? It is the evaluation or judgment that we make about situations relevant to our goals, concerns, and wellbeing, and it typically involves top-down processing.

Cognitive appraisal influences whether we experience guilt or anger in a given situation. According to Smith and Lazarus (1993), we experience guilt when the situation is related to our personal commitments, our goals are blocked, and we blame ourselves for what has happened. In contrast, we experience anger when the situation is related to our personal commitments, our goals are blocked, and we blame the other person for what has happened (other accountability).

From what has been said so far, it might seem that appraisal always involves deliberate conscious processing. However, most theorists argue that appraisal can also occur automatically without conscious awareness. For example, Smith and Kirby (2001) distinguished between appraisal based on reasoning (involving deliberate thinking) and appraisal based on activation of memories (involving automatic processes) (see Figure 12.4). Appraisal based on reasoning is slower and more flexible than appraisal based on memory activation. Evidence indicating that emotional experience can result from nonconscious cognitive processing is discussed later.

Findings

Most research in this area has used scenarios in which participants are asked to identify with the central character. The appraisal of any given situation is manipulated across scenarios to observe the effects on emotional experience. One scenario used by Smith and Lazarus (1993) involved a student who had

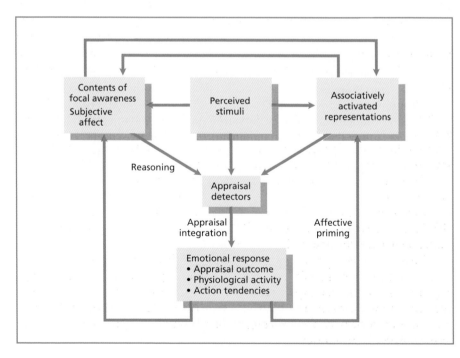

Figure 12.4 Mechanisms involved in the appraisal process. From Smith and Kirby (2001). Copyright © 2001 Oxford University Press. Reprinted with permission.

performed poorly in an examination. Participants reported that he would experience anger when he put the blame on the unhelpful teaching assistants. However, guilt was more common when the student blamed himself (e.g., for doing work at the last minute).

Subsequent research has indicated that any given emotion can be produced by several combinations of appraisals. Kuppens et al. (2003) studied four appraisals (goal obstacle; other accountability: someone else is to blame; unfairness; and control) believed to be relevant to the experience of anger. Participants described recently experienced unpleasant situations in which one of the four appraisals was present or absent. No appraisal component was essential for the experience of anger. Thus, for example, some participants felt angry *without* the appraisal of unfairness or the presence of a goal obstacle.

Tong (2010a) extended the research of Kuppens et al. (2003) by considering the four negative emotions of anger, sadness, fear, and guilt. Participants repeatedly indicated their negative emotions and their associated appraisals in everyday environments. No single appraisal (or combination of appraisals) was necessary or sufficient for the experience of any of the four emotional states.

The appraisal approach can be used to understand individual differences in emotional experience. Consider, for example, the personality dimension of neuroticism. Individuals high in neuroticism experience much more negative affect than low scorers. Tong (2010b) identified two reasons for this in a study on the four negative emotions of anger, sadness, fear, and guilt. First, those high in neuroticism used more negative appraisal styles than low-neuroticism individuals. Second, the relationships between appraisal and experienced emotion were greater among high-neuroticism individuals.

According to appraisal theories, appraisals *cause* emotional states rather than emotional states causing appraisals. However, most research has revealed only an association between appraisals and emotion and so doesn't directly address the issue of causality. Some appraisals may occur *after* a given emotion has been experienced and be used to justify that emotion.

In one study (Berndsen & Manstead, 2007), participants received various scenarios and rated their level of personal responsibility and guilt. The amount of guilt experienced seemed to determine appraisal (personal responsibility), whereas appraisal theories predict that the causality should be in the other direction.

If appraisals do cause emotions, appraisal judgments should be made *faster* than emotion judgments. In fact, however, appraisal judgments are generally made *more slowly* than emotion judgments (Siemer & Reisenzein, 2007). This finding may be less damaging to appraisal theories than it seems. It is possible that appraisal judgments are made very rapidly, but it is time-consuming to make *explicit* appraisal judgments.

Evaluation

➕ Appraisal is often of great importance in influencing emotional experience.

➕ Appraisal processes not only determine whether we experience emotion but also strongly influence which emotion is experienced.

- The links between appraisals and specific emotions are flexible and not especially strong.

- While it is assumed that appraisal causes emotional experience, the causality is probably sometimes in the opposite direction. More generally, appraisal and emotional experience often blur into each other. As Parkinson (2001, p. 181) pointed out, "It seems likely that a willingness to endorse items describing one's helplessness and feelings of loss [appraisal] implies a tendency to agree that one is also sad and sorrowful [emotional experience]."

- The scenario-based approach to appraisal and emotion treats life like a story that needs to be made sense of (Parkinson, 2007). This approach deemphasizes the social context in which most emotion is experienced – emotional experience generally emerges out of *active* social interaction.

NONCONSCIOUS EMOTIONAL PROCESSING

Suppose you were presented with a picture showing someone who had been seriously injured in a car accident. This would almost certainly trigger a negative emotional state in you. Suppose, however, that the same picture was shown very briefly so that you weren't consciously aware of it. Would you still experience a negative emotional state? As was mentioned earlier, Smith and Kirby (2001) argued that appraisal processes can be automatic and below the level of conscious awareness. They thus predicted that the answer to the question is "Yes" – an answer supported by the evidence.

Chartrand et al. (2006) presented positive (e.g., music; friends), negative (e.g., war; cancer), or neutral (e.g., building; plant) words repeatedly below the level of conscious awareness. Participants receiving the negative words reported a more negative mood state than those receiving the positive words.

Öhman and Soares (1994) presented pictures of snakes, spiders, flowers, and mushrooms so rapidly that they couldn't be identified consciously. Some of the participants were spider phobics (intense fear of spiders) and others were snake phobics (intense fear of snakes). The prediction was that pictures *relevant* to the individual's phobia would produce a more negative mood state than those that were irrelevant. That is what they found.

In Chapter 2, we discussed patients with damage to the primary visual cortex, as a result of which they lack conscious visual perception in parts of the visual field. However, they show some ability to respond appropriately to visual stimuli for which they have no conscious awareness (blindsight; see Glossary). Patients with blindsight have been tested for affective blindsight (see Glossary), in which different emotional stimuli can be discriminated in the absence of conscious perception. Several reports indicate the existence of affective blindsight (Tamietto & de Gelder, 2008).

Most research on affective blindsight has involved patients with lack of conscious perception in only part of the visual field. As a result, affective blindsight in these patients may have depended in part on the intact parts of their visual processing system. However, Pegna et al. (2005) studied a 52-year-old man who was entirely cortically blind. When he was presented with happy and angry faces he couldn't perceive consciously, he correctly reported the emotion on 59% of trials.

Pegna et al. (2005) also carried out a brain-imaging study in which the patient was presented with angry, happy, fearful, and neutral faces. There was greater activation in the right amygdala with the emotional faces than with neutral faces, with the greatest activation occurring in response to fearful faces. These findings suggest the patient was responding emotionally to the emotional faces.

Jolij and Lamme (2005) set out to show affective blindsight in healthy individuals. They used transcranial magnetic stimulation (TMS; see Glossary) to produce a brief disruption to functioning in the occipital area (involved in visual perception). On each trial, participants were presented with four faces (three neutral and one happy or sad). When the stimulus array was presented very briefly and followed by TMS, participants had no conscious perceptual experience. However, they were reasonably good at detecting the emotional expression. Thus, the participants showed a form of affective blindsight.

In sum, various emotions can be experienced in the absence of conscious awareness of the stimuli that triggered that emotion. It has also been found that different emotional stimuli can be discriminated without conscious awareness. It is unclear whether the underlying automatic processes should be regarded as appraisal processes.

Section Summary

Cognitive processes and the brain

- Emotional experience depends on bottom-up processes involving the occipital, parietal, and temporal lobes (including the amygdala). It also depends on top-down processes involving the medial and dorsolateral prefrontal cortex, the anterior cingulate, and amygdala.

Appraisal approach

- Cognitive appraisal processes are involved in determining which emotion is experienced in any given situation. Appraisal often involves deliberate conscious processing but can also involve relatively automatic processes. However, the links between appraisal and specific emotions are flexible and fairly weak, and appraisal and emotional experience often blur into each other.

Nonconscious emotional processing

- Stimuli that can't be consciously perceived can nevertheless trigger emotional experience. Patients with affective blindsight can discriminate among different emotional stimuli presented to parts of the visual field for which they lack conscious awareness.

EMOTION REGULATION

Many people feel they have little or no control over their emotions. In fact, however, we can (and do) use a range of cognitive processes to regulate and control our emotional states. This section is concerned with **emotion regulation**, which involves "a deliberate, effortful process that seeks to override people's spontaneous emotional responses" (Koole, 2009, p. 6).

There are many ways we can regulate emotion. As discussed earlier, we can use cognitive reappraisal to modify our emotional experience. Other emotion-regulation strategies include: controlled breathing; progressive muscle relaxation; stress-induced eating; and distraction (Koole, 2009).

Key Term
Emotion regulation: the use of deliberate and effortful processes to change a spontaneous emotional state (usually a negative one); examples of emotion regulation include cognitive reappraisal, use of distraction, and controlled breathing.

PROCESS MODEL

Gross and Thompson (2007) put forward a process model that allows us to categorize emotion-regulation strategies (see Figure 12.5). It is based on the crucial assumption that emotion-regulation strategies can be used at various points in time. For example, individuals suffering from social anxiety can regulate their emotional state by avoiding potentially stressful social situations (situation selection).

There are several other emotion-regulation strategies that socially anxious individuals can use. For example, they can change social situations by asking a friend to accompany them (situation modification). Alternatively, they can use attentional processes by, for example, focusing on pleasant distracting thoughts (attention deployment).

Socially anxious individuals can also use cognitive reappraisal to reinterpret the current situation (cognitive change). Finally, there is response modulation. For example, it is commonly believed it is best to express your angry feelings and so get them "out of your system." Alas, it turns out that expressing anger *increases* rather than decreases angry feelings (Bushman, 2002), because it facilitates the retrieval of angry thoughts.

ATTENTIONAL DEPLOYMENT

It is often claimed that a good way of reducing a negative mood state is via distraction or attending to something else. Much evidence supports that claim (Van Dillen & Koole, 2007).

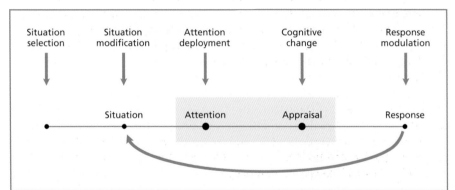

Figure 12.5 A process model of emotion regulation based on five major types of strategy (situation selection; situation modification; attention deployment; cognitive change; and response modulation). From Gross and Thompson (2007). Reproduced with permission from Guilford Press.

How does distraction reduce negative affect? According to Van Dillen and Koole, the working memory system (see Chapter 4) plays a central role. Working memory (involved in the processing and storage of information) has limited capacity. If most of its capacity is devoted to processing distracting stimuli, there is little capacity left to process negative emotional information.

Van Dillen and Koole (2007) tested the above working memory hypothesis. Participants were presented with strongly negative, weakly negative, or neutral photographs. After that, they performed an arithmetic task making high or low demands on working memory. Finally, they completed a mood scale. As predicted, participants' mood state following presentation of strongly negative photographs was less negative when they had just performed a task with high working memory demands than one with low demands.

Van Dillen et al. (2009) replicated the findings of Van Dillen and Koole (2007). In addition, they compared brain activity when task demands were high or low. The more demanding task was associated with greater activation in the prefrontal cortex (involved in working memory) but less activity in the amygdala (involved in fear and other negative emotions). Thus, the more demanding task produced more activation within the working memory system. This led to a dampening of negative emotion at the physiological (i.e., amygdala) and experiential (i.e., self-report) levels.

Rothermund et al. (2008) identified another strategy for emotion regulation that is useful when we feel the need to be cool, calm, and collected. Attentional counter-regulation involves the use of attentional processes to reduce positive and negative emotional states. More specifically, we attend to emotionally positive information when in a negative emotional state and to negative information when in a positive emotional state.

Wentura et al. (2009) obtained evidence of attentional counter-regulation. Participants played a modified version of TETRIS (a computer game in which "bricks" move down the screen and need to be rotated to fill complete rows). Descending bricks were sometimes accompanied by a smiley or sad-looking face. Participants instructed to adopt a positive outcome focus on the game attended more to the sad-looking face, whereas those adopting a negative outcome focus attended more to the smiley face.

COGNITIVE REAPPRAISAL AND DISTRACTION

A major way in which an individual can regulate his/her emotional state is by cognitive reappraisal. This involves "reinterpreting the meaning of a stimulus to change one's emotional response to it" (Ochsner & Gross, 2005, p. 245).

Another important strategy is distraction. Distraction can be behavioral (e.g., switching on the television) or cognitive (e.g., deliberately thinking about something other than the cause of the negative affect).

There is a large literature showing that cognitive reappraisal and distraction can have a considerable impact on the intensity and nature of emotional experience (Power & Dalgleish, 2008). Augustine and Hemenover (2009) carried out a meta-analysis combining the findings from numerous studies. Reappraisal and distraction were on average the most effective strategies for reducing negative affect.

In recent years, brain-imaging studies have served to clarify how cognitive reappraisal influences emotional states. Ochsner and Gross (2008) reviewed brain-imaging studies in which the emphasis was on two types of reappraisal strategy:

1. *Reinterpretation:* This involves changing the meaning of the context in which a stimulus is presented (e.g., imagining a picture has been faked).
2. *Distancing:* This involves taking a detached, third-person perspective.

Regardless of which strategy was used, the prefrontal cortex and the anterior cingulate were consistently activated. These brain areas are associated with executive processes that coordinate processing, and so it appears that emotion regulation involves executive processes.

Another general finding was that reappraisal strategies designed to reduce negative emotional reactions to stimuli produced reduced activation in the amygdala (strongly implicated in emotional responding). This is as predicted given that reappraisal reduces self-reported negative emotional experience. Koenigsberg et al. (2010) provide more details concerning the patterns of brain activation associated with distancing.

In one study (McRae et al., 2010), participants were presented with very negative pictures. They were instructed to use reappraisal (reinterpret the picture to make themselves feel less negative about it) or distraction (focus on remembering a six-letter string).

Both strategies reduced amygdala activation and negative affect, but reappraisal was more effective in reducing negative affect. Reappraisal was associated with greater increases than distraction in activation within the medial prefrontal cortex and anterior temporal regions (associated with processing affective meaning). Reappraisal was likely more effective than distraction because it was associated with more cognitive control of the individual's emotional state.

In sum, progress has been made in understanding why reappraisal is effective in reducing negative emotional states. Higher cognitive control processes associated with the prefrontal cortex are used rapidly and are followed by reduced emotional responses within the amygdala. Thus, cortical and subcortical processes are both heavily involved in successful reappraisal. The precise pattern of brain activation varies across cognitive strategies. This suggests that emotion regulation is complex and involves more different cognitive processes than previously assumed.

Section Summary

- Emotion regulation is the use of deliberate and effortful processes to override the individual's spontaneous emotional reaction. Such regulation can involve situation selection, situation modification, attentional deployment, cognitive change, or response modulation.

Cognitive reappraisal and distraction

- Cognitive reappraisal and distraction are two of the most effective strategies for reducing negative affect. Reappraisal is sometimes more effective than distraction because it involves greater cognitive control of the individual's emotional states.

EFFECTS OF EMOTION ON COGNITION

This section is concerned with the effects of emotion or mood on cognition. Our emotional state affects numerous aspects of cognition including perception, attention, interpretation, learning, memory, judgment, decision making, and reasoning (Blanchette & Richards, 2010). In what follows, we will consider some of the main findings in this area.

Much research in this area involves comparing cognitive processes and performance in groups differing in their mood state. *How* do researchers manipulate mood state? An increasingly popular approach involves asking participants to recall and then write about a personal event in which they experienced a given emotion. For example, Griskevicius et al. (2010) produced feelings of attachment love in some of their participants by telling them to write about a situation "when another person really took care of you and made you feel better."

Another technique was introduced by Velten (1968). Participants read a series of sentences designed to induce increasingly intense feelings of elation or depression. This technique is effective. However, it usually produces a blend of several mood states rather than just the desired one (Polivy, 1981). Other techniques include presenting emotionally positive or negative music or movie clips.

How important is it to assess the effects of emotion and mood on cognition and performance? There are two main reasons why such research is very important. First, mood states can have strong influences on behavior in everyday life. Car drivers very frequently listen to music, and so it is of interest to assess the effects of music on car-driving performance. Pecher et al. (2009) studied driving performance in a simulator while drivers listened to happy, sad, or neutral music. Happy music was the most distracting – there was an impaired ability to keep the car in lane and speed decreased by about 8 mph. In contrast, drivers found it easy to keep the car in lane when listening to sad music, but with a slight reduction in speed.

Second, there have been numerous studies concerned with the effects of mood on cognition and performance on a very wide range of tasks. The tasks used have included those assessing memory, judgment, decision making, and reasoning, and mood states have generally influenced performance. This is the case with positive mood states and with negative mood states as diverse as anxiety, sadness, and anger. Thus, we can only obtain a complete picture of human cognition by considering the impact of mood states and emotion.

MOOD AND MEMORY

How does mood affect what we remember? There is no single (or simple) answer to that question. Rather, several factors all contribute to determining the effects of mood on memory.

Attentional narrowing

An influential approach to understanding how memory is affected by mood is based on Easterbrook's (1959) hypothesis. According to this hypothesis, increases in arousal or anxiety produce a narrowing of attention in which fewer aspects of the environment are processed thoroughly. Levine and Edelstein (2009) modified this hypothesis slightly to explain the effects of emotion on memory. They argued that emotion enhances our memory for information central to our current goals but impairs it for peripheral or unimportant information.

There is reasonable support for the above hypothesis (Levine & Edelstein, 2009). For example, Cavenett and Nixon (2006) carried out a naturalistic study involving high levels of emotion. Skydivers learned words in anxiety-inducing conditions (on a plane shortly before jumping) or on the ground.

There was no difference between the groups in the number of words remembered when tested on the ground. However, those in the anxiety-inducing condition recognized more skydiving-relevant words (but fewer skydiving-irrelevant words) than those in the control condition. Thus, high arousal and anxiety led those about to skydive to increase their focus on relevant information.

Attentional narrowing depends on motivation as well as on emotion. Gable and Harmon-Jones (2010) argued that anxiety produces attentional narrowing because it involves high motivational intensity as well as negative affect. They found that sadness (a negative mood state associated with low motivational intensity) led to attentional *broadening* rather than narrowing. In contrast, disgust (a negative state associated with high motivational intensity) produced attentional narrowing. Thus, the presence or absence of high motivational intensity is important in determining whether there is attentional narrowing.

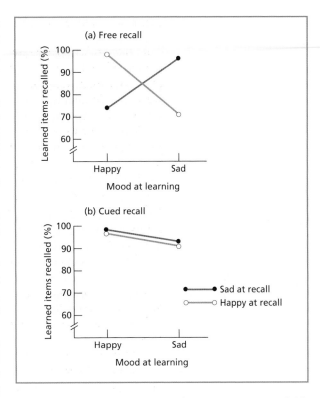

Figure 12.6 Free recall (a) and cued recall (b) as a function of mood state (happy or sad) at learning and at recall (b). Data from Kenealy (1997).

Mood-state-dependent memory

Mood-state-dependent memory is the finding that memory is better when the mood state at retrieval is the same as that at learning than when the two mood states differ. This effect was shown amusingly in the movie *City Lights*. In this movie, Charlie Chaplin saves a drunken millionaire from attempted suicide, and is befriended in return. When the millionaire sees Charlie again, he is sober and fails to recognize him. However, when the millionaire becomes drunk again, he catches sight of Charlie, treats him like a long-lost friend, and takes him home with him.

Pamela Kenealy (1997) provided evidence of mood-state-dependent memory. In one study, participants looked at a map and learned a set of instructions concerning a particular route. The next day they were given tests of free recall and cued recall (the cue consisted of the map's visual outline). Context was manipulated by using music to create happy or sad mood states at learning and at test.

As predicted, Kenealy (1997) found that free recall was better when the mood state was the same at learning and at testing than when it differed (see Figure 12.6). This finding resembles those discussed in Chapter 5 showing that memory is better when the context (here mood state) is the same at learning and at retrieval.

However, Kenealy (1997) found no evidence of mood-state-dependent memory (or context) with cued recall. *Why* was this? Eich (1995) argued that mood state exerts less influence when crucial information (the to-be-remembered material or the retrieval cues) is explicitly presented, as happens with cued recall. Eich talked about a "do-it-yourself principle" – memory is most likely to be mood-dependent when *effortful* processing at learning and/or retrieval is required.

The importance of the "do-it-yourself" principle was shown by Eich and Metcalfe (1989). At the time of learning, participants were assigned to read (e.g., *river–valley*) and generate (e.g., *river–v*) conditions. In the generate condition, they completed the second word in each pair during learning, and so it involved more effortful processing. Mood state was manipulated by having continuous music during learning and recall. The mood-state-dependent effect was *four* times greater in the generate condition than in the read condition.

Mood congruity

Consider what happens when you recall an emotional event (e.g., party) that occurred a few weeks previously. You may have found it easier to recall happy aspects of the event when you were in a positive (rather than negative or neutral) mood at the time of recall. This effect is known as **mood congruity**: Emotionally toned information is learned and retrieved best when there is agreement (or congruity) between its affective value and the learner's (or rememberer's) current mood state.

Miranda and Kihlstrom (2005) asked adults to recall childhood and recent autobiographical memories to pleasant, unpleasant, and neutral word cues. They did this in a musically induced happy, sad, or neutral mood. Mood congruity was shown – the retrieval of happy memories was facilitated when participants were in a happy mood and retrieval of sad memories was enhanced by a sad mood.

There is more evidence of mood-congruent retrieval with positive than with negative affect (Rusting & DeHart, 2000). How can we explain this? The most plausible reason is that individuals in a negative mood are much more likely to be motivated to *change* their mood, which reduces the accessibility of negative memories.

Rusting and DeHart (2000) obtained evidence supporting the above explanation. Participants were presented with positive, negative, and neutral words. After that, there was a negative mood induction in which participants imagined experiencing distressing events. Those who claimed to be successful at reducing negative moods showed less evidence of mood congruity than other participants.

Amygdala involvement

As discussed earlier, the amygdala is involved in the processing of emotional information. It has connections to nearly all cortical regions, and facilitates several memory processes. How can we show the role played by the amygdala in emotional learning and memory? An approach that has proved useful involves the study of patients with **Urbach-Wiethe disease**, in which the amygdala and adjacent areas are destroyed.

Key Terms

Mood congruity:
the finding that learning and retrieval are better when the learner's (or rememberer's) mood state is the same as (or congruent with) the affective value of the to-be-remembered material.

Urbach-Wiethe disease:
a disease in which the amygdala and adjacent areas are destroyed; it leads to the impairment of emotional processing and memory for emotional material.

Cahill et al. (1995) studied BP, a patient suffering from Urbach-Wiethe disease. He was told a story, in the middle of which was a very emotional event (a boy is severely injured in a traffic accident). Healthy controls showed much better recall of this emotional event than of the preceding emotionally neutral part of the story one week after learning. In contrast, BP recalled the emotional event *less* well than the preceding part of the story.

The amygdala is involved in memory for positive information as well as negative information. Siebert et al. (2003) compared long-term memory for positive, negative, and neutral pictures in healthy controls and 10 Urbach-Wiethe patients. The patients had poorer recognition memory than the controls for all picture categories, but their memory impairment was greatest for positive pictures and least for neutral ones.

Another approach to assessing the role of the amygdala in memory for emotional material is to use brain-imaging techniques. Individuals with the greatest amygdala activation during the learning of emotional material should have high levels of long-term memory for that material.

Murty et al. (2010) carried out a meta-analysis (see Glossary) of numerous studies, and found support for the above prediction. More specifically, successful learning of emotional material was associated with enhanced activation in a network of brain areas including the medial temporal lobe memory system as well as the amygdala.

In sum, similar findings have been reported in studies on patients with Urbach-Wiethe disease and on healthy individuals in brain-imaging studies. In both cases, there is much evidence that the amygdala plays an important role in enhanced memory for emotional information. This happens in part because the amygdala has connections to brain regions (e.g., hippocampus; prefrontal cortex) strongly involved in memory processes (LaBar & Cabeza, 2006).

JUDGMENT AND DECISION MAKING

Decision making (discussed in Chapter 11) involves choosing among various options, and is something we do every day. These decisions vary between the trivial (e.g., deciding which movie to see tonight) and the enormously important (e.g., deciding whether to get married; deciding which career path to follow).

Judgment (also discussed in Chapter 11) is an important aspect of decision making. It involves "assessing, estimating, and inferring what events will occur and what the decision-maker's evaluative reactions to those outcomes will be" (Hastie, 2001, p. 657). We might expect that the decisions made by those whose judgments about the future are pessimistic would differ from those made by individuals whose judgments about the future are optimistic.

In this section, we consider the influence of mood and personality on decision making. An important aspect of decision making is risk taking – are some moods and personality types associated with risk aversion? Common sense might suggest that individuals experiencing negative affect will be pessimistic and risk-averse, whereas those experiencing positive affect will be optimistic and more inclined to take risks. As we will see, however, reality is more complex than that.

Anxiety

Of all the negative emotional states, fear or anxiety is most consistently associated with pessimistic judgments about the future. For example, Lerner et al. (2003) carried out an online study very shortly after the 9/11 terrorist attacks. The participants were instructed to focus on aspects of the attacks that made them afraid, angry, or sad. The estimated probability of future terrorist attacks was higher in fearful participants than in sad or angry ones.

Lench and Levine (2005) presented participants with several hypothetical positive and negative events. They were asked to make judgments of the likelihood of each event happening to them compared to the average college student. Participants in a fearful mood were more pessimistic than those in a happy or neutral mood.

What are the effects of anxiety on decision making? Anxiety is often associated with impaired decision making. In one study (Preston et al., 2007), participants played the Iowa Gambling Task, which involves learning about the potential gains and losses associated with different decisions. Participants made anxious by anticipating that they would have to give a public speech showed slower learning than control participants.

Starcke et al. (2008) used the Game of Dice task, a decision-making task with explicit rules that requires the use of executive processes. Anxious participants (who anticipated giving a public speech) performed worse than control participants.

Why does anxiety impair decision making? Many decision-making tasks involve use of the working memory system (Baddeley, 1986, 2001; see Chapter 4), especially the attention-like central executive component. There is accumulating evidence that anxiety impairs the efficiency with which the central executive is used when performing complex tasks (Eysenck et al., 2007).

Anxiety is generally associated with less risky decision making (Maner et al., 2007; see Blanchette & Richards, 2010, for a review). In research by Maner et al. (2007), anxious individuals were more risk-averse than nonanxious ones on the computer-based balloon analog risk task. This involved gaining rewards for blowing up balloons provided that the balloon didn't burst.

Maner et al. (2007) also found that anxious individuals (clinical patients suffering from an anxiety disorder) scored much lower than healthy controls on the Risk-Taking Behaviors Scale. This scale has items referring to the willingness to behave in risky ways in several situations (e.g., health/safety; social interaction; gambling).

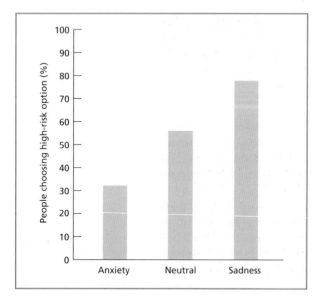

Figure 12.7 Effects of mood manipulation (anxiety, sadness, or neutral) on percentages of people choosing the high-risk job option. Based on data in Raghunathan & Pham (1999).

Raghunathan and Pham (1999) asked their participants to choose between two jobs. Job A offered a high salary with low job security (high risk), whereas job B offered an average salary with high security (low risk). Of participants in a neutral mood state, 56% chose the high-risk option compared to only 32% of those in an anxious mood state (see Figure 12.7). This happened because the anxious individuals attached more importance than those in a neutral mood to job security.

Why is anxiety associated with risk aversion? One reason is that anxious individuals are pessimistic about the likelihood of negative future events. Another reason follows from the finding that anxiety is often triggered by high uncertainty and low personal control over a situation (Frijda, 1986). Uncertainty can be minimized by making "safe" decisions.

Sadness

Individuals in a sad mood tend to be relatively pessimistic in their judgments about the likelihood of negative future events. Waters (2008) reviewed studies concerning the effects of mood state on likelihood estimates of health hazards and life events. The likelihood estimates of sad individuals were more pessimistic than those of individuals in a positive mood state.

We turn now to the effects of sadness on decision making. In a study already discussed, Raghunathan and Pham (1999) asked participants to choose between high-risk and low-risk jobs. Of participants in a sad mood state, 78% chose the high-risk option whereas only 56% of those in a neutral mood state did likewise. There was a marked difference between the decisions of sad participants and of anxious ones (see Figure 12.7).

Why did so many sad participants choose the high-risk option? The main reason was that they attached more importance to pay. According to Raghunathan and Pham, sad individuals experience the environment as being relatively unrewarding and so they are especially motivated to obtain rewards (e.g., high pay).

Further support for the notion that sad or depressed individuals are *less* risk-averse than anxious ones was reported by Maner et al. (2010). We have already seen that they found anxious patients were very risk averse on the Risk-Taking Behaviors Scale. However, clinically depressed patients were much less risk-averse than the anxious patients, and only slightly more risk averse than the healthy controls.

Anger

Anger is typically regarded as a negative affect. However, anger can be experienced as relatively pleasant, because it leads individuals to believe that they can control the situation and conquer those whom they dislike (Lerner & Tiedens, 2006). Consider *schadenfreude* (experiencing pleasure at the misfortune of disliked others). Anger increases *schadenfreude* (Hareli & Weiner, 2002). However, anger is also associated with negative affect. The events triggering anger are remembered as unpleasant, and it can lead to behavior (e.g., aggression; violence) causing substantial negative affect (Litvak et al., 2010).

In a review mentioned already, Waters (2008) found that anxiety and sadness were both associated with pessimistic judgments about the likelihood of negative events. In striking contrast to these negative moods, anger was associated with relatively *optimistic* judgments. Angry people are more likely than others to experience divorce, to have problems at work, and to have heart disease, but they rate themselves as less at risk (Lerner & Keltner, 2001).

Why is anger associated with optimistic judgments rather than the pessimistic ones associated with other negative mood states? Anger differs from other negative moods in being associated with a sense of *certainty* about what has happened and with perceived *control* over the situation (Litvak et al., 2010). These unique features of anger (especially high perceived control) explain why the effects of anger on judgment differ so much from those of other negative affective states.

We turn now to the effects of anger on decision making. Fessler et al. (2004) used a gambling task with substantial real stakes. Among men (but not women), induced anger was associated with increased risk taking.

It is often assumed that anger greatly impairs our ability to think straight. According to the American philosopher and essayist Ralph Waldo Emerson, anger "blows out the light of reason." This viewpoint has support. Bright and Goodman-Delahunty (2006) asked participants to act as mock jurors in a case in which the defendant was charged with murdering his wife.

The mock jurors were far more likely to return a guilty verdict when they had seen gruesome photographs than when they hadn't seen any photographs (41% vs. 9%, respectively). The distorting effect of the gruesome photographs occurred in part because they increased jurors' anger towards the defendant.

Why does anger impair decision making? An influential answer is that it leads to shallow processing based on heuristics (rules of thumb) rather than systematic or analytic processing (Litvak et al., 2010; see Chapter 11). Supporting evidence was reported by Lerner et al. (1998), who considered the effects of anger on fictional court cases. Angry participants used fewer cues than those in a neutral mood (suggesting the use of heuristic processing) when making their judgments. In addition, they recommended harsher punishment.

Small and Lerner (2008) presented participants with the fictitious case of Patricia Smith, a 25-year-old white female who was a divorced mother with three children. Those participants put into an angry mood decided she should receive less welfare assistance than those put into a neutral or sad mood.

In another condition, participants were given a second task (cognitive load) to perform at the same time as the decision-making task. This was done to reduce participants' ability to use systematic or analytic processing on the decision-making task. The added cognitive load had no effect on the decisions made by angry participants, suggesting they made little use of analytic processing in either condition.

Anger doesn't always lead to shallow or heuristic processing. Moons and Mackie (2008) presented participants in an angry or neutral mood with weak or strong arguments for the position that college students have good financial habits. Angry participants were more persuaded by strong than by weak arguments, indicating that they engaged in analytic or systematic processing. In contrast, participants in a neutral mood were equally persuaded by strong and weak arguments.

How can we reconcile these findings with other research? Moons and Mackie (2008) found that their angry and neutral participants didn't differ in self-reported arousal, suggesting that only fairly modest levels of anger were experienced. Low levels of anger may be associated with analytic or systematic processing, whereas extremely high levels of anger and arousal may prevent such processing from occurring.

Positive mood

Individuals in a positive mood state generally perceive the likelihood of negative events (e.g., health hazards) happening to them as smaller than individuals in a sad or anxious/fearful mood state (Waters, 2008). However, the effects are sometimes relatively weak. In a study discussed earlier, Lench and Levine (2005) presented participants with several hypothetical positive and negative events. Participants in a happy mood were more optimistic than fearful participants about the likelihood of these events happening to them. However, they weren't more optimistic than participants in a neutral mood.

A positive mood state typically leads individuals to adopt a less risky approach to decision making (Blanchette & Richards, 2010). In one study (Cahir & Thomas, 2010), participants in a positive mood made lower-risk decisions than those in a neutral mood when betting on hypothetical horse races. Mustanski (2007) carried out a study in the real world on men who have sex with other men. A key finding was that involvement in HIV risk behaviors was less among men experiencing positive affect.

In general, individuals in a positive mood state become increasingly risk-averse as the level of risk increases (Isen et al., 1988). A likely reason why those in a positive mood state are risk-averse is that they are motivated to maintain their current happy feelings.

What are the effects of positive mood on decision making? Some research (de Vries et al., 2008) has reported beneficial effects. Participants performed the Iowa Gambling Task. It involves decision making based on learning which decks of cards are financially advantageous and which are disadvantageous. Positive mood states speeded up learning on this task relative to negative mood states.

Much research has found that positive affect is associated with a tendency to process information in a more heuristic or shallow manner (Griskevicius et al., 2010). However, most of this research has been based on the assumption that all forms of positive affect have similar effects on cognitive processing.

Griskevicius et al. (2010) compared various types of positive affect including the following: anticipatory enthusiasm; amusement; attachment love; awe; nurturant love; and contentment. The task involved evaluating the persuasiveness of weak or strong arguments concerning a possible senior comprehensive exam in each major as a requirement for graduation.

What did Griskevicius et al. (2010) find? Participants experiencing three of the positive emotions (anticipatory enthusiasm; amusement; attachment love) were persuaded by the weak arguments, which is indicative of shallow or heuristic processing. It is noteworthy that these emotions are the ones most commonly studied in previous research. In contrast, two positive emotions (awe; nurturant love) were associated with *less* shallow or heuristic processing than a neutral mood state.

The above findings indicate there are important differences among positive emotions in their effects on information processing. In future research, it will be important to find out why this is the case.

Overview

Research on the effects of mood on judgment and decision making has indicated very clearly that the effects vary from mood to mood. Consider, for example, the three negative moods of anxiety, sadness, and anger. In general terms, anxiety is associated with pessimistic judgments and risk-averse decision making. Sadness is also associated with pessimistic judgments but (if anything) with risk taking in decision making. Finally, anger is associated with optimistic judgments and with risk taking in decision making.

Why does the pattern of findings differ so much between anger and the other negative mood states of anxiety and sadness? The most likely explanation is that anger is associated with high levels of perceived control, whereas anxiety and depression are not. Someone who feels in control is likely to be optimistic about the future and to avoid focusing on the possible negative consequences of making certain decisions.

Positive mood state is associated with slightly optimistic judgments and with risk-averse decision making. However, the evidence is limited because there have been very few attempts to see whether the precise effects obtained depend on the precise form of positive mood state involved.

REASONING

The ability to reason can be regarded as one of the greatest achievements of the human cognitive system. Much of the research on reasoning has involved syllogistic reasoning, in which two premises (statements) are followed by a conclusion (see Chapter 11). Syllogistic reasoning should depend *only* on logic – the task is to decide whether the conclusion follows logically from the premises regardless of the truth of the conclusion in the real world. In practice, individuals often fail to use logic when solving syllogistic-reasoning problems.

Syllogistic reasoning is a form of deductive reasoning in which the initial premises or statements are assumed to be valid and the conclusion that follows may be valid or invalid. There are two main ways in which the effects of emotion on deductive reasoning can be assessed:

1. Groups differing in emotion can be formed using mood manipulation techniques to induce negative, positive, or neutral mood states.
2. The emotionality of the content used for a reasoning task can be manipulated. For example, participants can reason about neutral topics or emotionally charged ones (e.g., terrorism).

It has often been assumed that the rational thinking needed for success in deductive reasoning is disrupted by emotion (Blanchette & Richards, 2010). There is support for that assumption. Blanchette et al. (2007) reviewed several studies in which negative emotion impaired deductive reasoning. In general, the adverse effects of emotion were greater when mood state was manipulated than when the emotional content of the reasoning task was manipulated.

Why does emotion impair reasoning? The answer varies from one emotion to another. Individuals who are anxious are easily distractible and devote some of their attention to task-irrelevant thoughts (e.g., "I am performing poorly"; "I can't do this task"). This uses up some of the resources of the central executive component, an attention-like component of the working memory system (Baddeley, 2007; see Chapter 4).

There is support for the above assumptions (Eysenck et al., 2007). For example, consider a study by Derakshan and Eysenck (1998). High-anxious and low-anxious individuals performed a simple verbal reasoning task. High-anxious and low-anxious participants had comparable levels of performance when the task was performed on its own. However, the performance of the high-anxious participants suffered much more than that of the low-anxious ones when they had to perform another central-executive task at the same time. Thus, the high-anxious individuals had fewer central executive resources available.

A similar explanation may help to explain the negative effects of sadness or depression on reasoning performance. Depression is associated with rumination (persistent focusing on symptoms of distress). In turn, rumination is associated with impaired performance on various cognitive tasks (Gotlib & Joormann, 2010).

Channon and Baker (1994) found that depressed individuals solved fewer syllogistic reasoning problems than nondepressed ones. The depressed participants were poorer than nondepressed ones at integrating information from the two premises. This integration requires much use of the processing resources of working memory.

Emotion isn't *always* associated with impaired reasoning performance. Johnson-Laird et al. (2006) presented individuals high and low in depressive symptoms with a reasoning task. Scenarios were presented, and participants listed logical possibilities.

High depressives produced many more valid possibilities than low depressives when the scenarios were likely to engage a feeling of depression. However, there were no group differences with other kinds of scenario. According to Johnson-Laird et al., depressed individuals spend much of their time thinking about the causes of their depression, and so they become expert at reasoning about depression.

In sum, anxiety and depression are both often associated with impaired reasoning performance. These negative effects are due to distractibility and worry in the case of anxiety and to rumination in the case of depression. Depression can produce enhanced reasoning performance when the task is *relevant* to depression. This is presumably because depressed individuals possess far more information about depression than do nondepressed ones.

Belief bias

One of the most important findings in research on syllogistic reasoning is belief bias (see Glossary). This bias involves accepting invalid conclusions that are believable and rejecting valid conclusions that are unbelievable (see Chapter 11). Vroling and de Jong (2009) wondered whether anxious individuals would show more belief bias than nonanxious ones when presented with syllogisms related to their social concerns and worries.

Here is one of the syllogisms used by Vroling and de Jong (2009):

Premises
Others find Person 1 less capable than Person A.
Others find Person A less capable than me.

Conclusion
Others find me less capable than Person 1.

The above conclusion is invalid because it doesn't follow logically from the premises. However, anxious individuals would probably find it more believable than nonanxious ones. Anxious individuals (but not nonanxious ones) took longer to produce the correct answer with syllogisms (like the one above) involving a conflict between validity and believability than when there was congruency between validity and believability. Thus, anxious individuals showed belief bias.

Blanchette et al. (2007) studied belief bias in participants in London (UK), Manchester (UK), and London (Canada) shortly after the terrorist attack on London, UK on July 7, 2005. They used syllogisms that were neutral, emotionally related to terrorism, or generally emotional. Unsurprisingly, the level of fear was greatest among the London (UK) participants. However, there was actually *less* belief bias on the terrorism-relevant syllogisms among the London (UK) participants than those from the other two cities.

Why was reasoning on terrorism-relevant syllogisms best in the group reporting the highest levels of fear? Londoners were most acutely aware of the potentially terrible *consequences* of terrorism. This led them to process information about terrorism in a more detailed and analytical way than other participants.

Section Summary

Introduction
- Mood states can be manipulated by asking participants to focus on emotional personal events or by presenting emotional music or movie clips. There are often clear-cut effects of mood state on cognition in the laboratory and real life.

Mood and memory
- Mood or emotion enhances our memory for information central to our current goals but impairs it for peripheral information. Memory is generally better when the mood state at retrieval is the same as that at learning, especially when effortful processing is needed at learning or retrieval. Emotionally toned information is learned and retrieved best when its affective value is congruent with the learner's or rememberer's current mood state. The amygdala plays an important role in enhanced memory for emotional information relative to neutral information.

Judgment and decision making
- Anxiety is more consistently associated with pessimistic judgments about the future than other negative mood states. Anxiety is often associated with impaired decision making and avoidance of risk. Sadness is associated with pessimistic judgments about the future, but not with risk aversion. Anger is associated with optimistic judgments about the future and can lead to impaired decision making based on shallow processing. Some of the differences between the effects of anger and other negative mood states are due to the greater sense of perceived control with anger. Positive mood is associated with modestly positive judgments about the future and a risk-averse approach to decision making, which may reflect the motivation to maintain their current mood state.

> **Reasoning**
> • Negative mood states often impair deductive reasoning because anxiety and depression increase distractibility. Belief bias, in which reasoning is influenced by the believability rather than the validity of conclusions, has been studied. There is some evidence that anxious individuals exhibit more belief bias than nonanxious ones when they find invalid conclusions more believable than nonanxious individuals.

ANXIETY AND COGNITIVE BIASES

Millions of people around the world suffer from long-lasting or chronic anxiety. Much research has been based on the assumption that this negative mood state is associated with various effects on cognition (discussed shortly), and that these effects may serve to maintain that negative mood state.

Some research in this area has focused on patients suffering from an anxiety disorder. Other research has involved studying healthy individuals high in the personality dimension of trait anxiety (related to the frequency and intensity of the experience of anxiety).

We have already seen that anxiety has several effects on cognitive processing and performance. However, the focus of this section is on two cognitive biases (attentional bias and interpretive bias) claimed to be of particular importance in clinical anxiety. *Why* are these cognitive biases important? A key assumption made by many researchers in this area (e.g., Eysenck, 1997; Williams et al., 1997) is that these biases may increase vulnerability to clinical anxiety and/or serve to maintain an existing anxiety disorder.

ATTENTIONAL BIAS

It seems reasonable to assume that anxious individuals would attend more than nonanxious ones to threat-related words (e.g., stupid; inept). We might also expect that those with a craving (e.g., for alcohol) would pay particular attention to stimuli related to their craving (e.g., beer; vodka). Supporting evidence has been obtained in studies using various modified versions of the Stroop task to assess **attentional bias**, which is the selective allocation of attention to threat-related stimuli.

For example, suppose individuals high and low in anxiety name the color in which words are printed as rapidly as possible. Some of the words are emotionally negative and relevant to anxiety whereas others are neutral (this is the emotional Stroop task). Only the anxious individuals take longer to name colors with emotionally negative than neutral words (Bar-Haim et al., 2007).

Attentional bias can also be assessed using the dot-probe task. In the original version of this task, two words were presented simultaneously. On critical trials, one word is threat-related and the other is neutral. The allocation of attention is assessed by recording speed of detection of a dot that can replace either word.

Detection times on the dot-probe task are shorter in attended areas. Thus, attentional bias is indicated by a consistent tendency for detection times to be shorter when the dot replaces the threat-related word rather than the neutral

> **Key Term**
>
> **Attentional bias:**
> the selective allocation of attention to threat-related stimuli when they are presented at the same time as neutral ones.

one. In some research, threat-related and neutral pictures have been used instead of words because they are likely to trigger a greater emotional response.

Attentional bias has been found in both the emotional Stroop and dot-probe tasks even when the threat stimuli are presented subliminally (below the level of conscious awareness) (Bar-Haim et al., 2007). Our current understanding of attentional bias is that it depends in part on a threat-detection mechanism. This mechanism is largely automatic and is activated by threat stimuli presented subliminally (below the level of conscious awareness). It also depends on a difficulty in disengaging attention from threat-related stimuli that is a mixture of automatic and controlled processing (Cister & Koster, 2010).

Attentional bias has been assessed in individuals with various kinds of craving using the emotional Stroop and dot-probe tasks. Individuals with a craving often show attentional bias for words relevant to their craving (Field et al., 2009), although the effects are typically rather modest. Attentional bias tends to be stronger in those with a craving for illicit drugs and caffeine than for alcohol and tobacco.

Attentional training

In recent years, there has been an exciting development in research on attentional bias. Suppose that attentional biases help to maintain an individual's high level of anxiety or craving for some substance. It follows that there might be beneficial effects of providing attentional training to reduce (or eliminate) those attentional biases.

How can we reduce attentional biases? We alter the dot-probe task so that the dot *always* (or nearly always) appears in the location in which the neutral word had been presented. As a result, individuals learn to avoid allocating attention to the threat word.

Attentional training on the dot-probe task has proved very effective in reducing attentional bias and in improving individuals' well-being. MacLeod et al. (2002) exposed students high in trait anxiety to more than 6000 training trials on the dot-probe task. The training significantly reduced attentional bias. More importantly, it also led to a significant reduction in the students' trait anxiety scores. In similar fashion, individuals with social anxiety showed less attention bias after training, and also showed reduced anxiety when engaged in public speaking (Amir et al., 2008).

Koster et al. (2010) considered the effects of attentional training in more detail. They presented threatening and neutral pictures together for 30, 100, or 1500 ms on each trial followed by a dot replacing the neutral picture. There was a significant reduction in attentional bias in the 1500 ms condition but not in the 30 or 100 ms conditions. These findings suggested that attentional training changes later or more controlled stages of threat processing but not early or more automatic ones.

Other studies on attentional training have focused on individuals with different problems. For example, Fadardi and Cox (2009) reduced attentional bias in harmful drinkers who consumed an average of 60 units of alcohol a week. After training, their alcohol consumption reduced to an average of 50 units per week, and this reduction was maintained at a three-month follow-up.

In sum, there are important individual differences in the extent to which our attention is attracted by threat-related stimuli. This is an important finding because most research on attention has largely ignored individual differences. Of great significance is that training designed to reduce attentional bias offers the prospect of benefiting people's lives by reducing a wide range of conditions including chronic anxiety and various cravings. However, most studies so far have considered only short-term effects of attention training and more research is needed to ascertain the extent of beneficial long-term effects.

INTERPRETIVE BIAS

In our everyday lives, we are often exposed to ambiguous events. For example, does a noise outside in the middle of the night indicate the presence of a burglar or a cat? If someone walks past you without acknowledging your presence, does that mean they dislike you or simply that they failed to notice you?

It has often been assumed that individuals differ considerably in the tendency to interpret such ambiguous situations in a threatening way. More specifically, it has been hypothesized that anxious individuals exhibit **interpretive bias** – the tendency to interpret ambiguous stimuli and events in a threat-related fashion.

Most research on interpretive bias in anxious individuals has focused on the interpretation of words and sentences. However, given that much anxiety occurs in social situations, there are good reasons for also considering interpretive bias with respect to facial expressions. Yoon and Zinbarg (2008) considered the interpretation of neutral facial expressions in individuals high and low in social anxiety. The socially anxious participants interpreted neutral faces as negative regardless of whether they anticipated a feared situation (giving a speech). In these participants, interpretive bias was due to their personality.

In contrast, Yoon and Zinbarg (2008) found that the nonanxious participants *only* showed interpretive bias when anticipating giving a speech. In these participants, interpretive bias was triggered by being in a situation creating anxiety rather than by their personality.

> **Key Terms**
>
> **Interpretive bias:**
> the tendency to interpret ambiguous stimuli and situations in a threatening fashion.
>
> **Homographs:**
> words that have a single spelling but at least two different meanings (e.g., maroon; throttle); used to study **interpretive bias**.

Research Activity 12.1: *Interpretive bias*

Some research on interpretive bias in anxious individuals has focused on the interpretation of **homographs**. These are words having a single spelling but two or more different meanings.

Have a look at the words in the column below (taken from Grey & Mathews, 2000). Write down in a word or two the *first* meaning of each word that comes to mind:

beat	nag
tank	maroon
stole	hang
strain	patient
lie	drop
break	throttle

When you have finished, have a look in the Appendix, and decide whether each interpretation was closer to the threatening or the neutral one. You might find it interesting to compare your responses to those of a friend.

Much research has considered the effects of anxiety on the interpretation of homographs such as those in the list. Healthy individuals with an anxious personality and patients with anxiety disorders are more likely than other people to produce threatening interpretations (Mathews & MacLeod, 2005).

An important issue concerns the stage of processing at which an interpretive bias occurs in anxious individuals (Blanchette & Richards, 2010). One possibility is that both (or all) meanings of an ambiguous word or sentence are activated initially, with anxious individuals favoring the threatening interpretation at a late stage of processing. Alternatively, anxious individuals may select the threatening interpretation relatively early in processing.

Most research favors the notion that interpretive bias occurs relatively late in processing. Calvo and Castillo (1997) presented ambiguous sentences relating to personal social threat to high-anxious and low-anxious individuals. There was clear evidence of an interpretive bias in high-anxious individuals 1250 ms after sentence presentation but not at 500 ms. These findings suggest that interpretive bias doesn't occur rapidly and automatically but rather that it depends on subsequent controlled processes.

Huppert et al. (2007) argued that the interpretation of ambiguous sentences involves successive stages of response generation and response selection. They presented participants with incomplete sentences such as, "As you walk to the podium, you notice your heart racing, which means you are __." Their task was to generate several sentence completions and then to select the one that seemed to fit the sentence the best. Socially anxious individuals (compared to nonanxious ones) showed evidence of interpretive bias at the generation and selection stages.

In the Real World 12.1: *Anxiety disorders and interpretive bias*

Here we will consider the role of interpretive bias in three of the main anxiety disorders: social phobia; panic disorder; and generalized anxiety disorder. Social phobia involves extreme fear and avoidance of social situations. Of central importance to social phobia is interpretive bias – social phobics interpret their own social behavior as substantially less adequate than it appears to observers (Rodebaugh et al., 2010).

Patients with panic disorder suffer from panic attacks, but *not* because they have heightened physiological responses to stressful events (Eysenck, 1997). The major reason is that patients with panic disorder are much more likely than other people to have catastrophic misinterpretations of their bodily sensations (Clark, 1986). Austin and Kiropoulos (2008) presented participants with questions such as, "You feel short of breath. Why?" Panic disorder patients gave more harm-related interpretations of such ambiguous internal stimuli than social phobics or healthy controls. They also regarded harm and anxiety outcomes as more catastrophic than did the other groups of participants.

Patients with generalized anxiety disorder exhibit excessive worrying about a wide range of issues. Some of this worrying undoubtedly reflects genuine personal problems, but part is due to an interpretive bias. In a study by Eysenck et al. (1991), patients with generalized anxiety disorder and healthy controls listened to ambiguous sentences such as the following:

1. At the refugee camp, the weak/week would soon be finished.
2. The doctor examined little Emma's growth.
3. They discussed the priest's convictions.

Only the anxious patients had an interpretive bias for these sentences.

So far we have seen that there is an *association* between having an anxiety disorder and the possession of an interpretive bias. However, this doesn't clarify whether anxiety disorder leads to interpretive bias or vice versa. If interpretive bias plays a role in producing or maintaining anxiety disorder, then therapy designed to reduce or eliminate interpretive bias should reduce anxiety levels.

Rodebaugh et al. (2010) asked social phobics to give two public speeches. After the first one, some social phobics were provided with video feedback of their performance to reduce their interpretive bias for their own social behavior. This feedback reduced their interpretive bias and made them

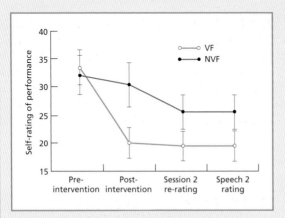

Figure 12.8 Self-ratings of speech performance (high scores are worse) as a function of video feedback intervention (VF) or no video feedback intervention (NVF). Self-ratings of Speech 1 were more positive following video feedback (i.e., Session 2 Re-rating) than before. From Rodebaugh et al. (2010). Copyright © 2010, with permission from Elsevier.

experience less anticipatory anxiety before giving the second speech (see Figure 12.8).

Hayes et al. (2010) trained patients with generalized anxiety disorder to produce nonthreatening interpretations of ambiguous homographs and scenarios. This intervention was effective in reducing their interpretive bias and their negative thought intrusions or worry.

The research we have been discussing is of direct relevance to cognitive therapy. Of crucial importance in such therapy is the attempt to eliminate patients' interpretive biases that lead them to exaggerate various potential threats.

In sum, interpretive bias in social phobics, panic disorder patients, and generalized anxiety disorder patients can be reduced or eliminated by training. Such training also reduces anxiety, which shows that at least some of the association between anxiety and interpretive bias occurs because interpretive bias maintains or increases anxiety. This makes sense – individuals who consistently interpret ambiguous situations in a threatening way are likely to perceive the world around them as threatening and dangerous and thus experience much anxiety.

The take-home message is that the emphasis that cognitive therapists place on reducing anxious patients' interpretive bias receives support from experimental research. Such research has also served to clarify the underlying mechanisms.

Section Summary

Attentional bias
- Anxious individuals show attentional bias on the emotional Stroop and dot-probe tasks. This attentional bias involves automatic and strategic or controlled processes. Attentional training reduces attentional bias and anxiety, mostly through its effects on later stages of processing.

Interpretive bias
- Anxious individuals exhibit interpretive bias for ambiguous facial expressions, words, and sentences. This interpretive bias depends mainly on later stages

of processing. Reducing interpretive bias reduces anxiety levels in patients with anxiety disorders, and shows that at least part of the association between anxiety and interpretive bias occurs because interpretive bias increases anxiety. Laboratory research supports the emphasis that cognitive therapists place on reducing interpretive bias in anxious patients.

Essay Questions

1. Discuss the role of appraisal in determining which emotion an individual experiences in any given situation.
2. Describe some of the main strategies used in emotion regulation. Which strategies tend to be especially effective?
3. In what ways does mood influence learning and memory?
4. What effects do various mood states have on judgment and decision making?
5. How do anxiety and depression or sadness influence reasoning performance?
6. Discuss the relevance of attentional and interpretive biases for an understanding of the anxiety disorders and depression.

Further Reading

- Blanchette, I., & Richards, A. (2010). The influence of affect on higher level cognition: A review of research on interpretation, judgment, decision making and reasoning. *Cognition & Emotion, 24*, 561–595. Isabelle Blanchette and Anne Richards discuss a wide range of effects of emotion on cognitive processes.
- Fox, E. (2008). *Emotion science*. New York, NY: Palgrave Macmillan. In this excellent book, Elaine Fox discusses at length relationships between cognition and emotion.
- Koole, S. (2009). The psychology of emotion regulation: An integrative review. *Cognition & Emotion, 23*, 4–41. This review paper provides a thorough discussion of the main strategies used to change emotional states.
- Litvak, P. M., Lerner, J. S., Tiedens, L. Z., & Shonk, K. (2010). Fuel in the fire: How anger impacts judgment and decision-making. In M. Potegal, G. Stemmler, & C. Spielberger (Eds.), *International handbook of anger: Constituent and concomitant biological, psychological, and social processes* (pp. 287–310). New York, NY: Springer. The reasons why the effects of anger on judgment and decision differ from those of other negative emotional states are analyzed in depth.
- Mathews, A., & MacLeod, C. (2005). Cognitive vulnerability to emotional disorders. *Annual Review of Clinical Psychology, 1*, 167–195. The role of attentional and interpretive biases in triggering anxiety and disorders and depression is discussed at length by Andrew Mathews and Colin MacLeod.
- Power, M., & Dalgleish, T. (2008). *Cognition and emotion: From order to disorder* (2nd ed.). New York, NY: Psychology Press. Mick Power and Tim Dalgleish provide a first-rate account of the ways in which cognitive processes influence emotional states.

Contents

Appendix

REBUS PUZZLES: SOLUTIONS
AND CLASSIFICATION (SEE FIGURE 10.4)

Solution	Number	Level	Explanation
Dark Ages	1	Subword	Interpret letters in bold font as word
Big bad wolf	1	Subword	Interpret capitalized letters as word
Capital punishment	1	Subword	Interpret capitalized letters as word
Little League	1	Subword	Interpret size of letters
Grave error	2	Subword	Letter anagram/acronym
Ambiguous	2	Subword	Interpret capitalized letter as "big"/ Interpret "big" letter as part of word
Excuse me	2	Subword	Interpret letters as word parts (twice)
Tea for two	2	Subword	Interpret letter as word/Identify as standing for missing element in number series
Go stand in the corner	1	Word	Interpret position of words
Round of applause	1	Word	Interpret orientation of word
Split personality	1	Word	Interpret dislocation of word
Waterfall	1	Word	Interpret orientation of word
Paralegal	2	Word	Interpret count of words/Use homonym
Too big to ignore	2	Word	Interpret count of words as homonym (twice)
Sit down and shut up	2	Word	Interpret orientation of word (twice)
Search high and low	2	Word	Interpret position of word (twice)
Somewhere over the rainbow	1	Supraword	Relation between words
Home (away) from home	1	Supraword	Relation between words
Beating around the bush	1	Supraword	Relation between words
Diamond in the rough	1	Supraword	Relation between words

(continued)

Solution	Number	Level	Explanation
A little on the large side	2	Supraword	Relation between words/Relative positions of words
Just between friends	2	Word/ Supraword	Interpret count of words as plural/ Relation between words
Lying down on the job	2	Word/ Supraword	Interpret position of word/Relation between words
Rock around the clock	2	Word/ Supraword	Identify distributed word/Relation between words

NOTES ON RESEARCH ACTIVITY 12.1: INTERPRETIVE BIAS

Homograph	Threatening interpretation	Neutral interpretation
beat	hit	drum
tank	war	reservoir
stole	theft	clothing
strain	injure	race
lie	false statement	be horizontal
break	smash	holiday
nag	find fault	horse
maroon	strand	color
hang	put to death	put up pictures/hold back
patient	in hospital	calm
drop	cease to associate with	rain
throttle	strangle	device regulating flow of fuel to an engine

Glossary

affective blindsight: the ability to discriminate among different emotional stimuli in spite of the absence of conscious perception.

amnesia: a condition caused by brain damage in which there are serious impairments of long-term memory (especially **declarative memory**).

amygdala: a part of the brain that is strongly associated with several emotions but especially fear or anxiety; it is buried deep within the temporal lobe.

analogical problem solving: a type of problem solving based on detecting analogies or similarities between the current problem and problems solved in the past.

anterograde amnesia: impaired ability of amnesic patients to learn and remember information acquired after the onset of **amnesia**.

Anton's syndrome: a condition in which blind patients mistakenly believe that visual imagery is actually visual perception.

aphasia: a condition due to brain damage in which the patient has severely impaired language abilities.

apperceptive agnosia: this is a form of visual agnosia in which there is impaired perceptual analysis of familiar objects.

apperceptive aphasia: a condition caused by brain damage in which object recognition is impaired mainly due to deficits in perceptual processing; see **associative aphasia**.

associative agnosia: this is a form of visual agnosia in which perceptual processing is fairly normal but there is an impaired ability to derive the meaning of objects.

associative aphasia: a condition caused by brain damage in which object recognition is impaired mainly due to problems in accessing relevant object knowledge stored in long-term memory; see **apperceptive aphasia**.

attentional bias: the selective allocation of attention to threat-related stimuli when they are presented at the same time as neutral ones.

autobiographical memory: a form of **declarative memory** involving memory for personal events across the lifespan.

availability heuristic: a rule of thumb in which the frequency of a given event is estimated (often wrongly) on the basis of how easily relevant information about that event can be accessed in long-term memory.

base-rate information: this is the relative frequency with which an event occurs in the population; it is often ignored (or deemphasized) when individuals make a **judgment**.

behaviorism: an approach to psychology that emphasized a rigorous experimental approach and the role of conditioning in learning.

belief bias: in syllogistic reasoning, mistakenly accepting believable conclusions that are invalid and rejecting unbelievable ones that are valid.

binocular rivalry: when two different visual stimuli are presented one to each eye, only one stimulus is seen; the stimulus that is seen tends to alternate over time.

blindsight: an apparently paradoxical condition often produced by brain damage to early visual cortex in which there is behavioral evidence of visual perception in the absence of conscious awareness.

body size effect: an extension of the **body swap illusion** in which the size of the body mistakenly perceived to be one's own influences the perceived size of objects in the environment.

body swap illusion: the mistaken perception that part or all of someone else's body is one's own; it occurs when, for example, shaking hands with someone else while seeing what is happening from the viewpoint of the other person.

bottom-up processing: processing that is determined directly by environmental stimuli rather than the individual's knowledge and expectations.

boundary extension: the finding that internal representations of visual scenes are more complete and extensive than the actual scene; dependent on perceptual **schemas** and expectations.

bounded rationality: thinking and decision making are only partially rational because of limited processing resources and complex environments; as a result, **heuristics** are often used.

categorical perception: the finding that when a sound is intermediate between two **phonemes**, the listener typically perceives one or other of the phonemes.

category: a set or class of objects that belong together (e.g., articles of furniture; four-footed animals).

central executive: the most important component of

working memory; it is involved in planning and the control of attention and has limited capacity.

change blindness: the failure to detect that a visual stimulus has moved, changed, or been replaced by another stimulus; see **inattentional blindness.**

change blindness blindness: the tendency of individuals to exaggerate greatly their ability to detect visual changes and so avoid **change blindness.**

Charles Bonnet syndrome: a condition in which individuals with eye disease form vivid and detailed visual hallucinations that are mistaken for visual perception.

child-directed speech: very short and simple utterances based on a limited vocabulary; designed to make it easy for young children to understand what is being communicated.

chunks: stored units formed from integrating smaller pieces of information.

clause: a group of words within a sentence that contains a subject and a verb; see **phrase.**

coarticulation: the finding that the production of a **phoneme** is influenced by the production of the previous sound and by preparations for the next sound; it provides a useful cue to listeners.

cognitive neuroscience: an approach that aims to understand human cognition by combining information from brain activity and behavior.

common ground: the shared knowledge and beliefs possessed by a speaker and a listener; its use assists communication.

computational modeling: this involves constructing computer programs that will simulate or mimic some aspects of human cognitive functioning.

concept: a mental representation representing a **category** of objects; stored in long-term memory.

conditional reasoning: a form of **deductive reasoning** in which an "if ... then" statement is followed by a conclusion that is logically valid or invalid.

confirmation bias: (1) distortions of memory caused by the influence of expectations concerning what is likely to have happened; (2) in **hypothesis testing**, a tendency to emphasize evidence that seems to confirm one's hypothesis and to ignore or reject evidence inconsistent with the hypothesis.

conjunction fallacy: the mistaken assumption that the probability of two events occurring in conjunction or combination is greater than one of these events on its own; most famously studied with the Linda problem.

connectionist networks: these consist of units or nodes that are connected in various layers with no direct connection from stimulus to response.

consolidation: a physiological process involved in establishing long-term memories; this process lasts several hours or more, and newly formed memories that are still being consolidated are fragile.

cross-modal attention: the coordination of attention across two or more sense modalities (e.g., vision and hearing).

cross-race effect: the finding that recognition memory for same-race faces is more accurate than for other-race faces.

decision making: this involves making a selection from various options; full information is often unavailable and so **judgment** is required.

declarative memory: also known as explicit memory, this is memory that involves conscious recollection of information; see **nondeclarative memory.**

deductive reasoning: an approach to reasoning in which conclusions can be categorized as valid or invalid given that certain statements or premises are assumed to be true; **conditional reasoning** and syllogistic reasoning are forms of deductive reasoning.

deliberate practice: a very useful form of practice in which the learner can repeat the task, correct his/her errors, and is given performance feedback.

deontic rules: in reasoning, rules in which the emphasis is on the detection of rule violations.

directed retrospection: a technique used in writing research in which writers categorize the process(es) in which they have just been engaged.

discourse: connected language that is a minimum of several sentences in length; it includes written text and connected speech.

discourse markers: words or phrases used by a speaker (e.g., "oh"; "so") that assist communication even though they are only of indirect relevance to his/her message.

dissociation: as applied to brain-damaged patients, intact performance on one task but severely impaired performance on a different task.

distinctiveness: this characterizes memory traces that are distinct or different from other memory traces stored in long-term memory; it leads to enhanced memory.

divided attention: a situation in which two tasks are performed at the same time; also known as **multitasking.**

double dissociation: the finding that some individuals (often brain-damaged) have intact performance on one task but poor performance on another task, whereas other individuals exhibit the opposite pattern.

dysexecutive syndrome: a condition in which damage to the frontal lobes causes impaired functioning of the **central executive** involving deficits in organizing and planning behavior.

dysrationalia: the failure of reasonably intelligent individuals to think and reason in a rational fashion.

ecological validity: the extent to which research findings (especially laboratory ones) can be generalized to the real world.

egocentric heuristic: a rule of thumb in which listeners rely solely on their own knowledge when interpreting what speakers are saying rather than on the **common ground** between them; it can inhibit effective communication.

emotion regulation: the use of deliberate and effortful processes to change a spontaneous emotional state (usually a negative one); examples of emotion regulation include cognitive reappraisal, use of distraction, and controlled breathing.

encoding specificity principle: the notion that retrieval depends on the *overlap* between the information available at retrieval and the information within the memory trace; memory is best when the overlap is high.

episodic buffer: a component of **working memory** that is used to integrate and to store briefly information from the **phonological loop**, the **visuo-spatial sketchpad**, and long-term memory.

episodic memory: a form of **declarative memory** concerned with personal experiences or episodes occurring in a given place at a given time; see **semantic memory**.

event-based prospective memory: a form of **prospective memory** in which some event (e.g., seeing a grocery store) provides the cue to perform a given action (e.g., buying fruit).

event-related potentials (ERPs): the pattern of electroencephalograph (EEG) activity obtained by averaging the brain responses to the same stimulus (or similar stimuli) presented repeatedly.

expertise: a very high level of thinking and performance in a given domain (e.g., chess) achieved from many years of practice.

expressive writing: writing in a heartfelt way on a topic of deep personal significance to the writer; it has beneficial effects on emotional states and health.

extinction: a disorder of visual attention in which a stimulus presented to the side opposite the brain damage is not detected when another stimulus is presented at the same time to the same side as the brain damage.

face-in-the-crowd effect: the finding that threatening (especially angry) faces can be detected more rapidly among other faces than faces with other expressions.

false memories: apparent **recovered memories** that refer to imagined rather than genuine events or experiences.

figure–ground organization: the division of the visual environment into a figure (having a distinct form) and ground (lacking a distinct form); the contour between figure and ground appears to belong to the figure, which stands out from the ground.

flashbulb memories: vivid and detailed memories of dramatic and significant events.

focused attention: a situation in which individuals try to attend to only one source of information while ignoring other stimuli; also known as selective attention.

framing effect: the finding that decisions are often influenced by aspects of the situation (e.g., precise wording of a problem) that are irrelevant to good decision making.

free will: the notion that we freely or voluntarily choose what to do from a number of possibilities; this notion has been challenged by those who claim that nonconscious processes determine our actions.

Freudian slip: a speech-production error that reveals the speaker's (often unconscious) sexual or other desires.

functional fixedness: the inflexible use of the usual function or functions of an object in problem solving.

functional magnetic resonance imaging (fMRI): a brain-imaging technique based on imaging blood oxygenation using an MRI scanner; it has very good spatial resolution and reasonable temporal resolution.

functional specialization: the assumption (only partially correct) that cognitive functions (e.g., color processing; face processing) occur in specific brain regions.

fusiform face area: an area within the inferotemporal cortex that is associated with face processing; the term is somewhat misleading given that the area is also associated with the processing of other categories of visual objects.

geons: basic shapes or components that are combined in object recognition; an abbreviation for "geometric ions" proposed by Biederman.

graphemes: basic units of written language; a word consists of one or more graphemes.

heuristics: these are rules of thumb that are easy to use and are much used in **judgment** and **decision making**; examples include the **representativeness heuristic**, **means–ends analysis**; and the **recognition heuristic**.

hill climbing: a simple **heuristic** used by problem solvers in which they focus on making moves that will apparently put them closer to the goal or problem solution.

hindsight bias: the tendency for people to exaggerate how accurately they would have predicted some event in advance after they know what actually happened.

homographs: words that have a single spelling but at least two different meanings (e.g., maroon; throttle); used to study **interpretive bias.**

hyperthymestic syndrome: an exceptional ability to remember the events of one's own life; in other words, outstanding **autobiographical memory.**

hypothesis testing: an approach to problem solving based on forming a hypothesis or tentative explanation which is then subjected to one or more tests.

ill-defined problems: problems in which the definition of the problem statement is imprecisely specified; the initial state, goal state, and methods to be used to solve the problem may be unclear; see **well-defined problems.**

illusory conjunction: mistakenly combining features from two different stimuli to perceive an object that isn't present.

implicit learning: a form of learning producing long-term memory in which there is no conscious awareness of what has been learned.

inattentional blindness: the failure to perceive the appearance of an unexpected object in the visual environment; see **change blindness.**

incubation: requiring participants to put a problem aside for some time to observe the effects on the subsequent likelihood of solving it; incubation generally enhances problem solving.

inferences: in sentence comprehension, going beyond what is said or written to make more complete sense of the speaker's or writer's intended meaning.

informal reasoning: a form of reasoning that involves arguments based on one's relevant knowledge and experience; it is prone to error and differs from **deductive reasoning** in not being based on logic.

insight: the experience of suddenly realizing how to solve a problem.

internal lexicon: information about the sounds, spellings, and meanings of words stored in long-term memory; it functions as a dictionary.

interpretive bias: the tendency to interpret ambiguous stimuli and situations in a threatening fashion.

introspection: a careful examination and description of one's own inner mental thoughts and states.

judgment: this involves an assessment of the likelihood of a given event occurring on the basis of incomplete information; it often forms the initial process in **decision making.**

knowledge effect: the tendency of writers to assume (often mistakenly) that those reading what they have written possess the same knowledge.

knowledge-lean problems: problems that can be solved without the use of much prior knowledge; most of the necessary information is provided by the problem statement; see **knowledge-rich problems.**

knowledge-rich problems: problems that can only be solved through the use of considerable amounts of relevant prior knowledge; see **knowledge-lean problems.**

law of Prägnanz: the notion that the simplest possible organization of the visual environment is what is perceived; proposed by the Gestaltists.

lesion: a structural alteration within the brain caused by disease or injury.

lexical bias effect: the tendency for speech errors to form words rather than nonwords; see **spoonerism.**

lexical decision task: strings of letters are presented, and the task is to decide as rapidly as possible whether each string is a word or a **nonword.**

life script: the typical major life events for individuals living within a given society; sample life events are getting married and having children.

linguistic universals: according to Chomsky, the features (e.g., word order) that are common to virtually all languages; there is controversy concerning the existence of such features.

loss aversion: the greater sensitivity to potential losses than to potential gains exhibited by most people in decision making.

magneto-encephalography (MEG): a noninvasive brain-scanning technique based on recording the magnetic fields generated by brain activity; it has excellent temporal resolution and reasonably good spatial resolution.

masking: suppression of the processing of stimulus (e.g., visual; auditory) by presenting a second stimulus (the masking stimulus) very soon afterwards.

matching bias: as applied to the Wason selection task, selection of cards simply because they match those contained within the rule whether they are correct or incorrect.

McGurk effect: when there is a conflict between a spoken **phoneme** and the speaker's lip movements, the sound that is heard combines the auditory and visual information.

means–ends analysis: a **heuristic** for solving problems based on creating a subgoal designed to reduce the difference between the current state of a problem and the end or goal state.

memory span: the number of items (e.g., digits; words) that an individual can recall immediately in the correct order; it is used as a measure of the capacity of short-term memory.

mental model: used in reasoning, an internal or mental representation of some possible situation or event in the world.

mental set: a readiness to think or act in a given way, often because this has been shown to be successful in the past.

meta-analysis: a form of statistical analysis based on combining the findings from numerous studies on a given issue.

metaphor: an expression in which something or someone is said to mean something it only resembles; for example, someone who is very brave may be described as a "lion in battle."

method of loci: a memory technique in which the items that are to be remembered are associated with various locations that are well known to the learner.

mixed-error effect: a type of speech error where the incorrect word is related in terms of both meaning and sound to the correct one.

mnemonics: these consist of numerous methods or systems that learners can use to enhance their long-term memory for information.

modularity: the assumption that the cognitive system consists of several fairly independent or separate modules or processors, each of which is specialized for a given type of processing (e.g., face processing).

mood congruity: the finding that learning and retrieval are better when the learner's (or remberer's) mood state is the same as (or congruent with) the affective value of the to-be-remembered material.

mood-state-dependent memory: the finding that memory performance is better when the individual's mood state is the same at learning and retrieval than when it differs.

morphemes: the basic units of meaning; words consist of one or more morphemes.

multitasking: performing two or more tasks at the same time by switching rapidly between them.

myside bias: in informal reasoning, the tendency to evaluate statements in terms of one's own beliefs and behavior rather than on their merits.

neglect: a disorder of visual attention in which stimuli or parts of stimuli presented to the side opposite the brain damage are undetected and not responded to; the condition resembles **extinction** but is more severe.

nondeclarative memory: also known as implicit memory, this is memory that doesn't involve conscious recollection of information; see **declarative memory**.

nonwords: letter strings that do not form words but are nevertheless pronounceable.

omission bias: a preference for risking harm through inaction compared to risking harm through action; it is shown even when the balance of advantage lies in action rather than inaction.

operation span: the maximum number of items (arithmetical questions + words) for which an individual can recall all the last words.

parallel processing: two or more processes occurring simultaneously; see **serial processing**.

parsing: identifying the grammatical structure of sentences that are read or heard.

phonemes: these are the basic units of sound; words consists of one or more phonemes.

phonemic restoration effect: the finding that listeners presented with a sentence including a missing **phoneme** use the sentence context to identify it and are not aware that it is missing.

phonics approach: a method of teaching young children to read in which they learn to link individual letters and groups of letters to the sounds of the language; see **whole-language approach**.

phonological dyslexia: a condition in which brain-damaged patients have difficulty in phonological processing; this causes them to find it hard to pronounce unfamiliar words and **nonwords** (but not familiar words) when reading aloud.

phonological loop: a component of **working memory** in which speech-based information is processed and stored and subvocal articulation occurs.

phonological similarity effect: the finding that immediate recall of word lists in the correct order is impaired when the words sound similar to each other.

phonology: the sounds of words; of importance in reading.

phrase: a group of words within a sentence that expresses a single idea; see **clause**.

positron emission tomography (PET): a brain-scanning technique based on the detection of positrons; it has reasonable spatial resolution but poor temporal resolution.

post-event misinformation effect: the distorting effect on eyewitness memory of misleading information provided after the crime or other event.

pragmatics: in sentence comprehension, using the social context and other information to work out the intended meaning of what is said.

preformulation: the production by speakers of phrases used frequently before; it is done to reduce the demands of speech production.

premises: in **deductive reasoning,** statements that participants are instructed to assume are true.

priming: this is a form of **nondeclarative memory** involving facilitated processing of (and response to) a target stimulus because the same or a related stimulus was presented previously.

principle of parsimony: in **deductive reasoning,** the tendency to form only one mental model even when additional ones could be constructed.

principle of truth: including what is true but omitting what is false from a mental representation or **mental model.**

proactive interference: disruption of memory by previous learning (often of similar material); see **retroactive interference.**

procedural memory: this is a form of **nondeclarative memory** involving learned skills and concerned with "knowing how."

progress monitoring: this is a heuristic used in problem solving in which insufficiently rapid progress towards solution leads to the adoption of a different strategy.

prosodic cues: various aspects of speech (e.g., rhythm; stress) used by speakers to assist communication; used most often by speakers when what they are saying is somewhat ambiguous.

prosopagnosia: a condition mostly caused by brain damage in which there is a severe impairment in face recognition with little or no impairment of object recognition; popularly known as "face blindness."

prospective memory: remembering to carry out some intended action in the absence of any explicit reminder to do so; see **retrospective memory.**

protocol analysis: the study and classification of the verbalizations of participants while performing some task.

prototype: a central description or conceptual core incorporating the major features of a **category,** with some features generally weighted more than others.

psychological refractory period (PRP) effect: the slowing of the response to the second of two stimuli when they are presented close together in time.

rationalization: in Bartlett's theory, the tendency in story recall to produce errors conforming to the cultural expectations of the rememberer; it is attributed to the influence of **schemas.**

reading span: the greatest number of sentences read for comprehension for which an individual can recall all the final words more than 50% of the time.

rebus problems: problems in which there are various verbal and visual cues to a well-known phrase; they are often solved by using **insight.**

recall: retrieving information from long-term memory in the presence or absence of cues.

recency effect: the tendency in free recall for the last few items (typically two or three) to be much more likely to be recalled than those from the middle of the list; this effect has been used to measure the capacity of short-term memory.

recognition heuristic: a rule of thumb in which a **judgment** has to be made between two objects (e.g., which city is larger?); it involves selecting the object that is recognized.

recognition memory: deciding whether a given stimulus was encountered previously in a particular context (e.g., the previous list).

reconsolidation: this is a new **consolidation** process that occurs when a previously formed memory trace is reactivated; it allows that memory trace to be updated.

recovered memories: childhood traumatic or threatening memories that are remembered many years after the relevant events or experiences.

rehearsal: subvocal reiteration of verbal material (e.g., words); often used in the attempt to increase the amount of information that can be remembered.

reminiscence bump: the tendency of older people to recall a disproportionate number of autobiographical memories from the years of adolescence and early adulthood.

repetitive transcranial magnetic stimulation (rTMS): the administration of **transcranial magnetic stimulation** several times in rapid succession.

representativeness heuristic: the rule of thumb that an object or individual belongs to a specified category because it is representative (typical) of that category; it is used in **judgment** and produces the wrong answer when it leads the individual to ignore **base-rate information.**

repression: motivated forgetting of traumatic or other very threatening events.

retroactive interference: disruption of memory for what was learned originally by other learning or processing during the retention interval; see **proactive interference.**

retrograde amnesia: impaired ability of amnesic patients to remember information and events (i.e., declarative memory) from the time period prior to the onset of **amnesia**.

retrospective memory: memory for events, words, people, and so on encountered or experienced in the past; see **prospective memory**.

rubber hand illusion: the misperception that a rubber hand is one's own; it occurs when the visible rubber hand is touched at the same time as the individual's own hidden hand.

saccades: rapid eye movements that are separated by eye fixations lasting about 250 ms.

satisficing: in decision making, a **heuristic** that involves selecting the first option that satisfies the individual's minimum requirements; formed from the words "satisfactory" and "sufficing."

schemas: organized knowledge of various kinds (e.g., about the world; typical sequences of events) stored in long-term memory; schemas facilitate perception and language comprehension, and allow us to form expectations (e.g., of likely events in a restaurant).

scripts: knowledge in the form of **schemas** of the typical actions associated with certain events (e.g., restaurant meals; football games).

segmentation problem: the listener's problem of dividing the almost continuous sounds of speech into separate **phonemes** and words.

self-reference effect: enhanced long-term memory for information if it is related to the self at the time of learning.

semantic dementia: a condition caused by brain damage in which there is initially mainly extensive loss of knowledge about the meanings of words and concepts.

semantic memory: a form of **nondeclarative memory** consisting of general knowledge about the world, concepts,

language, and so on; see **episodic memory**.

serial processing: this involves only one process occurring at any given moment; that process is completed before the next one starts; see **parallel processing**.

shadowing: repeating word for word one auditory message as it is presented while a second auditory message is also presented.

skill learning: see **procedural memory**.

source misattribution: errors in long-term memory that occur when the rememberer is mistaken about the source or origin of a retrieved memory.

split attention: allocation of attention to two (or more) nonadjacent regions of visual space.

split-brain patients: patients in whom most of the direct links between the two hemispheres have been severed; as a result, they can experience problems in coordinating their processing and behavior.

spoonerism: a speech error in which the initial letter or letters of two words (typically close together) are mistakenly switched to form; an example of **lexical bias**.

spreading activation: the notion that activation of a word or node within the brain causes some activation to spread to several related words or nodes.

stereotypes: **schemas** incorporating oversimplified generalizations (often negative) about certain groups.

Stroop effect: the finding that naming the colors in which words are printed takes longer when the words are conflicted color words (e.g., the word RED printed in green).

subliminal perception: perceptual processing occurring below the level of conscious awareness that can nevertheless influence behavior.

sunk-cost effect: the finding that individuals who have invested effort, time, or money to little avail tend to invest more resources in the hope of justifying the previous investment; it corresponds to "throwing good money after bad."

surface dyslexia: a condition in which brain-damaged patients have difficulty in accessing words in their internal lexicon or dictionary; this causes difficulties in reading irregular words aloud.

syllogism: a type of problem used in studies on **deductive reasoning**; there are two statements or **premises** and a conclusion that may or may not follow logically from the premises.

synesthesia: a sensory experience in which a stimulus in one sense modality (e.g., hearing) evokes an image in a second sense modality (e.g., vision).

syntactic priming: the tendency for the sentences produced by speakers to have the same syntactic structure as sentences they have heard or read shortly beforehand.

templates: organized abstract structures including information about several chess pieces; these structures (which are larger for chess experts) are useful when players decide on their next move.

testing effect: the finding that long-term memory is enhanced when some of the learning period is devoted to retrieving the to-be-remembered information.

textisms: the new abbreviations (often involving a mixture of symbols and letters) used when individuals produce text messages.

time-based prospective memory: a form of prospective memory in which time is the cue indicating that a given action needs to be performed.

tip-of-the-tongue state: the frustration experienced by speakers when they have an idea or concept in mind but can't find the appropriate word to express it.

top-down processing: stimulus processing that is determined by expectations, memory, and knowledge rather than directly by the stimulus.

transcranial magnetic stimulation (TMS): a technique in which magnetic pulses briefly disrupt the functioning of a given brain area, thus creating a short-lived **lesion**; when several pulses are given in rapid succession, the technique is known as repetitive transcranial magnetic stimulation (rTMS).

transfer-appropriate processing: this is the notion that long-term memory will be greatest when the processing at the time of retrieval is very similar to the processing at the time of learning.

typicality effect: the finding that the time taken to decide that a category member belongs to a **category** is less for more typical than for less typical members.

unconscious transference: the tendency of eyewitnesses to misidentify a familiar (but innocent) face as belonging to the person responsible for a crime.

unusualness heuristic: a rule of thumb used by scientists in which the emphasis is on unusual or unexpected findings that may lead to the development of new hypotheses and lines of experimentation.

Urbach-Wiethe disease: a disease in which the amygdala and adjacent areas are destroyed; it leads to the impairment of emotional processing and memory for emotional material.

vegetative state: a condition produced by brain damage in which there is wakefulness but an apparent lack of awareness and purposeful behavior.

ventriloquist illusion: the mistaken perception that sounds are coming from their apparent visual source, as in ventriloquism.

verb bias: the finding that some verbs occur more often within one particular syntactic or grammatical structure than within others.

visuo-spatial sketchpad: a component of **working memory** that is used to process visual and spatial information and to store this information briefly.

weapon focus: the finding that eyewitnesses pay so much attention to some crucial aspect of the situation (e.g., the weapon) that they ignore other details.

well-defined problems: problems in which the initial state, the goal, and the methods available for solving them are clearly laid out; see **ill-defined problems**.

whole-language approach: a method of teaching young children to read in which the emphasis is on understanding the meaning of text; it includes using sentence context to guess the identity of unknown words.

word-length effect: fewer long words than short ones can be recalled immediately after presentation in the correct order.

word superiority effect: the finding that a target letter is detected faster when presented in words than in **nonwords**.

working memory: a system that can store information briefly while other information is processed.

working memory capacity: an assessment of how much information can be processed and stored at the same time; individual differences in this capacity are associated with differences in intelligence and attentional control.

References

Abarbanell, L., & Hauser, M. D. (2010). Mayan morality: An exploration of permissible harms. *Cognition, 115,* 207–224.

Aberegg, S. K., Haponik, E. F., & Terry, P. B. (2005). Omission bias and decision making in pulmonary and critical care medicine. *Chest, 128,* 1497–1505.

Abrams, L. (2008). Tip-of-the-tongue states yield language insights: The process of turning thoughts into speech changes with age. *American Scientist, 96,* 234–239.

Abutalebi, J., & Green, D. W. (2008). Control mechanisms in bilingual language production: Neural evidence from language switching studies. *Language and Cognitive Processes, 23,* 557–582.

Acheson, D. J., Postle, B. R., & MacDonald, M. C. (2010). The interaction of concreteness and phonological similarity in verbal working memory. *Journal of Experimental Psychology: Learning, Memory, and Cognition, 36,* 17–36.

Addis, D. R., Wong, A. T., & Schacter, D. L. (2007). Remembering the past and imagining the future: Common and distinct neural substrates during event construction and elaboration. *Neuropsychologia, 45,* 1363–1377.

Aggleton, J. P. (2008). Understanding anterograde amnesia: Disconnections and hidden lesions. *Quarterly Journal of Experimental Psychology, 61,* 1441–1471.

Ahn, W. K., Kim, N. S., Lassaline, M. E., & Dennis, M. J. (2000). Causal status as a determinant of feature centrality. *Cognitive Psychology, 41,* 361–416.

Aizenstein, H. J., Stenger, V. A., Cochran, J., Clark, K., Johnson, M., Nebes, R. D., et al. (2004). Regional brain activation during concurrent implicit and explicit sequence learning. *Cerebral Cortex, 14,* 199–208.

Alais, D., & Burr, D. (2004). The ventriloquist effect results from near-optimal bimodal integration. *Current Biology, 14,* 257–262.

Albir, A. H., & Alves, F. (2009). Translation as a cognitive activity. In J. Munday (Ed.), *The Routledge companion to translation studies.* London, UK: Routledge.

Aleman, A., Schutter, D. L. G., Ramsey, N. F., van Honk, J., Kessels, R. P. C., Hoogduin, J. M., et al. (2002). Functional anatomy of top-down visuo-spatial processing in the human brain: Evidence from rTMS. *Cognitive Brain Research, 14,* 300–302.

Alexander, P. A., Schallert, D. L., & Hare, U. C. (1991). Coming to terms: How researchers in learning and literacy talk about knowledge. *Review of Educational Research, 61,* 315–343.

Allen, B. P., & Lindsay, D. S. (1998). Amalgamations of memories: Intrusion of information from one event into reports of another. *Applied Cognitive Psychology, 12,* 277–285.

Almashat, S., Ayotte, B., Edelstein, B., & Margrett, J. (2008). Framing effect debiasing in medical decision making. *Patient Education and Counseling, 71,* 102–107.

Altenberg, B. (1990). Speech as linear composition. In G. Caie et al. (Eds.), *Proceedings from the Fourth Nordic Conference for English Studies.* Copenhagen, Denmark: Copenhagen University Press.

Amir, N., Weber, G., Beard, C., Bomyea, J., & Taylor, C. T. (2008). The effect of a single-session attention modification program on response to a public-speaking challenge in socially anxious individuals. *Journal of Abnormal Psychology, 117,* 860–868.

Anaki, D., & Bentin, S. (2009). Familiarity effects on categorization levels of faces and objects. *Cognition, 111,* 144–149.

Anaki, D., Kaufman, Y., Freedman, M., & Moscovitch, M. (2007). Associative (prosop)agnosia without (apparent) perceptual deficits: A case-study. *Neuropsychologia, 45,* 1658–1671.

Anderson, J. R., Fincham, J. M., Qin, Y., & Stocco, A. (2008). A central circuit of the mind. *Trends in Cognitive Sciences, 12,* 136–143.

Anderson, J. R., & Lebiere, C. (2003). The Newell Test for a theory of cognition. *Behavioral and Brain Sciences, 26,* 587–640.

Anderson, R. C., & Pichert, J. W. (1978). Recall of previously unrecallable information following a shift in perspective. *Journal of Verbal Learning and Verbal Behavior, 17,* 1–12.

Anderson, S. W., Rizzo, M., Skaar, N., Cavaco, S., Dawson, J., & Damasio, H. (2007). Amnesia and driving. *Journal of Clinical and Experimental Neuropsychology, 29,* 1–12.

Andersson, U. (2010). The contribution of working memory capacity to foreign language comprehension in children. *Memory, 18,* 456–472.

Andrés, P. (2003). Frontal cortex as the central executive of working memory: Time to revise our view. *Cortex, 39,* 871–895.

Arkes, H. R., & Ayton, P. (1999). The sunk cost and Concorde effects: Are humans less rational than lower animals? *Psychological Bulletin, 125,* 591–600.

Arnold, J. E. (2008). Reference production: Production-internal and address-oriented processes. *Language and Cognitive Processes, 23,* 495–527.

Atkinson, R. L., & Shiffrin, R. M. (1968). Human memory: A proposed system and its control processes. In K. W. Spence & J. T. Spence (Eds.), *The psychology of learning and motivation* (Vol. 2). London, UK: Academic Press.

Augustine, A. A., & Hemenover, S. H. (2009). On the relative merits of affect regulation strategies: A meta-analysis. *Cognition & Emotion, 23,* 1181–1220.

Austin, D., & Kiropoulos, L. (2008). An internet-based investigation of the catastrophic misinterpretation model of panic disorder. *Journal of Anxiety Disorders, 22,* 233–242.

Awh, E., & Pashler, H. (2000). Evidence for split attentional loci. *Journal of Experimental Psychology: Human Perception and Performance, 26,* 834–846.

Baars, B. J. (1997). Consciousness versus attention, perception, and working memory. *Consciousness and Cognition, 5,* 363–371.

Baars, B. J., & Franklin, S. (2007). An architectural model of conscious and unconscious brain functions: Global Workspace Theory and IDA. *Neural Networks, 20,* 955–961.

Baars, B. J., Motley, M. T., & MacKay, D. G. (1975). Output editing for lexical status from artificially elicited slips of the tongue. *Journal of Verbal Learning and Verbal Behavior, 14,* 382–391.

Baddeley, A. D. (1986). *Working memory.* Oxford, UK: Clarendon Press.

Baddeley, A. D. (2000). The episodic buffer: A new component of working memory? *Trends in Cognitive Sciences, 4,* 417–423.

Baddeley, A. (2001). Is working memory still working? *American Psychologist, 56,* 851–864.

Baddeley, A. D. (2007). *Working memory, thought and action.* Oxford, UK: Oxford University Press.

Baddeley, A. D., & Andrade, J. (2000). Working memory and the vividness of imagery. *Journal of Experimental Psychology: General, 129,* 126–145.

Baddeley, A., Eysenck, M. W., & Anderson, M. C. (2009). *Memory.* New York, NY: Psychology Press.

Baddeley, A. D., & Hitch, G. J. (1974). Working memory. In G. H. Bower (Ed.), *Recent advances in learning and motivation* (Vol. 8, pp. 47–89). New York, NY: Academic Press.

Baddeley, A. D., Papagno, C., & Vallar, G. (1988). When long-term learning depends on short-term storage. *Journal of Memory and Language, 27,* 586–595.

Baddeley, A. D., & Wilson, B. (2002). Prose recall and amnesia: Implications for the structure of working memory. *Neuropsychologia, 40,* 1737–1743.

Bahrick, H. P. (1984). Semantic memory content in permastore: Fifty years of memory for Spanish learning in school. *Journal of Experimental Psychology: General, 113,* 1–29.

Bahrick, H. P., Bahrick, P. O., & Wittlinger, R. P. (1975). Fifty years of memory for names and faces: A cross-sectional approach. *Journal of Experimental Psychology: General, 104,* 54–75.

Bahrick, H. P., Hall, L. K., & Da Costa, L. A. (2008). Fifty years of memory of college grades: Accuracy and distortions. *Emotion, 8,* 13–22.

Ball, L. J., Lucas, F. J., Miles, J. N. V., & Gale, A. G. (2003). Inspection times and the selection task: What do eye movements reveal about relevance effects? *Quarterly Journal of Experimental Psychology, 56A,* 1053–1077.

Bandura, A. (1977). *Social learning theory.* Englewood Cliffs, NJ: Prentice Hall.

Bangert-Drowns, R. L., Kulik, J. A., & Kulik, C. L. C. (1991). Effects of frequent classroom testing. *Journal of Educational Research, 61,* 213–238.

Banks, W. P., & Isham, E. A. (2009). We infer rather than perceive the moment we decided to act. *Psychological Science, 20,* 17–21.

Banks, W. P., & Pockett, S. (2007). Benjamin Libet's work on the neuroscience of free will. In M. Velmans & S. Schinder (Eds.), *Blackwell companion to consciousness* (pp. 657–670). Malden, MA: Blackwell.

Barber, H. A., Donamayor, N., Kutgas, M., & Munte, T. (2010). Parafoveal N400 effect during sentence reading. *Neuroscience Letters, 479,* 152–156.

Bard, E. G., Anderson, A. H., Chen, Y., Nicholson, H. B. V. M., Havard, C., & Dalzel-Job, S. (2007). Let's you do that: Sharing the cognitive burdens of dialog. *Journal of Memory and Language, 57,* 616–641.

Bar-Haim, Y., Lamy, D., Pergamin, L., Bakermans-Kronenburg, M. J., & van IJzendoorn, M. H. (2007). Threat-related attentional bias in anxious and nonanxious individuals: A meta-analytic study. *Psychological Bulletin, 133,* 1–24.

Baron, J., & Ritov, I. (2004). Omission bias, individual differences, and normality. *Organizational Behavior and Human Decision Processes, 94,* 74–85.

Barrett, L. F., & Russell, J. A. (1998). Independence and bipolarity in the structure of current affect. *Journal of Personality and Social Psychology, 74,* 967–984.

Barrett, L. F., Tugade, M. M., & Engle, R. W. (2004). Individual differences in working memory capacity and dual-process theories of the mind. *Psychological Bulletin, 130*, 553–573.

Barsalou, L. W. (1985). Ideals, central tendency, and frequency of instantiation as determinants of graded structure in categories. *Journal of Experimental Psychology: Learning, Memory, & Cognition, 11*, 629–654.

Barsalou, L. W. (2003). Situated simulation in the human conceptual system. *Language & Cognitive Processes, 18*, 513–562.

Barsalou, L. W. (2008). Grounded cognition. *Annual Review of Psychology, 59*, 617–645.

Barsalou, L. W. (2009). Simulation, situated conceptualization, and prediction. *Philosophical Transactions of the Royal Society B: Biological Sciences, 364*, 1281–1289.

Barsalou, L. W., & Wiemer-Hastings, K. (2005). Situating abstract concepts. In D. Pecher & R. Zwaan (Eds.), *Grounding cognition: The role of perception and action in memory, language, and thought*. New York, NY: Cambridge University Press.

Bartlett, F. C. (1932). *Remembering: An experimental and social study*. Cambridge, UK: Cambridge University Press.

Bartolomeo, P. (2002). The relationship between visual perception and visual mental imagery: A reappraisal of the neuropsychological evidence. *Cortex, 38*, 357–378.

Bartolomeo, P. (2008). The neural correlates of visual mental imagery: An ongoing debate. *Cortex, 44*, 107–108.

Bartolomeo, P., & Chokron, S. (2002). Orienting of attention in left unilateral neglect. *Neuroscience and Biobehavioral Reviews, 26*, 217–234.

Barton, J. J. S., Press, D. Z., Keenan, J. P., & O'Connor, M. (2002). Topographic organization of human visual areas in the absence of input from primary cortex. *Journal of Neuroscience, 19*, 3619–2627.

Bauby, J.-D. (1997). *The diving bell and the butterfly*. New York, NY: Knopf.

Bavelas, J., Gerwing, J., Sutton, C., & Prevost, D. (2008). Gesturing on the telephone: Independent effects of dialog and visibility. *Journal of Memory and Language, 58*, 495–520.

Baxendale, S. (2004). Memories aren't made of this: Amnesia at the movies. *British Medical Journal, 329*, 1480–1483.

Baynes, K., & Gazzaniga, M. (2000). Consciousness, introspection, and the split-brain: The two minds/one body problem. In M. S. Gazzaniga (Ed.), *The new cognitive neurosciences*. Cambridge, MA: MIT Press.

Bays, P. M., Singh-Curry, V., Gorgoraptis, N., Driver, J., & Husain, M. (2010). Integration of goal- and stimulus-related visual signals revealed by damage to human parietal cortex. *Journal of Neuroscience, 30*, 5968–5978.

Bearman, C. R., Ball, L. J., & Ormerod, T. C. (2007). The structure and function of spontaneous analogizing in domain-based problem solving. *Thinking & Reasoning, 13*, 273–294.

Beck, M. R., Levin, D. T., & Angelone, B. (2007). Change blindness blindness: Beliefs about the roles of intention and scene complexity in change blindness. *Consciousness and Cognition, 16*, 31–51.

Behrman, B. W., & Davey, S. L. (2001). Eyewitness identification in actual criminal cases: An archival analysis. *Law and Human Behavior, 25*, 475–491.

Bereiter, C., Burtis, P. J., & Scardamalia, M. (1988). Cognitive operations in constructing main points in written composition. *Journal of Memory and Language, 27*, 261–278.

Bereiter, C., & Scardamalia, M. (1987). *The psychology of written composition*. Hillsdale, NJ: Lawrence Erlbaum Associates.

Berndsen, M., & Manstead, A. S. R. (2007). On the relationship between responsibility and guilt: Antecedent appraisal or elaborated appraisal? *European Journal of Social Psychology, 37*, 774–792.

Berman, M. G., Jonides, J., & Lewis, R. L. (2009). In search of decay in verbal short-term memory. *Journal of Experimental Psychology: Learning, Memory, & Cognition, 35*, 317–333.

Berndt, R. S., Mitchum, C. C., Haendiges, A. N., & Sandson, J. (1997). Verb retrieval in aphasia. I. Characterizing single word impairments. *Brain and Language, 56*, 69–106.

Berntsen, D. (1998). Voluntary and involuntary access to autobiographical memory. *Memory, 6*, 113–141.

Berntsen, D. (2010). The unbidden past: Involuntary autobiographical memories as a basic mode of remembering. *Current Directions in Psychological Science, 19*, 138–142.

Berntsen, D., & Hall, N. M. (2004). The episodic nature of involuntary autobiographical memories. *Memory & Cognition, 32*, 789–803.

Berntsen, D., & Rubin, D. C. (2002). Emotionally charged autobiographical memories across the life span: The recall of happy, sad, traumatic and involuntary memories. *Psychology and Ageing, 17*, 636–652.

Bickerton, D. (1984). The language bioprogram hypothesis. *Behavioral and Brain Sciences, 7*, 173–221.

Biederman, I. (1987). Recognition-by-components: A theory of human image understanding. *Psychological Review, 94*, 115–147.

Biederman, I., & Gerhardstein, P. C. (1993). Recognizing depth-rotated objects: Evidence for 3-D viewpoint invariance. *Journal of Experimental Psychology: Human Perception & Performance, 19*, 1162–1182.

Bilalić, M., McLeod, P., & Gobet, F. (2008a). Inflexibility of experts: Reality or myth? Quantifying the Einstellung effect in chess masters. *Cognitive Psychology, 56*, 73–102.

Bilalić, M., McLeod, P., & Gobet, F. (2008b). Why good thoughts block better ones: The mechanism of the pernicious Einstellung (set) effect. *Cognition, 108*, 652–661.

Bjork, R. A., & Bjork, E. L. (1992). A new theory of disuse and an old theory of stimulus fluctuation. In A. Healey, S. Kosslyn, & R. Shiffrin (Eds.), *From learning processes to cognitive processes: Essays in honor of William K. Estes* (Vol. 2). Hillsdale, NJ: Lawrence Erlbaum Associates.

Blanchette, I., & Richards, A. (2010). The influence of affect on higher level cognition: A review of research on interpretation, judgment, decision making and reasoning. *Cognition & Emotion, 24*, 561–595.

Blanchette, I., Richards, A., Melnyk, L., & Lavda, A. (2007). Reasoning about emotional contents following shocking terrorist attacks: A tale of three cities. *Journal of Experimental Psychology: Applied, 13*, 47–56.

Blandón-Gitlin, I., Przdek, K., Lindsay, D. S., & Hagen, L. (2009). Criteria-based content analysis of true and suggested accounts of events. *Applied Cognitive Psychology, 23*, 901–917.

Bleckley, M. K., Durso, F. T., Crutchfield, J. M., Engle, R. W., & Khanna, M. M. (2003). Individual differences in working memory capacity predict visual attention allocation. *Psychonomic Bulletin & Review, 10*, 884–889.

Boland, J. E., & Blodgett, A. (2001). Understanding the constraints on syntactic generation: Lexical bias and discourse congruency effects on eye movements. *Journal of Memory and Language, 45*, 391–411.

Bolden, G. B. (2006). Little words that matter: Discourse markers "so" and "oh" and the doing of other-attentiveness in social interaction. *Journal of Communication, 56*, 661–688.

Bolden, G. B. (2009). Implementing incipient actions: The discourse marker 'so' in English conversation. *Journal of Pragmatics, 41*, 974–998.

Bolognini, N., & Ro, T. (2010). Transcranial magnetic stimulation: Disrupting neural activity to alter and assess brain function. *Journal of Neuroscience, 30*, 9647–9650.

Boly, M., Phillips, C., Tschibanda, L., Vanhaudenhuyse, A., Schabus, M., Dange-Vu, T. T., et al. (2008). Intrinsic brain activity in altered states of consciousness: How conscious is the default mode of brain function? *Annals of the New York Academy of Sciences, 1129*, 119–129.

Bond, C. F., & DePaulo, B. M. (2008). Individual differences in judging deception: Accuracy and bias. *Psychological Bulletin, 134*, 477–492.

Bonnefon, J. F., Eid, M., Vautie, S., & Jmel, S. (2008). A mixed Rasch model of dual-process conditional reasoning. *Quarterly Journal of Experimental Psychology, 61*, 809–824.

Borges, J. L. (1964). *Labyrinths: Selected stories and other writing*. New York, NY: New Directions.

Borst, G., & Kosslyn, S. M. (2008). Visual mental imagery and visual perception: Structural equivalence revealed by scanning processes. *Memory & Cognition, 36*, 849–862.

Bourdais, C., & Pecheux, M.-G. (2009). Categorizing in 13- and 16-month-old infants: A comparison of two methods. *Année Psychologique, 109*, 3–27.

Bowden, E. M., & Beeman, M. J. (1998). Getting the right idea: Semantic activation in the right hemisphere may help solve insight problems. *Psychological Science, 9*, 435–440.

Bowden, E. M., & Jung-Beeman, M. (2007). Methods for investigating the neural components of insight. *Methods, 42*, 87–99.

Bowden, E. M., Jung-Beeman, M., Fleck, J., & Kounios, J. (2005). New approaches to demystifying insight. *Trends in Cognitive Sciences, 9*, 322–328.

Bower, G. H. (1973). How to ... uh ... remember!. *Psychology Today, 7*, 63–70.

Bower, G. H., Black, J. B., & Turner, T. J. (1979). Scripts in memory for text. *Cognitive Psychology, 11*, 177–220.

Bower, G. H., & Clark, M. C. (1969). Narrative stories as mediators for serial learning. *Psychonomic Science, 14*, 181–182.

Bowers, J. S. (2002). Challenging the widespread assumption that connectionism and distributed representations go hand-in-hand. *Cognitive Psychology, 45*, 413–445.

Bowers, J. S. (2009). On the biological plausibility of grandmother cells: Implications for neural network theories of psychology and neuroscience. *Psychological Review, 116*, 220–251.

Brandt, K. R., Gardiner, J. M., Vargha-Khadem, F., Baddeley, A. D., & Mishkin, M. (2006). Using semantic memory to boost "episodic" recall in a case of developmental amnesia. *NeuroReport, 17*, 1057–1060.

Bransford, J. D., Barclay, J. R., & Franks, J. J. (1972). Sentence memory: A constructive versus interpretive approach. *Cognitive Psychology, 3*, 193–209.

Bransford, J. D., Franks, J. J., Morris, C. D., & Stein, B. S. (1979). Some general constraints on learning and memory research. In L. S. Cermak & F. I. M. Craik (Eds.), *Levels of processing in human memory*. Hillsdale, NJ: Lawrence Erlbaum Associates.

Bransford, J. D., & Johnson, M. K. (1972). Contextual prerequisites for understanding. *Journal of Verbal Learning and Verbal Behavior, 11*, 717–726.

Brass, M., & Haggard, P. (2008). The what, when, and whether model of intentional action. *The Neuroscientist, 14*, 319–325.

Brédart, S., Brennen, T., Delchambre, M., McNeill, A., & Burton, A. M. (2005). Naming very familiar people: When retrieving names is faster than retrieving semantic biographical information. *British Journal of Psychology, 96*, 205–214.

Brennan, S. E. (1990). *Seeking and providing evidence for mutual understanding*. PhD dissertation, Department of Psychology, Stanford University, Stanford, CA.

Brewer, W. F., & Treyens, J. C. (1981). Role of schemata in memory for places. *Cognitive Psychology, 13*, 207–230.

Bright, D. A., & Goodman-Delahunty, J. (2006). Gruesome evidence and emotion: Anger, blame, and jury decision-making. *Law and Human Behavior, 30*, 183–202.

Broadbent, D. E. (1958). *Perception and communication*. Oxford, UK: Pergamon.

Brooks, R., Faff, R., Mulino, D., & Scheelings, R. (2009). Deal or no deal, that is the question: The impact of increasing stakes and framing effects on decision making under risk. *International Review of Finance, 9*, 27–50.

Brown, A. S., Bracken, E., Zoccoli, S., & Douglas, K. (2004). Generating and remembering passwords. *Applied Cognitive Psychology, 18*, 641–651.

Brown, R., & Kulik, J. (1977). Flashbulb memories. *Cognition, 5*, 73–99.

Brown, R., & McNeill, D. N. (1966). The "tip of the tongue" phenomenon. *Journal of Verbal Learning and Verbal Behavior, 5*, 325–337.

Brown, R. G., Jahanshahi, M., Limousin-Dowsey, P., Thomas, D., Quinn, N., & Rothwell, J. C. (2003). Pallidotomy and incidental sequence learning in Parkinson's disease. *NeuroReport, 14*, 1–4.

Brown-Schmidt, S. (2009). The role of executive function in perspective taking during online language comprehension. *Psychonomic Bulletin & Review, 16*, 893–900.

Bruce, K. R., & Pihl, R. P. (1997). Forget drinking to forget: Enhanced consolidation of emotionally charged memory by alcohol. *Experimental and Clinical Psychopharmacology, 5*, 242–250.

Bruce, V., Henderson, Z., Greenwood, K., Hancock, P., Burton, A. M., & Miller, P. (1999). Verification of face identities from images captured on video. *Journal of Experimental Psychology: Applied, 5*, 339–360.

Bruce, V., & Young, A. W. (1986). Understanding face recognition. *British Journal of Psychology, 77*, 305–327.

Bruner, J. S., Goodnow, J. J., & Austin, G. A. (1956). *A study of thinking*. New York, NY: Wiley.

Bruner, J. S., & Postman, L. (1949). On the perception of incongruity: A paradigm. *Journal of Personality, 18*, 206–223.

Bruno, N., Bernadis, P., & Gentilucci, M. (2008). Visually guided pointing, the Müller-Lyer illusion, and the functional interpretation of the dorsal–ventral split: Conclusions from 33 independent studies. *Neuroscience and Biobehavioral Reviews, 32*, 423–437.

Brunyé, T. T., & Taylor, H. A. (2008a). Extended experience benefits spatial mental model development with route but not survey descriptions. *Acta Psychologica, 127*, 340–354.

Brunyé, T. T., & Taylor, H. A. (2008b). Working memory in developing and applying mental models from spatial descriptions. *Journal of Memory and Language, 58*, 701–729.

Bryan, W. L., & Harter, N. (1897). Studies in the physiology and psychology of the telegraphic language. *Psychological Review, 4*, 27–53.

Bryan, W. L., & Harter, N. (1899). Studies on the telegraphic language. The acquisition of a hierarchy of habits. *Psychological Review, 6*, 345–375.

Bub, D. N., Masson, M. E. J., & Cree, G. S. (2008). Evocation of functional and volumetric gestural knowledge by objects and words. *Cognition, 106*, 27–58.

Bucciarelli, M., & Johnson-Laird, P. N. (1999). Strategies in syllogistic reasoning. *Cognitive Science, 23*, 247–303.

Bulbrook, M. E. (1932). An experimental inquiry into the existence and nature of 'insight'. *American Journal of Psychology, 44*, 409–453.

Burke, D., Taubert, J., & Higman, T. (2007). Are face representations viewpoint dependent? A stereo advantage for generalizing across different views of faces. *Vision Research, 47*, 2164–2169.

Burns, B. D. (2004). The effects of speed on skilled chess performance. *Psychological Science, 15*, 442–447.

Burns, B. D., & Wieth, M. (2004). The collider principle in causal reasoning: Why the Monty Hall dilemma is so hard. *Journal of Experimental Psychology: General, 133*, 434–449.

Burton, A. M., Bruce, V., & Hancock, P. J. B. (1999). From pixels to people: A model of familiar face recognition. *Cognitive Science, 23,* 1–31.

Bushman, B. J. (2002). Does venting anger feed of extinguish the flame? Catharsis, rumination, distraction, anger, and aggressive responding. *Personality and Social Psychology Bulletin, 28,* 724–731.

Byrne, R. M. J. (1989). Suppressing valid inferences with conditionals. *Cognition, 31,* 61–83.

Byrne, R. M. J., & Johnson-Laird. P. N. (2009). 'If' and the problems of conditional reasoning. *Trends in Cognitive Sciences, 13,* 282–287.

Caccappolo-van Vliet, E., Miozzo, M., & Stern, Y. (2004). Phonological dyslexia: A test case for reading models. *Psychological Science, 15,* 583–590.

Cahill, L., Babinsky, R., Markowitsch, H. J., & McGaugh, J. L. (1995). The amygdala and emotional memory. *Nature, 377,* 295–296.

Cahir, C., & Thomas, K. (2010). Asymmetric effects of positive and negative affect on decision making. *Psychological Reports, 106,* 193–204.

Caird, J. K., Willness, C. R., Steel, P., & Scialfa, C. (2008). A meta-analysis of the effects of cell phones on driver performance. *Accident Analysis and Prevention, 40,* 1282–1293.

Calabria, M., Cotelli, M., Adenzato, M., Zanetti, O., & Miniussi, C. (2009). Empathy and emotion recognition in semantic dementia: A case report. *Brain and Cognition, 70,* 247–252.

Calder, A. J., Young, A. W., Rowland, D., Perrett, D. I., Hodges, J. R., & Etcoff, N. L. (1996). Facial emotion recognition after bilateral amygdala damage: Differentially severe impairment of fear. *Cognitive Neuropsychology, 13,* 699–745.

Calvo, M. G. (2001). Working memory and inferences: Evidence from eye fixations during reading. *Memory, 9,* 365–381.

Calvo, M. G., & Castillo, M. D. (1997). Mood-congruent bias in interpretation of ambiguity: Strategic processes and temporary activation. *Quarterly Journal of Experimental Psychology, 50A,* 163–182.

Calvo, M. G., Castillo, M. D., & Schmalhof, F. (2006). Strategic influence on the time course of predictive inferences in reading. *Memory & Cognition, 34,* 68–77.

Calvo, M. G., & Eysenck, M. W. (1996). Phonological working memory and reading in test anxiety. *Memory, 4,* 289–305.

Calvo, M. G., & Marrero, H. (2009). Visual search of emotional faces: The role of affective content and featural distinctiveness. *Cognition & Emotion, 23,* 782–806.

Camerer, C., Babcock, L., Loewenstein, G., & Thaler, R. (1997). Labor supply of New York cab drivers: One day at a time? *Quarterly Journal of Economics, CXII,* 407–441.

Cappla, S. F. (2008). Imaging studies of semantic memory. *Current Opinion in Neurology, 21,* 669–675.

Caramazza, A., & Coltheart, M. (2006). Cognitive neuropsychology twenty years on. *Cognitive Neuropsychology, 23,* 3–12.

Carlesimo, G. A., Marfia, G. A., Loasses, A., & Caltagirone, C. (1996). Perceptual and conceptual components in implicit and explicit stem completion. *Neuropsychologia, 34,* 785–792.

Carlin, B. I., & Robinson, D. T. (2009). Fear and loathing in Las Vegas: Evidence from blackjack tables. *Judgment and Decision Making, 4,* 385–396.

Carr, T. H., Davidson, B. J., & Hawkins, H. L. (1978). Perceptual flexibility in word recognition – Strategies affect orthographic computation but not lexical access. *Journal of Experimental Psychology: Human Perception and Performance, 4,* 674–690.

Casper, C., Rothermund, K., & Wentura, D. (2010). Automatic stereotype activation is context-dependent. *Social Psychology, 41,* 131–136.

Casscells, W., Schoenberger, A., & Graboys, T. B. (1978). Interpretation by physicians of clinical laboratory results. *New England Journal of Medicine, 299,* 999–1001.

Cavaco, S., Anderson, S. W., Allen, J. S., Castro-Caldas, A., & Damasio, H. (2004). The scope of preserved procedural memory in amnesia. *Brain, 127,* 1853–1867.

Cavenett, T., & Nixon, R. D. V. (2006). The effect of arousal on memory for emotionally-relevant information: A study of skydivers. *Behaviour Research and Therapy, 44,* 1461–1469.

Centofanti, A. T., & Reece, J. (2006). The cognitive interview and its effect on misleading postevent information. *Psychology, Crime & Law, 12,* 669–683.

Chaigneau, S. E., Barsalou, L. W., & Zamani, M. (2009). Situational information contributes to object categorization and inference. *Acta Psychologica, 130,* 81–94.

Challis, B. H., Velichkovsky, B. M., & Craik, F. I. M. (1996). Levels-of-processing effects on a variety of memory tasks: New findings and theoretical implications. *Consciousness and Cognition, 5,* 142–164.

Chamberlain, E. (2003). Review of 'Behavioral assessment of the dysexecutive syndrome (BADS)'. *Journal of Occupational Psychology, 5,* 33–37.

Channon, S., & Baker, J. (1994). Reasoning strategies in depression: Effects of depressed mood on a syllogism task. *Personality and Individual Differences, 17,* 707–711.

Charlton, D., Fraser-Mackenzie, P. A. F., & Dror, I. E. (2010). Emotional experiences and motivating factors associated with fingerprint analysis. *Journal of Forensic Sciences, 55,* 385–393.

Charness, N. (1981). Search in chess: Age and skill differences. *Journal of Experimental Psychology: Human Perception and Performance, 7,* 467–476.

Charness, N., Tuffiash, M., Krampe, R., Reingold, E., & Vasyukova, E. (2005). The role of deliberate practice in chess expertise. *Applied Cognitive Psychology, 19,* 151–165.

Chartrand, T. L., van Baaren, R. B., & Bargh, J. A. (2006). Linking automatic evaluation to mood and information-processing style: Consequences for experienced affect, impression formation, and stereotyping. *Journal of Experimental Psychology: General, 135,* 7–77.

Chen, Y. W., Chen, C. Y., Lin, C. P., Chou, K. H., & Decety, J. (2010). Love hurts: An fMRI study. *NeuroImage, 51,* 923–929.

Chen, Z. (2002). Analogical problem solving: A hierarchical analysis of procedural similarity. *Journal of Experimental Psychology: Learning, Memory, & Cognition, 28,* 81–98.

Chen, Z., & Cowan, N. (2009). Core verbal working memory capacity: The limit in words retained without covert articulation. *Quarterly Journal of Experimental Psychology, 62,* 1420–1429.

Chen, Z. Y., Cowell, P. E., Varley, R., & Wang, Y.-C. (2009). A cross-language study of verbal and visuospatial working memory span. *Journal of Clinical and Experimental Neuropsychology, 31,* 385–391.

Chen, Z., & Klahr, D. (1999). All other things being equal: Children's acquisition of the control of variables strategy. *Child Development, 70,* 1098–1120.

Chenoweth, N. A., & Hayes, J. R. (2003). The inner voice in writing. *Written Communication, 20,* 99–118.

Cherney, I. D. (2008). Mom, let me play more computer games: They improve my mental rotation skills. *Sex Roles, 59,* 776–786.

Cherry, E. C. (1953). Some experiments on the recognition of speech with one and two ears. *Journal of the Acoustical Society of America, 25,* 975–979.

Cherubini, P., Castelvecchio, E., & Cherubini, A. M. (2005). Generation of hypotheses in Wason's 2–4–6 task: An information theory approach. *Quarterly*

Journal of Experimental Psychology Section A – Human Experimental Psychology, 58, 309–332.

Cherubini, P., & Mazzocco, A. (2004). From models to rules: Mechanization of reasoning as a way to cope with cognitive overloading in combinatorial problems. *Acta Psychologica, 116,* 223–243.

Chiappe, D. L., & Chiappe, P. (2007). The role of working memory in metaphor production and comprehension. *Journal of Memory and Language, 56,* 172–188.

Cho, S., Holyoak, K. J., & Cannon, T. D. (2007). Analogical reasoning in working memory: Resources shared among relational information, interference resolution, and maintenance. *Memory & Cognition, 35,* 1445–1455.

Chokron, S., Bartolomeo, P., & Sieroff, E. (2008). Unilateral spatial neglect: 30 years of research, discoveries, hope, and (especially) questions. *Revue Neurologique, 164,* S134–S142.

Chokron, S., Dupierrix, E., Tabert, M., & Bartolomeo, P. (2007). Experimental remission of unilateral spatial neglect. *Neuropsychologia, 45,* 3127–3148.

Chomsky, N. (1965). *Aspects of the theory of syntax.* Cambridge, MA: MIT Press.

Chomsky, N. (1986). *Knowledge of language: Its nature, origin, and use.* Westport, CT: Praeger.

Christiansen, M. H., & Chater, N. (2008). Language as shaped by the brain. *Behavioral and Brain Sciences, 31,* 489–512.

Christianson, K., Luke, S. G., & Ferreira, F. (2010). Effects of plausibility on structural priming. *Journal of Experimental Psychology: Learning, Memory, & Cognition, 36,* 538–544.

Christoffels, I. K. (2006). Listening while talking: The retention of prose under articulatory suppression in relation to simultaneous interpreting. *European Journal of Cognitive Psychology, 18,* 206–220.

Christoffels, I. K., de Groot, A. M. B., & Kroll, J. F. (2006). Memory and language skills in simultaneous interpreters: The role of expertise and language proficiency. *Journal of Memory and Language, 54,* 324–345.

Chrysikou, E. G., & Weisberg, R. W. (2005). Following the wrong footsteps: Fixation effects of pictorial examples in a design problem-solving task. *Journal of Experimental Psychology: Learning, Memory, and Cognition, 31,* 1134–1148.

Cister, J. M., & Koster, E. H. W. (2010). Mechanisms of attentional biases towards threat in anxiety disorders: An integrative review. *Clinical Psychology Review, 30,* 203–216.

Clancy, S. A., & McNally, R. J. (2005/2006). Who needs repression? Normal memory processes can explain "forgetting" of childhood sexual abuse. *Scientific Review of Mental Health Practice, 4,* 66–73.

Clancy, S. A., McNally, R. J., Schacter, D. L., Lenzenweger, M. F., & Pitman, R. K. (2002). Memory distortion in people reporting abduction by aliens. *Journal of Abnormal Psychology, 111,* 455–461.

Clark, D. M. (1986). A cognitive approach to panic. *Behaviour Research and Therapy, 24,* 461–470.

Clark, H. H., & Krych, M. A. (2004). Speaking while monitoring addressees for understanding. *Journal of Memory and Language, 50,* 62–81.

Cleary, M., & Pisoni, D. B. (2001). Speech perception and spoken word recognition: Research and theory. In E. B. Goldstein (Ed.), *Blackwell handbook of perception* (pp. 499–534). Malden, MA: Blackwell.

Cleland, A. A., & Pickering, M. J. (2003). The use of lexical and syntactic information in language production: Evidence from the priming of noun-phrase structure. *Journal of Memory and Language, 49,* 214–230.

Cleland, A.A., & Pickering, M.J. (2006). Do writing and speaking employ the same syntactic representations? *Journal of Memory and Language, 54,* 185–198.

Coch, D., Sanders, L. D., & Neville, H. J. (2005). An event-related potential study of selective auditory attention in children and adults. *Journal of Cognitive Neuroscience, 17,* 606–622.

Cohen, G. (2008). The study of everyday memory. In G. Cohen & M. A. Conway (Eds.), *Memory in the real world* (3rd ed., pp. 1–19). Hove, UK: Psychology Press.

Cole, S. A. (2005). More than zero: Accounting for error in latent fingerprinting identification. *Journal of Criminal Law & Criminology, 95,* 985–1078.

Coleman, M. R., Davis, M. H., Rodd, J. M., Robson, T., Ali, A., Owen, A. M., & Pickard, J. D. (2009). Towards the routine use of brain imaging to aid the clinical diagnosis of disorders of consciousness. *Brain, 132,* 2541–2552.

Coley, J. D., Medin, D. L., & Atran, S. (1997). Does rank have its privilege? Inductive inferences within folkbiological taxonomies. *Cognition, 64,* 73–112.

Collins, A. M., & Loftus, E. (1975). A spreading activation theory of semantic memory. *Psychological Review, 82,* 407–428.

Colman, A. M. (2001). *Oxford dictionary of psychology.* Oxford, UK: Oxford University Press.

Coltheart, M. (2001). *Assumptions and methods in cognitive neuropsychology.* Hove, UK: Psychology Press.

Coltheart, M., Rastle, K., Perry, C., Langdon, R., & Ziegler, J. (2001). The DRC model: A model of visual word recognition and reading aloud. *Psychological Review, 108,* 204–258.

Colvin, M. K., & Gazzaniga, M. S. (2007). Split-brain cases. In M. Velmans & S. Schneider (Eds.), *The Blackwell companion to consciousness.* Oxford, UK: Blackwell.

Coman, A., Manier, D., & Hirst, W. (2009). Forgetting the unforgettable through conversation: Socially shared retrieval-induced forgetting of September 11 memories. *Psychological Science, 20,* 627–633.

Conway, A. R. A., Kane, M. J., & Engle, R. W. (2003). Working memory capacity and its relation to general intelligence. *Trends in Cognitive Sciences, 7,* 547–552.

Conway, M. A. (2005). Memory and the self. *Journal of Memory and Language, 53,* 594–628.

Conway, M. A., & Pleydell-Pearce, C. W. (2000). The construction of autobiographical memories in the self-memory system. *Psychological Review, 107,* 261–288.

Conway, M. A., Wang, Q., Hanyu, K., & Haque, S. (2005). A cross-cultural investigation of autobiographical memory. *Journal of Cross-Cultural Psychology, 36,* 739–749.

Cook, G. I., Marsh, R. L., & Hicks, J. L. (2005). Associating a time-based prospective memory task with an expected context can improve or impair intention completion. *Applied Cognitive Psychology, 19,* 345–360.

Cooke, R., Peel, E., Shaw, R. L., & Senior, C. (2007). The neuroimaging research process from the participants' perspective. *International Journal of Psychophysiology, 63,* 152–158.

Copeland, D. E., & Radvansky, G. A. (2004). Working memory and syllogistic reasoning. *Quarterly Journal of Experimental Psychology, 57A,* 1437–1457.

Corbetta, M., Patel, G., & Shulman, G. L. (2008). The re-orienting system of the human brain: From environment to theory of mind. *Neuron, 58,* 306–324.

Corbetta, M., & Shulman, G. L. (2002). Control of goal directed and stimulus-driven attention in the brain. *Nature Reviews Neuroscience, 3,* 201–215.

Cosentino, S., Chute, D., Libon, D., Moore, P., & Grossman, M. (2006). How does the brain support script comprehension? A study of executive processes and semantic knowledge in dementia. *Neuropsychology, 20,* 307–318.

Cowan, N. (2000). The magical number 4 in short-term memory: A reconsideration of mental storage capacity. *Behavioral and Brain Sciences, 24,* 87–185.

Cowan, N., Elliott, E. M., Saults, J. S., Morey, C. C., Mattox, S., Hismjatullina, A., & Conway, A. R. A.

(2005). On the capacity of attention: Its estimation and its role in working memory and cognitive aptitudes. *Cognitive Psychology, 51,* 42–100.

Cowey, A. (2010). The blindsight saga. *Experimental Brain Research, 200,* 3–24.

Cowley, M., & Byrne, R. M. J. (2005). Chess masters' hypothesis testing. *Proceedings of the Twenty-Sixth Annual Conference of the Cognitive Science Society* (pp. 250–255). New York, NY: Psychology Press.

Craik, F. I. M., & Lockhart, R. S. (1972). Levels of processing: A framework for memory research. *Journal of Verbal Learning and Verbal Behavior, 11,* 671–684.

Craik, F. I. M., & Tulving, E. (1975). Depth of processing and the retention of words in episodic memory. *Journal of Experimental Psychology: General, 104,* 268–294.

Crawford, J. R., Smith, G., Maylor, E. A., Della Sala, S., & Logie, R. H. (2003). The Prospective and Retrospective Memory Questionnaire (PRMQ): Normative data and latent structure in a large nonclinical sample. *Memory, 11,* 261–275.

Cree, G. S., & McRae, K. (2003). Analyzing the factors underlying the structure and computation of the meaning of chipmunk, cherry, chisel, cheese, and cello (and many other such concrete nouns). *Journal of Experimental Psychology: General, 132,* 163–201.

Creem, S. H., & Proffitt, D. R. (2001). Grasping objects by their handles: A necessary interaction between cognition and action. *Journal of Experimental Psychology: Human Perception & Performance, 27,* 218–228.

Crystal, D. (1997). *A dictionary of linguistics and phonetics* (4th Ed.). Cambridge, MA: Blackwell.

Crystal, D. (2008). *Txtng: The Gr8 Db8.* New York, NY: Oxford University Press.

Cunningham, J. B., & MacGregor, J. N. (2008). Training insightful problem solving: Effects of realistic and puzzle-like contexts. *Creativity Research Journal, 20,* 291–296.

Cunningham, W. A., Preacher, K. J., & Banaji, M. R. (2001). Implicit attitude measures: Consistency, stability, and convergent validity. *Psychological Science, 12,* 163–170.

Cutler, A., & Butterfield, S. (1992). Rhythmic cues to speech segmentation: Evidence from juncture misperception. *Journal of Memory and Language, 31,* 218–236.

Dahan, D. (2010). The time course of interpretation in speech comprehension. *Current Directions in Psychological Science, 19,* 121–126.

Dalrymple, K. A., Kingstone, A., & Handy, T. C. (2009). Event-related potential evidence for a dual-locus model of global/local processing. *Cognitive Neuropsychology, 26,* 456–470.

Dalton, A. L., & Daneman, M. (2006). Social suggestibility to central and peripheral misinformation. *Memory, 14,* 486–501.

Danckert, J., & Ferber, S. (2006). Revisiting unilateral neglect. *Neuropsychologia, 44,* 987–1006.

Danckert, J., & Rossetti, Y. (2005). Blindsight in action: What can the different subtypes of blindsight tell us about the control of visually guided actions? *Neuroscience and Biobehavioral Reviews, 29,* 1035–1046.

Daneman, M., & Carpenter, P. A. (1980). Individual differences in working memory and reading. *Journal of Verbal Learning and Verbal Behavior, 19,* 450–466.

Daneman, M., & Merikle, P. M. (1996). Working memory and language comprehension: A meta-analysis. *Psychonomic Bulletin & Review, 3,* 422–433.

Darling, S., & Havelka, J. (2010). Visuo-spatial bootstrapping: Evidence for binding of verbal and spatial information in working memory. *Quarterly Journal of Experimental Psychology, 63,* 239–245.

Davis, J. P., & Valentine, T. (2009). CCTV on trial: Matching video images with the defendant in the dock. *Applied Cognitive Psychology, 23,* 482–505.

Dawes, R. M. (1988). *Rational choice in an uncertain world.* San Diego, CA: Harcourt Brace Jovanovich.

Dawson, E., Gilovich, T., & Regan, D. T. (2002). Motivated reasoning and performance on the Wason selection task. *Personality and Social Psychology Bulletin, 28,* 1379–1387.

Dean, I., Harper, N. S., & McAlpine, D. (2005). Neural population coding of sound level adapts to stimulus characteristics. *Nature Neuroscience, 8,* 1684–1689.

De Beni, R., & Moè, A. (2003). Imagery and rehearsal as study strategies for written or orally presented passages. *Psychonomic Bulletin & Review, 10,* 975–980.

De Beni, R., Moè, A., & Cornoldi, C. (1997). Learning from texts or lectures: Loci mnemonics can interfere with reading but not with listening. *European Journal of Cognitive Psychology, 9,* 401–415.

Deffenbacher, K. A., Bornstein, B. H., Penrod, S. D., & McGorty, E. K. (2004). A meta-analytic review of the effects of high stress on eyewitness memory. *Law and Human Behavior, 28,* 687–706.

De Groot, A. D. (1965). *Thought and choice in chess.* The Hague, The Netherlands: Mouton.

Dehaene, S., Changeux, J. P., Naccache, L., Sackur, J., & Sergent, C. (2006). Conscious, preconscious, and subliminal processing: A testable taxonomy. *Trends in Cognitive Sciences*, 10, 204–211.

Dehaene, S., Naccache, L., Cohen, L., Le Bihan, D., Mangin, J., Poline, J., et al. (2001). Cerebral mechanisms of word masking and unconscious repetition priming. *Nature Neuroscience*, 4, 752–758.

De Houwer, J., Teige-Mocigemba, S., Spruyta, A., & Moors, A. (2009). Implicit measures: A normative analysis and review. *Psychological Bulletin*, 135, 347–368.

De Jong, P. F., Bitter, D. J. L., van Setten, M., & Marinus, E. (2009). Does phonological recoding occur during silent reading, and is it necessary for orthographic learning? *Journal of Experimental Child Psychology*, 104, 267–282.

Delaney, P. F., Ericsson, K. A., & Knowles, M. E. (2004). Immediate and sustained effects of planning in a problem-solving task. *Journal of Experimental Psychology: Learning, Memory, and Cognition*, 30, 1219–1234.

Del Cul, A., Dehaene, S., Reyes, P., Bravo, E., & Slachevsky, A. (2009). Causal role of prefrontal cortex in the threshold for access to consciousness. *Brain*, 132, 2531–2540.

Dell, G. S. (1986). A spreading-activation theory of retrieval in sentence production. *Psychological Review*, 93, 283–321.

Dell, G. S., Burger, L. K., & Svec, W. R. (1997). Language production and serial order: A functional analysis and a model. *Psychological Review*, 93, 283–321.

Dell, G. S., Oppenheim, G. M., & Kittredge, A. K. (2008). Saying the right word at the right time: Syntagmatic and paradigmatic interference in sentence production. *Language and Cognitive Processes*, 23, 583–608.

DeLucia, P. R., & Hochberg, J. (1991). Geometrical illusions in solid objects under ordinary viewing conditions. *Perception & Psychophysics*, 50, 547–554.

Delvenne, J. F., Seron, X., Coyette, F., & Rossion, B. (2004). Evidence for perceptual deficits in associative visual (prosop)agnosia: A single-case study. *Neuropsychologia*, 42, 597–612.

De Martino, B., Camerer, C. F., & Adolphs, R. (2010). Amygdala damage eliminates monetary loss aversion. *Proceedings of the National Academy of Sciences of the United States of America*, 107, 3788–3792.

De Neys, W. (2006). Automatic-heuristic and executive-analytic processing during reasoning: Chronometric and dual-task considerations. *Quarterly Journal of Experimental Psychology*, 59, 1070–1100.

De Neys, W., & Glumicic, T. (2008). Conflict monitoring in dual process theories of thinking. *Cognition*, 106, 1248–1299.

De Neys, W., Schaeken, W., & d'Ydewalle, G. (2005). Working memory everyday conditional reasoning: Retrieval and inhibition of stored counterexamples. *Thinking & Reasoning*, 11, 349–381.

De Neys, W., Vartanian, O., & Goel, V. (2008). Smarter than we think: When our brains detect that we are biased. *Psychological Science*, 19, 483–489.

De Neys, W., & Verschueren, N. (2006). Working memory capacity and a notorious brain teaser – The case of the Monty Hall dilemma. *Experimental Psychology*, 53, 123–131.

DePaulo, B. M., Lindsay, J. J., Malone, B. E., Muhlenbruck, L., Charlton, K., & Cooper, H. (2003). Cues to deception. *Psychological Bulletin*, 129, 74–118.

Derakshan, N., & Eysenck, M. W. (1998). Working-memory capacity in high trait-anxious and repressor groups. *Cognition & Emotion*, 12, 697–713.

Destrebecqz, A., Peigneux, P., Laureys, S., Degueldre, C., Del Fiorem, G., Aerts, J., et al. (2005). The neural correlates of implicit and explicit sequence learning: Interacting networks revealed by the process dissociation procedure. *Learning and Memory*, 12, 480–490.

Deutsch, J. A., & Deutsch, D. (1963). Attention: Some theoretical considerations. *Psychological Review*, 93, 283–321.

De Vries, M., Holland, R. W., & Witteman, C. L. M. (2008). In the winning mood: Affect in the Iowa gambling task. *Judgment and Decision Making*, 3, 42–50.

Dewar, M. T., Cowan, N., & Della Sala, S. (2007). Forgetting due to retroactive interference: A fusion of Müller and Pizecker's (1900) early insights into everyday forgetting and recent research on retrograde amnesia. *Cortex*, 43, 616–634.

Dewar, M., Della Sala, S., Beschin, N., & Cowan, N. (2010). Profound retroactive amnesia: What interferes? *Neuropsychology*, 24, 357–367.

Diana, R. A., Yonelinas, A. P., & Ranganath, C. (2007). Imaging recollection and familiarity in the medial temporal lobe: A three-component model. *Trends in Cognitive Sciences*, 11, 379–386.

DiBonaventura, M. D., & Chapman, G. B. (2008). Do decision biases predict bad decisions? Omission bias, naturalness bias, and influenza vaccination. *Medical Decision Making*, 28, 532–539.

Dismukes, K., & Nowinski, J. (2007). Prospective memory, concurrent task management, and pilot error. In A. Kramer, D. Wiegmann, & A. Kirlik

(Eds.), *Attention from theory to practice*. New York, NY: Oxford University Press.

Ditto, P. H., Scepansky, J. A., Munro, G. D., Apanovitch, A. M., & Lockhart, L. K. (1998). Motivated sensitivity to preference-inconsistent information. *Journal of Personality and Social Psychology, 75*, 53–69.

Dodhia, R. M., & Dismukes, R. K. (2009). Interruptions create prospective memory tasks. *Applied Cognitive Psychology, 23*, 73–89.

Dorman, M. F., Raphael, L. J., & Liberman, A. M. (1979). Some experiments in the sound of silence in phonetic perception. *Journal of the Acoustical Society of America, 65*, 1518–1532.

Downing, P. E., Chan, A. W. Y., Peelen, M. V., Dodds, C. M., & Kanwisher, N. (2006). Domain specificity in visual cortex. *Cerebral Cortex, 16*, 1453–1461.

Drews, F. A., Pasupathi, M., & Strayer, D. L. (2008). Passenger and cell phone conversations in simulated driving. *Journal of Experimental Psychology: Applied, 14*, 392–400.

Driver, J., & Vuilleumier, P. (2001). Perceptual awareness and its loss in unilateral neglect and extinction. *Cognition, 79*, 39–88.

Dror, I. E., Charlton, D., & Péron, A. E. (2006). Contextual information renders experts vulnerable to making erroneous identifications. *Forensic Science International, 156*, 74–78.

Dror, I. E., & Mnookin, J. L. (2010). The use of technology in human expert domains: Challenges and risks arising from the use of automated fingerprint identification systems in forensic science. *Law, Probability and Risk, 9*, 47–67.

Dror, I. E., & Rosenthal, R. (2008). Meta-analytically quantifying the reliability and bias ability of forensic experts. *Journal of Forensic Sciences, 53*, 900–903.

Duchaine, B. (2006). Prosopagnosia as an impairment to face-specific mechanisms: Elimination of the alternative hypotheses in a developmental case. *Cognitive Neuropsychology, 23*, 714–747.

Duchaine, B., & Nakayama, K. (2006). Developmental prosopagnosia: A window to context-specific face processing. *Current Opinion in Neurobiology, 16*, 166–173.

Dudukovic, N. M., Marsh, E. J., & Tversky, B. (2004). Telling a story or telling it straight: The effects of entertaining versus accurate retellings on memory. *Applied Cognitive Psychology, 18*, 125–143.

Dumay, N., Frauenfelder, U. H., & Content, A. (2002). The role of the syllable in lexical segmentation in French: Word-spotting data. *Brain and Language, 81*, 144–161.

Dunbar, K. (1993). Concept discovery in a scientific domain. *Cognitive Science, 17*, 397–434.

Dunbar, K., & Blanchette, I. (2001). The in vivo/in vitro approach to cognition: The case of analogy. *Trends in Cognitive Sciences, 5*, 334–339.

Duncan, J., & Humphreys, G. W. (1989). A resemblance theory of visual search. *Psychological Review, 96*, 433–458.

Duncan, J., & Humphreys, G. W. (1992). Beyond the search surface: Visual search and attentional engagement. *Journal of Experimental Psychology: Human Perception & Performance, 18*, 578–588.

Duncker, K. (1945). On problem solving. *Psychological Monographs, 58* (Whole No. 270).

Eagly, A. H. (2001). Social role theory of sex differences and similarities. In J. Worrell (Ed.), *Encyclopedia of women and gender* (pp. 1069–1078). San Diego, CA: Academic Press.

Easterbrook, J. A. (1959). The effect of emotion on cue utilization and the organization of behavior. *Psychological Review, 66*, 183–201.

Ebbinghaus, H. (1885/1913). Über das Gedächtnis (Leipzig, Germany: Dunker) [translated by H. Ruyer & C. E. Bussenius]. New York, NY: Teachers College, Columbia University.

Echterhoff, G., Higgins, E. T., Kopietz, R., & Groll, S. (2008). How communication goals determine when audience tuning biases memory. *Journal of Experimental Psychology: General, 137*, 3–21.

Ehinger, K. A., Hidalgo-Sotelo, B., Torralba, A., & Oliva, A. (2009). Modelling search for people in 900 scenes: A combined source model of eye guidance. *Visual Cognition, 17*, 945–978.

Ehri, L. C., Nunes, S. R., Willows, D. M., Schuster, B. V., Yaghoub-Zadeh, Z., & Shanahan, T. (2001). Phonemic awareness instruction helps children learn to read: Evidence from the National Reading Panel's meta-analysis. *Reading Research Quarterly, 36*, 250–287.

Eich, E. (1995). Searching for mood-dependent memory. *Psychological Science, 6*, 67–75.

Eich, E., & Metcalfe, J. (1989). Mood-dependent memory for internal versus external events. *Journal of Experimental Psychology: Learning, Memory & Cognition, 15*, 443–455.

Eichenbaum, H. (2001). The hippocampus and declarative memory: Cognitive mechanisms and neural codes. *Behavioral Brain Research, 127*, 199–207.

Einstein, G. O., & McDaniel, M. A. (2005). Prospective memory: Multiple retrieval processes. *Current Directions in Psychological Science, 14*, 286–290.

Elder, J. H., & Goldberg, R. M. (2002). Ecological statistics of Gestalt laws for the perceptual organization of contours. *Journal of Vision, 2*, 324–353.

Ellis, J. A., & Cohen, G. (2008). Memory for intentions, actions, and plans. In G. Cohen & M. A. Conway (Eds.), *Memory in the real world* (pp. 141–172). Hove, UK: Psychology Press.

Engbert, R., Nuthmann, A., Richter, E. M., & Kliegl, R. (2005). SWIFT: A dynamical model of saccade generation during reading. *Psychological Review, 112*, 777–813.

Engel, H. (2007). *The man who forgot how to read.* Toronto, Canada: Harper Collins.

Engel, P. J. H. (2008). Tacit knowledge and visual expertise in medical diagnostic reasoning: Implications for medical education. *Medical Teacher, 30*, e184–e188.

Engelhardt, P. E., Bailey, K. G. D., & Ferreira, F. (2006). Do speakers and listeners observe the Gricean maxim of quantity? *Journal of Memory and Language, 54*, 554–573.

Ericsson, K. A. (1988). Analysis of memory performance in terms of memory skill. In R. J. Sternberg (Ed.), *Advances in the psychology of human intelligence* (Vol. 4, pp. 137–179). Hillsdale, NJ: Lawrence Erlbaum Associates.

Ericsson, K. A., & Chase, W. G. (1982). Exceptional memory. *American Scientist, 70*, 607–615.

Ericsson, K. A., Delaney, P. F., Weaver, G., & Mahadevan, R. (2004). Uncovering the structure of a memorist's superior "basic" memory capacity. *Cognitive Psychology, 49*, 191–237.

Ericsson, K. A., & Ward, P. (2007). Capturing the naturally occurring superior performance of experts in the laboratory: Toward a science of expert and exceptional performance. *Current Directions in Psychological Science, 16*, 346–350.

Eriksen, C. W., & St. James, J. D. (1986). Visual attention within and around the field of focal attention: A zoom lens model. *Perception & Psychophysics, 40*, 225–240.

Eriksson, J., Larsson, A., Ahlström, K. R., & Nyberg, L. (2006). Similar frontal and distinct posterior cortical regions mediate visual and auditory perceptual awareness. *Cerebral Cortex, 17*, 760–765.

Ervin-Tripp, S. (1979). Children's verbal turntaking. In E. Ochs & B. B. Schieffelin (Eds.), *Developmental pragmatics* (pp. 391–414). New York, NY: Academic Press.

Evans, J. S. T. (2002). Logic and human reasoning: An assessment of the deduction paradigm. *Psychological Bulletin, 128*, 978–996.

Evans, J. S. T. (2006). The heuristic-analytic theory of reasoning: Extension and evaluation. *Psychonomic Bulletin & Review, 13*, 378–395.

Evans, J. S. T. (2008). Dual-processing accounts of reasoning, judgment, and social cognition. *Annual Review of Psychology, 59*, 255–278.

Evans, J. St. B. T., Barston, J. L., & Pollard, P. (1983). On the conflict between logic and belief in syllogistic reasoning. *Memory and Cognition, 11*, 295–306.

Evans, N., & Levinson, S. C. (2009). The myth of language universals: Language diversity and its importance for cognitive science. *Behavioral and Brain Sciences, 32*, 429–448.

Eysenck M. W. (1979). Depth, elaboration, and distinctiveness. In L. S. Cermak & F. I. M. Craik (Eds.), *Levels of processing in human memory.* Hillsdale, NJ: Lawrence Erlbaum Associates.

Eysenck, M. W. (1997). *Anxiety and cognition: A unified theory.* Hove, UK: Psychology Press.

Eysenck, M. W., Derakshan, N., Santos, R., & Calvo, M. G. (2007). Anxiety and cognitive performance: Attentional control theory. *Emotion, 7*, 336–353.

Eysenck, M. W., & Eysenck, M. C. (1980). Effects of processing depth, distinctiveness, and word frequency on retention. *British Journal of Psychology, 71*, 263–274.

Eysenck, M. W., Mogg, K., May, J., Richards, A., & Mathews, A. (1991). Bias in interpretation of ambiguous sentences related to threat in anxiety. *Journal of Abnormal Psychology, 100*, 144–150.

Fadardi, J. S., & Cox, W. M. (2009). Reversing the sequence: Reducing alcohol consumption by overcoming alcohol attentional bias. *Drug and Alcohol Dependence, 101*, 137–145.

Fadiga, L., Craighero, L., Buccino, G., & Rizzolatti, G. (2002). Speech listening specifically modulates the excitability of tongue muscles: A TMS study. *European Journal of Neuroscience, 15*, 399–402.

Faigley, L., & Witte, S. (1983). Analyzing revision. *College Composition and Communication, 32*, 400–414.

Falk, R., & Lann, A. (2008). The allure of equality: Uniformity in probabilistic and statistical judgment. *Cognitive Psychology, 57*, 293–334.

Farah, M. J. (1994). Specialization within visual object recognition: Clues from prosopagnosia and alexia. In M. J. Farah & G. Ratcliff (Eds.), *The neuropsychology of high-level vision: Collected tutorial essays.* Hillsdale, NJ: Lawrence Erlbaum Associates.

Farah, M. J., & McClelland, J. L. (1991). A computational model of semantic memory impairment: Modality-specificity and emergent category-specificity. *Journal of Experimental Psychology: General, 120,* 339–357.

Farber, H. S. (2005). Is tomorrow another day? The labor supply of New York City cabdrivers. *Journal of Political Economics, 113,* 46–82.

Farivar, R. (2009). Dorsal–ventral integration in object recognition. *Brain Research Reviews, 62,* 144–153.

Farrell, S. (2010). Dissociating conditional recency in immediate and delayed free recall: A challenge for unitary models of recency. *Journal of Experimental Psychology: Learning, Memory & Cognition, 36,* 324–347.

Fehr, B. (2004). Intimacy expectations in same-sex friendships: A prototype interaction-pattern model. *Journal of Personality and Social Psychology, 86,* 265–284.

Feldman, J. (2003). The simplicity principle in human concept learning. *Current Directions in Psychological Science, 12,* 227–232.

Feldon, D. F. (2010). Do psychology researchers tell it like it is? A microgenetic analysis of research strategies and self-report accuracy along a continuum. *Instructional Science, 38,* 395–415.

Fellows, L. K., Heberlein, A. S., Morales, D. A., Shivde, G., Waller, S., & Wu, D. H. (2005). Method matters: An empirical study of impact in cognitive neuroscience. *Journal of Cognitive Neuroscience, 17,* 850–858.

Ferreira, F. (2003). The misinterpretation of noncanonical sentences. *Cognitive Psychology, 47,* 164–203.

Ferreira, F., Bailey, K. G. D., & Ferraro, V. (2002). Good enough representations in language comprehension. *Current Directions in Psychological Science, 11,* 11–15.

Ferreira, F., & Swets, B. (2002). How incremental is language production? Evidence from the production of utterances requiring the computation of arithmetic sums. *Journal of Memory and Language, 46,* 57–84.

Ferreira, V. S. (2008). Ambiguity, accessibility, and a division of labor for communicative success. *Psychology of Learning and Motivation, 49,* 209–246.

Ferreira, V. S., & Griffin, Z. M. (2003). Phonological influences on lexical (mis)selection. *Psychological Science, 14,* 86–90.

Ferreira, V. S., Slevc, L. R., & Rogers, E. S. (2005). How do speakers avoid ambiguous linguistic expressions? *Cognition, 96,* 263–284.

Fery, P., & Morais, J. (2003). A case study of visual agnosia without perceptual processing or structural descriptions' impairment. *Cognitive Neuropsychology, 20,* 595–618.

Fessler, D. M. T., Pillsworth, E. G., & Flamson, T. J. (2004). Angry men and disgusted women: An evolutionary approach to the influence of emotions on risk taking. *Organizational Behavior and Human Decision Processes, 95,* 107–123.

ffytche, D. H., Howard, R. J., Brammer, M. J., David, A., Woodruff, P., & Williams, S. (1998). The anatomy of conscious vision: An fMRI study of visual hallucinations. *Nature Neuroscience, 1,* 738–742.

Fiedler, K. (1988). The dependence of the conjunction fallacy on subtle linguistic factors. *Psychological Research, 50,* 123–129.

Fiedler, K., Brinkmann, B., Betsch, T., & Wild, B. (2000). A sampling approach to biases in conditional probability judgments: Beyond base-rate neglect and statistical format. *Journal of Experimental Psychology: General, 129,* 1–20.

Field, M., Munafo, M. R., & Franken, I. H. A. (2009). A meta-analytic investigation of the relationship between attentional bias and subjective craving in substance abuse. *Psychological Bulletin, 135,* 590–607.

Fields, A. W., & Shelton, A. L. (2006). Individual skill differences and large-scale environmental learning. *Journal of Experimental Psychology: Learning, Memory, and Cognition, 32,* 506–515.

Fleck, J. I. (2008). Working memory demands in insight versus analytic problem solving. *European Journal of Cognitive Psychology, 20,* 139–176.

Floro, M., & Miles, M. (2001). *Time use and overlapping activities – Evidence from Australia* (SPRC Discussion Paper No. 93). Sydney, Australia: Social Policy Research Center.

Foerde, K., & Poldrack, R. A. (2009). Procedural learning in humans. In L. R. Squire (Ed.), *The new encyclopedia of neuroscience, Vol. 7* (pp. 1083–1091). Oxford, UK: Academic Press.

Foley, M. A., Foley, H. J., & Korenman, L. M. (2002). Adapting a memory framework (source monitoring) to the study of closure processes. *Memory & Cognition, 30,* 412–422.

Foley, M. A., Foley, H. J., Scheye, R., & Bonacci, A. M. (2007). Remembering more than meets the eye: A study of memory confusions about incomplete visual information. *Memory, 15,* 616–633.

Folk, C. L., Remington, R. W., & Johnston, J. C. (1992). Involuntary covert orienting is contingent on attentional control settings. *Journal of Experimental Psychology: Human Perception and Performance, 18,* 1030–1044.

Forster, S., & Lavie, N. (2008). Failures to ignore entirely irrelevant distractors: The role of load. *Journal of Experimental Psychology: Applied, 14,* 73–83.

Forster, S., & Lavie, N. (2009). Harnessing the wandering mind: The role of perceptual load. *Cognition, 111,* 345–355.

Fortin, M., Voss, P., Lord, C., Lassande, M., Pruessner, J., Saint-Arnour, D., et al. (2008). Wayfinding in the blind: Large hippocampal volume and supranormal spatial navigation. *Brain, 131,* 2995–3005.

Foster, D. H., & Gilson, S. J. (2002). Recognizing novel three-dimensional objects by summing signals from parts and views. *Proceedings of the Royal Society of London B: Biological Sciences, 257,* 115–121.

Foulsham, T., Barton, J. J. S., Kingstone, A., Dewhurst, R., & Underwood, G. (2009). Fixation and saliency during search of natural scenes: The case of visual agnosia. *Neuropsychologia, 47,* 1994–2003.

Fox, E. (2008). *Emotion science.* New York, NY: Palgrave Macmillan.

Fox Tree, J. E. (2007). Folk notions of 'um' and 'uh', 'you know', and 'like'. *Text & Talk, 27,* 297–314.

Frank, M. C., & Ramscar, M. (2003). How do presentation and context influence representation for functional fixedness tasks? *Proceedings of the 25th Annual Meeting of the Cognitive Science Society* (p. 1345). Mahwah, NJ: Lawrence Erlbaum Associates.

Frattaroli, J. (2006). Experimental disclosure and its moderators: A meta-analysis. *Psychological Bulletin, 132,* 823–865.

Frazier, L., & Rayner, K. (1982). Making and correcting errors in the analysis of structurally ambiguous sentences. *Cognitive Psychology, 14,* 178–210.

Freud, S. (1925/1961). A note upon the "mystic writing pad." In J. Strachey (Ed.), *Standard edition of the collected works of Sigmund Freud, Vol. 19.* London: Hogarth Press. (Original work published 1925.)

Frick-Horbury, D., & Guttentag, R. E. (1998). The effects of restricting hand gesture production on lexical retrieval and free recall. *American Journal of Psychology, 111,* 43–62.

Friedman, A., Spetch, M. L., & Ferrey, A. (2005). Recognition by humans and pigeons of novel views of 3-D objects and their photographs. *Journal of Experimental Psychology: General, 134,* 149–162.

Friedman, N. P., & Miyake, A. (2004). The relations among inhibition and interference control functions: A latent variable analysis. *Journal of Experimental Psychology: General, 133,* 101–135.

Friedman-Hill, S. R., Robertson, L. C., & Treisman, A. (1995). Parietal contributions to visual feature binding: Evidence from a patient with bilateral lesions. *Science, 269,* 853–855.

Frijda, N. H. (1986). *The emotions.* Cambridge, UK: Cambridge University Press.

Frischen, A., Eastwood, J. D., & Smilek, D. (2008). Visual search for faces with emotional expressions. *Psychological Bulletin, 134,* 662–676.

Fuchs, A. H., & Milar, K. J. (2003). Psychology as a science. In D. F. Freedheim (Ed.), *Handbook of psychology (Vol. 1: The history of psychology)* (pp. 1–26). Hoboken, NJ: Wiley.

Fuller, J. M. (2003). The influence of speaker roles on discourse marker use. *Journal of Pragmatics, 35,* 23–45.

Fuselsang, J. A., Stein, C. B., Green, A. E., & Dunbar, K. N. (2004). Theory and data interactions of the scientific mind: Evidence from the molecular and the cognitive laboratory. *Canadian Journal of Experimental Psychology, 58,* 86–95.

Gable, P., & Harmon-Jones, E. (2010). The blues broaden but the nasty narrows: Attentional consequences of negative affects low and high in motivational intensity. *Psychological Science, 21,* 211–215.

Gainotti, G. (2000). What the locus of brain lesion tells us about the nature of the cognitive defect underlying category-specific disorders: A review. *Cortex, 36,* 539–559.

Galantucci, B., Fowler, C. A., & Turvey, M. T. (2006). The motor theory of speech perception reviewed. *Psychonomic Bulletin & Review, 13,* 361–377.

Galotti, K. M. (2002). *Making decisions that matter: How people face important life choices.* Mahwah, NJ: Lawrence Erlbaum Associates.

Galotti, K. M. (2007). Decision structuring in important real-life choices. *Psychological Science, 18,* 320–325.

Galotti, K. M., & Tinkelenberg, C. E. (2009). Real-life decision making: Parents choosing a first-grade placement. *American Journal of Psychology, 122,* 455–468.

Galpin, A., Underwood, G., & Crundall, D. (2009). Change blindness in driving scenes. *Transportation Research Part F: Traffic Psychology and Behavior, 12,* 179–185.

Galton, F. (1983). Enquiries into human faculty and its development. London: J. M. Dent & Co.

Ganis, G., Thompson, W. L., & Kosslyn, S. M. (2004). Brain areas underlying visual mental imagery and visual perception: An fMRI study. *Cognitive Brain Research, 20,* 226–241.

Ganong, W. F. (1980). Phonetic categorization in auditory word perception. *Journal of Experimental Psychology: Human Perception & Performance, 6,* 110–125.

Garcia-Marques, L., Santos, A. S. C., & Mackie, D. M. (2006). Stereotypes: Static abstractions or dynamic knowledge structures? *Journal of Personality and Social Psychology, 91*, 814–831.

Garnsey, S. M., Pearlmutter, N. J., Myers, E., & Lotocky, M. A. (1997). The contributions of verb bias and plausibility to the comprehension of temporarily ambiguous sentences. *Journal of Memory and Language, 37*, 58–93.

Gathercole, S. E., & Baddeley, A. D. (1993). Phonological working memory: A critical building-block for reading development and vocabulary acquisition. *European Journal of Psychology of Education, 8*, 259–272.

Gauthier, I., & Tarr, M. J. (2002). Unraveling mechanisms for expert object recognition: Bridging brain activity and behavior. *Journal of Experimental Psychology: Human Perception and Performance, 28*, 431–446.

Gazzaniga, M. S. (1992). *Nature's mind*. London, UK: Basic Books.

Gazzaniga, M. S., Ivry, R. B., & Mangun, G. R. (2009). *Cognitive neuroscience: The biology of the mind* (2nd ed.). New York, NY: W. W. Norton.

Gazzaniga, M. S., & Ledoux, J. E. (1978). *The integrated mind*. New York, NY: Plenum Press.

Gebauer, G. F., & Mackintosh, N. J. (2007). Psychometric intelligence dissociates implicit and explicit learning. *Journal of Experimental Psychology: Learning, Memory, and Cognition, 33*, 34–54.

Geis, M., & Zwicky, A. M. (1971). On invited inferences. *Linguistic Inquiry, 2*, 561–566.

Geiselman, R. E., & Fisher, R. P. (1997). Ten years of cognitive interviewing. In D. G. Payne & F. G. Conrad (Eds.), *Intersections in basic and applied memory research*. Mahwah, NJ: Lawrence Erlbaum Associates.

Geraerts, E., Lindsay, D. S., Merckelbach, H., Jelicic, M., Raymaekers, L., & Arnold, M. M. (2009). Cognitive mechanisms underlying recovered memory experiences of childhood sexual abuse. *Psychological Science, 20*, 92–98.

Geraerts, E., Schooler, J. W., Merckelbach, H., Jelicic, M., Hunter, B. J. A., & Ambadar, Z. (2007). Corroborating continuous and discontinuous memories of childhood sexual abuse. *Psychological Science, 18*, 564–568.

Gerwing, J., & Allison, M. (2009). The relationship between verbal and gestural contributions in conversation: A comparison of three methods. *Gesture, 9*, 312–336.

Geyer, T., von Mühlenen, A., & Müller, H. J. (2007). What do eye movements reveal about the role of memory in visual search? *Quarterly Journal of Experimental Psychology, 60*, 924–935.

Gick, M. L., & Holyoak, K. J. (1980). Analogical problem solving. *Cognitive Psychology, 12*, 306–355.

Gigerenzer, G., & Hoffrage, U. (1999). Overcoming difficulties in Bayesian reasoning: A reply to Lewis and Keren (1999) and Mellers and McGraw (1999). *Psychological Review, 102*, 684–704.

Ginet, M., & Verkampt, F. (2007). The cognitive interview: Is its benefit affected by the level of witness emotion? *Memory, 15*, 450–464.

Glanzer, M., & Cunitz, A. R. (1966). Two storage mechanisms in free recall. *Journal of Verbal Learning and Verbal Behavior, 5*, 351–360.

Glaser, W. R. (1992). Picture naming. *Cognition, 42*, 61–105.

Glenberg, A. M., Smith, S. M., & Green, C. (1977). Type I rehearsal: Maintenance and more. *Journal of Verbal Learning and Verbal Behavior, 16*, 339–352.

Glück, J., & Bluck, S. (2007). Looking back across the life span: A life story account of the reminiscence bump. *Memory & Cognition, 35*, 1928–1939.

Glushko, R. J. (1979). The organization and activation of orthographic knowledge in reading aloud. *Journal of Experimental Psychology: Human Perception and Performance, 5*, 674–691.

Glymour, C. (2001). *The mind's arrows: Bayes nets and graphical causal models in psychology*. Cambridge, MA: MIT Press.

Gobet, F., & Chass, P. (2009). Expertise and intuition: A tale of three theories. *Minds and Machines, 19*, 151–180.

Gobet, F., & Clarkson, G. (2004). Chunks in expert memory: Evidence for the magical number four … or is it two? *Memory, 12*, 732–747.

Gobet, F., de Voogt, A., & Retschitzki, J. (2004). *Moves in mind: The psychology of board games*. Hove, UK: Psychology Press.

Gobet, F., & Waters, A. J. (2003). The role of constraints in expert memory. *Journal of Experimental Psychology: Learning, Memory, and Cognition, 29*, 1082–1094.

Godden, D. R., & Baddeley, A. D. (1975). Context dependent memory in two natural environments: On land and under water. *British Journal of Psychology, 66*, 325–331.

Goldberg, A., Russell, M., & Cook, A. (2003). The effect of computers on student writing: A meta-analysis of studies from 1992 to 2002. *Journal of Technology, Learning, and Assessment, 2*, 1–52.

Goldenburg, G., Müllbacher, W., & Nowak, A. (1995). Imagery without perception: A case study of anosognosia for cortical blindness. *Neuropsychologia, 33*, 1373–1382.

Goldstein, D. G., & Gigerenzer, G. (2002). Models of ecological rationality: The recognition heuristic. *Psychological Review*, 109, 75–90.

Gomulicki, B. R. (1956). Recall as an abstractive process. *Acta Psychologica*, 12, 77–94.

Goodman, K. S. (1986). *What's whole in whole language*. Berkeley, CA: RDR Books.

Gorman, M. E. (1995). Hypothesis testing. In S. E. Newstead & J. S. T. Evans (Eds.), *Perspectives on thinking and reasoning: Essays in honor of Peter Wason*. Hove, UK: Lawrence Erlbaum Associates.

Gotlib, I. H., & Joormann, J. (2010). Cognition and depression: Current status and future directions. *Annual Review of Clinical Psychology*, 6, 285–312.

Gottfredson, L. S. (1997). Why g matters? The complexities of everyday life. *Intelligence*, 24, 79–132.

Grabner, R. H., Stern, E., & Neubauer, A. (2007). Individual differences in chess expertise: A psychometric investigation. *Acta Psychologica*, 124, 398–420.

Graf, P., & Schacter, D. L. (1985). Implicit and explicit memory for new associations in normal and amnesic subjects. *Journal of Experimental Psychology: Learning, Memory, & Cognition*, 11, 501–518.

Grainger, J., & Jacobs, A. M. (2005). Pseudoword context effects on letter perception: The role of word misperception. *European Journal of Cognitive Psychology*, 17, 289–318.

Gray, J. A., & Wedderburn, A. A. (1960). Grouping strategies with simultaneous stimuli. *Quarterly Journal of Experimental Psychology*, 12, 180–184.

Green, H. A. C., & Patterson, K. (2009). Jigsaws – A preserved ability in semantic dementia. *Neuropsychologia*, 47, 569–576.

Green, K. P., Kuhl, P. K., Melzoff, A. M., & Stevens, E. B. (1991). Integrating speech information across talkers, gender, and sensory modality: Female faces and male voices in the McGurk effect. *Perception & Psychophysics*, 50, 524–536.

Greenberg, J. H. (1963). *Some universals of grammar with particular reference to the order of meaningful elements*. Cambridge, MA: MIT Press.

Greene, J., & Cohen, J. (2004). For the law, neuroscience changes nothing and everything. *Philosophical Transactions of the Royal Society London B: Biological Sciences*, 359, 1775–1785.

Greenwald, A. G. (2003). On doing two things at once: III. Confirmation of perfect timesharing when simultaneous tasks are ideomotor compatible. *Journal of Experimental Psychology: Human Perception and Performance*, 29, 859–868.

Gregory, R. L. (1973). The confounded eye. In R. L. Gregory & E. H. Gombrich (Eds.), *Illusion in nature and art*. London, UK: Duckworth.

Grey, S., & Mathews, A. (2000). Effects of training on interpretation of emotional ambiguity. *Quarterly Journal of Experimental Psychology*, 53, 1143–1162.

Grice, H. P. (1967). Logic and conversation. In P. Cole & J. L. Morgan (Eds.), *Studies in syntax* (Vol. III). New York, NY: Seminar Press.

Grill-Spector, K., & Kanwisher, N. (2005). Visual recognition: As soon as you know it is there, you know what it is. *Psychological Science*, 16, 152–160.

Grill-Spector, K., Sayres, R., & Ress, D. (2006). High-resolution imaging reveals highly selective nonface clusters in the fusiform face area. *Nature Neuroscience*, 9, 1177–1185.

Griskevicius, V., Shiota, M. N., & Neufeld, S. L. (2010). Influence of different positive emotions on persuasive processing: A functional evolutionary approach. *Emotion*, 10, 190–206.

Gross, J. J., & Thompson, R. A. (2007). Emotion regulation: Conceptual foundations. In J. J. Gross (Ed.), *Handbook of emotion regulation*. New York, NY: Guilford Press.

Grossberg, S. (2003). Resonant neural dynamics of speech perception. *Journal of Phonetics*, 31, 423–445.

Guerin, B. (2003). Language use as social strategy: A review and an analytic framework for the social sciences. *Review of General Psychology*, 7, 251–298.

Guilbault, R. L., Bryant, F. B., Brockway, J. H., & Posavac, E. J. (2004). A meta-analysis of research on hindsight bias. *Basic and Applied Social Psychology*, 26, 103–117.

Gupta, P., & Cohen, N. J. (2002). Theoretical and computational analysis of skill learning, repetition priming, and procedural memory. *Psychological Review*, 109, 401–448.

Güss, C. D., Tuason, M. T., & Gerhard, C. (2010). Cross-national comparisons of complex problem-solving strategies in two microworlds. *Cognitive Science*, 34, 489–520.

Güss, C. D., & Wiley, B. (2007). Metacognition of problem-solving strategies in Brazil, India, and the United States. *Journal of Cognition and Culture*, 7, 1–25.

Gutschalk, A., Micheyl, C., & Oxenham, A. J. (2008). Neural correlates of auditory perceptual awareness under informational masking. *PLoS Biology*, 6, 1156–1165.

Hagoort, P., & van Berkum, J. (2007). Beyond the sentence given. *Philosophical Transactions of the*

Royal Society of London B: Biological Sciences, 362, 801–811.

Hahn, U., & Oaksford, M. (2007). The rationality of informal argumentation: A Bayesian approach to reasoning fallacies. *Psychological Review, 114,* 704–732.

Hamann, S. B., & Squire, L. R. (1997). Intact perceptual memory in the absence of conscious memory. *Behavioral Neuroscience, 111,* 850–854.

Hampton, J. A. (1981). An investigation of the nature of abstract concepts. *Memory & Cognition, 9,* 149–156.

Hampton, J. A. (2007). Typicality, graded membership, and vagueness. *Cognitive Science, 31,* 355–384.

Hampton, J. A. (2010). Concepts in human adults. In D. Mareschal, P. Quinn, & S. E. G. Lea (Eds.), *The making of human concepts* (pp. 293–311). Oxford, UK: Oxford University Press.

Hampton, J. A., Storms, G., Simmons, C. L., & Heussen, D. (2009). Feature integration in natural language concepts. *Memory & Cognition, 37,* 1150–1163.

Hancock, J. T. (2007). Digital deception: Why, where and how people lie online. In A. N. Joinson, K. McKenna, T. Postmes, & U. Reips (Eds.), *The Oxford handbook of internet psychology* (pp. 287–331). Cambridge, UK: Cambridge University Press.

Hannon, B., & Daneman, M. (2007). Prospective memory: The relative effects of encoding, retrieval, and the match between encoding and retrieval. *Memory, 15,* 572–604.

Hansen, C. H., & Hansen, R. D. (1988). Finding the face in the crowd – An anger superiority effect. *Journal of Personality and Social Psychology, 54,* 917–924.

Hardt, O., Einarsson, E. O., & Nader, K. (2010). A bridge over troubled water: Reconsolidation as a link between cognitive and neuroscientific memory research traditions. *Annual Review of Psychology, 61,* 141–167.

Hareli, S., & Weiner, B. (2002). Dislike and envy as antecedents of pleasure at another's misfortune. *Motivation and Emotion, 26,* 257–277.

Harley, T. A. (2008). *The psychology of language: From data to theory* (3rd ed.). Hove, UK: Psychology Press.

Harley, T. A., & Bown, H. E. (1998). What causes a tip-of-the-tongue state? Evidence for lexical neighborhood effects in speech production. *British Journal of Psychology, 89,* 151–174.

Harm, M. W., & Seidenberg, M. S. (2001). Are there orthographic impairments in phonological dyslexia? *Cognitive Neuropsychology, 18,* 71–92.

Harnsberger, J. D., Hollien, H., Martin, C. A., & Hollien, K. A. (2009). Stress and deception in speech: Evaluating layered voice analysis. *Journal of Forensic Sciences, 54,* 642–650.

Harris, I. M., & Miniussi, C. (2003). Parietal lobe contribution to mental rotation demonstrated with rTMS. *Journal of Cognitive Neuroscience, 15,* 315–323.

Hartley, J., Sotto, E., & Pennebaker, J. (2003). Speaking versus typing: A case-study of using voice-recognition software on academic correspondence. *British Journal of Educational Technology, 34,* 5–16.

Hartsuiker, R. J., Corley, M., & Martensen, H. (2005). The lexical bias effect is modulated by context, but the standard monitoring account doesn't fly: Related reply to Baars et al. (1975). *Journal of Memory and Language, 52,* 58–70.

Harvey, L. O. (1986). Visual memory: What is remembered? In F. Klix & H. Hagendorf (Eds.), *Human memory and cognitive capabilities.* The Hague, The Netherlands: Elsevier.

Haskell, T. R., & MacDonald, M. C. (2003). Conflicting cues and competition in subject–verb agreement. *Journal of Memory and Language, 48,* 760–778.

Hassabis, D., Kumaran, D., Vann, S. D., & Maguire, E. A. (2007). Patients with hippocampal amnesia cannot imagine new experiences. *Proceedings of the National Academy of Sciences of the United States of America, 104,* 1726–1731.

Hastie, R. (2001). Problems for judgment and decision making. *Annual Review of Psychology, 52,* 653–683.

Hauk, O., Johnsrude, I., & Pulvermüller, F. (2004). Somatotopic representation of action words in human motor and premotor cortex. *Neuron, 41,* 301–307.

Havelka, J., & Rastle, K. (2005). The assembly of phonology from print is serial and subject to strategic control: Evidence from Serbian. *Journal of Experimental Psychology: Learning, Memory, and Cognition, 31,* 148–158.

Hayes, J. R., & Bajzek, D. (2008). Understanding and reducing the knowledge effect: Implications for writers. *Written Communication, 23,* 135–149.

Hayes, J. R., & Chenoweth, N. A. (2006). Is working memory involved in the transcribing and editing of texts? *Written Communication, 23,* 135–149.

Hayes, J. R., & Flower, L. S. (1986). Writing research and the writer. *American Psychologist, 41,* 1106–1113.

Hayes, J. R., Flower, L. S., Schriver, K., Stratman, J., & Carey, L. (1985). *Cognitive processes in revision* (Technical Report No. 12). Pittsburgh, PA: Carnegie Mellon University.

Hayes, S., Hirsch, C. R., Krebs, G., & Mathews, A. (2010). The effects of modifying interpretation bias on worry in generalized anxiety disorder. *Behaviour Research and Therapy, 48,* 171–178.

Hayward, W. G. (2003). After the viewpoint debate: Where next in object recognition? *Trends in Cognitive Sciences, 7,* 425–427.

Heit, E. (1992). Categorization using chains of examples. *Cognitive Psychology, 24,* 341–380.

Henrich, J., Heine, S. J., & Norenzayan, A. (2010). Beyond WEIRD: Towards a broad-based behavioral science. *Behavioral and Brain Sciences, 33,* 111–135.

Herrmann, D. J., Yoder, C. Y., Gruneberg, M., & Payne, D. G. (Eds.). (2006). *Applied cognitive psychology: A textbook.* Mahwah, NJ: Lawrence Erlbaum Associates.

Herron, J. E., & Wilding, E. L. (2006). Brain and behavioral indices of retrieval model. *NeuroImage, 32,* 863–870.

Herschler, O., & Hochstein, S. (2009). The importance of being expert: Top-down attentional control in visual search with photographs. *Attention, Perception & Psychophysics, 71,* 1478–1486.

Hertwig, R., Pachur, T., & Kurzenhäuser, S. (2005). Judgments of risk frequencies: Tests of possible cognitive mechanisms. *Journal of Experimental Psychology: Learning, Memory, and Cognition, 31,* 621–642.

Heussen, D., & Hampton, J. A. (2007). 'Emeralds are expensive because they are rare': Plausibility of property explanations. In S. Vosniadou, D. Kayser, & A. Protopapas (Eds.), *Proceedings of Eurocogsci07: The European Cognitive Science Conference* (pp. 101–106). Hove, UK: Psychology Press.

Hicks, J. L., Marsh, R. L., & Cook, G. I. (2005). Task interference in time-based, event-based, and dual intention prospective memory conditions. *Journal of Memory and Language, 53,* 430–444.

Highley, J. R., Esiri, M. M., McDonald, B., Cortina-Borja, M., Herron, B. M., & Crow, T. J. (1999). The size and fiber composition of the corpus callosum with respect to gender and schizophrenia: A post-mortem study. *Brain, 122,* 99–110.

Hill, N. M., & Schneider, W. (2006). Brain changes in the development of expertise: Neuroanatomical and neurophysiological evidence about skill-based adaptations. In K. A. Ericsson, P. J. Feltovich, & R. R. Hoffman (Eds.), *The Cambridge handbook of expertise and expert performance.* Cambridge, UK: Cambridge University Press.

Hirst, W., Phelps, E. A., Buckner, R. L., Budson, A. E., Cuc, A., Gabrieli, J. D. E., et al. (2009). Long-term memory for the terrorist attack of September 11: Flashbulb memories, event memories, and the factors that influence their retention. *Journal of Experimental Psychology: General, 138,* 161–176.

Hobbs, S., & Burman, J. T. (2009). Is the 'cognitive revolution' a myth? *The Psychologist, 22,* 812–814.

Hoffrage, U., Lindsey, S., Hertwig, R., & Gigerenzer, G. (2000). Communicating statistical information. *Science, 290,* 2261–2262.

Hohwy, J., & Paton, B. (2010). Explaining away the body: Experiences of supernaturally caused touch and touch on non-hand objects within the rubber hand illusion. *PLoS One, 5,* e9416.

Hollingworth, A., & Henderson, J. M. (2002). Accurate visual memory for previously attended objects in natural scenes. *Journal of Experimental Psychology: Human Perception & Performance, 28,* 113–136.

Holliway, D. R., & McCutcheon, D. (2004). Audience perspective in young writers' composing and revising. In L. Allal, L. Chanquoy, & P. Largy (Eds.), *Revision of written language: Cognitive and instructional processes* (pp. 87–101). New York, NY: Kluwer.

Holtgraves, T. (1998). Interpreting indirect replies. *Cognitive Psychology, 37,* 1–27.

Holtgraves, T. (2008a). Automatic intention recognition in conversation processing. *Journal of Memory and Language, 58,* 627–645.

Holtgraves, T. (2008b). Conversation, speech acts, and memory. *Memory & Cognition, 36,* 361–374.

Horton, W. S., & Keysar, B. (1996). When do speakers take into account common ground? *Cognition, 59,* 91–117.

Hotopf, W. H. N. (1980). Slips of the pen. In U. Frith (Ed.), *Cognitive processes in spelling.* London, UK: Academic Press.

Howard, D., & Howard, J. H. (1992). Adult age differences in the rate of learning serial patterns: Evidence from direct and indirect tests. *Psychology & Aging, 7,* 232–241.

Howard, R. W. (2009). Individual differences in expertise development over decades in a complex intellectual domain. *Memory & Cognition, 37,* 194–209.

Hsiao, J. H. W., & Cottrell, G. (2008). Two fixations suffice in face recognition. *Psychological Science, 19,* 998–1006.

Hubel, D. H., & Wiesel, T. N. (1962). Receptive fields, binocular interaction and functional architecture in the cat's visual cortex. *Journal of Physiology, 160,* 106–154.

Hubel, D. H., & Wiesel, T. N. (1979). Brain mechanisms of vision. *Scientific American, 249,* 150–162.

Humphreys, G. W., Avidan, G., & Behrmann, M. (2007). A detailed investigation of facial expression processing in congenital prosopagnosia as compared to acquired prosopagnosia. *Experimental Brain Research, 176*, 356–373.

Humphreys, G. W., & Riddoch, M. J. (1987). *To see but not to see: A case study of visual agnosia*. Hove, UK: Psychology Press.

Humphreys, G. W., Riddoch, M. J., & Quinlan, P. T. (1985). Interactive processes in perceptual organization: Evidence from visual agnosia. In M. I. Posner & O. S. M. Morin (Eds.), *Attention and performance* (Vol. XI). Hillsdale, NJ: Lawrence Erlbaum Associates.

Hunt, R. R. (2006). The concept of distinctiveness in memory research. In R. R. Hunt & J. E. Worthen (Eds.), *Distinctiveness and memory* (pp. 3–25). New York, NY: Oxford University Press.

Hunt, R. R., & Smith, R. E. (1996). Accessing the particular from the general: The power of distinctiveness in the context of organization. *Memory & Cognition, 24*, 217–225.

Hunter, I. M. L. (2004). James, William. In R. L. Gregory (Ed.), *The Oxford companion to the mind* (2nd. ed., pp. 610–612). New York, NY: Oxford University Press.

Hupbach, A., Gomez, R., Hardt, O., & Nadel, L. (2007). Reconsolidation of episodic memories: A subtle reminder triggers integration of new information. *Learning & Memory, 14*, 47–53.

Hupbach, A., Gomez, R., & Nadel, L. (2009). Episodic memory reconsolidation: Updating or source confusion? *Memory, 17*, 502–510.

Hupbach, A., Hardt, O., Gomez, R., & Nadel, L. (2008). The dynamics of memory: Context-dependent updating. *Learning & Memory, 15*, 574–579.

Huppert, F. A., & Piercy, M. (1976). Recognition memory in amnesic patients: Effect of temporal context and familiarity of material. *Cortex, 4*, 3–20.

Huppert, J. D., Pasupuleti, R. V., Foa, E. B., & Mathews, A. (2007). Interpretation bias in social anxiety: Response generation, response selection, and self-appraisals. *Behaviour Research and Therapy, 45*, 1505–1515.

Husain, F. T., Fromm, S. J., Pursley, R. H., Hosey, L. A., Braun, A. R., & Horwitz, B. (2006). Neural bases of categorization of simple speech and nonspeech sounds. *Human Brain Mapping, 27*, 636–651.

Hyde, J. S. (2005). The gender similarities hypothesis. *American Psychologist, 60*, 581–592.

Hyde, K. L., Lerch, J., Norton, A., Forgeard, M., Winner, E., Evans, A. C., et al. (2009). Musical training shapes structural brain development. *Journal of Neuroscience, 29*, 3019–3025.

Hyman, I., Boss, S., Wise, B., McKenzie, K., & Caggiano, J. (2009). Did you see the unicycling clown? Inattentional blindness while walking and talking on a cell phone. *Applied Cognitive Psychology, 24*, 597–607.

Ihlebaek, C., Love, T., Eilertsen, D. E., & Magnussen, S. (2003). Memory for a staged criminal event witnessed live and on video. *Memory, 11*, 310–327.

Intraub, H. (2010). Rethinking scene perception: A multisource model. *Psychology of learning and motivation: Advances in research and theory, 52*, 231–264.

Intraub, H., Daviels, K. K., Horowitz, T. S., & Wolfe, J. M. (2008). Looking at scenes while searching for numbers: Dividing attention multiplies space. *Perception & Psychophysics, 70*, 1337–1349.

Intraub, H., & Dickinson, C. A. (2008). False memory 1/20th of a second later: What the early onset of boundary extension reveals about perception. *Psychological Science, 19*, 1007–1014.

Intraub, H., Gottesman, C. V., & Bills, A. J. (1998). Effects of perceiving and imagining scenes on memory for pictures. *Journal of Experimental Psychology: Learning, Memory & Cognition, 24*, 186–201.

Isen, A. M., Nygren, T. E., & Ashby, F. G. (1988). Influence of positive affect on the subjective utility of gains and losses – It is just not worth the risk. *Journal of Personality and Social Psychology, 55*, 710–717.

Ison, M. J., & Quiroga, R. Q. (2008). Selectivity and invariance for visual object recognition. *Frontiers in Bioscience, 13*, 4889–4903.

Isurin, L., & McDonald, J. L. (2001). Retroactive interference from translation equivalents: Implications for first language forgetting. *Memory & Cognition, 29*, 312–319.

Izard, C. E. (2007). Basic emotions, natural kinds, emotion schemas, and a new paradigm. *Perspective in Psychological Science, 2*, 260–280.

Jacobs, J. (1887). Experiments in "prehension". *Mind, 12*, 75–79.

Jacobs, N., & Garnham, A. (2007). The role of conversational hand gestures in a narrative task. *Journal of Memory and Language, 56*, 291–303.

Jacoby, L. L., Debner, J. A., & Hay, J. F. (2001). Proactive interference, accessibility bias, and process dissociations: Valid subjective reports of memory. *Journal of Experimental Psychology: Learning, Memory, & Cognition, 27*, 686–700.

Jahn, G., Knauff, M., & Johnson-Laird, P. N. (2007). Preferred mental models in reasoning about spatial relations. *Memory & Cognition, 35*, 2075–2087.

Jain, A. K., & Duin, R. P. W. (2004). Pattern recognition. In R. L. Gregory (Ed.), *The Oxford companion to the mind* (pp. 698–703). New York, NY: Oxford University Press.

Jain, A. K., Feng, J. J., & Nandakumar, K. (2010). Fingerprint matching. *Computer, 43*, 36–44.

James, W. (1890). *Principles of psychology*. New York, NY: Holt.

Janssen, N., Alario, F.-X., & Caramazza, A. (2008). A word-order constraint on phonological activation. *Psychological Science, 19*, 216–220.

Janssen, S. M. J., & Murre, J. M. J. (2008). Reminiscence bump in autobiographical memory: Unexplained by novelty, emotionality, valence or importance of personal events. *Quarterly Journal of Experimental Psychology, 61*, 1847–1860.

Jared, D., Levy, B. A., & Rayner, K. (1999). The role of phonology in the activation of word meanings during reading: Evidence from proof-reading and eye movements. *Journal of Experimental Psychology: General, 128*, 219–264.

Jiang, Y., Costello, P., Fang, F., Huang, M., & He, S. (2006). A gender- and sexual orientation-dependent spatial attentional effect of invisible images. *Proceedings of the National Academy of Sciences of the United States of America, 103*, 17048–17052.

Johnson, M. K., Hashtroudi, S., & Lindsay, D. S. (1993). Source monitoring. *Psychological Bulletin, 114*, 3–28.

Johnson-Laird, P. N. (1983). *Mental models*. Cambridge, UK: Cambridge University Press.

Johnson-Laird, P. N. (2004). Mental models and reasoning. In J. P. Leighton & R. J. Sternberg (Eds.), *The nature of reasoning*. Cambridge, UK: Cambridge University Press.

Johnson-Laird, P. N., Mancini, F., & Gangemi, A. (2006). A hyper-emotion theory of psychological illnesses. *Psychological Review, 113*, 822–841.

Jolij, J., & Lamme, V. A. F. (2005). Repression of unconscious information by conscious processing: Evidence for affective blindsight induced by transcranial magnetic stimulation. *Proceedings of the National Academy of Sciences of the United States of America, 102*, 10747–10751.

Jones, L. L. (2010). Pure mediated priming: A retrospective semantic matching model. *Journal of Experimental Psychology: Learning, Memory, & Cognition, 36*, 135–146.

Jonides, M. G., Lewis, R. L., Nee, D. E., Lustig, C. A., Berman, M. G., & Moore, K. S. (2008). The mind and brain of short-term memory. *Annual Review of Psychology, 59*, 193–224.

Josephs, R. A., Larrick, R. P., Steele, C. M., & Nisbett, R. E. (1992). Protecting the self from the negative consequences of risky decisions. *Journal of Personality and Social Psychology, 62*, 26–37.

Junghaenel, D. U., Smith, J. M., & Santner, L. (2008). Linguistic dimensions of psychopathology: A quantitative analysis. *Journal of Social and Clinical Psychology, 27*, 36–55.

Just, M. A., & Carpenter, P. A. (1992). A capacity theory of comprehension. *Psychological Review, 114*, 678–703.

Juth, P., Lundqvist, D., Karlsson, A., & Öhman, A. (2005). Looking for faces and friends: Perceptual and emotional factors when finding a face in the crowd. *Emotion, 5*, 379–395.

Kahneman, D. (2003). A perspective on judgment and choice: Mapping bounded rationality. *American Psychologist, 58*, 697–720.

Kahneman, D., & Frederick, S. (2005). A model of heuristic judgment. In K. J. Holyoak & R. G. Morrison (Eds.), *The Cambridge handbook of thinking and reasoning*. Cambridge, UK: Cambridge University Press.

Kahneman, D., & Tversky, A. (1984). Choices, values and frames. *American Psychologist, 39*, 341–350.

Kalakoski, V., & Saariluoma, P. (2001). Taxi drivers' exceptional memory of street names. *Memory & Cognition, 29*, 634–638.

Kaliski, S. Z. (2009). 'My brain made me do it!' – How neuroscience may change the insanity defense. *South African Journal of Psychiatry, 15*, 4–6.

Kane, M. J., & Engle, R. W. (2003). Working-memory capacity and the control of attention: The contribution of goal neglect, response competition, and task set to Stroop interference. *Journal of Experimental Psychology: General, 132*, 47–70.

Kanwisher, N., & Yovel, G. (2006). The fusiform face area: A cortical region specialized for the perception of faces. *Philosophical Transactions of the Royal Society B: Biological Sciences, 361*, 2109–2128.

Kaplan, G. A., & Simon, H. A. (1990). In search of insight. *Cognitive Psychology, 22*, 374–419.

Karpicke, J. D., Butler, A.C., & Roediger III, H. L. (2009). Metacognitive strategies in student learning: Do students practise retrieval when they study on their own? *Memory, 17*, 471–479.

Kaufer, D., Hayes, J. R., & Flower, L. S. (1986). Composing written sentences. *Research in the Teaching of English, 20*, 121–140.

Kaup, B., Yaxley, R. H., Madden, C. J., Zwaan, R. A., & Lüdtke, J. (2007). Experiential simulations of negated text information. *Quarterly Journal of Experimental Psychology, 60*, 976–990.

Kay, K. N., Naselaris, T., Prenger, R. J., & Gallant, J. L. (2008). Identifying natural images from human brain activity. *Nature, 452*, 352–355.

Keane, M. (1987). On retrieving analogs when solving problems. *Quarterly Journal of Experimental Psychology, 39A*, 29–41.

Kellogg, R. T. (1988). Attentional overload and writing performance: Effects of rough draft and outline strategies. *Journal of Experimental Psychology: Learning, Memory, & Cognition, 14,* 355–365.

Kellogg, R. T. (1994). *The psychology of writing.* Oxford, UK: Oxford University Press.

Kellogg, R. T. (2001a). Long-term working memory in text production. *Memory & Cognition, 29,* 43–52.

Kellogg, R. T. (2001b). Competition for working memory among writing processes. *American Journal of Psychology, 114,* 175–191.

Kellogg, R. T. (2008). Training writing skills: A cognitive developmental perspective. *Journal of Writing Research, 1,* 1–26.

Kellogg, R. T., & Mueller, S. (1993). Performance amplification and process restructuring in computer-based writing. *International Journal of Man–Machine Studies, 39,* 33–49.

Kellogg, R. T., Olive, T., & Piolat, A. (2007). Verbal, visual, and spatial working memory in written language production. *Acta Psychologica, 124,* 382–397.

Kelly, S. D., Barr, D. J., Church, R. B., & Lynch, K. (1999). Offering a hand to pragmatic understanding: The role of speech and gesture in comprehension and memory. *Journal of Memory and Language, 40,* 577–592.

Kelly, S. D., Creigh, P., & Bartolotti, J. (2010a). Integrating speech and iconic gestures in a Stroop-like task: Evidence for automatic processing. *Journal of Cognitive Neuroscience, 22,* 683–694.

Kelly, S. D., Ozyurek, A., & Maris, E. (2010b). Two sides of the same coin: Speech and gesture mutually interact to enhance comprehension. *Psychological Science, 21,* 260–267.

Kelly, S. W. (2003). A consensus in implicit learning? *Quarterly Journal of Experimental Psychology, 56A,* 1389–1391.

Kemp, R., Towell, N., & Pike, G. (1997). When seeing should not be believing: Photographs, credit cards and fraud. *Applied Cognitive Psychology, 11,* 211–222.

Kendeou, P., Savage, R., & van den Broek, P. (2009). Revisiting the simple view of reading. *British Journal of Educational Psychology, 79,* 353–370.

Kenealy, P. M. (1997). Mood-state-dependent retrieval: The effects of induced mood on memory reconsidered. *Quarterly Journal of Experimental Psychology, 50A,* 290–317.

Keppel, G., & Underwood, B. J. (1962). Proactive inhibition in short-term retention of single items. *Journal of Verbal Learning and Verbal Behavior, 1,* 153–161.

Keren, G., & Schul, Y. (2009). Two is not always better than one: A critical evaluation of two-system theories. *Perspectives on Psychological Science, 4,* 533–550.

Kertesz, A., Jesso, S., Harciarek, M., Blair, M., & McMonagle, P. (2010). What is semantic dementia? A cohort study of diagnostic features and clinical boundaries. *Archives of Neurology, 67,* 483–489.

Key, W. B. (1980). *The clam-plate orgy: And other subliminals the media use to manipulate your behavior.* Englewood Cliffs, NJ: Prentice Hall.

Keysar, B., Barr, D. J., Balin, J. A., & Brauner, J. S. (2000). Taking perspectives in conversation: The role of mutual knowledge in comprehension. *Psychological Science, 11,* 32–38.

Keysar, B., & Henly, A. S. (2002). Speakers' overestimation of their effectiveness. *Psychological Science, 13,* 207–212.

Khetrapal, N. (2010). Load theory of selective attention and the role of perceptual load: Is it time for revision? *European Journal of Cognitive Psychology, 22,* 149–156.

Kim, P. Y., & Mayhorn, C. B. (2008). Exploring students' prospective memory inside and outside the lab. *American Journal of Psychology, 121,* 241–254.

King, W. R., & Dunn, T. M. (2010). Detecting deception in field settings: A review and critique of the criminal justice and psychological literatures. *Policing: An International Journal of Police Strategies & Management, 33,* 305–320.

Kintsch, W. (2000). Metaphor comprehension: A computational theory. *Psychonomic Bulletin & Review, 7,* 257–266.

Kirchhoff, B. A., Schapiro, M. L., & Buckner, R. L. (2005). Orthographic distinctiveness and semantic elaboration provide separate contributions to memory. *Journal of Cognitive Neuroscience, 17,* 1841–1854.

Klahr, D., & Dunbar, K. (1988). Dual-space search during scientific reasoning. *Cognitive Science, 12,* 1–48.

Klahr, D., & Simon, H. A. (2001). What have psychologists (and others) discovered about the process of scientific discovery? *Current Directions in Psychological Science, 10,* 75–79.

Klauer, K. C., & Zhao, Z. (2004). Double dissociations in visual and spatial short-term memory. *Journal of Experimental Psychology: General, 133,* 355–381.

Klein, L., Dubois, J., Mangin, J.-F., Kherif, F., Flandin, G., Poline, J.-B., et al. (2004). Retinopic organization of visual mental images as revealed by functional magnetic resonance imaging. *Cognitive Brain Research, 22,* 26–31.

Klein, S. B., & Kihlstrom, J. F. (1986). Elaboration, organization, and the self-reference effect in memory. *Journal of Experimental Psychology: General, 115,* 26–38.

Knoblich, G., Ohlsson, S., Haider, H., & Rhenius, D. (1999). Constraint relaxation and chunk decomposition in insight. *Journal of Experimental Psychology: Learning, Memory, and Cognition, 25,* 1534–1555.

Knowlton, B. J., & Foerde, K. (2008). Neural representations of nondeclarative memories. *Current Directions in Psychological Science, 17,* 107–111.

Koch, C., & Tsuchiya, N. (2007). Attention and consciousness: Two distinct brain processes. *Trends in Cognitive Sciences, 11,* 16–22.

Koehler, J. J. (1996). The base rate fallacy reconsidered: Descriptive, normative, and methodological challenges. *Behavioral & Brain Sciences, 19,* 1–17.

Koenigsberg, H. W., Fan, J., Ochsner, K. N., Liu, X., Guise, K., Pizzarello, S., et al. (2010). Neural correlates of using distancing to regulate emotional responses to social situations. *Neuropsychologia, 48,* 1813–1822.

Köhnken, G., Milne, R., Memon, A., & Bull, R. (1999). The cognitive interview: A meta-analysis. *Psychology of Crime Law, 5,* 3–27.

Kolko, J. D. (2009). The effects of mobile phones and hands-free laws on traffic fatalities. *Berkeley Electronic Journal of Economic Analysis & Policy, 9,* No. 10.

Koller, S. M., Drury, C. G., & Schwaninger, A. (2009). Change of search time and non-search time in X-ray baggage screening due to training. *Ergonomics, 52,* 644–656.

Kondo, Y., Suzuki, M., Mugikura, S., Abe, N., Takahashi, S., Iijima, T., et al. (2004). Changes in brain activation associated with use of a memory strategy: A functional MRI study. *NeuroImage, 15,* 1154–1163.

Koole, S. (2009). The psychology of emotion regulation: An integrative review. *Cognition & Emotion, 23,* 4–41.

Kornilova, L. N. (1997). Vestibular function and sensory interaction in altered gravity. *Advances in Space Biological Medicine, 6,* 275–313.

Kosslyn, S. M. (1994). *Image and brain: The resolution of the imagery debate.* Cambridge, MA: MIT Press.

Kosslyn, S. M. (2004). Mental imagery: Depictive accounts. In R. L. Gregory (Ed.), *The Oxford companion to the mind* (pp. 585–587). New York, NY: Oxford University Press.

Kosslyn, S. M. (2005). Mental images and the brain. *Cognitive Neuropsychology, 22,* 333–347.

Kosslyn, S. M., Pascual-Leone, A., Felician, O., Camposano, S., Keenan, J. P., Thompson, W. L., et al. (1999). The role of Area 17 in visual imagery: Convergent evidence from PET and rTMS. *Science, 284,* 167–170.

Kosslyn, S. M., & Thompson, W. L. (2003). When is early visual cortex activated during visual mental imagery? *Psychological Bulletin, 129,* 723–746.

Koster, E. H. W., Baert, S., Bockstaele, M., & De Raedt, R. (2010). Attentional retraining procedures: Manipulating early or late components of attentional bias? *Emotion, 10,* 230–236.

Kraljic, T., & Brennan, S. E. (2005). Prosodic disambiguation of syntactic structure: For the speaker or for the addressee? *Cognitive Psychology, 50,* 194–231.

Krauss, S., & Wang, X. T. (2003). The psychology of the Monty Hall problem: Discovering psychological mechanisms for solving a tenacious brain teaser. *Journal of Experimental Psychology: General, 132,* 3–22.

Kreiner, H., Sturt, P., & Garrod, S. (2008). Processing definitional and stereotypical gender in reference resolution: Evidence from eye-movements. *Journal of Memory and Language, 58,* 239–261.

Króliczak, G., Heard, P., Goodale, M. A., & Gregory, R. L. (2006). Dissociation of perception and action unmasked by the hollow-face illusion. *Brain Research, 1080,* 9–16.

Krupinsky, E. A., Tillack, A. A., Richter, L., Henderson, J. T., Bhattacharyya, A. K., Scott, K. M., et al. (2006). Eye-movement study and human performance using telepathology and differences with experience. *Human Pathology, 37,* 1543–1556.

Krynski, T. R., & Tenenbaum, J. B. (2007). The role of causality in judgment under uncertainty. *Journal of Experimental Psychology: General, 136,* 430–450.

Kubovy, M., & van den Berg, M. (2008). The whole is greater than the sum of its parts: A probabilistic model of grouping by proximity and similarity in regular patterns. *Psychological Review, 115,* 131–154.

Kuefner, D., Jacques, C., Prieto, E. A., & Rossion, B. (2010). Electrophysiological correlates of the composite face illusion: Disentangling perceptual and decisional components of holistic face processing in the human brain. *Brain and Cognition, 74,* 225–238.

Kuiper, K. (1996). *Smooth talkers.* Mahwah, NJ: Lawrence Erlbaum Associates.

Kulatunga-Moruzi, C., Brooks, L. R., & Norman, G. R. (2004). Using comprehensive feature lists to bias medical diagnosis. *Journal of Experimental Psychology: Learning, Memory, and Cognition, 30,* 563–572.

Kulkarni, D., & Simon, H. A. (1988). The processes of scientific discovery – The strategy of experimentation. *Cognitive Science, 12*, 139–175.

Kunar, M. A., Carter, R., Cohen, M., & Horowitz, T. S. (2008). Telephone conversation impairs sustained visual attention via a central bottleneck. *Psychonomic Bulletin & Review, 15*, 1135–1140.

Kundel, H. L., Nodine, C. F., Conant, E. F., & Weinstein, S. P. (2007). Holistic component of image perception in mammogram interpretation: Gaze-tracking study. *Radiology, 242*, 396–402.

Kuppens, P., van Mechelen, I., Smits, D. J. M., & De Broeck, P. (2003). The appraisal basis of anger: Specificity, necessity and sufficiency of components. *Emotion, 3*, 254–269.

Kurt, S., Deutscher, A., Crook, J. M., Ohl, F. W., Budinger, E., Moeller, C. K., et al. (2008). Auditory cortical contrast enhancing by global winner-take-all inhibitory interactions. *PLoS One, 3*, e1735.

Kurtz, K. J., & Loewenstein, J. (2007). Converging on a new role for analogy in problem solving and retrieval: When two problems are better than one. *Memory & Cognition, 35*, 334–341.

Kvavilashvili, L., & Fisher, L. (2007). Is time-based prospective remembering mediated by self-initiated rehearsals? Role of incidental cues, ongoing activity. age, and motivation. *Journal of Experimental Psychology: General, 136*, 112–132.

LaBar, K. S., & Cabeza, R. (2006). Cognitive neuroscience of emotional memory. *Nature Reviews Neuroscience, 7*, 54–64.

Lamme, V. A. F. (2003). Why visual attention and awareness are different. *Trends in Cognitive Sciences, 7*, 12–18.

Lampinen, J. M., Copeland, S. M., & Neuschatz, J. S. (2001). Recollections of things schematic: Room schemas revisited. *Journal of Experimental Psychology: Learning, Memory, & Cognition, 27*, 1211–1222.

Lamy, D., Salti, M., & Bar-Haim, Y. (2009). Neural correlates of subjective awareness and unconscious processing: An ERP study. *Journal of Cognitive Neuroscience, 21*, 1435–1446.

Landman, R., Spekreijse, H., & Lamme, V. A. F. (2003). Large capacity storage of integrated objects before change blindness. *Vision Research, 43*, 149–164.

Langenburg, G., Champod, C., & Wertheim, P. (2009). Testing for potential contextual bias during the verification stage of the ACE-V methodology when conducting fingerprint comparisons. *Journal of Forensic Sciences, 54*, 571–582.

Larsen, J. D., Baddeley, A., & Andrade, J. (2000). Phonological similarity and the irrelevant speech effect: Implications for models of short-term memory. *Memory, 8*, 145–157.

Latorella, K. A. (1998). Effects of modality on interrupted flight deck performance: Implications for data link. *Proceedings of the Human Factors and Ergonomics Society 42nd Annual Meeting* (Vols 1 and 2, pp. 87–91). Chicago, IL: HFES.

Lavric, A., Forstmeier, S., & Rippon, G. (2000). Differences in working memory involvement in analytical and creative tasks: An ERP study. *NeuroReport, 11*, 1613–1618.

Leahey, T. H. (1992). The mythical revolutions of American psychology. *American Psychologist, 47*, 308–318.

Leahey, T. H. (2003). Cognition and learning. In D. F. Freedheim (Ed.), *Handbook of psychology, Vol. 1: The history of psychology* (pp. 109–133). Hoboken, NJ: Wiley.

Lee, A. C. H., Graham, K. S., Simons, J. S., Hodges, J. R., Owen, A. M., & Patterson, K. (2002). Regional brain activations differ for semantic features but not for categories. *NeuroReport, 13*, 1497–1501.

Lehle, C., Steinhauser, M., & Hubner, R. (2009). Serial or parallel processing in dual tasks: what is more effortful? *Psychophysiology, 46*, 502–509.

Lench, H. C., & Levine, L. J. (2005). Effects of fear on risk and control judgments and memory: Implications for health promotion messages. *Cognition & Emotion, 19*, 1049–1069.

Lenton, A. P., & Stewart, A. (2008). Changing her ways: The number of options and mate-standard strength impact mate choice strategy and satisfaction. *Judgment and Decision Making Journal, 3*, 501–511.

Lerner, J. S., Goldberg, J. H., & Tetlock, P. E. (1998). Sober second thought: The effects of accountability, anger, and authoritarianism on attributions of responsibility. *Personality and Social Psychology Bulletin, 24*, 563–574.

Lerner, J. S., Gonzalez, R. M., Small, D. A., & Fischhoff, B. (2003). Effects of fear and anger on perceived risks of terrorism: A national field experiment. *Psychological Science, 14*, 144–150.

Lerner, J. S., & Keltner, D. (2001). Fear, anger, and risk. *Journal of Personality and Social Psychology, 81*, 146–159.

Lerner, J. S., & Tiedens, L. Z. (2006). Portrait of the angry decision maker: How appraisal tendencies shape anger's influence on cognition. *Journal of Behavioral Decision Making, 19*, 115–137.

Lescroart, M. D., Biederman, I., Yue, X. M., & Davidoff, J. (2010). A cross-cultural study of the representation of shape: Sensitivity to generalized cone dimensions. *Visual Cognition, 18*, 50–66.

Levelt, W. J. M., Roelofs, A., & Meyer, A. S. (1999). A theory of lexical access in speech production. *Behavioral and Brain Sciences, 22,* 1–38.

Levin, D. T., Drivdahl, S. B., Momen, N., & Beck, M. R. (2002). False predictions about the detectability of visual changes: The role of beliefs about attention, memory, and the continuity of attended objects in causing change blindness blindness. *Consciousness and Cognition, 11,* 507–527.

Levin, D. T., & Simons, D. J. (1997). Failure to detect changes to attended objects in motion pictures. *Psychonomic Bulletin and Review, 4,* 501–506.

Levine, L. J., & Edelstein, R. S. (2009). Emotion and memory narrowing: A review and goal-relevance approach. *Cognition & Emotion, 23,* 833–875.

Levine, M. (1971). Hypothesis theory and nonlearning despite ideal S–R reinforcement contingencies. *Psychological Review, 78,* 130–140.

Levy, C. M., & Ransdell, S. E. (1995). Is writing as difficult as it seems? *Memory & Cognition, 23,* 767–779.

Levy, D. M., & Ransdell, S. E. (2001). Writing with concurrent memory loads. In T. Oliver & C. M. Levy (Eds.), *Contemporary tools and techniques for studying writing.* Dordrecht, The Netherlands: Kluwer Academic Publishers.

Levy, J., Pashler, H., & Boer, E. (2006). Central interference in driving: Is there any stopping the psychological refractory period? *Psychological Science, 17,* 228–235.

Liberman, A. M., Cooper, F. S., Shankweiler, D. S., & Studdert-Kennedy, M. (1967). Perception of the speech code. *Psychological Review, 74,* 431–461.

Libet, B., Gleason, C. A., Wright, E. W., & Pearl, D. K. (1983). Time of conscious intention to act in relation to onset of cerebral activity (readiness potential): The unconscious initiation of a freely voluntary act. *Brain, 106,* 623–642.

Lichtenstein, S., Slovic, P., Fischhoff, B., Layman, M., & Coombs, J. (1978). Judged frequency of lethal events. *Journal of Experimental Psychology: Human Learning and Memory, 4,* 551–578.

Lief, H., & Fetkewicz, J. (1995). Retractors of false memories: The evolution of pseudo-memories. *Journal of Psychiatry & Law, 23,* 411–436.

Lin, L. (2009). Breadth-biased versus focused cognitive control in media multitasking behaviors. *Proceedings of the National Association of Sciences of the United States of America, 106,* 15521–15522.

Lindholm, T., & Christianson, S.-A. (1998). Intergroup biases and eyewitness testimony. *Journal of Social Psychology, 138,* 710–723.

Lippa, R. A., Collaer, M. L., & Peters, M. (2010). Sex differences in mental rotation and line angle judgments are positively associated with gender equality and economic development across 53 nations. *Archives of Sexual Behavior, 39,* 990–997.

Litvak, P. M., Lerner, J. S., Tiedens, L. Z., & Shonk, K. (2010). Fuel in the fire: How anger impacts judgment and decision-making. In M. Potegal, G. Stemmler, & C. Spielberger (Eds.), *International handbook of anger: Constituent and concomitant biological, psychological, and social processes* (pp. 287–310). New York, NY: Springer.

Liu, L., Uttal, D., & Newcomb, N. (2008). *A meta-analysis of training effects on spatial skills: What works, for whom, why and for how long?* Paper presented at the Conference on Research Training in Spatial Intelligence, Evanston, IL.

Locke, S., & Kellar, L. (1973). Categorical perception in a nonlinguistic mode. *Cortex, 9,* 355–369.

Loftus, E. F., & Davis, D. (2006). Recovered memories. *Annual Review of Clinical Psychology, 2,* 469–498.

Loftus, E. F., Loftus, G. R., & Messo, J. (1987). Some facts about "weapons focus". *Law and Human Behavior, 11,* 55–62.

Loftus, E. F., & Palmer, J. C. (1974). Reconstruction of automobile destruction: An example of the interaction between language and memory. *Journal of Verbal Learning and Verbal Behavior, 13,* 585–589.

Loftus, E. F., & Zanni, G. (1975). Eyewitness testimony – Influence of wording of a question. *Bulletin of the Psychonomic Society, 5,* 86–88.

Logie, R. H. (1999). State of the art: Working memory. *The Psychologist, 12,* 174–178.

Logie, R. H., Baddeley, A. D., Mane, A., Donchin, E., & Sheptak, R. (1989). Working memory and the analysis of a complex skill by secondary task methodology. *Acta Psychologica, 71,* 53–87.

Logie, R. H., & Della Sala, S. (2005). *Disorders of visuo-spatial working memory.* New York, NY: Cambridge University Press.

Logie, R. H., & van der Meulen, M. (2009). Fragmenting and integrating visuo-spatial working memory. In J. R. Brockmole (Ed.), *Representing the visual world in memory.* Hove, UK: Psychology Press.

Loukopoulos, L. D., Dismukes, R. K., & Barshi, I. (2009). *The multitasking myth: Handling complexity in real-world operations.* Burlington, VT: Ashgate.

Loverock, D. S. (2007). Object superiority as a function of object coherence and task difficulty. *American Journal of Psychology, 120,* 565–591.

Luchins, A. S. (1942). Mechanization in problem solving: The effect of Einstellung. *Psychological Monographs, 54,* 248.

Luchins, A. S., & Luchins, E. H. (1959). *Rigidity of behavior*. Eugene, OR: University of Oregon.

Luria, A. (1968). *The mind of a mnemonist*. New York, NY: Basic Books.

Lustig, C., & Hasher, L. (2001). Implicit memory is not immune to interference. *Psychological Bulletin, 127*, 618–628.

Lustig, C., Konkel, A., & Jacoby, L. L. (2004). Which route to recovery? Controlled retrieval and accessibility bias in retroactive interference. *Psychological Science, 15*, 729–735.

Lynch, E. B., Coley, J. D., & Medin, D. L. (2000). Tall is typical: Central tendency, ideal dimensions, and graded category structure among tree experts and novices. *Memory & Cognition, 28*, 41–50.

MacDonald, A. W., Cohen, J. D., Stenger, V. A., & Carter, C. S. (2000). Dissociating the role of the dorsolateral prefrontal cortex and anterior cingulate cortex in cognitive control. *Science, 288*, 1835–1838.

MacDonald, M. C., Pearlmutter, N. J., & Seidenberg, M. S. (1994). Lexical nature of syntactic ambiguity resolution. *Psychological Review, 101*, 676–703.

MacGregor, J. N., & Cunningham, J. B. (2008). Rebus puzzles as insight problems. *Behavior Research Methods, 40*, 263–268.

MacGregor, J. N., & Cunningham, J. B. (2009). The effects of number and level of restructuring in insight problem solving. *Journal of Problem Solving, 2*, 130–141.

MacGregor, J. N., Ormerod, T. C., & Chronicle, E. P. (2001). Information processing and insight: A process model of performance on the nine-dot and related problems. *Journal of Experimental Psychology: Learning, Memory, and Cognition, 27*, 176–201.

Mack, M. L., Gauthier, I., Sadr, J., & Palmeri, T. J. (2008). Object detection and basic-level categorization: Sometimes you know it is there before you know what it is. *Psychonomic Bulletin & Review, 15*, 28–35.

Mackintosh, N. J. (1998). *IQ and human intelligence*. Oxford, UK: Oxford University Press.

MacLeod, C. M. (2005). The Stroop task in cognitive research. In A. Wenzel & D. C. Rubin (Eds.), *Cognitive methods and their application to clinical research* (pp. 17–40). Washington, DC: American Psychological Association.

MacLeod, C., Rutherford, E., Campbell, L., Ebsworthy, G., & Holker, L. (2002). Selective attention and emotional vulnerability: Assessing the causal basis of their association through the experimental manipulation of attentional bias. *Journal of Abnormal Psychology, 111*, 107–123.

Macpherson, R., & Stanovich, K. E. (2007). Cognitive ability, thinking dispositions, and instructional set as predictors of critical thinking. *Learning and Individual Differences, 17*, 115–127.

Macrae, C. N., & Bodenhausen, G. V. (2000). Social cognition: Thinking categorically about others. *Annual Review of Psychology, 51*, 93–120.

Macrae, C. N., Milne, A. B., & Bodenhausen, G. V. (1994). Stereotypes as energy-saving devices: A peak inside the cognitive toolbox. *Journal of Personality and Social Psychology, 66*, 37–47.

Maguire, E. A., Nannery, R., & Spiers, H. J. (2006). Navigation around London by a taxi driver with bilateral hippocampal lesions. *Brain, 129*, 2894–2907.

Mandel, D. R. (2005). Are risk assessments of a terrorist attack coherent? *Journal of Experimental Psychology: Applied, 11*, 277–288.

Maner, J. K., Richey, J. A., Cromer, K., Mallott, M., Lejuez, C. W., Joiner, T. E., et al. (2007). Dispositional anxiety and risk-avoidant decision-making. *Personality and Individual Differences, 42*, 665–675.

Manktelow, K. I. (1999). *Reasoning and thinking*. Hove, UK: Psychology Press.

Mann, S. A., Vrij, A., Fisher, R. P., & Robinson, M. (2008). See no lies, hear no lies: Differences in discrimination accuracy and response bias when watching or listening to police suspect interviews. *Applied Cognitive Psychology, 22*, 1062–1071.

Manns, J. R., Hopkins, R. O., & Squire, L. R. (2003). Semantic memory and the human hippocampus. *Neuron, 38*, 127–133.

Marian, V., & Kaushanskaya, M. (2007). Language context guides memory content. *Psychonomic Bulletin & Review, 14*, 925–933.

Marsh, E. J. (2007). Retelling is not the same as recalling – Implications for memory. *Current Directions in Psychological Science, 16*, 16–20.

Marsh, E. J., & Tversky, B. (2004). Spinning the stories of our lives. *Applied Cognitive Psychology, 18*, 491–503.

Martin, A., & Caramazza, A. (2003). Neuropsychological and neuroimaging perspectives on conceptual knowledge: An introduction. *Cognitive Neuropsychology, 20*, 195–221.

Martin, A., & Chao, L. L. (2001). Semantic memory and the brain: Structure and processes. *Current Opinion in Neurobiology, 11*, 194–201.

Martin, R. C., Crowther, J. E., Knight, M., Tamborello, F. P., & Yang, C. L. (2010). Planning in sentence production: Evidence for the phrase as a default planning scope. *Cognition, 116*, 177–192.

Martin, R. C., Miller, M., & Vu. H. (2004). Lexical–semantic retention and speech production: Further evidence from normal and brain-damaged participants for a phrasal scope of planning. *Cognitive Neuropsychology, 21*, 625–644.

Martinez, A., Anllo-Vento, L., Sereno, M. I., Frank, L. R., Buxton, R. B., Dubowitz, D. J., et al. (1999). Involvement of striate and extrastriate visual cortical areas in spatial attention. *Nature Neuroscience, 4*, 364–369.

Marzi, C. A., Girelli, M., Natale, E., & Miniussi, C. (2001). What exactly is extinguished in unilateral visual extinction? *Neuropsychologia, 39*, 1354–1366.

Marzi, C. A., Smania, N., Martini, M. C., Gambina, G., Tomelleri, G., Palamara, A., et al. (1996). Implicit redundant-targets effect in visual extinction. *Neuropsychologia, 34*, 9–22.

Massen, C., & Vaterrodt-Plünnecke, B. (2006). The role of proactive interference in mnemonic techniques. *Memory, 14*, 189–196.

Massen, C., Vaterrodt-Plünnecke, B., Krings, L., & Hilbig, B. E. (2009). Effects of instruction on learners' ability to generate an effective pathway in the method of loci. *Memory, 17*, 724–731.

Mather, G. (2009). *Foundations of sensation and perception* (2nd ed.). New York: Psychology Press.

Mathews, A., & MacLeod, C. (2005). Cognitive vulnerability to emotional disorders. *Annual Review of Clinical Psychology, 1*, 167–195.

Matlin, M. W. (2009). *Cognitive psychology: International student version* (7th ed.). New York, NY: Wiley.

Mattys, S. L., Brooks, J., & Cooke, M. (2009). Recognizing speech under a processing load: Dissociating energetic from informational factors. *Cognitive Psychology, 59*, 203–243.

Mattys, S. L., & Liss, J. M. (2008). On building models of spoken-word recognition: When there is as much to learn from natural "oddities" as artificial normality. *Perception & Psychophysics, 70*, 1235–1242.

Mattys, S. L., White, L., & Melhorn, J. F. (2005). Integration of multiple speech segmentation cues: A hierarchical framework. *Journal of Experimental Psychology: General, 134*, 477–500.

Matuszewski, V., Piolino, P., Belliard, S., de la Sayette, V., Laisney, M., Lalevée, C., et al. (2009). Patterns of autobiographical memory impairment according to disease severity in semantic dementia. *Cortex, 45*, 456–472.

Maylor, E. A., & Logie, R. H. (2010). A large-scale comparison of prospective and retrospective memory development from childhood to middle age. *Quarterly Journal of Experimental Psychology, 63*, 442–451.

Mazzone, M., & Lalumera, E. (2010). Concepts: Stored or created? *Minds and Machines, 20*, 47–68.

McCarley, J. S., Kramer, A. F., Wickens, C. D., & Boot, W. R. (2004). Visual skills in airport-security screening. *Psychological Science, 15*, 302–306.

McCarthy, R. A., Kopelman, M. D., & Warrington, E. K. (2005). Remembering and forgetting of semantic knowledge in amnesia: A 16-year follow-up investigation of RFR. *Neuropsychologia, 43*, 356–372.

McCarthy, R. A., & Warrington, E. K. (1984). A two-route model of speech production. *Brain, 107*, 463–485.

McCauley, C., & Stitt, C. L. (1978). An individual and quantitative measure of stereotypes. *Journal of Personality and Social Psychology, 36*, 929–940.

McClelland, J. L. (1991). Stochastic interactive processes and the effect of context on perception. *Cognitive Psychology, 23*, 1–44.

McClelland, J. L., & Elman, J. L. (1986). The TRACE model of speech perception. *Cognitive Psychology, 18*, 1–86.

McClelland, J. L., Rumelhart, D. E., & The PDP Research Group (1986). *Parallel distributed processing: Vol. 2. Psychological and biological models*. Cambridge, MA: MIT Press.

McCloskey, M. E., & Glucksberg, S. (1978). Natural categories: Well defined or fuzzy sets? *Memory & Cognition, 26*, 121–134.

McDonald, J. L. (2008). Differences in the cognitive demands of word order, plural, and subject–verb agreement constructions. *Psychonomic Bulletin & Review, 15*, 980–984.

McEvoy, S. P., Stevenson, M. R., & Woodward, M. (2007). The contribution of passengers versus mobile use to motor vehicle crashes resulting in hospital attendance. *Accident Analysis and Prevention, 39*, 1170–1176.

McGlone, M. S., & Manfredi, D. (2001). Topic–vehicle interaction in metaphor comprehension. *Memory & Cognition, 29*, 1209–1219.

McGugin, R. W., & Gauthier, I. (2010). Perceptual expertise with objects predicts another hallmark of face perception. *Journal of Vision, 10*(4), Article No. 15.

McGurk, H., & MacDonald, J. (1976). Hearing lips and seeing voices. *Nature, 264*, 746–748.

McKone, E., Kanwisher, N., & Duchaine, B. C. (2007). Can generic expertise explain special processing for faces? *Trends in Cognitive Sciences, 11*, 8–15.

McKoon, G., & Ratcliff, R. (1992). Inference during reading. *Psychological Review, 99*, 440–466.

McLaughlin, K., Remy, M., & Schmidt, H. G. (2008). Is analytic information processing a feature of expertise in medicine? *Advances in Health Sciences Education*, 13, 123–128.

McMurray, B., Dennhardt, J. L., & Struck-Marcell, A. (2008). Context effects on musical chord categorization: Different forms of top-down feedback in speech and music? *Cognitive Science*, 32, 893–920.

McNally, R. J., & Geraerts, E. (2009). A new solution to the recovered memory debate. *Perspectives on Psychological Science*, 4, 126–134.

McNamara, D. S., & Magliano, J. (2009). Toward a comprehensive model of comprehension. *Psychology of Learning and Motivation*, 51, 297–384.

McNamara, T. P. (1992). Priming and constraints it places on theories of memory and retrieval. *Psychological Review*, 99, 650–662.

McPherson, F. (2004). *The memory key: Unlock the secrets to remembering*. New York, NY: Barnes & Noble.

McQueen, J. M. (1991). The influence of the lexicon on phonetic categorization: Stimulus quality in word-final ambiguity. *Journal of Experimental Psychology: Human Perception & Performance*, 17, 433–443.

McRae, K., Hughes, B., Chopra, S., Gabrieli, J. D. E., Gross, J. J., & Ochsner, K. N. (2010). Neural systems supporting the control of affective and cognitive conflicts. *Journal of Cognitive Neuroscience*, 22, 248–262.

McWilliam, L., Schepman, A., & Rodway, P. (2009). The linguistic status of text message abbreviations: An exploration using a Stroop task. *Computers in Human Behavior*, 25, 970–974.

Medin, D. L., & Atran, S. (2004). The native mind: Biological categorization and reasoning in development and across cultures. *Psychological Review*, 111, 960–983.

Meister, I. G., Wilson, S. M., Delieck, C., Wu, A. D., & Iacobini, M. (2007). The essential role of premotor cortex in speech perception. *Current Biology*, 17, 1692–1696.

Menchaca-Brandan, M., A., Liu, A. M., Oman, C. M., & Natapoff, A. (2007). Influence of perspective-taking and mental rotation abilities in space teleoperation. *Proceedings of the 2007 ACM Conference on Human–Robot Interaction*, Washington, DC, March 9–11, pp. 271–278.

Menneer, T., Cave, K. R., & Donnelly, N. (2009). The cost of search for multiple targets: Effects of practice and target similarity. *Journal of Experimental Psychology: Applied*, 15, 125–139.

Mercier, H., & Sperber, D. (2011). Why do humans reason? Arguments for an argumentative theory. *Behavioral and Brain Sciences*, 34, 57–111.

Merikle, P. M., Smilek, D., & Eastwood, J. D. (2001). Perception without awareness: Perspectives from cognitive psychology. *Cognition*, 79, 115–134.

Metcalfe, J., & Kornell, N. (2007). Principles of cognitive science in education: The effects of generation, errors, and feedback. *Psychonomic Bulletin & Review*, 14, 225–229.

Metcalfe, J., & Wiebe, D. (1987). Intuition in insight and noninsight problem solving. *Memory & Cognition*, 15, 238–246.

Meteyard, L., & Patterson, K. (2009). The relation between content and structure in language production: An analysis of speech errors in semantic dementia. *Brain and Language*, 110, 121–134.

Meulemans, T., & Van der Linden, M. (2003). Implicit learning of complex information in amnesia. *Brain and Cognition*, 52, 250–257.

Meyer, A. S. (1996). Lexical access in phrase and sentence production: Results from picture–word interference experiments. *Journal of Memory and Language*, 35, 477–496.

Meyer, A. S., & Damian, M. F. (2007). Activation of distractor names in the picture–picture interference paradigm. *Memory & Cognition*, 35, 494–503.

Meyer, D. E., & Schvaneveldt, R. W. (1976). Meaning, memory structure, and mental processes. *Science*, 192, 27–33.

Miles, C., & Hardman, E. (1998). State-dependent memory produced by aerobic exercise. *Ergonomics*, 41, 20–26.

Miller, G. A. (1956). The magical number seven, plus or minus two: Some limits on our capacity for processing information. *Psychological Review*, 63, 81–97.

Milner, A. D., & Goodale, M. A. (1998). The visual brain in action. *Psyche*, 4, 1–14.

Milner, A. D., & Goodale, M. A. (2008). Two visual systems re-viewed. *Neuropsychologia*, 46, 774–785.

Miranda, R., & Kihlstrom, J. F. (2005). Mood congruence in childhood and recent autobiographical memory. *Cognition & Emotion*, 19, 981–998.

Mirman, D., McClelland, J. L., Holt, L. L., & Magnuson, J. S. (2008). Effects of attention on the strength of lexical influences on speech perception: Behavioral experiments and computational mechanisms. *Cognitive Science*, 32, 398–417.

Mitchell, D. B. (2006). Nonconscious priming after 17 years. *Psychological Science*, 17, 925–929.

Mitchell, K. J., Johnson, M. K., & Mather, M. (2003). Monitoring and suggestibility to misinformation: Adult age-related differences. *Applied Cognitive Psychology*, 17, 107–119.

Mitterer, H., & de Ruiter, J. P. (2008). Recalibrating color categories using world knowledge. *Psychological Science*, 19, 629–634.

Miyake, A., Friedman, N. P., Emerson, M. J., Witzki, A. H., Howerter, A., & Wager, T. (2000). The unity and diversity of executive functions and their contributions to complex "frontal lobe" tasks: A latent variable analysis. *Cognitive Psychology, 41,* 49–100.

Moè, A. (2009). Are males always better than females in mental rotation? Exploring a gender belief explanation. *Learning and Individual Differences, 19,* 21–27.

Mol, L., Krahmer, E., Maes, A., & Swerts, M. (2009). The communicative import of gestures: Evidence from a comparative analysis of human–human and human–machine interactions. *Gesture, 9,* 97–126.

Molholm, S., Martinez, A., Shpanker, M., & Foxe, J. J. (2007). Object-based attention is multisensory: Co-activation of an object's representations in ignored sensory modalities. *European Journal of Neuroscience, 26,* 499–509.

Moons, W. G., & Mackie, D. M. (2008). Thinking straight while seeing red: The influence of anger on information processing. *Personality and Social Psychology Bulletin, 33,* 706–721.

Moors, A., & de Houwer, J. (2006). Automaticity: A theoretical and conceptual analysis. *Psychological Bulletin, 132,* 297–326.

Morawetz, C., Holz, P., Baudewig, J., Treue, S., & Dechent, P. (2007). Split of attentional resources in human visual cortex. *Visual Neuroscience, 24,* 817–826.

Moray, N. (1959). Attention in dichotic listening: Affective cues and the influence of instructions. *Quarterly Journal of Experimental Psychology, 11,* 56–60.

Moro, V., Berlucchi, G., Lerch, J., Tomaiuolo, F., & Aglioti, S. M. (2008). Selective deficit of mental visual imagery with intact primary visual cortex and visual perception. *Cortex, 44,* 109–118.

Morris, C. D., Bransford, J. D., & Franks, J. J. (1977). Levels of processing versus transfer appropriate processing. *Journal of Verbal Learning and Verbal Behavior, 16,* 519–533.

Morris, P. E., Fritz, C. O., Jackson, L., Nichol, E., & Roberts, E. (2005). Strategies for learning proper names: Expanding retrieval practice, meaning and imagery. *Applied Cognitive Psychology, 19,* 779–798.

Morris, P. E., Jones, S., & Hampson, P. (1978). An imagery mnemonic for the learning of people's names. *British Journal of Psychology, 69,* 335–336.

Morris, P. E., & Reid, R. L. (1970). Repeated use of mnemonic imagery. *Psychonomic Science, 20,* 337–338.

Morrison, R. G., Holyoak, K. J., & Truong, B. (2001). Working-memory modularity in analogical reasoning. In J. D. Moore & K. Stenning (Eds.), *Proceedings of the Twenty-third Annual Conference of the Cognitive Science Society.* Mahwah, NJ: Lawrence Erlbaum Associates.

Moscovitch, M. (2008). Commentary: A perspective on prospective memory. In M. Kliegel, M. A. McDaniel, & G. O. Einstein (Eds.), *Prospective memory: Cognitive, neuroscience, developmental, and applied perspectives.* New York, NY: Lawrence Erlbaum Associates.

Moscovitch, M., Nadel, L., Winocur, G., Gilboa, A., & Rosenbaum, R. S. (2006). The cognitive neuroscience of remote episodic, semantic and spatial memory. *Current Opinion in Neurobiology, 16,* 179–190.

Moscovitch, M., Winocur, G., & Behrmann, M. (1997). What is special about face recognition? Nineteen experiments on a person with visual object agnosia but normal face recognition. *Journal of Cognitive Neuroscience, 9,* 555–604.

Motley, M. T. (1980). Verification of "Freudian slips" and semantic prearticulatory editing via laboratory-induced spoonerisms. In V. A. Fromkin (Ed.), *Errors in linguistic performance: Slips of the tongue, ear, pen, and hand.* New York, NY: Academic Press.

Mottaghy, F. M. (2006). Interfering with working memory in humans. *Neuroscience, 139,* 85–90.

Möttönen, R., & Watkins, K. E. (2009). Motor representations of articulators contribute to categorical perception of speech sounds. *Journal of Neuroscience, 29,* 9819–9825.

Moulton, S. T., & Kosslyn, S. M. (2009). Imagining predictions: Mental imagery as mental emulation. *Philosophical Transactions of the Royal Society B: Biological Sciences, 364,* 1273–1280.

Mueller, S. T., Seymour, T. L., Kieras, D. E., & Meyer, D. E. (2003). Theoretical implications of articulatory duration, phonological similarity, and phonological complexity in verbal working memory. *Journal of Experimental Psychology: Learning, Memory & Cognition, 29,* 1353–1380.

Müller, N. G., Bartelt, O. A., Donner, T. H., Villringer, A., & Brandt, S. A. (2003). A physiological correlate of the "zoom lens" of visual attention. *Journal of Neuroscience, 23,* 3561–2565.

Munro, G. D., & Stansbury, J. A. (2009). The dark side of self-affirmation: Confirmation bias and illusory correlation in response to threatening information. *Personality and Social Psychology Bulletin, 35,* 1143–1153.

Münsterberg, H. (1908). *On the witness stand: Essays on psychology and crime.* New York: Doubleday.

Murphy, G., & Kovach, J. K. (1972). *Historical introduction to modern psychology.* London, UK: Routledge & Kegan Paul.

Murray, J. D., & Burke, K. A. (2003). Activation and encoding of predictive inferences: The role of reading skill. *Discourse Processes, 35*, 81–102.

Murty, V. P., Ritchey, M., Adcock, R. A., & LaBar, K. S. (2010). fMRI studies of successful emotional memory encoding: A quantitative meta-analysis. *Neuropsychologia, 48*, 3459–3469.

Mustanski, B. (2007). The influence of state and trait affect on HIV risk behaviors: A daily diary study of MSM. *Health Psychology, 26*, 618–626.

Muter, P. (1978). Recognition failure of recallable words in semantic memory. *Memory & Cognition, 6*, 9–12.

Naccache, L., Blandin, E., & Dehaene, S. (2002). Unconscious masked priming depends on temporal attention. *Psychological Science, 13*, 416–424.

Nadel, L., & Moscovitch, M. (1997). Memory consolidation, retrograde amnesia and the hippocampal complex. *Current Opinion in Neurobiology, 7*, 217–227.

Nahmias, E. (2005). Agency, authorship, and illusion. *Consciousness and Cognition, 14*, 771–785.

Nairne, J. S. (2002). The myth of the encoding–retrieval match. *Memory, 10*, 389–395.

Nairne, J. S., Whiteman, H. L., & Kelley, M. R. (1999). Short-term forgetting of order under conditions of reduced interference. *Quarterly Journal of Experimental Psychology, 52A*, 241–251.

Nation, K., & Cocksey, J. (2009). The relationship between knowing a word and reading it aloud in children's word reading development. *Journal of Experimental Child Psychology, 103*, 296–308.

Navon, D. (1977). Forest before trees: The precedence of global features in visual perception. *Cognitive Psychology, 9*, 353–383.

Neisser, U. (1964). Visual search. *Scientific American, 210*, 94–102.

Newell, A., Shaw, J. C., & Simon, H. A. (1958). Elements of a theory of human problem solving. *Psychological Review, 65*, 151–166.

Newell, A., & Simon, H. A. (1972). *Human problem solving*. Englewood Cliffs, NJ: Prentice Hall.

Newman, M. L., Groom, C. J., Handelman, L. D., & Pennebaker, J. W. (2008). Gender differences in language use: An analysis of 14,000 text samples. *Discourse Processes, 45*, 211–236.

Newman, M. L., Pennebaker, J. W., Berry, D. S., & Richards, J. M. (2003). Lying words: Predicting deception from linguistic styles. *Personality and Social Psychology Bulletin, 29*, 665–675.

Nieuwland, M. S., & van Berkum, J. J. A. (2006). When peanuts fall in love: N400 evidence for the power of discourse. *Journal of Cognitive Neuroscience, 18*, 1098–1111.

Nijboer, T. C. W., McIntosh, R. D., Nys, G. M. S., Dijkerman, H. C., & Milner, A. D. (2008). Prism adaptation improves voluntary but not automatic orienting in neglect. *NeuroReport, 19*, 293–298.

Nisbett, R. E., & Wilson, T. D. (1977). Telling more than we can know: Verbal reports on mental processes. *Psychological Review, 84*, 231–259.

Noice, H., & Noice, T. (2007). The non-literal enactment effect: Filling in the blanks. *Discourse Processes, 44*, 73–89.

Nolan, M. S. (2010). *Fundamentals of air traffic control* (5th ed.). Florence, KY: Delmar Cengage Learning.

Nooteboom, S., & Quené, H. (2008). Self-monitoring and feedback: A new attempt to find the main cause of lexical bias in phonological speech errors. *Journal of Memory and Language, 58*, 837–861.

Norman, G. (2005). Research in clinical reasoning: Past history and current trends. *Medical Education, 39*, 418–427.

Norris, D., McQueen, J. M., Cutler, A., & Butterfield, S. (1997). The possible-word constraint in the segmentation of continuous speech. *Cognitive Psychology, 34*, 191–243.

Nosek, B. A., Greenwald, A. G., & Banaji, M. R. (2005). Understanding and using the Implicit Association Test: II. Method variables and construct validity. *Personality and Social Psychology Bulletin, 31*, 166–180.

Nosek, B. A., & Hansen, J. J. (2008). Personalizing the Implicit Association Test increases explicit evaluation of target concepts. *European Journal of Psychological Assessment, 24*, 226–236.

Nosek, B. A., Smyth, F. L., Sriram, N., Lindner, N. M., Devos, T., Ayala, A., et al. (2009). National differences in gender-science stereotypes in science and math achievement. *Proceedings of the National Association of Sciences of the United States of America, 106*, 10593–10597.

Novick, L. R. (2003). At the forefront of thought: The effect of media exposure on airplane typicality. *Psychonomic Bulletin & Review, 10*, 971–974.

Novick, L. R., & Sherman, S. J. (2003). On the nature of insight solutions: Evidence from skill differences in anagram solution. *Quarterly Journal of Experimental Psychology, 56A*, 351–382.

Oaksford, M., & Hahn, U. (2004). A Bayesian approach to the argument from ignorance. *Canadian Journal of Experimental Psychology, 58*, 75–85.

Oatley, K., & Djikic, M. (2008). Writing as thinking. *Review of General Psychology, 12*, 9–27.

Obleser, J., Scott, S. K., & Eulitz, C. (2006). Now you hear it, now you don't: Transient traces of consonants and their nonspeech analogs in the human brain. *Cerebral Cortex, 16*, 1069–1076.

O'Brien, E. J., Cook, A. E., & Guerand, S. (2010). Accessibility of outdated information. *Journal of Experimental Psychology: Learning, Memory, & Cognition, 36*, 979–991.

Ochsner, K. N., & Gross, J. J. (2005). The cognitive control of emotion. *Trends in Cognitive Sciences, 9*, 242–249.

Ochsner, K. N., & Gross, J. J. (2008). Cognitive emotion regulation: Insights from social cognitive and affective neuroscience. *Current Directions in Psychological Science, 17*, 153–158.

Ochsner, K. N., Ray, R. R., Hughes, B., McRae, K., Cooper, J. C., Weber, J., et al. (2009). Bottom-up and top-down processes in emotion generation: Common and distinct neural mechanisms. *Psychological Science, 20*, 1322–1331.

Ohlsson, S. (1992). Information processing explanations of insight and related phenomena. In M. T. Keane & K. J. Gilhooly (Eds.), *Advances in the psychology of thinking*. London, UK: Harvester Wheatsheaf.

Öhman, A., & Soares, J. J. F. (1994). "Unconscious anxiety": Phobic responses to masked stimuli. *Journal of Abnormal Psychology, 103*, 231–240.

Olive, T. (2004). Working memory in writing: Empirical evidence from the dual-task technique. *European Psychologist, 9*, 32–42.

Olive, T., Alves, R. A., & Castro, S. L. (2009). Cognitive processes in writing during pause and execution periods. *European Journal of Cognitive Psychology, 21*, 758–785.

Olive, T., & Kellogg, R. T. (2002). Concurrent activation of high- and low-level production processes in written composition. *Memory & Cognition, 30*, 594–600.

Olive, T., & Piolat, A. (2002). Suppressing visual feedback in written composition: Effects on processing demands and coordination of the writing process. *International Journal of Psychology, 37*, 209–218.

Ollinger, M., Jones, G., & Knoblich, G. (2008). Investigating the effect of mental set on insight problem solving. *Experimental Psychology, 55*, 269–282.

Ophir, E., Nass, C., & Wagner, A. D. (2009). Cognitive control in media multitaskers. *Proceedings of the National Association of Sciences, 106*, 15583–15587.

Oppenheimer, D. M. (2003). Not so fast! (and not so frugal!). Rethinking the recognition heuristic. *Cognition, 90*, B1–B9.

Oppenheimer, D. M. (2004). Spontaneous discounting of availability in frequency judgment tasks. *Psychological Science, 15*, 100–105.

Orban, P., Peigneux, P., Lungu, O., Albouy, G., Breton, E., Laberenne, F., et al. (2010). The multifaceted nature of the relationship between performance and brain activity in motor sequence learning. *NeuroImage, 49*, 694–702.

Ostojic, P., & Phillips, J. G. (2009). Memorability of alternative password systems. *International Journal of Pattern Recognition and Artificial Intelligence, 23*, 987–1004.

Overgaard, M., Fehl, K., Mouridsen, K., Bergholt, B., & Cleermans, K. (2008). Seeing without seeing? Degraded conscious vision in a blindsight patient. *PLoS One, 3*, e3028.

Owen, A. M., Coleman, M. R., Boly, M., Davis, M. H., Laureys, S., & Pickard, J. D. (2006). Detecting awareness in the vegetative state. *Science, 313*, 1402.

Pacheco-Cobos, L., Rosetti, M., Cuatianquiz, C., & Hudson, R. (2010). Sex differences in mushroom gathering: Men expend more energy to obtain equivalent benefits. *Evolution and Human Behavior, 31*, 289–297.

Pachur, T., & Hertwig, R. (2006). On the psychology of the recognition heuristic: Retrieval primacy as a key determinant of its use. *Journal of Experimental Psychology: Learning, Memory, & Cognition, 32*, 983–1002.

Palmer, S. E. (1975). The effects of contextual scenes on the identification of objects. *Memory & Cognition, 3*, 519–526.

Papagno, C., Valentine, T., & Baddeley, A. D. (1991). Phonological short-term memory and foreign language vocabulary learning. *Journal of Memory and Language, 30*, 331–347.

Parker, E. S., Cahill, L., & McGaugh, J. L. (2006). A case of unusual autobiographical remembering. *Neurocase, 12*, 35–49.

Parkin, A. J. (2001). The structure and mechanisms of memory. In B. Rapp (Ed.). *The handbook of cognitive neuropsychology: What deficits reveal about the human mind*. Hove, UK: Psychology Press.

Parkinson, B. (2001). Putting appraisal in context. In K. R. Scherer, A. Schorr, & T. Johnstone (Eds.), *Appraisal processes in emotion: Theory, methods, research*. Oxford, UK: Oxford University Press.

Parkinson, B. (2007). Getting from situations to emotions: Appraisal and other routes. *Emotion, 7*, 21–25.

Parton, A., Mulhotra, P., & Husain, M. (2004). Hemispatial neglect. *Journal of Neurology, Neurosurgery and Psychiatry, 75*, 13–21.

Pashler, H. (1993). Dual-task interference and elementary mental mechanisms. In D. E. Meyer & S. Kornblum (Eds.), *Attention and performance* (Vol. XIV). London, UK: MIT Press.

Patterson, K., Nestor, P. J., & Rogers, T. T. (2007). Where do you know what you know? The representation of semantic knowledge in the human brain. *Nature Reviews Neuroscience, 8,* 976–987.

Paulus, M., Lindemann, O., & Bekkering, H. (2009). Motor simulation in verbal knowledge acquisition. *Quarterly Journal of Experimental Psychology, 62,* 2298–3305.

Payne, J. (1976). Task complexity and contingent processing in decision making: An information search and protocol analysis. *Organizational Behavior and Human Performance, 16,* 366–387.

Pearson, J., Clifford, C. W. G., & Tong, F. (2008). The functional impact of mental imagery on conscious perception. *Current Biology, 18,* 982–986.

Pecher, C., Lemercier, C., & Cellier, J.-M. (2009). Emotions drive attention: Effects on driver's behaviour. *Safety Science, 47,* 1254–1259.

Pegna, A. J., Khateb, A., Lazeyras, F., & Seghier, M. L. (2005). Discriminating emotional faces without primary visual cortices involves the right amygdala. *Nature Neuroscience, 8,* 24–25.

Peissig, J. J., & Tarr, M. J. (2007). Visual object recognition: Do we know more now than we did 20 years ago? *Annual Review of Psychology, 58,* 75–96.

Pennebaker, J. W. (1993). Putting stress into words: Health, linguistic, and therapeutic implications. *Behaviour Research and Therapy, 31,* 539–548.

Peretz, I., & Coltheart, M. (2003). Modularity of music processing. *Nature Neuroscience, 6,* 688–691.

Perfect, T. J., Wagstaff, G. F., Morre, D., Andrews, B., Cleveland, V., Newcombe, S., et al. (2008). How can we help witnesses to remember more? It's an (eyes) open and shut case. *Law and Human Behavior, 32,* 314–324.

Perre, L., Pattamadilok, C., Montant, M., & Ziegler, J. C. (2010). Orthographic effects in spoken language: On-line activation or phonological restructuring? *Brain Research, 1275,* 73–80.

Perre, L., & Ziegler, J. C. (2008). On-line activation of orthography in spoken word recognition. *Brain Research, 1188,* 132–138.

Perry, C., Ziegler, J. C., & Zorzi, M. (2007). Nested incremental modeling in the development of computational theories: The CDP+ model of reading aloud. *Psychological Review, 114,* 273–315.

Persaud, N., & Cowey, A. (2008). Blindsight is unlike normal conscious vision: Evidence from an exclusion task. *Consciousness and Cognition, 17,* 1050–1055.

Persaud, N., & McLeod, P. (2008). Wagering demonstrates subconscious processing in a binary exclusion task. *Consciousness and Cognition, 17,* 565–575.

Pessiglione, M., Schmidt, L., Draganski, B., Kalisch, R., Lau, H., Dolan, R. J., & Frith, C. D. (2007). How the brain translates money into force: A neuroimaging study of subliminal motivation. *Science, 316,* 904–906.

Pessoa, L. (2008). On the relationship between emotion and cognition. *Nature Reviews Neuroscience, 9,* 148–158.

Peters, D. P. (1988). Eyewitness memory in a natural setting. In M. M. Gruneberg, P. E. Morris, & R. N. Sykes (Eds.), *Practical aspects of memory: Current research and issues: Vol. 1. Memory in everyday life.* Chichester, UK: Wiley.

Peterson, L. R., & Peterson, M. J. (1959). Short-term retention of individual verbal items. *Journal of Experimental Psychology, 58,* 193–198.

Petkova, V. I., & Ehrsson, H. H. (2008). If I were you: Perceptual illusion of body swapping. *PLoS One, 3,* e3832.

Pezdek, K. (2003). Event memory and autobiographical memory for the events of September 11, 2001. *Applied Cognitive Psychology, 17,* 1033–1045.

Philipp, A. M., Gade, M., & Koch, I. (2007). Inhibitory processes in language switching: Evidence from switching language-defined response sets. *European Journal of Cognitive Psychology, 19,* 395–416.

Pickel, K. L. (2009). The weapon focus effect on memory for female versus male perpetrators. *Memory, 17,* 664–678.

Pickering, M. J., & Ferreira, V. S. (2008). Structural priming: A critical review. *Psychological Bulletin, 134,* 427–459.

Pickering, M. J., & Garrod, S. (2004). Toward a mechanistic psychology of dialog. *Behavioral and Brain Sciences, 27,* 169–226.

Pickford, R. W., & Gregory, R. L. (2004). Bartlett, Sir Frederic Charles. In R. L. Gregory (Ed.), *The Oxford companion to the mind* (2nd. ed., pp. 86–87). New York, NY: Oxford University Press.

Pinker, S. (1984). *Language learnability and language development.* Cambridge, MA: Harvard University Press.

Pinker, S. (1997). *How the mind works.* New York, NY: W. W. Norton.

Pinkham, A. E., Griffin, M., Baron, R., Sasson, N. J., & Gur, R. C. (2010). The face in the crowd effect: Anger superiority when using real faces and multiple identities. *Emotion, 10,* 141–146.

Pisoni, D. B., & Tash, J. (1974). Reaction times to comparisons within and across phonetic categories. *Perception & Psychophysics, 15,* 285–290.

Piwnica-Worms, K. E., Omar, R., Hailstone, J. C., & Warren, J. D. (2010). Flavor processing in semantic dementia. *Cortex, 46,* 761–768.

Plaut, D. C., McClelland, J. L., Seidenberg, M. S., & Patterson, K. (1996). Understanding normal and impaired word reading: Computational principles in quasi-regular domains. *Psychological Review, 103,* 56–115.

Plester, B., Wood, C., & Joshi, P. (2009). Exploring the relationship between children's knowledge of text message abbreviations and school literacy outcomes. *British Journal of Developmental Psychology, 27,* 145–161.

Pohl, R. F., & Hell, W. (1996). No reduction in hindsight bias after complete information and repeated testing. *Organizational Behavior and Human Decision Processes, 67,* 49–58.

Poldrack, R. A., & Gabrieli, J. D. E. (2001). Characterizing the neural mechanisms of skill learning and repetition priming: Evidence from mirror reading. *Brain, 124,* 67–82.

Polivy, J. (1981). On the induction of emotion in the laboratory: Discrete moods or multiple affect states? *Journal of Personality and Social Psychology, 41,* 803–817.

Polka, L., Rvachew, S., & Molnar, M. (2008). Speech perception by 6- to 8-month-olds in the presence of distracting sounds. *Infancy, 13,* 421–439.

Pollatsek, A., Reichle, E. D., & Rayner, K. (2006). Tests of the E-Z Reader model: Exploring the interface between cognition and eye-movement control. *Cognitive Psychology, 52,* 1–56.

Poole, B. J., & Kane, M. J. (2009). Working memory capacity predicts the executive control of visual search among distractors: The influences of sustained and selective attention. *Quarterly Journal of Experimental Psychology, 62,* 1430–1454.

Popper, K. R. (1968). *The logic of scientific discovery.* London, UK: Hutchinson.

Porter, S., & ten Brinke, L. (2010). The truth about lies: What works in detecting high-stakes deception? *Legal and Criminological Psychology, 15,* 57–75.

Posner, M. I. (1980). Orienting of attention: The VIIth Sir Frederic Bartlett lecture. *Quarterly Journal of Experimental Psychology, 32A,* 3–25.

Power, M., & Dalgleish, T. (2008). *Cognition and emotion: From order to disorder* (2nd ed.). New York, NY: Psychology Press.

Pozzulo, J. D., Crescini, C., & Panton, T. (2008). Does methodology matter in eyewitness identification research? The effect of live versus video exposure on eyewitness identification of accuracy. *International Journal of Law and Psychiatry, 31,* 430–437.

Prat, C. S., Keller, T. A., & Just, M. A. (2007). Individual differences in sentence comprehension: A functional magnetic resonance imaging investigation of syntactic and lexical processing demands. *Journal of Cognitive Neuroscience, 19,* 1950–1963.

Preston, S. D., Buchanan, T. W., Stansfield, R. B., & Buchanan, A. (2007). Effects of anticipatory stress on decision making in a gambling task. *Behavioral Neuroscience, 121,* 257–263.

Price, J. (2008). *The woman who can't forget: A memoir.* New York, NY: Free Press.

Prince, S. E., Tsukiura, T., & Cabeza, R. (2007). Distinguishing the neural correlates of episodic memory encoding and semantic memory retrieval. *Psychological Science, 18,* 144–151.

Pyers, J. E., Gollan, T. H., & Emmorey, K. (2009). Biomodal bilinguals reveal the source of tip-of-the-tongue states. *Cognition, 112,* 323–329.

Pylyshyn, Z. W. (2002). Mental imagery: In search of a theory. *Behavioral and Brain Sciences, 25,* 157–238.

Pylyshyn, Z. W. (2003). Return of the mental image: Are there really pictures in the brain? *Trends in Cognitive Sciences, 7,* 113–118.

Quinlan, P. T. (2003). Visual feature integration theory: Past, present, and future. *Psychological Bulletin, 129,* 643–673.

Quinlan, P. T., & Wilton, R. N. (1998). Grouping by proximity or similarity? Competition between the Gestalt principles in vision. *Perception, 27,* 417–430.

Quiroga, R. Q., Reddy, L., Kreiman, G., Koch, C., & Fried, I. (2005). Invariant visual representation by single neurons in the human brain. *Nature, 435,* 1102–1107.

Raghunathan, R., & Pham, M. T. (1999). All negative moods are not equal: Motivational influences of anxiety and sadness on decision making. *Organizational Behavior and Human Decision Processes, 79,* 56–77.

Raichle, M. E., & Snyder, A. Z. (2007). A default model of brain function: A brief history of an evolving idea. *NeuroImage, 37,* 1083–1090.

Raizada, R. D. S., & Poldrack, R. A. (2007). Selective amplification of stimulus differences during categorical processing of speech. *Neuron, 56,* 726–740.

Ramsey, J. D., Hanson, S. J., Hanson, C., Halchenko, Y. O., Pokdrack, R. A., & Glymour, C. (2010). Six problems for causal inference from fMRI. *NeuroImage, 49,* 1545–1558.

Rapp, D. N., & Kendeou, P. (2009). Noticing and revising discrepancies as texts unfold. *Discourse Processes, 46,* 1–24.

Rascovsky, K., Growdon, M. E., Pardo, I. R., Grossman, S., & Miller, B. L. (2009). The quicksand of forgetfulness: Semantic dementia in *One Hundred Years of Solitude. Brain, 132,* 2609–2616.

Rasmussen, A. S., & Berntsen, D. (2009). The possible functions of involuntary autobiographical memories. *Applied Cognitive Psychology, 23,* 1137–1152.

Rastle, K., & Brysbaert, M. (2006). Masked phonological priming effects in English: Are they real? Do they matter? *Cognitive Psychology*, *53*, 97–145.

Rayner, K., Li, X. S., & Pollatsek, A. (2007). Extending the E-Z model of eye-movement control to Chinese readers. *Cognitive Science*, *31*, 1021–1033.

Raz, A., Packard, M. G., Alexander, G. M., Buhle, J. T., Zhu, G. M., Yu, S., & Peterson, B. S. (2009). A slice of pi: An exploratory neuroimaging study of digit encoding and retrieval in a superior memorist. *Neurocase*, *15*, 361–372.

Reali, F., & Christiansen, M. H. (2005). Uncovering the richness of the stimulus: Structure dependence and indirect statistical evidence. *Cognitive Science*, *29*, 1007–1028.

Reber, A. S. (1993). *Implicit learning and tacit knowledge: An essay on the cognitive unconscious.* Oxford, UK: Oxford University Press.

Recanzone, G. H., & Sutter, M. L. (2008). The biological basis of audition. *Annual Review of Psychology*, *59*, 119–142.

Reddy, L., Tsuchiya, N., & Serre, T. (2010). Reading the mind's eye: Decoding category information during mental imagery. *NeuroImage*, *50*, 818–825.

Redelmeier, C., Koehler, D. J., Liberman, V., & Tversky, A. (1995). Probability judgment in medicine: Discounting unspecified alternatives. *Medical Decision Making*, *15*, 227–230.

Redelmeier, D. A., & Tibshirani, R. J. (1997). Association between cellular-telephone calls and motor vehicle collisions. *New England Journal of Medicine*, *336*, 453–458.

Reder, L. M., Park, H., & Kieffaber, P. D. (2009). Memory systems do not divide on consciousness: Reinterpreting memory in terms of activation and binding. *Psychological Bulletin*, *135*, 23–49.

Rees, G. (2007). Neural correlates of the contents of visual awareness in humans. *Philosophical Transactions of the Royal Society B: Biological Sciences*, *362*, 877–886.

Reese, C. M., & Cherry, K. E. (2002). The effects of age, ability, and memory monitoring on prospective memory task performance. *Aging, Neuropsychology, and Cognition*, *9*, 98–113.

Rehder, B., & Kim, S. (2009). Classification as diagnostic reasoning. *Memory & Cognition*, *37*, 715–729.

Reicher, G. M. (1969). Perceptual recognition as a function of meaningfulness of stimulus material. *Journal of Experimental Psychology*, *81*, 274–280.

Reichle, E. D., Rayner, K., & Pollatsek, A. (2003). The E-Z Reader model of eye- movement control in reading: Comparisons to other models. *Behavioral and Brain Sciences*, *26*, 445–526.

Rensink, R. A. (2002). Change detection. *Annual Review of Psychology*, *53*, 245–277.

Rensink, R. A., O'Regan, J. K., & Clark, J. J. (1997). To see or not to see: The need for attention to perceive changes in scenes. *Psychological Science*, *8*, 368–373.

Repovš, G., & Baddeley, A. (2006). The multi-component model of working memory: Explorations in experimental cognitive psychology. *Neuroscience*, *139*, 5–21.

Reverberi, C., Toraldo, A., D'Agostini, S., & Skrap, M. (2005). Better without (lateral) frontal cortex? Insight problems solved by frontal patients. *Brain*, *128*, 2882–2890.

Reynolds, D. J., Garnham, A., & Oakhill, J. (2006). Evidence of immediate activation of gender information from a social role name. *Quarterly Journal of Experimental Psychology*, *59*, 886–903.

Ricco, R. B. (2003). The macrostructure of informal arguments: A proposed model and analysis. *Quarterly Journal of Experimental Psychology: Human Experimental Psychology*, *56A*, 1021–1051.

Ricco, R. B. (2007). Individual differences in the analysis of informal reasoning fallacies. *Contemporary Educational Psychology*, *32*, 459–383.

Richter, T., & Späth, P. (2006). Recognition is used as one cue among others in judgment and decision making. *Journal of Experimental Psychology: Learning, Memory, & Cognition*, *32*, 150–162.

Riddoch, G. (1917). Dissociations of visual perception due to occipital injuries, with especial reference to appreciation of movement. *Brain*, *40*, 15–57.

Riddoch, M. J., & Humphreys, G. W. (2001). Object recognition. In B. Rapp (Ed.), *The handbook of cognitive neuropsychology: What deficits reveal about the human mind.* Hove, UK: Psychology Press.

Riddoch, M. J., Humphreys, G. W., Akhtar, N., Allen, H., Bracewell, R. M., & Scholfield, A. J. (2008). A tale of two agnosias: Distinctions between form and integrative agnosia. *Cognitive Neuropsychology*, *25*, 56–92.

Rinck, M., & Weber, U. (2003). Who, when and where: An experimental test of the event-indexing model. *Memory & Cognition*, *31*, 1284–1292.

Rinne, J. O., Tommola, J., Laine, M., Krause, B. J., Schmidt, D., Kaasinen, V., et al. (2000). The translating brain: Cerebral activation patterns during simultaneous interpreting. *Neuroscience Letters*, *294*, 85–88.

Rips, L. J., & Collins, A. (1993). Categories and resemblance. *Journal of Experimental Psychology: General, 122,* 468–486.

Rips, L. J., Shoben, E. J., & Smith, E. E. (1973). Semantic distance and the verification of semantic relations. *Journal of Verbal Learning and Verbal Behavior, 12,* 1–20.

Ritov, J., & Baron, J. (1990). Reluctance to vaccinate: Omission bias and ambiguity. *Journal of Behavioral Decision Making, 3,* 263–277.

Rizzi, C., Piras, F., & Marangolo, P. (2010). Top-down projections to the primary visual areas necessary for object recognition: A case study. *Vision Research, 50,* 1074–1085.

Robbins, T., Anderson, E, Barker, D., Bradley, A., Fearneyhough, C., Henson, R., et al. (1996). Working memory in chess. *Memory and Cognition, 24,* 83–93.

Robertson, S. I. (2001). *Problem solving.* Hove, UK: Psychology Press.

Robinson, B. L., & McAlpine, D. (2009). Gain control mechanisms in the auditory pathway. *Current Opinion in Neurobiology, 19,* 402–407.

Rodebaugh, T. L., Heimberg, R. G., Schultz, L. T., & Blackmore, M. (2010). The moderated effects of video feedback for social anxiety disorders. *Journal of Anxiety Disorders, 24,* 663–671.

Roediger, H. L. (2008). Relativity of remembering: Why the laws of memory vanished. *Annual Review of Psychology, 59,* 225–254.

Roediger, H. L., & Karpicke, J. D. (2006). Test-enhanced learning: Taking memory tests improves long-term retention. *Psychological Science, 17,* 249–255.

Rogers, T. B., Kuiper, N. A., & Kirker, W. S. (1977). Self-reference and the encoding of personal information. *Journal of Personality and Social Psychology, 35,* 677–688.

Rogers, T. T., & McClelland, J. L. (2005). A parallel distributed processing approach to semantic cognition: Applications to conceptual development. *Carnegie Mellon Symposia on Cognition,* 335–387.

Rogers, T. T., & Patterson, K. (2007). Object categorization: Reversals and explanations of the basic-level advantage. *Journal of Experimental Psychology: General, 136,* 451–469.

Rosch, E., & Mervis, C. B. (1975). Family resemblances: Studies in the internal structure of categories. *Cognitive Psychology, 7,* 573–605.

Rosch, E., Mervis, C. B., Gray, W. D., Johnson, D. M., & Boyes-Braem, P. (1976). Basic objects in natural categories. *Cognitive Psychology, 8,* 382–439.

Rosen, L. D., Chang, J., Erwin, L., Carrier, L. M., & Cheever, N. A. (2010). The relationship between "textisms" and formal and informal writing among young adults. *Communication Research, 37,* 420–440.

Rosenbaum, R. S., Köhler, S., Schacter, D. L., Moscovitch, M., Westmacott, R., Black, S. E., et al. (2005). The case of KC: Contributions of a memory-impaired person to memory theory. *Neuropsychologia, 43,* 989–1021.

Rosenblum, L. D. (2008). Speech perception as a multimodal phenomenon. *Current Directions in Psychological Science, 17,* 405–409.

Rosielle, L. J., & Scaggs, W. J. (2008). What if they knocked down the library and nobody noticed? The failure to detect large changes to familiar scenes. *Memory, 16,* 115–124.

Ross, D. F., Ceci, S. J., Dunning, D., & Toglia, M. P. (1994). Unconscious transference and mistaken identity: When a witness misidentifies a familiar but innocent person. *Journal of Applied Psychology, 79,* 918–930.

Rossetti, Y., Rode, G., Pisella, L., Boisson, D., & Perenin, M. T. (1998). Prism adaptation to a rightward optical deviation rehabilitates left hemispatial neglect. *Nature, 395,* 166–169.

Rothermund, K., Voss, A., & Wentura, D. (2008). Counter-regulation in affective attentional biases: A basic mechanism that warrants flexibility in emotion and motivation. *Emotion, 8,* 34–46.

Roussey, J. Y., & Piolat, A. (2008). Critical reading effort during text revision. *European Journal of Cognitive Psychology, 20,* 765–792.

Royden, C. S., Wolfe, J. M., & Klempen, N. (2001). Visual search asymmetries in motion and optic flow fields. *Perception & Psychophysics, 63,* 436–444.

Rubin, D. C., Berntsen, D., & Hutson, M. (2009). The normative and the personal life: Individual differences in life scripts and life story events among US and Danish undergraduates. *Memory, 17,* 54–68.

Rubin, D. C., Rahhal, T. A., & Poon, L. W. (1998). Things learned in early childhood are remembered best. *Memory & Cognition, 26,* 3–19.

Rubinstein, J. S., Meyer, D. E., & Evans, J. E. (2001). Executive control of cognitive processes in task switching. *Journal of Experimental Psychology: Human Perception and Performance, 27,* 763–797.

Ruchkin, D. S., Berndt, R. S., Johnson, R., Grafman, J., Ritter, W., & Canoune, H. L. (1999). Lexical contributions to retention of verbal information in working memory. *Journal of Memory and Language, 41,* 345–364.

Rumelhart, D. E., McClelland, J. L., & the PDP Research Group (1986). *Parallel distributed processing, Vol. 1: Foundations.* Cambridge, MA: MIT Press.

Rumelhart, D. E., & Ortony, A. (1977). The representation of knowledge in memory. In R. C. Anderson, R. J. Spiro, & W. E. Montague (Eds.), *Schooling and the acquisition of knowledge*. Hillsdale, NJ: Lawrence Erlbuam Associates.

Russell, B., Perkins, J., & Grinnell, H. (2008). Interviewees' overuse of the word "like" and hesitations: Effects in simulated hiring decisions. *Psychological Reports, 102*, 111–118.

Russell, M. (1999). Testing writing computers: A follow-up study comparing performance on computer and on paper. *Educational Policy Analysis Archives, 7* (20).

Russell, R., Duchaine, B., & Nakayama, K. (2009). Super-recognizers: People with extraordinary face recognition ability. *Psychonomic Bulletin & Review, 16*, 252–257.

Rusting, C. L., & DeHart, T. (2000). Retrieving positive memories to regulate negative mood: Consequences for mood-congruent memory. *Journal of Personality and Social Psychology, 78*, 737–752.

Ryan, J. D., Althoff, R. R., Whitlow, S., & Cohen, N. J. (2000). Amnesia is a deficit in relational memory. *Psychological Science, 11*, 454–461.

Sanchez, C. A., & Wiley, J. (2006). An examination of the seductive details effect in terms of working memory capacity. *Memory & Cognition, 34*, 344–355.

Sacks, H., Schegloff, E. A., & Jefferson, G. (1974). A simplest systematics for the organization of turn-taking in conversation. *Language, 50*, 696–735.

Santhouse, A. M., Howard, R. J., & ffytche, D. H. (2000). Visual hallucinatory syndromes and the anatomy of the visual brain. *Brain, 123*, 2055–2064.

Sato, H., & Matsushima, K. (2006). Effects of audience awareness on procedural text writing. *Psychological Reports, 99*, 51–73.

Schacter, D. L. (1999). The seven sins of memory – Insights from psychology and cognitive neuroscience. *American Psychologist, 54*, 182–203.

Schacter, D. L., & Addis, D. R. (2007). The cognitive neuroscience of constructive memory: Remembering the past and imagining the future. *Philosophical Transactions of the Royal Society B: Biological Sciences, 362*, 773–786.

Schacter, D. L., Wig, G. S., & Stevens, W. D. (2007). Reductions in cortical activity during priming. *Current Opinion in Neurobiology, 17*, 171–176.

Schenk, T., & McIntosh, R. D. (2010). Do we have independent visual streams for perception and action? *Cognitive Neuroscience, 1*, 52–62.

Scherer, K. R., Schorr, A., & Johnstone, T. (Eds.). (2001). *Appraisal processes in emotion: Theory, methods, research*. Oxford, UK: Oxford University Press.

Schneider, W., & Shiffrin, R. M. (1977). Controlled and automatic human information processing: I. Detection, search, and attention. *Psychological Review, 84*, 1–66.

Schriver, K. (1984). *Revised computer documentation for comprehension: Ten lessons in protocol-aided revision* (Technical Report No. 14). Pittsburgh, PA: Carnegie Mellon University.

Schumacher, E. H., Seymour, T. L., Glass, J. M., Fencsik, D. E., Lauber, E. J., Kieras, D. E., et al. (2001). Virtually perfect time sharing in dual-task performance: Uncorking the central cognitive bottleneck. *Psychological Science, 12*, 101–108.

Schunn, C. D., & Klahr, D. (1996). The problem of problem spaces: When and how to go beyond a 2-space model of scientific discovery. *Proceedings of the Eighteenth Annual Conference of the Cognitive Science Society*, San Diego, CA, pp. 25–26.

Schwartz, B. (2004). *The paradox of choice: Why more is less*. New York, NY: HarperCollins.

Schwartz, B. (2009). Incentives, choice, education and well-being. *Oxford Review of Education, 35*, 391–403.

Schwartz, B. L., & Hashtroudi, S. (1991). Priming is independent of skill learning. *Journal of Experimental Psychology: Learning, Memory, & Cognition, 17*, 1177–1187.

Schwartz, J. A., Chapman, G. B., Brewer, N. T., & Bergus, G. B. (2004). The effects of accountability on bias in physician decision making: Going from bad to worse. *Psychonomic Bulletin & Review, 11*, 173–178.

Schwarzkopf, D. S., Zhang, J. X., & Kourtzi, Z. (2009). Flexible learning of natural statistics in the human brain. *Journal of Neurophysiology, 102*, 1854–1867.

Scott, S. K., Young, A. W., Calder, A. J., Hellawell, D. J., Aggleton, J. P., & Johnson, M. (1997). Impaired auditory recognition of fear and anger following bilateral amygdala lesions. *Nature, 385*, 254–257.

Scullin, M. K., McDaniel, M. A., Shelton, J. T., & Lee, J. H. (2010). Focal/nonfocal cue effects in prospective memory: Monitoring difficulty or different retrieval processes? *Journal of Experimental Psychology: Learning, Memory, and Cognition, 36*, 736–749.

Seghier, M. L., Lee, H. L., Schofield, T., Ellis, C. L., & Price, C. J. (2008). Inter-subject variability in the use of two different neuronal networks for reading aloud familiar words. *NeuroImage, 42*, 1226–1236.

Sejnowski, T. J., & Rosenberg, C. R. (1987). Parallel networks that learn to pronounce English text. *Complex Systems, 1*, 145–168.

Sekuler, R., & Blake, R. (2002). *Perception* (4th ed.). New York, NY: McGraw-Hill.

Sellen, A. J., Lowie, G., Harris, J. F., & Wilkins, A. J. (1997). What brings intentions to mind? An *in situ* study of prospective memory. *Memory, 5*, 483–507.

Senghas, A., Kita, S., & Özyürek, A. (2004). Children creating core properties of language: Evidence from an emerging sign language in Nicaragua. *Science, 305*, 1779–1782.

Seo, M.-G., & Barrett, L. F. (2007). Being emotional during decision making: Good or bad? An empirical investigation. *Academy of Management Journal, 50*, 923–940.

Seymour, P. H. K., Aro, M., Erskine, J. M., Wimmer, H., Leybaert, J., Elbro, C., et al. (2003). Foundation literacy acquisition in European orthographies. *British Journal of Psychology, 94*, 143–174.

Shah, A. K., & Oppenheimer, D. M. (2008). Heuristics made easy: An effort-reduction framework. *Psychological Bulletin, 134*, 207–222.

Shallice, T., & Warrington, E. K. (1970). Independent functioning of verbal memory stores: A neuropsychological study. *Quarterly Journal of Experimental Psychology, 22*, 261–273.

Shallice, T., & Warrington, E. K. (1974). The dissociation between long-term retention of meaningful sounds and verbal material. *Neuropsychologia, 12*, 553–555.

Shanks, D. R. (2005). Implicit learning. In K. Lamberts & R. Goldstone (Eds.), *Handbook of cognition* (pp. 202–220). London, UK: Sage.

Shanks, D. R., & St. John, M. F. (1994). Characteristics of dissociable human learning systems. *Behavioral & Brain Sciences, 17*, 367–394.

Share, D. L. (2008). On the Anglocentricities of current reading research and practice: The perils of over-reliance on an "outlier" orthography. *Psychological Bulletin, 134*, 584–615.

Sharpe, D. (1997). Of apples and oranges, file drawers and garbage: Why validity issues in meta-analysis will not go away. *Clinical Psychology Review, 17*, 881–901.

Shepard, R. N., & Metzler, J. (1971). Mental rotation of three-dimensional objects. *Science, 171*, 701–703.

Sheth, B. R., Sandkühler, S., & Bhattacharya, J. (2009). Posterior beta and anterior gamma oscillations predict cognitive insight. *Journal of Cognitive Neuroscience, 21*, 1269–1279.

Shiffrin, R. M., & Schneider, W. (1977). Controlled and automatic human information processing: II. Perceptual learning, automatic attending, and a general theory. *Psychological Review, 84*, 127–190.

Shiv, B., Loewenstein, G., Bechera, A., Damasio, H., & Damasio, A. R. (2005). Investment behavior and the negative side of emotion. *Psychological Science, 16*, 435–439.

Shrager, Y., Levy, D. A., Hopkins, R. O., & Squire, L. R. (2008). Working memory and the organization of brain systems. *Journal of Neuroscience, 28*, 4818–4822.

Shriver, E. R., Young, S. G., Hugenberg, K., Bernstein, M. J., & Lanter, J. R. (2008). Class, race, and the face: Social context modulates the cross-race effect in face recognition. *Personality and Social Psychology Bulletin, 34*, 260–274.

Shuell, T. J. (1969). Clustering and organization in free recall. *Psychological Bulletin, 72*, 353–374.

Sides, A., Osherson, D., Bonini, N., & Viale, R. (2002). On the reality of the conjunction fallacy. *Memory & Cognition, 30*, 191–198.

Siebert, M., Markowitsch, H. J., & Bartel, P. (2003). Amygdala, affect and cognition: Evidence from 10 patients with Urbach-Wiethe disease. *Brain, 126*, 2627–2637.

Siemer, M., & Reisenzein, R. (2007). The process of emotion inference. *Emotion, 7*, 1–20.

Silvanto, J. (2008). A re-evaluation of blindsight and the role of striate cortex (V1) in visual awareness. *Neuropsychologia, 46*, 2869–2871.

Silverman, I., Choi, J., & Peters, M. (2007). The hunter-gatherer theory of sex differences in spatial abilities: Data from 40 countries. *Archives of Sexual Behavior, 36*, 261–268.

Simmons, C. L., & Hampton, J. A. (2006). *Essentialist beliefs about basic and superordinate level categories.* Poster presented at the 47th Annual Meeting of the Psychonomic Society, Houston, TX, November.

Simner, J., Mayo, N., & Spiller, M. J. (2009). A foundation for savantism? Visuo-spatial synesthetes present with cognitive benefits. *Cortex, 45*, 1246–1260.

Simon, D., Krawczyk, D. C., & Holyoak, K. J. (2004). Construction of preferences by constraint satisfaction. *Psychological Science, 15*, 331–336.

Simon, H. A. (1957). *Models of man: Social and rational.* New York, NY: Wiley.

Simon, H. A. (1966). Scientific discovery and the psychology of problem solving. In H. A. Simon (Ed.), *Mind and cosmos: Essays in contemporary science and philosophy.* Pittsburgh, PA: University of Pittsburgh Press.

Simon, H. A. (1974). How big is a chunk? *Science, 183*, 482–488.

Simon, H. A. (1978). Rationality as a process and product of thought. *American Economic Association, 68*, 1–16.

Simons, D. J., & Chabris, F. (1999). Gorillas in our midst: Sustained inattentional blindness for dynamic events. *Perception, 28*, 1059–1074.

Simons, D. J., & Levin, D. T. (1998). Failure to detect changes to people during a real-world interaction. *Psychonomic Bulletin & Review, 5,* 644–649.

Simons, D. J., & Rensink, R. A. (2005). Change blindness: Past, present, and future. *Trends in Cognitive Sciences, 9,* 16–20.

Simonson, I., & Staw, B. M. (1992). De-escalation strategies: A comparison of techniques for reducing commitment to losing courses of action. *Journal of Applied Psychology, 77,* 419–426.

Simonton, D. K. (2008). Scientific talent, training, and performance: Intellect, personality, and genetic endowment. *Review of General Psychology, 12,* 28–46.

Sio, U. N., & Ormerod, T. C. (2009). Does incubation enhance problem solving? A meta-analysis review. *Psychological Bulletin, 135,* 94–120.

Skinner, E. I., & Fernandes, M. A. (2007). Neural correlates of recollection and familiarity: A review of neuroimaging and patient data. *Neuropsychologia, 45,* 2163–2179.

Slatcher, R. B., & Pennebaker, J. W. (2006). How do I love thee? Let me count the words: The social effects of expressive writing. *Psychological Science, 17,* 660–664.

Slepian, M. L., Weisbuch, M., Rutchick, A. M., Newman, L. S., & Ambady, N. (2010). Shedding light on insight: Priming bright ideas. *Journal of Experimental Social Psychology, 46,* 696–700.

Slezak, P. (1991). Can images be rotated and inspected? A test of the pictorial medium theory. *Program of the Thirteenth Annual Conference of the Cognitive Science Society,* Chicago, IL, pp. 55–60.

Slezak, P. (1995). The 'philosophical' case against visual imagery. In T. Caelli, P. Slezak, & R. Clark (Eds.), *Perspectives in cognitive science: Theories, experiments and foundations* (pp. 237–271). New York, NY: Ablex.

Sloboda, J. A., Davidson, J. W., Howe, M. J. A., & Moore, D. G. (1996). The role of practice in the development of performing musicians. *British Journal of Psychology, 87,* 287–309.

Small, D. A., & Lerner, J. S. (2008). Emotional policy: Personal sadness and anger shape judgments about a welfare case. *Political Psychology, 29,* 149–168.

Smania, N., Martini, M. C., Gambina, G., Tomelleri, G., Palamara, A., Natale, E., et al. (1998). The spatial distribution of visual attention in hemineglect and extinction patients. *Brain, 121,* 1759–1770.

Smith, C. A., & Kirby, L. D. (2001). Toward delivering on the promise of appraisal theory. In K. R. Scherer, A. Schorr, & T. Johnstone (Eds.), *Appraisal processes in emotion: Theory, methods, research.* Oxford, UK: Oxford University Press.

Smith, C. A., & Lazarus, R. S. (1993). Appraisal components, core relational themes, and the emotions. *Cognition & Emotion, 7,* 233–269.

Smith, E. E., & Jonides, J. (1997). Working memory: A view from neuroimaging. *Cognitive Psychology, 33,* 5–42.

Smith, J. D., & Minda, J. P. (2000). Thirty categorization results in search of a model. *Journal of Experimental Psychology: Learning, Memory, & Cognition, 26,* 3–27.

Smith, M. (2000). Conceptual structures in language production. In L. Wheeldon (Ed.), *Aspects of language production.* Hove, UK: Psychology Press.

Smith, R. E. (2003). The cost of remembering to remember in event-based prospective memory: Investigating the capacity demands of delayed intention performance. *Journal of Experimental Psychology: Learning, Memory, and Cognition, 29,* 347–361.

Smith, R. E., & Bayen, U. J. (2005). The effects of working memory resource availability on prospective memory: A formal modeling approach. *Experimental Psychology, 52,* 243–256.

Smith, R. E., & Hunt, R. R. (2000). The effects of distinctiveness require reinstatement of organization: The importance of intentional memory instructions. *Journal of Memory and Language, 43,* 431–446.

Smith, R. E., Hunt, R. R., McVay, J. C., & McConnell, M. D. (2007). The cost of event-based prospective memory: Salient target events. *Journal of Experimental Psychology: Learning, Memory, and Cognition, 33,* 734–746.

Snedeker, J., & Trueswell, J. (2003). Using prosody to avoid ambiguity: Effects of speaker awareness and referential context. *Journal of Memory and Language, 48,* 103–130.

Soon, C. S., Brass, M., Heinze, H. J., & Haynes, J. D. (2008). Unconscious determinants of free decisions in the human brain. *Nature Neuroscience, 10,* 257–261.

Sorqvist, P. (2010). High working memory capacity attenuates the deviation effect but not the duplex-mechanism account of auditory distraction. *Memory & Cognition, 38,* 651–658.

Spelke, E. S., Hirst, W. C., & Neisser, U. (1976). Skills of divided attention. *Cognition, 4,* 215–230.

Spence, I., Yu, J. J., Feng, J., & Marshman, J. (2009). Women match men when learning a spatial skill. *Journal of Experimental Psychology: Learning, Memory and Cognition, 35,* 1097–1103.

Sperber, D., & Girotto, V. (2002). Use or misuse of the selection task? Rejoinder to Fiddick, Cosmides, and Tooby. *Cognition, 85,* 277–290.

Spiers, H. J., Maguire, E. A., & Burgess, N. (2001). Hippocampal amnesia. *Neurocase, 7,* 357–382.

Spinney, L. (2010). The fine print. *Nature, 464,* 344–346.

Spivey, M. J., Tanenhaus, M. K., Eberhard, K. M., & Sedivy, J. C. (2002). Eye movements and spoken language comprehension: Effects of visual context on syntactic ambiguity resolution. *Cognitive Psychology, 45,* 447–481.

Stanovich, K. E. (2009). The thinking that IQ tests miss. *Scientific American,* November/December, 34–39.

Stanovich, K. E., & West, R. F. (2007). Natural myside bias is independent of cognitive ability. *Thinking & Reasoning, 13,* 225–247.

Stanovich, K. E., West, R. F., & Toplak, M. E. (2011). Individual differences as essential components of heuristics and biases research. In K. Manktelow, D. Over, & S. Elqayam (Eds.), *The science of reason: A Festschrift for Jonathan St. B. T. Evans.* Hove, UK: Psychology Press.

Starcke, K. W., lf, O. T., Markowitsch, H. J., & Brand, M. (2008). Anticipatory stress influences decision making under explicit risk conditions. *Behavioral Neuroscience, 122,* 1352–1360.

Steller, M., & Köhnken, G. (1989). Critera-based content analysis. In D. C. Raskin (Ed.), *Psychological methods in criminal investigation and evidence* (pp. 217–245). New York, NY: Springer-Verlag.

Sternberg, R. J., & Ben-Zeev, T. (2001). *Complex cognition: The psychology of human thought.* Oxford, UK: Oxford University Press.

Stirman, S. W., & Pennebaker, J. W. (2001). Word use in the poetry of suicidal and nonsuicidal poets. *Psychosomatic Medicine, 63,* 517–522.

Storms, G., De Boeck, P., & Ruts, W. (2000). Prototype and exemplar-based information in natural language categories. *Journal of Memory and Language, 42,* 51–73.

Stottinger, E., Soder, K., Pfusterschmied, J., Wagner, H., & Perner, J. (2010). Division of labor within the visual system: Fact or fiction?. Which kind of evidence is appropriate to clarify this debate? *Experimental Brain Research, 202,* 79–88.

Strayer, D. L., & Drews, F. A. (2007). Cell-phone induced driver distraction. *Current Directions in Psychological Science, 16,* 128–131.

Stroop, J. R. (1935). Studies of interference in serial verbal reactions. *Journal of Experimental Psychology: General, 106,* 404–426.

Stuss, D. T., & Alexander, M. P. (2007). Is there a dysexecutive syndrome? *Philosophical Transactions of the Royal Society B: Biological Sciences, 362,* 901–1015.

Subramaniam, K., Kounios, J., Parrish, T. B., & Jung-Beeman, M. (2009). A brain mechanism for facilitation of insight by positive affect. *Journal of Cognitive Neuroscience, 21,* 415–432.

Sulin, R. A., & Dooling, D. J. (1974). Intrusion of a thematic idea in retention of prose. *Journal of Experimental Psychology, 103,* 255–262.

Sun, R., Zhang, X., & Mathews, R. (2009). Capturing human data in a letter-counting task: Accessibility and action-centeredness in representing cognitive skills. *Neural Networks, 22,* 15–29.

Svenson, O., Salo, I., & Lindholm, T. (2009). Post-decision consolidation and distortion of facts. *Judgment and Decision Making, 4,* 397–407.

Sweller, J., & Levine, M. (1982). Effects of goal specificity on means–ends analysis and learning. *Journal of Experimental Psychology: Learning, Memory, and Cognition, 8,* 463–474.

Swets, B., Desmet, T., Clifton, C., & Ferreira, F. (2008). Underspecification of syntactic ambiguities: Evidence from self-paced reading. *Memory & Cognition, 36,* 201–216.

Symons, C. S., & Johnson, B. T. (1997). The self-reference effect in memory: A meta-analysis. *Psychological Bulletin, 121,* 371–394.

Szpunar, K. K. (2010). Episodic future thought: An emerging concept. *Perspectives on Psychological Science, 5,* 142–162.

Takahashi, M., Shimizu, H., Saito, S., & Tomayori, H. (2006). One percent ability and ninety-nine percent perspiration: A study of a Japanese memorist. *Journal of Experimental Psychology: Learning, Memory, & Cognition, 32,* 1195–1200.

Talarico, J. M., & Rubin, D. C. (2003). Confidence, not consistency, characterizes flashbulb memories. *Psychological Science, 14,* 455–461.

Talarico, J. M., & Rubin, D. C. (2009). Flashbulb memories result from ordinary memory processes and extraordinary event characteristics. In O. Luminet & A. Curci (Eds.), *Flashbulb memories: New issues and new perspectives* (pp. 79–97). New York, NY: Psychology Press.

Talmi, D., Hurlemann, R., Patin, A., & Dolan, R. J. (2010). Framing effect following bilateral amygdala lesion. *Neuropsychologia, 48,* 1823–1827.

Tamietto, M., & de Gelder, B. (2008). Affective blindsight in the intact brain: Neural interhemispheric summation for unseen fearful expressions. *Neuropsychologia, 46,* 820–828.

Tanaka, J. W., & Taylor, M. E. (1991). Object categories and expertise: Is the basic level in the eye of the beholder? *Cognitive Psychology, 15,* 121–149.

Tanenhaus, M. K., Spivey-Knowlton, M. J., Eberhard, K. M., & Sedivy, J. C. (1995). Integration of visual and linguistic information in spoken language comprehension. *Science, 268,* 1632–1634.

Tarr, M. J., & Bülthoff, H. H. (1995). Is human object recognition better described by geon structural descriptions or by multiple views? Comment on Biederman and Gerhardstein (1993). *Journal of Experimental Psychology: Human Perception & Performance, 21,* 1494–1505.

Tarr, M. J., Williams, P., Hayward, W. G., & Gauthier, I. (1998). Three-dimensional object recognition is viewpoint-dependent. *Nature Neuroscience, 1,* 195–206.

Taubert, J., & Alais, D. (2009). The composite illusion requires composite face stimuli to be biologically plausible. *Vision Research, 49,* 1877–1885.

Teigen, K. H., & Keren, G. (2007). Waiting for the bus: When base-rates refuse to be neglected. *Cognition, 103,* 337–357.

Terlecki, M. S., & Newcombe, N. S. (2005). How important is the digital divide? The relation of computer and videogame usage to gender differences in mental rotation ability. *Sex Roles, 53,* 433–441.

Tetlock, P.E. (2002). Social functionalist frameworks for judgment and choice: Intuitive politicians, theologians, and prosecutors. *Psychological Review, 109,* 451– 471.

Thagard, P. (1998). Explaining disease: Correlations, causes, and mechanisms. *Minds and Machines, 8,* 61–78.

Thagard, P. (2005). How to be a successful scientist. *Scientific and Technological Thinking,* 159–171.

Thomas, L. E., & Lleras, A. (2009). Covert shifts of attention function as an implicit aid to insight. *Cognition, 111,* 168–174.

Thompson, C. P., Cowan, T., Frieman, J., Mahadevan, R. S., Vogl, R. J., & Frieman, R. J. (1991). Rajan – A study of a memorist. *Journal of Memory and Language, 30,* 702–724.

Thompson, V. A., Evans, J. St. B. T., & Handley, S. J. (2005). Persuading and dissuading by conditional argument. *Journal of Memory & Language, 53,* 238–257.

Thompson, W. L., Slotnick, S. D., Burrage, M. S., & Kosslyn, S. M. (2009). Two forms of spatial imagery: Neuroimaging evidence. *Psychological Science, 20,* 1245–1253.

Thornton, T. L., & Gilden, D. L. (2007). Parallel and serial processes in visual search. *Psychological Review, 114,* 71–103.

Todd, N. P. M., Lee, C. S., & O'Boyle, D. J. (2006). A sensorimotor theory of speech perception: Implications for learning, organization, and recognition. In S. Greenberg & W. A. Ainsworth (Eds.), *Listening to speech: An auditory perspective*

(pp. 351–373). Mahwah, NJ: Lawrence Erlbaum Associates.

Todd, P. M., & Gigerenzer, G. (2007). Environments that make us smart. *Current Directions in Psychological Science, 16,* 167–171.

Tollestrup, P. A., Turtle, J. W., & Yuille, J. C. (1994). Actual victims and witnesses to robbery and fraud: An archival analysis. In D. F. Ross, J. D. Read, & M. P. Toglia (Eds.), *Adult eyewitness testimony: Current trends and developments.* New York, NY: Wiley.

Tolman, E. C. (1948). Cognitive maps in rats and men. *Psychological Review, 55,* 189–208.

Tomasino, B., Borroni, P., Isaja, A., & Rumiati, R. I. (2005). The role of the primary motor cortex in mental rotation: A TMS study. *Cognitive Neuropsychology, 22,* 348–363.

Tomasino, B., Weiss, P. H., & Fink, G. R. (2010). To move or not to move: Imperatives modulate action-related verb processing in the motor system. *Neuroscience, 169,* 246–258.

Toms, M., Morris, N., & Foley, P. (1994). Characteristics of visual interference with visuo-spatial working memory. *British Journal of Psychology, 85,* 131–144.

Tong, E. M. W. (2010a). The sufficiency and necessity of appraisals for negative emotions. *Cognition & Emotion, 24,* 692–701.

Tong, E. M. W. (2010b). Personality influences in appraisal–emotion relationships: The role of neuroticism. *Journal of Personality, 78,* 393–417.

Treisman, A. M. (1960). Contextual cues in selective attention. *Quarterly Journal of Experimental Psychology, 12,* 242–248.

Treisman, A. M. (1964). Verbal cues, language, and meaning in selective attention. *American Journal of Psychology, 77,* 206–219.

Treisman, A., & Gelade, G. (1980). A feature integration theory of attention. *Cognitive Psychology, 12,* 97–136.

Treisman, A. M., & Riley, J. G. A. (1969). Is selective attention selective perception or selective response? A further test. *Journal of Experimental Psychology, 79,* 27–34.

Trickett, S. B., & Trafton, J. G. (2007). "What if …": The use of conceptual simulations in scientific reasoning. *Cognitive Science, 31,* 843–875.

Trout, J. D. (2001). The biological basis of speech: What to infer from talking to the animals. *Psychological Review, 108,* 523–549.

Tuckey, M. R., & Brewer, N. (2003a). How schemas affect eyewitness memory over repeated retrieval attempts. *Applied Cognitive Psychology, 7,* 785–800.

Tuckey, M. R., & Brewer, N. (2003b). The influence of schemas, stimulus ambiguity, and interview schedule on eyewitness memory over time. *Journal of Experimental Psychology: Applied*, 9, 101–118.

Tuffiash, M., Roring, R. W., & Ericsson, K. A. (2007). Expert performance in Scrabble: Implications for the study of the structure and acquisition of complex skills. *Journal of Experimental Psychology: Applied*, 13, 124–134.

Tulving, E. (1979). Relation between encoding specificity and levels of processing. In L. S. Cermak & F. I. M. Craik (Eds.), *Levels of processing in human memory*. Hillsdale, NJ: Lawrence Erlbaum Associates.

Tulving, E. (1985). How many memory systems are there? *American Psychologist*, 40, 385–398.

Tulving, E. (2002). Episodic memory: From mind to brain. *Annual Review of Psychology*, 53, 1–25.

Tulving, E., & Schacter, D. L. (1990). Priming and human-memory systems. *Science*, 247, 301–306.

Tulving, E., Schacter, D. L., & Stark, H. A. (1982). Priming effects in word-fragment completion are independent of recognition memory. *Journal of Experimental Psychology: Learning, Memory, & Cognition*, 17, 595–617.

Turner, M. L., & Engle, R. W. (1989). Is working memory capacity task dependent? *Journal of Memory and Language*, 28, 127–154.

Tversky, A. (1972). Elimination by aspects: A theory of choice. *Psychological Review*, 79, 281–299.

Tversky, A., & Kahneman, D. (1983). Extensional versus intuitive reasoning: The conjunction fallacy in probability judgment. *Psychological Review*, 91, 293–315.

Tversky, A., & Kahneman, D. (1987). Rational choice and the framing of decisions. In R. Hogarth & M. Reder (Eds.), *Rational choice: The contrast between economics and psychology*. Chicago, IL: University of Chicago Press.

Tversky, A., & Koehler, D. J. (1994). Support theory: A nonextensional representation of subjective probability. *Psychological Review*, 101, 547–567.

Tversky, A., & Shafir, E. (1992). The disjunction effect in choice under uncertainty. *Psychological Science*, 3, 305–309.

Tweney, R. D., & Chitwood, S. C. (1995). Scientific reasoning. In S. Newstead & J. S. T. Evans (Eds.), *Perspectives on thinking and reasoning: Essays in honor of Peter Wason* (pp. 241–260). Hove, UK: Lawrence Erlbaum Associates.

Uddin, L. Q., Rayman, J., & Zaidel, E. (2005). Split-brain reveals separate but equal self-recognition in the two cerebral hemispheres. *Consciousness and Cognition*, 14, 633–640.

Underwood, B. J., & Postman, L. (1960). Extra-experimental sources of interference in forgetting. *Psychological Review*, 64, 49–60.

Underwood, G. (1974). Moray vs. the rest: The effect of extended shadowing practice. *Quarterly Journal of Experimental Psychology*, 26, 368–372.

Unsworth, N. (2010). Interference control, working memory capacity, and cognitive abilities: A latent variable analysis. *Intelligence*, 38, 255–267.

Unsworth, N., Redick, T. S., Lakey, C. E., & Young, D. L. (2010a). Lapses in sustained attention and their relation to executive control and fluid abilities: An individual differences investigation. *Intelligence*, 38, 111–122.

Unsworth, N., Schrock, J. C., & Engle, R. W. (2004). Working memory capacity and the antisaccade task: Individual differences in voluntary saccade control. *Journal of Experimental Psychology: Learning, Memory and Cognition*, 30, 1302–1321.

Unsworth, N., & Spillers, G. J. (2010). Working memory capacity: Attention control, secondary memory, or both? A direct test of the dual-component model. *Journal of Memory and Language*, 62, 392–406.

Unsworth, N., Spillers, G. J., & Brewer, G. A. (2010b). The contributions of primary and secondary memory to working memory capacity: An individual differences analysis of immediate free recall. *Journal of Experimental Psychology: Learning, Memory & Cognition*, 36, 240–247.

Uttl, B. (2008). Transparent meta-analysis of prospective memory and aging. *PLoS One*, 3, No. e1568.

Valentine, E. R. (1992). *Conceptual issues in psychology* (2nd ed.). London, UK: Routledge.

Vallée-Tourangeau, F., & Payton, T. (2008). Graphical representation fosters discovery in the 2–4–6 task. *Quarterly Journal of Experimental Psychology*, 61, 625–640.

Van Boxtel, J. J. A., Tsuchiya, N., & Koch, C. (2010). Opposing effects of attention and consciousness on afterimages. *Proceedings of the National Academy of Sciences of the United States of America*, 107, 8883–8888.

Vandenberghe, M., Schmidt, N., Fery, P., & Cleeremans, A. (2006). Can amnesic patients learn without awareness? New evidence comparing deterministic and probabilistic sequence learning. *Neuropsychologia*, 44, 1629–1641.

Vanderberg, R., & Swanson, H. L. (2007). Which components of working memory are important in the writing process? *Reading and Writing*, 20, 721–752.

Van der Hoort, B., Guterstam, A., & Ehrsson, H. (2011). Being Barbie: The size of one's own body determines the perceived size of the world. *PLoS One*, 6(5), e20195.

Van-Dillen, L. F., Heselenfeld, D. J., & Koole, S. L. (2009). Turning down the emotional brain: An fMRI study of the effects of cognitive load on the processing of affective images. *NeuroImage, 45*, 1212–1219.

Van Dillen, L. F., & Koole, S. L. (2007). Clearing the mind: A working memory model of distraction from negative mood. *Emotion, 7*, 715–723.

Van Gompel, R. P. G., Pickering, M. J., Pearson, J., & Liversedge, S. P. (2005). Evidence against competition during syntactic ambiguity resolution. *Journal of Memory and Language, 52*, 284–307.

Van Harreveld, F., Wagenmakers, E. J., & van der Maas, H. L. J. (2007). The effects of time pressure on chess skills: An investigation into fast and slow responses underlying expert performance. *Psychological Research, 71*, 591–597.

Van Orden, G. C. (1987). A rows is a rose: Spelling, sound and reading. *Memory & Cognition, 14*, 371–386.

Vargha-Khadem, F., Gadian, D. G., & Mishkin, M. (2002). Dissociations in cognitive memory: The syndrome of developmental amnesia. In A. Baddeley, M. Conway, & J. Aggleton (Eds.), *Episodic memory: New directions in research* (pp. 153–163). New York, NY: Oxford University Press.

Vargha-Khadem, F., Gadian, D. G., Watkins, K. E., Connelly, A., Van Paesschen, W., & Mishkin, M. (1997). Differential effects of early hippocampal pathology on episodic and semantic memory. *Science, 277*, 376–380.

Velten, E. (1968). A laboratory task for induction of mood states. *Behaviour Research and Therapy, 6*, 473–482.

Viggiano, M. P., Giovannelli, F., Borgheresi, A., Feurra, M., Berardi, N., Pizzorusso, T., et al. (2008). Disruption of the prefrontal cortex by rTMS produces a category-specific enhancement of the reaction times during visual object identification. *Neuropsychologia, 46*, 2725–2731.

Vigliocco, G., & Hartsuiker, R. J. (2002). The interplay of meaning, sound, and syntax in sentence production. *Psychological Bulletin, 128*, 442–472.

Vingerhoets, G., Vermeule, E., & Santens, P. (2005). Impaired intentional content learning but spare incidental retention of contextual information in non-demented patients with Parkinson's disease. *Neuropsychologia, 43*, 675–681.

Vogel, E. K., Woodman, G. F., & Luck, S. J. (2001). Storage of features, conjunctions, and objects in visual working memory. *Journal of Experimental Psychology: Human Perception and Performance, 27*, 92–114.

Voss, J. L., Reber, P. J., Mesulam, M. M., Parrish, T. B., & Paller, K. A. (2008). Familiarity and conceptual priming engage distinct cortical networks. *Cerebral Cortex, 18*, 1712–1719.

Vousden, J. L., & Maylor, E. A. (2006). Speech errors across the lifespan. *Language and Cognitive Processes, 21*, 48–77.

Vrij, A. (2008). Nonverbal dominance versus verbal accuracy in lie detection: A plea to change police practice. *Criminal Justice and Behavior, 35*, 1323–1336.

Vrij, A., Mann, S. A., Fisher, R. P., Leal, S., Milne, R., & Bull, R. (2008). Increasing cognitive load to facilitate lie detection: The benefit of recalling an event in reverse order. *Law and Human Behavior, 32*, 253–265.

Vroling, M. S., & de Jong, P. J. (2009). Deductive reasoning and social anxiety: Evidence for a fear-confirming belief bias. *Cognitive Therapy & Research, 33*, 633–644.

Vuilleumier, P., Schwartz, S., Clark, K., Husain, M., & Driver, J. (2002). Testing memory for unseen visual stimuli in patients with extinction and spatial neglect. *Journal of Cognitive Neuroscience, 14*, 875–886.

Vuilleumier, P., Schwartz, S., Verdon, V., Maravita, A., Hutton, C., Husain, M., et al. (2008). Abnormal attentional modulation of retinotopic cortex in parietal patients with spatial neglect. *Current Biology, 18*, 1525–1529.

Vul, E., & Pashler, H. (2007). Incubation benefits only after people have been misdirected. *Memory & Cognition, 35*, 701–710.

Wagner, U., Gais, S., Haider, H., Verleger, R., & Born, J. (2004). Sleep inspires insight. *Nature, 427*, 352–355.

Wagner, V., Jescheniak, J. D., & Schriefers, H. (2010). On the flexibility of grammatical advance planning: Effects of cognitive load on multiple lexical access. *Journal of Experimental Psychology: Learning, Memory, and Cognition, 36*, 423–440.

Walker, M. P., Brakefield, T., Hobson, J. A., & Stickgold, R. (2003). Dissociable stages of human memory consolidation and reconsolidation. *Nature, 425*, 616–620.

Walton, D. (2010). Why fallacies appear to be better arguments than they are. *Informal logic, 30*, 159–184.

Wang, A. Y., & Thomas, M. H. (2000). Looking for long-term mnemonic effects on serial recall: The legacy of Simonides. *American Journal of Psychology, 113*, 331–340.

Wang, X. T. (1996). Domain-specific rationality in human choices: Violations of utility axioms and social contexts. *Cognition, 60*, 31–63.

Wang, X. T., Simons, F., & Brédart, S. (2001). Social cues and verbal framing in risky choice. *Journal of Behavioral Decision Making, 14*, 1–15.

Ward, J. (2010). *The student's guide to cognitive neuroscience* (2nd ed.). Hove, UK: Psychology Press.

Warren, R. M. (2006). The relation of speech perception to the perception of nonverbal auditory patterns. In S. Greenberg & W. A. Ainsworth (Eds.), *Listening to speech: An auditory perspective* (pp. 333–349). Mahwah, NJ: Lawrence Erlbaum Associates.

Warren, R. M., & Warren, R. P. (1970). Auditory illusions and confusions. *Scientific American, 223*, 30–36.

Wason, P. C. (1960). On the failure to eliminate hypotheses in a conceptual task. *Quarterly Journal of Experimental Psychology, 12*, 129–140.

Wason, P. C. (1968). Reasoning about a rule. *Quarterly Journal of Experimental Psychology, 20*, 63–71.

Wason, P. C., & Shapiro, D. (1971). Natural and contrived experience in reasoning problems. *Quarterly Journal of Experimental Psychology, 23*, 63–71.

Waters, E. A. (2008). Feeling good, feeling bad, and feeling at risk: A review of incidental affect's influence on likelihood estimates of health hazards and life events. *Journal of Risk Research, 11*, 569–595.

Watson, D., & Clark, L. A. (1992). Affects separable and inseparable: On the hierarchical arrangement of the negative affects. *Journal of Personality and Social Psychology, 62*, 489–505.

Watson, D., & Tellegen, A. (1985). Toward a consensual structure of mood. *Psychological Bulletin, 98*, 219–235.

Watson, J. B. (1913). Psychology as the behaviorist views it. *Psychological Review, 20*, 158–177.

Watson, J. M., & Strayer, D. L. (2010). Supertaskers: Profiles in extraordinary multitasking ability. *Psychonomic Bulletin & Review, 17*, 479–485.

Wegner, D. M. (2003). The mind's best trick: How we experience conscious will. *Trends in Cognitive Sciences, 7*, 65–69.

Wegner, D. M., & Wheatley, T. (1999). Apparent mental causation: Sources of the experience of will. *American Psychologist, 54*, 480–492.

Weinman, J., Ebrecht, M., Scott, S., Walburn, J., & Dyson, M. (2008). Enhanced wound healing after emotional disclosure intervention. *British Journal of Health Psychology, 13*, 95–102.

Weiskrantz, L. (1980). Varieties of residual experience. *Quarterly Journal of Experimental Psychology, 32*, 365–386.

Weiskrantz, L. (2004). Blindsight. In R. L. Gregory (Ed.), *Oxford companion to the mind*. Oxford, UK: Oxford University Press.

Weiskrantz, L., Warrington, E. K., Sanders, M. D., & Marshall, J. (1974). Visual capacity in the hemianopic field following a restricted occipital ablation. *Brain, 97*, 709–728.

Weisstein, N., & Harris, C. S. (1974). Visual detection of line segments – Object superiority effect. *Science, 186*, 752–755.

Weisstein, N., & Wong, E. (1986). Figure–ground organization and the spatial and temporal responses of the visual system. In E. C. Schwab & H. C. Nusbaum (Eds.), *Pattern recognition by humans and machines* (Vol. 2). New York, NY: Academic Press.

Wentura, D., Voss, A., & Rothermund, K. (2009). Playing TETRIS for science: Counter-regulatory affective processing in a motivationally "hot" context. *Acta Psychologica, 131*, 171–177.

Werker, J. F., & Tees, R. C. (1992). The organization and reorganization of human speech perception. *Annual Review of Neuroscience, 15*, 377–402.

Wheeler, M. A., Stuss, D. T., & Tulving, E. (1997). Toward a theory of episodic memory: The frontal lobes and autonoetic consciousness. *Psychological Bulletin, 121*, 331–354.

White, P. A. (2009). Property transmission: An explanatory account of the role of similarity information in causal inference. *Psychological Bulletin, 135*, 774–793.

Whithaus, C., Harrison, S., & Midyette, J. (2008). Keyboarding compared with handwriting on a high-stakes assessment: Student choice of composing medium, raters' perceptions and text quality. *Assessing Writing, 13*, 4–25.

Wilding, J., & Valentine, E. (1994). Memory champions. *British Journal of Psychology, 85*, 231–244.

Wilkinson, L., & Jahanshahi, M. (2007). The striatum and probabilistic implicit sequence learning. *Brain Research, 1137*, 117–130.

Wilkinson, L., Khan, Z., & Jahanshahi, M. (2009). The role of the basal ganglia and its cortical connections in sequence learning: Evidence from implicit and explicit learning in Parkinson's disease. *Neuropsychologia, 47*, 2564–2573.

Wilkinson, L., & Shanks, D. R. (2004). Intentional control and implicit sequence learning. *Journal of*

Experimental Psychology: Learning, Memory, & Cognition, 30, 354–369.

Williams, J. M. G., Watts, F. N., MacLeod, C. M., & Mathews, A. (1997). *Cognitive psychology and emotional disorders* (2nd ed.). Chichester, UK: Wiley.

Wilmer, J. B., Germine, L., Chabris, C. F., Chatterjee, G., Williams, M., Loken, E., et al. (2010). Human face recognition ability is specific and highly heritable. *Proceedings of the National Academy of Sciences of the United States of America, 107*, 5238–5241.

Winningham, R. G., Hyman, L. E., Jr., & Dinnel, D. L. (2000). Flashbulb memories? The effects of when the initial memory report was obtained. *Memory, 8*, 209–216.

Winograd, E., & Soloway, R. M. (1986). On forgetting the locations of things stored in special places. *Journal of Experimental Psychology: General, 115*, 366–372.

Wixted, J. T. (2004). The psychology and neuroscience of forgetting. *Annual Review of Psychology, 55*, 235–269.

Woike, B., Gershkovich, I., Piorkowski, R., & Polo, M. (1999). The role of motives in the content and structure of autobiographical memory. *Journal of Personality and Social Psychology, 76*, 600–612.

Wolfe, J. M. (2007). Guided search 4.0: Current progress with a model of visual search. In W. Gray (Ed.), *Integrated models of cognitive systems* (pp. 99–119). New York, NY: Oxford University Press.

Wolfe, J. M., Horowitz, T. S., Van-Wert, M. J., Kenner, N. M., Place, S. S., & Kibbi, N. (2007). Low target prevalence is a stubborn source of errors in visual search tasks. *Journal of Experimental Psychology: General, 136*, 623–6638.

Woollett, K., & Maguire, E. A. (2009). Navigational expertise may compromise anterograde associative memory. *Neuropsychologia, 44*, 1088–1095.

Woollett, K., Spiers, H. J., & Maguire, E. A. (2009). Talent in the taxi: A model system for exploring expertise. *Philosophical Transactions of the Royal Society B: Biological Sciences, 364*, 1407–1416.

Wright, D. B., & Loftus, E. F. (2008). Eyewitness memory. In G. Cohen & M. A. Conway (Eds.), *Memory in the real world* (3rd ed.). Hove, UK: Psychology Press.

Wright, G. (1984). *Behavioral decision theory.* Harmondsworth, UK: Penguin.

Wroe, A. L., Bhan, A., Salkovskis, P., & Bedford, H. (2005). Feeling bad about immunizing our children. *Vaccine, 23*, 1428–1433.

Wu, L. L., & Barsalou, L. W. (2009). Perceptual simulation in conceptual combination: Evidence from property generation. *Acta Psychologica, 132*, 173–189.

Xu, Y., & Chun, M. M. (2009). Selecting and perceiving multiple visual objects. *Trends in Cognitive Sciences, 13*, 167–174.

Yantis, S. (2008). The neural basis of selective attention: Cortical sources and targets of attentional modulation. *Current Directions in Psychological Science, 17*, 86–90.

Yates, M. (2005). Phonological neighbors speed visual word processing: Evidence from multiple tasks. *Journal of Experimental Psychology: Human Perception and Performance, 34*, 1599–1606.

Yates, M., Friend, J., & Ploetz, D. M. (2008). Phonological neighbors influence word naming through the least supported phoneme. *Journal of Experimental Psychology: Human Perception and Performance, 21*, 996–1014.

Ye, L., Cardwell, W., & Mark, L. S. (2009). Perceiving multiple affordances for objects. *Ecological Psychology, 21*, 185–217.

Yonelinas, A. P. (2002). The nature of recollection and familiarity: A review of 30 years of research. *Journal of Memory and Language, 46*, 441–517.

Yoon, K. L., & Zinbarg, R. E. (2008). Interpreting neutral faces as threatening is a default mode for socially anxious individuals. *Journal of Abnormal Psychology, 117*, 680–685.

Young, A. W., Hay, D. C., & Ellis, A. W. (1985). The faces that launched a thousand slips: Everyday difficulties and errors in recognizing people. *British Journal of Psychology, 76*, 495–523.

Young, A. W., Hellawell, D., & Hay, D. C. (1987). Configurational information in face perception. *Perception, 16*, 747–759.

Young, A. W., Newcombe, F., de Haan, E. H. F., Small, M., & Hay, D. C. (1993). Face perception after brain injury: Selective impairments affecting identity and expression. *Brain, 116*, 941–959.

Zacks, J. M. (2008). Neuroimaging studies of mental rotation: A meta-analysis and review. *Journal of Cognitive Neuroscience, 20*, 1–19.

Zago, S., Corti, S., Bersano, A., Baron, P., Conti, G., Ballabio, E., et al. (2010). A cortically blind patient with preserved visual imagery. *Cognitive and Behavioral Neurology, 23*, 44–48.

Zangwill, O. L. (2004). Ebbinghaus. In R. L. Gregory (Ed.), *The Oxford companion to the mind* (2nd ed., p. 276). New York, NY: Oxford University Press.

Zanon, M., Busan, P., Monti, F., Pizzolato, G., & Battaglini, P. P. (2010). Cortical connections between dorsal and ventral visual streams in humans: Evidence by TNS/EEG co-registration. *Brain Topography, 22*, 307–317.

Zeki, S., & Romaya, J. P. (2010). The brain reaction to viewing faces of opposite- and same-sex romantic partners. *PLoS One, 5,* e15802.

Zelko, H., Zammar, G. R., Ferreira, A. P. B., Phadtare, A., Shah, J., & Pietrobon, R. (2010). Selection mechanisms underlying high impact biomedical research – A qualitative analysis and causal model. *PLoS One, 5,* e10535.

Zevin, J. D., & Seidenberg, M. S. (2006). Simulating consistency effects and individual differences in nonword naming: A comparison of current models. *Journal of Memory and Language, 54,* 145–160.

Zhou, X. L., Ye, Z., Cheung, H., & Chen, H.-C. (2009). Processing the Chinese language: An introduction. *Language and Cognitive Processes, 24,* 929–946.

Ziemann, U. (2010). TMS in cognitive neuroscience: Virtual lesion and beyond. *Cortex, 46,* 124–127.

Zimmer, H. D. (2008). Visual and spatial working memory: From boxes to networks. *Neuroscience and Biobehavioral Reviews, 32,* 1373–1395.

Zwaan, R. A. (1994). Effects of genre expectations on text comprehension. *Journal of Experimental Psychology: Learning, Memory, & Cognition, 20,* 920–933.

Zwaan, R. A. (2009). Mental simulation in language comprehension and social cognition. *European Journal of Social Psychology, 39,* 1142–1150.

Zwaan, R. A., & Madden, C. J. (2004). Updating situation models. *Journal of Experimental Psychology: Learning, Memory, and Cognition, 30,* 283–288.

Zwaan, R. A., & Radvansky, G. A. (1998). Situation models in language comprehension and memory. *Psychological Bulletin, 123,* 162–185.

Zwaan, R. A., Stanfield, R. A., & Yaxley, R. H. (2002). Language comprehenders mentally represent the shapes of objects. *Psychological Science, 13,* 168–171.

Zwaan, R. A., & van Oostendorp, U. (1993). Do readers construct spatial representations in naturalistic story comprehension? *Discourse Processes, 16,* 125–143.

Author index

Subject index

Page numbers in **bold** indicate glossary definitions.